G000232065

COLLINS
BIBLE COMPANION

is a book with extraordinary strengths, designed to
meet the needs of today. It is a unique companion, a
useful tool to help Christians and non-Christians
discover the Bible in a new and attractive way: loving
it, reading it, understanding it and applying it in their
lives. ... I commend it to the whole spectrum of
readers and specifically to students and young people
around the world.

Dr DANIEL BOURDANNÉ
International Fellowship
of Evangelical Students (IFES)

This well-produced, easy-to-read
Bible compendium is a basic book for
all would-be disciples of Jesus Christ.
I commend it most heartily.

JIM PACKER

It is almost impossible to exaggerate the
importance of studying the great truths of
the Bible. I warmly commend this programme
of teaching – it will meet a great need and give
clear insight into the Bible's teaching.

BILLY GRAHAM
(on the BIBLE TEACHING section)

COLLINS
BIBLE
COMPANION

THE ONLY BOOK YOU
NEED BESIDE THE BIBLE

Martin H. Manser · *Editor*
Tony Cantale · *Designer*
Robert F. Hicks · *Project director*

Collins

A division of HarperCollins*Publishers*
77–85 Fulham Palace Road, London W6 8JB

www.bookarmy.com

Martin H. Manser · *Editor*
Tony Cantale · *Designer*
Robert F. Hicks · *Project director*

1

Copyright © 2009
Creative 3 International, Bath

A catalogue record for this book is available from the British Library

ISBN 978 0 00 733980 8

Printed and bound in China by Leo Paper Products Ltd

Introductory articles
Andrew Stobart
Keith J. White

The Bible Book by Book
David Barratt
Mike Beaumont
Pieter Lalleman
Richard Littledale
Debra Reid
Andrew Stobart
Derek Williams

Bible outlines from *NIV Thematic Study Bible*, copyright Hodder & Stoughton, reproduced by permission of Hodder & Stoughton Publishers, an Hachette UK company

Extracts at Mark, 1 Corinthians, Galatians, Ephesians, Philippians, Colossians, 1 and 2 Thessalonians, 1 and 2 Timothy, Titus, from *Critical Companion to the Bible*, edited by Martin H. Manser (Facts on File, 2009) by permission of Facts on File

Bible Teaching
Richard Bewes
Robert F. Hicks

Living the Christian Life
Derek Williams
Robert F. Hicks
Andrew Stobart

Key People and Places
Text from *NIV Comprehensive Concordance*, copyright Hodder & Stoughton, reproduced by permission of Hodder & Stoughton Publishers, an Hachette UK company

How the Bible Developed
Some source material from The Bible Society *Timeline*, used with permission

What the Bible Says About ...
James Collins

In Times of Need
Nick Gatzke

Editorial assistant
Nicola L. Bull

Contents

The Bible in its Setting

Pages 12–55
**About the Bible – why it was written, its
history, geography and cultural setting**

Contents
continued

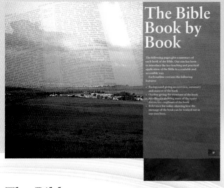

The Bible
Book by Book

Bible
Teaching

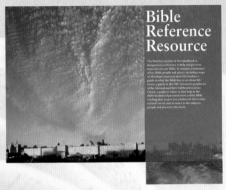

Living the Christian Life

Pages 464–579
**How to work out and apply
the message of the Bible**

Bible Reference Resource

Pages 580–718
**Where to find information in the Bible,
what the Bible has to say about life issues,
where to find help in the Bible, a plan for
daily Bible reading**

POWERPOINT AND PRESENTATIONS
How to use the material in this book

This book is a resource for those who want to study the Bible and for those who seek to teach others.

Material is presented throughout using headings, subheadings and explanation. It can be adapted for PowerPoint or overhead projection by copying or extracting the headings and subheadings for display.

You will find that some material is presented in "bullet points"; other material readily subdivides into teaching points. By listing and displaying what is suitable for display and using your own notes for explanation, a teaching session can easily be developed. Because of the consecutive nature of the material whole teaching programmes can be created relatively simply.

Material in this book may be freely used for such study and teaching purposes in a non-commercial personal, church or teaching setting.

Those who have worked on this book want people to be helped in their faith and understanding of God and his ways.

ABBREVIATIONS
Abbreviations for the books of the Bible used in this book are:

Old Testament		New Testament	
Genesis	Ge	Matthew	Mt
Exodus	Ex	Mark	Mk
Leviticus	Lev	Luke	Lk
Numbers	Nu	John	Jn
Deuteronomy	Dt	Acts	Ac
Joshua	Jos	Romans	Ro
Judges	Jdg	1 Corinthians	1Co
Ruth	Ru	2 Corinthians	2Co
1 Samuel	1Sa	Galatians	Gal
2 Samuel	2Sa	Ephesians	Eph
1 Kings	1Ki	Philippians	Php
2 Kings	2Ki	Colossians	Col
1 Chronicles	1Ch	1 Thessalonians	1Th
2 Chronicles	2Ch	2 Thessalonians	2Th
Ezra	Ezr	1 Timothy	1Ti
Nehemiah	Ne	2 Timothy	2Ti
Esther	Est	Titus	Tit
Job	Job	Philemon	Phm
Psalms	Ps	Hebrews	Heb
Proverbs	Pr	James	Jas
Ecclesiastes	Ecc	1 Peter	1Pe
Song of Songs	SS	2 Peter	2Pe
Isaiah	Isa	1 John	1Jn
Jeremiah	Jer	2 John	2Jn
Lamentations	La	3 John	3Jn
Ezekiel	Eze	Jude	Jude
Daniel	Da	Revelation	Rev
Hosea	Hos		
Joel	Joel		
Amos	Am		
Obadiah	Ob		
Jonah	Jnh		
Micah	Mic		
Nahum	Na		
Habakkuk	Hab		
Zephaniah	Zep		
Haggai	Hag		
Zechariah	Zec		
Malachi	Mal		

Foreword

I believe you hold in your hand a wonderful tool. *Collins Bible Companion* will enable you to dig into and explore the greatest treasure entrusted to the human race, the very words of God. Speaking as a pastor and theological educator, I am personally tremendously excited about the appearance of this book. Speaking as a preacher, allow me to share three reasons to explain my enthusiasm.

Firstly, this volume is an amazingly comprehensive book. A cursory glance at the contents will immediately confirm that observation – the Bible book by book, its major themes, its key people, and how to put it all into practice in actually living the Christian life, etc.

Secondly, this companion is creative. In our highly visually oriented age, you will immediately appreciate its clear, colourful and beautiful production. You have, at your fingertips, a superb aid for teaching and learning.

Thirdly, this manual is unashamedly Christ-centred. It is all too possible to approach the word of the Lord and miss the Lord of the word. This guide will encourage you to hear Christ's footfall and see his face through the pages of the Bible, Old and New Testaments alike.

When the concept of this book was mentioned to the students of my college, something unprecedented happened: such was their enthusiasm that many of them ordered a copy there and then, without even having seen the finished article! Now you can share their "faith" and judge for yourself how well-placed it is!

Welcome to this excellent tool. May the Lord Jesus bless you as this guide helps you to discover some of the rich treasures of his holy word.

Rev Dr Steve Brady
Principal
Moorlands College
Christchurch, UK

Introduction

Welcome to *Collins Bible Companion*. This book is an all-in-one guide to the Bible that is both a comprehensive reference book and an exciting companion. Here you will have opportunity to:

- discover the contents of the Bible
- explore the truth of the Bible
- believe and experience the message of the Bible

In all, your life will be enriched as you allow God to speak to you through his word. But we want more for you than that: this book's special task is to enable teachers and preachers around the world to communicate the message of the Bible to others effectively.

The text is user-friendly to enable the busy teacher to grasp subjects in an accessible way and to make the most of their time. Whether you teach in a church service, a student group or home group, we know that you will find life-giving information in these pages. Pass it on!

As those involved in creating this book, we believe it to be unique. Its various approaches all have one underlying aim: to help you know your Bible more thoroughly.

We believe the Bible is an essential ingredient of the Christian life – to appreciate the content of the whole sweep of the books of the Bible, to know its basic doctrines and to know how to apply its message – there is enough here for a lifetime of study!

The core parts of *Collins Bible Companion* are:

- **The Bible in its Setting** (see pages 12–55) – giving background information on the whole Bible, including how and why it was written, and its history, geography and cultural context. Here are included general charts, eg on biblical feasts and festivals, covenants, the calendar, money, and weights and measures.
- **The Bible Book by Book** (see pages 56–329) – provides an overview of the essentials of each book of the Bible. Sometimes we can be so immersed in the details of a particular verse that we do not realise the purpose and importance of each Bible book, so this summary of each whole book of the Bible gives a summary, an outline and the

key teachings, plus application to work out its relevance for today.

- **Bible Teaching** (see pages 330–463) – explores the essential truths of Christianity, such as God, Jesus Christ, the Holy Spirit and Humanity, in a clear and methodical way, to lay and develop a solid foundation for your Christian life.
- **Living the Christian Life** (see pages 464–579) – shows how we are to work out and apply the message of the Bible at every stage in our growth and progress as Christians.
- **Bible Reference Resource** (see pages 580–718) – provides an alphabetical listing of key Bible people and places, a concise explanation of what the Bible has to say about a variety of subjects – for example, choices, integrity, patience – that we face as we live in the world, a plan for daily Bible reading to give you a balanced diet of taking in God's word, a guide to Old Testament prophecies of the Messiah and their fulfilment in Jesus Christ, a guide to where to find help in the Bible in times of personal need and an index to the whole book.

We've also included many other resources to help you get even more out of your Bible: 36 maps and charts as background information, for example, maps of Abraham's travels; the exile; charts such as Old Testament festivals; a guide to the Old Testament prophecies of the Messiah and their fulfilment in Jesus Christ; a summary of key people and places; a guide to helps in time of personal need; a daily Bible reading plan to give you a balanced diet when taking in God's word.

As you read through this book, you will find it helpful to look up the references in your Bible: this will help reinforce the words of the Bible in your heart and mind. This book is designed for use with any translation of the Bible such as the New International Version.

The contemporary approach and design of this book will help make the Bible as accessible as possible. We live in a visual age, so the use of full-colour text and illustration is an important aspect of this book's preparation.

For many people, the Bible is a closed book: it does not mean anything. As you use this book next to your Bible, our hope is that you will be challenged: you will see the way God wants you to live and we trust this book will equip you to serve him even more effectively in his world. Our prayer and hope is that you will hear God speak in a fresh way as you explore and apply its message, first to yourself and then to the lives of those you teach.

Tony Cantale
Martin Manser
Robert Hicks

The Bible in its Setting

This section is designed as an introduction that provides background information to the Bible: its authority and inspiration; its significance and relevance to today's world; its different parts and how they came to be written; and a summary of how its message may be understood.

We then explore the world setting of the Old and New Testaments, including maps and charts on certain cultural aspects to help our understanding of the Bible text: festivals and feasts; the calendar; sacrifice; covenants; the tabernacle and its furnishings; and money, weights and measures, and distances.

The Authority and Inspiration of the Bible

The terms "authority" and "inspiration" together help us to understand the significance of the Bible for the Christian faith.

The term "authority" describes the fact that the Bible is uniquely capable of leading people from every generation and situation to faith in God through Jesus Christ. No other book in the world has this authority. The Bible, in both the Old and New Testaments, faithfully presents the character of the creator God and declares his invitation for the world to come to him for salvation. The Bible is said to be authoritative in all matters of faith, which means that when it comes to finding out about having a relationship with God, the Bible can be trusted.

The Bible's authority was recognised by the early church. The New Testament documents were originally collected together because they were considered to be an accurate account of the events and significance of the life, death and resurrection of Jesus Christ. The church realised that when the apostles who had been with Jesus and seen him after his resurrection had themselves died, it was vital that the young church was able to pass on their testimony about God's good news. From the beginning, the church also accepted the Jewish Scriptures as an authority for their faith. These were the Scriptures that Jesus himself had known and quoted from, and as the first Christians studied the writings and prophecies, they discovered that they also pointed faithfully to what had happened in Jesus Christ. The Jewish Scriptures became the "Old" Testament, while the new documents became a "New"

Testament. Together, these Scriptures were the official documents of the church, called a *canon* (from the Latin and Greek for "rule", which referred to the church's decision to recognise the authority the documents already had in church life and thought).

Thus, the Bible is said to have authority because God's people have already identified it as being a faithful (written) messenger of God's good news. This is why the Bible is often called "the word of God". Christians understand that the Bible is not filled simply with human messages or accounts of religious experiences, but that through the different human authors of the various books, God declares his word. The authority of the Bible for faith thus leads straight to our second term. The fact that God's message is heard through human words is called the Bible's "inspiration".

Using the term "inspired" about the Bible does not mean that God dictated the words of Scripture to the human authors, who simply acted as secretaries. In that case the human authors would have contributed nothing at all. But on the other hand, calling Scripture "inspired" does not mean that the human authors merely had a good idea, which they wrote down as being a message from God. In actual fact, the inspiration of the Bible does not say much about how the text itself came about. There may have been many different ways by which the authors received God's message and wrote it down. This variety would fit well with the multiple genres we find in Scripture.

Inspiration is not so much a theory of the Bible's composition as an affirmation of what

the Bible is. Inspiration describes the Bible by referring to both its divine and human authorship at the same time. The Bible is inspired because the message we receive from it is both a collection of human words – with cultural, literary and stylistic characteristics – and the words of the eternal God! The term "inspiration" helps Christians to affirm equally that the Bible is human, and so requires study and effort in order to be understood, and that it is divine, so its message can only be received as the Spirit of God enables faith and understanding.

It can be said that the Bible is infallibly inspired. This means that when it comes to matters of God and faith, the Bible does not mislead us – its human words truly are God's words. However, it is entirely different to say that the Bible is inerrant, as this usually means that every statement the Bible makes about every subject is completely true. This may be an unhelpful way to look at the Bible, since, for example, it does not claim to be a textbook of science.

The terms "inspiration" and "authority" help us to understand what our relationship with the Bible should be. By calling the Bible inspired, we recognise that the Bible is given to us by God and through it he meets with us today. Because God himself speaks through the human words, the Bible really does reveal God's character and his works in the world. As this unique revelation, the Bible is supremely authoritative for the Christian life. By recognising the Bible's authority, we are acknowledging that it is God's word, and not ours, and that is decisively significant for our lives and for the world. We must therefore listen to Scripture, and seek the enlightenment of God's Spirit, to help us understand and apply God's message to our lives.

The Bible
for Today's World

Today's world

Contemporary societies around the world are increasingly cosmopolitan, cross-cultural and multi-ethnic: in and through them the global and the local interact in a kaleidoscopic variety of ways; there are tensions between religions and what have been called clashes between civilisations; electronic communication and visual images are coming to be preferred to narrative; the era is post-colonial; and it has been described as "post-modern". Set in this context if we ask who the reader of a Bible is, increasingly we must conclude that it is potentially everyone.

This article therefore seeks to hold in mind people of all ages, male and female, rich and poor, literate and illiterate, individuals, households and groups, Christian and non-Christian. A guiding principle of Bibles in the 21st century may well be that they should be conceived of as accessible to all.

What is the Bible?

Paradoxically for a volume whose Greek name, *biblos*, means "book", that is precisely what it is not. It certainly looks like a book, but in fact it is a library, what has been called a book of books, or perhaps more accurately, a collection of manuscripts. These manuscripts include chronicles, stories, poems, letters, census data, oracles, household codes, genealogies and laws.

How does this clarification help in today's world? It means that the Bible as a whole is able to speak into situations and cultures in a way that a single book, preacher or pastor could never do. This is because it connects in a range of different forms, and communicates from a range of different perspectives. It has coherence in and through the Lord Jesus Christ, and a glorious meta-narrative starting with creation and culminating in the new creation, but these are revealed in what resembles a glorious tapestry woven from a stunning array of threads of varying textures and hues. And of course different parts speak to very different communities in quite contrasting situations: some readers are effectively persecuted minorities like the Hebrews in Egypt and the early Christians, others are exiles (migrants) like the Jews in exile, and still others enjoy influence and power like the Jews who settled in the Promised Land and established a kingly rule.

How to handle the Bible with care?

How to interpret the Bible is one of the issues that continue to divide Christians. Perhaps we can demystify things a little for non-specialists by dropping the term *hermeneutics* (literally, "interpretation"), and replacing it with the idea of handling the Bible (reading and interpreting it) with care. There are those who see this handling ultimately in the hands of the church or denomination, and others who see the individual reader as the valid interpreter. There are huge matters of control at stake here worldwide. Denominations, creeds and doctrines all relate to this matter: who decides what is the correct interpretation, and against what criteria? Without attempting to set out a definitive position here, maybe we can agree that if individual readers do not have a Bible they can understand, the matter has already

been decided: in their case others will determine how it is interpreted, pastors, priests, teachers, those from other cultures.

And where there are notes they should be written inclusively, rather than creating the impression of an "us" and "them" polarity. The notes in this book have been written and edited with care to encourage readers to dig deeper and wider into the Bible for themselves. The notes provide helpful information, not with the aim of seeking to close arguments down, but with the aim of nurturing an intelligent reading of the text by asking focused questions.

The whole, or parts of the whole?

A third question concerns the matter of the whole and its parts. Put simply, how valid is it to present a part of the Bible, rather than the whole canon (acknowledging that there are different canons in the worldwide church) to readers? It follows from what has already been argued that there is the strongest possible case for presenting the Bible as a whole. Any selection is potentially risky both in relation to doing justice to the text, but also in relation to the global readership. How would an editor avoid a colonial approach that assumes he or she knows what is most relevant to which readers worldwide?

Is the Bible still relevant?

Given the fact that the Bible is a collection of manuscripts over 2000 years old, and is presented as a book in an age of visual, digital technology and communication, is the Bible (still) relevant in every culture and for every age of person, particularly the emerging younger generations? And here we are thinking about the Bible per se, not about living it out, preaching from it, or repackaging it for children and others.

We do well to ponder the question not just in general terms, but starting at home: is it still relevant for churches? Judging by many worship services not informed and constrained by lectionaries and liturgy that I

have attended in recent years around the world the Bible is used less prominently than it once was; there has even been a significant and seemingly inexorable decline in the reading aloud from the Bible during acts of worship. It is as if there has been a crisis of confidence in God's revealed word, and that by using other more modern or culturally appropriate means we can do better. The reading of Scripture, and actively listening to and pondering it, belong in this view, to a bygone age.

It would be strange if we believed it still relevant for "others" if we have decided or accepted that it no longer speaks with authority and relevance in our own worshipping communities! If, on the other hand, we believe that it is still relevant (and by the "we" I do not restrict myself to Bible societies, the Gideons, and those committed to translating and disseminating the Bible) then why is that so? Presumably, as Christians committed to a high view of Scripture we would argue that the Bible is still relevant to men and women, children and young people of every people group and culture, because it is God-breathed: it communicates in a unique and authoritative way God's word. It is an essential part, perhaps the primary vehicle of his revelation of himself.

And if we are to maintain that Jesus Christ is the Lord of our faith, the one in whom all things hold together, the exact image of God the Father, and the one through whom salvation comes, then where else can we turn to discover the revelation of who this Jesus is?

If we view the Bible as a relic of a bygone age, then what of our Lord and Master? Do we then rely on alternative revelations of his person, teaching and grace?

It does not take long with this question in mind to realise that Christians have nowhere else to go: it is in and through this particular text that we have discovered the one who has the words of eternal life.

In what form is it most relevant?

If we answer in the affirmative, as I believe we must, then a subsequent question immediately follows (if we answered in the negative, than I think we have come to the wrong place or are reading the wrong book). The question is, "In what form is it relevant?" By this I mean, not how is it translated (we have good and increasing examples of excellent translation into the languages of more and more people groups), but in what form should it best be presented to people of different ages and cultures? Traditionally it has been done in the form of a single book, divided into two parts, the Old and New Testaments, where the 66 "books" within the Bible look much alike, with double columns, chapters and verses. We have become so wedded to the overriding virtue of accurate translation into local languages (sometimes using a dynamic equivalent), that we have seen presentation as a second-rank issue. At the turn of the 21st century we do well to rethink this question radically and thoroughly.

So what do we take for granted about the presentation of the Bible? This calls for a breadth of response for which there is not space in this current article. But among the things we tend to take for granted is the idea of niche marketing that sees Bibles designed for very particular readerships and purposes (children, study, devotion etc). We have also accepted that we may include illustrations, charts, boxes of information, introductions about an organisation, and so on. The text is no longer "sacred" in a way that it once was.

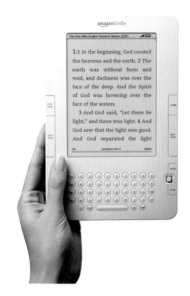

Many means of accessing and reading the Scriptures are now available, including hand-held portable reader devices such as the Kindle

How does it compare with other sacred texts?

If we need jolting in this respect, then we would do well to look at presentations of the Koran, where the publishers do not believe they have the right to treat the text as the producers of some presentations of the Bible. Increasingly, readers will find they have some knowledge of more than one set of sacred texts. And so we need to ask how the Bible compares with other sacred texts in the way it is presented, received and used. If we are thinking about a global readership of the Bible, we need to have in our minds the different ways in which people see and handle their sacred texts. People learn Arabic in order to read the Koran; the Hindu Scriptures exist in a number of different forms and texts, never as far as I know being bound in a single volume. If we are to present the Bible to people of these cultures we must consider very carefully how we present it, and what messages its very presentation will convey even before the covers have been opened.

Searching the Scriptures: Cambodia

Recently I was teaching theology in the Far East, when the students commented that I held the Bible differently to other westerners. On enquiring where the difference lay they said it was in that I handled it as if it were a sacred text: with reverence and respect. Perhaps we have become so used to Bibles all around us, in various translations and editions that a sense of awe has departed from the handling and reading of the Bible.

And then there is a big distinction to make between the Bible and other sacred texts: whereas the Koran is interpreted (and guarded carefully) by Muslims, the Bible is the property of no one group or sect. It is not "ours" if we are Christians, Jews or westerners: rather it belongs to God and is freely available and accessible to the whole world. Perhaps Christians have unconsciously given the impression that we are the guardians and interpreters, whereas God's Spirit takes God's word way beyond the confines of church and Christianity.

What examples are there from around the world?

I conclude with a few examples, to which many more can be added from around the world, where the Bible is respected, read and relevant.

Groups that sit in circles with Bibles open beginning with their own stories and seeking to identify questions that they need to ask of God, determined to wrestle with his word. (Latin America)

Street children who find trusted adults willing to spend time with them listening to their stories; then pictures that evoke a response that leads to the telling of the stories of Jesus. (The Pavement Project, Philippines)

Children in "Sunday School" sitting in a circle listening to a Bible story told simply and without deviation by a trained teacher who will not come between the children and the Bible. The children are then given quality equipment with which to explore the story in their own way. (Godly Play and Bible Play around the world)

Families reading through the narrative of the whole Bible each day at the meal table, and exploring other parts of the Bible at special times of the year like Advent, Easter or on holidays. (UK through *The Bible Narrative and Illustrated*.)

Churches where in worship the Bible is read aloud and everyone including the children is given space in silence to reflect upon it, to ponder it and allow it into the deep recesses of their lives and souls. (Mukti, India)

Courses in theology where students gather to listen to whole stories from the Bible before reflecting on them silently for an hour as a prelude to discussing them reverently together. (Penang, Malaysia)

People in China who have been restricted to one or two pages of the Bible, or to memorising passages, and through them coming to and being sustained in their faith.

Members of a house group discussing how to apply the Bible to parenting, work, neighbourliness, Christian fellowship, mission, and citizenship.

Bible study participants facing up to claims of Christ for the first time.

Student pastors working out the meaning and challenge of radical Christian leadership, where worldly values and priorities are replaced by those of the cross.

The examples could be multiplied, but they have in common a deep respect for the Scriptures, and the power of the Holy Spirit to go between the text of the Scriptures and the text of the life of the hearers. The primary task of the communicator is to get out of the way of the Bible, and certainly not to defend it! It will do its own work if, and only if, it is allowed to speak.

Conclusion

With these threads or perspectives in mind what might we tentatively conclude? In our enthusiasm for a variety of imperatives which may charitably be said to come under the general rubric of "mission" (community development, evangelism, sponsorship, education, health, purpose driven and other methods...) we have probably tended to take the Bible for granted. We (that is the "missioners") all know about that: we have moved on and are now implementing what we believe it inspires us to do. We risk losing God's voice, his challenge and his reformation and recreation in this process. And what we offer to others tends to downgrade the Bible's significance.

How can we counteract this tendency? By presenting the whole Bible in ways that reinforce the sacredness of the text itself. By reshaping life and worship so that reading, listening to and discussing the Bible become more central to all our activities. By having a diet of the whole Bible, rather than being restricted to denominational or personal preferences. And we must always begin at home; the challenge is to us all: how much time is spent reading the Scriptures together and how much do we assume that we know the Bible already?

This handbook is offered as a resource to those around the world, individually or in groups, who wish to study the whole Bible carefully and intelligently in their local and global contexts. It does not seek to direct the reader, but to enable the reader to understand and interpret the text with care.

The Bible Library

The Bible is not one book but a collection of writings by people from many and varied backgrounds: king, priest, shepherd, tent-maker, farmer, doctor, tax-collector, wine-taster, fisherman, prophet, prince .... Each writer was guided by the Holy Spirit of God, yet their individuality and character is still evident.

It is all one story however – about God, who loves his creation so much that he himself paid the price that would restore humanity to fellowship with God. The Old Testament looks forward to, and the New Testament centres on, the life, death and resurrection of God's Son, Jesus Christ.

The purpose of the Bible is to show us who God is, what God is like and what he has done. As we read its words we understand more of what God in his love requires from us.

"All Scripture is God-breathed and is useful for teaching, rebuking, correcting and training in righteousness, so that the man of God may be thoroughly equipped for every good work."
2 Timothy 3:16,17

OLD TESTAMENT

THE LAW

OLD TESTAMENT HISTORY

POETRY AND WISDOM LITERATURE

THE PROPHETS

NEW TESTAMENT

THE LIFE OF JESUS

THE EARLY CHURCH

LETTERS TO EARLY CHRISTIANS

PROPHETIC VISIONS

Genesis Exodus Leviticus Numbers Deuteronomy			The Jewish Torah, or Book of the Law, is really one book divided into five. It spans the beginnings of time through creation, the fall of humanity, the growth of nations, the start of the Jewish nation and God's dealings with them, the giving of laws, and wanderings to the land promised to the new nation.

Joshua   1 Chronicles
Judges   2 Chronicles
Ruth   Ezra
1 Samuel   Nehemiah
2 Samuel   Esther
1 Kings
2 Kings

An account of the entry, conquest and settlement of the Promised Land, how the nation continually turned away from God, eventual division of the land, destruction, exile and return.

Job
Psalms
Proverbs
Ecclesiastes
Song of Songs

Varied styles of writing include drama, poetry, songs, wise sayings and a love poem. Imagery is used to portray emotion from the highest praise to the depths of despair.

Isaiah   Joel   Habakkuk
Jeremiah   Amos   Zephaniah
Lamentations Obadiah   Haggai
Ezekiel   Jonah   Zechariah
Daniel   Micah   Malachi
Hosea   Nahum

A record of prophetic words given by the messengers called by God to speak to his people. Messages of encouragement and warning, sometimes telling of events yet to happen.

Matthew
Mark
Luke
John

Four biographies of the life of Jesus that show us who he is and what he came to do. Written by, and from accounts of, those who were closest to him. They show us that it is possible to know God personally.

Acts

An account of the early days of the church and how the Holy Spirit enabled the good news of God's kingdom to become available to all of God's creation.

Romans   1 Thessalonians   James
1 Corinthians   2 Thessalonians   1 Peter
2 Corinthians   1 Timothy   2 Peter
Galatians   2 Timothy   1 John
Ephesians   Titus   2 John
Philippians   Philemon   3 John
Colossians   Hebrews   Jude

Written by Christian leaders to churches and individuals, to give Christian teaching, correction and encouragement, with lessons and instruction that apply for all time.

Revelation

A unique account of visions given to John, looking to the future end times, to encourage the early Christians and followers of God through the ages.

Understanding the Message

The Bible was written centuries ago over a long period of time by many different people from all walks of life, in a setting different from our own.

When we read a portion of Scripture we should consider:
- the type of writing
- the context it was written in and for
- the reason it was written
- what can it now say to me?

We will discover the joy of reading the Bible:
- if we read while dependent on the Holy Spirit to help us understand it
- if we sincerely want to know more about God and his ways
- if we prayerfully read it to discover its message, rather than primarily as literature or for information
- if we allow our reading to lead us to worship God through prayer and praise and apply what we have learnt, with God's help, to our daily life.

When reading a portion of Scripture we must:
- not take a verse or one part of Scripture out of its context
- not create an opinion based only on one verse or portion – this is the error of cults and those who want to twist the meaning for their own ends
- not think of it as anything other than the word of God – the Scriptures were written by real people in many real situations, under the Holy Spirit's inspiration.

"... these are written that you may believe that Jesus is the Christ, the Son of God, and that by believing you may have life in his name."
John 20:31

OLD TESTAMENT

What am I reading?

"Your word is a lamp to my feet and a light for my path."
Psalm 119:105

NEW TESTAMENT

"Above all, you must understand that no prophecy of Scripture came about by the prophet's own interpretation. For prophecy never had its origin in the will of man, but men spoke from God as they were carried along by the Spirit."
2 Peter 1:20,21

LAW

Genesis–Deuteronomy

A moral law, for all time? Sacrificial or social law? Is there a general principle to consider?

"The unfolding of your words gives light; it gives understanding to the simple."

Psalm 119:130

HISTORY

Joshua–Esther

What was the original setting – what did it mean to the first hearers?

What happened, where? Why is this story here? Is there a lesson for me?

POETRY AND WISDOM

Job–Song of Songs

Poetry is not prose – it is picture language. Allow yourself to enter into the emotion of the words you read.

PROPHECY

Isaiah–Malachi

What is the setting? Is the language symbolic or direct? What response should the passage evoke?

How can I apply the same message to my situation?

HISTORY
Four accounts of the life of Jesus

Matthew–John

The life and teachings of Jesus from four viewpoints. What do I learn about the person of Jesus – how can this affect my life?

HISTORY
The beginning of the church

Acts

What was the original setting – what did it mean to the first hearers?

What was the setting? What can I learn or apply from this?

LETTERS

Romans–Jude

Who wrote, to whom? Why was the letter as a whole written? Can I apply a particular lesson to my situation?

PROPHECY

Revelation

Written in "apocalyptic" style: poetic imagery, giving a foretaste of what is yet to be. What questions are raised?

How the Bible Developed

C. 2000 BC
Oral tradition: Abraham obeys God's call and journeys from Mesopotamia (Iraq) to Canaan. Stories of the patriarchs preserved mainly through storytelling and song.

C. 1300 BC
Moses receives God's instructions on Mt Sinai.

C. 1000 BC
The earliest parts of the Bible, and sources it draws from, believed to be recorded on scrolls.

10th–2nd C BC
Books of the Old Testament compiled from oral tradition, archives, memoirs, genealogies, laws and poetry. Mostly completed by the time of the return from exile around 430 BC.

Mt Sinai in southern Sinai: most probable site of the giving of the Law

A fragment of a papyrus copy of the Gospel of John dated about 130 BC

400 BC
Pentateuch (Genesis–Deuteronomy) established.

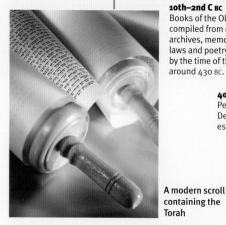

A modern scroll containing the Torah

3rd–2nd C BC
Septuagint started in the time of the Ptolemies (after 285 BC) and completed in 1st C BC. The first and most authoritative of several translations from Hebrew into Greek.

2nd C BC
The Old Testament list of books (canon) established by AD 100.

One of the clay jars that helped preserve the Dead Sea Scrolls

2nd C BC–1st C BC
Dead Sea Scrolls. Preserved by the Qumran community (20 BC–AD 70). Now the oldest surviving Hebrew copies of complete Bible texts. They confirm the accuracy of copies made 1,000 years later.

14th C AD
John Wycliffe and followers translate the complete Bible from Latin into English. Copied by hand and circulated widely. >>>

10th C AD
Masoretes complete a 300-year work on Old Testament Hebrew text to remove ambiguities in meaning – becomes the reference source for future scholars and translators.

John Wycliffe

8th C AD
The Venerable Bede translates most of the Gospels into Anglo-Saxon.

4th C AD
In order to settle disputes St Athanasius compiles a definitive list of New Testament books that is accepted by most churches.

mid-4th C AD
Pope Damascus commissions official church version of the Bible for use in the Latin-speaking Empire. Jerome revises Gospel texts and translates the Old Testament from Hebrew: the Vulgate. Completed in 405.

2nd C AD
The first codex (book form) made – more compact than scrolls.

Hebrew text containing jots and tittles

The Codex Sinaiticus: a 4th C Greek codex

2nd C AD
Many copies of the New Testament texts made and circulated: first in Greek, then other languages as the church spreads.

Jerome, by El Greco

mid-late 1st C AD
The four Gospels, Acts, letters: written, copied and circulated widely. First-hand accounts from those who knew Jesus and his contemporaries.

1st C AD
Letters to churches by Paul and other apostles to give advice and encouragement. Copied, collected together and circulated to the wider Christian community.

Bede, a medieval illustration

How the Bible Developed
(CONTINUED)

A woodcut of 1568 showing Gutenberg's invention of the screw-press in operation

AD 1455
Gutenberg completes the first printed Bible (the Latin Vulgate), using movable type, in Germany

AD 1516
Erasmus brings together the Greek New Testament for printing – accepted as "the received text" and forms the basis of the later King James Version.

AD 1522
Martin Luther produces a translation of the whole Bible from the original languages into everyday German.

Martin Luther

AD 1526
Tyndale's New Testament translated from Hebrew and Greek. Smuggled into England in the face of opposition to a "plain man's" text. Only able to complete a small part of the Old Testament before his betrayal and death at the stake in 1536 for heresy.

Tyndale was burnt at the stake for his actions

AD 1535
The first complete printed Bible in English by Miles Coverdale.

AD 1539
Henry VIII of England commands that a Bible revised by Coverdale should be available in every church building.

Title page of an edition of the Coverdale Bible

AD 1569
Against the Spanish Inquisition ban on Spanish-language Bibles, the de Reina complete Bible is published in Switzerland

AD 1580–1602
Revision of the de Reina text – in 1602 the Reina-Valera Spanish Bible published in Amsterdam because of continued opposition.

The de Reina Bible of 1569

Pandita Ramabai

AD 2000
The Bible, in complete or
partial form, known to be
available in 2,261 languages.

AD 1947
The Dead Sea Scrolls
discovered – they pre-date
other Hebrew manuscripts
by 1,000 years

AD 1922
India – Pandita Ramabai
completes her translation of
the complete Bible from the
original Hebrew and Greek
into Marathi.

Cave 4, Qumran,
where the first of
the Dead Sea
Scrolls were
discovered

20th C AD
Further translations and
revisions as a result of the
discovery of previously
unknown manuscripts and
greater understanding of the
biblical text.

William Carey
and his colleague –
a period engraving of
1853

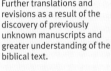

AD 1804
British and Foreign Bible
Society formed to encourage
the spread of the Scriptures
worldwide.

18th C AD
Missionary translation work gathers pace:
India – William Carey and colleagues learn and
translate Scriptures into 45 languages and
dialects.
China – Joshua Marshman and John Lassar
translate and publish complete Bible.
South Africa – Robert Moffatt translates whole
Bible into Setswana.

The pioneer John Eliot preaching
to Algonquin Indians

AD 1663
N America: the Puritan
John Eliot's translation of
the Bible into Algonquin
published for the
indigenous Indians. The
first American printed
Bible.

AD 1604–1611
A new revision of the English Bible
welcomed by James I – completed
and published in 1611. (The King
James Version becomes the most
widely read book in the English
language.)

The Old Testament in its World Setting

EGYPTIAN supremacy

Most older dates are approximate and conjectural; many are disputed.
Dates of individuals indicate their period of influence or power.
Dating for each Bible book indicates the setting in time, not the date of writing.

7000 BC Known settlement in Katal Huyuk, Anatolia
c. 6500 Farming begins
6500 Beginnings of communal living in towns and cities
6000 Farming in N Mesopotamia and Syria
5900 Ubaid culture rises in S Mesopotamia
5500 Mesopotamia: irrigation developed
4800 China: communal culture develops
4500 Ur becomes permanent settlement
4200 Oman, Arabia: copper mining
4000 W Asia: potter's wheel developed; E Asia: silk production
c. 3800 Writing developed
3800 E Asia: jade production
3500 Mesopotamia: the wheel in use; S Asia: rice cultivation
3300 City-states in Syria and Palestine
3200 Bronze in widespread use
3100 Cuneiform writing in Sumer
2700 Gilgamesh, king of Uruk, Sumer
2500 Writing developed: Indus civilisation, W Pakistan, N India
2400 Akkadians rule Mesopotamia
2300 Trading between Indus, Mesopotamia and Arabian Gulf; Sargon of Akkad conquers Sumer, Syria and W Iran
2100 Uruk: ziggurat building; Amorite nomads move into Mesopotamia
2094 Shulgi reigns over all Mesopotamia
2060 Ur sacked by Elamites from the east and Amorites from the west
2004 Elamites take over Sumer
2000 Crete: Minoan palaces built

•c. 2000 Palestine: potter's wheel in use

•Abraham leaves Ur in Mesopotamia

•c. 1800 Troy established as major city

🧍**c. 1790** Hammurabi king of Mesopotamia

•1780 Hammurabi law-code

•c. 1700 Canaanites enter Nile delta

•1700 Hittite Emp Anatolia

•c. 1700 Crete: Minoans develop ea▸ script writir

c. 1650 Hittites settle in Asia Minor

1665 ✕ Hyksos from Asia take control of Egypt

Farmers and hunters, Egypt, c. 1400 BC

🧍**?Isaac**

🧍**?Abraham**

🧍**?Jacob**

🧍**?Joseph**

•Jacob's family settle Egypt

📜 **Genesis**

1301–1234
Pharaoh
Ramesses II
rules Egypt

1365
Ashur-ubalit I of
Assyria

•1200
Farming in S
India

•c. 1600
Aryans enter
India

•1250
Egyptian building
projects: Abu Simbel,
Karnak, Thebes

1150
Nebuchadnezzar I
of Babylon invades
Elam – Susa sacked

•1550
Hyksos
forced out of
Egypt

•1450
Egypt:
sundial in
use

1365
Hittites
conquer
Mittani
kingdom

1300
Assyria and
Elam
threaten
Babylon

esopotamia:
ass-making

c. 1200
The Trojan Wars

reece:
ycenean
vilisation
ourishes

•c. 1500
Sabeans
settle in
Arabia

•1420 +
Hittite
law-codes
written

1334
Egypt: Pharaoh
Tutankhamun

1100 •
Phoenician
city-states

ttites
evelop iron
chnology

•c. 1300
Indus
civilisation
declines

c. 1200
Sea peoples invade
Egypt and Syro-
Palestine

1482
Battle of
Megiddo

1274
Battle of Kadesh –
Ramesses II
of Egypt defeats
King Muwatalli of
Hittites

c. 1200
Assyria conquers
Hittite empire

**•Exodus from
Egypt**

• Jacob's descendants
multiply in Egypt but are
forced into slave labour

Hittite Lion Gate, Hattusha,
Turkey

1240
Jericho falls:
conquest of
Canaan begins

**•Moses
receives the
Law on Mt
Sinai**

Samson

Moses

Joshua

Deborah

Deuteronomy

Gideon

Numbers

Karnak, Temple of Ramesses
II

Leviticus

Exodus

Ruth

Judges

Joshua

ASSYRIAN Supremacy

>>>

CHALDEA
(Babylon

c. 600 •
India:
Mahabharata
epic poem

• **c. 1000**
Phoenician trade
around the
Mediterranean

858–824
Shalmaneser III
of Assyria

• **771**
China
fragments
into smaller
states

• **720**
Egypt
under
Kushite
control

✗ **668**
Assyria
invades
Egypt

563–4
Sidhar
Gauta
(Budd

c1114–1076
Tiglath-pileser I
of Assyria, self-
declared "king of
the world"

883–859
Ashurnasirpal II
of Assyria

705–681
Assyria:
Sennacherib
reigns

✗ **626**
Nabopolas
captures
Babylon

• **1100**
Phoenician
city-states

✗ **880**
Assyria attacks
Levant cities

• **760**
Nubian
kingdom
of Kush
established

• **680**
Babylon:
Ishtar Gate
built

✗ **612**
Medes
Babylo
sack As
cities

✗ **924**
Shishak
invades
Palestine

✗ **729**
Assyria
conquers
Babylon

660
Jimmu
– first
Japanese
emperor

609
✗ Babylo
defeat
Assyri

✗ **732**
Damascus
falls to
Assyria

622 •
Josiah's reforms

✗ **701**
Assyrians
besiege
Lachish

668–630
Assyria:
Ashurbanipal
reigns

✗ **605**
Egypt
taken
Baby

• **928**
Kingdom of
Israel split in
two

• **647**
Babylon
destroyed

✗ **598**
E G
citi
up
Per

✗ **701**
Sennacherib
attacks
Jerusalem

• **c. 966**
First temple
built

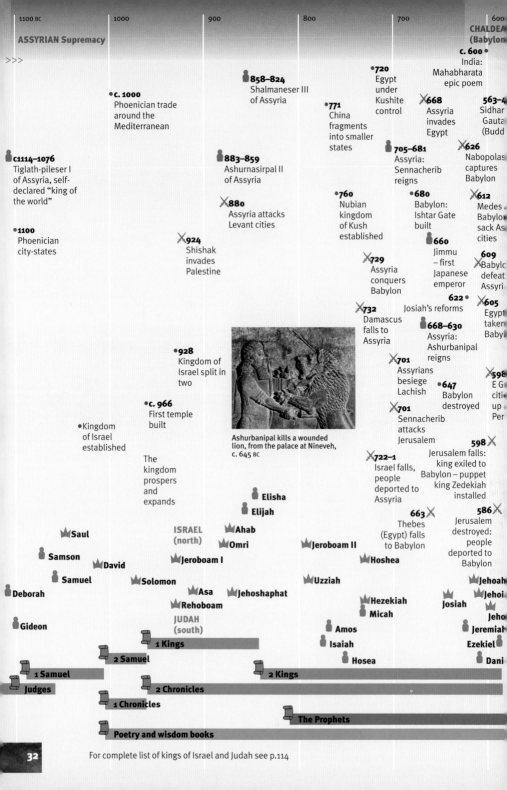

Ashurbanipal kills a wounded
lion, from the palace at Nineveh,
c. 645 BC

598 ✗
Jerusalem falls:
king exiled to
Babylon – puppet
king Zedekiah
installed

• Kingdom
of Israel
established

The
kingdom
prospers
and
expands

✗ **722–1**
Israel falls,
people
deported to
Assyria

663 ✗
Thebes
(Egypt) falls
to Babylon

586 ✗
Jerusalem
destroyed:
people
deported to
Babylon

👑 Saul

👑 Ahab

👑 Jeroboam II

👤 Samson

👑 Omri

👑 Hoshea

ISRAEL
(north)

👑 Jeroboam I

👤 Samuel

👑 David

👤 Deborah

👑 Solomon

👑 Asa

👑 Jehoshaphat

👑 Uzziah

👑 Jehoah

👑 Jehoi

👑 Rehoboam

👑 Hezekiah

👑 Josiah

👑 Micah

👤 Gideon

JUDAH
(south)

👤 Amos

👤 Isaiah

👤 Hosea

Jeho

👤 Jeremiah

👤 Ezekiel

👤 Dani

Elisha

Elijah

📖 1 Kings

📖 2 Samuel

📖 2 Kings

📖 1 Samuel

📖 Judges

📖 2 Chronicles

📖 1 Chronicles

📖 The Prophets

📖 Poetry and wisdom books

For complete list of kings of Israel and Judah see p.114

RSIAN (Achaemid)   **GREEK/SELEUCID**   **ROMAN**

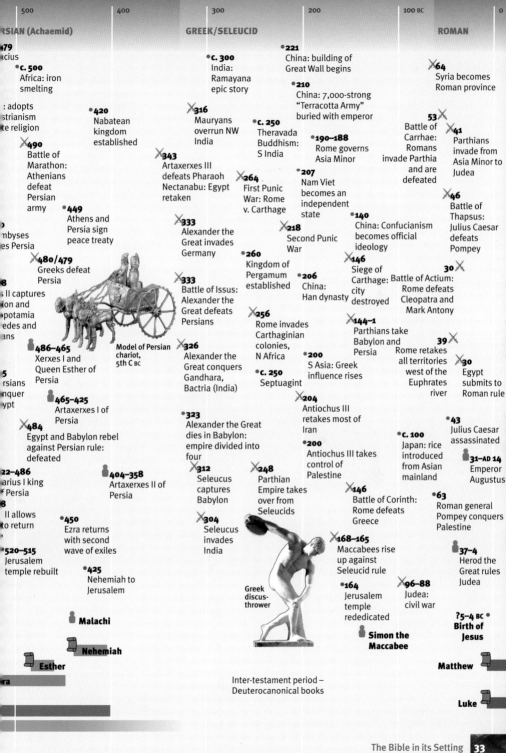

79
cius

c. 500
Africa: iron
smelting

: adopts
strianism
te religion

490
Battle of
Marathon:
Athenians
defeat
Persian
army

449
Athens and
Persia sign
peace treaty

mbyses
es Persia

480/479
Greeks defeat
Persia

ll captures
lon and
potamia
edes and
ans

486–465
Xerxes I and
Queen Esther of
Persia

Model of Persian
chariot,
5th C BC

465–425
Artaxerxes I of
Persia

484
Egypt and Babylon rebel
against Persian rule:
defeated

22–486
arius I king
Persia

ll allows
o return

404–358
Artaxerxes II of
Persia

450
Ezra returns
with second
wave of exiles

520–515
Jerusalem
temple rebuilt

425
Nehemiah to
Jerusalem

420
Nabatean
kingdom
established

316
Mauryans
overrun NW
India

343
Artaxerxes III
defeats Pharaoh
Nectanabu: Egypt
retaken

333
Alexander the
Great invades
Germany

333
Battle of Issus:
Alexander the
Great defeats
Persians

326
Alexander the
Great conquers
Gandhara,
Bactria (India)

323
Alexander the Great
dies in Babylon:
empire divided into
four

312
Seleucus
captures
Babylon

304
Seleucus
invades
India

c. 300
India:
Ramayana
epic story

c. 250
Theravada
Buddhism:
S India

264
First Punic
War: Rome
v. Carthage

260
Kingdom of
Pergamum
established

256
Rome invades
Carthaginian
colonies,
N Africa

c. 250
Septuagint

248
Parthian
Empire takes
over from
Seleucids

221
China: building of
Great Wall begins

210
China: 7,000-strong
"Terracotta Army"
buried with emperor

190–188
Rome governs
Asia Minor

207
Nam Viet
becomes an
independent
state

218
Second Punic
War

206
China:
Han dynasty

200
S Asia: Greek
influence rises

204
Antiochus III
retakes most of
Iran

200
Antiochus III takes
control of
Palestine

140
China: Confucianism
becomes official
ideology

146
Siege of
Carthage:
city
destroyed

144–1
Parthians take
Babylon and
Persia

146
Battle of Corinth:
Rome defeats
Greece

168–165
Maccabees rise
up against
Seleucid rule

164
Jerusalem
temple
rededicated

c. 100
Japan: rice
introduced
from Asian
mainland

96–88
Judea:
civil war

64
Syria becomes
Roman province

53
Battle of
Carrhae:
Romans
invade Parthia
and are
defeated

41
Parthians
invade from
Asia Minor to
Judea

46
Battle of
Thapsus:
Julius Caesar
defeats
Pompey

30
Battle of Actium:
Rome defeats
Cleopatra and
Mark Antony

39
Rome retakes
all territories
west of the
Euphrates
river

30
Egypt
submits to
Roman rule

43
Julius Caesar
assassinated

31–AD 14
Emperor
Augustus

63
Roman general
Pompey conquers
Palestine

37–4
Herod the
Great rules
Judea

?5–4 BC
Birth of
Jesus

Malachi

Nehemiah

Esther

ra

Greek
discus-
thrower

**Simon the
Maccabee**

Inter-testament period –
Deuterocanonical books

Matthew

Luke

The World of the Old Testament

Black Sea

Adriatic Sea

Rome • ITALY

MACEDONIA

THRACIA

PONTUS

LYDIA

• Hattusha

Aegean Sea

PHRYGIA

CAPPADOCIA

ACHAIA

CILICIA

SICILY

• Athens

Taurus Mountains

Haran
Genesis 12

• Sparta

CARIA

R.
Eup.

CAPHTOR

KITTIM

The Great Sea
(Mediterranean Sea)

ARAM

• Damascus
Isaiah 7

• Cyrene

CANAAN
Jerusalem •
2 Samuel 6

• Jericho
Joshua 6

PUT

Alexandria

• Rameses
Exodus 1

KEDAR

LIBYA

• Memphis

Sinai
Exodus 19–20

MIDIAN

DEDAN

EGYPT

River Nile

Red Sea

• Thebes

Country, regional and place names changed constantly
because of the rise and fall of dominant powers.
The map shows selective place names to aid
identification with various biblical accounts.

• Abu Simbel

ETHIOPIA
(CUSH)

0   100   200 miles

0   100   200 kilometres

SCYTHIA

Caspian
Sea

SCYTHIA

Caucasus
Mountains

RMENIA

AT
TU) Ararat
Genesis 8

Kara
Kum

MEDIA

PARTHIA

Nineveh
Jonah
Asshur

Ecbatana

River
Tigris

Zagros
Mountains

BABYLONIA

ELAM
(PERSIA)

Babylon
Genesis 10

Susa
Nehemiah 1

Ur
Genesis 10

ian
ert

Lower
Sea

Erythraean
Sea

OKTAN

River
Indus

INDIA

GANDHARA

Arabian
Sea

HAZARMAVETH

SHEBA

Inset map:

0   10   20 miles

0   10   20 kilometres

Mt
Hermon

Tyre

Laish
(Dan)

Kedesh

Misrephoth-maim

Hazor

Merom

Acco

Aphek   Chinnereth

Sea of
Chinnereth

The
Great Sea

Mt
Carmel

R Kishon

BASHAN

Shunem

Dor

Megiddo

Taanach

Beth-shean

Migdal

Dothan

Socoh

Tirzah

Jabesh
Gilead

Mt Ebal

Shechem

Succoth

Mt
Gerizim

Penuel

Joppa

Aphek

Shiloh

Gath

Beth-
horon

Bethel

Gezer

Jericho

Gilgal

Shittim

Ekron

Aijalon

Gibeon

Makkedah

Kiriath
Jearim

Jerusalem

Mt
Nebo

Ashdod

Beth-
jeshimoth

Libnah

Bethlehem

Ashkelon

Adullam

Ataroth

Eglon

Lachish

Kiriathaim

Gaza

Debir

Hebron

Salt Sea
(Sea
of the
Arabah)

HILL
COUNTRY

R Arnon

Beersheba

CANAAN

THE
NEGEV

Hormah

MOAB

CANAAN

PLAIN OF SHARON

THE ARABAH

AMORITES

THE SHEPHELAH

River Jordan

R Jordan

Between the Testaments: the Struggle for Power

Alexandria, Egypt: Scriptures translated from Hebrew into Greek for the benefit of Greek-speaking Jews. (The Septuagint)

Antiochus IV Epiphanes

Alexander the Great at the Battle of Issus

PERSIAN EMPIRE

350 BC

ALEXANDER

THE PTOLEMIES

300 BC

200 BC

SELEUCID CONTROL

223–187 BC
Antiochus III: a time of some freedom for the Jews

323 BC
Alexander dies: empire divided into four. Judea ruled by Ptolemies (Egypt)

331 BC
Battle of Gaugamela, Iraq: Alexander crushes the Persians. Greek political and cultural domination

333 BC
Battle of Issus, NE Syria: Alexander the Great of Macedonia defeats Darius III of Persia

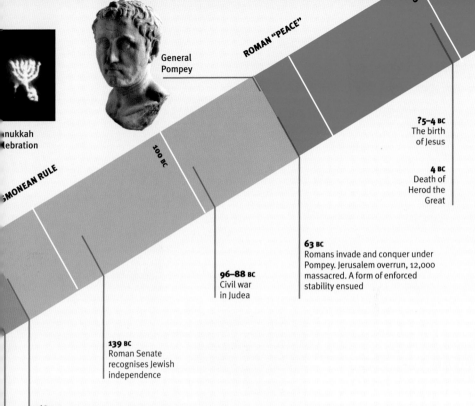

General
Pompey

ROMAN "PEACE"

?5–4 BC
The birth
of Jesus

nukkah
ebration

100 BC

4 BC
Death of
Herod the
Great

MONEAN RULE

63 BC
Romans invade and conquer under
Pompey. Jerusalem overrun, 12,000
massacred. A form of enforced
stability ensued

96–88 BC
Civil war
in Judea

139 BC
Roman Senate
recognises Jewish
independence

168 BC
The Maccabean revolt – Jewish uprising
sparked by Mattathias, led by Judas.
Seleucid army defeated. Temple
restored to proper use. Hasmonean
rule. Hanukkah (Festival of Lights)
inaugurated

175–164 BC
Antiochus IV Epiphanes
subjugates the Jews. Jerusalem
temple ransacked, profane
worship. Judea Hellenised.

98 BC
Battle of Paneon: Antiochus III
defeats General Scopus (Ptolemy).
Seleucids (Greeks) take control of
he Empire

THE DEUTEROCANONICAL BOOKS

Christian Bibles include the 39 books of the Hebrew
Scriptures. Some also contain the Apocrypha, or
Deuterocanonical books. These were never part of the
Hebrew canon but were introduced when the Scriptures
were translated by Jewish scholars into Greek – the
Septuagint – and other ancient versions. Most were Greek
in origin.

Some of the apocryphal books tell the story of the
Jewish nation in the intertestamental period, or add to the
accounts in other Bible books. Others are designed to
encourage faithful observance of religious duty. Some
contain wisdom literature similar to Proverbs.

The New Testament in its World Setting

ROMAN domination

Many dates are approximate and conjectural; some are disputed.
Dates of individuals indicate their period of influence or power.
Dating for each Bible book indicates its setting in time, not the date of writing.

✕41
Parthians invade from Asia Minor to Judea

✕30
Battle of Actium: Octavian defeats Mark Antony and Cleopatra: Egypt submits to Roman rule

✕17
Rome invades Germany

✕36
Rome attacks Mesopotamia: forced to retreat

✕18
Roman conquest of Hispania

•c. 1
Mexico: hieroglyphic writing in use by Mayans

c. 33•
Christianity introduced into Egypt

The River Jordan at Bethany beyond Jordan, supposed site of Jesus' baptism

•6
Quirinius orders tax census

37
Emperor Ga (Calig

26–36
Pontius Pilat procurator ov Judea

•43
Julius Caesar assassinated

•19
Building of Herod's temple commences

•6
Samaria & Judea become Roman provinces

C. 27–AD 14
Emperor Augustus

14–37
Emperor Tiberius

•Step marty

37–4
Herod the Great rules Judea

4 BC–AD 39
Herod Antipas rules Judea

33•
Conversion of Saul (Paul)

18–37
Caiaphas high priest

4 BC–AD 6
Archelaus governs Judea

• Jesus is baptised

?5–4 BC
Birth of Jesus

Jesus'•
death and resurrection;
Pentecost

Acts

Mark

Matthew

John

Luke

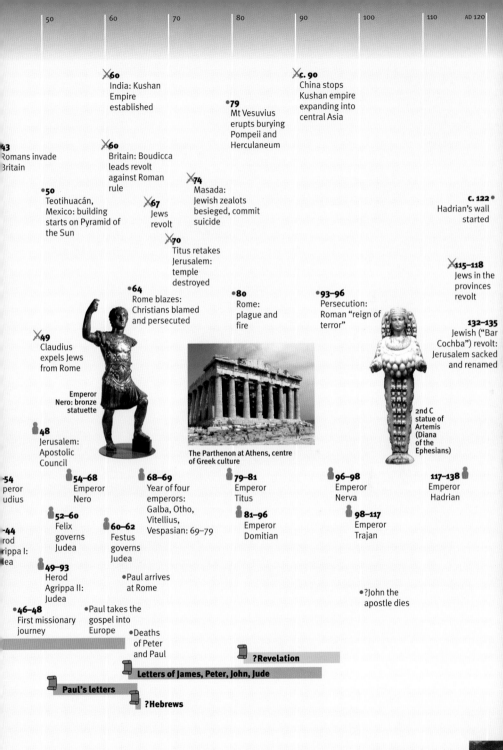

×60
India: Kushan Empire established

•79
Mt Vesuvius erupts burying Pompeii and Herculaneum

×c. 90
China stops Kushan empire expanding into central Asia

43
Romans invade Britain

×60
Britain: Boudicca leads revolt against Roman rule

×74
Masada: Jewish zealots besieged, commit suicide

•50
Teotihuacán, Mexico: building starts on Pyramid of the Sun

×67
Jews revolt

c. 122 •
Hadrian's wall started

×70
Titus retakes Jerusalem: temple destroyed

•64
Rome blazes: Christians blamed and persecuted

•80
Rome: plague and fire

•93–96
Persecution: Roman "reign of terror"

×115–118
Jews in the provinces revolt

×49
Claudius expels Jews from Rome

132–135
Jewish ("Bar Cochba") revolt: Jerusalem sacked and renamed

Emperor Nero: bronze statuette

2nd C statue of Artemis (Diana of the Ephesians)

48
Jerusalem: Apostolic Council

The Parthenon at Athens, centre of Greek culture

-54
peror udius

54–68
Emperor Nero

68–69
Year of four emperors: Galba, Otho, Vitellius, Vespasian: 69–79

79–81
Emperor Titus

96–98
Emperor Nerva

117–138
Emperor Hadrian

52–60
Felix governs Judea

60–62
Festus governs Judea

81–96
Emperor Domitian

98–117
Emperor Trajan

-44
rod rippa I: lea

49–93
Herod Agrippa II: Judea

•Paul arrives at Rome

•?John the apostle dies

•46–48
First missionary journey

•Paul takes the gospel into Europe

•Deaths of Peter and Paul

?Revelation

Letters of James, Peter, John, Jude

Paul's letters

?Hebrews

The World of the New Testament

BRITANNIA

BELGICA

GERMANIA

NORICUM

RHACTIA

GAUL

PANNONIA

Genua

NARBONENSIS

ILLYRICUM

Sea of
Adria

CORSICA

Rome ● ITALIA

Appian Way

Puteoli

Brundis

HISPANIA

SARDINIA

Tyrrhenean
Sea

Sea
Adr

Rhegium

SICILIA

Syracuse

Malaca

Carthage

MALTA

The Great Sea
(Mediterranean S

AFRICA

NUMIDIA

(Lesser
Syrtis)

Atlas
Mountains

Lepsis Magna

TRIPOLITANIA

(Grea
Syrti

By the time of the birth of Jesus the Roman empire had all
but conquered the "known world" and a time of uncertain
peace ensued – the *pax Romana*. Judea was at this time a client
kingdom of Rome – allowed a modest level of independence.
The road-building programmes that the Romans introduced
made travel easier, aiding the spread of the good news of the
kingdom.

Sahara Desert

Roman empire at AD 14, at the death
of Emperor Augustus

Later expansion

0   100   200 miles

0   100   200 kilometres

SARMATIA

SCYTHIA

DACIA

BOSPORAN KINGDOM

MOESIA

*Euxine Sea
(Black Sea)*

*Caspian
Sea*

THRACE

COLCHIS

*Caucasus
Mountains*

NIA

Philippi

Byzantium

PONTUS

Egnatian Way

Thessalonica

BITHYNIA

ARMENIA

SALY

Troas

MYSIA

A   S   I   A   M   I   N   O   R

*Aegean
Sea*

Pergamum

PHRYGIA

is

LYDIA

GALATIA

Athens

Ephesus

CAPPADOCIA

Corinth

*Aegean
Sea*

CARIA

PISIDIA

LYCAONIA

Lystra

MESOPOTAMIA

MEDIA

Miletus

LYCIA

PAMPHYLIA

CILICIA

Tarsus

CRETE

Antioch

*Fair
Havens*

CYPRUS

Salamis

SYRIA

Paphos

Dura-Europus

*River
Euphrates*

*River
Tigris*

rene

PHOENICIA

ICA

Tyre

Damascus

JUDEA

Jericho

Jerusalem

Babylon

Alexandria

NABATAEA

*Arabian
Desert*

LIBYA

Petra

Memphis

A   R   A   B   I   A

*Persian
Gulf*

E   G   Y   P   T

River Nile

Thebes

*Red
Sea*

ETHIOPIA
(CUSH)

Festivals and Feasts

	Time	Description	Reason	Bible reference
Sabbath	7th day of the week	Day of rest, no work	Rest for people and livestock	Ex 20:8-11
Sabbath year	Every 7th year	Year of rest, fields left fallow	Rest for the land, help for the poor, debts cancelled	Ex 23:10-11 Dt 15:1-6
Year of Jubilee	Every 50th year	Debts cancelled, slaves liberated, land returned to its rightful owner	Help for the poor, social stability, rest for the land	Lev 25:8-55
Passover	14 Abib (1st month)	Slaying and eating a lamb with bitter herbs and bread without yeast, in each household	To remember the sparing of Israel's firstborn and the nation's deliverance from Egypt	Dt 16:1-7
Unleavened Bread	15–21 Abib (1st month)	Eating bread without yeast, assemblies, offerings	To remember how the Lord brought out Israel from Egypt in haste	Ex 12:15-20; 13:3-10; 23:15
Firstfruits	16 Abib (1st month) A wave	offering of a sheaf from the first of the barley harvest, a burnt offering and a grain offering	To recognise God's provision	Lev 23:9-14
Weeks (Pentecost/ Harvest)	6 Sivan (3rd month)	A time of joy. Freewill and compulsory offerings, including the firstfruits of the wheat harvest	To joyfully give thanks for God's blessing in the harvest	Ex 23:16
Trumpets (Rosh Hashanah/ New Year)	1 Ethanim (7th month)	Assembly on a day of rest, marked by trumpet blasts and sacrifices	To present all Israel as a people before the Lord	Lev 23:23-25
Day of Atonement (Yom Kippur)	10 Ethanim (7th month)	Day of rest, fasting, sacrifices of atonement for priests and people	To cleanse people and priests from their sin and to purify the Holy Place	Lev 16; 23:26-32

Observing feasts and festivals is an important part of Hebrew religion. They were viewed as gifts from God regulating the people's communal life as God's people and have preserved the memories of God's interaction with his people throughout their history, especially in terms of his miraculous deliverance or his daily provision for their physical and spiritual needs.

Times of joy: children dressed up for Purim celebration; gathering firstfruits of wheat for the Festival of Weeks

	Time	Description	Reason	Bible reference
Tabernacles (Booths/ Ingathering)	15–21 Ethanim (7th month)	Week of celebration for harvest, building and living in temporary shelters, offering sacrifices	To remember the journey to the Promised Land and to give thanks for the bounty of Canaan	Ex 23:16
Sacred Assembly	22 Ethanim (7th month)	A day of gathering together, rest and sacrifices	To close the cycle of feasts	Lev 23:36; Nu 29:35-38
Hanukkah (Dedication/ Festival of Lights)	25 Kislev (9th month)	Family celebration of lighting of oil or candles in a 9-branched menorah	To celebrate the rededication of the temple and altar by the Maccabees	(Referred to in Jn 10:22)
Purim	14, 15 Adar (12th month)	Day of happiness, feasting and giving presents	To remember the preservation of the Jews under Persian rule in the time of Queen Esther	Est 9:18-32
		The first day of each month was designated as new moon, and was celebrated with sounding of trumpets and festivity		Nu 10:10; 1 Sa 20:5

The Calendar Year

The Jewish calendar, as in all early civilisations, grew out of the agricultural cycle and the phases of the moon. Religious rites and festivals were associated with both the farmer's year and commemoration of the great events in Jewish history.

In order that the lunar calendar would relate to the solar year an extra month (Second Adar) was added about every three years.

A limestone "notepad" found at Gezer in central Israel shows the calendar inscribed in Hebrew. Dated at around 900 BC, it is known as the "Gezer Calendar"

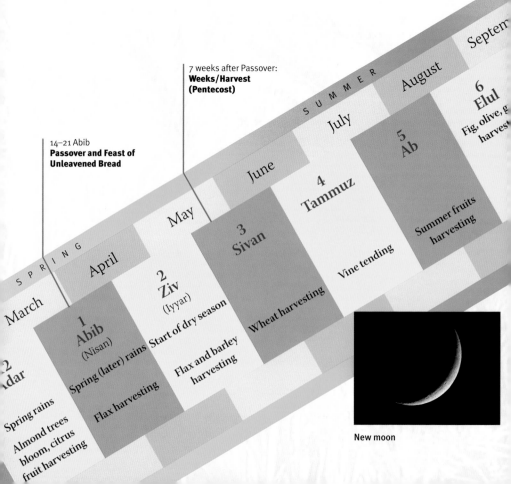

7 weeks after Passover:
**Weeks/Harvest
(Pentecost)**

14–21 Abib
**Passover and Feast of
Unleavened Bread**

September

6
Elul
Fig, olive, g
harvest

SUMMER

July

August

5
Ab

June

4
Tammuz

Summer fruits
harvesting

May

3
Sivan

Vine tending

SPRING

April

2
Ziv
(Iyyar)

Wheat harvesting

March

1
Abib
(Nisan)

Start of dry season

Flax and barley
harvesting

2
Adar

Spring (later) rains

Flax harvesting

Spring rains

Almond trees
bloom, citrus
fruit harvesting

New moon

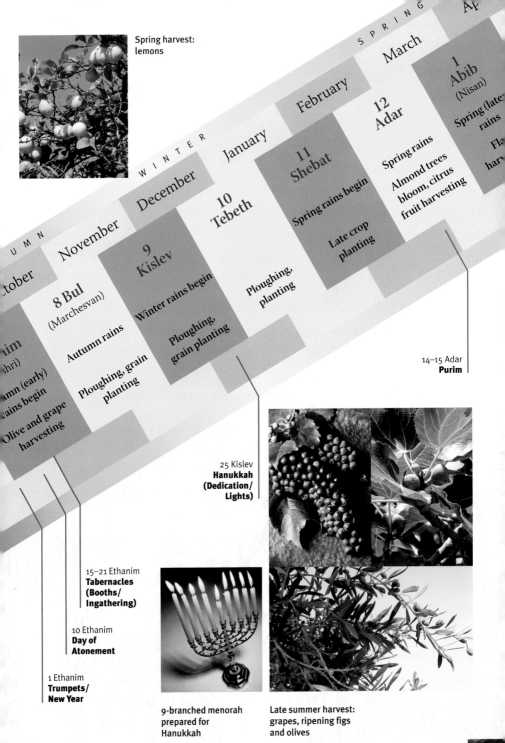

Spring harvest:
lemons

SPRING

March

February

1
Abib
(Nisan)

12
Adar

Spring (late)
rains

WINTER

January

11
Shebat

Spring rains

Almond trees
bloom, citrus
fruit harvesting

Fla
harv

December

10
Tebeth

Spring rains begin

Late crop
planting

Spring rains begin

...UMN

November

9
Kislev

Winter rains begin

Ploughing,
planting

Octob er

8 Bul
(Marchesvan)

Autumn rains

Ploughing,
grain planting

Ploughing,
grain planting

...im
...shri)

...mn (early)
...ins begin

Ploughing, grain
planting

Olive and grape
harvesting

14–15 Adar
Purim

25 Kislev
**Hanukkah
(Dedication/
Lights)**

15–21 Ethanim
**Tabernacles
(Booths/
Ingathering)**

10 Ethanim
**Day of
Atonement**

1 Ethanim
**Trumpets/
New Year**

9-branched menorah
prepared for
Hanukkah

Late summer harvest:
grapes, ripening figs
and olives

Sacrifice

Sacrifice and offering in the Old Testament

Sacrifice and offering are woven into the fabric of the Jewish way of life. Rules for sacrifice were given to Moses by God himself, with provision for all aspects of life. Each sacrifice was to be carried out in a specified way outlined in Leviticus 1–7. But the annual sacrifice of the Day of Atonement (16:1-34) reminds us that none of these sacrifices could ever atone for sin (only unintentional sin was provided for; there was no sacrifice for deliberate sin). The New Testament sees this as anticipating Christ's sacrifice, which alone can do away with all sin (Hebrews 9:1–10:14).

In the New Testament

All the writers in the New Testament stress the significance of Jesus' death as superseding the sacrifices of the Old Testament. As God's perfect high priest, Jesus Christ himself became the perfect sacrifice – one offering for sin, valid for all time. Human sin is atoned for once and for all. The former system could not do this. His sacrifice has made the way open for people to come to God – no further sacrifice is required.

Israelite practice and observance was distinct from that of the nations around them because:

- Jews believed in one God;
- people were to seek to live pure lives in obedience to God's law and to respect others;
- repentance and atonement were necessary because sin created separation between God and humanity;
- practices of magic and sorcery were forbidden;
- there was to be no human sacrifice, sexual deviation or frenzied activity.

In Jesus' time sheep from the Shepherds' Fields at Bethlehem were used for ritual sacrifice in the temple at Jerusalem

Each year on Mount Gerizim the Samaritans still publicly sacrifice a Passover lamb

	Description	Purpose	Bible reference
Burnt offering	A bull, ram or male bird, without defect, or for the poor a dove or young pigeon. (The only offering where the whole animal was consumed)	A freewill act of worship, an atonement for unintentional sin, a token of devotion and dedication to God	Lev 1; 6:8-13
Cereal or grain offering	Grain, fine flour, olive oil, incense, baked bread, salt, often offered with a burnt or peace offering	A freewill act of worship recognising God's goodness and provision	Lev 2; 6:14-18
Peace or fellowship offering	An animal from the herd or flock, without defect	A freewill act of worship to re-establish fellowship with God or others, or a thank offering. Accompanied by a communal meal	Lev 3; 7:11-36
Sin offering	Either a young bull (for the high priest and gathering); a male goat (for a senior figure); a female goat or lamb (for a commoner); a dove or pigeon (for the poor); a tenth of an ephah of fine flour (for the destitute)	A requirement to obtain forgiveness for unintended sin, to be accompanied by confession; and for cleansing from defilement	Lev 4:1–5:13; 6:24-30
Guilt or repayment offering	A ram or a lamb	A requirement for atonement for unintended sin needing restitution: to be accompanied by making good the wrong and paying a fine	Lev 5:14–6:7; 7:1-10
The Day of Atonement	Once each year, on the 10th day of Ethanim, the high priest was allowed into the Most Holy Place, where the ark of the covenant was. He was to obtain forgiveness and cleansing for his own sin, then offer on behalf of the sins of the nation. A bull and a goat would be sacrificed, while another goat would have the sins of the people confessed over it and then released in the desert		Lev 16; Heb 9–10

Covenants

A covenant is a binding promise; it cannot be broken and stands for all time.

Covenants were the basis of all forms of relationship in the ancient Near East, covering both personal and commercial life. It was natural that God's relationship to his people should be seen in the same terms.

Although they could be made between equals, the strength of some covenants lies in the ability of the dominant partner to fulfil their obligation to the benefit of the other partner. A covenant has been compared to a treaty made between a king and his subject.

God chose to reach out to humanity first through Noah and to Abraham, offering unconditional promises. The promise to Noah was sealed by the placing of the rainbow in the sky. Abraham's agreement was sealed through the act of circumcision.

However, agreements carry responsibilities and, while God promised blessing and security, this was conditional upon the Jewish nation keeping their part of the agreement.

The most significant covenant took place on Mount Sinai, when God called the nation of Israel to be holy and dedicated solely to him, promising particular blessing as they obeyed.

TYPES OF COVENANT

Royal
Without conditions.
A king grants benefits to a loyal, faithful servant on account of exceptional service. Perpetual, unconditional: heirs benefit only as long as they continue to be loyal.

Equal (Parity)
Between equals – cementing mutual friendship or respect.

Conditional
Regulating relationship between master or king and his subjects.
Demands total loyalty, subservience, pledge of protection of realm/dynasty. Cemented by act of dependence/obedience.

Established in the Old Testament between God and his people

Noah
Never again would a flood destroy earth; seasons in their time
Ge 9:8-17

Abraham
Land preserved for future generations
Ge 15:4-21
Descendants uncountable, like the stars
Ge 15:5; 17:4-8

Moses
Commitment to Israel as his chosen people
Ex 19–24

Phinehas
Priestly line established through him alone
Nu 25:10-13

David
Kingly line established through David's house for ever
2Sa 7:5-16

New
Promise of a new covenant to come: an inward change, where God's law becomes internal, the knowledge of God dwells within and God will pardon sin by his grace
Jer 31:31–34

Fulfilled in the New Testament

Jesus
Jesus seals the new covenant through his blood
Mt 26:28; Heb 8:8-12

God promised Abraham that his descendants would be uncountable, like the stars

The Sinai desert was the unpromising setting for God's meeting with Moses

Main picture: The rainbow is a permanent reminder to all humanity of God's promise through Noah that he would never again destroy the earth through flood

The Tabernacle

After the people of Israel had come out of Egypt and the terms of covenant had been laid down, God gave instructions for a tent to be built. There God would make a home with them and would guide and watch over them at all times. Prefabricated portable shrines were known in Egypt even before this time, and training and trades learnt in Egypt would have been used in its construction.

The instructions in the Bible are detailed but not a complete blueprint, leading to dispute on the actual appearance. Carrying-poles were used to transport the various elements when the nation was on the move.

Materials for crafting and decoration were given willingly by the people. Acacia wood, local to the Sinai desert, was used in its construction, and the Israeli herds provided animal skins and hides for the coverings. The most skilled craftspeople were used, creating a place of great beauty. Bezalel and Oholiab were chosen by God and given special abilities for the task and to teach others.

The site was surrounded by an outer wall, separating the people from the courtyard area.

On the day the tabernacle was completed, as the people looked on, the Lord in his glory came and filled the tabernacle. The cloud that settled over the Tent of Meeting showed everyone that God had indeed come to dwell with them. From then on the cloud by day, and fire in the cloud by night, became the visible presence of God and the nation's guide through the desert.

Ex 25:1–31:11; 35:4–40:38

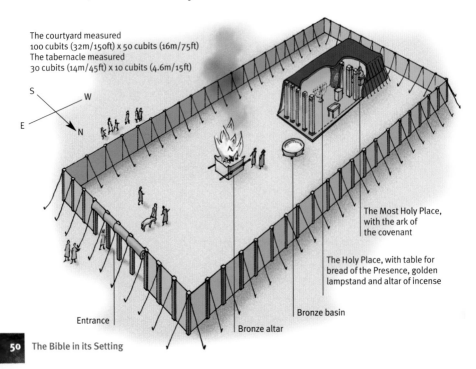

The courtyard measured
100 cubits (32m/150ft) x 50 cubits (16m/75ft)
The tabernacle measured
30 cubits (14m/45ft) x 10 cubits (4.6m/15ft)

S
W
E
N

The Most Holy Place, with the ark of the covenant

The Holy Place, with table for bread of the Presence, golden lampstand and altar of incense

Bronze basin

Entrance

Bronze altar

The Tabernacle Furnishings

When the people settled, the tabernacle was set up at the centre of the encampment. There were specific instructions for the positioning of the people in their tribal communities around the tabernacle area. Nu 2

The main elements within the tabernacle

- The Most Holy Place contained the ark of the covenant, which held the tablets of the law and Aaron's rod that budded;
- The Holy Place held the gold-covered table on which the bread of the Presence, the golden lampstand and the altar of incense were placed;
- The courtyard held the bronze altar of burnt offering and the basin.

There was nowhere for the priests to sit, signifying that their work could never be completed. Heb 10:11-12

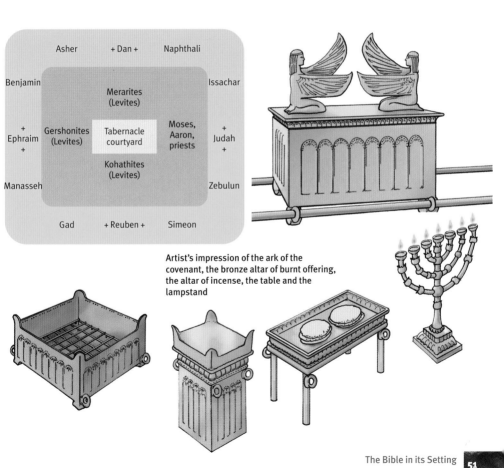

	Asher	+ Dan +	Naphtali	
Benjamin		Merarites (Levites)		Issachar
+ Ephraim +	Gershonites (Levites)	Tabernacle courtyard	Moses, Aaron, priests	+ Judah +
Manasseh		Kohathites (Levites)		Zebulun
	Gad	+ Reuben +	Simeon	

Artist's impression of the ark of the covenant, the bronze altar of burnt offering, the altar of incense, the table and the lampstand

A House for God

Once the nation had settled in the Promised Land and tribal areas had been established, the focal point of worship became Shiloh, where a permanent tent was erected. David wanted to build a permanent house for God's presence in his capital Jerusalem, but because of his warlike lifestyle he was forbidden, the temple being built in peacetime by his son Solomon. The pattern and layout of furniture echoed the style set for the original tabernacle.

Solomon's temple was destroyed by the Babylonians and partially rebuilt under Zerubbabel after the return from exile.

During the intertestamental period the temple fell more and more into disrepair. In 20 BC Herod the Great started a programme of rebuilding in Jerusalem that had as its centrepiece a new temple. This was the temple that Jesus visited. The whole site was completed in AD 64 but destroyed just three years later in the Roman destruction of Jerusalem.

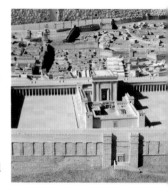

Solomon's temple. The colonnaded outer courtyard held an enormous altar for burnt offerings and a large cast metal basin, or Sea, that was supported by 12 metal bulls

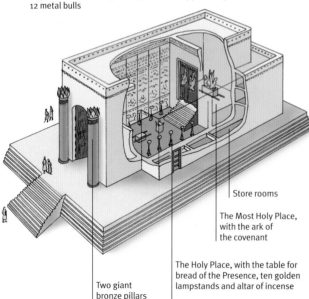

Scale model of Herod's temple, as viewed from the Mount of Olives; frieze from the Arch of Titus in Rome, showing the removal of the sacred objects from the temple after the sacking of Jerusalem

Store rooms

The Most Holy Place, with the ark of the covenant

The Holy Place, with the table for bread of the Presence, ten golden lampstands and altar of incense

Two giant bronze pillars

Images similar to this Phoenician ivory may well have been used as part of the decoration of Solomon's temple

Money and Values

The exchange of goods gradually gave way from around the 7th C BC to the exchange of precious metals by weight, then much later to coinage that represented weight and worth. There was no constant standard, and values varied according to time, place and personal honesty. International trade brought a degree of understanding of values across cultures. Some coinage bore the mark or seal of the local overlord.

In New Testament times, Roman standards took hold, although money-changers in Israel did a brisk business due to the circulation of Roman, Greek and local currencies.

Old Testament values
(Measured by weight which eventually related to value)

	Approx weight	
Shekel	11.5g	(50 shekels = 1 mina)
Mina	500g	(60 minas = 1 talent)
Talent	30kg	

There was a silver standard and a gold standard for the wealthy

New Testament values in Israel
Showing comparative values across the currencies, approximate

Roman	Greek	Jewish
		Lepton
Quadrans		= 2 lepta
As		= 4 lepta
4 asses (= 1 sestertius)		
Denarius (= 16 asses)	Drachma	
2 denarii =	Didrachma (2 drachmae)	Half-shekel
4 denarii =	Stater/tetradrachma	Shekel
Aureus (gold)	(25 drachmae)	
100 denarii =	Mina*	= 30 shekels
240 aurei =	Talent* (60 minas)	

*An amount of money, not a coin

Money was minted in brass, copper, silver and gold.
A lepton was the widow's offering: Mk 12:42
One as was the value of two sparrows: Mt 10:29
A denarius was a day's wages: Mt 20:9,10
A half-shekel was the standard temple-tax: Mt 17:24

Silver shekel of Darius 1, Persian, c. 500 BC; Roman copper quadrans, c. 230 BC; legionary denarius of Marc Antony, 32 BC; Jewish copper lepton (a "widow's offering"); Jewish half-shekel; tetradrachmae from Antioch, Syria, showing the busts of Nero c. AD 68 and Claudius c. AD 52

Weights and Measures

Most transaction in ancient times would have been by exchange of goods. For paying in silver, scales and weights were used. These had to be standardised, although the system was open to abuse by the unscrupulous. Many weights were formed into shapes and marked.

Measures were used for selling and storage of harvest produce and liquids. A fair and full measure of grain was said to be "running over".

All equivalents shown are approximate.

Liquid container, Egyptian, holding a hin

Amphorae, discovered near Athens, dated c. 500 BC

WEIGHT

Old Testament
Gerah (0.6g)
Bekah (6g)
Shekel (11g)
Royal shekel (13g)
Mina (600g)
Talent (34kg)
Double standard talent (60kg)

New Testament
Litra/pound (327g)
Talent (20–40kg)

DRY MEASURES

Old Testament
Log (0.3 litres)
Kab (1.2 litres)
Omer (2.2 litres)
Seah (7.3 litres)
Ephah (22 litres)
Lethek (110 litres)
Cor, Homer (220 litres)

LIQUID MEASURES

Old Testament
Log (0.3 litres)
Kab (1.2 litres)
Hin (4 litres)
Bath (22 litres)

Duck-shaped basalt weight from Mesopotamia, c. 1000 BC. Part of a set of standardised weights

Bronze lion-weight from Nimrud. Assyrian, inscribed with the king's name

Length and Distance

A Finger/digit (19mm/0.75in)

B Palm/handbreadth (8cm/3in)

C Span (23cm/9in), equivalent to half a cubit

Old Testament cubit measured from elbow to fingertips (44.5cm/17.5in)

The long cubit added a handbreadth (52cm/20.4in)

A New Testament cubit measured (55cm/21.6in)

A fathom/orygia was the width of the outstretched arms (1.85m/6ft)

The New Testament stadion/furlong was 185m/202yds

The New Testament milion (mile) of 1,000 paces by Roman measure was 1,478m/1,618yds

Jewish law permitted travel on the sabbath day to be a maximum of 2,000 cubits (914m/1,000yds)

Because of the extensive influence of the Mesopotamian culture, Hebrew measurements were based from very early times on the Babylonian system. Original measures came from the human body: finger, hand, arm, span, foot. Some sculptures inscribed with scales have been found: these provided a standard to overcome the problem of difference in individuals.

After Roman occupation, Graeco-Roman measures were introduced, bringing in the milion and stadion.

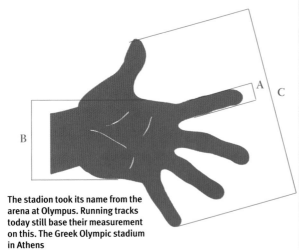

The stadion took its name from the arena at Olympus. Running tracks today still base their measurement on this. The Greek Olympic stadium in Athens

Measuring a field. Scene from a tomb in the Valley of the Kings, Egypt, c. 1500 BC

passed the city, going about
once; and they came into the
mp; and lodged in the camp.
And Joshua rose early in
morning, and the priests
k up the ark of the LORD.
And seven priests bearing
ore the ark of the LORD went
continually, and blew with
trumpets: and the armed
n went before them; but the
eward came after the ark of
LORD, *the priests going on,*
blowing with the trumpets.
And the second day they
passed the city once, and
urned into the camp: so they
six days.
And it came to pass on
seventh day, that they rose
ly about the dawning of the
, and compassed the city
r the same manner seven
es: only on that day they
passed the city seven times.
And it came to pass at the
th time, when the priests
w with the trumpets, Joshua
d to the people, Shout; for

b He. 11. 30.
1 Heb.,
under it.

b Nu. 4. 15.
c Deu. 7. 2.

shouted with a great shout, that
the wall fell down flat, so that
the people went up into the
city, every man straight before
him, and they took the city.
21 And they utterly destroyed
all that was in the city, both
man and woman, young and
old, and ox, and sheep, and ass,
with the edge of the sword.
22 But Joshua had said unto
the two men that had spied out
the country, Go into the har-
lot's house, and bring out thence
the woman, and all that she
hath, as ye sware unto her.
23 And the young men that
were spies went in, and brought
out Rahab, and her father, and
her mother, and her brethren,
and all that she had; and the
brought out all her kindred, a
left them without the camp

and they burnt the c
th fire, and all that
therein: only the silver,
the gold, and the vessels
of brass and of iron, they put
... of the house of the
LORD.

25 And Joshua saved R
the har... and her fa
... and all that s

The Bible Book by Book

The following pages give a summary of
each book of the Bible. Our aim has been
to introduce the key teaching and practical
application of the Bible in a readable and
accessible way.

Each outline contains the following
features:

- Background giving an overview, summary
  and context of the book
- Outline giving the structure of the book
- Key themes showing some of the major
  distinctive emphases of the book
- Relevance for today: showing how the
  message of the book can be worked out in
  our own lives.

The Bible Book by Book

CONTENTS

This page is arranged in the order of the 66 books of the Bible. An alphabetical list is given on the facing page.

OLD TESTAMENT

NEW TESTAMENT

THE BOOKS OF THE BIBLE
IN ALPHABETICAL ORDER

Genesis

GREAT BEGINNINGS

OVERVIEW

Genesis reveals how everything began, and what went wrong with it. The problems started when humanity made wrong choices, ruining a perfect world, but a loving God had a plan to bring people back to himself and restore his creation.

SUMMARY

Genesis ("origins" or "beginnings") is a story of beginnings. Most major Bible themes are first found here.

The beginnings of everything

Genesis begins with creation and early human history (1:1–11:32). It doesn't explain *how* things were made, simply *who* made them and *why*. Creation (1:1–2:3) climaxes with the first humans, Adam and Eve, created to know God (1:26-27) and rule everything (1:28-30). Their freedom was limited by just one command: not to eat from a particular tree (2:2-17). Yet this was the very thing they did, leading to expulsion from the Garden of Eden (3:1-24). Human society continued to develop but, without God's presence, deteriorated rapidly (4:1–11:32). Even God's judgement through a flood (6:1–9:29) didn't restrain human arrogance and sin (11:1-4). But God had a plan.

The beginnings of a family

Through Abram, God would build a new family who would love and obey him. Although Abram's wife was barren (11:30) and, being Chaldeans (11:31), they were moon-worshippers, God nevertheless revealed himself, promising to bless him and make him into a nation that would bless all nations (12:1-3). Abram responded in faith (15:1-6) and God made a covenant with him (15:7-20; 17:1-22). Abraham – see 17:5 for the change of his name from Abram – wasn't perfect

(12:10-20; 20:1-18) and tried to help God's plan (16:1-16); but he finally learned that God does things in his own way and time. Only then was Isaac, the promised son, born (21:1-7).

Under Isaac and his son Jacob, God's people grew in numbers and prosperity, living as nomads in Canaan (chs.24–36). Jacob's twelve sons became the twelve tribes of Israel, the name Jacob was given after wrestling with God (32:22-32). Through one of those sons, Joseph (37:1-36; 39:1–41:57), Israel went to Egypt to avoid a famine (42:1–50:26). The growing family was now safe, but in the wrong place! It would be centuries before they returned to the Promised Land, a key feature in Old Testament history.

Author

The traditional view is that Moses wrote the Bible's first five books ("the Pentateuch" or "five-volume book"), though some think his stories were only written down much later. But since Moses kept written records (Exodus 17:14; 24:4; 34:27), there seems no good reason for doubting his authorship, as Jesus himself confirmed (Mark 7:10; 12:26).

Date

Although recording events from much earlier in history, Genesis was probably written during the wilderness wanderings (c.1446–1406 BC), though some later editing may have taken place.

OUTLINE – GENESIS

The creation

Abraham

Isaac

Jacob

Joseph

KEY THEMES – GENESIS

God

The Bible's opening verse focuses us on God – *eternal* (21:33), *unique* (1 Timothy 1:17), *all-powerful*, creating everything from nothing (Hebrews 11:3). However, he is no mere force or power, but *personal*, making humans in his image (1:26-27) for relationship with him (2:7-24). As Genesis unfolds, we see that he is also gracious (12:1-3), caring (16:7-16), sovereign (50:20), and yet he judges sin (3:23; 6:7; 11:8; 19:23-29).

Humanity

Although made on the same day as animals, humans are distinct and superior, reflected in their separate creation (1:24-26), dominion over the animal world (1:28), and creation in God's image (1:26-27) – an image reflected fully and equally in both sexes.

Creation

Creation is "good" (1:4,10,12,18,21,25, 31) and to be enjoyed, but not to the exclusion of its Creator, nor by being made into god (Exodus 20:4-5). As God's stewards, humanity is to care for creation on his behalf (1:28; 2:15; 9:1-3; Psalm 8:3-8; 115:16).

Sin

Adam and Eve's disobedience had widespread consequences, affecting relationship with God (3:8-10), one another (3:7,12), and creation itself (3:17-19), yet excusing its guilt by hiding and explaining things away (3:7-13). Their sin spread deeply into their descendants (eg 4:1-8) and the rest of humanity (6:1-6) so that "every inclination of his heart is evil from childhood" (8:21). The Bible says that "all have sinned and fall short of the glory of God" (Romans 3:23).

Covenant

While covenants (solemn, unbreakable contracts between two parties) were common, biblical covenants were distinct by being entirely at God's initiative. So all Abraham could do when God made covenant with him was stand by and watch (15:1-21). Only after it was made could he respond. God made covenants with his people at key times (eg 9:8-17; 15:9-21; 17:1-27; 19:3-8), but the prophets looked forward to a new covenant, written in people's hearts (Jeremiah 31:31-34; Ezekiel 37:25-27), which the New Testament says happened through Jesus (Matthew 26:26-28; Hebrews 9:15-28).

Election

Election is God's gracious and sovereign calling of people for his greater purpose. In Genesis he chooses Israel through Abraham (12:1-3; 15:1-18; 17:1-16) rather than another nation, Isaac rather than Ishmael (17:19-21; Romans 9:6-9), Jacob rather than Esau (25:23; 27:1-40; Romans 9:10-16). This choice isn't out of favouritism, but love (Deuteronomy 7:7-8), in order to bring about his bigger salvation purposes. Those chosen can therefore never be proud (Romans chapters 9-11), and even those not chosen can still find blessing, as Ishmael (21:17-20) and Esau (36:6-8) discovered.

RELEVANCE FOR TODAY – GENESIS

Sin is always exposed
Sin's deceitfulness makes us think we can hide sin; but we can't. Adam and Eve tried to hide (3:8-10); Cain claimed to know nothing of what had happened to Abel (4:8-12); Abraham lied about Sarah (12:10-20; 20:1-18); but all were exposed. We don't find forgiveness for sin by hiding it, but by confessing it (eg 1 John 1:8-9).

Faith is always rewarded
Abraham wasn't perfect; what put him right with God was not behaviour, but faith (15:6). Despite setbacks and mistakes, he kept faith in God's promise and was therefore blessed (21:1-5; 22:1-18). The New Testament sees him as an example to follow (eg Romans 4:1-25; Galatians 3:1-18; Hebrews 11:8-19).

Promises are always fulfilled
God promised Abraham he would be "very fruitful" (17:6) and become a great nation. Genesis shows how this promise was kept, as Abraham's descendants grew in numbers and wealth, eventually becoming twelve tribes. When Canaan experienced a famine, God took them to safety in Egypt where they "were fruitful and increased greatly in number" (47:27). This continued until, by Exodus, Pharaoh was fearful of their size (Exodus 1:1-10).

Obedience is always blessed
Abraham responded to God's call to "Go to the land I will show you" (12:1) even though he didn't know where it was, trusting God's promise that he would be blessed and be a blessing (12:2). This mission call to "go" is still relevant today for all God's people (Matthew 28:18-20). As Jesus' followers obeyed it, they too were blessed (eg Mark 16:20; Acts 2:38-41; 8:4-8), as we ourselves will be.

> "You intended to harm me, but God intended it for good to accomplish what is now being done, the saving of many lives."
>
> **Genesis 50:20**

Purposes are always worked out
Right from the Garden of Eden, Satan has tried to oppose God's purposes, but Genesis shows how God's providence – his unceasing watch over his people and his shaping of all events and circumstances for his own purposes – ensures that things always come out right in the end. While we see this at several points in the lives of the patriarchs, nowhere is it clearer than in the story of Joseph. He trusted God was at work even when everything seemed to go wrong (37:36; 39:1–41:57), assuring his fearful brothers that God had been working through everything (50:20-21). Still today God is the one who "in all things works for the good of those who love him" (Romans 8:28).

Exodus
A PEOPLE FREED, A NATION FORMED

OVERVIEW

Oppressed by Egypt's Pharaoh and forced into slavery, God's people cried out for freedom. But God's plan was far bigger than theirs. They were simply hoping for freedom from a cruel nation, but God planned to transform them into a nation of his own.

SUMMARY

Exodus (meaning "exit" or "way out") opens with Abraham's descendants still in Egypt, where we left them in Genesis. 430 years have passed (12:40) and new rulers (1:8), who knew nothing about how Joseph had saved Egypt from famine, felt threatened by their growing numbers. So they made them slaves (1:9-14) and killed their firstborn sons (1:15-22).

Responding to their cries (2:23-25), God called Moses to free them. Moses felt inadequate (3:10–4:17), but was just the man God needed. Although born a Hebrew, he grew up in Pharaoh's palace (2:1-10) learning skills like leadership and writing. However he would also have worshipped Egypt's gods, so first needed to meet the living God. God revealed himself to Moses when he was 80 (7:7) in a burning bush, not just as his ancestors' God, but also as "I AM", and sent him back to Egypt (3:1–4:31).

Pharaoh refused to free his slaves (5:1-21); but through ten plagues (7:14–12:30), climaxing in the death of Egypt's firstborn sons, his hardened heart was broken. He freed the Israelites, then changed his mind and pursued them, trapping them by the Red Sea. However God miraculously parted the waters, letting them escape (14:1-31).

The joy of freedom quickly gave way to grumbling because of desert hardships, despite God's miraculous provision (15:22–17:7). Three months later, they arrived at Mount Sinai where they stayed for almost a year. Here God made a covenant with them (19:1-8; 24:1-18), giving them the Ten Commandments (20:1-17) and other laws (20:22–23:19). This Law was placed in the ark of the covenant and kept in a special tent (the tabernacle). In the courtyard surrounding it, priests could offer sacrifices (27:1–30:38) to re-establish the covenant when people broke it.

While Moses was still up Mount Sinai, Aaron made a golden calf (a pagan symbol) which the people worshipped in a wild party (32:1-8). It was only because of Moses' prayer that God didn't abandon them (32:9–33:22). God honoured Moses' faith by revealing what he is really like: a God who wants to forgive rather than judge (34:6-7). This revelation transformed Moses (34:29-35).

With the ark and tabernacle completed (35:4–40:33), God visited his people in a cloud of glory (40:34-38). Now the journey could continue.

Author

Traditionally seen by both Jews and Christians as Moses. There are suggestions within the text itself that this is the case (see 17:14; 24:4; 34:27). See handbook at Genesis, p.60.

Date

Written some time after the exodus, usually dated c.1446 BC, during the wilderness wanderings, though some later editing may have taken place.

OUTLINE – EXODUS

Israel in bondage in Egypt

The exodus

Israel at Sinai

MOSES AND THE EXODUS

Under Joseph's patronage Jacob and his family were welcomed into Egypt and settled there (Ge 39–50). A later pharaoh pressed his descendants into bondage and slavery. An order to dispose of all male Hebrew infants could not prevent the birth and survival of Moses, who was raised in the royal court as an Egyptian noble.

After killing an Egyptian who was beating a Hebrew, Moses fled for his life to Midian, where he lived and raised a family. God called him to return to Egypt to lead his people out of slavery (Ex 3:1–4:20). Eventually, after God's power had been evidenced through plagues (Ex 7–10), the Hebrews left, after 430 years in Egypt.

The route taken is open to debate and some place names are uncertain. Because the Hebrew people both questioned Moses' authority and continually disobeyed God, their journey from Egypt to their promised home took a further 40 years, allowing the generation who left Egypt to die and their children to inherit the Promised Land.

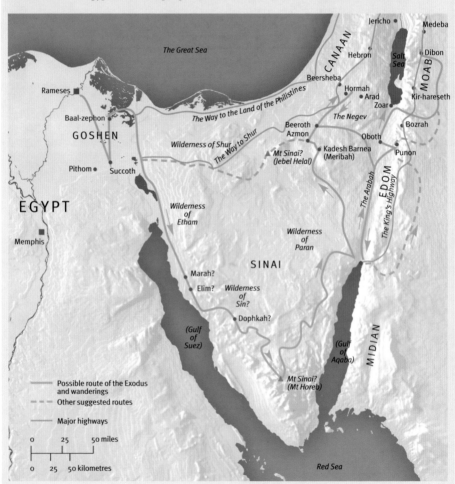

Possible route of the Exodus and wanderings

Other suggested routes

Major highways

0   25   50 miles

0   25   50 kilometres

KEY THEMES – EXODUS

Revelation

God's appearing to Moses through the burning bush (3:1–4:17) is an expression of *revelation* – God revealing himself, entirely at his own initiative, to people not looking for him and without hope of finding him (eg Genesis 12:1-4; 35:6-7; Ezekiel 1:1–2:2; Acts 9:1-18; Hebrews 1:1-3). Revelation is essential because God is so transcendent and so holy that we ourselves could never find him or discover his character and purposes.

God revealed not only himself, but his name – the LORD, or Yahweh (3:15) – which is a play on words with the Hebrew "I AM" (3:14) – showing he is both a personal God and one who is always "there".

Remembering

Knowing how easily people forget, God commanded Israel to remember the exodus through the annual festival of *Passover* (12:1-20), still celebrated by Jews today. In this key Old Testament festival, they remembered how God "passed over" their homes, spared their firstborn, and freed them (12:21-42).

Passover (or *Feast of Unleavened Bread*) was one of three annual festivals God established to help Israel remember him (23:14-17). The other two were *The Feast of Harvest* (or *Feast of Weeks* or *Pentecost*), celebrating God's provision through the grain harvest in May/June, and *The Feast of Ingathering* (or *Feast of Tabernacles*), celebrating the fruit harvest in September/October and recalling their life in "tabernacles" (tents) in the wilderness.

Redemption

God described his freeing Israel as a *redemption* (6:6-8), which becomes a model of salvation for God's people. The Bible often looks back to this event as the greatest redemption in Israel's history (eg Deuteronomy 7:7-8; 15:12-15; 2 Samuel 7:22-24; Isaiah 43:1-4).

In the New Testament Jesus' death is seen as the ultimate price to redeem humanity from their sin (eg Romans 3:23-24; Galatians 3:13-14; Ephesians 1:7).

Response

Having established his covenant with Israel and made them his people, a holy God expected them to now lead holy lives (19:3-8; 22:31). The Ten Commandments (20:1-1-17), the very heart of the covenant he made with them, sum up fundamental responses to God and one another, and are still a sound basis for any society. The laws that follow (20:22–23:19) unpack these basic commandments, governing Israel's life in the wilderness and the Promised Land, and establishing a pattern of worship for them (chapters 25-40). Trying to live by these laws would reveal the impossibility of living up to God's holy standards.

RELEVANCE FOR TODAY – EXODUS

The God of history

Exodus shows that God acts within history to save his people. No circumstance is outside his control.

- Israel's slavery was transformed by God who always remembers his people (2:23-25; 3:7-10) and works all things together for good (Romans 8:28).
- Jesus holds the scroll of history, not Satan (Revelation 5:1-10). When Satan tried to destroy the Jewish babies, God intervened and protected Moses right under Pharaoh's nose (2:1-10; Acts 7:20-22).

> "I will free you ...
> I will redeem you ...
> I will take you as my own
> people, and I will be
> your God."
>
> Exodus 6:6-7

The God of promise

No matter how long we might wait, God always keeps his promises. He revealed himself as the God of Abraham, Isaac and Jacob (3:6) because the promises to them were about to be fulfilled (3:15-17). It was this promise that kept Moses going (eg 33:14; Numbers 10:29), together with God's constant promise that he was with him (eg 3:12; 4:15).

The God of power

More miracles happen in Exodus than probably any other Old Testament book, reminding us that God doesn't just speak, he also acts. When Pharaoh didn't respond to his word (7:8-13), God demonstrated his power though ten plagues (7:14–12:30), each one challenging an Egyptian god (for everything struck either represented a god or was seen as a god). God's power always prevails.

The God of grace

Although containing God's laws, Exodus is also full of God's grace: his undeserved kindness. We see this in:

- God's revelation and call to Moses (3:1-10)
- God's provision of co-leaders through Jethro's wise counsel when Moses was weary with the responsibilities of leadership (18:13-27)
- God's forgiveness of Israel when Moses prayed (32:17–33:17)
- God's revelation of himself as, first and foremost, "compassionate and gracious" (34:6).

The God of guidance

God did not free Israel and then let them get on with life. He carefully guided them, both by his presence (the cloud and fiery pillar, 13:21-22) and his word (the Law). God never leaves us alone. All we have to do is follow, even when it looks like a wilderness ahead.

The God of hope

Exodus is full of hope in the midst of hopeless situations (eg 3:7-10; 14:15-18; 15:22-25; 33:123). The prophets often looked back to the exodus as a model of hope for God's people (eg Isaiah's seeing the return from exile as a new exodus, Isaiah chapters 40–55). The New Testament focuses our ultimate hope in the return of Jesus Christ.

Leviticus
HOLY GOD, HOLY PEOPLE

OVERVIEW
The nation that a holy God had redeemed from slavery in Egypt now needed to learn what it meant to be holy (different) themselves, not just in their worship and religion, but in the whole of life.

SUMMARY
Leviticus ("relating to the Levites") was given this title because much of it concerns the work of the Levites and the priests that assisted in worship. In Exodus the holy God had made Israel his "holy nation" (Exodus 19:6) and given them instructions for building the tabernacle. Now in Leviticus he gives them laws regulating worship in that tabernacle and describing the holy lifestyle that should follow. These instructions were given during the year that Israel was camped at Mount Sinai.

God describes to Moses the sacrificial system (chapters 1-7) through which fellowship with him could be maintained or restored. Five key sacrifices are outlined: the burnt offering (1:1-17; 6:8-13), expressing devotion to God; *the grain offering* (2:1-16; 6:14-23), expressing gratitude for God's provision; *the fellowship offering* (3:1-17; 7:11-21), re-establishing friendship between the worshipper and God or others; *the sin offering* (4:1-35; 6:24-30), covering unintentional sin against God; *the guilt offering* (5:14–6:7; 7:1-6), covering unintentional sin against others. Each sacrifice was carried out in different and precise ways, underlining that sinners couldn't rush into a holy God's presence. Only *unintentional* sin was covered; there was no provision for *deliberate* sin. The annual sacrifice of the Day of Atonement (16:1-34) reminded God's people that none of these sacrifices were ever sufficient to really deal with sin. The New Testament sees this as a foreshadowing of Christ's sacrifice, which alone can atone for sin (eg Hebrews 9:1–10:14).

Holy sacrifices to a holy God needed holy priests to offer them, and so God outlined the qualifications and characteristics of the priesthood (8:1-9:24). Throughout Leviticus, God's people are reminded that because God is holy they too must be holy. One important reminder of this comes in the deaths of Aaron's sons Nadad and Abihu because of their disobedience. In this instance God speaks to affirm that he will be show his holiness (10:1-3).

The need for holiness was further stressed by excluding anything unclean or imperfect from God's presence (11:1–15:33). Only when ritually cleansed could the defiled person return. The New Testament says that Jesus has now done this cleansing for us (eg Hebrews 9:11-14).

Chapters 17–27 describe how the national life of Israel was to reflect their holiness. They were to be seen as different from the people around them. Practical issues are specified including sexual relationships (18:1-30), the poor (19:9-10), gossip (19:16), respect for the elderly (19:32), honesty in business (19:35-36) and care for the land (25:1-7).

Author
Traditionally seen by both Jews and Christians as Moses. See handbook at Genesis, p.60.

Date
Written some time between 1446 and 1406 BC, during the wilderness wanderings, though some scholars think later editing may have taken place. See handbook at Genesis, p.60.

OUTLINE – LEVITICUS

The sacrificial system

The consecration of priests

Clean and unclean

The Day of Atonement

The regulation of the life of Israel

KEY THEMES – LEVITICUS

Holy priests
God permitted only certain people to work in the tabernacle. These people were priests, Aaron's descendants (Numbers 3:10), to offer sacrifices and Levites, Levi's descendants, to assist them (Numbers 3:5-9). Priests, ordained for their work (8:1-9:24), stood between sinful people and holy God.

Christ alone is now our High Priest (Hebrews 2:17; 3:1; 4:14–5:10; 10:19-23) and so we need no other. *All* Christians are now priests (eg 1 Peter 2:4-10).

Holy sacrifices
What made these sacrifices different was that they were not *people's gifts* to the gods (like in other religions), but *God's gift* to them (17:11). This was *God's* way of dealing with sin. Adam and Eve had tried to hide sin (Genesis 3:7-11); sacrifice brought it into the open.

The sinner killed the sacrifice himself (eg 1:3-5; 3:1-2), underlining that "the wages of sin is death" (Romans 6:23). The priest then took its blood to the altar (eg 1:5; 3:2) to "make atonement" (eg 1:4; 4:20). The Hebrew word means "to cover". It is only as sins are covered or dealt with that sinners can approach a Holy God and become "at one" with him.

Sacrifices were always:
- *Animals* (eg 1:2; 4:3), substituting for humans through the laying-on of hands (eg 1:4)
- *Male* (eg 1:3; 4:3), underlining the cost because males, with their breeding potential, were more valuable
- *Perfect* (eg 1:3; 4:3), reflecting God's perfection and that only the best was good enough.

The inadequacy of these sacrifices, however, was shown by the Day of Atonement (16:1-34) when atonement was made for the nation's sins. The high priest killed one goat, sprinkling its blood on the ark in the Most Holy Place (which he could enter only once a year), and then laid hands on a second goat, confessing the people's sins and sending it into the desert. Through these two aspects – wiping away and sending away – the assurance of God's forgiveness was declared.

Holy living
Much of Leviticus concerns the way that God wanted his people to live – different (the meaning of "holy") from those around. No area of life was exempt – worship, health, work, sex, attitudes, justice, business – all expressions of the command to "love your neighbour as yourself" (19:18).

RELEVANCE FOR TODAY – LEVITICUS

The way we live

A holy God wants holy people, and holiness must affect the *whole* of life, Leviticus shows; and the New Testament agrees (eg 1 Corinthians 6:9-20; Ephesians 4:17–5:20; 1 Peter 1:13–2:12). If people claim to be saved but are not changed, we may doubt whether they are truly saved.

Holiness is not a list of behaviours that must be followed or avoided, however. Jesus rejected this approach to holiness (adopted by the Pharisees), stressing that it was primarily a matter of the heart (Mark 7:1-23).

> "'Consecrate yourselves and be holy, because I am the LORD your God. Keep my decrees and follow them. I am the LORD, who makes you holy.'"
>
> Leviticus 20:7-8

The way we worship

Sacrifices were costly (animals were not cheap!), bringing home that sin cannot be dealt with cheaply and that true worship will always cost us. We no longer need to bring animal sacrifices, for Christ's sacrifice fulfilled them all. They were just shadows, while his was the real thing (Hebrews 10:1-14). We can now freely enter God's presence to worship at any time (Hebrews 4:14-16).

The way we care

Leviticus shows the need to demonstrate our love for God through practical expressions of love for others (19:18). This is reflected in laws about gleaning (19:9-10) and the Jubilee Year (25:8-55), when all land was to be returned to its original owner every fiftieth year to give everyone a fresh start in life.

Jesus commanded his followers to demonstrate their love for God in practical care for others (Luke 10:27) and James doubted the reality of anyone's faith who didn't (James 2:1-17).

The way we rest

The holy God gave his people a holy day, the Sabbath (23:3) which was to be different from other days. Everyone had to stop work so they could be refreshed and remember God.

By Jesus' day, the Pharisees had made the Sabbath a burden rather than a blessing by filling it with rules, something Jesus criticised (Mark 2:23-28; Luke 14:1-6; John 9:13-34). However, he never undermined the Sabbath itself, and its principle of rest and refreshment remain part of God's wise pattern for life, going back to creation itself (Genesis 2:2-3; Exodus 20:8-11).

The first Christians changed this day of rest and remembrance from Saturday to Sunday to celebrate the resurrection.

Numbers
FROM GRATITUDE TO GRUMBLING

OVERVIEW
Continuing the journey begun in Exodus and Leviticus, Numbers describes how the Israelites moved on from Mount Sinai towards the Promised Land. Sadly they didn't respond with gratitude, but with grumbling, and so forfeited the right to enter it. A two-week journey would now take 38 years, and only their children would ever reach it.

SUMMARY
After a census (1:1-54) the twelve tribes were assigned positions around the ark (2:1-34). God assigned responsibilities to the Levites (3:1–4:49; 8:5-26), gave instructions for keeping the camp pure (5:1-31), and established a trumpet-alert system (10:1-10). Now they could leave Sinai (10:11-36). But they quickly grumbled about their hardships, idealising life in Egypt and wishing they were back (11:1-6). God provided manna (11:7-9) and quail (11:31-34) and gave Moses 70 elders when he found the burden of leadership too great (11:10-35). Even Miriam and Aaron joined in the criticism (12:1-16). Clearly life in the desert was a strain.

Spies were sent into Canaan and returned with mixed reports (13:1-33). The land was fertile, they said, but its inhabitants were too strong to dislodge. Their report prompted a desire to return to Egypt (14:1-4), and only Joshua and Caleb stood firm (11:6-9). Moses and Aaron prayed (11:5), appealing to God's reputation (11:13-16) and character (11:17-19) as reasons for him not abandoning Israel. God heard their prayer but said everyone over 20 years old, except Joshua and Caleb, would die in the desert and never enter Canaan (11:29-30; Hebrews 3:7-11).

The journey was a mixture of good and bad. On the bad side, a rebellion had to be crushed (16:1-50); Edom refused permission to cross their territory (20:14-21); Aaron died because of disobedience (20:22-29). On the good side, Aaron's rod blossomed as a sign (17:1-13); water miraculously gushed from a rock (20:1-13); God provided healing from snake bites (21:4-9; John 3:14-15). God might have been judging his people, but he had certainly not abandoned them.

The opposition of Moab, east of the Dead Sea, was overcome as the prophet Balaam, hired to curse them, found he could only bless (23:1–24:25). Temptations to sexual immorality were not as easily overcome however (25:1-17).

God appointed Joshua to succeed Moses, excluded from entering Canaan because of his own disobedience (27:12-23). Two tribes were allowed to settle east of the Jordan provided they helped the others take their land first (32:1-42). Moses made a record of their journey (33:1-55) and God defined the boundaries of the land (34:1–36:13). Now they were ready for the final stage of the journey.

Author
Traditionally seen by both Jews and Christians as Moses. See handbook at Genesis, p.60.

Date
Written some time between 1446 and 1406 BC, during the wilderness wanderings, though some scholars think later editing may have taken place. See handbook at Genesis, p.60.

OUTLINE – NUMBERS

KEY THEMES – NUMBERS

The kingdom of God

Israel left Sinai not as a bunch of escaping slaves, but as an advancing army with God in their midst, symbolised by the ark of the covenant at the centre (2:1-31; 10:11-33). Here is a picture of God's kingdom advancing, about to invade part of fallen humanity and from which God would expand that kingdom into the whole world. The heart of Jesus' message was that God's kingdom is here, advancing, and cannot be stopped (Matthew 4:17,23; 9:35-38; 13:1-52; 16:18-19; 24:14).

The discipline of God

God had made a covenant with Israel at Sinai, but that didn't mean they could now do as they pleased simply because God was with them. Grumbling and rebellion was a breach of that covenant and a lack of trust; so God, like any good father (Hebrews 12:5-11), disciplined his children (11:1-10; 12:1-15; 14:35; 16:1-50).

The promises of God

Hundreds of years earlier God had promised Canaan to Abraham (Genesis 12:1; 15:12-20; 17:1-8). Now at last his descendants were on their way to possess that promise. Their constant disobedience and lack of faith in the desert could have led God to abandon his promise, however, for they had failed to keep their part of the covenant – to "obey me fully" (Exodus 19:5). But Numbers shows us how God stays faithful to his promises even when we aren't faithful. Those who had not trusted would be excluded from entering the Promised Land; but God would maintain his part of the promise and fulfil it through their children (14:29-35).

The miracles of God

Like in Exodus, there are many miracles in Numbers, for this was a crucial time when God's power needed to be experienced. There are significant miracles of provision – some of them supernatural, like the mysterious manna (11:4-9), some an overruling of natural forces, like the wind blowing quail towards them (11:31-32). God is the sovereign God of both.

One of the strangest miracles is Balaam's talking donkey (20:21-35). Whether this was (impossible as it may seem) a literal talking donkey (after all, there is a talking snake in the Garden of Eden, Genesis 3:1-4), or whether it was what Balaam thought was happening (for magicians from this part of the ancient world believed in animal divination), it brings home the fact that God is prepared to do anything to get his message across to people.

RELEVANCE FOR TODAY – NUMBERS

Beware of grumbling

Grumbling occurs often in Numbers (11:1-10; 12:1-15; 14:1-2,27-45; 16:1-50; 17:1-13) and each time God judges it. Paul told the Corinthians, "Do not grumble", referring back to these stories (1 Corinthians 10:1-11). See also Hebrews 3:17-19; James 5:9.

Beware of living in the past

Whenever life got hard, the Israelites wished they were back in Egypt, forgetting what life had been like there and idealising the past (11:4-6; 14:1-4). It is always easy to think the past was better, but it rarely was. And anyway, God does not want us living in the past but in the present.

Beware of thinking God's rules don't apply to you

No one is exempt from obeying God, not even (especially) leaders. Both Aaron (20:23-29) and Moses (Deuteronomy 34:1-12) learnt this the hard way. God wasn't prepared to let them require certain behaviour of others but then not live up to that themselves. The New Testament says leaders will be judged by higher standards (James 3:1).

Beware of jealousy in ministry

Miriam and Aaron became jealous of Moses, feeling they were as good as him (12:1-3). While their criticism had some basis (he had married a Cushite woman), it was really a cover for their jealousy of his prophetic ministry (12:2). But God saw through this and rebuked them (12:4-15). God wants leaders who aren't jealous of others but who see their need of one another and work together (1 Corinthians 3:3-7; 12:27-31; Ephesians 4:7-13).

Beware of getting in a rut

Once we have experienced God working in a particular way, it is easy to think this is how he will work next time. This is what Moses did. He had seen God provide water previously (Exodus 17:1-7). That time God had told him to *strike* the rock; surely that was how God would do it again. But in fact, this time God told him to *speak* to the rock, not strike it (20:8). In doing it like he had before, he disobeyed God, out of frustration with the people it seems (20:10-11). But God rebuked him and said he could not now enter the Promised Land.

> "We should go up and take the possession of the land, for we can certainly do it." But the men who had gone up with him said, "We can't..."
>
> Numbers 13:30-31

Deuteronomy
FINAL PREPARATIONS

OVERVIEW

With the journey from Egypt completed, Moses made his farewell speech. Forbidden to enter Canaan himself, he encouraged the people to occupy the land God had promised long before and prepared them for their new life by reminding them of God's laws and renewing the covenant. His work done, Moses then died.

SUMMARY

Deuteronomy (meaning "second law") follows the ancient pattern of a covenant renewal document:

Recollection

Covenant renewal treaties began by recounting the history of the parties involved, just like here. Moses looked back over the 38 years since leaving Mount Sinai, recalling key events, both good and bad (1:1–3:29), and urging continued obedience to God (4:1-40).

Requirements

Moses then outlined the terms Israel must follow as their part of the covenant. The Ten Commandments were given central place (5:1-33) and were then summed up in one short commandment: "Hear, O Israel: The LORD our God, the LORD is one. Love the LORD your God with all your heart and with all your soul and with all your strength" (6:4-5). Jesus himself would say that this commandment summed up all the others (Mark 12:28-31).

This absolute allegiance to God was then underlined by instructions to destroy the Canaanites who might otherwise turn their hearts to their gods (7:1-26). (In fact, this was exactly what would happen.) Warned not to forget God and all he had done (8:1-20), they were reminded that they would conquer Canaan, not because of their own goodness or abilities, but because God was with them. If they feared God alone (10:12-22) and

remained obedient, they would indeed be blessed (11:1-32).

Chapters 12-26 then give a wide range of religious, social and legal laws governing life in the Promised Land.

Ratification

Having outlined the terms of the covenant, Moses listed curses that would follow if they disobeyed (27:1-26; 28:15-68) and blessings if they obeyed (28:1-14). The covenant was then ratified (renewed) (29:1–30:20).

The covenant renewed, Moses' work was complete and he handed over leadership to Joshua, who had been alongside him since leaving Egypt, encouraging him to be strong and courageous for the task ahead (31:1-8). He praised God for all he had done (32:1-43), blessed the twelve tribes (33:1-29) and then died, being buried on Mount Nebo on the very edge of the Promised Land (34:1-12) – so close, and yet so far.

Author

Traditionally seen by both Jews and Christians as Moses, apart from the final chapter which records his death. See handbook at Genesis, p.60.

Date

Written some time between 1446 and 1406 BC, during the wilderness wanderings, though some scholars think later editing may have taken place. See handbook at Genesis, p.60.

OUTLINE – DEUTERONOMY

KEY THEMES – DEUTERONOMY

Deuteronomy is one of the most quoted books in the New Testament, with almost 100 quotations and references to it. Jesus himself quoted it to resist the devil (Luke 4:4,8,12). Clearly Deuteronomy was much loved by Jesus and the first Christians.

A unique God
Yahweh, the living God, is the one and only God (eg 4:35-39; 6:4-5), something that needed emphasising before Israel entered Canaan with its many gods and idols. Israel was to have no other gods (5:6-7) nor make any idols (4:15-19; 5:8-10). Monotheism (belief in one God), not polytheism (belief in many gods), is upheld for God's people.

A loving God
Deuteronomy is about the people's relationship with God. God and his people are bound together not just by a treaty, but by love. Love led God to choose Israel, rescue them and bring them to the Promised Land (4:35-38; 7:7-9; 10:14-15; 23:5). 13 times Israel is called to love God in return, and to show their love for him through love for one another and through obedience to the detailed laws governing every aspect of life.

A blessing God
God wants to bless his people (eg 1:11; 7:13-15; 15:4-6,10,18; 28:1-14); but to experience this, they must live a life of total commitment to him. Only obedience will lead to blessing (28:1-14) while disobedience will lead to curse (27:1-26; 28:15-68).

A holy God
All this talk of God loving and blessing people could lead them think they could do as they like and God would turn a blind eye. But Deuteronomy shows this is not the case, as we see in the command to destroy the Canaanites (7:1-6; 9:1-6). To human thinking, this seems unjust. But it was to do with both God's holiness (7:6) and human wickedness (9:5). Canaanite religion, which was not only idolatrous but also included temple prostitution and child sacrifice at times, was an offence to the holy God. But God knew it was also attractive to sinful people and would be a snare to Israel (9:16). God wanted to stop the infection of Canaanite religion getting in to them, for through Israel salvation would come for all the nations.

RELEVANCE FOR TODAY – DEUTERONOMY

The blessing of serving God
Once we realise there is only one true God, it is logical to love and serve him alone (6:4-5). No room is left for other gods or idols (4:15-19), whether literal or metaphorical; all are empty, false and should be destroyed (12:2-4).

The blessing of obedience
God blesses those who say, "We will listen and obey" (11:27). While his blessings are often material, we cannot assume they will always be so, or that they will come immediately. Even Jesus, who obeyed God like no other, experienced homelessness (Matthew 8:20). God's blessing may sometimes be spiritual rather than physical, and may even be delayed until heaven (eg Mark 10:21; Hebrews 11:24-26; Revelation 22:12).

> "Hear, O Israel:
> The LORD our God,
> the LORD is one.
> Love the LORD your God
> with all your heart and
> with all your soul
> and with all your
> strength."
>
> Deuteronomy 6:4-5

The blessing of having a successor
Moses' faithful service for 80 years would have been of little value if he had no successor. Joshua had been alongside Moses all that time and had witnessed first hand how he had prayed, trusted God, performed miracles, and led God's people. Now it was his turn (31:1-8).

Real success is not simply doing things yourself, but producing others who can continue after you, taking God's work to its next stage, just like Joshua. Success is producing successors.

The blessing of purity
God's purity should be reflected in the purity of our own lives. The world says we are missing out if we stay pure, especially in the area of sexual relationships, but God says that sex is special, solely for one man and one woman within marriage. Every sexual relationship outside of this – sex before marriage, outside of marriage, instead of marriage – is impure in God's eyes (22:13-30) and cannot bring his blessing. Thinking we can live in sexual impurity and still be blessed is to deceive ourselves (eg 1 Corinthians 6:9-10).

The blessing of compassion
While underlining God's compassion to us, Deuteronomy shows that if we want to experience that compassion we ourselves must demonstrate it. Chapters 17-25 therefore contain laws calling for compassion in matters as varied as law (16:18-20; 17:8-11; 21:1-9), provision for God's servants (18:1-8), warfare (20:1-20) and even nature itself (22:6-8).

PALESTINE IN THE EARLY OLD TESTAMENT

0   10   20 miles

0   10   20 kilometres

Sidon

Zarephath

Mt Lebanon

Damascus

ARAM
(SYRIA)

Mt Hermon

Tyre

Laish (Dan)

Kedesh

Hazor

R. Jordan

Merom

The Great Sea

Acco

Chinnereth

Sea of Chinnereth

Ashtaroth

BASHAN

Mt Carmel

R. Kishon

Jokneam

Aphek

Dor

Shunem

Edrei

Megiddo

Ramoth Gilead

Beth-shean

CANAAN

Migdal

Socoh

Dothan

Tirzah

HILL COUNTRY OF ISRAEL

Mt Ebal

Shechem

Succoth

R. Jabbok

Mt Gerizim

Penuel

Mahanaim

THE ARABAH

River Jordan

PLAIN OF SHARON

Joppa

Aphek

Rabbah

AMMON

Lod

Bethel

Beth-horon

Ai

Gilgal

Shittim

Gezer

Jericho

Ekron

Aijalon

Gibeon

Mt Pisgah

Heshbon

Beth-shemesh

Jerusalem

Beth-jeshimoth

Medeba

Timnah

Ashdod

Socoh

Bethlehem

Ashkelon

Lachish

Adullam

Mamre

Ataroth

Kiriathaim

Eglon

Debir

Hebron

Salt Sea (Sea of the Arabah)

R Arnon

City of Moab

Gaza

CANAAN

HILL COUNTRY OF JUDAH

THE SHEPHELAH

Rapha

Beersheba

Ar

MOAB

Hormah

The Valley of Siddim

Kir-hareseth

Possible region of cities of Sodom, Gomorrah, Admah, Zeboiim, Zoar.

Rehoboth

THE NEGEV

Zoar?

Ziph

Brook Zered

EDOM

Beeroth

Hazazon-tamar

WILDERNESS OF ZIN

AMORITES

Joshua
TAKING THE LAND

OVERVIEW

After Moses' death, Joshua ("the Lord saves") succeeds Moses as leader of the Israelites. His task to lead them into the Promised Land was not easy. Canaan was occupied by many independent states and fortified cities. It was therefore only through dependence on God that he could lead God's people to claim their inheritance.

SUMMARY

Call

With Moses dead, God called Joshua to his new task (1:1-2), promising him success (1:3-5) and challenging him to be courageous and obedient (1:6-9). Joshua then prepared the Israelites (1:10-18) and sent spies to reconnoitre Jericho (2:1-24).

Crossing

The spies had forded the river the previous day (2:23), but it was now in flood (3:15), which the Canaanites probably interpreted as Baal (their weather god) protecting them. God told the priests to carry the ark into the river, and as they did, the water stopped so people could cross (3:14-17). Stones were erected to remember what God had done (4:1-24).

Circumcision

Before fighting, the men needed circumcising (something neglected in the wilderness) to remind them they were God's people (5:2-9). Once the Passover was celebrated (5:10-12) they were ready for battle. Joshua was reminded that this was God's battle (5:13-15).

Conquest

Joshua began by capturing cities along the road that cut Canaan into two. Jericho was taken, not by fighting but through a noisy religious procession (6:1-27). Moving west, they found themselves unexpectedly defeated at Ai (7:1-9). The reason was sin: Achan had

taken plunder from Jericho designated for God alone. With his sin exposed (7:10-26), Ai was taken (8:1-35).

In phase two, Joshua turned south. The Gibeonites tricked Israel into becoming allies (9:1-27) and five Amorite kings marched against them (10:1-6). God miraculously defeated them (10:7-15), allowing Joshua to conquer the rest of the south (10:16-43).

In phase three, Joshua turned north, defeating the King of Hazor and his allies (11:1-23). The conquest was now over, some 30 years after it began, and God allocated land to each tribe (13:8–21:45), but pockets of resistance remained for many years (13:1-7).

For map of the division of the land into tribal territories, see p.98.

Covenant

The conquest over, Joshua made his farewell speech (23:1-16) and led the people in an act of covenant renewal (24:1-27), reminding Israel of all God had done and urging wholehearted obedience. His work complete, he died, aged 110 (24:28-33).

Author

The book does not give the author, but the word "we" (eg 5:1) indicates an eye-witness. While Joshua kept records (eg 18:8; 24:25), the frequent use of "to this day" (eg 7:26) suggests the final version was written later, perhaps during the monarchy, by an unknown author.

Date

Traditionally, the invasion of Canaan is dated as beginning in 1406 BC and lasting some 30 years. Some archaeological evidence has been interpreted as making a date as late as 1250 BC possible for Joshua's invasion. The surrounding nations – Hittites, Egyptians and Babylonians – were weak by this time, leaving Canaan (situated between them) vulnerable to Joshua's army.

THE CONQUEST OF CANAAN

1 Moses dies in sight of the Promised Land (Dt 34)
2 God commissions Joshua (Jos 1)
3 Spies are sent from Shittim to Jericho (2)
4 The nation cross the Jordan on dry ground (3–4)
5 Jericho falls (6)
6 Ai attacked – Israelites routed (7)
7 Ai attacked again and destroyed (8)
8 Words of the law read at Mt Ebal and the covenant restored (8)
9 Gibeonites deceive Joshua (9)
10 The sun stands still at Gibeon to prolong the light for battle (10)
11 Five Amorite kings routed and put to death at Makkedah (10)
12 The southern cities overcome (10)
13 Coalition of northern kings defeated at the Waters of Merom (11)
14 The land is divided between the tribes of the nation (13–19)
15 The covenant renewed yet again at Shechem (24)
16 Joshua dies and is buried at Timnath Serah (16)

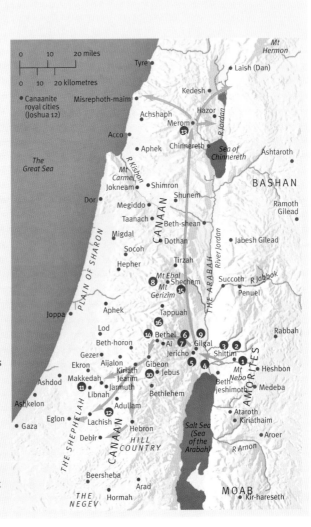

OUTLINE – JOSHUA

KEY THEMES – JOSHUA

The God of faithfulness

It was almost 600 years earlier that God had promised to make Abraham into a great nation and to give him Canaan (Genesis 12:1-2; 15:7-21; 17:3-8). God hadn't rushed to fulfil that promise, but it had now surely happened, as Joshua reminded the people (24:2-15). God always keeps his promises.

The God of battle

Joshua contains some hard stories, with commands to wipe out whole peoples – genocide. Why was this?

First, God had given the Canaanites a long time to repent, just as he promised (Genesis 15:16); but they had continued with their corrupt religion and morality. God is patient; but his patience doesn't last for ever and judgement eventually comes.

Second, these were commands for specific times and purposes, limited in *extent* to Canaan (they weren't allowed to attack neighbours or build an empire) and in *execution* (they weren't allowed to use captured chariots to fight more aggressively, 11:6). God wanted Canaan, and only Canaan, as a base for his people from whom Messiah would come to save *all* the nations.

Third, in those days, victory in battle reflected the greatness of your God. A God who wasn't victorious was considered weak; so God was demonstrating who he was in the language of that time.

Fourth, the taking of the Promised Land is a picture of God's advancing kingdom that cannot be stopped and that one day will overcome all the peoples of this world (eg Daniel 2:44; 7:13-14). God is a God of battle; but that battle is now spiritual (John 18:36).

These stories cannot be taken as justification today for every fight we think is right. When Joshua asked the angel if he was on their side or their enemies, he replied "Neither!" God is on his own side, not ours (5:13-14).

The God of detail

Joshua contains much material that we might (if we are honest) consider boring: lists of defeated kings (12:1-24), descriptions of how the land was to be divided (13:1–19:51), cities of refuge (20:1-9), towns for the Levites who had no land of their own (21:1-45). While we might not see this as the most inspiring part of Scripture, they bring home God's infinite care for the details of life, no matter how trivial they might seem. God wanted to ensure that no one was left out in experiencing his promise.

RELEVANCE FOR TODAY – JOSHUA

Be obedient

The key to success, Joshua was told, was absolute obedience to God and his word, something God underlined to him at the beginning (1:7-8). The fact that the people were quick to obey Joshua (1:17-18) probably reflects the fact that they saw obedience in his own life first. Leaders cannot ask of others what they will not do themselves.

Be strong

Three times God tells Joshua to "be strong and courageous" (1:6,7,9), just as Moses had told him (Deuteronomy 31:6-7), and even the people say this to him too (1:18). This appeal is based on God's presence "for I will be with you" (see also 8:1; 10:8; 11:6). Presumably this was because Joshua didn't feel very strong and courageous at that moment. His life-long mentor, Moses, was dead, and only Caleb and himself remained of those who had left Egypt 40 years earlier and had seen God's power in overcoming an enemy. Would people believe God could do it again – and through him? Little wonder he felt anxious. But leadership means taking hold of God yourself in order to inspire confidence in others.

Be radical

Israel failed to completely drive out the Canaanites, as God had commanded. Pockets of resistance were left in the shape of towns they felt unable to conquer (13:1-7), and these would prove to be a source of trouble and temptation to Israel for many years to come.

> "… choose for yourselves this day whom you will serve."
>
> Joshua 24:15

When we are not radical in removing potential problems from our lives, we can guarantee things will go wrong at some point in the future. Jesus urged his followers to be radical in dealing with things that might lead them astray (Mark 9:43-48).

Be fair

Joshua cast lots to divide the land between the tribes (18:1-10) so no one could accuse him of unfairness or favouritism. While every family was given their own plot of land, the Levites were excluded to remind them that their inheritance was their service to God (18:7). So Joshua provided towns where they could live and pasture lands for their flocks (21:1-45). He also provided cities of refuge, spread across the country, where anyone guilty of manslaughter could flee to ensure a fair trial before the elders (20:1-9). Although he was responsible for the whole nation, Joshua was thoughtful in recognising particular needs. We too should always be fair concerning the needs of others, especially if we are a leader.

Judges
THE SAD DECLINE

OVERVIEW

By the end of Joshua's life, Canaanite power had been broken, but the Canaanite presence still remained. The people of Israel needed to complete their work, cleansing Canaan of its godless people and religion. But with no clear leader to unite them, Israel's life fragmented and spiralled downhill for the next 300 years. They forgot their God, but God had not forgotten them.

SUMMARY

Setting the scene

Judges begins by showing that the conquest was incomplete (1:1–2:5) and the Israelites were beginning to accept Canaanite life, rather than destroy it (2:6-13). God didn't abandon them, however, first disciplining them through attacks from enemies (2:14-15), then delivering them as they called to him (2:16). He did this through "judges" (2:16), Spirit-anointed leaders whose task was to judge God's enemies by overcoming them. However, the people always reverted to wicked ways (2:6-23), and this cycle of disobedience, distress and deliverance continued for over 300 years.

Stories of twelve judges

The author tells of twelve judges, from Othniel (1367–1327 BC) to Samson (1075–1055 BC). He constructed his story very carefully, selecting the judges he wrote about. Right in the centre are two contrasting stories: Gideon, who didn't want to be king (6:1–8:35), and Abimelech his son, who did (9:1-57). On either side come Deborah (4:1-5:31), from the west, and Jephthah (10:6–12:7), from the east, both of whom were not highly regarded in their culture, the first because she was a woman and the second because he was a prostitute's son. And then on either side of these stories come two loners: Ehud from the south (Benjamin) and Samson from the north (Dan). The point

the author is making is that right across Israel, the nation had gone astray, going round in ever-descending circles. But although Israel had abandoned God, God had not abandoned Israel.

Spiritual and social decline

Chapters 17-21 show how bad life had become. Micah established an idolatrous shrine and unofficial priest (17:1-12), and the Danites stole both (18:1-31). A homosexual gang demanded sex with a visiting Levite (19:16-22) and raped and murdered the woman with him (19:23-29), leading to civil war among God's people (20:1–21:24). The concluding verse sums up the darkness: "In those days Israel had no king; everyone did as he saw fit" (21:25).

Author

While the author is unknown, the expression "in those days Israel had no king" (17:6; 18:1; 19:1; 21:25) indicates it was written during the monarchy and looking back to life before it. Samuel may have gathered some of the original material.

Date

Judges covers the period between the Joshua's death (around 1375 BC) and Saul's rise as king (around 1050 BC). This fits in with Jephthah, a later judge, saying that Israel had been in Canaan for 300 years (11:26).

OUTLINE – JUDGES

The occupation of the land

The judges

Later developments

THE JUDGES OF ISRAEL

Once the nation of Israel was settled in the land of Canaan, they soon forgot that God had brought them there and established them. They started to become like the nations about them, so God allowed neighbouring nations to discipline them. Each time the nation recognised their wrongdoing and cried to God for help, he raised up individuals to protect and guide his people in the power of his Spirit.

1. Othniel (of Judah) drove out invading nomads from the east led by Cushan-Rishathaim (Judges 3:7-11).

2. Ehud (of Benjamin) defeated the Moabite king Eglon (3:12-30).

3. Shamgar was victorious over the Philistines (3:31).

4. Deborah the prophetess (of Ephraim) and **Barak** (of Naphthali) led the northern tribes to defeat the Canaanites led by Jabin and Sisera (4–5).

5. Gideon (of Manasseh) drove out Midianite and Amalekite invaders (6–8).

6. Tola (of Issachar) led the nation (10:1-2).

7. Jair (of Gilead) led Israel (10:3-5).

8. Jephthah (of Gilead) led the people to drive out the Ammonites (11:1–12:7).

9. Ibzan (of Zebulun) led the nation (12:8-10).

10. Elon (of Zebulun) led the nation (12:11-12).

11. Abdon (of Ephraim) led Israel (12:1-15).

12. Samson (of Dan) warred against the Philistines (13–16).

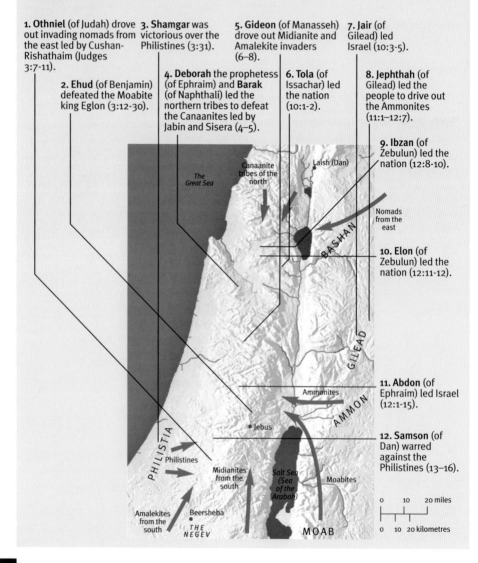

The Great Sea

Canaanite tribes of the north

Laish (Dan)

BASHAN

Nomads from the east

GILEAD

Ammonites

AMMON

Jebus

PHILISTIA

Philistines

Midianites from the south

Salt Sea (Sea of the Arabah)

Moabites

Amalekites from the south

Beersheba

THE NEGEV

MOAB

0   10   20 miles

0   10   20 kilometres

KEY THEMES – JUDGES

The king they forgot

A central theme is that Israel had forgotten that God was their king and they were bound to him by covenant. When they wanted to make Gideon king (thinking this would solve their problems), he had to remind them of this (8:23); but they constantly forgot and "everyone did as he saw fit" (17:6), a clear breaking of the covenant (Deuteronomy 12:8). They therefore forfeited the covenant's blessings (Deuteronomy 28:1-14) and experienced its curses instead (Deuteronomy 28:15-68). It was only God's mercy and patience that kept them from being completely destroyed.

The leaders they followed

Although sometimes fulfilling legal functions (eg 4:4-5), the judges were primarily leaders God raised up and empowered by his Spirit to rescue Israel from its current enemy. Even the best had weaknesses, however: Gideon was fearful (6:11) and unbelieving (6:13); Ehud was deceptive 3:15-27); Samson was ruled by sexual passions (14:1-7; 16:1,4) and was angry (14:19) and vindictive (15:1-5). The fact that God used such people was not a sign of his approval, simply a reflection of how bad things had got. These were the best God could find!

The gods they embraced

While the Canaanites were a very cultured civilisation (contrary to common belief), they practised fertility religion in which nature's powers were worshipped. Baal, the son of El (the chief god) was a god of fertility and weather. He was often portrayed on a bull's back with a lightning spear. Together with Asherah (El's wife) and Ashtoreth (Baal's wife) they were worshipped through ritual prostitution, which was thought to bring fertility to the land. It is therefore easy to see why Canaanite religion was so attractive and why God commanded its removal. It was Israel's failure to do so that led to problems for over 300 years.

The discipline they experienced

Israel's apostasy (turning from God) broke the covenant and was grounds for God abandoning them, but he didn't. Rather, he used loving discipline through permitting surrounding peoples to attack Israel, trying to bring them to their senses and bring them back to him. While they did return, it was always short-lived, and as soon as the latest crisis was over, they went back to their old ways. But God never gave up; he kept disciplining them for their good (eg Hebrews 12:5-11).

RELEVANCE FOR TODAY – JUDGES

Called to live differently

God called Israel to be "a holy nation" (Exodus 19:6), living differently from those around. But rather than change the world, they were distracted from their allegiance to Yahweh. They began to worship other gods and as a consequence, the downward spiral of religious, moral and social decline gained momentum.

Christians too are told not to love the world or anything in it (1 John 2:15), but to live a holy life, different from the culture around (eg Ephesians 5:3-16; Colossians 3:1-17; 1 Thessalonians 4:3-8). We are here to influence the world, not the other way around.

> "In those days Israel had no king; everyone did as he saw fit."
>
> Judges 21:25

Called to live by the Spirit

The judges were empowered for God's work by God's Spirit (eg 3:10; 6:34; 11:29; 13:25; 14:6, 19; 15:14). When his Spirit was working, they were not dependent on human resources, as Gideon discovered when God reduced his army from 32,000 to just 300 (7:1-7), nor limited by human abilities (14:5-6; 15:11-17). Their anointing was only temporary, however, the Spirit coming on them for the occasion and then leaving again. By contrast, since Pentecost, Christians can experience a permanent anointing of God's Spirit (1 John 2:27), empowering them for Christ's work (Acts 1:8).

Called to trust God

Gideon didn't feel up to the task, making excuses and full of doubt, despite God's reassurances (6:11-16). Yet God called him to trust, and patiently bore with his requests for signs (6:17-18, 36-40). God didn't see his doubt as sin, however; he patiently dealt with it, just as he did with Moses (Exodus 3:10-17).

We too are called to trust God (Proverbs 3:5-6; Isaiah 26:3-4; John 14:1) and he may even graciously give us signs to encourage and guide us along the way (Isaiah 30:21). Note however that Gideon's fleece was a lack of trust, rather than a measure of faith!

Called to keep going

Judges brings home the importance of keeping going, especially when the work is not yet completed, something the Israelites failed to do. When the Promised Land wasn't taken as quickly as they thought it might be, many got discouraged and never possessed their possessions, settling for less than God's best. By contrast, Caleb was a man who wouldn't give up and so got what he was promised (1:20; Joshua 14:6-15).

God calls his people to keep going (Hebrews 10:35-39; 12:1-2; James 1:2-12), especially when things don't happen overnight.

Ruth

FAITHFULNESS REWARDED

OVERVIEW

Named after one of its main characters, Ruth shows how things never get too bad for God to come and change them. In the dark days of the judges (1:1), a ray of sunshine breaks out through this story of love, faithfulness and redemption.

SUMMARY

Ruth begins with a prologue of 71 words in Hebrew (1:1-5) and ends with an epilogue of 71 words. In between there are four scenes, with a turning point right in the middle: "That man is our close relative; he is one of our kinsman-redeemers" (2:20). This is the key to the story: it is a story of redemption.

Scene 1: The return (1:1-22)

A famine led Elimelech, Naomi and their two sons to leave Bethlehem, seeking refuge in Moab (1:1-2). Elimelech died there, so Naomi married her sons to Moabites, Orpah and Ruth; but the sons also died and the three women were left abandoned (1:3-5). Naomi decided to return to Bethlehem, urging her daughters-in-law to stay in Moab (1:6-9). Orpah stayed, but Ruth insisted on accompanying Naomi home (1:10-18), with a wonderful expression of commitment (1:16). Naomi arrived home bitter from her experiences (1:19-22).

Scene 2: The reunion (2:1-23)

Quite accidentally (humanly speaking), Ruth went gleaning (picking up harvest leftovers) in the field of a kind landowner who was Naomi's relative (2:1-18) and therefore able to be a kinsman-redeemer (2:19-23).

Scene 3: The request (3:1-18)

Naomi told Ruth to visit Boaz (3:1-6). That night, Ruth lay at his feet and, when he awakened suddenly, requested his protection (3:9) – an invitation to marriage. Boaz saw this

as kindness, for although younger than him (3:10), Ruth had put Naomi's needs first. But there was a problem: a closer relative had rights before Boaz (3:11-18).

Scene 4: The redemption (4:1-12)

Before the elders, Boaz explained Naomi's situation to this relative (4:1-3). At first he was eager for marriage since he would get Elimelech's land; on discovering it carried responsibilities for Ruth too, and any future children, he quickly declined (4:5-6). This released a delighted Boaz to marry Ruth (4:7-12).

The epilogue (4:13-17) tells how their marriage was blessed with a son (4:13-17). Not only had Ruth been redeemed, along with Naomi, but also she had become the ancestor of Kind David, from whom Jesus, the great Redeemer, would come – an amazing story of redemption, underlined in a final genealogy (4:18-22).

Author

While Jewish tradition points to Samuel, this is unlikely since the story mentions King David. We simply do not know the author.

Date

The mention of David (4:17,22) and the style of writing suggests that Ruth was written during the period of the monarchy.

OUTLINE – RUTH

Naomi left desolate

Ruth and Boaz

Boaz marries Ruth

KEY THEMES – RUTH

God's remnant

No matter how bad things get, God always keeps some who stay faithful to him. This "remnant" is represented by Boaz who was faithful and did things God's way, even in these dark days. Not only was he personally rewarded for his faithfulness, but through him came Jesus, the Saviour of the world.

God always has a faithful remnant through whom he works his purpose (Genesis 45:7;

2 Kings 19:1-4; Ezra 9:5-15; Isaiah 10:20-22; Jeremiah 23:1-4; Romans 11:1-5).

God's grace

God's grace is shown not just to Naomi, a daughter of Israel, but also to Ruth, a Moabite. The Moabites had been enemies ever since forbidding Israel to pass through their territory on the way to the Promised Land (Judges 11:14-18), and the Law excluded them from God's presence (Deuteronomy 23:3-6; Nehemiah 13:1-3). But Ruth shows that Gentiles too can experience God's grace, as Jesus' ministry would show (Matthew 28:19; Mark 7:24-30). Becoming part of God's people has nothing to do with our race, circumstances or efforts, but everything to do with God's grace received by faith (Romans 1:5; Ephesians 2:8-18).

God's covenant love

God's covenant love (NIV, *kindness*) is a recurring theme (1:8; 2:20; 3:10). It is reflected in the commitment Ruth makes to Naomi: "Where you go I will go, and where you stay I will stay. Your people will be my people and your God my God" (1:16) – a commitment to stand by another come what may. Boaz shows the same kindness to his distant relatives when he acts as their kinsman-redeemer, reflecting God's covenant love to his people when they didn't deserve it.

God's redemption

In ancient literature, the key to understanding a book was often right at the centre. The centre of the Hebrew text in Ruth is 2:20, "That man is our close relative, he is one of our kinsman-redeemers", showing that redemption is the key theme. The word occurs (in various forms) 23 times in this short story. It is significant in various ways: Naomi is redeemed from bitterness to joy; Ruth is redeemed from being an outsider to being part of God's people; Boaz is redeemed from being alone to having his own family; Bethlehem is redeemed from famine to plenty. Everything in the story shouts out the message that God is a redeemer God (Exodus 6:6-8; 2 Samuel 7:22-24; Job 19:25; Isaiah 43:1-13; Galatians 3:13-14; 1 Peter 1:18-19).

Looking across the Judean hills to Bethlehem, home to Naomi and Ruth and birthplace of Jesus

RELEVANCE FOR TODAY – RUTH

Be patient

Naomi and Ruth had to patiently wait and trust Boaz to act (3:18); Boaz too had to wait and see whether the nearer kinsman-redeemer would act instead of him. They may well have felt anxious, wondering whether things would turn out right; but none of them tried to make things happen by manipulating the circumstances. If God is going to act, we can wait patiently for him; he does not need our help. The Bible commends patient waiting for God to act (Proverbs 8:34; Isaiah 64:4; Hebrews 6:15; James 5:11).

Be redemptive

Nothing and no one is ever beyond God's ability to redeem them, as the story of the desolate Naomi and Ruth show us. In hundreds of stories in the Bible we see God redeeming or rescuing people from their situations (Exodus 3:7-10; Deuteronomy 4:32-40; Psalm 34:22; Isaiah 41:10-14; Jeremiah 50:34; Luke 1:67-75; 1 Peter 1:18-19). As his people, therefore, we too should never write off anyone or anything, but rather always look to bring the best out of every situation.

Be committed

Naomi's situation was transformed through Ruth's commitment to her. Her expression of commitment – "Where you go I will go, and where you stay I will stay. Your people will be my people and your God my God" (1:16) – is one of the most beautiful expressions of commitment in the Bible and is still a powerful example for Christians to follow in their commitment to one another. If we are members of Christ's body, how can we not be committed to one another (Romans 12:4-5; 1 Corinthians 12:12-27; Ephesians 4:3-16)?

Be trusting

No matter how bad things look, this story shows us that we can trust in God who is always at work behind the scenes and who "in all things works for the good of those who love him, who have been called according to his purpose" (Romans 8:28). Nothing can separate us from the love of God in Christ (Romans 8:32-39). Trusting him in the hard times isn't always easy, but it is always blessed (Psalm 40:1-5; 84:5-12; Jeremiah 17:5-8).

Be considerate

Putting others first is more important than our own personal comfort, as Ruth demonstrated. Jesus did not consider himself when he went to the cross, but rather us (Philippians 2:3-11). We are therefore called to always be considerate towards others (Titus 3:1-2; James 3:13-18; 1 Peter 3:7).

> "That man is our close relative; he is one of our kinsman-redeemers."
>
> **Ruth 2:20**

1 Samuel
THE SEARCH FOR A KING

OVERVIEW

Named after the man God used to establish kingship in Israel, Samuel describes Israel's transition from theocracy (ruled directly by God) to monarchy (ruled by a king). But Israel's king also had a king – the Lord God. Saul, their first king, forgot that fact and was destroyed; David, the second, remembered it and was blessed.

SUMMARY

Samuel's story

Miraculously born to godly parents (1:1-20) at the end of the period of the judges, Samuel was handed over to God's service (1:21–2:11). It was while serving Eli the priest that he was called to be a prophet (3:1-21). Around this time the Philistines, coastal dwellers who were pressing inland for more territory, fought Israel and captured the ark (4:1-22), though quickly returning it (5:6–7:1). This increased Philistine threat, the failure of Eli's sons and Samuel's increasing age, led Israel to ask for a king (8:1-5).

Saul's story

Although Samuel was angry with the people's request, God told him to proceed (8:6-21). God chose Saul, an ideal man, at least according to their standards (9:2), and Samuel anointed him king (9:3–10:7), but tested his obedience (10:8). While making a good start (11:1-15), Saul became independent, and Samuel rebuked him when he disobeyed God's command. Saul claimed it was because his soldiers were afraid and Samuel had not come to offer the sacrifice on time (13:5-12), but Samuel said this disobedient action meant God had taken the kingdom from him (13:13-14). Even when given a second chance, Saul failed the test, once again protesting his innocence (15:1-21). So Samuel abandoned him to his fate (15:22-35).

David's story

In looking for Saul's replacement, Samuel looked for the wrong qualities initially (16:1-7). God led him to David, probably just 15 years old, and anointed him as Israel's new king (16:13). David quickly proved himself, as a musician (16:14-23), fighter (17:1-58) and friend (18:1-4). This made Saul jealous and he tried to kill David (18:5–19:24). For the next ten years, David was on the run from Saul, hiding in the hills and even among the Philistines (27:1-12; 29:11). Amazingly he spared Saul's life twice (24:1-22; 26:1-25). Abandoned by God, Saul resorted to a witch (28:1-25). Defeated in battle, he killed himself, (31:1-13) ending a life once so full of potential.

Author

The author of 1 and 2 Samuel, originally one book but separated when translated from Hebrew into Greek, is unknown. It was not Samuel since he dies in 1 Samuel 25; the books are simply named in honour of him.

Date

Written after Solomon's death (930 BC) as the author refers to "Israel and Judah", names used only after the nation divided (1 Kings 12:1-20).

OUTLINE – 1 SAMUEL

The birth and early life of Samuel

The institution of the monarchy

The failure of Saul's kingship

The rise of David

KEY THEMES – 1 SAMUEL

The king

Until now, Israel had been ruled directly by God, through his appointed spokesmen (like Moses), but now, kings would govern Israel on his behalf. Unlike the nations around, however, their king was not free to do as he pleased; he too was subject to God's Law and God's prophetic word. It was when Saul showed he would not do this that God replaced him with "a man after his own heart" (13:14) – David.

Samuel felt that God didn't want Israel to have a king (8:8), though this may simply have been self-pity, for God assured him it is not him they have rejected (8:7). However, God had already made provision for kingship in the Law given to Moses 400 years earlier (Deuteronomy 17:14-20); so it may have been, not that Israel asked for the wrong thing, but they asked it for the wrong reason – to bring them security.

The prophet

Miraculously born to a barren woman (1:1-20), Samuel quickly grew in faith (2:26) and prophetic gifting (3:19-21). His first prophetic word was really hard to deliver: he had to tell Eli, his friend and mentor, that his godless family would be judged (3:11-14). But Samuel was not only a prophet but also the last of the judges (7:15-17) and he led Israel in a significant battle against the Philistines (7:2-14). He was not afraid of challenging disobedience to God's word, even disobedience by the king (13:13; 15:22-26). Throughout the Bible the prophet is given the task of boldly proclaiming what he believes God is saying, and God's people, having tested it, are then to obey (Deuteronomy 18:14-21; 1 Corinthians 14:29-33).

The covenant

The appointment of a king was not the end of the covenant God made with Israel at Sinai, but rather a new *expression* of it. That was why Samuel called Israel to renew their allegiance to God when Saul was appointed king (11:14–12:25). Israel's first obedience was still to God, but through the king; but the king himself also had to obey God and was not above the covenant. This is why Samuel wrote down rules for kingship, explaining them to both king and people and placing them before the LORD in the sanctuary as a covenant act (10:25). When Saul failed to obey that covenant, he was removed from office, for no one is higher than God's word.

RELEVANCE FOR TODAY – 1 SAMUEL

God's servant

True servants don't simply start the race well, they also finish it well. Saul began well, with every advantage: physically strong, popular, Spirit-anointed; under pressure, however, he yielded to others' fears (13:7-9) and ideas (15:13-15) and so was disqualified. Meanwhile, despite many obstacles during his ten years on

TRIBAL TERRITORIES

Under Joshua, the land of Canaan was divided into regions and allotted to each of the tribes. The main bulk of the land was taken including the Negev, the Shephelah, the Arabah, from Kadesh Barnea in the very south to beyond Laish in the north, but much remained unconquered, including the land of the Philistines.

In the allotment of land, the region east of the River Jordan was given to Reuben, Gad and half the tribe of Manasseh. To the west of the Jordan the regions given to Judah, Ephraim and Manasseh were decided by casting of lots at Gilgal. The remaining regions were decided at Shiloh. As the priestly tribe, Levi was allotted 48 cities across the land, of which six were appointed as cities of refuge.

Because Joshua had not been able to drive out all other nations from the land, they became an ongoing problem for the new nation of Israel, continually at war and attempting to reclaim territory. Further, inter-marriage with the surrounding nations led to religious compromise and led the people away from observing the law given to Moses. As a result, the nation suffered God's judgement at the hand of invaders throughout its history.

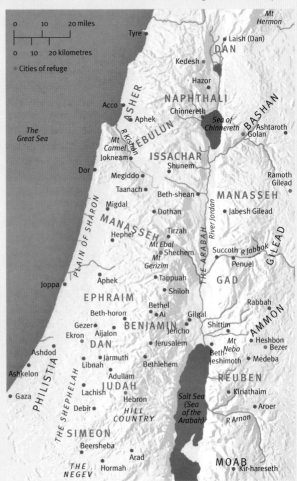

the run, David kept going, which is what all God's servants are encouraged to do (Hebrews 12:1-3).

God's voice

The living God speaks (15:10; Job 33:13-14), in contrast to dumb idols (12:21; Isaiah 44:12-20). However, God does not waste his words, and God stops speaking when we stop listening. He gave Saul repeated opportunities to hear and obey his voice, but when he would not listen, Samuel abandoned him to his fate (15:34-35). At the end, Saul was desperate to hear God, but God wouldn't answer (28:5-6). "Today if you hear his voice, do not harden your hearts" (Hebrews 3:7, 15; 4:7).

> "The LORD
> has sought out a man
> after his own heart."
>
> 1 Samuel 13:14

God's timing

God's timing is generally much slower than ours. Hannah had to wait for many years, living under provocation (1:6-7), before God heard her prayer and gave her Samuel (1:17-20). David, although anointed king (16:12-13), had to wait for ten years before seeing that become reality. But their waiting was not wasted. Hannah learned how to pray; David learned how to endure, fight and lead. With God, waiting time is never wasted time.

God's boundary

It is understandable when people want to know their deceased loved-ones are at peace or want to contact them, but this is a boundary God says we must not cross. The Bible forbids all spiritism, divination, mediumship and sorcery (Leviticus 19:31; 20:6; Deuteronomy 18:9-13; Isaiah 8:19-22; Acts 13:6-12; Galatians 5:19-20), for they open us up to demonic powers.

Saul knew this, and had previously outlawed mediums and spiritists (28:3). However, in his hour of desperation, he ignored God's command and consulted a medium, with terrifying results (28:4-25). Was it Samuel he saw, permitted by God, as an exception, to return from the dead? Or a deceiving spirit (1 Kings 22:21-23; 1 Timothy 4:1) impersonating him? Whatever it was, the medium was terrified (28:12) and Samuel went home even more afraid and depressed (28:20-23).

We engage with evil spiritual powers to our peril, as Saul was about to discover. In crossing this final boundary, the ultimate one of many he had crossed, he stepped towards a shameful death (31:1-4), his life ruined by fear, greed and jealousy – so much potential, wasted.

2 Samuel
THE MAN AFTER GOD'S HEART

OVERVIEW

Continuing where 1 Samuel finished, this book shows how Saul's death opened
the way for David to become king, at first of Judah, then later of all Israel. Unlike Saul,
here was a man after God's heart who wanted to rule God's way. But that didn't mean
he was perfect, as we often discover.

SUMMARY

New king

David was heartbroken to hear of Saul and
Jonathan's death (1:17-27), killing the
Amalekite who claimed (falsely) to have killed
Saul (1:1-16). This reverent attitude towards
kingship made David seek God (2:1) rather
than hastily claiming what God had promised.
Although welcomed as king by Judah at this
point (2:2-4), it was seven antagonistic years
before Israel accepted David (5:1-5) – after
Saul's son, Ishbosheth, was murdered (4:1-12).

New capital

David captured Jerusalem, strategically
situated on the border between north and
south, making it his new capital (5:6-12). He
strengthened its importance by bringing the
ark there (6:1-5). However, disobedience in
transporting it (Exodus 25:12-14) led to
disaster and David became angry with God
(6:6-11). It was months before David brought
it back to Jerusalem, with great rejoicing
(6:12-23).

New victories

God's favour was seen in David's military
victories (5:17-25; 8:1-14; 10:1-19). He
established the kingdom in a way Saul had
never done and honoured God for it (22:1-51).

New covenant

David felt it strange that, while he lived in a
palace, God had only a tent (7:1-2). So he
decided to build a temple. But God said that he
didn't want David to build a house for him;
rather he would build a house for David
(7:4-11), promising him an eternal kingdom
(7:12-16). These words of promise are known
as the Davidic covenant. David responded to
God's words with a prayer of humble gratitude
and praise (7:18-29).

New problems

Even the greatest leader is only human, and
the second half of 2 Samuel is all about David's
failures.

- **Failure in his personal life**, through
  adultery and conspiracy to murder (11:1-27).
  Through confessing quickly, however (in
  contrast to Saul who excused sin or blamed
  others), David was forgiven (12:1-25).
- **Failure in his family life**, through weak
  fathering. David failed to discipline Amnon
  when he raped Tamar (13:1-21), and
  Absalom when he avenged her (13:23-39).
  When David eventually allowed Absalom to
  return from self-imposed exile (14:1-33),
  Absalom interpreted this as weakness and
  gathered people (15:1-6), finally leading a
  coup (15:7-12). David fled, leaving his
  country in civil war (15:13–17:29). It fell to
  Joab to deal with Absalom (18:1-18) and
  persuade David to return (18:19–20:26).
- **Failure in leadership**, through counting his
  soldiers. Whether an act of pride, or lack of
  trust in God, he was judged for it (24:1-25).

Not even the king was exempt from God's discipline (7:14).

Author
See handbook at 1 Samuel, p.95.

Date
See handbook at 1 Samuel, p.95.

OUTLINE – 2 SAMUEL

David anointed as king over Israel

1:1-16	David informed of Saul's death
1:17-27	David's lament for Saul and Jonathan
2:1-7	David anointed as king over Judah at Hebron
2:8–3:39	The rivalry between David and Ish-Bosheth
4:1-12	The death of Ish-Bosheth
5:1-5	David anointed as king over all Israel
5:6-15	David conquers Jerusalem
5:16-25	The defeat of the Philistines
6:1-23	The ark of the Lord brought to Jerusalem

The reign of David

7:1-29	God's promise that David's dynasty will last for ever
8:1-18	Records of victories and officials
9:1-13	David's dealings with Mephibosheth, son of Jonathan
10:1-19	The defeat of the Ammonites and their allies
11:1-5	David's affair with Bathsheba
11:6-25	The elimination of Uriah
11:26-27	David's marriage to Bathsheba and the birth of their child
12:1-14	Nathan's parable against David's adultery
12:15-31	The death of David's child; birth of Solomon

The rebellion of Absalom

13:1-22	Amnon's rape of Tamar
13:23-29	Absalom murders Amnon
13:30-39	David learns of Amnon's death
14:1-33	Absalom gains entry to David's presence
15:1-6	The growing influence of Absalom
15:7-12	Absalom seizes power
15:13–16:14	David flees from Jerusalem
16:15–17:14	Absalom determines to kill David and his army
17:15-29	David warned of Absalom's plans
18:1–19:8	The battle between the armies of David and Absalom; Absalom killed by Joab

The final period of David's reign

19:9-43	David returns to Jerusalem
20:1-13	The rebellion of Sheba, son of Bicri
20:14-26	The death of Sheba
21:1-14	The Gibeonites avenged on the family of Saul
21:15-22	The defeat of Philistine warriors by David's army
22:1-51	David's song of victory
23:1-7	David's final poem
23:8-39	The list of David's warriors
24:1-17	The census of Israel
24:18-25	David builds an altar to the Lord

KEY THEMES – 2 SAMUEL

The Davidic king

David is the focal point in 2 Samuel, presented as the ideal king who took his responsibilities before God seriously, unlike Saul who so often put his own interests first. Under his godly leadership, Israel reached the boundaries that God had promised his ancestors long before and experienced security and blessing. The Bible presents him as a "type" or model of the coming Messiah (eg Jeremiah 23:5-6; Ezekiel 34:23-24). Jesus' kingship is often linked with David's (eg Matthew 22:41-46; Luke 1:31-33) and Jesus is even called the Son of David (eg Matthew 12:22-23; 21:9).

The Davidic covenant

God would not allow David to build a house for him because of the blood on his hands from battle (1 Chronicles 28:2-3). Nevertheless, God recognised the integrity of David's devotion to him and promised to build a house for David instead – a house not of stones but of descendants. God covenanted with David that, in contrast to Saul, he would always have a descendant on the throne (7:11-16).

At a purely human level, this promise seems to have failed, for there has not been a descendant of David on Israel's throne for well over 2000 years. However, the New Testament says this descendant is Jesus, the Son of David, who reigns on an eternal throne in heaven (eg Luke 1:32-33; Revelation 22:16).

The Davidic city

Knowing the jealousies that could have arisen if he had chosen a capital in either the northern or southern territories, David wisely chose a city on the boundary between the two, a city that had not been taken when Joshua entered the Promised Land or since. Entering Jerusalem by its water shaft, David overcame its inhabitants, the Jebusites, and made it his

capital and personal property, calling it the City of David (5:6-9). It was also known as Zion (5:7), after the hill on which it was built.

Because the temple would be built here, Zion became known as "the city of God" (eg Psalm 46:4-5; 87:1-7) and also as a symbol for the people of God (eg Hebrews 12:22-23; 1 Peter 2:4-6; Revelation 14:1).

DAVID'S CONQUESTS

Under David's kingship, the kingdom of Israel was extended from the Gulf of Aqaba in the south to the upper Euphrates River in the north.

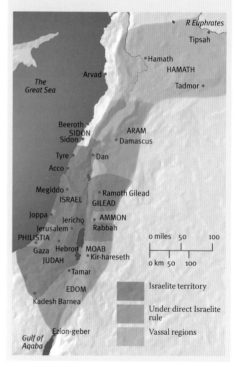

RELEVANCE FOR TODAY – 2 SAMUEL

Don't be presumptuous

God had promised David the throne
(1 Samuel 16:1-13), but David didn't assume
Saul's death meant this was his moment.
Rather he prayed, asking if this was God's time
and only proceeding when God spoke (2:1-4).
He then waited seven years before Israel asked
him to be their king too (5:1-3). If God is at
work, we don't need to make things happen, as
David discovered.

Don't be judgemental

David expressed his delight at the ark's return
to Jerusalem (6:9-19) through extravagant
worship. However, his wife Michal despised
what she felt was his undignified behaviour
(6:20). But David said he would "become even
more undignified than this" (6:22), such was
his love for God. Michal's judgemental attitude
was itself judged: she remained childless (6:23)
and David was vindicated. The Bible often
warns us against judging others (Matthew
7:1-5; Romans 2:1-4; 14:1-23; James 2:1-4,
4:11-12).

Don't be casual about temptation

None of us can ever afford to be casual about
temptation, like David was (11:1-5). When he
should have been fighting, he took it easy and
stayed home (11:1). From his roof he caught
sight of Bathsheba bathing and, rather than
turning away quickly, he slid down the spiral of
temptation into sin ("saw … sent … get … slept
with her"). At any point he could have turned
away, but didn't; and so Bathsheba became
pregnant and her husband ended up dead
(11:6-27).

Temptation is common to everyone
(Luke 17:1; Romans 7:15-25; 1 Corinthians
10:12-13), so we should always be alert and flee
temptation quickly when it comes
(1 Corinthians 6:18-20; 1 Timothy 6:9-12;
2 Timothy 2:22; James 4:4-10).

Don't be slow to confess

While David's sin (11:1-27) seems worse than
anything Saul did, David was forgiven while
Saul wasn't. Why? Because Saul never took
responsibility for his sin, always blaming
others (1 Samuel 13:11-12; 15:15-21), while
David confessed quickly (12:13). Hidden sin
cannot be forgiven; but if brought into the
light, God will forgive it, as David experienced
(Psalm 32:1-5; 51). Hiding sin harms me;
confessing sin frees me (Proverbs 28:13; 1 John
1:6-9).

Don't be disloyal

Despite experiencing David's forgiveness and
being allowed to return to Jerusalem, Absalom
started to secretly gather supporters around
himself with the specific aim of stealing their
hearts from David and taking over the
kingdom (15:1-6). Such deceptive and ungodly
behaviour should never be part of how we live,
especially if we are a leader. God hates
disloyalty (Numbers 12:1-15; Psalm 78:56-59).

> "The LORD himself
> will establish a house
> for you."
>
> **2 Samuel 7:11**

1 Kings
FROM BLESSING TO DIVISION

OVERVIEW

Looking back over history, 1 Kings surveys the events that led Israel from Solomon's glorious reign (970–930 BC) to division, decline, and (in 2 Kings) disaster, asking: "How did we end up here in exile?" The author's answer is simple: because we were disobedient.

SUMMARY

Years of blessing

The transition of kingship from David to Solomon, just as promised (1 Chronicles 22:6-10), was somewhat unsteady (1:1–2:46). Solomon's reign was characterised by:

- **Wisdom.** When invited to choose his blessing, Solomon chose wisdom (3:5-15). His wisdom was both down-to-earth (3:16-28) and far-reaching (4:29-34). Proverbs records many of his sayings.
- **Worship.** Solomon built the temple David had planned (5:1–7:51). God's presence filled it as Solomon dedicated it to God (8:1-66). God reaffirmed his covenant, but reminded Solomon to obey him (9:1-9). The temple remained the focus of worship until destroyed by Babylon in 586 BC.
- **Wealth.** Solomon became extremely wealthy (10:14-29), as the Queen of Sheba witnessed (10:1-13). Some wealth came from trade, but some from taxes.
- **Wives.** Solomon showed his wealth by having 700 wives and 300 concubines. This inability to rule his sexual appetite would be his downfall, for his foreign wives brought their foreign gods which stole Solomon's heart (11:1-13).

Years of division

Sadly, Solomon sowed the seeds of Israel's destruction, through crippling taxes and compulsory labour, which bore fruit in the reign of his son, Rehoboam. Rejecting the elders' wisdom, he threatened to make things even harder for the northern tribes, on whom the greatest burden had fallen (12:1-15). They therefore rejected him, crowning instead Jeroboam, one of Solomon's officials, and established a separate kingdom (12:16-24). God's people split into two – Judah in the south and Israel in the north – never to come together again. To prevent people going to Jerusalem to worship, Jeroboam established shrines (12:25-33), a sin rebuked by prophets (13:1–14:20) and known thereafter as "the sin of Jeroboam".

The author then deals with these two kingdoms in parallel – Judah first and then Israel. Israel's kings were wicked; most of Judah's were good.

Years of challenge

A major focus is Elijah (17:1–21:29; 2 Kings 2), who challenged Israel for adopting Baal worship, or at least trying to blend worshipping Baal with worshipping the living God. Miracles are associated with Elijah's ministry, showing God's provision (17:1-6), compassion (17:7-24; 21:1-29) and supremacy (18:16-46).

Author

Originally one book, 1 and 2 Kings were written by an unknown author who based his accounts on court sources (11:41; 14:19; 14:29) and probably prophetic records (referred to in Chronicles).

Date

Written some time after the fall of Jerusalem (586 BC), during Israel's exile.

OUTLINE – 1 KINGS

The reign of Solomon

1:1-53	The accession of Solomon
2:1-12	The death of David
2:13-46	The consolidation of Solomon's position
3:1-28	The wisdom of Solomon
4:1-28	Details of Solomon's administration
4:29-34	Further details of Solomon's wisdom
5:1–6:38	The building of the temple at Jerusalem
7:1-12	The building of Solomon's palace
7:13-51	The manufacture of the temple furnishings
8:1-21	The transfer of the ark from Zion to the temple
8:22-66	The dedication of the temple
9:1-28	Details of Solomon's activities
10:1-13	The visit of the Queen of Sheba
10:14–11:13	Solomon's possessions and wives
11:14-25	The rise of Solomon's enemies
11:26-40	The rebellion of Jeroboam against Solomon
11:41-43	The death of Solomon

The division of the kingdom

12:1-24	The northern tribes rebel against Rehoboam
12:25–13:34	Jeroboam re-establishes paganism in Israel
14:1-18	Ahijah's prophecy against Jeroboam
14:19-20	The death of Jeroboam
14:21-31	The reign of Rehoboam (Judah)
15:1-8	The reign of Abijah (Judah)
15:9-24	The reign of Asa (Judah)
15:25-31	The reign of Nadab (Israel)
15:32–16:7	The reign of Baasha (Israel)
16:8-14	The reign of Elah (Israel)
16:15-20	The reign of Zimri (Israel)
16:21-22	The reign of Tibni (Israel)
16:23-28	The reign of Omri (Israel)
16:29-34	The accession of Ahab (Israel)

The ministry of Elijah

17:1-24	Elijah and the ravens; Elijah and the widow
18:1-15	Elijah and Obadiah
18:16-40	Elijah slaughters the prophets of Baal at Mount Carmel
18:41-46	The end of the drought
19:1-8	Elijah flees from Jezebel
19:9-18	God speaks to Elijah at Horeb
19:19-21	The call of Elisha
20:1-34	Ahab defeats the king of Aram
20:35-43	A prophet condemns Ahab
21:1-29	The incident of Naboth's vineyard
22:1-28	The prophecy of Micaiah against Ahab
22:29-40	The death of Ahab
22:41-50	The reign of Jehoshaphat (Judah)
22:51-53	The accession of Ahaziah (Israel)

KEY THEMES – 1 KINGS

The message

The underlying message of Kings is that *obedience leads to blessing.* Not a social or political history, but rather a spiritual one, Kings focuses on one key truth: that whenever a king obeyed the covenant, Israel was blessed; whenever he didn't, or simply observed it in theory, it was cursed. The dividing line is always between kings who were faithful to God and the covenant and those who were not. Most attention is focused on kings that demonstrate this "Deuteronomic principle", so called because it is the principle God gave to Moses in Deuteronomy 28. It is the guiding light of our author's analysis of Israel's history.

The messengers

This message is reinforced by the prophets who challenged the kings when they disobeyed the covenant and encouraged them when they obeyed. Most important is Elijah, with his challenge to obey God alone; but other prophets are also mentioned, including Ahijah (11:29-39; 14:1-18), Shemaiah (12:22-24), Micaiah (22:1-28), and in 2 Kings Jonah (14:25), Isaiah (19:1–20:19), and Huldah (22:14-20), and Elisha (2:1-9:1; 13:14-21). As God's messengers, the prophets were to be listened to and obeyed.

Elijah and Elisha's authority was underlined by the miracles they performed, the most significant outbreak of the miraculous since the exodus. These were needed because these were very dark days, and true worship was in danger of disappearing, especially in the north.

The mess

Solomon's sowing of the seeds of the nation's destruction (both through his importing of foreign gods and his unreasonable demands for the building of his palace and temple), together with his son Rehoboam's lack of wisdom, led the country into a complete mess from which it never recovered. God's one people divided into two nations, Judah and Israel, never to come back together again, and often to be at odds with one another.

The books of Kings show us how Israel was unstable, with 20 different rulers from nine different dynasties over 210 years, before being finally destroyed by Assyria. Meanwhile Judah had 20 rulers from just one dynasty (David's) over 345 years, making it much more stable. Judah, with its temple to help focus on the living God, stayed for the most part true to Yahweh, but Israel was constantly seduced to the worship of Baal with its sensuous fertility rituals.

RELEVANCE FOR TODAY – 1 KINGS

The need for obedience

The constant message is that obedience leads to blessing and disobedience leads to curse. We cannot expect blessing if living in disobedience. Obedience is the first call on God's people (eg Leviticus 25:18; Deuteronomy 26:16-19; 1 Samuel 15:22-23; John 14:15; Romans 6:15-18; 1 Peter 1:13-16).

The need for wisdom

Solomon was famous for his wisdom (10:24), but he was also foolish. In marrying foreign wives, he not only disobeyed God (11:2), his heart was stolen as they introduced their gods to him (11:1-13). His son, Rehoboam, was unwise for not listening to the elders' advice (12:1-15), with catastrophic results (12:16-24) which never healed.

The Bible encourages us to seek wisdom above everything else (eg Proverbs 1:7; 2:1-22; 3:13-20; 4:1-9; 8:1-36; 24:3-6; James 1:5).

The need for dedication

Although initially passionate for God, Solomon became lukewarm after marrying unbelieving wives, something the Bible forbids (Deuteronomy 7:3-4; 2 Corinthians 6:14-18). Solomon's desire for personal pleasure, sexual satisfaction and a comfortable life gradually became more important than God and he end up drifting away. No one suddenly decides, "I think I'll become lukewarm today"; it is something we gradually drift into, usually by explaining away God's word. The Bible warns us about becoming lukewarm (Revelation 3:14-22).

The need for unity

When Solomon died, disunity erupted. Both sides were in the wrong: Rehoboam for not being a servant to his people (12:7), the northern tribes for rejecting their God-appointed ruler (12:16). The results of their disunity lasted for 350 years and led to Israel being destroyed by Assyria.

It is so easy to divide when things don't go

> "The LORD became angry with Solomon because his heart had turned away from the LORD ..."
>
> **1 Kings 11:9**

the way we think they should; but God hates division, and the Bible urges us to maintain unity (Romans 15:1-7; 1 Corinthians 12:21-26; Ephesians 4:1-13; Philippians 4:2-3; Colossians 3:12-14). Jesus prayed for unity among his followers (John 17:20-23) for it carries the blessing of God (Psalm 133:1-3).

The need for wholeheartedness

The Ten Commandments reveal that there is only one God and he alone is worthy of our devotion (Exodus 20:1-6). However, many kings in this period tried to blend worship of God with worship of other gods (syncretism). The Bible says that God finds this utterly unacceptable (Deuteronomy 7:1-6; Joshua 23:16; Jeremiah 19:1-15; Hosea 2:2-15; 1 Corinthians 8:1-13; 10:21).

2 Kings
JUDGEMENT TIME

OVERVIEW
Continuing the story of 1 Kings, the divided people of God continued to reject his call through the prophets. For Israel, this led to destruction by Assyria; for Judah, exile in Babylon. But the reason for both lay, not in the rise of these superpowers, but in the judgement of God.

SUMMARY
Elisha picks up Elijah's mantle (2:1-18) and a series of miracles, mostly personal rather than national, confirm his God-given authority (2:19-22,23-25; 3:14-20; 4:1-7,8-37, 38-41, 42-44; 5:27; 6:1-7,8-23; 6:24–7:20; 8:1-6,7-15). The author then returns to the history of Judah and Israel and, as in 1 Kings, alternates between the two.

Israel
Israel's godlessness continued, characterised by:

- **religious syncretism**, as they "persisted in all the sins of Jeroboam and did not turn away from them" (17:22). (See 10:28-31; 13:1-3, 10-11; 14:23-24; 15:8-9,17-18, 23-24,27-28). They also blended worship of God with worship of Baal (17:7-17).
- **political instability**, as one dynasty replaced another, often through bloodshed (eg 10:1-17). Every northern king, except Omri and Jeroboam II, was weak, and even these two are dismissed in a few verses because of their godlessness. Several kings tried to prop up the nation through political alliances with other nations.

Prophets like Jonah (785–775 BC), Amos (760–750 BC) and Hosea (750–715 BC) challenged both king and nation, reminding them of God's character and covenant, denouncing sin, and warning that unless people repented, judgement would come. That judgement came through Assyria.

Assyria wanted more territory and, after several years of dominating Israel from a distance, it finally besieged its capital Samaria in 722 BC (17:1-4). Israel was conquered and many citizens were deported across the Assyrian empire (17:3-6; 18:9-12). The history of the ten northern tribes was now over, the deportees being scattered among other races and religions to be lost without trace.

Judah
Meanwhile down south, David's descendants continued to rule, challenged and encouraged by Obadiah (855–840 BC, or 605–586 BC), Isaiah (740–681 BC), Micah (750–686 BC) and Jeremiah (628–585 BC). Two good kings were Hezekiah (715–687 BC), who reformed worship and trusted God when Assyria attacked Jerusalem (18:1–20:21), and Josiah (640–609 BC), who refurbished the temple, rediscovered part of God's Law, and renewed the covenant (22:1–23:30). Especially bad was Manasseh (687–642 BC), who returned to Baal worship, erecting pagan altars in the temple and even sacrificing his son (21:1-18).

Jeremiah (626–585 BC) warned that judgement was coming. If Judah didn't repent, it would be judged, like Israel, and even the temple would be destroyed. No one believed him, but when Babylon conquered Assyria (605 BC), it invaded Judah and appointed Zedekiah as king (24:1-17). When he tried to rebel, Babylon marched against Jerusalem, capturing it in 586 BC. The city and temple were destroyed and the population exiled to Babylon (25:1-21; 2 Chronicles 36:15-21; Jeremiah 52:1-30).

Author
See handbook at 1 Kings, p.104.

Date
See handbook at 1 Kings, p.104.

OUTLINE – 2 KINGS

The ministry of Elisha

1:1-18	Ahaziah and Elijah
2:1-18	Elijah taken to heaven in a whirlwind
2:19-25	The early ministry of Elisha
3:1-27	The accession of Joram (Israel); revolt of Moab
4:1–6:7	Elisha's miracles
6:8-23	The Arameans attempt to capture Elisha
6:24–7:20	The famine in Samaria
8:1-6	The restoration of the Shunammite woman's land
8:7-15	The murder of the king of Aram
8:16-29	The reigns of Jehoram and Ahaziah (Judah)
9:1-13	The anointing of Jehu (Israel)
9:14-37	The death of Joram and Ahaziah; death of Jezebel
10:1-27	The slaughter of Ahab's family and the Baal worshippers
10:28-36	Jehu's sin and death
11:1-3	The reign of Athaliah (Judah)
11:4-21	Joash (Judah) replaces Athaliah
12:1-21	The reign of Joash
13:1-9	The reign of Jehoahaz (Israel)
13:10-25	The reign of Jehoash (Israel); death of Elisha

Israel and Judah from the death of Elisha to the exile of Israel

14:1-20	The reign of Amaziah (Judah)
14:21-22	Azariah (Judah) replaces Amaziah
14:23-29	The reign of Jeroboam II (Israel)
15:1-7	The reign of Azariah (Judah)
15:8-12	The reign of Zechariah (Israel)
15:13-16	The reign of Shallum (Israel)
15:17-22	The reign of Menahem (Israel)
15:23-26	The reign of Pekahiah (Israel)
15:27-31	The reign of Pekah (Israel)
15:32-38	The reign of Jotham (Judah)
16:1-20	The reign of Ahaz (Judah)
17:1-2	The accession of Hoshea (Israel)
17:3-6	The fall of Samaria to the Assyrians
17:7-23	The deportation of Israel to captivity
17:24-41	The settlement of foreigners in Samaria

From the exile of Israel to the exile of Judah

18:1-8	The accession of Hezekiah (Judah)
18:9-16	Judah pays tribute to Assyria
18:17-37	Sennacherib's attack against Judah
19:1-34	Isaiah predicts deliverance from the attack
19:35-37	Assyria withdraws from Judah; death of Sennacherib
20:1-21	Hezekiah's illness and death
21:1-18	The reign of Manasseh (Judah) >>>

KEY THEMES – 2 KINGS

The God of miracles

Many miracles happened through Elijah and Elisha. With Elijah, they generally demonstrated God's supremacy over Baal; with Elisha, God's compassion for those in need. Miracles are generally restricted in the Old Testament to crucial moments, like at the exodus and during these dark days when the prophets were fighting for the survival of Israel's faith. In the New Testament, miracles become much more common, not only in Jesus' and the apostles' ministry, but throughout the early church.

The God of judgement

Kings shows that, while God loves his people, if they continue in sinful ways he has no alternative, as a holy God, but to judge them. We see this, first in the destruction of Israel by Assyria, and then in the exile of Judah by Babylon.

Jeremiah, prophesying at the end of this period, described God's wrath – his righteous anger against sin – as being stored up in a goblet, ready to be poured out in judgement (Jeremiah 25:15-29), not just on God's enemies, but also on God's people unless they changed. It is this cup that Jesus saw himself drinking for us at the cross (Matthew 26:39).

The God we can trust

Hezekiah showed how God can be trusted (18:5). When Assyria, now only a few miles from Jerusalem after its invasion of Israel, threatened to invade Judah too (18:17-37), Hezekiah turned to God, rather than Egypt, spreading out Assyria's threatening letter before God in the temple (19:14-19). Isaiah encouraged him to stand firm (19:20-34) and "that night the angel of the LORD went out and put to death a hundred and eighty-five thousand men in the Assyrian camp" (19:35). Whenever the kings trusted God, and returned to his covenant like Josiah did (eg 22:1–23:25), he rescued them; whenever they depended on themselves or human resources, he left them to experience the consequences.

What happened to Israel?

Many Israelites were dispersed across the Assyrian Empire, while other conquered peoples were transported to Israel, thus mixing up these nations and destroying any powerbase that might rebel. Many fanciful ideas grew up about what happened to the ten lost tribes of Israel. However, while some probably fled to Judah, most were either dispersed (and we have no idea what happened to them) or were left behind and intermarried with other peoples. These eventually became the Samaritans, despised by Jews in New Testament times because of their racial and religious impurity.

RELEVANCE FOR TODAY – 2 KINGS

God's people

God uses all kinds of people. **Elijah** ("My God is the LORD") was from Gilead, a backwater, and his rough manner and blunt message made him look like a nobody. He preferred to work alone, and could be something of a depressive (1 Kings 19:1-5). By contrast, **Elisha** ("My God saves") was a quieter character who came from a wealthy family and gave up everything to respond to God's call. While sometimes involved in national affairs, he was more concerned with individuals, wanting them to know that God, not Baal, was their provider.

God still uses different characters and personalities. We don't have to imitate others to be used by him.

God's portion

Before Elijah was taken into heaven, Elisha asked for "a double portion" (2:9). He wasn't asking to be twice as powerful or anointed, but rather to be his successor. When a father died, the eldest son received a double share of the inheritance because he was now responsible for the wider family. Elisha was saying he was now ready to pick up Elijah's responsibilities.

God is looking for those who are not eager to get special anointing for themselves, but for others. His portion is for service not for selfishness.

God's perspective

God wants us to look with spiritual eyes. When Elisha's servant saw the Arameans who were sent to capture his master, Elisha asked God to open his eyes "and he looked and saw the hills full of horses and chariots of fire all around Elisha" (6:17). Elisha understood that God's angels are always around, always protecting us. See Psalm 91:9-13.

> "... the LORD removed them from his presence, as he had warned through all his servants the prophets..."
>
> **2 Kings 17:23**

God's love

The story of the healing of Naaman (chapter 5), an Aramean commander with leprosy, shows that God's love reaches beyond those who are already his people. Damascus was a proud city and Elisha challenged his pride by telling him to bathe in the Jordan, a river much inferior to the rivers of Damascus. While at first he struggled with this, the wisdom of a young Israelite girl prevailed and he obeyed. He was healed and became a believer (5:14-15).

God wants us to always be ready to look beyond our own kind – whether people, tribe, town or nation – remembering that his salvation really is for all.

1 Chronicles

UNDERSTANDING YOUR HISTORY

OVERVIEW

1 Chronicles (originally one book with 2 Chronicles, but separated by the Greek translators of the Old Testament) tells the history of Israel with a particular emphasis on the role of the temple and its priests. It emphasises God's ongoing purposes for his people in the light of his promises in the past, especially to David.

SUMMARY

The history of God's people

To establish the identity of God's people, 1 Chronicles opens with long genealogies (chapters 1-9). For people returning from exile to reclaim their heritage, this was immensely important. Going right back to Adam, through the development of twelve tribes from Jacob's twelve sons, and right up to their recent experience of God's judgement (9:1-2), the Chronicler sets the scene for new hope.

The history of God's king

Having dealt quickly with Saul (10:1-14), the Chronicler focuses on Israel's ideal king, David. Omitting Saul's opposition (1 Samuel chapters 18-31) and David's seven-year rule over just Judah (2 Samuel 2:1-4; 5:1-5), he tells how David became king over "all Israel" (11:1) because both God and Israel wanted it (11:2-3). David demonstrated his leadership by capturing Jerusalem, making it his capital (11:4-9), and gathering warriors (11:10–12:40). Bringing the ark there reinforced Jerusalem's importance, though disaster interrupted the process (13:1-14). Realising this was because they had violated God's holiness by not having Levites carry it (15:1-2, 13; see Exodus 25:12-14), the ark was returned properly, amid great rejoicing (15:1–16:43). The irony of God's ark being in a tent while David lived in a palace provoked a desire to build a temple (17:1-2). However, God turned David's desire on its head: God would build a "house" for him

instead (17:3-10), one that would last for ever (17:11-14), and David responded with gratitude (17:16-27). David's victories (18:1–20:8) were followed by Satan's attack, provoking David to pride by taking a military census (21:1-6). God was angry with David and sent a plague as judgement (21:7-14). However, the place where God stopped the plague – where his judgement and mercy met – was designated as the future temple's site (21:15–22:1). The remaining chapters are devoted to David's preparations for building the temple: his charge to Solomon and explanation of why he himself couldn't build it (22:2-19); the Levites' roles (23:1–26:32); arrangements for military and administrative service (27:1-34); David's plans (28:1-21) and gifts (29:1-9) for the temple. The book closes with David's prayer of amazement (29:10-20) and the anointing of Solomon as king (29:21-25). This done, David's life work is over (29:26-30).

Author

The author of Chronicles ("the Chronicler") is unknown, although ancient Jewish tradition suggests Ezra wrote Chronicles, and Ezra and Nehemiah, which complete the story.

Date

Written after Judah's return from exile in Babylon in the fifth or fourth century BC.

OUTLINE – 1 CHRONICLES

KEY THEMES – 1 CHRONICLES

God's purpose

While Kings, written in exile, answers the question, "How did we end up here?" Chronicles, written after the return from exile, answers the question, "Is God still with us?" The Chronicler answers, "Yes!" For even though there was no Davidic king ruling and Israel was subject to Persia, God still had a purpose for them. Assuming his readers knew Samuel and Kings (eg 2 Chronicles 27:7), he focuses on events that demonstrated this ongoing purpose to provoke them to faith for the future.

God's covenant

David acknowledged that God "remembers his covenant for ever, the word he commanded, for a thousand generations" (16:15). It was this covenant, rather than present circumstances, that was Israel's basis of hope. When this covenant was obeyed, its blessings were experienced; when it wasn't, disaster came (eg 15:2, 13). The consequences of obedience and disobedience are seen especially in 2 Chronicles.

God's king

The Chronicler sees David as the ideal king. Whereas in 2 Samuel we see his failures (eg his adultery and weak fathering), Chronicles presents him in a better light, omitting his bad points and highlighting his good ones. The prophets saw David as a "type" of the Messiah who would fulfil God's promises to David (eg Isaiah 9:6-7; Jeremiah 23:5-6; Ezekiel 34:23-24), and the Chronicler also sees David as typifying that messianic king.

God's temple

The Chronicler emphasises David's preparations for the temple, and 2 Chronicles Solomon's actual building of it. He draws parallels between David-Solomon and Moses-Joshua, the "preparer" and the "doer" (eg compare 22:11-16; 28:2-10 with Deuteronomy 1:37-38; 31:2-8). When the Chronicler was writing, the temple was probably still in ruins; but his work ends with Cyrus' edict about its rebuilding (2 Chronicles 36:22-23), demonstrating hope for its future. The temple represents continuity with the past. It, rather than king, is now the focus of Israel's identity.

God's people

The term "all Israel" is used repeatedly, even when referring to the divided kingdom. This is because the returned exiles were now all that was left of God's people. In 2 Chronicles he records how, after the kingdom divided, godly people left Israel for Judah (eg 2 Chronicles 11:14; 15:9; 30:1-20; 34:9). So the post-exilic remnant could truly be called "all Israel" since representatives from the other tribes were among them.

KINGS OF ISRAEL AND JUDAH

Dates are approximate; overlapping dates indicate periods of co-regency

The united kingdom		Israel		Judah	
1050–1010	Saul	931–910	Jeroboam I	931–913	Rehoboam
1010–970	David			913–911	Abijah
970–931	Solomon	910–909	Nadab	911–870	Asa
(931 The kingdom divides)		909–886	Baasha		
		886–885	Elah		
		885	Zimri		
		885–880	Tibni		
		880–874	Omri		
		874–853	Ahab	873–848	Jehoshaphat
		853–852	Ahaziah		
		852–841	Jehoram	848–841	Jehoram
		841–814	Jehu	841	Ahaziah
				841–835	Queen Athaliah
		814–798	Jehoahaz	835–796	Joash
		798–782	Jehoash	796–767	Amaziah
		793–753	Jeroboam II	792–740	Uzziah
		753–752	Zechariah	740–735	Jotham
		752	Shallum		
		752–742	Menahem		
		742–740	Pekahiah		
		740–732	Pekah	735–715	Ahaz
		732–722	Hoshea		
		(722 Israel falls, people exiled)		715–687	Hezekiah
				687–642	Manasseh
				642–640	Amon
				640–609	Josiah
				609	Jehoahaz
				609–598	Jehoiakim
				597	Jehoiachin
				597–586	Zedekiah
				(586 Jerusalem falls)	

RELEVANCE FOR TODAY – 1 CHRONICLES

The Chronicler underlines keys to our moving into God's future at a time of change and challenge:

Knowing who we are

Although genealogies (like the one in chapters 1-9) can seem quite boring to us (if we're honest!), they were important to people at the time. Here, at the beginning of Chronicles, they establish the identity of the returning exiles, for people can only know where they are going when they know who they are and where they have come from. Jesus himself underlined this principle. "Jesus knew ... that he had come from God (*identity*) and was returning to God (*destiny*), so he got up ... and began to wash his disciples' feet" (John 13:3-5). His security in his identity and destiny meant he could undertake any task, even washing feet, for neither was affected by it. We cannot serve God and move ahead into his future for us unless we are secure about who we are in Christ. It was Jabez' confidence in who he was that enabled him to confidently ask God for more (4:10).

Learning from history

By retelling Israel's history (to people who already had Samuel and Kings) the Chronicler was showing that we can always learn from the past, especially from different perspectives, and if we don't learn, we will commit the same errors again. By emphasising some facts and omitting others, he underlined his message that only obedience leads to ongoing blessing. Comparing Chronicles with Samuel and Kings often highlights what important lesson he was trying to underline.

Needing one another

Despite his gifts and calling, David was not a "one-man ministry". He not only gathered great warriors (11:10–12:40), he also released them in their gifting (eg 11:14, 20-21, 22-25; 12:1-2, 8, 14). This in turn produced loyalty as they "gave his kingship strong support" (11:10) and committed themselves to his success (12:18). Good leaders do not do everything themselves but release the gifts in all God's

> "Now, who is willing to consecrate himself today to the LORD?"
>
> 1 Chronicles 29:5

people. The Chronicler knew that, in this period after the return from exile, God's people desperately needed that.

Planning for the future

Most politicians (and many pastors) think only of their own immediate success, but David thought to the future and made plans for the success of his son Solomon. David prepared everything for the building of the temple, but he knew it would be Solomon who built it. Good leaders plan for the future and for their successor's success, not simply their own.

2 Chronicles
FROM DEDICATION TO DISASTER

OVERVIEW

Continuing the history of Israel begun in 1 Chronicles, the book surveys the kings of Judah from its third king, Solomon, to its last one at the time of the exile showing that, despite the hard time God's people have been through, there is still hope for the future.

SUMMARY

Solomon

Invited to choose a blessing, Solomon chose wisdom, but was given wealth too (1:1-17). He built the temple (3:1–5:1), brought the ark there (5:2-14) and dedicated it (6:1-42). Fire fell (7:1), showing God's acceptance. God appeared to him in a dream (7:11-12), promising that repentance and obedience would produce blessing (7:13-18) but disobedience would always bring curse (7:19-22), a principle seen throughout Chronicles. In Solomon the writer sees temple and throne coming together, which is why he avoids mentioning his errors, noted in Kings.

The divided kingdom

Lacking Solomon's wisdom, Rehoboam ignored Israel's plea for relief (10:1-15). Israel therefore split away, crowning Jeroboam (10:15-19). Rehoboam strengthened Judah by reinforcing its border towns (11:5-12), and some northern priests and Levites joined him because of Jeroboam's idolatry (11:13-17). But Judah too adopted idolatry (12:1, 5) and was punished by Egypt robbing the temple (12:1-11). Rehoboam repented and Judah was spared (12:12).

The Chronicler then recalls Judah's succeeding kings, ignoring Israel completely except where its story affected Judah. The message is clear: only obedient kings were blessed.

Good kings

These include:

- Jehoshaphat (17:1–20:37), who taught God's word and defeated his enemies through praise, but who later allied with Israel and didn't remove high places.
- Joash (24:1-16), who restored the temple and worship, but who later adopted Baal worship (24:17-27).
- Uzziah (26:3-23), who was a great soldier, farmer and administrator, but who became proud and contracted leprosy.
- Hezekiah (29:1–32:33), who restored both temple and worship and followed Isaiah's counsel when Sennacherib threatened Jerusalem, seeing it spared, but who became proud.
- Josiah (34:1–35:27), who purged Judah of idolatry and refurbished the temple. During repair works "the Book of the Law" (probably Deuteronomy) was found (34:14-15) which Josiah immediately implemented.

Wicked kings

These include:

- Ahaz (28:1-27), who developed pagan worship and was judged through military defeats. His appeal to Assyria ended in humiliation, but this didn't turn him back to God.
- Manasseh (33:1-20), the longest reigning (52 years) and most wicked of Judah's kings, who utterly embraced Baal worship, including child sacrifice (33:1-9). He finally repented in exile in Assyria.

End of the kings

With Assyria's overthrow, Judah was eyed up by both Egypt and Babylon. After years of uncertainty, God allowed Babylon to destroy Jerusalem (36:15-19). Many were massacred, while the rest were taken into exile (36:20) to give the land rest from the people's wickedness (36:21).

The author concludes with a summary of the return from exile, which is expanded further in Ezra.

Author
See handbook at 1 Chronicles, p.112.

Date
See handbook at 1 Chronicles, p.112.

THE DIVIDED KINGDOM

After Solomon died, his son Rehoboam was appointed king over Judah, continuing the same overbearing hold over the country as his father. Jeroboam returned from Egypt and led demands for a less oppressive approach. Rehoboam refused, causing Jeroboam to be appointed king over the tribes of the north.

Shechem became the capital of Israel in the north while Jerusalem ruled over Judah. During Jeroboam's reign he relocated his capital to Tirzah, but years later Omri had Samaria built as his seat of power.

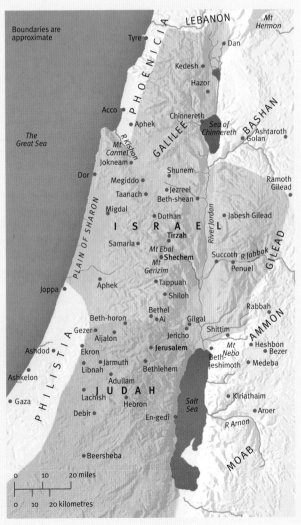

OUTLINE – 2 CHRONICLES

KEY THEMES – 2 CHRONICLES

See handbook at 1 Chronicles, p.113.

God's temple

The temple is given priority because the writer wants to encourage the returned exiles to give priority to it as a symbol of the priority God must have. Although based on the tabernacle, Solomon wanted the temple to reflect God's greatness in size and magnificence (3:3–5:1). God's acceptance of it was shown in his coming in cloud (6:13-14) and fire (7:1), symbols of his presence at the exodus.

God's priests

The Chronicler records faithful work by priests, like preparing the temple and bringing the ark to it (4:1–5:14). Northern priests and Levites are commended for abandoning idolatrous Israel and coming to Jerusalem (11:13-17). Priests were involved in praising in battle (13:13-18; 20:18-23) and collecting offerings (24:4-5, 8-11; 31:4-13). The work of the chief priest Jehoiada as counsellor to Joash is particularly noted, and he was rewarded by being buried alongside kings (22:10–24:16).

God's law

Whether the temple existed or not, it was according to their allegiance to the covenant that every king was judged. Those who "did what was right in the eyes of the LORD" (eg 20:32; 24:2; 26:4; 27:2; 29:2; 34:2) were blessed; those who didn't were judged, as God said (7:14-22). The rediscovery of "the Book of the Law" (probably Deuteronomy) is highlighted (34:14-33), with Josiah quick to implement its requirements, leading to another reform.

God's prophets

The prophets' role was not primarily to predict the future, but to call people back to the covenant and encourage them in face of difficulties. Their importance is reflected in the many prophets mentioned, including: Shemaiah (12:5, 15), Iddo (13:22), Azariah (15:8), Micaiah (18:1-27) and Oded (28:9-11). Canonical prophets linked with kings were:

- Micah (750–686 BC) – Jotham, Ahaz, Hezekiah
- Isaiah (740–681 BC) – Hezekiah
- Jeremiah (628–585 BC) – Josiah, Jehoiakim, Jehoiachin, Zedekiah
- Zephaniah (640–609 BC) – Josiah
- Nahum (663–612 BC) – Josiah
- Habakkuk (640–598 BC) – Josiah, Jehoiakim
- Daniel (605–530 BC) – Jehoiakim and exile
- Ezekiel (593–571 BC) – Jehoiakim, Jehoiachin, Zedekiah and exile
- Obadiah (possibly 855–840 BC) – Jehoshaphat, Jehoram; (or 605–586 BC) – Jehoiakim, Jehoiachin, Zedekiah

God's kings

Kings were appointed by God, but they couldn't do as they pleased. They were constrained by God's Law (eg 7:17-22), and were judged by whether they lived according to it. For the Chronicler, kings' disobedience always met with immediate retribution (eg 12:5; 16:7-9; 19:1-2; 21:12-15; 24:20; 25:14-15; 28:1-5; 34:22-25).

RELEVANCE FOR TODAY – 2 CHRONICLES

Understanding God's promises

God's promises aren't always worked out as we expect. The Chronicler (and prophets like Haggai, Zechariah and Malachi) saw that God's promise of an eternal Davidic kingdom (1 Chronicles 17:10-14), apparently now broken, wasn't dependent on David's descendants reigning. Rather, "ideal" kings, like David, Solomon, Jehoshaphat, Hezekiah and Josiah, were "types" of the coming Messiah and his everlasting kingdom. God's ways of working things out is often different (eg Isaiah 55:8-9).

> "If my people,
> who are called by
> my name, will humble
> themselves and pray and
> seek my face and turn from
> their wicked ways,
> then will I hear from heaven
> and will forgive their sin
> and will heal
> their land."
>
> **2 Chronicles 7:14**

Seeking God's resources

Invited to choose any gift (1:7), Solomon chose wisdom (1:10); and because he didn't grasp for things for himself, God added wealth too (1:11-12). Good leaders seek nothing for themselves, only for those they lead; so it is sad when they prioritise personal prestige or possessions. God's blessing of prosperity is for others through us, not for us through others.

Finding God's heart

No matter how far we have drifted from God, there is always a way back. Even Manasseh, one of Judah's worst kings, discovered this. Although involved in idolatry, child-sacrifice, sorcery, witchcraft and spiritism (33:6), he made a dramatic U-turn when taken into exile (33:12). Despite all he had done and led others into doing, God not only forgave him, but restored him (33:13), as he promised (7:14). His repentance shows it's never too late for anyone to find God's heart.

Building God's house

Solomon wanted his temple to reflect God's greatness (2:5) and impress unbelievers (9:6), and it did. But it was also a snare, eventually becoming a source of pride. Judah thought that, as "God's house", God was bound to protect it and Jerusalem; but they were wrong (36:15-19), as Jeremiah warned (Jeremiah 7:3-15). Buildings are not God's house; we are (eg 1 Peter 2:4-5). Buildings make good servants but poor masters.

Experiencing God's revival

Revivals are exciting times; but for them to be long-lasting, the change in lives must be profound; when it isn't, the revival is shallow and short-lived, as Hezekiah discovered. While revival led to the speedy renewal of the temple (29:36) and even touched people's pockets (31:4-10), the change was not deep: priests weren't ready for the challenge (30:2-3), Hezekiah became proud (32:24-26), and his son Manasseh, clearly untouched by the revival, quickly led the nation back into paganism (33:1-9), showing how superficial the revival had been. Revivals are not about superficial excitement, but deep and lasting change. Key principles for revival can be found in Solomon's prayer (7:14).

Ezra
GOD'S PROMISE IS KEPT

OVERVIEW

Picking up where 2 Chronicles finished, Ezra tells how God's people returned to Judah and how, despite many struggles and obstacles, they succeeded in rebuilding the temple and re-establishing themselves in the land God had promised them so long before.

SUMMARY

Return

Having conquered Babylon, Cyrus allowed the Jews in 538 BC to return to the home from which Babylon had exiled them 70 years earlier (1:1-4), fulfilling Jeremiah's prophecy (Jeremiah 25:8-14; 29:4-14). They were given resources and livestock to begin life again (1:6) and Cyrus returned the temple's treasure (1:7-11). The returning exiles, under Zerubbabel, are carefully listed (2:1-70).

Rebuilding

Three months after their return, they rebuilt the altar and recommenced sacrifices (3:1-6) "despite their fear of the peoples around them" (3:3). Then the temple's foundation was relaid, a moment of great emotion (3:7-9).

Resistance

Their return was resented by those Assyria had resettled, for this was now their home. So, with offers of help to rebuild the temple rejected (4:1-3), they turned against the Jews, undermining them (4:4-5) and warning the Persian king how dangerous a restored Jerusalem would be (4:6-22). Further work was then prohibited (4:23-24) and stopped for 16 years – too long for Haggai and Zechariah who stirred them into action (5:1-2). Further threats in the form of opposition represented by the governor of the Trans-Euphrates (Tattenai) and Shethar-Bozenai and their associates (5:3) and an appeal to Darius followed (5:3-17), but God frustrated this and Darius confirmed Cyrus'

permission (6:1-12), leading to the completion of rebuilding and dedicating the temple (6:13-22) on March 12, 516 BC, almost 70 years exactly after its destruction.

Renewal

Between chapters 6 and 7, 30 years pass about which we know nothing. But in 458 BC Ezra, an expert in God's Law (7:10), returned with another group (7:1-10; 8:1-14), with authority to implement God's Law (7:11-28). Having fasted before the journey to seek God's protection (8:15-23) and entrusted resources to twelve priests and twelve Levites (8:24-30), he celebrated their safe arrival with sacrifices (8:31-36). He was appalled at the spiritual state of God's people, especially how many, including priests and leaders, had married unbelievers (9:1-5), prayerfully recalling that this was the root of the backsliding that had led to exile (9:6-15). All the men were called to Jerusalem (10:1-8) where, in pouring rain (10:9), Ezra confronted them (10:9-17). Over the coming days (10:12-17), a list of those who had intermarried was drawn up (9:18-44).

While most of Ezra is written in Hebrew, parts quoting official documents or letters (4:8–6:18; 7:12-26) are written in their original Aramaic, the international language of the day.

Author

Literary parallels suggest the same author as Chronicles, possibly Ezra himself.

Date

Written after Judah's return from exile around 440 BC.

OUTLINE – EZRA

The return from exile
1:1-4	The edict of Cyrus
1:5-11	The return to Jerusalem
2:1-70	The list of returning exiles

The rebuilding of the temple
3:1-13	The rebuilding of the altar
4:1-24	Opposition to the rebuilding of the temple
5:1–6:12	Darius' decree that the temple shall be rebuilt
6:13-15	The rebuilding of the temple
6:16-18	The dedication of the temple
6:19-22	The celebration of the Passover

Ezra's return to Jerusalem
7:1-26	Artaxerxes authorises Ezra to return
7:27-28	Ezra's act of praise
8:1-14	The list of those returning with Ezra
8:15-20	Ezra's search for Levites to serve in the temple
8:21-30	Preparations for the return
8:31-36	The journey to Jerusalem
9:1–10:44	The religious reforms introduced by Ezra on his arrival

KEY THEMES – EZRA

God's sovereignty

Ezra opens with a great declaration of God's sovereignty. Cyrus, King of Persia, may have conquered Babylon and swallowed its empire, but what really lay behind his victory was the sovereign timing of God who had counted the 70 years Jeremiah had prophesied and had determined that now was the time for his people to go home, just as promised (1:1). Cyrus may not have known God, but God knew Cyrus and moved him to do what he wanted.

God's temple

The importance of the temple, as the new focus of religious and cultural identity, is underlined by detailing the long and difficult process of rebuilding it in the face of constant opposition (4:1-24; 5:3-17). The opposition almost succeeded, the people becoming so discouraged that they stopped work for 16 years. It took the provocation of Haggai and Zechariah to stir them into action again (5:1-2; see handbook at Haggai and Zechariah, p.216, 219). The mixed emotions at the foundation-laying (3:10-13) show how important re-establishing the temple was to them.

God's word

Ezra was a scribe (religious teacher) who was "well versed in the Law of Moses, which the LORD, the God of Israel, had given" (7:6). His knowledge led King Artaxerxes to send him to Judah to teach this law to God's people. His desire to give God's word first place is seen in his challenging people to put right their disobedience to it concerning mixed marriages (9:10-15; Exodus 34:15-16) and his later week-long reading it to them (Nehemiah 8:1-18). Reading the Scriptures had found new importance during the exile when they did not have the temple and its sacrifices, and it helped shape modern Judaism.

God's people

God's people are called to be holy – distinct and different – even as God himself is (Leviticus 11:44-45; 19:2; 20:26; 1 Peter 1:15-16). The first group of returning exiles had intermarried with the residents of the land put there by Babylon. No doubt it was with good intentions, perhaps because there weren't enough Jewish women to provide every Jewish man with a wife to have children to continue the nation; however, good intentions are no substitute for obedience, so Ezra challenged this fundamental breach of holiness. God's people are called to maintain their holiness, their distinctiveness through everything – worship, lifestyle, character and beliefs.

RELEVANCE FOR TODAY – EZRA

Keeping holy
While most Christians genuinely want to lead lives that are pleasing to God, it gets harder to be holy in times of pressure. The lack of Jewish

"There is still hope for Israel..."

Ezra 10:2

women led many Jewish men, and even some leaders, to forget the demands of holiness in marriage – that God's people may only marry believers (eg 2 Corinthians 6:14-18) – in favour of "being practical". After all, without children, they no doubt thought, how would the Jewish race ever continue? But following God's holiness will always be for our best, even though we may have to trust God on the way.

Keeping going
It's hard to keep going when everything is against us, and even harder when God's promises aren't working out as quickly or easily as we had hoped. That's what the returning exiles experienced. Discouraged by opposition and lack of progress, they eventually gave up and focused on their homes instead of God's house. So God sent Haggai and Zechariah to stir them up (5:1-2). God wants his people to learn stickability and not give up (Galatians 6:9; Hebrews 12:1-13).

Keeping focused
Ezra believed in the value of fasting – abstaining from food to focus on God. It was practised at crucial times in the Bible or on solemn occasions to show complete dependence on God. Ezra fasted before undertaking the long and hazardous journey back to Judah (8:21-23). Others who fasted include David (2 Samuel 12:16), Daniel (9:3), Esther (4:3, 16), Nehemiah (1:4), Paul (Acts 13:2-3) and Jesus (Matthew 4:2). When prayer doesn't seem to be working, or the challenge ahead seems great, fasting still helps us focus on God and his ability to provide a solution to our needs.

Keeping sincere
Sincerity and integrity are important for God's people, and even more so for leaders. There is nothing more shameful than leaders being exposed for having secretly done the very things they have been preaching against. Jesus condemned the Pharisees for living this way (eg Matthew 23:1-39). Ezra, by contrast, was very careful to keep his integrity. "Ezra had devoted himself to the study and observance of the Law of the LORD, and to teaching its decrees and laws in Israel" (7:10). Notice that studying and observing (for himself) came before teaching (for others).

Nehemiah
BUILDING FOR GOD

OVERVIEW
Continuing the story begun in Ezra, Nehemiah recounts the story of the amazing rebuilding of the walls of Jerusalem and the reorganising of the life of God's people under the inspiring leadership of Nehemiah.

SUMMARY

Requesting permission
On hearing of the returned exiles' struggles (1:1-3), Nehemiah, a Jew in Persian royal service, was devastated and immediately fasted and prayed (1:4-11). While wanting an answer "today" (1:11), it was four months (2:1) before it came. Noticing his sad face, the king asked what was wrong (2:1-2). Nehemiah explained about Jerusalem, seeking permission to go and rebuild it (2:3-5). The king agreed, but made it clear he wanted Nehemiah to return to his job as king's cupbearer (2:6).

Rebuilding walls
Having inspected the walls by night to keep his plans secret (2:11-16), Nehemiah challenged the leaders (2:17-18). As the work began, they faced opposition: threats (2:19-20), ridicule (4:1-3), anger (4:7-8), rumour-mongering (6:1-9) and intimidation (6:10-13), but Nehemiah encouraged them to keep building.

Dividing the task between 42 groups, he involved everyone, assigning them sections near their homes (3:1-32) and ensuring they were protected (4:16-18). Through his single-minded determination, the work was completed in just 52 days (6:15), an amazing timescale after 90 years of relative inactivity. With guards placed on the gates (7:1-3), the city was at last secure and censuses could be taken (7:4-73; 11:1-24, 25-36; 12:1-26).

Re-ordering life
Nehemiah never lost sight of people in the midst of the project, implementing social reforms for the poor. Not only had many sold land, some were now selling their children to raise money (5:1-5). Nehemiah demanded an end to interest on loans and the return of family land (5:6-13), setting a self-restrained example (5:14-19).

With the walls secure, Ezra read God's Law in a great ceremony (8:1-18), leading to immediate recognition of the need for repentance (8:9) and the restoration of the week-long Festival of Tabernacles (8:13-18). Two weeks later, they gathered again for a ceremony of repentance and rededication (9:1-38). Finally the walls were dedicated to God (12:27-43).

Returning home
Nehemiah's first tour of duty lasted twelve years (5:14) after which he returned to Persia. But he then came back, discovering many abuses: mixed marriages (13:1-3, 23-29), an Ammonite living in the temple (13:4-5, 8-9), the Levites not supported (13:10-14), and Sabbath observance neglected (13:15-22). He took swift action to correct all this, so restoring Israel's distinctiveness.

Author
The opening words suggest the author was Nehemiah. However the book was combined

with Ezra in the earliest Jewish manuscripts, suggesting the same editor, possibly Ezra, worked on both.

Date
Written almost 100 years after the return of the first exiles, around 430 BC.

EXILE AND RETURN

The story of the middle eastern nations was one of continually fluctuating power.

From c. 1350–625 BC Assyria held the ascendancy. During this time Tiglath-pileser III claimed Syria, Phoenicia and Galilee as Assyrian provinces.

King Hoshea of Israel revolted but was attacked and defeated by Sargon II in 721. The whole of the northern kingdom was exiled, never to return: foreign peoples from Syria and Babylonia were imported to replace them.

In 701 Sennacherib overran Phoenicia and many of the cities of Judah; Hezekiah in Jerusalem was forced to pay a heavy tribute.

In 626 Babylon won independence from Assyria but in 614 became part of the Medes and Babylonian empire.

In 597 Nebuchadnezzar conquered Jerusalem: Jehoiachin and the leading men of Judah were exiled to Babylon and Zedekiah installed as puppet king. Ten years later Zedekiah revolted – Jerusalem was besieged again and destroyed (587/6).

The nation remained in exile until the decree of Persian king Cyrus allowed many to return with Zerubbabel in 538. Haggai and Zechariah encouraged rebuilding of the temple in Jerusalem (520).

In 458 Ezra returned with a large group. He reinstated the Law and marriage reforms. Nehemiah followed from Susa in 445. The walls of Jerusalem were rebuilt and life began again in their homeland.

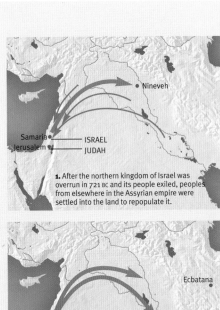

1. After the northern kingdom of Israel was overrun in 721 BC and its people exiled, peoples from elsewhere in the Assyrian empire were settled into the land to repopulate it.

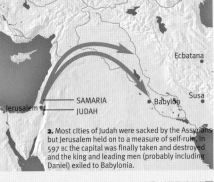

2. Most cities of Judah were sacked by the Assyrians but Jerusalem held on to a measure of self-rule. In 597 BC the capital was finally taken and destroyed and the king and leading men (probably including Daniel) exiled to Babylonia.

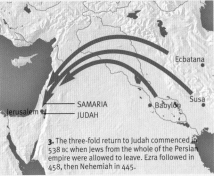

3. The three-fold return to Judah commenced in 538 BC when Jews from the whole of the Persian empire were allowed to leave. Ezra followed in 458, then Nehemiah in 445.

OUTLINE – NEHEMIAH

The rebuilding of the walls of Jerusalem

Ezra's preaching and the resulting revival

The process of resettlement of the returning exiles

The outbreak of abuse during Nehemiah's absence

KEY THEMES – NEHEMIAH

God's man
Nehemiah shows us that it's not just religious leaders (prophets and pastors) that God can use. He had a "secular" job in Persia as "cupbearer to the king" (1:11) – in other words, the poison tester! His faithful and trusted service over the years opened a door for God to use him for much bigger purposes.

God's city
Nehemiah was appalled at Jerusalem's condition and gave himself unstintingly to its restoration. The detailed description of who built various sections of the wall (chapter 3) underlines the Jerusalem's importance for re-establishing the identity of God's people. With no Davidic king ruling, the restored city and temple took on new importance, as Nehemiah understood.

God's remnant
With only a small remnant of God's people returning to Judah (many decided to stay in Persia), it was crucial they maintained a distinct lifestyle to mark them out as God's people. This was why Nehemiah was so shocked when he returned for a second period of office (13:6-7) and found the Jews had disregarded Ezra's teaching and backslidden in many areas, such as mixed marriages (13:1-3, 23-29) and neglecting the Sabbath (13:15-22). His swift, firm action was designed to re-establish the distinctiveness of God's people, crucial to their future survival.

God's justice
True faith, the Bible says, will always overflow into social justice and compassion (eg Jeremiah 22:2-3; Amos 5:21-24). Nehemiah understood this, and so was quick to act when the poor were being abused by the rich (5:1-13), setting a personal example of simple living (5:14-19). Jesus said that it was impossible to love God without loving those in need (eg Luke 10:25-37).

God's Law
As in Ezra, God's Law has a central place in Nehemiah. Having completed his task of getting the wall and gates rebuilt, Nehemiah gave way to Ezra for him to bring God's Law to God's people. An initial morning's reading from the Law (8:1-12) turned into a week-long reading (8:13-18). But just hearing the word of God isn't enough; it's important that people understand it, which is why the Levites were involved in "making it clear and giving the meaning so that the people could understand what being read" (8:8). This central place of God's Law was crucial to establishing and maintaining the identity of the people of God.

RELEVANCE FOR TODAY – NEHEMIAH

The importance of being prayerful

Nehemiah was clearly a man of prayer, knowing both how to spend lengthy times of prayer (1:4) and how to send up "arrow prayers" in moments of need (2:4; 6:9). Both are needed if we are truly to keep dependent on God and not ourselves or our own abilities.

The importance of being ready

Between Nehemiah praying (1:4) and God answering his prayer (2:1), four months passed. God doesn't always answer our prayers immediately so it is important to be ready at the time when he does.

The importance of good administration

Some people seem to think that it isn't spiritual to prepare or plan, but Nehemiah wouldn't have agreed. He prepared by making a secret night-time survey of the wall (2:12) which enabled him to win over the leaders the next day (2:17-18). He then organised the workforce, with everyone working on a section of the wall near their home to ensure the work was done well (chapter 3). With the work completed, he then made careful listings of people and things. Good administration does not need
to quench the Spirit; indeed good administration is a gift of the Holy Spirit (1 Corinthians 12:28).

The importance of team work

Nehemiah was not a "one-man ministry". He knew the importance of getting everyone involved and making them feel part of the team. He did this by carefully assigning people to work together on areas of the wall near their home. Note the recurrence of the phrase "next to him/them" in chapter 3 (3:7,17,18,19,20,21, 22,23,24,25,27,29,30,31). "Team" ensures that "Together Everyone Achieves More". (See also 1 Corinthians 12.)

> "Come,
> let us rebuild
> the wall of Jerusalem,
> and we will no longer
> be in disgrace."
>
> **Nehemiah 2:17**

The importance of clear teaching

Ezra was keen that people should not only hear God's word but also understand it. He involved the Levites in instructing the people in the word and in "making it clear and giving the meaning so that the people could understand what was being read" (8:8). "Making it clear" can also mean "translating it", probably from classical Hebrew into the local language. This and the teaching almost certainly happened in small groups around the temple courtyard. The true measure of teaching is not how well teachers feel they have taught but how well the listeners have learnt.

Esther
THE POWER BEHIND THE THRONE

OVERVIEW
While some Jews went home after the exile, others chose to stay in Persia where they had established new lives. Esther tells how a Jewish orphan there became Queen of Persia and, through her position, foiled a plot to exterminate the Jews.

SUMMARY

A new queen
When King Xerxes' wife refused to be displayed as royal treasure (1:1-12), he deposed her, to teach both her and all wives a lesson (1:13-22). Esther, a Jewish orphan, was chosen to replace her (2:1-18), though her uncle Mordecai told her not to reveal her Jewish nationality (2:10,19-20). She established her new position as queen by passing on Mordecai's warning concerning an assassination plot (2:21-23).

A new problem
Four years later, Haman became chief courtier, but Mordecai refused to bow down to him (3:1-4). Furious, Haman decided to exact revenge by destroying not just him but all Jews (3:6) and persuaded the king to issue a decree for their extermination (3:7-15). Mordecai appealed for Esther's intervention (4:1-14), saying that perhaps this was the very reason God had made her Queen (4:14).

A new deliverance
Esther organised a banquet for Haman and the king (5:1-8). Haman's delight that he was honoured in this way was spoilt when he saw Mordecai at the king's gate. So Haman built a gallows for Mordecai's execution (5:9-14). That night the king couldn't sleep and sent for the royal records and discovered he had never rewarded Mordecai for saving his life (6:1-3). The king asked Haman what should be done for a man he wanted to honour and, thinking it

was for himself, Haman suggested a procession (6:4-9). He was devastated to find it was for Mordecai (6:10-14). That evening at the banquet, Esther explained what Haman had planned against her people, the Jews (7:1-6). The king was angry, and even angrier when he thought Haman was molesting her. He ordered Haman's execution on the very gallows built for Mordecai (7:7-10). Haman's job was given to Mordecai who immediately issued a law allowing Jews to defend themselves (8:1-17). Since Persian laws couldn't be repealed, the earlier decree permitting their extermination still stood; but with permission to defend themselves, they took this opportunity to deal with their enemies (9:1-17).

A new remembrance
The Festival of Purim was instituted to remember this example of deliverance (9:18-32). Mordecai himself would be remembered as a Jew who served the secular authorities but who through it had "worked for the good of his people" (10:3).

Author
Unknown, though clearly someone who understood both Judaism and life at the Persian court.

Date
Shortly after the events narrated, around 460 BC.

OUTLINE – ESTHER

The background to the plot to destroy the Jews

1:1-22   Queen Vashti deposed
2:1-18   Esther made queen
2:19-23 Mordecai uncovers a plot to assassinate the king

The plot to destroy the Jews

3:1-15   Haman's decision to destroy the Jews
4:1-17   Mordecai asks Esther to help him foil the plot
5:1-8   Esther's banquet
5:9-14   Haman builds a gallows to hang Mordecai
6:1-14   The king honours Mordecai
7:1-10   Haman hanged on his own gallows

The institution of the feast of Purim

8:1-17   The king gives the Jews religious freedom and privileges
9:1-17   The Jews kill their enemies in Susa
9:18-32 The institution of Purim
10:1-3   The greatness of Mordecai

King Xerxes of Persia ruled over his kingdom from the twin capitals of Susa and Persepolis. He built the Gate of All Nations in Persepolis as the grand entrance to the city

KEY THEMES – ESTHER

God's presence

While God is never mentioned in Esther, it is clear that he is at work on every page. His apparent absence is the author's technique for showing that God is in control of life – everything in life – even when it isn't obvious. For example, the "coincidences" in chapter 6: the king not being able to sleep, his requesting the court records to read, his discovering what Mordecai had done for him, Haman's entering the court – all this speaks of a God at work at just the right moment.

God's people

Archaeological discoveries show that Jews were still in Persia long after the exile. It is estimated that only 50,000 returned to Judah, a handful compared to those who left. Many stayed where they were because they had settled into a new life, while others moved to other parts of Persia. This dispersion (the "Diaspora") helped the rapid spread of Judaism and, ultimately, of Christianity too, since Christian missionaries often began their evangelism at the synagogues.

God's protection

Haman's edict was the final attempt in the Old Testament period to exterminate the Jews. Haman was an Agagite (3:1), meaning he was probably descended from Agag, King of the Amalekites. This would explain his intense hatred of Jews, since the Amalekites had been Israel's traditional enemy ever since the exodus (Exodus 17:8-16; Deuteronomy 25:17-19). Haman clearly saw this as his moment to "get even", but the God who neither slumbers nor sleeps (Psalm 121:3-4) had his watchful eye on his people to protect them. God's complete reversal of this situation for his people is still celebrated by Jews today in the Festival of Purim, as commanded in this story (9:23-32). In this joyful festival, the story of Esther is read, people dress up in costumes representing the key people in the story, and a celebratory meal is enjoyed together.

God's parallels

The Bible contains a number of remarkable parallels, as God repeats things he has done in the past. The author of Esther seems to have noticed the parallels between Esther and Joseph (Genesis chapters 37–50), parallels reflected in both the language used and the details given. For example, both stories are set in foreign royal courts and both have heroes who rise to a significant position within it which God was then able to use for the deliverance of his people.

Jews celebrate the feast of Purim each year in honour of Queen Esther. Children dress up and special food is prepared

RELEVANCE FOR TODAY – ESTHER

Aligning your life

God wants us to line up our lives completely with him and his purposes, even if that seems risky. Both Mordecai and Esther were prepared to stand and be counted for God, and God honoured them both. Jesus himself underlined this principle (eg Matthew 10:26-33).

Acknowledging your rulers

Esther, like Joseph and Daniel, acknowledged the authority of her ruler, because that was where God had placed her. It can't have been easy because women in the Persian court were merely royal playthings, but she trusted Mordecai's counsel that God had brought her here for a greater purpose (4:14-16). Before the exile Jeremiah urged the Jews to seek the good of the nation they were being taken into because if it prospered, they too would prosper (Jeremiah 29:4-7). Paul urged Christians to submit to secular authorities, support them, pay taxes and pray for them (Romans 13:1-7; 1 Timothy 2:1-4; Titus 3:1).

Appreciating your workplace

Joseph's gifts of administration and dream-interpretation were developed in Egypt; Moses' gift of leadership was learnt in Pharaoh's palace; Daniel's prophesying grew in the service of Babylon; Nehemiah's servant-heart was learnt in Persia – all underlining that God's training of us happens as much in the secular sphere as among God's people. If Esther had despised her position and tried to escape it, it is highly likely the Jews would have been almost exterminated.

Accepting your delays

Most of us hate delays, wanting to rush in and get things done now, but Esther learned how to wait for God's moment. She didn't tell the king immediately she was Jewish (2:10); she didn't rush to tell him of Haman's plan but called people to prayer (4:15-16); when he asked what he could give her, she didn't tell him straight away (5:3-4). She knew that "there is a time for everything, and a season for every activity under heaven" (Ecclesiastes 3:1). Waiting and delays are hard, but they are always worth it, bringing us in line with "the God who acts on behalf of those who wait for him" (Isaiah 64:4).

> "The tables were turned and the Jews got the upper hand over those who hated them."
>
> **Esther 9:1**

Affirming your joy

Our author loved feasting, there being ten banquets in Esther (1:3-4; 1:5-8; 1:9; 2:18; 3:15; 5:1-8; 7:1-10; 8:17; 9:17; 9:18-32). In fact, every key point happens at banquets – probably to underline the importance of Purim, one of Judaism's most joyful holidays. Jesus himself was not afraid to express his joy in life through feasting (eg Matthew 9:10-13; John 2:1-11), despite the Pharisees' objections (eg Matthew 9:14-15). Jesus knew how to feast, just as he knew how to fast.

Job
DEALING WITH DISASTER

OVERVIEW

When Job's life fell apart, he dared to question God. Job's suffering ultimately leads him to a deeper and first hand understanding of God (42:5). This enables him to accept his period of suffering rather than to be obsessed by trying to understand the reasons for it.

SUMMARY

The book of Job begins with two scenes. The first is on earth: Job is a godly man who has a large family and many possessions (1:1-5). The second is in heaven: Satan talks to God about Job, and suggests that Job only follows God because life is going well for him (1:6-11). God allows Satan to test Job (1:12) by taking away all his possessions and his children (1:13-19). However, Job remains faithful to God (1:20-22). Satan then tries to test Job's trust in God by giving him a painful skin disease (2:1-8).

Job still did not lose faith in God (2:9-10), but tries to understand what has happened to him (3:1-26). Much of the book is in the form of a conversation with his friends (2:11-13; 32:1-5). Eliphaz, Bildad and Zophar try to convince Job that he is suffering as a result of some secret wickedness (eg 8:1-22; 11:1-20; 15:1-35; 22:1-30). Job should accept his suffering as the discipline of God (eg 4:1-5:27). However, Job maintains his innocence and accuses God of bringing suffering on him unjustly (eg 6:1–7:21; 9:1-10:22; 23:1–24:25). A fourth friend, Elihu, rebukes Job and the other friends (32:1-5). For Elihu, Job's suffering is a warning, to keep Job close to God, and so Job should not have complained (32:6–35:16).

Finally, God speaks (38:1). He overwhelms Job with his ability to create and sustain the world, and asks Job a series of unanswerable questions to show that his wisdom and power are beyond human understanding (38:2–41:34).

These questions leave Job with nothing to say (40:3-5). But after God has finished speaking, Job reaffirms his complete trust in God (42:1-4). Eliphaz, Bildad and Zophar are rebuked by God for their unwise counsel (42:7-9). In the final scene, God blesses Job with another large family, great wealth and a long life (42:10-17).

Author

An Israelite, but otherwise unknown.

Date

The date when Job was written down is unknown – probably between 7th and 2nd centuries BC, though the story itself is much older.

Job is set a long time ago, perhaps in the age of the patriarchs of Genesis. Its story, however, is relevant for everyone who struggles with seemingly unjust suffering.

OUTLINE – JOB

Introduction

Job's conversation with his three friends

Elihu's speeches

God's response

Conclusion

KEY THEMES – JOB

Understanding God's justice

Like other wisdom literature in the Bible (such as Proverbs, Ecclesiastes, and James), the book of Job is interested in reflections on the right way to live in "the fear of the Lord" (wisdom). Job's friends express the standard understanding of God's justice: God punishes the wicked but rewards the righteous (eg 4:7-9; 8:3,20; 20:1-29). Job's suffering, however, causes him to question this understanding. Job is convinced that he is innocent of any wrongdoing (see 31:1-40) and so it appears that God is bringing disaster to the godly while letting the wicked prosper (eg 10:2-3; 12:4). Job cries out in complaint to God that God is being unjust: God is treating the righteous Job as if he were wicked (9:22). Job wishes he could confront God and present his complaint in person (13:22-27; 23:1–24:12).

In the end, God confronts Job and declares that he remains just (40:8). Although God does not explain to Job why he has been suffering, Job accepts God's response and confesses that he should not have spoken about God's ways when he did not know them (42:1-6). The standard view of God's justice remains: God rewards Job for his faithfulness (42:10-17). However, the book of Job has shown that understanding God's justice is not straightforward. Suffering and wickedness, and blessing and righteousness are not always automatically linked.

The mystery of suffering

Despite his righteous life, Job experiences great suffering: he loses all his possessions (1:13-17), his children are killed (1:18-19) and he is struck down with a painful skin disease (2:7-8). As a result of this, Job wishes he had never been born (3:1-19; 10:18-19) and he experiences the darkness of depression (eg 3:20-26; 6:1-3), feeling that he has been rejected by both God (6:4; 16:7-14; 19:7-12) and his friends (6:14-23; 19:13-22). Job's friends presume that Job must have sinned in order to bring this suffering upon himself as the discipline of God (eg 22:4-11). However, Job is sure that he is right with God, and his woes are undeserved (eg 27:2-6).

When God speaks, he does not accuse Job of being an evildoer. All suffering does not come as a result of sin. But neither does God answer Job's complaint and tell him why he has suffered so much. God does not even mention that he had allowed Satan to test Job (1:6-12; 2:1-6). Suffering remains a mystery. What Job does learn, though, is that God is wiser and far more powerful than Job had ever imagined (42:2-5).

RELEVANCE FOR TODAY – JOB

Staying faithful through suffering

Throughout his sufferings, Job was unaware of the conversation that had taken place between God and Satan (1:6-12; 2:1-7). The readers of the book, however, know that Job's terrible circumstances are the result of Satan's desire to test Job's faith (1:9-11; 2:4-5). Satan expects Job to curse God, once his possessions, family and health are taken away – and Job's wife agrees (2:9)!

Job, however, remains faithful to God throughout his troubles. Although Job does not understand why he is going through suffering, and even accuses God of some injustice in allowing him to suffer, he still declares that God is the creator of the universe (9:4-10; 10:8-12), full of wisdom (12:13; 21:22), and the only hope for the future (19:25-27). Job's faithfulness is ultimately revealed by the end point he reaches: he seals his lips (40:4-5), confirms his faith, confesses his sin (42:1-6) and forgives those who have accused him of wrong (42:7-9).

> "The LORD gave
> and the LORD has taken away;
> may the name of the LORD
> be praised."
>
> **Job 1:21**

The honesty of prayer

At the end of the book, God commends Job for how he has spoken of God (42:7,8). God did not agree with all that Job had said in the rest of his conversation with his friends (see eg 38:2; 40:8), but he is pleased that Job has been honest. Job did not curse God (2:10) or give up on God, but rather expressed his bewilderment at his suffering and complained that God did not seem to be listening to him (19:7).

God wants us to be honest in our relationship with him. Job teaches us that God allows himself to be questioned. He may not give the answers we expect (Job was overwhelmed by God's answer in 38:1–41:34), but our questions and complaints show that we are still holding on to our faith in him, and struggling to relate what we know of God's justice and goodness to the suffering we are experiencing.

The danger of speaking out about God's ways

In another situation, the advice of Job's friends may have been entirely appropriate. Their belief in God's justice (eg 8:2-22; 34:10-30) was admirable. However, they failed to recognise that their rigid beliefs did not apply in every situation: in this situation, Job was innocent and his suffering was simply a mystery. God rebukes Job's friends for what they had said to Job (42:7,8).

The book of Job reminds us that God's ways can never be contained by simple human formulas. Whenever we speak out about God's ways – especially in pastoral situations – we should remember that our understanding is always limited.

Psalms
THE HEARTBEAT OF FAITH

OVERVIEW
A relationship with God embraces all human emotions and experiences.
The book of Psalms is the songbook of God's people – through the Psalms they can find words to express their hope, trust, despair, thanks, sorrow and praise to God.

SUMMARY
Psalms is a collection of 150 poems, arranged into five books.

Book 1 (Psalms 1–41) is a collection of David's psalms. It begins with an introduction to the entire collection, describing the blessing of those who delight in God rather than following evil (1). Most of the psalms in Book 1 are personal prayers for help (eg 5, 10, 22) or expressions of confidence in God (eg 3, 18, 23, 27). Some give praise to God for his greatness in the world (eg 8, 29, 33).

Book 2 (Psalms 42–72) is a compilation of psalms from different authors. They include personal prayers of praise and thanksgiving (eg 46, 47, 66), petition (eg 51, 55, 64) and devotion to God (eg 42, 62, 63).

The psalms of Book 3 (Psalms 73–89) are mainly written by Asaph, the worship leader in Jerusalem. They seem to refer mostly to the life of Israel as a nation (eg prayer for restoration in 85).

Psalms 90–106 (Book 4) give praise to God for his faithfulness to Israel, particularly around the time of the exodus from Egypt (eg 105).

The final book (Psalms 107–150) includes a meditation on God's law (119) and a small collection of songs for pilgrims on the way to Jerusalem (120–134). Although there are a few petitions (eg 102, 140), most of the psalms in this section are hymns of praise to God (eg 100, 103, 134, 144–150).

Author
The Psalms were written by a number of different authors. Around half are attributed to David, but other authors include Moses (90) and the leaders of worship at the temple in Jerusalem – the sons of Korah (eg 42; see 1 Chronicles 6:31-33) and Asaph (eg 50; see 1 Chronicles 6:39, 15:17, and 16:5). The authors of other psalms remain unknown.

Date
The Psalms were written over most of the Old Testament period – from the time of Moses and the exodus from Egypt to the exile in Babylon (c1300–586 BC). Some Psalms might even come from the period after the exile. Most, however, were probably written after David's reign as king in Jerusalem (c.1000 BC).

The book of Psalms spans nearly the whole of Israel's history, and touches upon almost every major event from creation, the patriarchs, and the exodus to the exile. Some relate to a specific incident, which is noted in the psalm's title (eg 3, 30, 34).

OUTLINE – PSALMS

Book 1

1 The righteous and the wicked
2 The king is enthroned
3 Trust in the middle of trouble
4 Confidence in God's goodness
5 Assurance of acceptance by God
6 Prayer for healing
7 Prayer for deliverance
8 Praise of God's majesty in creation
9 Praise for God's justice
10 Lament of the oppressed
11 God is the only refuge
12 Prayer to be kept safe
13 Call for God to answer prayer
14 Reflection on foolish people
15 Reflection on the righteous person
16 Confidence in God
17 Prayer to be kept close to God
18 The great ways of God
19 The glory of God's creation and law
20 Confidence that God will save
21 The king praises God
22 Prayer for help in distress
23 Confidence in God's guidance
24 Entering God's house
25 Celebration of God's character
26 Prayer for vindication
27 Putting trust in the Lord
28 Prayer for mercy
29 God is awesome!
30 Praise to God for salvation
31 Trust in times of distress
32 Encouragement to trust in God's forgiveness
33 Praise for God's faithfulness
34 God's deliverance
35 Prayer for God's help
36 Godlessness and God's love
37 Trusting in the Lord
38 Prayer for forgiveness
39 Prayer for wisdom, help and forgiveness
40 Prayer and thanks for rescue
41 Prayer for healing

Book 2

42 Putting hope in God
43 Prayer for rescue and guidance
44 Prayer for God to come to Israel's aid
45 Praise for the king at his wedding
46 The strength of God's presence
47 Praise to God the King
48 God and his city
49 Wealth and wisdom
50 Acceptable sacrifices
51 Confession and cleansing
52 The wicked and the righteous
53 Reflection on foolish people
54 Prayer for salvation
55 Deliverance from enemies
56 Fear of enemies and God's salvation
57 God's love and faithfulness
58 The judgement of the wicked
59 Deliverance from the wicked
60 Lament over God's rejection
61 Prayer for safety, and for the king
62 Finding rest in God
63 Seeking God
64 Complaint about the wicked
65 Praise for God's creation
66 Declaration of God's power in salvation
67 Prayer for blessing
68 The great majesty of God
69 Prayer for salvation from enemies
70 Prayer for help
71 God is refuge and hope
72 Prayer for the king to rule with justice and blessing

Book 3

73 The wicked perish but the righteous are held by God
74 Lament because of enemies' success
75 Thanks for God's judgement
76 God is great and to be feared
77 Calling to God in time of need
78 The history of Israel
79 Lament for the destruction of Jerusalem

SONGS OF PRAISE AND THANKS

The book of Psalms is best known for its songs of praise and thanks to God, many of which are still used regularly in the worship of God's people today.

The Hebrew title for this book means "praises".

KEY THEMES

Praise for who God is

Hymns of praise declare the majesty and greatness of God. There are a number of common themes:

- **God is awesome.** In many hymns of praise, the psalmist is overwhelmed by the greatness of God. God's power is able to make the earth shake (29:3-8), and he sits on the throne of the universe, surrounded by fire and thick cloud and lightning (97:2-4) – symbolising his unapproachable majesty!
- **God is Creator.** The world and everything in it belong to God because he has created it all (24:1,2). The psalms of praise delight in the wonders of God's creation (104:2-26).
- **God is King.** Compared to the heavenly angels and the gods of other nations, the God of Israel is the mighty King of kings and Lord of lords (89:6-7; 135:5). God rules over the nations (47:7-9) – to him alone belongs all authority and power.
- **God is near.** The songs of praise often contrast the majestic power of God in creation with his gentle tenderness to his people. God is praised for his grace, compassion, mercy, and love (145:8,9). He is faithful and righteous (145:13,17) and is especially close to those who are in need (145:14-16,18).

Thanks for what God has done

God's people always have so much to thank God for! The songs of thanks are declarations of the mighty deeds of God:

- **The salvation of Israel.** Many psalms give thanks to God for rescuing Israel out of difficult situations. In particular, God is thanked for bringing Israel out of Egypt at

> "Shout with joy to God, all the earth! Sing the glory of his name; make his praise glorious!"
>
> **Psalm 66:1-2**

the Exodus (136:10-15) and giving them the land of promise (136:16-22).

- **Personal deliverance.** God kept safe not only the nation of Israel, but also individuals. David and his fellow Israelites could be personally thankful to God for delivering them out of many different situations: despair, danger, sickness and sin (see eg 30:1-12).
- **Faithfulness, justice and care.** God's people thank him for being faithful to them (117:2) and listening to their prayers (118:21). God especially cares for those who are helpless, such as the oppressed, the poor and the lonely (146:7-9).

RELEVANCE FOR TODAY

Joining with creation

The Psalms make it clear that humans are not alone when they give praise to God. The whole of creation – including heavenly angels and all the creatures of the earth – is already praising God for his great goodness (148:1-2,7,10). The natural world of the skies, the stars and the mountains declare God's glory (19:1; 148:3,4,8,9). Even the rivers clap their hands (98:8)!

Our praise may often seem to be very small in comparison with the greatness of God. But by our songs of thanks and praise we join with the rest of creation, both heavenly and earthly, to worship the Lord our God. Praise reminds us that we are not the only people who have been blessed by God: he has a worldwide family and an entire universe to praise him!

A celebration of praise

The Psalms give us a glimpse of the worship of the Israelites. Some psalms would have been read by a leader, others included responses for the congregation to join in (see eg 136). Many were songs to be sung (108:1). The hymns of praise mention dancing, tambourines, harps, trumpets, flutes, strings, and cymbals (149:3; 150:3-5) – this worship was joyful and enthusiastic, encouraging the whole congregation of Israel to join in praise of their God.

There are certainly times for quietness and solemnity in our worship. But the Psalms teach us to praise God with reverence and joy. We must avoid losing either aspect in our worship today: God is great and to be feared, but he is also so wonderful that we must burst out in joy!

The worthiness of God

There is always something for which we can be thankful. Even when our situation seems bleak, the Psalms teach us that we can still bring praise to God for who he is and what he has done. God never ceases to be worthy of worship (48:1).

The focus of praise should always be God. So, whatever we may feel like, it is always fitting for us to praise him (33:1). In the Psalms, praise will always be pleasant to us also (135:3; 147:1)! Our praise should be overwhelmed by the sheer awesomeness and greatness of God.

Joyful celebration, Ghana

PRAYERS TO GOD

The most common type of psalm is a prayer to God.
These psalms cover the whole spectrum of human experience.

KEY THEMES

Crying out to God

Many of the Psalms are passionate cries to God from the middle of difficult and distressing circumstances. These psalms come from almost every imaginable situation – from being attacked by enemies (25:2,19) to suffering from a deadly sickness (41:8). The psalmist feels alone (31:11-12), close to death (31:10), and full of anxiety (31:9). At times, the psalmist goes through the darkness of depression. On occasion, even faith in God seems to falter, and the psalmist feels abandoned by the very God to whom the prayer is made (22:1-2).

These psalms plead for God's intervention and help, whether for help, whether in the form of protection from enemies (25:20), healing (41:4) or guidance (27:11). Some ask God to save the psalmist because of his righteous life (26:1,11) and to destroy the enemies who ridicule and attack them (35:4-8). Others simply make a complaint to God, because of evil in the world (64:1-6) or because God himself seems to be far away (22:1).

Confessing sin

Sometimes, the problem the psalmist faces is not something external, like trouble or sickness, but internal – the guilt and power of sin. Many psalms speak about Israel's rebellion against God, which has led to God's rejection of them (74:1). Others refer to the personal sins of the psalmist (6:1-7). In Psalm 51, David confesses his sin with Bathsheba (see 2 Samuel 11:2-27). In each case, the psalm recognises that sin destroys relationship with God, and so asks for God's forgiveness and cleansing (51:1-2,9-10). The psalmist prays that God will also restore the life of Israel, after her rebellion (85:4-7).

Trusting and hoping

A common theme in the prayer psalms is the confidence that the psalmist has in God. God is a place of safety and security (18:2), who can always be trusted to be good, just, merciful and faithful (86:15-17). The Psalms express a deep longing to be with God (63:1), and constantly encourage the reader to trust and hope in him (43:5).

RELEVANCE FOR TODAY

Expressing life to God

The diversity of the prayer psalms shows that all the experiences and emotions of life can be expressed to God. The Psalms range from great joy and confidence in God (31:7) to deep despair about life (55:4,5). Some psalms even express frustration at God, complaining that he seems far away (22:1). Others speak about the desire for revenge on enemies and oppressors (eg 58:6; 137:8,9), about which we might feel uncomfortable. However, it is appropriate for God's people to call out to him whatever their situation and feelings, because he is their loving Father who cares for them. It is certainly better to direct our desire for revenge against evildoers to God in prayer, rather than to take God's justice into our own hands.

Reading the Psalms regularly can help us to express the depths of human experience in our faith and worship.

Appealing to God's faithfulness

According to the prayers of the book of Psalms, the basis for confidence that God will help in the present is his past faithfulness. The Psalms often recount scenes from the history of Israel – particularly the exodus from Egypt and entry into the Promised Land – as a way of reminding both the users of the psalm and

God himself of God's mighty acts to help his people in the past (eg 44:1-4; 80:8-11). If God is to be true to himself, and to the covenant he has made, he will surely come to rescue his people in their present trouble. This gives the psalmist confidence to appeal directly to God for help (83:1-18).

The psalmist's confidence in the face of difficulty is an example for Christian prayer also. After the death and resurrection of Jesus Christ, we have even more reason to appeal to God's faithfulness and ask for his strength for our problems and weaknesses. The basis of our present help is what God has already accomplished in Jesus Christ.

Being transformed by prayer

The Psalms are difficult to categorise, because the emotions and experiences they express can change in the space of one psalm. Petition can turn into praise (compare 28:1-5 and 6-9, or 69:1-29 and 30-36), while initial confidence and thanksgiving can lead to further petition

> "Hear my voice when I call, O LORD, be merciful to me and answer me. My heart says of you, 'Seek his face!' Your face, LORD, I will seek."
>
> Psalm 27:7-8

(compare 40:1-10 and 11-17). Prayer is truly a conversation with God, in which we both express our own feelings and also receive an assurance of God's faithfulness, holiness or justice. The Psalms show that prayer itself can lead to relief from trouble, or to deeper reflection on the mystery of life or to a fresh acknowledgement of our need for God's help.

PSALMS OF INSTRUCTION

Some psalms instruct the reader in the type of life that is pleasing to God. To know God's blessing, there are both things to avoid and things to do.

KEY THEMES

God's life-giving law

The book of Psalms begins with a meditation on the goodness of God's law (1:2). In fact, the division of the Psalms into five books could be a way of accompanying the five books of the law (Genesis to Deuteronomy) with five books of songs. Whether or not this is so, God's law recurs throughout the Psalms as the way to enjoy life with God (19:7-11). Psalm 119, the longest chapter in the Bible, is a long poem of delight in God's law. The law is God's eternal word (119:89) that gives direction to life (119:105,133). By obeying this law, God's people will be pure and righteous (119:9). It is

therefore very precious (119:127) and evokes the love of God's people (119:167). This picture of God's law corrects the image many people have of dry, meaningless commands.

Wisdom and purity before God

As with wisdom literature, some Psalms make a contrast between foolish and wise people. Foolish people are those who turn away from God's law and do not seek him (14:1-3; 53:1-3). Wise people, on the other hand, desire to follow God's will (1:2; 40:8) and so are righteous. God will watch over the righteous while letting the wicked go to their destruction (1:6).

The wise person will seek to be pure before God. Wisdom shows that real purity is not ritual obedience to the letter of the law, and does not come from simply offering sacrifices (40:6). The purity God delights in is purity of the heart (51:6). This can only come as humans confess their sin to God (51:3-5) and receive God's cleansing (51:7,10). This purity is expressed by a righteous life, which is marked by honesty, integrity, mercy and kindness (15:1-5).

The Psalms show that true righteousness is a matter of the heart, and not of following the right rituals.

Warnings from Israel's history

Some psalms were written in order to pass on the history of Israel to future generations (78:1-6). This history was not simply a repetition of historical facts, but was also a warning to avoid the sins of previous generations and instead to trust in God (78:7,8; 95:7-11).

RELEVANCE FOR TODAY

Singing and learning

The book of Psalms may have been Israel's songbook, but it was also her textbook too. By memorising and reciting these songs, Israelites learned to express their relationship with God. Alongside the rest of Scripture, the Psalms have a valuable role in Christian nurture and education. Sung worship and poetry have a huge role to play in informing and shaping each new generation. The Psalms should inspire us to be creative in expressing our relationship with the eternal God, as we find new songs to praise him (96:1)!

The faith of God's people

The Psalms remind us that God's people in the Old Testament were not simply a political nation, with civic and social laws – they were also a worshipping people. The Psalms found their place in Israelite corporate liturgical life. Other parts of the Old Testament focus on the historical rise of the nation, or the specifics of laws for religious practices. The Psalms, though, are the heartbeat of God's people. They remind us that God's people in every age have a living faith: they were real people with real struggles, doubts, joys and hopes. This faith may not be expressed in dry history books, but it can be found in the songs, poems and prayers they write and use. The book of Psalms encourages us to appreciate and learn from the spirituality of our forefathers in the faith (78:5-8).

Learning and loving

The Psalms are about devotion – faith in and love for God that leads to an overflow of praise, or petition, or thanks, or confession. Whether a psalm was written by the great King David, or an unknown poet, its value is not in who wrote it, but in its ability to lead us to a deeper understanding of and trust in God. The Psalms teach us to love God's law (119:167), because it is pleasing (119:103).

SONGS FOR SPECIAL OCCASIONS

**Some psalms were written with a particular occasion in mind,
including the royal psalms and the songs of pilgrimage.**

ROYAL PSALMS

Key theme

The royal psalms (eg 2, 45, 110) focus on the king of Israel. Some celebrate the enthronement of the king (2:6-7; 110:1), while another celebrates the king's wedding (45:17). The king is described as just and righteous (72:1-7); he trusts in God (21:7) and his kingdom will become great and will last for ever (72:8-11). The psalmist prays for the king to be blessed (20:9; 72:15-17).

Relevance for today

Although these psalms were originally written for David and his successors in Jerusalem, some of the statements made about the king were not fulfilled by the Old Testament kings (eg 72:17; 110:4). These words look forward to the true king and Son of God, Jesus Christ. Jesus used the words of Psalm 110 to describe his own relationship with his heavenly Father (110:1; see Matthew 22:43-45). Early Christians used quotations from the royal psalms to show that Christ was the true king promised by the Old Testament (eg see Acts 2:34,35; Hebrew 1:5,13). These psalms help us to express our worship of Christ as king of the universe.

SONGS OF PILGRIMAGE TO ZION

Key theme

Psalms 120–134 are known as the "songs of ascent". They were probably sung by faithful Israelites on their way to Jerusalem for the major religious festivals at the temple. Other psalms also speak of coming to worship at Jerusalem (eg 24:3-4; 100:4). Others declare the greatness of Jerusalem, because it is the city where Zion, the temple mount, is situated, and so for the Israelites the earthly location of God's heavenly rule (eg 87:1-6).

> "I rejoiced with those who said to me, 'Let us go to the house of the LORD.'"
>
> **Psalm 122:1**

Relevance for today

We no longer worship God in a particular location (see John 4:21,23). These psalms, however, are not just about the temple in Jerusalem, but about the seriousness in which Israelites came to worship. They wanted to prepare themselves to be in God's presence (15:1-5), and they sang songs of joy as they looked forward to being in God's house (122:1-5). We should approach worship of God with the same deep and joyful faith.

Proverbs
WISDOM FOR LIFE

OVERVIEW

How can you learn to live well in the world? Proverbs is full of practical advice to help you in all kinds of situations. Readers of Proverbs will gain insight about life if they pursue wisdom by fearing the Lord.

SUMMARY

Proverbs introduces itself as a useful instruction manual for gaining wisdom (1:1-6). After identifying the basic principle of wisdom (1:7), Proverbs continues with a long poem in which the reader is persuaded to follow the path of wisdom rather than the way of folly (1:8–9:18). Wisdom and Folly are both described as women, who invite the reader to come to them (1:20-33; 8:1-9:12; 9:13-18). The reader should go to Lady Wisdom, because wisdom is the most valuable possession you can acquire (2:1–4:27). By contrast, adultery (5:1-23; 6:20–7:27), laziness (6:1-11) and corruption (6:12-19) are to be avoided at all costs.

   The rest of Proverbs (10:1–31:9) contains collections of short pieces of wisdom on a wide range of topics: wealth, work, eating and drinking, family life, conversation, education, friends, marriage, reputation, ruling a nation, generosity, charity and many other topics. Most are short, two-line couplets, which compare, contrast or highlight wise and foolish actions. There is often no discernible order between the sayings, and many repeat the same idea, but the reader is encouraged to take them all to heart in order to become wise and godly (eg 23:19,22-26). Proverbs ends with a description of a godly woman, who is worthy of great honour (31:10-31).

Author

Proverbs is mainly a collection of Solomon's wise sayings (1:1; 10:1–22:16; 25:1–29:27), but some sayings from Agur (30:1-33) and King Lemuel (31:1-31) are also included. Other sayings are simply from "the wise" (22:17–24:22; 24:23-34). It is likely they were collected together by unknown scribes (see eg 25:1).

Date

Most of the proverbs come from the time of King Solomon (c. 961–922 BC), but were probably collected at a later date – some at the time of King Hezekiah (c. 715–687 BC) and some even later after the exile.

   Proverbs seems to have been written in the royal court in Jerusalem. The court would have had international contacts, so it is not surprising that some parts of Proverbs are similar to other works of wisdom in the ancient world. Proverbs, however, sets wisdom within the context of faith in Israel's God. It may have first been used to train the children of important courtiers, but its value for those in all walks of life was soon recognised outside the court.

OUTLINE – PROVERBS

KEY THEMES – PROVERBS

The fear of the Lord

Wisdom, knowledge and understanding begin with the fear of the Lord (1:7; 9:10). "Fear", in this statement, does not mean being frightened of God, but rather being aware that the whole of life is lived in his presence and that carefully following his ways leads to blessing. To fear God means to respect him, as a child would respect loving parents who know what is best. To live in the fear of God means to avoid sin (3:7; 14:16) and to do what is right (14:2). This is more important than great wealth (15:16).

According to Proverbs, fearing God leads to long and blessed life (10:27; 14:27; 19:23; 22:4). Those who fear God can be confident that he will keep them safe (14:26; 29:25) and should receive honour from others (31:30).

Proverbs shows the reader that wisdom can only be gained as the gift of God to those who fear him (2:1-8).

Wisdom and foolishness

Proverbs contrasts the way of wisdom (8:1–9:12) with the way of foolishness (9:13-18). The difference between these ways is not in the amount of information a person knows, but in whether or not a person is able to live well in the world. In Proverbs, foolishness is a moral problem: the foolish person rejects God's wisdom (1:7,29,30), despises instruction (15:5), is controlled by anger (12:16; 14:16,17) and is deceitful (11:3), lazy (6:9-11), dishonest (17:23) and proud (13:10). A fool brings dishonour to their family (10:1) and harm to their friends (13:20). A fool does whatever they think is right.

A wise person, by contrast, is always willing to listen to advice (1:2-6; 4:1, 10; 5:1,2; 12:15; 23:22). They will learn from the experiences of others and from observing the natural world (eg 6:6). Most of all, the wise person will trust in God's judgements rather than their own (3:5-6). This type of wise life pleases God (3:4), and leads to success and contentment (24:3-6,14).

Proverbs describes many more differences between the wise and the foolish person in order to encourage the reader to seek wisdom.

The rewards of wisdom

The proverbs act as mini parables that teach a general straightforward observation of God's character and how life works: wisdom and the fear of the Lord bring life and success, while foolishness brings death and hardship (eg 1:32,33; 8:35,36). Although the rewards of wisdom may often seem to be missing at the moment, Proverbs expresses strong faith in the just judgement of God (eg 15:3), expecting the foolish to end in disaster while the wise will enjoy God's blessing.

RELEVANCE FOR TODAY – PROVERBS

Faith and life

Proverbs does not make a distinction between a person's attitude toward God and their behaviour in the world. It is taken for granted that a godly person will be wise, and an ungodly person will be foolish (1:7). Proverbs assumes that faith is not just for special occasions or special places, but is to be lived out in every situation. We should not pretend that our faith is only important in church!

Wisdom in the world

Although our world may seem very different from that of Solomon and the other authors, Proverbs gives wise advice on many contemporary issues:

- **Work and wealth.** Proverbs encourages diligence and hard work (6:6-11; 10:4-5). Those who work hard should be allowed to enjoy what they have earned, while those who are unwilling to work will not stay rich (eg 10:4; 12:27). Wealth itself is not as important as what you do with it (11:4): a wise person will be generous (11:25).
- **Authority.** Proverbs expects wise people to respect authority and to receive instruction willingly (eg 13:13). When a wise person is in a position of authority, they will not abuse that position but act justly and do what is right (eg 28:2,3,16). Proverbs warns against the abuse of power.
- **Friends.** Friends are very important, and a wise person will choose their friends carefully (13:20). Wise friends will not lead one another astray.
- **Speech.** Proverbs reminds its readers to avoid malicious (11:12), angry (12:16) or deceitful (12:19) conversations. Sometimes, it may be better to say nothing at all, than to speak untruthfully or without proper thought (10:19).

Wisdom in the home

Proverbs also has much to say about the intimate relationships of family life:

- **Marriage.** Marriage is the closest of human relationships. It is therefore important that the husband or wife we choose is godly (31:10-31), so that this relationship can be blessed by God (18:22). Because of the importance of marriage, Proverbs is very concerned that its readers avoid adultery (5:1-20; 6:24-29). However appealing it may seem, it is the worst form of foolishness (7:10-27).
- **Parents and children.** Parents and children should respect each other (17:6). Parents are responsible for the wellbeing and instruction of their children (19:18; 22:6; 23:13,14), and children should receive this gladly (23:22). Other people, such as Solomon himself, also act as instructors in wisdom. Proverbs shows the importance of wise and godly teachers and mentors, who will show how to live a faithful life by their example.

> "Trust in the LORD with all your heart and lean not on your own understanding; in all your ways acknowledge him, and he will make your paths straight."
>
> **Proverbs 3:5-6**

Ecclesiastes
THE TENSION OF FAITH

OVERVIEW

Ecclesiastes encourages us to take a long, hard look at the world. What we find is often not very comforting: people build up wealth and wisdom, only to lose it when they die; sometimes the wicked do better than the wise and the good. There seems to be no discernible order to life; it is meaningless. Ecclesiastes helps us to face up to this reality of life.

SUMMARY

Ecclesiastes begins with a description of how the author, who is known as "Teacher" (Hebrew, *Qoheleth*) sees the world: life is meaningless, and is full of repetitive experiences (1:1-11). The Teacher had become wise through much study and learning, but his knowledge of the world only made him more certain that it is meaningless (1:12-18). He tried to find meaning in many things: pleasure (2:1-3), great building projects (2:4-6), wealth and greatness (2:7-10), and hard work (2:17-26), but he realised that all these things were worthless, because despite them he would die, just like everyone else (2:11-16).

The Teacher reflects on the seasons of life (3:1-8) and suggests that people should enjoy life because it would soon be over (3:9-22). It is pointless to strive to accumulate great wealth; it is better to be content and to enjoy what is already possessed (4:7-8; 5:10–6:12).

Although it is good to be wise and righteous (7:11,12), the Teacher notes that it often does not bring the expected reward: wicked people live long while righteous people die early (7:15; 8:14). So he encourages people simply to be obedient citizens (8:2-8), neither being overly wicked or overly righteous (7:16,17)! They should enjoy this life, because death is the end of everything (9:1-12).

Ecclesiastes ends with a series of short proverbs about wisdom (9:17–11:6), and a call to remember that God will judge all people (11:7–12:14).

Author

Qoheleth, often translated as "the Teacher". He claims to be king of Israel, with his court in Jerusalem (1:1,12). Whoever it was, this anonymous author was building upon the tradition of Solomon's wisdom.

Date

Ecclesiastes was probably compiled after Israel's exile, sometime in the fifth to third centuries BC.

The first readers of Ecclesiastes were Israelites who knew the promises of God and the type of wisdom found in the book of Proverbs. Ecclesiastes reminded them that despite their faith in God, life was sometimes confusing and meaningless. Many of the Teacher's observations of life are true of every generation and culture.

OUTLINE – ECCLESIASTES

Introduction

Observations of the absurdity of life

Conclusion

KEY THEMES – ECCLESIASTES

Life is meaningless!

Throughout Ecclesiastes, the Teacher exclaims that life is meaningless (eg 1:2,14; 2:11,15,23,26; 4:4,7,16; 5:7; 6:2,9; 7:15; 8:14; 12:8). "Meaningless" is a translation of the Hebrew word hebel, which expresses the Teacher's deep confusion about life. He has looked at life "under the sun" (1:14) and realised that all the things humans busy themselves doing come to nothing in the end (2:11).

Observations of the world

The Teacher's conclusion that life is meaningless is not an irrational outburst, but the result of his careful observation of the world (1:13-14) and study of conventional wisdom (1:17). Like other wisdom literature, Ecclesiastes places great weight on human experience, but in the Teacher's case, he is unable to find a discernible order. His honest observation of life led him to note several things that seem to call the meaning of life into question:

- **The reality of death.** Death comes to everyone, whether they have been wise or foolish, wealthy or poor, wicked or godly (2:14,16; 9:2). For the Teacher, living before the knowledge of the resurrection of Christ, there is nothing beyond death – it is the end of all hope and knowledge (9:4-6). Whatever advantage a person may have enjoyed in life, whether riches or wisdom, it is all taken away by death (2:16; 5:15). When death comes, someone else will receive the riches that a person has worked hard to gain (5:18,21). For the Teacher, the finality of death means that all the effort humans put into their lives is meaningless. At death, humans are no better than animals (3:18-20).

- **The reality of human inadequacy.** Although humans are able to do great things (2:4-5), amass huge wealth (2:7-9), and gain much wisdom (1:16), their power and knowledge is limited (1:15). All humans, whatever their status in life, are subject to time and chance (9:11). Even the wisest person cannot explain the mystery of life (8:17; 11:5) or tell what the future will hold (7:14; 11:2,6). Complete wisdom, according to the Teacher, is unattainable (7:23,24), and it is impossible to understand the ways of God (3:11).

- **The reality of injustice.** Faith in Israel's God includes the belief that he will bring all people to judgement (3:17; 11:9; 12:14). However, experience shows that often the wicked enjoy success in life while the righteous suffer (7:15; 8:14). Oppressors appear to get away without judgement (4:1,2) and wicked rulers pervert justice (3:16; 5:8,9). If death is truly the end, as the Teacher thinks, then the lack of judgement in this world makes faith in God's justice meaningless.

RELEVANCE FOR TODAY – ECCLESIASTES

Being honest

We might be surprised that the book of Ecclesiastes is in the Bible! Its message seems to be very different from the confident tones of faith we find in other books. The repeated statement that "everything is meaningless" (1:2; 12:8) is perhaps a little disconcerting for our faith. But that is the value of Ecclesiastes for us. It is a reminder that God allows us to be honest in our faith. We do not have to pretend that we can make complete sense of the world, when in fact our experience of it leads us to confusion. As Christians, we cannot ignore the horrors of natural disasters, terrible illnesses or intense emotional or physical suffering. Sometimes we will want to cry out with the Teacher that life is meaningless!

Living with tension

The Teacher writes as a believing Israelite. His exclamation of the absurdity of life does not come from a rejection of faith. In fact, it is because of his faith in God and God's justice, and his refusal to give that faith up (see 12:13,14), that he finds the injustice of the world so troublesome (8:13,14).

When the promises of faith and the experiences of reality contradict each other, it is tempting to resolve this tension by either denying the problems are real, or by denying God himself. The Teacher takes neither of these routes. He can speak one moment of the meaninglessness of life (3:9,10), and the next moment of the beauty of God's creation (3:11). For the Teacher, faith lives with a real tension: our experience of the world throws surprising things in our way (9:11), but God is still worthy of worship and obedience (3:14; 12:13). We must learn to live with the same tension.

Enjoying life

Throughout Ecclesiastes, the Teacher encourages his readers to enjoy their lives (2:24; 3:12,13,22; 5:18,19; 8:15; 9:7-10; 11:9). He has observed that many people spend so much of their time striving for wealth or success that they do not have time to enjoy what they have worked for before they die (eg 4:8; 6:3). Instead of this meaningless activity, the Teacher tells his readers to be content with what they have

> "When times are good, be happy; but when times are bad, consider: God has made the one as well as the other."
>
> **Ecclesiastes 7:14**

(4:6) because it comes from God (7:14). God wants us to enjoy what he has given us (9:7), and our enjoyment and contentment is a gift from him (2:24-26; 3:13; 5:19).

Of course, Christians can look forward to resurrection life after death, which was not a part of the Teacher's faith. However, it is a good thing for us also to enjoy our lives now. However meaningless life may seem, we still have much to be thankful to God for.

Song of Songs
THE JOY OF LOVE

OVERVIEW
Love and romance are important aspects of all human life – but do they have a place within the life of faith? Song of Songs answers "yes", with a dramatic celebration of the romantic love between a man and a woman.

SUMMARY
Song of Songs, which means "the best song", is a dramatic poem about a developing relationship. The exact plot of the unfolding drama is a little unclear, and even the identity of the speakers is uncertain. The male character appears to be very important and wealthy, and is possibly even the king (see 1:4,12; 6:8,9; 7:5). Some scholars have seen him as a dramatic representation of Solomon (see 1:1; 3:7,9) while others think he is just a wealthy shepherd (eg 1:7). The other main character is a young Shulammite woman (6:13). There is also a chorus of friends.

The drama begins with the young woman entering the king's court in Jerusalem. She is anxious to attract the attention of the man and win his love (1:2-7). When he sees the young woman, he is immediately impressed (1:9-11).

The young woman tells her friends how amazing her lover is (2:3-7), and she is delighted when he comes to her again (2:8-11). It is now obvious that they are committed to each other (2:16). When the man is away, the young woman longs for his presence (3:1-3).

Next, the man is seen on his wedding day, dressed in all the splendour of Solomon (3:6-11). He praises the beauty of the young woman (4:1-15). They delight in their union with each other (4:16–5:1).

In the next scene, the husband apparently arrives home late, to find his wife already in bed. She delayed opening the door for him, and he leaves (5:2-6). She goes to search for him (5:7) and asks her friends to help her find her lover (5:9-16). Eventually, the couple are reunited and delight once more in each other (6:4–8:7). The book ends with a meditation on the delight of pure love (8:8-14).

Author
The book is linked to Solomon (1:1; see also 3:7,9,11; 8:12), though it was not necessarily written by him. It is likely that an unknown author was using Solomon's royal court as the setting for this dramatic poem.

This style of dramatic literature would fit well in the high society of the royal court in Jerusalem. It also makes many references to the surrounding countryside.

Date
Date of composition is unknown, but it was at least not before the reign of Solomon (mid 10th century BC), and could have been much later.

OUTLINE – SONG OF SONGS

The first scene: the table

1:1	The title
1:2-8	The young woman and the daughters of Jerusalem
1:9–2:2	The man and the young woman talk

The second scene: the spring fields

2:3-7	The young woman describes her experience
2:8-13	The man comes to meet the young woman
2:14-17	The lovers delight in each other

The third scene: the city in the night

3:1-3	The young woman's search
3:4-5	The meeting in the night

The fourth scene: the wedding

3:6-11	The entrance of the groom
4:1-15	The man's song of praise for his bride
4:16–5:1	The wedding night

The fifth scene: the young woman's bedroom

5:2-6	The young woman delays opening the door for her husband
5:7-8	She searches for him in vain
5:9-16	She describes him to the daughters of Jerusalem
6:1	The daughters of Jerusalem help in the search

The sixth scene: the garden and the road

6:2-3	The young woman and the man meet
6:4-9	The man accepts and praises his wife
6:10-12	The young woman is at the side of the man in his chariot
6:13	The couple leave the city

The seventh scene: the countryside

7:1–8:4	The lovers delight in each other
8:5-7	The strength of love
8:8-12	The purity of love
8:13-14	A final delight in each other

KEY THEMES – SONG OF SONGS

Celebrating love

The central theme of the Song of Songs is love. The colourful descriptions the book uses have caused embarrassment for some readers, who have interpreted it simply as a picture of God's love for Israel, or Christ's love for the church. However, the love that is the main theme of the book is really romantic human love, including its sexual expression.

- **Love has a rich language.** Song of Songs is full of lively descriptions of the delight lovers find in each other's bodies. Most of the imagery comes from the worlds of shepherding (eg 1:8; 4:1,2) and gardening (eg 4:12-15), and while some references may seem a little obscure today, it is obviously a very exuberant way of describing human love.

- **Love itself is passionate.** From the very beginning, the relationship described in the Song of Songs is full of passion. The young woman longs to kiss the man (1:2), and sets out to win his affection (1:7). Once he sees the young woman, he is captivated, and lavishes her with gifts (1:11). They long for each other when they are apart (2:9; 3:1) and delight in each other when they are together (eg 4:1-7).

Loving exclusively

It seems strange that this celebration of the exclusive relationship between the man and the young woman is set in the royal court and associated with Solomon. 1 Kings records that Solomon had 700 wives and 300 concubines, who between them led Solomon astray from the Lord (1 Kings 11:1-4). Here in the Song of Songs, it is noted that there are 60 wives and 80 concubines in the royal court (6:8).

In contrast to Solomon's many marriages, Song of Songs holds on to the importance of exclusive relationship. Both the man (6:8,9) and the woman (5:10) think that their lover is beyond all comparison with other people. The young woman is even better that the many wives and concubines of the royal court (6:9)! The couple say that they have given themselves to each other completely (2:16; 4:9; 6:3).

Whoever wrote Song of Songs wanted to celebrate exclusive love. Perhaps it was also a way of criticising Solomon himself, whose accumulation of wives had led him astray from God (1 Kings 11:3,4)!

RELEVANCE FOR TODAY – SONG OF SONGS

Sexuality and faith

The existence of the Song of Songs as part of Scripture shows that the passion of sexual love is part of God's good creation. God himself is not mentioned in the Song of Songs, but the background for the work is the royal court in Jerusalem, and so faith in Israel's God is presumed. It is important to emphasise, particularly in today's society, that delighting in sexuality is not incompatible with Christian faith. The moral boundary for sexual activity – marriage – does not deny the goodness of intimacy, but rather affirms that it is God's gift to be enjoyed in the proper context.

Lessons in love

Although an ancient poem, the reality of human love does not change, and so Song of Songs has much to say to today's world:

- **Patience and strength.** Three times in Song of Songs, the young woman comments, "Do not arouse or awaken love until it so desires" (2:7; 3:5; 8:4). This is simple advice to be patient with the development of a loving relationship, and the advice is repeated throughout the book as the man and his beloved grow closer together. Despite the pressure of society to jump immediately into a sexual relationship, Scripture advises giving a relationship time and space to grow so that when the sexual element is added within marriage, it is fulfilling (5:1). In this way, love will grow strong, and will not fail (8:6,7).
- **Purity.** The young woman is seen as a locked garden, to which the husband has exclusive access (4:12,16). It is revealed at the end of the book that the young girl has been protected from sexual activity (8:8,9) until she can give it exclusively to her husband (8:12). This standard of purity, of course, applies to both men and women.

The love of God and Christ

While the Song of Songs is actually speaking about a human relationship, it has been understood to refer also to God's relationship with his people. It was often read at the beginning of the celebration of the Jewish Passover, as a reminder that God's covenant with Israel was not simply a matter of words and laws, but a relationship of passionate love. Christians have often seen the Song of Songs as a picture of Christ's love for the church, which is compared in the New Testament to the marriage relationship (see eg Ephesians 5:25). The richness of human love should remind us of the God who has created it – and of his great, passionate love for the world.

> "Love is as strong as death, its jealousy unyielding as the grave. It burns like blazing fire, like a mighty flame."
>
> **Song of Songs 8:6**

Isaiah
PROPHET OF SALVATION

OVERVIEW

Isaiah's comprehensive message to God's people addresses them in prosperity, exile and restoration. He brings to them messages of warning, comfort and hope in some of the deepest insights into God's character and purposes in the Old Testament, insights that proved to be foundational to New Testament thinking about Jesus and the nature of salvation.

Isaiah is the longest of the prophetic books, slightly longer than Jeremiah. It is the prophetic book most quoted in the New Testament. Its poetic language suggests deep revelation and great inspiration of the human spirit

SUMMARY

Part one (chapters 1–39)

The book falls into two parts. The first part (chapters 1–39) covers the time of four major reigns in Judah, the southern kingdom of the divided country of Israel. The opening section (chapters 1–12) includes an account of the prophet's own calling (chapter 6), probably the most dramatic of all accounts of prophetic calling (see also 1 Samuel 3, Ezekiel 1 and Jeremiah 1).

Interestingly, however, this account is preceded by five chapters that outline many of the main themes of the book: God is "the Holy One of Israel". He is deeply offended by the immoral behaviour of his people, for which there will be punishment in terms of invasion and devastation of the now prosperous land. But after punishment will come restoration and good government. The delay in giving an account of Isaiah's calling has the effect of concentrating our minds on the message and its authenticity, not on the messenger.

Isaiah's prophecies have a political dimension in warning against any sort of alliances with other countries. Instead they must trust in God alone for political as well as spiritual salvation (chapters 7–11). The section concludes with a psalm (chapter 12).

The second section of the first part is a series of oracles against neighbouring countries (chapters 13–24). This is a common prophetic practice. Parallels can be found, for example, in Jeremiah 46–51 and Ezekiel 25–32. God is Lord of the whole earth and his people's destiny is not separate from other nations, though different from theirs. In Isaiah's day, the dominant threat to Judah's security was Assyria (14:24-27); its false security was Egypt (19:1–20:6).

But the strongest woes and denunciations seem to be against Babylon (13:1–14:23; 21:1-10), which in Isaiah's time was for some periods an independent but small state (see chapter 39). Only in the following century did Babylon rise to be a devastating force enabling it to destroy Jerusalem. The taunting language used against its pride (14:12-23) reminds us of Ezekiel's language against Tyre (Ezekiel 28).

In chapter 22, Isaiah turns the denunciations back on his home city, Jerusalem. In the final chapter of the section, there is a concluding apocalyptic description of worldwide destruction, and the restoration of God's kingly rule from Jerusalem.

The third section (chapters 25–35) elaborates on the preceding themes. Chapters 25–26 form an apocalyptic bridge with the preceding section. The fourth section is a historical one, narrating three interventions into King Hezekiah's life (chapters 36-39), including a threat to Jerusalem by the Assyrians. Some of this material also occurs in 2 Kings 18:17–20:19.

Part two (chapters 40–66)

The second part of the book can be further divided into two sections. The first section (chapters 40–55) deals with Judah in exile in Babylon and the promise of restoration, not in terms of a great king or future leader, but in terms of Israel as servant. This section includes the famous servant songs that are often related to the ministry of Jesus Christ. The Persian king, Cyrus, is mentioned as deliverer, but only as a minor player in the drama of salvation.

The final section (chapters 56–66) paints a picture of universal deliverance and justice. At the same time it acknowledges that return from exile had not or would not mean perfect spirituality. The same old faults are all too likely to recur. In fact, the final chapter parallels the opening chapter in placing the hope of a new rule of God alongside the destruction on those who had rebelled. We are reminded that holiness is both glory and fire.

Tile frieze of the Babylonian god Marduk from the Ishtar Gate, Babylon. The city was denounced by Isaiah for its idolatry and pride

Author

Isaiah is mentioned in 2 Kings 19:2-7,20-34 and 20:1-19. These chapters, together with Isaiah 6 and 36–39, give us a picture of a prophet in the mainstream of national life. This has led some scholars to think he was well-born, unlike his village contemporary, Micah. He was married, his wife possibly having a prophetic ministry in her own right. They had two boys, both symbolically named.

The shift of emphasis between the first and second parts has led to the supposition that Isaiah only wrote the first part, and the second part was written by someone living in the exile some 150 years later. Isaiah is not mentioned by name in the second part. However, if this is the case, then someone had obviously immersed himself in the writings of his predecessor. While some of the language and ideas are different, much is similar.

Date

Isaiah lived through the reigns of Uzziah (or Azariah, 792–740 BC), Jotham (740–735 BC), Ahaz (735–715 BC), and Hezekiah (715–687 BC). This is the period of Assyrian domination. For example, Sennacherib reigned 705–681 BC. The northern kingdom fell to the Assyrians in 722 BC and Sennacherib besieged Jerusalem in 701 BC. It is supposed Isaiah died during the reign of Manasseh (687–642 BC). The second part of the book covers the period of the exile in Babylon (from 598 BC), ending when the Persian King Cyrus allowed the Jews to return to Jerusalem in 538 BC after his conquest of Babylon.

OUTLINE – ISAIAH

Present judgement and future glory

Threats against Judah

Woes against the nations

Parenthesis: God's future kingdom

Woes and blessings on Judah

Isaiah helps king Hezekiah

Release from exile and a new beginning

The restored community

KEY THEMES – ISAIAH

The Holy One of Israel

This phrase is distinctive to the book of Isaiah. It forms one of the unifying key phrases of the prophecy, being found in every part (eg 1:4; 5:19, 24; 8:13; 10:17, 20; 12:6; 17:7; 37:23; 47:4; 57:15; 60:9, 14). Most of the prophetic books speak of God's holiness, but it is Isaiah who perhaps has the deepest sense of it. For modern people, it is a much harder concept to understand than, say, the New Testament teaching "God is love" and therefore close attention has to be paid to this book in order to understand what the phrase means.

Isaiah's great vision (6:1-7) is a good starting place. The otherness and transcendence of God is stressed, as it is in 40:12-14. His ways are not our ways (55:8-9), as Job 38 also reminds us. However, that does not prevent him from forming the closest relationships with humans, either as individuals or as a chosen nation.

But holiness is more than otherness: it is also purity and freedom from all sin and imperfection. That is why holiness is typically associated with God's anger, since that is part of the divine reaction to deliberate sin, especially pride, rebellion and false religion. False religion lowers standards, covers over sin too easily (1:13-17). However, God's anger does not prevent him from approaching sinful people

(1:18-20). Isaiah 53 in fact is a startling revelation of the lengths God will go to deal with people's sinful behaviour or "transgressions".

Holiness is also closely linked to God's sovereignty, in that there is simply "no other god" (43:10; 45:5-6; 46:9). This is the offence of idolatry, which claims that there are other gods (40:18-20). Chapter 40 stresses God's unique creative power and his rule of the cosmos, including the nations of the earth. But it finishes on a profoundly personal note of promise, that his greatness does not prevent his appreciation of human weakness nor his desire to provide help for it (40:28-31).

The Holy City

The concept of holiness is applied to an earthly city, variously called Jerusalem or Zion, the capital of Israel. In the book, we see it actually besieged and then miraculously saved (chapters 36–37). In fact, this becomes a metaphor for the spiritual deliverance from earthly power and pride that God desires. He wants his kingdom to have an earthly basis, but one that shares in his own nature of holiness. This theme again runs through the book (eg 1:26; 2:3; 4:3; 25:6; 52:8; 54:11; 60).

As such, the holy city can become a spiritual centre for the whole world. It is a provision for all who seek God, not just the Jewish people. Its approaches are spoken of as "the way of holiness" (35:8) which needs preparation (42:16), the turning of spiritual darkness into light. This holy city is the place where the remnant will return from exile (37:32; 51:11). In the New Testament, the book of Revelation speaks of this as the "new Jerusalem" and sees it as the new paradise of God (Revelation 21–22).

The Servant

The second part of Isaiah contains a group of "Servant Songs", the most famous of which is 52:13–53:12, which became central to early Christian formulations of who Jesus Christ was and how his death had been redemptive.

These songs represent one of the most significant shifts between the two parts of the book. In the first part, there are prophecies of a king from the line of David who will become God's chosen leader or *Messiah* (meaning, literally, "the anointed one") (eg 9:1-7; 11). In the second part, specifically chapters 40–55, these are replaced by this figure of the servant. At first, the servant appears to be the whole nation (41:8-9; 43:1-13), but then becomes an individual (42:1), whose mission is to bring justice and understanding (42:4,7), "release from the dungeon". In 49:5-6 and 50:10 he appears to be the prophet himself, as representative of the nation, with a mission of being "a light for the Gentiles".

However, in the last servant song, 52:13–53:12, he is portrayed as an individual who can bring actual salvation "for the transgression of my people". His suffering leads to an actual death, which becomes a substitute death, allowing comparison with animal sacrifices laid down in the Mosaic rituals of guilt offerings (53:10). The notion of justification is introduced, which became so important for Paul in the New Testament (see Romans 6), as he sees Christ as the embodiment of the suffering servant.

Redemption and salvation

Though other prophets speak of redemption, ransoming and salvation, it is Isaiah who speaks most coherently and fully on these. 43:1-28 is perhaps one of the most poetic expressions of this. The simplest notion is that of deliverance from punishment, as in conquest, captivity and exile. However, the book extends the notion from return from exile to a holy city and fertile land, with a restored covenant with God, to an inner state of salvation. In this inner state there is righteous living, joy (35:10; 52:8,9), peace (57:2), and justice (56:1). God himself takes on the title "Saviour" (43:3; 60:16) and "Redeemer" (43:1,14; 44:6), and the terms are human and personal, not legal (46:3,4; 61:10). This is a personal, loving act of God (54:5,8).

RELEVANCE FOR TODAY – ISAIAH

A new thing

Like the Psalms, Isaiah speaks to us about a whole range of human experience of God as well as a whole range of God's attributes. Our spiritual experiences often find themselves defined by the images and expressions to be found among the many prophecies of the book. This is its relevance for today.

One such experience is that of the new birth of salvation and redemption. Isaiah is emphatic in its sense that God wants to do "a new thing" (43:19, compare 42:9; 48:6). The first part of the book traces the failure of God's people, despite threats of punishment and promises for reform. The exile becomes a sort of death experience, out of which new hope, a new thing arises. In this new thing, God wants to draw a line under the past. This is expressed in various ways. For example, 43:25 talks of "I am he who blots out your transgressions … and remembers your sins no more." The only thing we need to remember is that "I am God, and there is no other" (46:9). Another way is in terms of healing and peace (57:18-19); another the sense of being born in the new holy city, as part of a redeemed citizenship (66:7-11).

A new spirit

But to be able to live in the light of this we need a new spirit within us. Isaiah prefigures New Testament teaching on the Holy Spirit in various passages. 44:3 promises the outpouring of "my Spirit on your offspring" and the new covenant is defined in terms of the Spirit being on us in 59:21 (see also 32:15). Both the new Davidic leader and "the servant" are promised the Spirit (11:1-2; 42:1), the former passage giving a formulation of the Holy Spirit which is still used today as the "sevenfold Spirit". The prophet himself senses the Spirit on him to preach the message of deliverance and comfort (61:1-2), quoted by Jesus in Luke 4:18. Ezekiel follows Isaiah in promising a new spirit (Ezekiel 11:19; 18:31; 36:26).

Living waters

In the Gospels, the Holy Spirit is likened to springs of running waters (John 4:10-14; 7:38,39). The imagery comes largely from Isaiah, "I will pour water on the thirsty land" (44:3). Water imagery is central to all the Old Testament prophets: the land was typically fertile but arid. Water would therefore bring prosperity and fruitfulness, but the failure of rains or irrigation would mean desert-like conditions.

Many people have described times of their life as deserts: a lack of fruitfulness, joy, life even. Conversely, many have described their experience of the Holy Spirit in their lives as being showered, baptised, flooded – all words that refer to water (see also John 7:37-39).

Isaiah speaks to all these conditions. In 55:1-3, the prophet invites the thirsty to drink of "the waters", which are then linked to "the everlasting covenant" and "my faithful love promised to David". 35:1-7; 41:18-19 and 44:3-4 describe a new fertility in the desert, an image literally fulfilled in the state of Israel today, but for most people, a metaphor of emotional and spiritual renewal (32:2). 48:21 takes us back to when God led the Israelites out of Egypt and did not allow them to go thirsty. The many images of God as "the Rock" in the book have a subtext rooted in this time, when Moses struck the rock for water to gush out.

Peace

One of the water images refers to peace: "your peace would have been like a river" (48:18). Peace is a concept with which we identify readily – both as an inner state and an outer one. Isaiah talks of "the covenant of peace" (54:10). This implies not just that God will protect his people from wars, but that he is no longer at enmity with them. It is both the peace of God and peace with God that we need, and is here promised (see also 26:12).

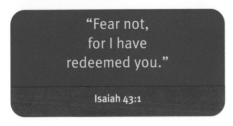

> "Fear not,
> for I have
> redeemed you."
>
> Isaiah 43:1

Elsewhere, the Messiah is called "Prince of Peace" (9:6,7; see also 32:16-18; 60:17). His reign will be marked by peace when swords shall become ploughshares (2:4) and wolves shall lie down with lambs (11:6; 65:25).

Deep waters

Isaiah also uses the image of water to express our experience of being overwhelmed by circumstances: that is, rivers in flood and "waters of affliction" (30:20). 43:2 describes passing "through the waters" in parallel with walking "through the fire". Both are images of testing and trial. The promise of God's presence in such circumstances is one that many Christians have held on to rather like a rescue rope or life belt. The following verses suggest not just a survival by the skin of our teeth, but a divine love that allows these experiences as "a ransom". Such verses are a small aspect of the whole theme of deliverance running through the book, expressed here as redemption, calling and summoning.

Jeremiah
THE HEART-BROKEN PROPHET

OVERVIEW

Jeremiah lived through the last days of the southern kingdom of Judah. He consistently warns of impending disaster, brought about by the nation's neglect of true religion, its turning to pagan practices and its social injustice. Its blind trust in its covenant relationship with God is a delusion, as are its false prophets with their messages of peace. But no-one listens to the prophet. He is heart-broken and argues with God about his seemingly impossible mission to make people listen. He also believes the Babylonians are God's instrument of punishment and advises cooperation with them. This is seen as treasonable, and he is thrown into prison, in danger of his life. His last warning is not to trust Egypt. Ironically, this is where he ends up, forced there after Jerusalem's destruction.

SUMMARY

Jeremiah's ministry

Jeremiah's ministry extended through the reigns of five kings, in a constantly deteriorating spiritual and political situation. However, the many prophecies contained in the book are not arranged in any chronological order. They were first given orally; but at some point, Jeremiah felt the need to write them down with the help of Baruch his assistant, and show them to the king (chapter 36). The king cynically took each page as it was read, cut it up with a knife and threw the fragments into the fire. It took Jeremiah and Baruch a year to rewrite them, adding a number of other prophecies at the same time. Then they had to flee the fall of Jerusalem, the written scrolls ending up in Egypt or Babylon. The wonder is that so much has survived, not that it appears chaotically arranged!

Included in the book are a series of denunciations against surrounding nations (chapters 46–51), and a historical account of the last days of Jerusalem (chapters 34–45; 52), the last chapter containing the same material as 2 Kings 25 and 2 Chronicles 36. These two topics form discreet sections in the latter part of the book.

Jeremiah's pleadings to a deaf city

The first ten chapters introduce some of the book's central themes. Chapter 1 is an account of Jeremiah's young calling, and the signs to confirm it, similar to the callings of Isaiah and Ezekiel. The remaining nine chapters speak against the fashionable syncretistic religion. It is not that the people had abandoned their traditional worship of God; they had added all sorts of pagan elements, the worst feature of which was child sacrifice (2:1–3:6; 7:16–8:17).

The people had a false sense of security from the presence of Solomon's temple in Jerusalem. It was seen as where God literally dwelt and while it was there, they felt safe (7:1-15). But there was no moral sense to this, and social injustice ran rife (5:1-31; 6:13-21; 9:3-26). In some prophecies, Jeremiah suggests there was still time to repent, return to true worship and restore justice (3:11–4:4; 5:18). In this, Jeremiah is similar to many of his predecessors, Amos, Hosea, Isaiah and Micah, for example. But if they did not repent, then God had appointed the Babylonians, the enemy from the north, to wipe Jerusalem from the map and disperse its people (4:5-31; 6:1-12,22-30).

This message was really heartbreaking for him to give, and in this he reflected God's

DOMINANT POWERS OF BIBLE TIMES

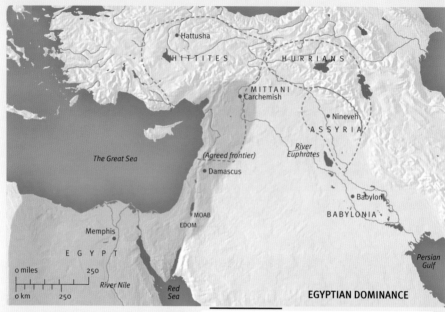

EGYPTIAN DOMINANCE

C. 3000–1200 BC
Egypt had dominated since around 3000 BC and, with its extensive trade interests, was at its height at this period. Other great nations were attempting to expand their borders. Later the decline of Egypt and the absence of one supreme power enabled the people of Israel to settle in Canaan.

C. 1350–650 BC
The Assyrians arose as the leading power from c. 1350 BC until the capture of Nineveh by King Nabopolassar of Babylon in 612 BC. Despite their aggression towards other nations, they built great cities, palaces and temples. Literature too played a significant part in Assyrian life.

THE ASSYRIANS

C. 600 BC
By around 1850 BC Babylonia was one of the earliest centres of civilisation in the Middle East and had developed sophisticated skills like writing and irrigation. After 612 BC the empire expanded to take control of the area from the Persian Gulf to the border with Egypt. The reign of supreme power was relatively short-lived, with Cyrus II of Persia taking Babylon in 539 BC.

THE BABYLONIANS

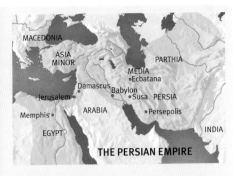

THE PERSIAN EMPIRE

539–333 BC
Cyrus the Great established Persian domination west into Babylonia, Egypt and Asia Minor, expanding into Macedonia, and east to India, using wise administration and rule to control the vast area. Magnificent buildings and skilled craftsmanship are testament to the Persian love of beauty and refinement. Alexander the Great of Macedonia conquered the empire in 333 BC.

GREEK DOMINATION

333–167 BC
Alexander the Great was a brilliant general, but he was also keen to unify the peoples he ruled by imposing Greek culture and ideals on them. In twelve years he changed the face of the whole Middle East. After his death the empire was divided into four regions which eventually fought against themselves, bringing about their own downfall to Rome.

THE ROMANS

167 BC–AD 475
Rome's power increased steadily, gradually expanding from Italy into surrounding nations, including north Africa, and establishing a provincial system to control its interests. The prevailing Greek culture was absorbed into the Roman way of life. Soon the whole of the Mediterranean area was under Roman rule.

heart (4:9; 8:18–9:2; 10:19-25). Other prophets, especially Hosea, had spoken similarly. But Jeremiah allows us to see his own emotions much more: we sense the drama and the anguish of his own soul.

Jeremiah's inner conflict

The second group of chapters (chapters 11–20) shows this inner conflict even more, where growing outer conflict parallels it. The section has five utterances beginning "The word of the LORD came to me" or something similar (11–12; 13; 14–15; 16–17; 18–20). The themes of the first section are repeated, though in chapters 11–12, Jeremiah introduces specific reference to the covenant relationship between God and his people. We also hear about the plot against Jeremiah by his fellow-villagers and Jeremiah's complaint to God about them. This was the first of many attacks on the prophet. Another occurs in 20:1-18, where one of the priests attacked Jeremiah physically.

We also see a number of enacted prophecies, where Jeremiah was told to do some rather strange action, which was then interpreted symbolically. So here he had to bury some brand-new linen undergarments (13:1-11); take a vow of celibacy (16:1-4); go to a potter's workshop (18:1-11) and buy a jug and take it to the city gates (19:1-13).

Denunciation of faithless kings and false prophets

The third section comprises a series of denunciations against faithless kings and false prophets (chapters 21–29). Jeremiah's uncompromising message to the people, who wanted to hear only that God would save them from Nebuchadnezzar, the Babylonian king, was that Nebuchednezzar was God's chosen instrument over all the immediate nations, and so it was useless to resist him. He also writes to those already in exile (Jerusalem was attacked twice), telling them to expect 70 years of exile. Jeremiah's condemnation of kings and the prophets who gave false messages of security is quite specific.

The promise of restoration
However, chapters 30–33 counterbalance this with promises of restoration. Though such promises are typical of the prophets, what is here remarkable is that they were made while Jeremiah was in prison and the city under siege. At one point, there was a brief respite and Jeremiah went out to buy a field, to show there would be a future life in the land (32:1-25).

The last days of Jerusalem
The prophecies against Jerusalem cease at this point, to be replaced by a historical account of its siege and fall, and the chaotic conditions after. Jeremiah was carried off against his will to Egypt, where he must have died. He had actually seen many of his prophecies come true, including the death of a number of his opponents.

Judgements against surrounding nations
A series of woes and denunciations against neighbouring states is then added (chapters 46–51), including a major one against Babylon herself. Though she had been God's instrument, she was condemned because of her pride. The final note, however, is that the Davidic kingship had survived in exile (52:31-34). A remnant had been kept safe. God's purposes with his people continued.

Author
Jeremiah was born in the village of Anathoth, where his father Hilkiah was a priest. The village lay in the territory of Benjamin, north of Jerusalem, and part of the southern kingdom of Judah. He was called to be a prophet at a young age, in the reign of the reforming king Josiah, over whose untimely death he wrote a lament (2 Chronicles 35:25).

He is often referred to as the "weeping prophet" (9:1). He is revealed as a complex character, uncompromising and consistent, realistic yet visionary, pessimistic yet hopeful of the future. He is worn down by constant opposition and rejection, and laments his calling. Yet heroically he continues at great danger to himself, suffering beatings, imprisonment and near death, finally being carried off against his will to Egypt, after having refused safe passage to Babylon. As a true prophet, he wishes to intercede for his people, but is forbidden to pray for them. As a "prophet to the nations" (1:5) he also speaks out against the surrounding nations.

Date
The book describes events from shortly before the death of King Josiah in 609 BC till several years after the fall of Jerusalem in 586 BC. Jeremiah's ministry lasted some 30 years, following Nahum's and Zephaniah's, and then contemporary with Ezekiel's and Daniel's, these two already being in exile.

In 612 BC the Babylonians defeated the Assyrians, and in 605 BC, at the battle of Carchemish, the Egyptians, though the Egyptians would make comebacks. The Egyptians replaced Josiah's son, Jehoahaz, with their own puppet king, Jehoiakim (609–598 BC). He rebelled against the Babylonians in 602 BC, but died before they could respond. His son Jehoiachin (or Jeconiah or Coniah) was seized with a large number of leading families and deported to Babylon in 598 BC (Jeremiah 52:31). The Babylonians put in Zedekiah as their puppet, but he too rebelled in 587 BC, leading to the final siege and burning of the city of Jerusalem.

OUTLINE – JEREMIAH

KEY THEMES – JEREMIAH

False security

7:1-15 is a key passage in the book. The Israelites, in their spiritual confusion, were imagining that because "the temple of the LORD" was in the centre of their capital, Jerusalem, God was actually living in it and therefore they were invulnerable to outside attack. This sense of false security enabled them to "steal and murder, commit adultery and perjury" without any scruples on the one hand while on the other they "burn incense to Baal and follow other gods", the whole time saying "we are safe".

Jeremiah demolishes this security by pointing out the fate of Shiloh, the place where the precursor of the temple, the tabernacle, was given a temporary home (Judges 18:31). Shiloh was now deserted, the northern tribes from around the area were already in exile. Sacred space may be necessary for the divine presence (see Haggai), but that presence is dependent on a holy people as much as on a God who wishes to dwell among them. There can be no security outside a holy God *and* a holy people. 9:23-24 pushes this even further: there can be no dependence on anything except a true understanding of who God is, that is a God who loves justice and righteousness.

Social injustice

The exposure of social injustice runs through many of the prophetic books (see Isaiah, Joel, Amos, Micah, Habakkuk and Zephaniah). Chapter 5 is a dramatic plea for it. 6:13-21 sets God's hatred of injustice against the vain attempts by the people to mask it by making ritual offerings, again a central theme of other prophets. Whilst social and personal morality are not the same as holiness, they are not separate, either. This is what Jeremiah's audience could not understand. They felt as long as they made the required sacrifices in their ritual worship, it didn't matter how they behaved to each other. It became a "buying God off" – but we cannot buy God off. The message is that social justice and personal morality authenticate worship and sacrifice and render it acceptable.

Punishment as refinement

9:7 is typical of many verses. Such is the spiritual blindness of the people that they need their eyes opening. Only drastic punishment will bring this about. If they are willing to accept such punishment, that is to accept the Babylonians as God's instrument of punishment, and accept the consequent exile as its form, then there will be a continued promise and future. Otherwise, punishment moves from being refinement to being a sentence of death. That is not God's purpose, but a realistic consequence.

What may amaze us is that even in the nearness of Babylonian attack, King Zedekiah imprisoned Jeremiah rather than receive his message (37:16). But then having imprisoned him, he secretly asked Jeremiah if he had a word from God (37:17; 38:14). At first, Jeremiah merely asked him where the false prophets were who had prophesied peace (37:19) but then urged him again to surrender and take his punishment (38:17). God was willing to have mercy till the last moment. Even so, the king refused (compare 18:12).

Restoration and the new covenant

Like other prophets who prophesied exile and punishment, for example Isaiah, Jeremiah also prophesied restoration (for example 30:3-24). But he went further. He saw that God's people needed a new covenant. The old one had not led to any permanent change of heart (11:1-13). 31:31-34 are the crucial verses here. The law is now to be written on their hearts, rather than on stone tablets, as given to Moses on Mount Sinai; and put "in their minds" – an internalised covenant. Judgement gives way to salvation here (chapters 30–33), and is Jeremiah's consolation.

The New Testament means the new covenant, so we can see Jeremiah's prophecy anticipates God's plan for the future. Jeremiah's verses are, in fact, quoted in the Letter to the Hebrews (Hebrews 8:8-12) as a central part of the writer's argument about this new and better covenant. What the New Testament shows is that it needs the revelation of Jesus Christ to the individual believer by the Holy Spirit to bring about this new "writing" on our hearts (2 Corinthians 3:3-18). This revelation brings about inner transformation (the new birth), made possible by the once-for-all perfect sacrifice of Christ (Hebrews 9:11-15).

The promise of restoration, therefore, can be interpreted at two levels. Firstly, in terms of the Old Testament, there was indeed a return from exile and a return to the Holy Land. Secondly, in terms of the New Testament, there was a new return to a covenant relationship with God, not in terms of a geographical sacred land, but still as a new people of God, a holy nation (1 Peter 2:9).

RELEVANCE FOR TODAY – JEREMIAH

Complaints

The Bible shows us prophets arguing with or complaining to God on several occasions. In Habakkuk, for example, the prophet cannot understand God's purposes in using the Babylonians as his instrument of justice (Habakkuk 1:12-17). So he argues it out with God, the result being a deeper understanding of God's immediate and his long-term purposes. The point is, God does not mind our arguing (called a "complaint" in literary terms), as long as we accept the answer when it comes.

Jeremiah makes a number of complaints. The most relevant, perhaps, is that voiced in 12:1-4, a complaint repeated in Gerard Manley Hopkins' famous sonnet "Thou art indeed just, Lord". Hopkins talks of his failure to prosper in his ministry, while the wicked seem to have successful careers. Jeremiah offers some of this complaint: why do the ways of the wicked prosper? People are then saying, "God will not see what happens". The psalmist had similar problems (for example, Psalm 73:12-14).

God's answer to Jeremiah is not quite what he expected. It is basically that problems like

these are training to toughen up Jeremiah in his prophetic role. The image is of an athlete (12:5), an unusual image for the Old Testament, when athletic competitions were not known. Athletes need tough courses to train on to build up their stamina. Jeremiah will have to get used to problems like this: there are far harder ones down the road (12:7-13). Certainly, we can see Jeremiah's life as a prophet was exemplary in the mental toughness required over a sustained period of time.

A second complaint was in 15:10, enlarged upon in 20:7-18: Jeremiah had simply had enough! No one listened to him, he was attacked and his ministry seemed to be having no effect. He says at first he delighted in it (15:16) but now it is a pain (15:18). If he tries to keep quiet, the message burns like a fire inside him (19:9).

To the second complaint there is no easy answer given. He is promised his life, that is, he will know God's protection. 1 Corinthians 4:2 provides some sort of answer: God requires faithfulness in ministry, not success. Jeremiah stuck at a hopeless task, and is quite rightly viewed as one of the greatest prophets, even though in terms of audience response he must seem the least. But God's word is truth, and it is the truth-tellers whom history vindicates.

This leads to the answer to the first complaint: evildoers did not prosper. All they had was eventually looted and burned, and they were hauled into exile if they were lucky. Again, the long-term purposes of God are the ones that have to be looked to.

The potter and the clay

Another way of expressing some of the dilemmas discussed in the previous section is through the extended analogy used in chapters 18–21. God is the potter; we are the clay. The clay cannot demand anything of the potter; and if the potter decides to rework the clay, that is entirely up to him. In the end, therefore, we do have to submit to the will of God. This is not fatalism, however, since fate is blind and unfeeling, whilst God is loving and creative, like the potter. A pot has some purpose and some beauty to it, some order and design. Ultimately, Jeremiah needed to give the prophecy to himself, as we often need to.

> "I will put my law in their minds and write it on their hearts."
>
> Jeremiah 31:33

Plans to prosper

Despite the many prophecies of impending judgement and destruction, the book makes clear that this is not God's purpose for his people. 29:10-14 give a summary of what those plans are: to restore and to prosper. The condition is that the LORD is sought with the whole heart.

Such promises are relevant to any time. We have an inbuilt need to "prosper", to receive some fruit for our labours. The irony is that only the prophet himself seemed excluded, in that his prophecies did not seem to prosper but brought him into trouble. However, in the long term, his words too have prospered, because we prosper by believing them as truth. Isaiah 55:11 reinforces this: "my word … will accomplish what I desire".

There is always a choice

Jeremiah's prophecies were often given in extreme conditions, for example, with the Babylonians closing in on a besieged city. But even in the most extreme conditions, Jeremiah insists we always have a choice. 21:8 is the clearest expression of this: "the way of life and the way of death" – this is the most basic choice possible. The choice did seem extreme: stay in the city and die; surrender and live (38:17-19). The "no surrender" brigade won the vote over Jeremiah and duly died, for no good purpose. Those who made the right choice lived to take God's purposes into exile. In such difficult circumstances, we need to trust God to give us a prophetic word as to what the choice is set before us.

Lamentations

DEATH OF A CITY

OVERVIEW

The book of Lamentations mourns the death of the holy city, Jerusalem.
Her people have gone into exile as part of the punishment God has sent them
for their sins. Sometimes the city herself speaks; sometimes the writer.
The last chapter pleads with God to remember the survivors and to restore them.

SUMMARY

There are a number of examples of laments in
the Old Testament, for example 2 Samuel 1:19-
27; Psalms 38, 79, 88; and Amos 5:2. This is the
only book of the Bible given wholly over to
lamentation. Its five chapters are separate,
carefully crafted poems. The first four chapters
are acrostics, each verse of chapters 1, 2 and 4
beginning with a successive letter of the
Hebrew alphabet, 22 in all. Chapter 3 devotes
three verses to each letter, whilst chapter 5
retains 22 verses, though not the acrostic form.

The tight structure gives form to what
would otherwise be a devastating grief that
would overwhelm the writer. The acrostic
form is used, it has been suggested, to show
that the grief is all-inclusive, omitting nothing.
Chapter 3 reaches a climax at the book's midpoint as the writer is able to catch a glimpse of
a compassionate God behind the force of his
destruction of the city (3:22-30). There is no
protest to God: the reasons for the punishment
are too well known, too obviously deserved.
But the implications are enormous: the
enemies of God's people scorn them (2:16;
3:46); the whole ritual of worship has been
abandoned (2:6); the survivors have suffered
dreadfully (5:10-13) and are having to do
dreadful things, even eat their dead children
(2:20; 4:10).

Author

No writer is mentioned by name. The
commonest assumption is that he is the
prophet Jeremiah, who certainly saw the
destruction of Jerusalem, and was not
immediately taken into exile to Babylon. He
would therefore have had time to have seen the
aftermath of the burning of the city, and to
have composed this lament then or soon
afterwards. There are many echoes of the book
of Jeremiah, in terms of the city's failures and
its predicted doom, as well as various verbal
echoes (eg Jeremiah 4:27-31; 6; 9; 13:18-27).
And we know Jeremiah had written other
laments (2 Chronicles 35:25; see Jeremiah
9:10f.; 14:17f.)

Date

The destruction of Jerusalem was in 587 BC, so
the composition of this book must have been
shortly after this time. The destroyed city is
named variously *Jerusalem*, *Zion*, and *daughter
of Zion*.

OUTLINE – LAMENTATIONS

KEY THEMES – LAMENTATIONS

God as enemy

There is a saying, "With friends like these, who needs enemies?" The poet here feels much the same: "The LORD is like an enemy" (2:5). The whole section 2:1-5 deals with God's hostility towards the city. However, there is a difference between "like an enemy", as here, and "the enemy", as in 2:7. The poet feels there is also a human enemy, who should be punished, too, for their destructiveness and mockery (1:21; 3:61-66).

This builds on the viewpoint of the book of Jeremiah: that God is using the Babylonians to punish Jerusalem for her wickedness. Yet in turn, the Babylonians will be punished for their pride. But here, the sense is that God is first and foremost the enemy, the first cause of the destruction, the Babylonians only the second cause. That is why here the enemy is left anonymous and unnamed. What matters is God's enmity. So does God actually send evil, or merely permit it?

We need to realise this is a human, academic question. From God's standpoint, in

this case, the alternatives are meaningless. What we need to realise is that God is both friend and enemy at the same time. "Faithful are the wounds of a friend" (Proverbs 27:6) is the nearest we can get to this paradox in human terms, but the truth is stronger even than this. The behaviour and attitudes of God's covenant people have outraged him. God's people have, in fact, become his enemies, declaring war on him. So he responds. This is terrible, but in God's mercy, such anger does not last for ever (3:31-32). Enmity is not his permanent disposition, but compassion is. So in the final verse, when the poet asks, "Unless you … are angry at us without measure", we know, even if it is only from the pages of history, that God never is.

Failure of priests and prophets

In any catastrophe, we usually want to know who is to blame. Here, the prophet-poet singles out the priests and prophets (4:13). This fits in with the book of Jeremiah, which attacks the false prophets for their saying "peace, peace, where there was no peace" (Jeremiah 6:14; 8:11; see also 23:1-40), and the priests, who at one point physically attack Jeremiah (Jeremiah 20:1-2; 26:8).

In other words, the failure is one of spiritual leadership. The very people appointed by God to keep the people in covenant faithfulness are the ones who have led them astray in a false security and into syncretism, or false worship. In biblical terms, judgement must always start with the household of God (1 Peter 4:17).

RELEVANCE FOR TODAY – LAMENTATIONS

Crying from the depths
At some time in our lives, it is almost certain we will feel like we are crying to God "from the depths" (3:55). It is difficult to imagine a more devastating scenario than that which faced the poet: the whole present and future seemed wiped out; the survivors suffering dreadful things (5:8-13) and doing dreadful things (2:20; 4:10).

At such times, it is only too easy to see God as our enemy, or as indifferent to our prayers. Our suffering seems uniquely terrible (1:12). We are reminded of the book of Job, whose afflictions seemed more than he could bear, or of Jonah, crying from the belly of the great fish, or of the psalmist, at his wits' end (Psalm 130:1). In such circumstances, all we can do is to cry out. The one note of assurance that comes from this book is that God does hear such cries (3:57-58), just as he heard Christ's desolating cry on the cross: "My God, my God, why have you forsaken me?" (Matthew 27:46). In a very real sense, it is because of Christ's cry of desolation, that our similar cries *are* heard. He has gone down into the depths and has risen again from them.

Unfailing compassion
The climax of the book is undoubtedly 3:22-23, since it represents a moment of faith in the midst of despair. It is a moment that is given to the poet in God's mercy, and so is part of the compassion that he witnesses.

The secret is acceptance (3:26). This is a just punishment; it is not outside what God said he

> "... for his compassions never fail. They are new every morning..."
>
> Lamentations 3:22-23

would do. Not all our depths will be because of this, of course. Many depths come from outside ourselves, perhaps the behaviour of those we love dearly, or they are caused by natural disasters. But after all the cries, laments and anger we need to come to a place of acceptance. This is where the divine compassion must envelop us, to save us from our own self-despair, bitterness or hopelessness.

Significantly, the poet cannot hold this moment for long – but the very fact he does reach it at all is a triumph of faith. Other prophets (especially Isaiah and Ezekiel) take up the story of God's compassion.

Grieving and restoration
In a sense, the book is incomplete. "What happened?" we ask. Later books of the Bible (Daniel, Ezekiel, Zechariah, Malachi) tell us. Life does go on; God's purposes are not thwarted by even the direst catastrophe.

This book does not tell us these things. But what it does do is show us how we must enter into the grief of the situation without losing all our faith. Such grieving will allow God to continue to work out his compassionate purposes. This is the new morning.

Ezekiel
STANDING IN THE GAP

OVERVIEW

Ezekiel, in exile in Babylon, addresses his fellow exiles and the remnants of Jerusalem before its final fall. In a series of visionary statements, he denounces the failure of its moral and spiritual life, but also offers hope for the future. In an apocalyptic conclusion, he foresees God's kingdom established in a perfect form.

SUMMARY

The book of Ezekiel may be divided into two parts, with a transition between both parts. The first part consists of a series of powerful visions, appearances of God in his glory (chapters 1–3), which affected Ezekiel powerfully. They lead to a series of woes spoken against the priests still ministering in the Jerusalem temple, and then against the inhabitants of the doomed city, the capital of Judah. Their failures were both historical and present (chapters 8–21). God's glory was seen to leave the city. Ezekiel's language is dramatic, often emphasised by acting out his message (chapters 4–7).

The transition passage condemns in equally forceful terms those nations round about Judah who were eagerly awaiting its downfall (chapters 25–32). The strongest denunciations are against Tyre and Egypt. Both would fail even more completely than Judah.

Finally, Ezekiel offered hope for the future in terms of a renewed covenant with God (chapters 33–39) and a restored holy temple, city and land (chapters 40–48). The tone here is eschatological, looking towards the end times, after a restoration from exile in Babylon and further battles, after which God's glory would be seen to have returned.

Author

Ezekiel was both a priest and a prophet, hence his concern with both present and future temples in Jerusalem. At the opening of the book, he was probably about 30, the age when priests began their service. At the end, he would be about 50. During the book, his wife died, though he could not mourn her death, any more than he could mourn the death of Jerusalem.

Date

The book's prophecies are very precisely dated. The period indicated is from the time of the first Babylonian assault on Judah and the taking of a first group of exiles to Babylon, about 593 BC, to 571 BC. This would make him contemporary with Jeremiah, who stayed behind in Jerusalem, and perhaps the young Daniel. His wife's death is dated to the final fall of Jerusalem in 586 BC.

OUTLINE – EZEKIEL

The call of Ezekiel

Prophecies against Jerusalem

Prophecies against Israel

Prophecies against surrounding nations

Prophecies of restoration

KEY THEMES – EZEKIEL

Visions of glory

Of all the written prophets, Ezekiel was, with Daniel and Zechariah, the most visionary. Some of his visions recall those of Elisha's vision of the horses and chariots of God (2 Kings 6:17), especially the opening vision which is as spectacular as any SciFi film. They reveal God in his heavenly glory, veiled in unapproachable light.

However, typically, God's glory was linked to the Jerusalem temple, such as when it was dedicated by Solomon (2 Chronicles 7:2). This is where Isaiah had his commissioning vision (Isaiah 6:4). The significance of Ezekiel's opening vision was that God's glory was universal, not confined to the temple. One could have glimpses of it anywhere. The significance of his vision of the glory leaving the temple (10:1-22) is that neither God's presence nor his glory was automatically fixed there. He would not leave his glory in a polluted building. However, Ezekiel has a further vision of the future, when that glory returns (43:1-27). God wants his glory to be in the midst of his people, though it cannot be contained there.

Prophetic responsibility

The book of Ezekiel gives clear teaching on the responsibilities of prophecy, both in terms of its giving and reception. In its giving, the responsibility is to declare it, no matter what the reception. The prophet is he who stands in the gap or breach for God, when the spiritual walls would otherwise be broken (3:4-27; 22:30). Interestingly, the book of Nehemiah literally shows just such a man.

The responsibility of reception is not just to hear, repent and obey, but to remain in that obedience (33:1-20). Even last-minute repentance will be acceptable, just as last-minute reneging will lead to death. But reception is individual (18:1-32). Here, Ezekiel modifies the older teaching of punishment extending to later generations (Exodus 20:5, but see also Deuteronomy 24:16; Jeremiah 31:29-30). The effect of sin may be generational, but the responsibility – the guilt – is on the present individual.

RELEVANCE FOR TODAY – EZEKIEL

Dry bones

One of the most well-known visions of Ezekiel is that of the Valley of Dry Bones (37:1-14). God asks Ezekiel in a rhetorical question: "Can these bones live?" (verse 3). The answer is re-enacted in the vision, at the end of which God tells Ezekiel: "I will put my spirit in you and you will live." At the literal level, this refers to God's promise of restoration to the scattered exiles, a promise made in many other prophecies and by many other prophets, and fulfilled, as the Ezra-Nehemiah account tells us.

> "The name of the city from that time on will be: THE LORD IS THERE."
>
> Ezekiel 48:35

However, the promise of renewal is an ongoing spiritual one in God's plan. At one level, our natural life needs God's spirit to make us a spiritual person, that is, regeneration. But even as believers, we have periods when our spiritual life feels dried up and in need of renewal. Water is the commonest symbol of such renewal, standing at the opposite extreme to the arid valley of Ezekiel's vision. In John 4:14, Jesus promises us a spring of water "welling up to eternal life". We need to hold to this as an ongoing promise, not just a once-off experience of grace.

Apocalyptic writing and the fall of the great city

Chapters 26–28 have puzzled many scholars and ordinary readers. They appear to be woes directed against a fairly small city and its trading empire. Why should the prophet use such poetic and forceful language at such length on these small objects?

One of the answers is that Ezekiel was speaking to more than he knew, in an apocalyptic way. Put simply, it means that Tyre becomes a type of the modern, commercial (or secular) world empire, which in its pride thinks it is self-sustaining and unconquerable, as also in Isaiah 23. In Ezekiel's day, this would have been Babylon, but Ezekiel could not easily have said this directly. In the book of Revelation, it *is* called Babylon (Revelation 18). In its pride and self-sufficiency, it comes under God's judgement (see Isaiah 14 for a similar prophecy).

But interpretations have gone further. In the language used of the King of Tyre in Ezekiel 28, we have references that can be applied to Satan himself, who is elsewhere called the prince of this world (John 12:31). He, too, is judged (John 16:11), along with the great city. Behind such imperial forces lies this satanic power, always doomed, but always needing to be recognised and opposed.

Daniel
ORDEALS AND VISIONS

OVERVIEW

Daniel was an exile in Babylon after the fall of Jerusalem. He found favour with a series of kings during the course of a long and distinguished life, even though he was a Jew and even though he refused to compromise his beliefs. At times he and his three friends underwent terrible ordeals; at other times he was given terrifying visions of the future. But in every conflict situation, God's truth and kingdom emerged triumphant.

SUMMARY

In this highly literary book, the twelve chapters fall neatly into two halves. Chapters 1–6 deal with Daniel and his three friends in a series of memorable stories. Over a lifetime, they underwent a series of ordeals, which tested their faith to the limits. Firstly, they refused as Jews to go against their strict dietary laws (chapter 1). Daniel's three friends then refused to worship an idol and were thrown into a furnace (chapter 3). The final ordeal for Daniel came when he refused to pray to King Darius. He was thrown into a den of lions, but again survived (chapter 6).

In between these chapters, Daniel is presented with a series of tests, which challenge his ability as a wise man. In one case he actually had to reveal the content of a dream before interpreting it (chapter 2). In another dream interpretation, he had to predict the future disgrace of the king (chapter 4). Finally, he interpreted a sign about the fall of King Belshazzar, after he had used sacred drinking vessels from the Jerusalem temple (chapter 5).

Chapters 7–12 are more apocryphal, interpreting dreams of future kingdoms and their fall. Here, Daniel becomes the dreamer,

needing an angelic helper to interpret. The second part again divides into two: the first three chapters (7–9) are three distinct but fairly general visions, not dissimilar to that in chapter 2. The second part (chapters 10–12) is one long detailed vision of the future world kingdoms, until God's kingdom breaks in.

The two parts of the book illustrate that the God who is in control of the nations is also the God who cares for and protects individuals in times of need.

Author

Daniel was a well-born young man at the beginning of the story, who was trained in all the wisdom of the Babylonians. Much of this wisdom is to do with dreams and signs, as well as the more practical wisdom of law and administration.

Date

There exists a great deal of controversy over the date. The exile period from 605–530 BC is the traditional date, but some scholars have suggested the period of the Maccabees around 175–160 BC, another period of great suffering for the Jewish people.

OUTLINE – DANIEL

Stories of exile and testing

Visions of the future

KEY THEMES – DANIEL

Deliverance

The theme of deliverance is seen in two ways in the book. Firstly, there is actual physical deliverance, from the furnace (3:27) and the den of lions (6:20-22). These deliverances are as miraculous as the crossing of the Red Sea, when God delivered the Israelites from the Egyptian army (9:15; see Exodus 14:14-31). The mysterious presence of the fourth person in the furnace (3:25) suggests God's direct intervention.

But the theme of deliverance runs right through the second part also. Daniel sees a time when God's people, the "saints" (7:18), will be persecuted (7:21; 8:24; 9:26; 11:31-35; 12:7). However severe the persecution, deliverance is promised (7:22; 8:25; 9:27; 12:1). The strength of apocalyptic writing is to give hope to God's people when their enemies seem to have the upper hand completely. And indeed history shows also that no period of persecution goes on for ever: the tyrants are overthrown and God's people are delivered.

The term "deliverance" is used specifically in the Bible in regards to evil. Sometimes today the term is used where the Bible would use the term exorcism or the "throwing-out" of evil spirits (eg Matthew 7:22).

Repentance for the past

The exile happened as a result of Israel's failure to follow God. Jeremiah prophesied a 70-year exile (9:2; see Jeremiah 25:11; 29:10). Daniel comes to terms with this in a remarkable chapter (9:1-19). Though he personally was faultless, he repents for the sins of his people in the past. Nehemiah does the same (Nehemiah 1), as does Ezra (Nehemiah 9), all in the same situation. So Daniel shows us that we need to repent not only of our personal sins: repentance has corporate dimensions too.

An everlasting kingdom

One of the main messages of apocalyptic writing is that although earthly kingdoms, whether Babylon, Persia, Greece, or even Rome (probably meant by the fourth beast), might seem impregnable, in the grand scheme of things they are short-lived and will inevitably fail. Only God's kingdom, the final kingdom, will last for ever (2:44; 7:14, 27). This is our historical perspective as believers. The point is its certainty.

Angels

Although angels are mentioned throughout the Bible as messengers from God, they are seen in a wider context in Daniel as interpreters and revealers (8:16), and also as fighters (10:13). At his trial, Jesus acknowledges this (Matthew 26:53).

RELEVANCE FOR TODAY – DANIEL

Don't compromise

Daniel and his three companions, Hananiah, Mishael, and Azariah, find themselves in exile, having lost everything, it would appear. Even their names are taken from them, being replaced by Babylonian ones. Then suddenly, they are given an opportunity to make good in a strange culture with a strange religion and a tyrannical ruler. But the demand is always to obey the rules of the conquerors, rather than their own religious beliefs.

The temptation must have been overwhelming, but the book makes it clear that no temptation to compromise beliefs is overwhelming. It is possible to withstand, even on pain of death, whether from burning, execution or wild animals. But the book goes much further in its stories: God will vindicate those who refuse to compromise, not only by delivering them, but also by honouring them and giving them victory over their enemies. In the end, Daniel lives to a ripe old age, respected and honoured. This is the consequence of true wisdom.

But Daniel also refuses to compromise in regards to his message. Despite its unpopular content he delivers it. He tells Nebuchadnezzar to his face (4:27) to repent otherwise he will go mad. He tells Belshazzar his kingdom has been judged and found wanting. He could have watered down the message. He didn't and such is the authority of truth that his message was received, even if it was not believed.

Serve God in an alien culture

Daniel proves it is possible to serve God fully in an alien culture without compromising your beliefs and practices. Daniel continued praying towards Jerusalem till he was an old man (6:10). Yet he was honoured and promoted by no fewer than three kings (2:48; 5:29; 6:28).

For all his uncompromising attitude, however, Daniel is shown to be wise and tactful. In 1:12 he suggests a way out for the nervous official; 2:20 shows due humility and deference; in 4:19 he tries to soften the blow. It is God who caused Daniel to find favour. But he still had to do his part by displaying a caring and truthful attitude.

> "Daniel,
> I have now come
> to bring you insight
> and understanding."
>
> Daniel 9:22

God gives wisdom

James 1:15 tells us that God will willingly give us wisdom if we ask. This is what the book of Daniel shows in practice. For example, 2:23 shows wisdom given at a crucial moment. In this case it was by direct revelation (2:19,28), but this is not necessarily the only way. Patient thinking and praying about a situation or person will often bring a new love or sympathy, which will then bring its own wisdom. Taking advice from people who are more godly or less involved in a situation than we are can also bring wisdom.

Hosea

THE DIVINE LOVER

OVERVIEW

Hosea, the first of the twelve Minor Prophets, was a prophet primarily to the northern kingdom of Israel, like his predecessor Amos. Whereas Amos stresses God's justice and righteousness, Hosea presents God as divine lover. Thus, Israel's sinfulness is seen in terms of unfaithfulness as much as unrighteousness; and he uses terms of complaint, wooing and pleading as much as terms of denunciation. Remarkably, his own marriage becomes an enactment of the message he preaches: motivated by love, God will restore Israel just as Hosea takes back his faithless wife.

SUMMARY

The book falls into two somewhat unequal parts. The first part (chapters 1–3) tell of Hosea's unhappy marriage. Hosea is told to marry a woman, Gomer, who proved to be unfaithful to him. She bore him three children, all of whom were symbolically named. The first was a son called Jezreel, after the incident recorded in 2 Kings 9:13-37, prefiguring a final wiping out of the royal line of Israel. The second child, a daughter, was named Lo-Ruhamah, ("not loved"), signifying the withdrawal of God's love to Israel; and the third, a boy, was named Lo-Ammi ("not my people"), meaning that Israel was no longer to be considered the people of God. Hosea is then told to reclaim Gomer from the prostitution she had fallen into, but to set her apart for a time to prove her faithfulness (chapters 1 and 3). Chapter 2 summarises the themes and prophecies that run through the second part of the book.

The second part (chapters 4–14) consists of a series of highly poetic prophecies to Israel and sometimes Judah, the southern kingdom. These prophecies outline both the nature and possible consequences of Israel's

unfaithfulness, which includes idolatry and a whole range of moral, social and political wrongs, and hold out the promise of God's forgiveness and restoration when Israel truly repents. Running through the descriptions of present failings are accounts of God's faithfulness in history.

Author

Nothing much is known about Hosea. Unlike Amos, he was a native of the northern kingdom. His imagery is entirely natural, whereas Amos' is partly urban, suggesting Hosea lived and worked on the land. His prophecies were most likely given over a number of years.

Date

The kings mentioned as reigning in the southern kingdom of Judah in 1:1 are the same as named in the book of Isaiah. Jeroboam II, the northern king, lived 793–753 BC, and is mentioned by Amos also. No reference is made to the eventual fall of Samaria, Israel's capital, which was in 722 BC, so the general conclusion is he was writing between 755–725 BC.

OUTLINE – HOSEA

KEY THEMES – HOSEA

Spiritual adultery

Hosea's marital experiences, commented on initially in chapter 2, form the basis for his messages. The foremost theme in them is that of Israel's unfaithfulness to God, seen in terms of covenant breaking (4:1; 5:7; 6:4-7; 9:1,10). He speaks of a "spirit of prostitution" (4:12f.; 5:4; 6:10). This is then more specifically defined as idolatry (8; 9:15; 13:1-2), which is helped on by the priests (4:6-9; 5:1f.;10:5) in their refusal to hear the prophets (9:7-8; 12:10). This has led to a failure of true repentance (6:1-3; 8:2,11; 11:5,7), and instead to seeking outside help in their need for assistance and protection (5:13; 7:11; 8:9; 12:1; 14:3). The linking of idolatry to sexuality was more natural than we might think today. The worship of Baal, which was the prevalent form of idolatry in Israel, was basically a fertility cult, and there would be temple prostitutes (4:14) and a man and his son could lie with the same girl. Hence the curse of barrenness (9:11,14) and images of difficult birth (13:13) and illegitimacy (5:7). The word *Baal* itself can mean either "lord" or "husband".

God's faithfulness

Balanced against Israel's failings is a list of God's responses. Firstly, God longs to redeem and be merciful (6:11; 7:13; 11:4-9;14:4f.); but if there is no response to him, then punishment will inevitably follow (5:10-14; 9:7-9; 10:2-15; 13:7-8). This may be in the form of ecological disaster (5:7f.; 8:7; 9:2), military defeat (5:8-9; 11:5-6; 13:16) or exile (9:17; 10:5-6). Included in this theme is a series of reviews of God's faithful dealings in the past (9:10; 10:9; 12:3-10; 13:4-6). For the Old Testament writers, history is covenant history, and covenant is based on *hesed*, the Hebrew term meaning faithfulness, promise-keeping. Marriage, too, is a form of covenant (2:18-20); hence, again, the centrality of the marriage analogy in Hosea's writings.

God as divine lover

The previous theme, then, leads naturally into seeing God as divine lover. Hosea literally has to model this first by marrying Gomer, then rescuing her, literally redeeming her as he has to buy her out of prostitution. God is then seen doing the same thing: marrying Israel, and then having to woo her again out of her Baal prostitution (11:8). Chapter 2 has some ambiguity: does it refer to Hosea and Gomer, or God and Israel? The answer is both. Israel's other acts of unfaithfulness have been to trust Egypt and Assyria to protect her, instead of the LORD alone (8:9,13; 9:3).

RELEVANCE FOR TODAY – HOSEA

God's heart of mercy

One of the striking features of Hosea is the constant interchange between God's anger and frustration at Israel's unfaithfulness, and his pleas for her to turn back to him. Thus in chapter 2, we begin with "Rebuke your mother" (2:2) and "I will take back … and I will expose" (2:9,10). But then in 2:14 comes "Therefore I am going to allure her" and "I will respond …" (2:21). At the end of the book there is a final appeal (14:1) and a final promise of unconditional love (14:4). Similar promises of restoration close other prophetic books (eg Amos 9:11-15; Joel 3:17-21). The LORD's last word is one of mercy, forgiveness and restoration.

This should encourage us. In the prophetic writings, Israel is typically a stubborn and faithless nation, and so divine anger is turned full force on it. But there is no need for us to be like this. God wishes, far more than we do, a covenant relationship of intimacy and love. His yearning heart reaches out to gather us in. We tend to see our failings in a disproportionate way, either as huge or quite minor. Sin is sin to God, but what should matter to us is the greatness of his merciful love.

Cheap grace

On the other hand, it is possible to repent too superficially. This is what Hosea sees Israel doing in 6:1-3. God responds, "Your love is like the morning mist" (6:4). The term "cheap grace" was termed by the German theologian Dietrich Bonhoeffer to describe this sort of attitude. God's grace in forgiving us our sin

> "Maintain love and justice, and wait for your God always."
>
> **Hosea 12:6**

freely was obtained at tremendous cost, the death of his own Son, Jesus Christ. True repentance, then, is to realise what it actually cost God. This is not to prevent us from repenting, but to cause us to mean it as deeply as we can and seriously change what caused our sin in the first place.

The church as the bride of Christ

Although the intimate language of love might not always be associated with Old Testament prophecy, it is part of an ongoing revelation of God's covenant relationship with his people that culminates in the New Testament image of the church as the bride of Christ (Revelation 21:2,9; 22:17). A number of Christ's parables are about wedding feasts or bridegrooms (Matthew 25:1-13; Luke 5:34-35; John 3:29).

At present, it would be difficult to see the present-day church as a pure and beautiful bride. We are all too aware of spots and stains and ugly blemishes. But we need to see that for all its imperfections, Christ loves the church and is seeking to present her spotless and faultless at the day of his coming again. We should pray for it in that light.

Joel
DISASTER TO BLESSING

OVERVIEW

A dreadful plague of locusts becomes for Joel a picture of the coming Day of the Lord. He calls for national repentance. As the nation truly repents, then God pronounces judgements against the nations that have oppressed them, an outpouring of his Spirit, and a restoration of all they have lost and more.

SUMMARY

Joel's message has three parts. The first is a vivid and dramatic description of the worst plague of locusts experienced by Judah in living memory. Although locusts were a recurring menace in the Middle East (for example, Amos 7:1-2), this was obviously far worse than the normal experience. It seemed to have been accompanied by an equally devastating drought (1:1-20). Such a natural calamity needed to be met by a national call to prayer and repentance.

The second part interprets this plague as a type or picture of the Day of the LORD. The stage is widened from the local to the cosmic. The scenario becomes apocalyptic. The need for true repentance is even greater (2:1-17).

The final part has two elements. As the nation repented, the LORD promised to "repay for the years the locusts have eaten" (2:25), manifesting itself in both material restoration (3:17-21) and in spiritual gifts (2:28-32). But also there would be a day of judgement on the nation's enemies (3:1-16). The place of judgement is located as "the Valley of Jehoshaphat" (3:2) lying outside the walls of Jerusalem. God promises that "never again" would the land be devastated (3:17).

Author

Nothing is known at all about the writer apart from 1:1, where he is named as the "son of Pethuel". None of the other prophets mention him, though there are many echoes of his message scattered throughout the other prophetic books, including Zephaniah, Zechariah, Isaiah, and Daniel.

Date

There is no decisive clue within the text to give an accurate dating of the book. The compilers of the Hebrew Bible felt it should go between Amos and Hosea, presumably because they thought it belonged to the time around 770–740 BC. Some scholars agree. Some put it a generation earlier, which would make the book the first of the written prophets in time. By contrast, others put it much later, after the exile round 450 BC, the time of Malachi, or even later. There are good reasons for all these dates, but none is decisive.

OUTLINE – JOEL

The Day of the LORD:
a day of judgement

1:1	Title
1:2-4	The plague of locusts
1:5-8	Drunks called to mourning – no more wine
1:9-10	No more sacrifices for the priests to make
1:11-12	No more crops for the farmers
1:13-14	First call to fasting and repentance
1:15	The Day of the LORD is near
1:16-18	Effects of plague and drought
1:19-20	The prophet calls to God
2:1-2a	The alarm needs sounding
2:2b-11	The coming of a destroying army
2:12-14	God promises true repentance will be met by mercy
2:15-17	Second call to national repentance

The Day of the LORD:
a day of salvation

2:18-20	The LORD will have mercy on his people
2:21-24	A call to rejoicing
2:25-27	Promise of restoration
2:28-32	Promise of an outpouring of God's Spirit
3:1-8	Judgement on the nations
3:9-11	Preparations for war
3:12-16	Punishment on the nations for oppressing Judah
3:17-21	Future blessings and prosperity

KEY THEMES – JOEL

National repentance

Many prophets attacked specific sins and failings in the people of God. Zephaniah, for example, attacked spiritual apathy, syncretism and idolatry, social injustice and oppression. Repentance, therefore, had to include those sins specifically. Joel, however, makes no mention of any specific sins on the part of the nation. Instead there is general repentance. Its manifestations are sackcloth (1:13), a fast (1:14), weeping and mourning (2:12), tearing garments (2:13). This is in the context of a sacred assembly (1:14; 2:15). However, Joel realises God will not be impressed by these physical acts alone. They must be accompanied by a genuine inner repentance, figuratively expressed as "rend your heart" (2:13; compare Zechariah 7:5). Such repentance must include the sense of utter dependence on God, and human unworthiness.

Apocalypse now

The national calamity is expressed very dramatically in terms of an invading army (2:2-9) as the locusts advance inexorably. They are so thick that they darken the sky (2:10-11). Such cosmic manifestations are a picture of the Day of the LORD – a wake-up call to the nation that God's final intervention will be *the* decisive culmination of history (see also Zephaniah).

Judgement against the nations

Again, many of the prophetic books envisage specific judgement on other nations (see for example, Zephaniah 2:4-15). Joel is more general, mentioning by name only Tyre and Sidon, and Philistia (3:4). Nations are judged according to how they have treated Israel, that is, God's covenant people (3:4-8). Joel reverses Isaiah's picture of beating swords into ploughshares (3:10; see Isaiah 2:4; Micah 4:3).

The images of the harvest and vintage of wrath (3:13) are truly disturbing. Only after such judgement can true prosperity come (3:18-19).

Never again
This apocalyptic time will also be different from the present by being a time of eternal security for God's people (3:17). Joel shares this conviction with many other prophets: there does really come a time when God brings a full end to his people's suffering and/or punishment (2:18, 26; compare Amos 9:15). Here Joel makes it seem like an Eden, once lost (2:3), now regained (3:18). The book of Revelation closes with the same note (Revelation 22:1-5).

RELEVANCE FOR TODAY – JOEL

> "Everyone who calls on the name of the Lord will be saved."
>
> **Joel 2:32**

The years the locusts have eaten
One of the most widely quoted verses in Joel is 2:25, sometimes translated "I will restore …" rather than "repay" as in the NIV. Locusts wipe out the land in an unimaginably devastating way: literally nothing remains. The word that is striking here is "years" rather than "places". Many people feel that their life has had periods of total devastation, where they have nothing to show except barrenness and waste. This promise then becomes particularly important. Restoration is something God will do for them. A similar biblical image is of the barren woman rejoicing more than those women with children (Isaiah 54:1-3).

The generosity of God
The book begins with total poverty – nothing is left economically. The second part of the book not only restores this lost prosperity, but also reveals God's heart as overwhelmingly generous. The promise of restoration is filled out in detail (2:19, 22-24; 3:18). Such images of plenty and fertility remind us of God's original promise to the Israelites to give them a land overflowing with milk and honey (Exodus 3:8). We tend to see God as someone who has to be persuaded to measure out his blessings one by one. This reflects our poverty of spirit rather than a true picture of the generous God who gives feasts to his returning prodigals (Luke 15:23).

Pouring out the Spirit
The promise of the outpouring of the Spirit was one of the key passages quoted at length by Peter on the Day of Pentecost (Acts 2:17-21), which was seen by the early church as the fulfilment of this prophecy. But each generation has to reclaim this prophecy for itself.

Three things need to be noted about it:
- The promise was to "all people", not just to Israel
- There were to be supernatural prophetic manifestations
- God would do the "pouring".

The Acts of the Apostles is full of such manifestations, which extend beyond the prophetic to healing and exorcisms also. Most obvious, perhaps, is the prophetic boldness of the early apostles; the outpouring was a transforming experience (Acts 2:37–3:10).

Different churches have different explanations of how this outpouring of the Spirit should be experienced today. Whatever explanation is made, it should line up with Joel's prophecy as interpreted through the New Testament.

Amos

A FAILING STATE

OVERVIEW

Amos prophesied to the northern kingdom of Israel, even though he was a southerner, from Judah. He spoke out against the luxurious lifestyle of the ruling classes, the moral and spiritual apathy this had brought about, and the injustice and corruption he saw. He viewed the exile as God's judgement on this, resulting in the near total destruction of the nation. Only a handful would be saved. Amos' message was not well received and he was told to go back to Judah (7:12-13).

SUMMARY

The prophecy falls into three sections: chapters 1–2, 3–6 and 7–9. The first two chapters consist of a brief introduction, followed by a series of woes directed at Israel's seven neighbours (1:3–2:5). The climax of this series of denunciations is one against Israel, the northern kingdom of the once unified country (2:6-16). Such attacks on other countries are common in the prophetic writings (see also Isaiah 13–23; Jeremiah 46–51; Zephaniah 2:4-15). Amos focuses on the atrocities against other countries.

The second section consists of a series of oracles, or prophecies, again mainly denunciations of evils in the land, with the retribution God is placing on them. To Amos, God is a God of righteousness, so all forms of injustice come under his judgement. Amos speaks out particularly against a corrupt legal system, bribery and failure to distribute wealth (5:11-12). Moneymaking took precedence over a true practice of religion. In fact, religion had become an empty shell of ritual with no moral force to it at all. Amos warns people to change their ways.

The final section consists of a series of five visions or pictures (7:1-9; 8:1-3; 9:1-5). The warning of judgement is rather more apocalyptic this time (8:9-14). The book finishes with the promise of a remnant and their future restoration (9:13-15).

Author

Amos came from the village of Tekoa, in the plateau south of Bethlehem, where he was both a shepherd and a tender of sycamore-figs (1:1; 7:14-15). He emphasises he was not a professional prophet. Amos was thus an outsider twice over. Nevertheless, his language is highly rhetorical.

Date

Amos preached in the reigns of Uzziah of Judah (792–740 BC) and Jeroboam II of Israel (793–753 BC). The earthquake of 1:1 cannot be dated, though it was remembered two hundred years later (Zechariah 14:5). The prophecy was received two years before it, though obviously the book was not written till after. The likeliest date for Amos' ministry is thus 775–755 BC, a little before Hosea, Micah and Isaiah.

OUTLINE – AMOS

Oracles against the nations

1:1-2   Title and announcement of God's judgement
1:3-5   Denunciation of Damascus (Syria)
1:6-8   Denunciation of Gaza (Philistia)
1:9-10   Denunciation of Tyre (Phoenicia)
1:11-12   Denunciation of Edom
1:13-15   Denunciation of Ammon
2:1-3   Denunciation of Moab
2:4-5   Denunciation of Judah
2:6-16   Denunciation of Israel herself

The judgement against Israel

3:1-15   Witness against Israel's failure to be God's chosen people
4:1-13   Israel unrepentant of her sins despite previous punishment
5:1-17   Luxury and injustice widespread
5:18-27   The Day of the Lord will bring judgement
6:1-14   The inevitability of judgement

The visions of Amos

7:1-3   Vision of the plague of locusts
7:4-6   Vision of judgement by fire
7:7-9   Vision of the plumb-line
7:10-13   Amaziah, the high priest, tells Amos to go home
7:14-17   Judgement against Amaziah and his family
8:1-3   The vision of the basket of ripe fruit
8:4-6   Condemnation of social injustice
8:7-10   Signs of the Day of the Lord
8:11-14   Coming spiritual hunger
9:1-6   Vision of the Lord at the altar
9:7-10   A righteous remnant will survive the coming punishment
9:11-12   Restoration promised
9:13-15   Return from exile and future prosperity

KEY THEMES – AMOS

What God wants in a nation: justice

Israel was what is termed today a "failing state", almost a "failed state". But unlike today, the reasons were not economic or administrative. Quite the contrary, for the state was prosperous, made so by taking over much of the trade from its defeated northern neighbour, Syria. Marks of luxury, for example, the expensive houses and furnishings (6:4-6) and lush vineyards (5:11), struck the itinerant shepherd Amos forcibly. There was a legal system and religious ritual was observed (5:21-23).

Israel was failing because its very prosperity had blinded the people to the demands of justice and true worship demanded by God. Amos saw God's righteousness should be reflected in a righteous nation (3:2-3; 5:24). This should be seen in a fair legal system (5:15), and in fair treatment of the poor. Israel's failure is denounced by Amos (5:7, 11, 12; 6:12; 8:4).

Such failure will meet with God's judgement. Unfortunately, a corrupt society becomes morally blind, and unable to see possible judgement coming from God. Amos points out examples of other formerly prosperous states now in ruins (6:1-3). 9:1-6 paints a terrible and dramatic picture of the inevitable result of such blindness.

What God wants in a nation: true spirituality

The prophets did not simply denounce idolatry, the worship of false gods (5:26), nor syncretism (mixing worship of God with worship of idols). They also denounced worship meant for God which was mere gesture and outward show. God abhors this (8:10; compare Isaiah 1:11-17). For Amos and the other prophets, worship is a moral activity as much as a spiritual (5:24). The plumb-line image is the clearest expression of this (7:7-9): the plumb-line is a symbol of uprightness and honesty. Israel fails the test and so her high-places and sanctuaries, that is, her spiritual centres of worship, will be destroyed.

The inevitability of judgement

The first two visions show Amos pleading with God not to impose punishment (7:5). We are reminded of Abraham pleading for Sodom and Gomorrah to be saved (Genesis 18:16-33). God agrees yet in both cases judgement came. God is willing to show mercy (5:14-15), but he sees more clearly than the prophets that the unrighteous, blind inhabitants are not in a position to receive such grace. The inevitability, therefore, is as much a law of human moral blindness as God's imposition of a punishment after repeated warning. There seems to be a point of no return. Grace can then only be given after judgement (9:11-15).

Hong Kong fish market. Amos and other prophets spoke out strongly against injustice and unfair dealings against the poor

RELEVANCE FOR TODAY – AMOS

Setting lifestyle priorities

The clearest picture of the Israelites' lack of true spirituality lies in the corruption depicted in 8:5-6. The people cannot wait to get back from worship service to make more money as dishonestly as possible.

But a society or an individual does not just get to such a position at once. At some stage, wrong decisions about priorities must have been taken. Making money and grasping the economic opportunities suddenly made available must have been a decision, at some level, made consciously. Today we too can be lured by moneymaking as a prestigious undertaking. We need to take heed of the warning of Amos to avoid the moral progression downwards. From prosperity comes a carelessness over moral standards, cutting corners, manipulating the legal system, stepping over those who are weaker, bribery. As material rewards come, a love of luxury is developed. Formerly positive religious acts can become meaningless, a front, even a false security. Warnings, either from other people's failure, or more direct confrontations, are ignored. Ultimately, spiritual bankruptcy and God's judgement come.

> "Seek me
> and live."
>
> Amos 5:4

Speaking out for justice

A prophet's ministry is likely to be confrontational; deafness and rejection the likely response. Jonah's preaching was quite unusually successful; Haggai's likewise. But more typical is Jeremiah's ministry with no obvious positive results, only repeated rejection. Amos suffered similarly, being told to go back home. However, his prophecies were fulfilled and the northern kingdom was wiped out some 30 years later, when the people were taken into exile by the Assyrians, disappearing without trace – the "ten lost tribes of Israel".

When Amaziah told Amos to stop prophesying, it was something Amos simply could not do: he was so conscious of God calling him (7:15) and speaking to him (3:7-8). But the Israelites had a tradition of silencing their prophets (2:11-12) and thought they could do the same to Amos. After all, "the prudent man keeps quiet in such times, for the times are evil" (5:13). In God's grace, Amos was not prudent, and we have his book as record of his imprudence and a permanent judgement against a society that wants to shut its prophets up.

Our own society does not care for any Christian prophetic voice. It discusses whether such prophets are mad, "hearing voices". But we have to speak out against those things we know offend God's righteousness if we are to keep our integrity as Christians.

Obadiah
FALL OF A PROUD NATION

OVERVIEW

Obadiah condemns the nation of Edom for its pride. Edom feels impregnable in its mountain fortress. Worse, it has betrayed Judah when Jerusalem fell, cutting off its refugees. It will be devastated in even worse measure, whilst Jerusalem will be restored as the centre of God's blessing.

SUMMARY

Obadiah predicted the fall of Edom (verses 1-7). At present, they felt invincible, giving rise to pride and false wisdom. The prophet foretold the breaking of this pride. But God was not just simply punishing pride: Edom as a nation was related to Judah, but had now betrayed Judah by siding with the invading enemy, cutting down those fleeing the burning city of Jerusalem, plundering and invading the territory of Judah (verses 8-14).

The Day of the LORD was now upon all nations: there would be divine retribution and restoration (verses 15-18). Edom and Philistia would both disappear as nations, whilst Judah would be restored as exiles repossess their stolen territories (verses 19,20). Jerusalem would once more be the city of God (verse 21).

Author

Obadiah's prophecy is the shortest of all the Old Testament prophets. We know nothing about him outside this single chapter. He sees himself as a mouthpiece of God only; his name meaning "servant of God", could be a name he gave himself. His language is both poetic and passionate.

Date

Six of his verses are very close to some in Jeremiah (verses 1-6 = Jeremiah 49:9,14-16). This leads many to presume Obadiah is referring to the fall of Jerusalem in 586 BC. Ezekiel, writing at much the same time, refers to the misdeeds of the Edomites as well (Ezekiel 25:12f.; compare Psalm 137:7; Lamentations 4:21). The prophecy is usually therefore dated within the exilic period.

OUTLINE – OBADIAH

Against Edom

1a	Obadiah's vision
1b-2	A prediction of disaster against Edom
3-4	Her pride will be brought low
5-7	Her destruction will be total
8-9	The wise and the military will be destroyed
10-14	Edom's shameful treatment of Judah
15-21	The coming Day of the Lord: retribution and restoration

KEY THEMES – OBADIAH

Pride will be brought down

The boast of impregnability is not new to Edom. In 2 Samuel 5:6-7 we read of the Jebusites boasting that Jerusalem was impregnable. That did not prevent King David capturing it and then using it as his new capital. Edom, a little nation on the edge of the Negev desert, part of modern-day Jordan, thought its mountains were its protection. But God says, "The pride of your heart has deceived you" (verse 3). It is God himself who "will bring you down" (verse 4).

This is a theme common to other prophets also. Isaiah talks of "the pride of men brought low" (Isaiah 2:11). To the Greeks, pride was termed "hubris" and meant putting oneself beyond the reach of fate. It was considered the worst of sins. The Bible does not list sins in rank order quite like this, but certainly no one and no nation is beyond the reach of God's judgement.

Chaos and God's sovereignty

The Babylonian invasion, which led to the destruction of Jerusalem, produced a chaotic aftermath, well described in Jeremiah 39–44. It is amazing any prophetic writing survived. Its survival is symbolic, however, of God's order being established in the middle of chaos and the breaking of relationships. Obadiah is able to see a return to order in terms of restoration, of exiles returning to their land, and Jerusalem once again being established as the centre of God's rule (verses 19-21).

Justice and fulfilment

Part of God's judgement is the equalising of guilt and punishment. The phrase "in the day of their (Judah's) disaster" is repeated as the reason for God's punishment, leading to the climax "your deeds will return on your own head" (verse 15).

As a matter of history, Edom did not fall quickly, probably not till the time of the Maccabees (1 Maccabees 5:3), some 400 years later, though they were displaced from the mountains earlier than that. God does not put a timetable on the execution of his justice. But history has proved how complete the punishment was. By New Testament times, there was no sign left of Edom.

Wasting the inheritance

It might appear that Edom had always been enemies of Israel. But in fact, the Edomites were descended from Esau, Jacob's brother (Genesis 25:24-26; 36:1). As such, there was potentially a residual blessing available for them. But they opposed Israel, especially when the Israelites were escaping Egypt (Numbers 20:18-21). Although later incorporated into King David's empire (1 Kings 11:14-22), they soon rebelled (2 Kings 8:20-21). Even so, their betrayal of Judah is seen as a brotherly betrayal by Obadiah (verse 10).

> "But on Mount Zion will be deliverance."
>
> Obadiah 17

Many people think that because their country has had a Christian past, it will still enjoy God's blessing. But actually it is possible for that country to oppose God's laws and rule and to waste its inheritance actively, not just passively. At that stage it will certainly come under God's judgement.

Courage and trust

World affairs sometimes seem chaotic, and certainly out of God's control. That may be true for our personal lives, including even betrayal by close family members. Like Obadiah, we need to re-assert our vision of God's control, order and restoration. This takes courage, especially when discouragement becomes our greatest enemy. It also takes trust in God's purposes, looking afresh at our circumstances with a view to seeing God's purposes.

Jonah
MAN WITH A MISSION

OVERVIEW
The book of Jonah is quite unlike those of the other Minor Prophets, since it tells
a story of a prophet, rather than gives his message. The story itself becomes the message.
Jonah is given a commission, runs away from it and almost dies as a consequence.
He is recommissioned, has great success, but still cannot find fulfilment in what he
has accomplished.

SUMMARY
The story divides into two halves, both of
which can be subdivided to form the four
chapters of this dramatic little book. The story
line is not difficult – it is often retold as a
children's story – but the meaning has been
argued over. It contains different layers of
meaning, and uses irony as a central device.

Jonah is given a commission from God to
preach judgement to the city of Nineveh, the
main city of the great Assyrian Empire. Unlike
other prophets, such as Nahum, he is to give
his denunciation in person in the country (1:2).
Jonah ran away as far as he could, to Tarshish,
generally supposed to have been a Phoenician
colony in Spain (1:3-4).

The boat he sailed in ran into a massive
storm. The superstitious sailors saw this as
divine in origin and sought its cause.
Eventually Jonah's disobedience came to light,
and he told the sailors to throw him overboard
(1:4-12). They hesitated at first, but eventually
had to (1:13-15).

The storm abated at once, causing the
sailors to believe in Jonah's God. Meanwhile, a
great fish swallowed Jonah (1:17). Within the
fish's stomach, Jonah worshipped God (2:1-9).
Finally, Jonah was vomited up on dry land
(2:10).

Jonah now went to Nineveh, and such was
the force of his preaching, the whole city
repented. God's judgement was averted
(3:1-10). But instead of being pleased, Jonah
became very angry with God, wishing to die.
In the final chapter, God and Jonah argue
about God's apparent change of mind. Jonah is
challenged for his inconsistency: he is more
upset at a plant dying than with the thought of
a whole city's population being destroyed.

Author
There is no general agreement about the
author. There is a prophet named Jonah son of
Amittai mentioned once in 2 Kings 14:25
during the reign of Jeroboam II of Israel. But
there is no certainty that the writer of the book
and the prophet are one and the same person.

Date
Nor is there any general agreement about the
date. The earliest date would have to be
between 793–753 BC, the dates of Jeroboam II.
It was a period of Assyrian weakness. But 3:3
suggests Nineveh's greatness was in the past,
which would suggest a date after 612 BC, when
the city fell (see Nahum).

OUTLINE – JONAH

Jonah flees from God

1:1-2	God commissions Jonah
1:3	Jonah's flight to Tarshish
1:4	The great storm at sea
1:5-10	Jonah exposed as the cause of the storm
1:11-15	Jonah is thrown overboard by the crew
1:16	The crew worship the Lord
1:17	Jonah swallowed by a great fish

Jonah's prayer

2:1	Jonah prays inside the great fish
2:2-7	From his holy temple, God hears Jonah's plea
2:8	The futility of idolatry
2:9	Jonah's thanksgiving
2:10	The fish throws up Jonah

Jonah's mission to Nineveh

3:1-2	God recommissions Jonah
3:3	Jonah goes to Nineveh
3:4	Jonah's message to its inhabitants
3:5-9	The repentance of the Ninevites
3:10	God spares Nineveh

Jonah's reaction to God's mercy

4:1	Jonah's anger at God's decision
4:2-4	God questions Jonah over his anger
4:5-7	Jonah and the vine
4:8-9	Jonah's anger at the vine withering
4:10-11	God's concern for the city

KEY THEMES – JONAH

The mercy of God

The most obvious book to compare is that of Nahum. Nahum preaches judgement over Nineveh; Jonah preaches judgement, too, but sees God's mercy. The two books together reveal "the kindness and sternness of God" (Romans 11:22): once the people repent then God "relents from sending calamity" (4:2).

Such an act is entirely in keeping with what the earlier books of the Old Testament show about God's character. Time and again, Israel disobeyed God, often abandoning the faith altogether, yet when they do eventually turn again and repent, God continues to have mercy on them and restore them.

This is the single most difficult thing for Jonah. In 4:2 he finally states why he fled: he was afraid that God would "change his mind" and leave him looking foolish. The irony here is that Jonah is the faithless prophet, not for running away, but for understanding only half his message – or rather, understanding what God was like, yet refusing to accept it. It is the same attitude as the older brother's in the parable of the prodigal son (Luke 15:25-32).

The universality of salvation

It could be argued that God's mercy to Israel was because of his covenant relationship with them as his special people. But here it is clearly shown that God has mercy on other people who were outside this covenant – in other words, God's offer of forgiveness for sins is available to everyone.

It is sometimes pointed out that this would have been the real difficulty for the original Jewish readers of the book. Their belief that God only had a plan of salvation for one nation would have been challenged. Certainly, the New Testament teaching is that "Christ died for all" (2 Corinthians 5:14).

Prophecy as a warning

Jonah wanted his message to be predictive, just as Nahum's apparently was. But in fact, any prophetic utterance of judgement is meant to pronounce a warning, not a fate. This distinction is not as easy as it sounds. The great prophet Ezekiel wrestled with understanding this (Ezekiel 18). What emerges from Jonah and the other prophets is that prophecy is a function of God's mercy (4:2); and the desired end is always repentance and faith.

RELEVANCE FOR TODAY – JONAH

Mission and motives

One of the great ironies of the book is that Jonah brought people to repentance despite his best efforts not to! His actions convinced the mariners that his God was the one to worship (1:16); and his preaching brought the Ninevites to repentance in a quite spectacular way (3:5-9).

The calling was the key element, rather than his willingness or right motive. If God calls us, he will anoint us, and it is his anointing. There is therefore no room for pride in our individual endeavours, even in our obedience.

But if we do want some personal sense of fulfilment in serving God, then right motives are essential. Jonah only got misery from his reluctance and his unloving attitudes.

> ## "Should I not be concerned about that great city?"
>
> ### Jonah 4:11

Second chances

God is often said to be the God of second chances. Jonah proves the point here, just as Peter proved the point after his denial of Jesus (John 21:15-19). The great fish is a sign of mercy rather than judgement, and the time spent in its stomach was the space Jonah needed to find God's presence and purposes. In the parable of the prodigal son, it is a pig-sty (Luke 15:15-17). Second chances are given, and in his grace he provides the heart space for us to receive them.

Death and resurrection

Jesus Christ refers to the book of Jonah once in connection with repentance (Luke 11:29-32), and in connection with death and resurrection, using the three days in the fish's stomach as a sign of his time in the grave (Matthew 12:39-41; 16:4).

The whole structure of the book reinforces this. In chapter 1, Jonah descends deeper and deeper into death: he sleeps (a type of death) in the bowels of the ship; is thrown into the sea to sink; is swallowed by what could be symbolic of death. But then in the grave he comes to, and begins to rise again, thrown on to the beach as new-born. This then also signifies our rebirth, for which baptism is another water sign.

In your anger do not sin (Ephesians 4:26)

Interestingly, the end of the book is not another rising. The book finishes in an open-ended way: will Jonah come to personal sorrow for his anger against God? We don't know.

What can we do when we have anger, especially when it is against God for being seemingly "unfair" to us? The book suggests anger hurts no one but ourselves. God will argue with us, but he always has the last word (4:11). We have to give our anger to God for him to transform it.

Micah
HUMAN INJUSTICE: GOD'S JUSTICE

OVERVIEW

Micah sees the many failings rampant in his society, naming perversions of power, money, false prophecy and false religion. This is not only his case, but God's, and God pronounces judgement, like for like. But in his mercy, God does not stop there: he promises a generous restoration and a renewed hope for his people's future.

SUMMARY

Chapters 1–3 and 6 deal with the deep failures within the societies of the northern and southern kingdoms of the Holy Land. The northern kingdom is called variously Israel, Ephraim, and Samaria, the name of its capital. The southern kingdom is called Judah or Jerusalem, its capital. Sometimes the term Israel is used of the whole country, north and south.

The book particularly singles out for repeated mention sins of social injustice, maladministration by corrupt leaders, idolatry, and false priests and prophets (1:3-7; 2:1-11; 3:1-3,8-11; 6:9-12). Such failures would lead to dire consequences, which God would either bring about or allow to happen, namely lack of prosperity, military defeat, destruction of towns and finally exile (1:8-16; 2:3-4; 3:4-7,12; 6:13-16). But even in the prediction of destruction, a promise of hope in a restored remnant is given (2:12-13).

This latter promise is then expanded in the other chapters (4-5, 7). Restoration (4:6-8; 5:7-9; 7:18-20) would be accompanied by power over other nations (4:11-13; 5:10-15;

7:11-17). But the power will be primarily spiritual. In his most exalted vision midpoint in the book, Micah saw a restored Jerusalem as the centre for worldwide worship of God (4:1-5). These chapters also contain references to the same failures as the other chapters (4:9-12; 5:3; 7:1-10). The first and last chapters book-end the prophecy, summarising the main themes and emphases.

Author

The book contains a selection of the prophecies of Micah of Moresheth-Gath (1:14), a village lying in the hilly country west of Jerusalem. Unlike Isaiah, Micah seems to have more of a country background and to have travelled widely in both kingdoms.

Date

Micah lived through the reigns of Jotham (740–735 BC), Ahaz (735–715 BC) and Hezekiah (715–687 BC). This makes him a younger contemporary of Isaiah, and a generation or so after Amos and Hosea. Some scholars think that certain small sections, which talk of the enemy as Babylon rather than Assyria (4:10), may have been added later.

OUTLINE – MICAH

Judgement and deliverance for Israel and Judah

1:1   Title
1:2   The Lord is putting his people on trial
1:3-7   Punishment on Samaria will be destruction
1:8-16   Lament for Judah in her punishment
2:1-11   Sins named and judgement given
2:12-13   Deliverance for a remnant
3:1-8   Corruption of leaders and prophets
3:9-12   Punishment on Jerusalem will be her destruction

Future hope in the face of despair

4:1-5   Peace and security will be restored to Jerusalem
4:6-7   Even the weakest exiles will return
4:8   Jerusalem will reign
4:9-13   Despite appearances, this is God's plan
5:1-6   The shepherd-king of Israel will save his people
5:7-9   Foes will be defeated
5:10-11   Destruction of all militarism in the land
5:12-15   Destruction of all occult practices

The LORD's case against Israel

6:1-5   God has cared for his people
6:6-9   God requires justice and mercy
6:10-16   Nature of God's just punishment against Israel
7:1-6   Lament over Israel's sins

Expectations of restoration

7:7-10   After punishment, Israel will have her case for mercy made by God himself
7:11-13   Israel will prosper as other nations fail
7:14-15   The shepherd will pasture his people
7:16-17   The nations will submit to God
7:18-20   God is a God of mercy

KEY THEMES – MICAH

God the just judge

The book begins and ends with a courtroom drama: "the Sovereign LORD may witness against you" (1:2); "until he pleads my case"(7:9). 6:2 states "the LORD has a case against his people" (see also Malachi for this structure). The need for a just judge is especially acute when "rulers of the house of Israel … despise justice" (3:9). Only God, and the prophet as God's mouthpiece (3:8), can make the case against his people fairly, and give a right judgement (4:3). This is because in the past God has shown himself to be merciful. 6:3-5 is the evidence for this, based on the covenant oath taken long ago (7:20).

The punishments are like for like, and therefore in due measure. The elaborate series of puns on place names in 1:8-15 in a strange way demonstrates this. The punishment fits the place, symbolic of the actual crime. Thus pride and arrogance (2:1-2) are punished by humiliation and despoliation (2:2-5). Exile (4:10) is fitting in that God's people have exiled themselves from him; they have dispossessed themselves by their robbery of land from those weaker than themselves. God's justice is truly seen in "a man reaps what he sows" (Galatians 6:7), as shown most clearly in 6:9-16.

The future shepherd

There are some passages in Micah that have a striking similarity with Isaiah. Just as Isaiah, and other prophets, attacked the country's injustices, so they also prophesied future restoration under a leader appointed by God. These prophecies were later seen as "messianic", that is, predicting a future great leader to bring salvation and deliverance. The New Testament writers quote many such prophecies as being fulfilled in Jesus Christ.

For example, Matthew 2:6 quotes Micah 5:2, which parallels Isaiah 11:1. The shepherd image of Micah 5:4 echoes that in Isaiah 40:11, and is taken up, with other Old Testament references, in Jesus' claim to be the good shepherd (John 10:14). Micah 4:1-3 parallels Isaiah 2:2-4 in predicting this future restoration, using the image of God as judge, and the peaceful one of beating swords into ploughshares. But that is after the shepherd has brought victory over his enemies (5:5-6).

God's continuing purposes

These predictions of restoration are always linked in the Old Testament prophets with prophecies concerning a righteous remnant. This is because human failure and its punishment cannot ultimately derail God's purposes. God is not at the mercy of human sin! Thus future purposes are seen as brought about by his forgiveness, intervention and provision of divine leadership – all anticipating the new covenant in Jesus Christ. In Micah we have many passages that emphasise this: 4:1-8; 5:1-15; 7:8-20.

RELEVANCE FOR TODAY – MICAH

True prosperity

Micah, like Haggai (Haggai 1:5-10) and
Malachi (Malachi 3:8-12), spells out why God's
people do not prosper. Most people want to
prosper, and feel that God should somehow
help them in this. It certainly is God's will for
us to know prosperity of some sort (Psalm
35:27), even though the preaching of the so-
called "Prosperity Gospel" recently has given
the concept a bad name. We cannot, of course,
reduce it to simple material terms, "paying
God in order for him to pay you back". Micah
suggests the failure of prosperity in terms of
human efforts achieving nothing. It is a moral
failure, in that we try to achieve success in
wrong ways. 2:1-2 is a blatant example of this;
6:9-15 almost as obvious a list.

If the verse "You will store up but save
nothing" (6:14) seems to describe our

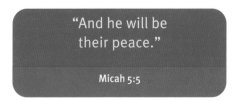

"And he will be
their peace."

Micah 5:5

situation, the first place to seek redress is to
check our ways of "storing up" against the
prophetic checklists. There are other reasons,
of course, from practical mismanagement to a
"spirit of poverty", but Micah gives us
somewhere to start.

What does God want?

6:6-8 is a prophecy backed up by statements
from other prophets about what God truly
wants. Here, Micah makes it clear God is not
really interested in our sacrifices as such, as if
somehow he needed them. The system of
sacrifices in the Old Testament was partly to
deal with sin and partly as an expression of
gratitude. What had happened in Micah's day
was that sacrifices were made more as an
insurance policy, or to keep God on their side;
that is from wrong motives, with no intention
of moral reform.

Micah makes it clear the three true
requirements God wants are:
- To act justly
- To love mercy
- To walk humbly.

Today, sacrifices could, for example, be
seen as giving money or hours of working
hard, even hours of prayer. But if these do not
come from a merciful, humble and just heart,
they are of no real value.

What is God like?

However much Micah has expressed his
message in terms of charges, evidence,
sentencing, he returns at the end to what is
most deeply on his heart: God's pardoning and
merciful nature. "You delight to show mercy"
(7:18; see also 7:20) is something we need to
hang on to, whether in the middle of a sense of
our own failures, or in the middle of other
people's. Again, Micah echoes Isaiah, this time
Isaiah 43:25. Such mercy is true evidence of
God's loving purposes for us.

Nahum
AN EVIL EMPIRE OVERTHROWN

OVERVIEW
The prophet Nahum delivers a series of blistering attacks on the evil empire of Assyria and announces that its capital, Nineveh, will soon be unexpectedly and utterly destroyed by God. The result will be that Judah will have respite.

SUMMARY
The prophecy of Nahum is unusual in that it consists almost entirely of a series of mocking denunciations of a foreign power, rather than messages directed to the spiritual life of God's people. Although Nineveh is often addressed directly, obviously the main audience would have been the Israelites, probably living in mortal dread of this foreign power. The prophecy thus becomes a source of hope for them.

The book opens with a song of praise to God as divine warrior (1:2-14). This sets the theme of warfare and victory. For Judah this meant hope, but for Nineveh it meant total destruction. "Who can endure his fierce anger?" Nahum asks (1:5).

The second chapter consists of a vivid and dramatic description of Nineveh's final destruction, with the battle raging within its walls. Although the Assyrians might summon their picked soldiers, it would make no difference. Nahum uses images of lions, an animal the Assyrians often used symbolically: "Where now is the lions' den?" he asks rhetorically (2:11).

The final chapter is addressed to the city itself. In a highly poetic, impressionistic description, Nahum paints a picture of chaos and the humiliation of defeat.

Author
All we know about Nahum is that he came from the village of Elkosh, which was probably in Judah. He has a "burden" (1:1), as the KJV puts it, which means a heavy message of impending doom, and he gives it in a dramatic and poetic style, full of literary devices and vivid description.

Date
The Assyrians had previously attacked Jerusalem in 701 BC (2 Kings 18:17–19:36), and before that had destroyed the northern kingdom of Israel in 722 BC (2 Kings 17:1-5; 18:9-10). At the time of the writing of the prophecy, Assyria still seemed invincible and was dreaded.

However, it did fall in 612 BC, when it was attacked from the north by the Medes, and from the south and east by the Babylonians. Nahum must have been writing before this, but after the fall of No-Amon, or Thebes (in 663 BC) mentioned in 3:8.

OUTLINE – NAHUM

Title

KEY THEMES – NAHUM

God as warrior

This is a theme that runs through much of the Old Testament. Its commonest form is in the use of the title "LORD of Hosts", which is the term Nahum uses in 2:13. The NIV translates this phrase as "LORD Almighty".

"Hosts" is an older English word meaning "armies", "military forces". Instances of this phrase are in 2 Kings 19:31, where Isaiah predicts the defeat of the Assyrian army when besieging the city of Jerusalem, and in Isaiah 37:32, where Isaiah predicts a remnant of Israel surviving. In both cases, the meaning is that God will literally fight for his people against the enemy.

Elsewhere, God as a strong warrior is described in Habakkuk 3:5-15, and in Zechariah 9:1-15; 14:1, 3, 5. Zechariah forms the theme into two hymns, which include references to a theophany (or appearance of God to humans) and the cosmic disturbances brought about as God fights for his people. Psalm 98 contains similar pictures, in a tradition that goes right back to Exodus 15:3

and Joshua 5:13-15.

Nahum mentions similar disturbances to Habakkuk and Zechariah (1:3-5). He fights for his people (1:8, 13) to bring them peace (1:15) and restoration (2:2). The whole book is perhaps the most military one of all the prophets.

The severity of God

Nahum was writing about the same time as the young Jeremiah, a little after Zephaniah and a little before Habakkuk. However, the most obvious prophet to link him with is Jonah. Both prophets devoted their prophecies to Nineveh, which is the centre of power of the brutal Assyrian regime.

What is immediately striking is how different Nahum and Jonah are. In Jonah's case, the message is a message of salvation to a wicked city, a message that appears to have been received. Nahum brings a message of punishment and judgement. Taken both together, the two books represent "the goodness and the severity of God" (Romans 11:22 KJV).

God does not punish Nineveh just because they have attacked his people. Their cruelty in their own day was notorious and mentioned specifically by Nahum (2:1-4; 3:19). The taunt in 3:4 suggests they were deeply involved in witchcraft and sexual immorality.

RELEVANCE FOR TODAY – NAHUM

Who writes history?

Many great empires feel themselves invulnerable. It is said that conquerors write history. Clearly Assyria thought so. Nahum reminds them of the fall of another great empire, Egypt, and one of its main cities (3:8-11). It is not the conqueror who writes history; it is God.

Over the last century, we have seen great evil empires defeated, often quite catastrophically. The feeling of relief at, for example, the defeat of Nazi Germany and Hitler's death, or the breaking of the Berlin Wall, must be similar to what Nahum was seeking to convey to his listeners. The relief is that there is a God who does bring down evil.

History continues to be written. It is almost inevitable other evil empires and leaders will emerge, thinking their destiny is in their hands, that they can write history to their will. We need to have Nahum's vision that at some stage, God will demonstrate his judgement over them. We look to him today to deal with countries that govern with brutality and injustice.

> "The LORD is good,
> a refuge in times
> of trouble."
>
> Nahum 1:7

Spiritual warfare

The prophecy focuses our minds on battle and fighting. What is the spiritual relevance of this? At one level, we are all too aware of inner forces at war within ourselves, just as Paul was in Romans 7:23. We cannot escape this battle between good and evil within ourselves.

The New Testament, however, suggests a much wider arena for such warfare. Interestingly, the lion image is used again to describe it: "your enemy the devil like a roaring lion" (1 Peter 5:8). That is why Paul tells us to wear armour (1 Thessalonians 5:8) and fight back against an evil which is a cosmic principle, not just a set of inner urges.

But there is also a realm of warfare at a "national" level, where countries and cultures, at certain times at least, are engaged in warfare that has a spiritual and cosmic dimension. God does fight for his people and for godly nations, to bring down mighty powers that oppose his purposes of righteousness and justice.

Proclaiming peace

In the middle of the fighting language, Nahum can still talk of proclaiming peace and protection (1:15). In this he echoes Isaiah 52:7. God fights for the peace, protection and deliverance for his people. We need to realise how much Nahum's vision was a great step of faith for him. But we need that same sort of faith, to know that God is for us, for our peace and our deliverance. Otherwise we become overwhelmed by the sheer amount of evil in this world.

Habakkuk
HARD QUESTIONS

OVERVIEW
Habakkuk asks hard questions of God, questions about injustice and corruption in his society. He receives even harder answers. At first he is shocked by God. Then, as he waits, the answers begin to make sense. Finally, he comes to understand God's purposes and finds faith again despite what appears an uncertain future.

SUMMARY

Habakkuk the prophet found himself living in an unjust society. He cried out to God about this, asking God to send justice and punishment, but God did not seem to be listening. The book opens with Habakkuk's lodging a serious complaint against God (1:2-4).

God answered, but in a way that Habakkuk was totally unprepared for: God planned to send the Babylonians to destroy Habakkuk's society (1:5-11). The Babylonian army is vividly described in images of leopards, vultures, a desert wind. It is a terrifying picture of an unstoppable force.

Habakkuk was appalled (1:12-17). His moral sense was outraged: however bad his own society, the Babylonians were far worse. The Babylonians' victims are described as shoals of fish that have no leader and can be scooped up helplessly in nets. It would seem might is right. In a sort of challenge to God, Habakkuk set himself to wait for a full explanation (2:1).

The answer came. Habakkuk must take the long-term view. In the end, all unjust societies and nations will fail, and the oppressed will have the last word (2:2-20). Meanwhile, Habakkuk needs to live as a man of faith: he might not see the end result, but he must believe in God's plans and purposes. In a series of four woes, God universally condemns all forms of injustice and idolatry.

In a concluding prayer, Habakkuk asked God to renew his people (3:2). He remembered how God often reveals his power through nature, and how he saved his people out of Egypt (3:3-15). So whatever might happen in the immediate future, however terrible the coming invasion, Habakkuk would rejoice in God, his justice and his purposes (3:16-19).

Author

Habakkuk was a prophet (1:1; 3:1) about whom nothing is known outside this book. His name means "someone who clings or embraces". His prophecy is technically known as an "oracle". Unusually, he is told to write it down, rather than deliver it orally, as many of the prophets did (2:2). The fact that he finished with a psalm may mean that he was a "singing prophet" connected to the temple in Jerusalem (see 1 Chronicles 25:1).

Date

The Babylonians (or Chaldeans) came to power in the region after the battle of Carchemish (605 BC), when they defeated the hitherto dominant Assyrians and Egyptians. But they did not invade Judah, that is, the surviving southern kingdom of Israel, until 598 BC (2 Kings 24:1-4,8-17). This places Habakkuk between these two dates, living at the same time as the prophet Jeremiah, perhaps under King Jehoiakim. Jeremiah, too, spoke out against injustice, in considerably more detail, and predicted the coming invasion of the Babylonians (Jeremiah 5:1-13; 27:6-11).

OUTLINE – HABAKKUK

Title
1:1   Habakkuk receives a prophecy

Habakkuk's first complaint
1:2-4   Sin goes unpunished, justice remains perverted

God's reply
1:5-6   God is going to use the Babylonians
1:7-11   Dramatic descriptions of the Babylonians

Habakkuk's second complaint
1:12-13   God is too holy to look on evil
1:14-17   So why does he employ a merciless and wicked nation?

The prophet as watchman
2:1   The prophet is going to watch out for God's reply

God's reply
2:2-3   God's pronouncements will be fulfilled
2:4-5   For now the Babylonians are oppressors
2:6-8   A taunt song: the oppressed will turn the tables
2:9-19   A series of woes: injustice will be punished
2:20   God is on the throne

A psalm of praise
3:1-2   Plea for revival
3:4-15   God's mighty acts in nature and his deliverance from Egypt is remembered
3:16-18   The prophet will rejoice no matter what happens
3:19   God alone will be his strength

KEY THEMES – HABAKKUK

Protesting against injustice

Habakkuk, like most of the other Bible prophets, was revolted by his society's evil ways. His immediate concern is with the violence, injustice and conflict all around him. Wrongdoers are not brought to justice; the system is run by the wicked. Some prophets, such as Isaiah or Jeremiah, directly speak to their corrupt society. Habakkuk, it seems, has cried out to God for divine intervention.

For Habakkuk, the problem is compounded when God tells him that the Babylonians will be sent as punishment on this corrupt society. Yet "they are a law to themselves"(1:7), their "own strength is their god"(1:11). They are merciless to their enemies (1:17).

Habakkuk keeps protesting to God. The book's message is that God does hear these protests against injustice. He does not remain passive: in the long term his purposes will be revealed to those who passionately seek him.

God's strange purposes

These purposes, however, are not what Habakkuk expected. It is always good to know that injustice will be punished, but the prophet cannot dictate the mode of punishment. Being a prophet involves commitment to the people of God, however off-track. Their punishment has, to some extent, to be shared by the prophet. It also involves being prepared to lay aside previous convictions about how God works. It is not comfortable being a prophet, either physically or spiritually.

Isaiah realised this when he preached the coming of the Assyrians (Isaiah 10:5-10).

Jeremiah realised this too, though his discomfort was more in the total rejection of his message (Jeremiah 36:20-32). Jonah's discomfort was more with the idea that God would forgive the very people he had been denouncing (Jonah 4:1).

For Habakkuk, the core of the problem lay in his idea of God's holiness (1:13). But God's holiness sometimes expresses itself in strange ways (Isaiah 55:8-9). All such expressions prefigure God's purposes in Jesus Christ. His own death was the strangest expression of God's holiness of all, the use of tremendous injustice to bring about justice and deliverance for humankind (Acts 2:22-39).

Living by faith

God's strange and mysterious purposes will be revealed eventually (2:3). In the meanwhile, the wicked may be "puffed up", but the righteous must hang on to their faith, and that is how they will live (2:4). The New Testament writers found in this verse the very essence of our relationship with God and they quote it three times (Romans 1:17; Galatians 3:11; Hebrews 10:38-39). For them it implies both faith in Jesus Christ and faith in God's good purposes. Hebrews states that God is not pleased with those who hang back because they cannot trust God. The choice is between allowing our faith to be constantly challenged, and receiving the revelation of God that comes with that, or "playing it safe", refusing to go beyond what can be understood.

RELEVANCE FOR TODAY – HABAKKUK

Arguing with God

Habakkuk's dialogue with God is technically known as a "complaint". Jeremiah complained to God, too (Jeremiah 12:1-6), as did Job (Job 3:1-26), and Jonah (Jonah 4:1-3). The Bible suggests that God does not mind his servants arguing, as long as they are prepared to sit still and wait for an answer. So often in our complaining we are so full of self-pity, we only want to rehearse a list of grievances.

God answered Habakkuk twice, and through his complaints, Habakkuk actually received a deeper revelation than if he had kept quiet. However, at some point, we do have to keep quiet (2:20, also in Zechariah 2:13). Injustice and evil will inevitably baffle us; as will God's ways of dealing with them. We have to accept that we live in a fallen world, but that God is in charge of all nations and of history. This can lead us to a place of trust, even if only at the end of a process of arguing and listening.

Discerning God's purposes

If arguing is one way to gain revelation, watching is another. The prophets saw themselves as watchmen (2:1; Isaiah 21:8-12; Ezekiel 3:17; 33:1-20). When every city had walls, they were only as good as the watchmen on them. Hence the imagery the prophets used. Habakkuk uses the image not in terms of an approaching enemy, but of waiting for God's revelation or answer. It is when he receives this that he is committed to communicate it.

Habakkuk discerns that God is actively in control of the whole world. He intervenes. So we have the choice as watchmen. Either we believe what the media tell us is happening in the world, or we discern what God is doing. The Bible record, especially in the prophetic writings, helps us to do this. But we have to wait in prayer, too. In that way we become people of faith, knowing what to say in troubled times.

Longing for renewal

Habakkuk cries out for renewal (3:2). He wants God's deeds to become obvious to everyone. Then he wants God's glory to be seen (2:14). That is what we should still want. Above all, God will be known through his church, the society of God's people. We need to cry to God for his church to be renewed. The KJV expresses 3:2 as "O LORD, revive thy work in the midst of the years."

Habakkuk also prays for mercy rather than anger, or even mercy out of anger. Sometimes in our prayers against injustice, we want punishment and our hearts become angry. We need to plead for mercy as we pray that our hearts would be kept tender and responsive.

Trusting God no matter what

Habakkuk's final statement is that he will rejoice in God whatever happens (3:16-18). Even if he has to suffer the devastation of Babylonian invasion, with no crops, no harvest, nothing left, he will still keep rejoicing in God.

This is tough. But this is what living by faith actually means: however hard the circumstances, yet we still rejoice. After the arguing, after the silence, after the discernment, Habakkuk reaches the stage of rejoicing unconditionally.

> "The Sovereign LORD
> is my strength;
> he makes my feet
> like the feet of a deer,
> he enables me to go
> on the heights."
>
> Habakkuk 3:19

Zephaniah
THE DAY OF THE LORD

OVERVIEW

**This book is a forthright condemnation of the spiritual state of Judah and Jerusalem.
Zephaniah preaches the Day of the Lord as a day of catastrophic judgement.
However, those who turn to God will be saved as a treasured and protected remnant.**

SUMMARY

The book of Zephaniah can be divided into two rather unequal parts. First comes a series of judgements (1:1-3:8); which is then followed by a promise of restoration for a remnant (3:9-20).

The judgements are focused on Jerusalem, but begin as a worldwide judgement (1:2-3), then narrowing down to Judah, the southern kingdom of Israel (1:4–2:3). The book then delivers a series of judgements on Judah's neighbours (2:4-15), before returning to focus on Jerusalem, the capital of Judah, and the centre of its religious life (3:1-7). This part of Zephaniah concludes by a further brief worldview (3:8).

The judgements are delivered as woes and denunciations of specific sins, delivered as if God were speaking directly, using the prophet as his mouthpiece. The sins range from social injustice and oppression to idolatry and spiritual apathy. The coming judgement is spoken of in terms of "the Day of the LORD", which is depicted in hyperbolic terms of total destruction and cataclysm.

However, the message is tempered by the possibility of safety and deliverance in this day if the "humble of the land" seek God (2:3). These would be sheltered and become a righteous remnant, who would not only be rescued, but would also know God's pleasure and prosperity. There would be a total restoration for them.

Author

The only information we have of Zephaniah is given in 1:1, where he traces his ancestry back four generations, to Hezekiah, presumably the righteous king of Judah who reigned 715–687 BC, which would mean Zephaniah is one of the upper class of Jerusalem upon whom his prophecies pronounce judgement.

Date

The opening verse established the date as within the reign of King Josiah (640–609 BC). However, the widespread idolatry associated with the two intervening kings between Hezekiah and Josiah, Manasseh and Amon, still seems to be prevalent. Josiah introduced widespread reforms from 622 BC, though they may not have been immediately effective. The denunciation of Assyria (2:13-15) suggests a date before 612 BC, which is when that country fell. A date between 639–612 BC would make Zephaniah a contemporary of Nahum, preceding the ministry of Jeremiah.

OUTLINE – ZEPHANIAH

The coming of the Day of the LORD

God's judgement against the nations

Judgement and mercy on God's people

KEY THEMES – ZEPHANIAH

The Day of the LORD

Each of the Minor Prophets has some emphasis which makes them unique. Zephaniah's emphasis is "the Day of the LORD" (1:7), a phrase which recurs some 14 times in the next 15 verses, either in that form or as "that day", "a day", "the great day of the LORD" or "the day of the LORD's wrath".

The phrase is used in earlier prophets, such as Amos (Amos 5:18-20), Joel (Joel 1:15), and Isaiah (Isaiah 2:6-22), but it is Zephaniah who uses it most emphatically and centrally in his message. Through Zephaniah, it became an accepted and widely understood phrase for later writers to use, often in an apocalyptic context.

Basically, the term means the time when God will intervene directly in some obvious way. Typically, it means a day of judgement, but as the last section demonstrates, it can also refer to an intervention of deliverance and restoration.

The remnant

The idea of a righteous remnant to be restored by God is absolutely central to Old Testament prophetic writing. Isaiah 1:9 states "Unless the LORD Almighty had left us some survivors, we would have become like Sodom". This points out two things:

- At times the Israelites were no better than the wicked nations that surrounded them and fully deserved the same judgement
- God's relationship with Israel was different. They were the people chosen by him to demonstrate his purposes to the world, and established by covenant.

This means that God chooses to preserve a people through whom he makes himself known. The pattern of Noah is similar: a remnant had to be preserved from the flood (Genesis 8:21). In Zephaniah, the remnant of Israel will be virtuous (3:12-13), and God will actively rejoice over them (3:17). The idea of gathering from exile is also typical, as in Joel 3:1-2 and Jeremiah 31.

God's anger

Again, God's anger is central to an understanding of his nature as revealed throughout the Old Testament. In Zephaniah, the emphasis is on a holy God in an unholy city (3:5). God's choice of Jerusalem as his holy city, where his temple would be situated, meant that in some sense it was his earthly dwelling place. Though he was God of the whole world (1:2-3), Jerusalem was the place where evil would be especially repugnant to him, since his presence would give it special holiness. Zephaniah's description of particular places within the city (1:10-12) shows that God's anger is not just of a general nature, but quite specific. Jesus' cleansing of the temple shows something of this anger (Matthew 21:13). In 3:8 God's anger is directed towards the whole world, for the sake of giving all the opportunity to "call on the name of the LORD" (3:9).

RELEVANCE FOR TODAY – ZEPHANIAH

The reality of judgement

Many people today shudder at the whole idea of God's anger. Either they reject the whole Christian idea of God, because they see anger in terms of arbitrary force or emotion or they reject the Old Testament depiction of God, as they see it opposing a concept of God as love. Even some Christians are guilty of this, failing to see the necessary connection between divine (in contrast to human) anger, judgement, justice, and discipline.

In terms of the reality of Zephaniah's prophecy, Assyria was devastated soon afterwards, and Judah and the city of Jerusalem a generation later. The typical attitude towards Zephaniah's message is seen in 1:12 – God will not get involved in our lives. But he did – and does. We need, then, to keep a clear sense of sin and judgement to keep our moral and spiritual senses sharp, as well as being God's instruments of righteousness in a society increasingly indifferent to moral absolutes.

No judgement without hope

The language used by the Old Testament prophets is dramatic, provocative and often deliberately exaggerated to make people listen, as in chapter 1. It does not mean it is harsh, cruel or inexorably negative. It is Satan who is "the accuser of our brothers" (Revelation 12:10). In Zephaniah, there is both promise (2:3; 3:9-12) and a picture of God rejoicing over his righteous remnant (3:17). This is followed by promises of restoration (3:18-20). "I will bring you home" (3:20) has very deep resonance, implying not only acceptance in the Father's household, but also coming to a right state of mind and heart – finding ourselves, too. This is what is often called the "father heart" of God.

> "The LORD has taken away your punishment."
>
> Zephaniah 3:15

The same old sins

The list of sins in Zephaniah shows us that the same sins occur in every generation even if they find new variations and expressions. Even what may seem the oddest of sins, "avoiding stepping on the threshold" (1:9) is a pagan variation of acts to avoid bad luck (see 1 Samuel 5:5). The syncretism of today is seen in 1:5: a bit of God and a bit of Molech, one of the local pagan gods, to live by. The pride of the rich and the betrayal of those who are meant to be spiritual leaders (3:4) are similarly, unfortunately, only too familiar to us.

Haggai
RIGHT PRIORITIES

OVERVIEW

Haggai urges the exiles who have returned from Babylon to get their priorities right. At present, they are putting their efforts into their own affairs, whilst the temple of God still lies in ruins. The people respond and Haggai encourages them with promises of God's blessings on their lives and their leaders.

SUMMARY

The book of Haggai consists of four separate prophecies, addressed variously to Zerubbabel, the prince; Shealtiel, the high priest; and the people in general. The prophecies are given over a very short time span, and we can trace the progress of the task Haggai urged them to carry out.

The first prophecy (1:1-11) is an explanation of why the people's lives had not prospered since their return from exile in Babylon. God had withheld blessing on their crops and commerce because they had failed to put his affairs first. This meant that the temple, burnt down at the destruction of Jerusalem in 586 BC, still lay in ruins, when it should have been their first priority.

Haggai's words had an instant effect and work was restarted (1:12-15). Haggai promised that God really was with them and would bless them. In his second prophecy (2:1-9), Haggai encouraged those especially who remembered the previous temple, which was a much bigger construction. Nevertheless, God's glory would be greater in this temple than the previous one.

In the third prophecy, addressed to priests and in the form of a series of questions and answers, Haggai reminded the people of the strict rules of ceremonial holiness. The

implication is that the people have been even more defiled by the presence of the ruins (2:10-14).

Before the final prophecy addressed to Zerubbabel, which assured him of God's favour (2:20-23), Haggai asked the people to consider whether God had blessed their affairs since they had started the rebuilding programme (2:15-19).

Author

Haggai was one of two prophets who had accompanied the first group returning from exile, the other being Zechariah. The two prophets both urged the same thing, but in very different ways. Haggai is practical and direct; Zechariah is visionary and poetic. Their inspiration led to the temple being finished in five years. Haggai is mentioned in this connection in Ezra 5:1,2; 6:14.

Date

The writer is very particular to give exact dates for each prophecy. The exiles returned in 539 BC, and began some reconstruction work (Ezra 1–3). Then they ran into local opposition (Ezra 4:1-5), effectively halting the building for the next sixteen years, till the second year of the Persian King Darius (522–486 BC). The prophecies were thus delivered in 520 BC.

OUTLINE – HAGGAI

Title
1:1 Dating of Haggai's first message

The first message: the call to rebuild the temple
1:2-8 A call to rebuild the temple
1:9-11 Failure to do this has led to withdrawal of God's blessings
1:12 The people respond to Haggai
1:13 Haggai's message of encouragement
1:14-15 Work begins on the temple

The second message: the promise of glory
2:1-3 Apparent loss of glory from first to second temple
2:4-5 Encouragement to the leaders
2:6-9 The promise of greater glory

The third message: the need for purity
2:10-12 Can holiness be transmitted by contact?
2:13 Can uncleanness be transmitted by contact?
2:14 The people have become defiled
2:15-19 Promise of purification and blessings

The fourth message: God's promise to Zerubbabel
2:20-22 God will overthrow the foreign powers
2:23 Zerubbabel chosen by God

KEY THEMES – HAGGAI

Sacred space

In the Old Testament, there was a deep sense that God's presence should be visibly in the midst of his people. For this to occur, there needed to be sacred space: a building set apart entirely for God to inhabit and for his worship to take place in. At first, a tabernacle was built when the Israelites were in the desert, fleeing from Egypt. This was a tent-like structure with fencing around it. In Solomon's time, a temple was built and set apart in an awesome ceremony.

When the Babylonians captured the city and exiled its people, the Israelites learnt to live without a temple. On their return from exile, the urgency to recreate this sacred space was further lessened by opposition and their own need to make a living. It was Haggai's task to instil again into their consciousness this sense of the vital importance of the temple if God was really going to be with his people. Not till Jesus' time was this consciousness again displaced, when he stated his body was now the new temple (Matthew 24:2; 26:61; 27:40).

Covenant faithfulness

Zerubbabel was in the lineage of King David, and so inherited the Davidic covenant, as it was known (2:23, see 1 Kings 9:5). But there was a longer standing covenant, too, made during the exodus from Egypt (2:5, see Exodus 24:8), that God would be with his people. God is faithful to his covenant promises. The other aspect of covenant faithfulness is what is demanded of the people in terms of purity (2:10-14).

RELEVANCE FOR TODAY – HAGGAI

Re-ordering priorities

We all want God's blessings in our lives. We know we cannot earn them, for all blessings are by grace. Yet there are certain things that can hinder us from knowing God's blessing. The returning exiles were finding this out: whatever they tried to do to prosper failed (1:6,10; 2:16-17). Haggai's message is clear: get your priorities right. Honour God first, a message repeated by Jesus (Matthew 6:33). Malachi gave the same message in terms of giving (Malachi 3:8-12), as did Micah (Micah 6:14). Haggai widens the concept to include all our best efforts and endeavours (2:18-19).

> "From this day on I will bless you."
>
> **Haggai 2:19**

Don't procrastinate

It wasn't as if the exiles were consciously refusing to rebuild the temple. But because of wrong time priorities, they were merely putting it off. But Haggai suggests this is, in effect, a refusal of God's purposes, and a dishonouring of God, since the temple, the most obvious sign of his presence, remains a ruin (1:9). The relevance in today's hectic and disordered world is clear: we are to stop making excuses and resisting God's purposes and we are to honour him by getting on with what we know he wants us to do.

Zechariah
THE CITY OF TRUTH

OVERVIEW

The prophecy of Zechariah looks towards the future of Jerusalem after the return from exile. He sees the temple rebuilt and a high priest firmly established. He also sees God's presence and blessing on the whole city and that all nations will be drawn to it. However, there will also be fierce conflict around the city before the final Day of the Lord.

SUMMARY

The book divides into two parts. Chapters 1–8 describe eight visions the prophet Zechariah received. He was in the presence of an angelic being, who gave the interpretation for each one of the visions. They vary widely in topic and symbolism, but most deal with the immediate future of Jerusalem and its temple, which was in urgent need of rebuilding after the 70-year exile in Babylon.

God promised favour again to his holy city (1:12-17), and favour and authority to the high priest, Joshua (3:1-10; 6:9-15). The city would attract many nations (2:11; 8:23) because of God's presence (2:10-13). But it needed to become a city of truth and righteousness for it to enjoy God's blessing (8:1-23).

The second part (chapters 9–14) is somewhat different. There is no named prophet and there are no angel interpreters. Instead, the series of prophecies is more apocalyptic, about the Day of the Lord. Some of the themes of the prophecies are as the first part: nations would come to Jerusalem (14:16-21); God would protect the city (9:14-17; 12:8; compare 2:4-5). But there are also negative prophecies: nations would attack Jerusalem (12:1-5; 14:1-2), and spiritual leadership would fall into the wrong hands (11:4-17; 13:7-9). These prophecies should not be seen as sequential.

Many verses are used by New Testament writers in relation to the coming of Jesus Christ (6:13; 9:9; 11:12,13; 12:10). The prophecies also echo earlier prophecies found in the Old Testament (for example, 1:2-6, 12, 17; compare Hosea 14:1-7; Isaiah 54; Jeremiah 3:15).

Author

Zechariah is mentioned in Ezra 5:1 as one of the two prophets urging Joshua, Zerubbabel the governor, and the people, to rebuild the temple. The other prophet is Haggai. Both Ezra and Haggai show that their encouragement was successful.

Date

1:1,7; 7:1 help us date the first part of the book precisely to 520 BC. The second part was probably written some 40 years later, since Greece is mentioned, a power that arose around 480 BC.

OUTLINE – ZECHARIAH

KEY THEMES – ZECHARIAH

Rebuilding Jerusalem as the city of truth

Much of the first part of Zechariah has to do with rebuilding after the devastation of the Babylonian attack on Jerusalem in 586 BC (1:12). Haggai concentrates on the practicality of getting the work restarted after the returned exiles had lost heart. Zechariah is more mystical and apocryphal as he envisions a wider context and wider purposes (eg 1:10-14; 6:5-8).

He sees that the city will be repopulated (2:4; 8:4-8), but lessons have to be learnt from the past for this renewal to be permanent (1:1-6). So true justice must be dispensed (7:9-10). The city must become a city of truth (8:3,16-17), then it will be a witness to the whole world (8:20-23). Zechariah is moving towards the image of the Holy City, the new Jerusalem, which fills the final pages of the Bible (Revelation 21–22).

The kingly priest

Whereas Haggai is content to encourage the existing high priest, Joshua, Zechariah has a loftier vision of what the role of high priest is to become (3:8). The enacted prophecy of fashioning a crown (6:9-15) is symbolic of the priest actually reigning, something that had never happened before. Here the term "the Branch" is used (3:8; 6:12), a term used in earlier prophecies to denote messianic rule in the line of King David (Isaiah 4:2; 11:1; Jeremiah 23:5-6; 33:15-16).

In the New Testament, the concept of the royal priest is taken to refer to Jesus Christ in the Letter to the Hebrews, by using the figure of Melchizedek (Hebrews 5:6, 10; 6:20; 7:1-21; see Genesis 14:18; Psalm 110:4).

The true shepherd

Whereas the first part of the book sees the need for truth, the second part shows it has to be fought for. The rather mysterious account of the true and false shepherds depicts such a struggle. Typically at this period of the Old Testament, the term "shepherd" meant kings and rulers, rather than pastors. The true shepherd is rejected (11:8-15), prophetically being paid off with thirty pieces of silver (11:12). Later, the people "look on me, the one they have pierced" (12:10), which could be identified with the rejected shepherd, as Revelation 1:7 suggests. Christ's claim to be the true or good shepherd (John 10:14) is thus a claim to be the Messiah.

The divine warrior

The victory of good over evil will not just be gained by establishing the true city. It has to be defended, and in such a cosmic battle that only the revelation of God as the divine warrior fighting for his city will bring victory (12:1-9; 14:1-5). For further material on the divine warrior, see Nahum.

RELEVANCE FOR TODAY – ZECHARIAH

Not by power

Zechariah 4:6 is an often quoted verse. In the context of the book, it does not mean no power is required. Far from it: the real question is, whose power? The words are addressed to Zerubbabel, the governor or secular head of the tiny state re-established in the midst of hostile neighbours. It is not going to be by his power or might that the city will be established, but by the Spirit of God.

This is a fundamental biblical principle. There are many examples in the Bible of small forces, humanly speaking, overcoming much more powerful enemies, solely because God was fighting for them by the power of his spirit (eg Gideon in Judges 7). Thus, we must not look simply in human terms at the spiritual battle that we often feel rages round us, or at the opposition we have to face at times to advance God's kingdom.

> **"'Not by might nor by power, but by my Spirit,' says the LORD Almighty."**
>
> Zechariah 4:6

Marks of leadership

Of all the Minor Prophets, Zechariah and Haggai address the need for firm leadership. Joshua needs to see himself standing in the righteousness given to him by God, and not in his own guilt (3:1-5): this is to be his confidence and source of courage. Zechariah needs to see himself standing in the power God will give him, not his own (4:1-6). Both need to see their anointing from God (4:11-14). No reliance on human competence alone will withstand Satan's accusations and undermining (3:2).

Fasting and feasting

The book spends nearly two chapters discussing this topic, so it must be of some real importance. The question given to Zechariah was whether the old traditions of fasting should be continued in the new city (7:3). Zechariah's answer is unequivocal. He asks what good their fasting did in the past, since it was done out of habit and tradition (7:4-7). He chimes in with the older prophets in declaring what God is really looking for is justice and truth (7:9-10; compare Isaiah 58:4-5). But he goes further: fasting will give way to feasting (8:18-19). It is this joy, combined with truth and peace, which would attract outsiders to God's people. It still does.

The end of prophecy

13:2-6 seems a rather strange set of verses. How can a prophet welcome the end of prophecy? Some interpreters see it as referring to the false shepherds of 10:17. False shepherds bring false prophecy. Some see it as anticipating 1 Corinthians 13:8, that when full knowledge and revelation come, there will be no need of prophecy. However we understand these verses, to be a prophet now needs to be done in humility by people who are pure, certainly not by anyone who promotes themselves and considers it their "job".

Malachi
SECOND-RATE RELIGION

OVERVIEW

Malachi holds the post-exilic nation to account for its second-rate religion. Its priests are leading the people poorly, offering substandard sacrifices in the temple rituals. The people are failing to give God his due; they are intermarrying with non-believers and divorcing without the slightest scruple. The book predicts the coming of a great messenger who will restore true religion.

SUMMARY

The book of Malachi stands as a bridge from Old to New Testament by anticipating the coming of a new messenger, taken later to be John the Baptist. It also brings together two great sections of the Old Testament, the Law, personified in Moses, and the Prophets, personified in Elijah.

Its 55 verses can be divided into seven sections, with a brief prologue and epilogue. Most sections can be taken as a courtroom investigation: a statement is made, it is questioned and evidence is brought. A verdict is given and a likely sentence. God is both judge and prosecutor, the prophet his recorder and mouthpiece. Rhetorical questions are a central stylistic feature.

The first section establishes Israel as his chosen people, with whom he has formed a covenant. The evidence comes from looking at Edom (or Esau), Jacob's (or Israel's) twin (1:2-5). Edom has fared, and will fare, badly, just because it was not loved by God in the same way that God loved Israel. The next two sections form accusations against the priests, who both offered substandard sacrifices (1:6-14) and failed to be true messengers for God to the people (2:1-9).

Malachi then turns to the people. They have broken faith by allowing easy divorce (2:13-16) and intermarriage with non-believers (2:10-12). A new messenger would come to bring God's verdict on their sins of injustice and witchcraft (3:1-5; 4:5). The people have failed to give God his due, the tithe or tenth part of their income, as the law of Moses requires (3:6-12). They see religion purely as something they can benefit from (3:13-18). But judgement will come. A righteous remnant will be restored (4:1-6).

Author

The name means "My Messenger", and so it is not entirely clear whether that is his real name, his title or his pen-name. Some traditions equate him with the priest Ezra, but this is not generally accepted. Nothing else is known about him.

Date

References to a governor suggest a post-exilic time, when the temple has been rebuilt in Jerusalem. The failures of the Israelites are similar to those exposed by Ezra and Nehemiah, so it is generally assumed the book was written about their time or just before, some time between 520–458 BC.

OUTLINE – MALACHI

KEY THEMES – MALACHI

God's elective love

The whole emphasis of the Old Testament is that God has chosen a people for himself, to be called his people. He entered into a covenant with them, which was renewed in various forms. The concept of covenant is mentioned a number of times in the book, in connection with marriage (2:14) and the Levites, or priestly clan (2:4). The covenant, whilst a mutual agreement, is not a covenant of equals. God offered the terms of the agreement, he did the choosing (or electing), and there was no merit on the part of the Israelites to be somehow more worthy of the election than any other nation.

The argument of 1:2-5 establishes this principle by using Esau, the forefather of the Edomites, as an example. Esau and Israel were twin brothers (Genesis 25:24-26; 27:36; 28:6; 36:43), but it was Israel that enjoyed the blessing and the promise. However, Edom was not punished because it was not chosen; rather it was punished because of its unbrotherly acts against Israel, as the book of Obadiah demonstrates (see also Isaiah 34; 63:1-6; Jeremiah 49:7-22; Ezekiel 25:12-14; Amos 1:11-12). The rest of the book goes on to show that covenant blessings require responsive accountability, not a half-hearted fulfilment of duties.

The priests' responsibility

Numbers 18:21-24 is the clearest expression of the covenant with the Levites. Clearly the people have been failing in giving them their tithes, but the Levites also failed the people by not giving clear teaching (2:8-9), and they failed God by not presenting the best animals to sacrifice (1:13-14).

Malachi presents a picture of the ideal priest (2:5-7), which includes the function of teaching and being God's messenger, a role usually reserved for the prophets. In the case of Ezra, we see priests were willing to give instruction of the law (Nehemiah 8), and in the case of Ezekiel, acting as prophets (Ezekiel 1:3).

True messages

These days, our lives are full of texts and messaging. The importance of texts as true messages from God is central in this book, as is the equally important emphasis on the truth of the messenger. The prophet is messenger; so is the priest. And significantly, so is the one who is to come, to proclaim the Day of the LORD.

3:1 echoes Isaiah 40:3. It is not clear whether 3:2 refers to the appearance of the messenger or that of God. However, 4:5-6 gives a fuller account of this messianic messenger. He is seen as Elijah, the great prophet. In the New Testament, John the Baptist, the messenger of Jesus Christ, is seen as fulfilment of this verse (Matthew 11:7-15; 17:1-13; Mark 6:14-16).

RELEVANCE FOR TODAY – MALACHI

Divorce and family life

There is clear teaching on several aspects of family life in this book. The secular world sees marriage more and more as a contract. Obviously breaking a contract leads to penalties, but it is not seen as more than a legal and financial matter. Malachi teaches clearly that marriage is covenant, part of the wider covenant God establishes with his people. God therefore regards divorce as he would other acts of covenant-breaking such as idolatry: something sacred has been defiled.

This does not mean there is a total ban. But it does suggest repentance and the need for forgiveness from God. Above all, it suggests marriage should not be entered into lightly, but as a sacred trust. And it should not be with unbelievers (2:11). One of the messenger's most significant tasks will be to turn "the hearts of the fathers to the children" and the reverse. Divorce, above all, alienates. If there is no reconciliation, the land is liable to be cursed (4:6). This is strong language indeed and we need to take due note of it. It is the Old Testament's last word.

Tithing

Tithing, the giving of a tenth of your income to God, is another principle the book talks very specifically about. In the Old Testament instructions over the tithe, it was to be both the first and the best tenth. Nehemiah 13:10-14 suggests failure had become acute and was affecting the whole spiritual life of the community. The principle outlined in 3:10-12 is an echo of Haggai 1:5-6. A failure to give to God will mean lack of prosperity for the person; a willingness to give will mean God's blessing financially. It is a simple covenant equation.

Worship and covenant faithfulness

Whilst failure to tithe may seem less serious than divorce, both are symptomatic of a failure to see the Christian life in covenant terms. We

> "So guard yourself in your spirit, and do not break faith."
>
> Malachi 2:15

are under the new covenant of grace, sealed by Christ's blood, and therefore we are under something even more precious than the old covenant, to which Malachi is referring.

True heart worship is also part of this covenant. Ideally, worship should bring glory to God among the nations (1:11). But a half-hearted, second-rate worship brings dishonour (1:12-14). For us, worship services should be a witness to our deepest responses to God's love. Covenant faithfulness means living the Christian life with a hundred per cent commitment to the "great king", our God.

Matthew

THE DISCIPLES' GOSPEL

OVERVIEW

Matthew, written for Jewish Christians, focuses on who Jesus is, why he came, and how he fits into God's bigger purposes, showing he is the long-expected Messiah, the bringer of God's kingdom.

SUMMARY

Who Jesus was (1:1-17)

Matthew begins by recording Jesus' key ancestors, starting with Abraham and going through King David (1:1-17), to show he had the legal right to fulfil God's promises to them.

How Jesus came (1:18–3:17)

Matthew describes Jesus' miraculous conception and the events surrounding his birth (1:18–2:23). Passing over the next 30 years in complete silence, he comes to John the Baptist who prepared the way for Jesus (3:1-12). At his baptism, God confirmed Jesus as his Son and filled him with his Spirit (3:13-17), empowering him for his mission.

What Jesus taught (4:1–25:46)

Having overcome the devil (4:1-11), Jesus moved to Capernaum where he began his ministry and called his disciples (4:12-25). Matthew records Jesus' key teaching, organising it thematically into five main blocks (chapters 5–7; 10; 13; 18; 24–25) and interspersing this teaching with accounts of what Jesus did. Jesus' focus was always God's kingdom, his miracles serving as a *demonstration* of it and his parables an *explanation* of it. But while the Jews were expecting Messiah to establish God's kingdom with a sword, Matthew shows Jesus came to do it through a cross.

Why Jesus died (26:1–28:20)

Angered by Jesus' teaching, his religious and political opponents plotted together to get rid of him (26:3-5), finding the perfect opportunity when Judas agreed to betray him (26:14-16). Having shared the Passover with his disciples (26:17-29) and predicted Peter's denial (26:31-35), Jesus went to Gethsemane where he prayed and was betrayed (26:36-56). After several trials through the night (26:57–27:26), Jesus was crucified and buried (27:27-65). This wasn't the end of the story, however, for Jesus rose from the dead (28:1-15), proving that he was truly the Messiah. He then sent his disciples into the whole world to share his good news with others (28:16-20).

Author

Since the days of the early church it has been believed that this Gospel was written by the tax collector who appears in 9:9. This is supported by other evidence. Matthew is the only Gospel writer who identifies this tax collector as "Matthew". Furthermore, his writing shows both the interest in numbers and the local knowledge that you would expect of a tax collector living in that place at that time. This Matthew was one of the twelve disciples of Jesus (10:2-4).

Date

Since Matthew quotes extensively from Mark, it seems obvious he wrote his Gospel later, probably in the 60s, but almost certainly before the destruction of Jerusalem in AD 70.

OUTLINE – MATTHEW

Introduction – the birth of Jesus

The background to the ministry of Jesus

The ministry of Jesus

The final week of Jesus' earthly ministry

KEY THEMES – MATTHEW

Jesus the Messiah

Matthew demonstrates that Jesus was the Messiah through his genealogy (1:1-17), titles (like Son of David and Messiah), parallels with Israel (eg 2:15), and fulfilment of prophecy. He quotes the Old Testament extensively, showing how events in Jesus' life fulfilled what was written (1:22; 4:14; 8:17; 12:17; 21:24), authenticating his messianic claims. He also draws parallels between Moses and Jesus. For example, just as Moses left Egypt, so did Jesus; just as Moses received God's commandments on a mountain, so Jesus explained those commandments on a mountain (the Sermon on the Mount).

Jesus the King

Matthew portrays Jesus as the ultimate King, descended from David (1:1-17) and honoured by the Gentile Magi seeking the King of the Jews (2:2), underlining the global nature of his kingship. Jesus claimed the King's right to judge everyone at the End (25:31-46) and he delegated his kingly authority over all nations to his disciples (28:16-20).

This kingship is also seen in Matthew's emphasis on "the kingdom of God"; writing for Jewish readers, he generally calls it "kingdom of heaven" since Jews avoided using God's name. The Jews believed God's kingdom would come powerfully at the End, bringing judgement on God's enemies; but Jesus said it had started to come right now, because he the King was here. His kingdom has both present (eg 12:28) and future (eg 24:36-51) dimensions.

Jesus the fulfilment and foundation

Matthew's extensive quotations from the Old Testament (eg 2:5,6; 3:3; 4:4,6,7,10; 11:10; 13:13-15; 15:7; 21:4,5,9,13,16) together with his use of the phrase "in order to fulfil" (eg 1:22,23; 4:14-16; 8:17; 12:17-21; 21:4,5) confirm his view of Jesus as the fulfilment of the Jewish hopes for a Messiah, that is, a liberator sent by

God himself. He further emphasises this belief about Jesus as the fulfilment of that hope by drawing parallels, both explicit and implicit, between Moses as the bringer of the Old Covenant and Jesus as the bringer of the new. Thus, just as Moses leaves Egypt, so Christ comes from there. Just as Moses receives the Ten Commandments on a mountain (Exodus 19:20-20:1), so Jesus explains those commandments through the Sermon on the Mount. Just as Moses encountered a shocking lack of faith (Exodus 32:1-20), when he descended from the mountain, so did Jesus (17:14-20).

Jesus the Teacher

Matthew gathers Jesus' teaching into five main sections, recalling Moses and his five books of the Law and showing that Jesus is not just a teacher but a new Moses who would bring about a new deliverance. These five main sections cover:

- Kingdom living – the Sermon on the Mount (5:1–7:29)
- Kingdom mission – instruction on mission (10:1-42)
- Kingdom principles – the parables of kingdom (13:1-58)
- Kingdom attitudes – caring for the weak and forgiving others (18:1-35)
- Kingdom perspective – God's plan for history, including the imminent destruction of Jerusalem and Christ's return at the end of the age (24:1–25:46)

The centre of gravity in Matthew's Gospel, therefore, both in the straightforward teaching and in the parables, is the new community of the kingdom of God. Whilst Jewish mystics were talking about the location and physical appearance of heaven, Christ was talking about the essence of the kingdom of heaven, especially in the parables of chapter 13. As that kingdom's true king, he calls others to his royal service. This communal focus shows itself, too,

THE BE-ATTITUDES

Matthew 5:1-16: the distinctive, inner, spiritual qualities that are to mark us out as citizens of the kingdom.

"Blessed are the poor in spirit, for theirs is the kingdom of heaven" (v. 3)
Are we humble? What is our response when we meet God (Isaiah 57:15)?

"Blessed are those who mourn, for they will be comforted" (v. 4)
Are we aware of our own inner corruption (Romans 7:24)?

"Blessed are the meek, for they will inherit the earth" (v. 5)
How much do we assert ourselves; how sensitive are we (Numbers 12:3)?

"Blessed are those who hunger and thirst for righteousness, for they will be filled" (v. 6)
Do we have a supreme desire to know God and have fellowship with him (Philippians 3:10)?

"Blessed are the merciful, for they will be shown mercy" (v. 7)
Are we merciful to others (Luke 10:36,37)?

"Blessed are the pure in heart, for they will see God" (v. 8)
Do we have a sincere, undivided heart that seeks God above all else (Psalm 86:11)?

"Blessed are the peacemakers, for they will be called sons of God" (v. 9)
How "touchy" are we, insisting on our own rights? Are we prayerful, doing all we can to bring peace, including being silent at times (Hebrews 12:14)?

"Blessed are those who are persecuted for righteousness, for theirs is the kingdom of heaven" (vs. 10-12)
Are our lives different from those around us (2 Timothy 3:12)?

Jesus said that as citizens of the kingdom we should build our lives, not just by listening to his teaching but by putting it into practice

in that this is the only Gospel to mention the church itself (16:18; 18:17). Readers of Matthew's Gospel will find themselves developing a keen awareness of their own place within God's timeless and eternal plan.

Jesus the Judge
Because Jesus is the King, he is also the ultimate judge. While Jesus' message is good news, he was not afraid to speak of God's coming judgement on those who did not believe his message (eg 11:20-24; 12:22-42; 23:1–25:46). This judgement underlines the need to make good decisions about Jesus right now or to risk losing our life for ever (eg 10:32,33; 16:24-27).

Using God's word

Many preachers today just use the New Testament, but Matthew shows how Old and New Testaments fit perfectly together. Jesus didn't come to abolish the Old Testament but to fulfil it (5:17,18), as Matthew shows by often quoting from it. He wanted us to see the unbroken line of God's activity in history, stretching back to Abraham and Moses and forward to the end of this age. Wise preachers will reflect that in their preaching.

Depending on God's word

For Jesus, God's word was not something to be preserved and locked up like the Pharisees did, but a dynamic reality that changes life. He modelled his trust of it (5:18) and dependence on it (4:1-11). God's word is still living and active.

> "Jesus went throughout Galilee, teaching in their synagogues, preaching the good news of the kingdom, and healing every disease and sickness among the people."
>
> Matthew 4:23

Teaching God's word

While Matthew gives us five main blocks of Jesus' teaching, it is clear Jesus taught much more, backing it up with his miracles (4:23-25) and amazing the crowds with his authority (7:28,29). He used simple illustrations to teach profound truths (eg the parables) and made them memorable through simple structures (eg the Beatitudes, 5:3-11). Good teaching is concerned for the needs of those who are taught.

Following God's word

Jesus said we should build our lives, not just on listening to his teaching but putting it into practice (7:24-27). Matthew constantly stresses the demands of discipleship, involving seeking God's kingdom first (6:25-34) and risking everything to follow Jesus (eg 4:19; 8:18-22; 10:32-39; 16:24, 25). But those who do will find they are richly rewarded (eg 19:27-30).

Trusting God's word

We don't always see the fruit of what we sow immediately, and so it is with God's word (13:1-23). However, because it is *God's* word, the word of his kingdom, there is power within it and it *will* grow (13:31-33). If we live by the principles of God's kingdom, God will always vindicate what we do, just as he did in Jesus' life.

Sharing God's word

Although Matthew focuses primarily on Jesus' mission to the Jews (eg 10:5-6), he knew that Jesus' message was for everyone, whatever their racial or social background (2:1-12; 8:5-13; 21:43; 28:18-20). Our preaching the gospel can never be just kept to "our kind" of people.

PALESTINE IN NEW TESTAMENT TIMES

--- Political division

● City of the Decapolis
(the Ten Cities): self-governing
city

0   10   20 miles

0   10   20 kilometres

Sidon

Zarephath

Mt Lebanon

ABILENE • Damascus

Mt Hermon

PROVINCE   *ITURAEA*   **OF SYRIA**

Tyre

PHOENICIA

● Caesarea Philippi

Lake Huleh

R Jordan

GAULANITIS   *TRACHONITIS*
TETRARCHY OF PHILIP

Ptolemais

GALILEE

Chorazin
Capernaum
Gennesaret

● Bethsaida-Julias

● Raphana

Cana

Sea of Galilee

AURANITIS

Mediterranean Sea

Sepphoris

Mt Carmel

Tiberias

?Dion

Hippos ●

Nazareth

● Abila

Dor

Nain

Gadara

Caesarea

The Great Plain

Scythopolis

DECAPOLIS

Salim
Aenon

Pella ●

Hill Country

River Jordan

Gerasa ●

Sebaste
(Samaria)

SAMARIA

Mt Ebal Sychar
Mt Gerizim

The Arabah

R Jabbok

Joppa

Aphek

Alexandrium

A N D   P E R E A

Lydda
Beth-horon

Bethel

● Ephraim

Jericho

Rabbah
(Philadelphia) ●

Ekron

?Emmaus

● Jerusalem

Azotus

Bethlehem
Herodium

Mt Pisgah

Ashkelon

J U D E A

● Medeba

Gaza

Hebron

Hill Country of Judea

En-gedi

Wilderness of Judea

Dead Sea

Machaerus ●

Rapha

The Shephelah

IDUMEA
Beersheba

Malatha

Masada

R Arnon

● Areopolis

Rehoboth

The Negev

NABATEAN KINGDOM

● Beeroth

● Hazazon-tamar

WILDERNESS OF ZIN

Mark
JESUS FOR BEGINNERS

OVERVIEW
The shortest and earliest Gospel, Mark is written in simple language and is an action-packed, fast-moving account of the life and teaching of Jesus, the Messiah (8:29) and Son of God (15:39), who was rejected by his own people but vindicated by God through his resurrection.

SUMMARY

In his Gospel, Mark paints a vivid picture of Jesus as a Messiah (Saviour) whom we dare not ignore. He has largely organised his material chronologically, with much emphasis on Jesus' work in Galilee and on the final week of his life. He was writing for those who were not of Jewish background, as he often explains Jewish history and traditions. In fact, his may well have been a Roman readership.

Mark is the only Gospel to contain the actual word *Gospel*, which means "good news", and he clearly sees Christ as good news for all: good news prophesied by Isaiah (1:2-3) and prepared for by John the Baptist (1:2-8). After his baptism and overcoming Satan's temptations (1:9-13), Jesus started to announce this good news: God's kingdom had arrived; and that demanded a response (1:14-20). This kingdom would affect the whole of life, as Mark immediately demonstrates through a string of stories showing Jesus' authority over everything: demons (1:21-28), sickness (1:29-34), uncleanness (1:40-45), sin (2:1-12), exclusion (2:13-18), religious traditions (2:18-22), even the Sabbath (2:23–3:6). All this drew huge crowds (3:7-12), and Jesus now called 12 apostles to work alongside him (3:13-19). Continuing his ministry, first in Galilee and around the lake (3:20–7:23) and then in Gentile territory (7:24–9:32), he reached pagan Caesarea Philippi where he asked his disciples who they thought he was. Peter acknowledged him as the Christ, or Messiah (8:27-30). From this point, Jesus began explaining what sort of Messiah he would be, establishing God's kingdom not through force, but through suffering and death (8:31-38).

After his transfiguration (9:2-13), Jesus moved south (10:1), teaching about discipleship and predicting his death with increasing clarity (10:32-34). The final third of Mark's Gospel is devoted to the last week of Jesus' life: his triumphant entry into Jerusalem and cleansing the temple (11:1-19), his teaching and opposition to him (11:20–13:37), his anointing (14:1-11), the Last Supper (14:12-26), his arrest in Gethsemane (14:32-52) and his trials, crucifixion and burial (14:53–15:47). The Gospel ends on a note of hope, however, as the women find the tomb empty and angels proclaiming Jesus has risen (16:1-8).

The final section (16:9-20) was probably not written by Mark (the Greek is different) but added by an early church leader.

Author
The early church was unanimous that the author was John Mark (see Acts 12:12; 15:37-40; Colossians 4:10; 2 Timothy 4:11; Philemon 24; 1 Peter 5:13). Tradition says he recorded Peter's preaching in Rome. Some think he is the man mentioned in 14:51-52.

Date
Most believe this was the first Gospel, written in the late 50s or early 60s when Roman persecution of Christians was increasing.

OUTLINE – MARK

The revelation of Jesus as the Messiah

The revelation of the suffering of Jesus the Messiah

KEY THEMES – MARK

The person of Jesus

Mark introduces his Gospel by focusing on "Jesus Christ, the Son of God" (1:1), immediately declaring who he was:

- *Christ* (Greek) or *Messiah* (Hebrew), meaning "anointed one", God's deliverer. While Jesus' contemporaries expected a military Messiah, Jesus would bring deliverance in a very different way (8:27-32).
- *Son of God*, just as God himself declared (1:11; 9:7) and the soldier at the cross recognised (15:39).

Jesus' favourite title for himself, however, was *Son of Man* because its meaning wasn't immediately obvious. Drawing together two key Old Testament ideas – the Son of Man as a glorious heavenly figure (Daniel 7:13-14) and as a lowly earthly figure (Psalm 8:4) – this summed up exactly both aspects of Jesus' nature as God and man.

The problem of Jesus

Jesus was a problem to many. His family thought he was mad (3:20,21), religious leaders thought he was demonised (3:22), his townsfolk were confused by him (6:1-6), and even his disciples didn't understand him (4:13; 8:14-21,31-34). Only the demons grasped who he was (1:24,34; 5:7)! But this was no accident. Jesus didn't make his identity obvious, and often told those who worked it out *not* to tell others (1:44; 5:43; 8:30) because of current wrong expectations of what Messiah would be and do. Only when it was unmistakable what sort of Messiah he was claiming to be did he openly acknowledge it (14:60-64). Of course, after the resurrection, this messianic secret need remain secret no longer.

The power of Jesus

Jesus backed up his claims by demonstrating his authority. He defeated demons (1:21-28), healed sickness (1:29-45), forgave sin (2:1-12), controlled nature (4:35-41) and even overcame death (5:35-43). Even in his encounter with Pilate, he maintained his quiet authority – the prisoner ruling over his captor (15:1-15, especially verse 5). His ultimate power was displayed at the resurrection where death itself could not hold him.

The passion of Jesus

While Mark doesn't over-dwell on the details of Jesus' "passion" (sufferings), summing up the crucifixion in the simple words "and they crucified him" (15:24), it is clear this is the focus and climax of his Gospel and of all that Jesus predicted (8:31; 9:12; 10:33,34; 14:21).

The path of Jesus

The disciples are often reminded that they too must walk the path of Jesus, ready to resist the attraction of greatness (9:33-36) and to suffer like him (8:34-37). When Mark was read across the Roman Empire, where many Christians suffered for their faith, his words must have had a great impact.

RELEVANCE FOR TODAY – MARK

Jesus' authority

Mark presents Jesus as the powerful Saviour with authority over every aspect of life. Nothing is greater than him, whether sickness, sin, nature or death. Yet he never used this authority for selfish advantage (eg 14:44-50). Our use of God's authority should be the same.

Jesus' challenge

Mark shows that those who believe in Jesus must be ready to deny themselves and follow him with their whole being (8:34,35; 12:29-31). When Jesus asked his disciples about different perceptions of him (8:27-29), he was interested in what they themselves believe, rather than the opinions they had gathered from other people. Mere admiration of Jesus is insufficient; only a costly and wholehearted following of him would do, as the rich young man discovered (10:17-31).

> "Surely this man was the Son of God."
>
> Mark 15:39

Jesus' message

Mark opens his story by describing it as "the beginning of the gospel about Jesus Christ" (1:1). The word *Gospel* means "good news": the good news that God's kingdom is here and the door to it is open to everyone. As Jesus' followers, we too are called to focus on his good news as we share his message with others.

Jesus' love

Jesus mixed with all kinds of people, especially those that the religious leaders avoided and whom they described as "sinners", meaning either immoral people or simply those who didn't keep all their religious rules and rituals. They despised Jesus for this, but he said these were the very ones who needed him (2:15-17). Our ministry should reach out to all kinds of people, not just nice people or the sort we like.

Jesus' way

Jesus' message wasn't just preached by words, but was backed up with clear demonstrations of God's love and power through his miracles of healing, and he sent out his disciples to do the same (3:14-15; 6:6-13). In the longer ending of the Gospel, this challenge is repeated (16:15-18), and even if that section wasn't written by Mark himself, it shows that such things were still expected in the early church and are a challenge to us today.

Jesus' action

Mark presents Jesus as a real man of action who doesn't sit around thinking about things but who gets on with it. One of Mark's favourite words is "immediately", which connects one story to the next and keeps things moving rapidly. His action appealed to ordinary people who had no time for the long religious debates of the scribes and Pharisees. How active are we?

MARK'S USE OF THE WORD "IMMEDIATELY"

Mark writes his account of Jesus in direct, forceful language. He includes relatively long stories and a limited amount of teaching by Jesus. The Gospel is action-packed and often uses the word "immediately" ("at once") to connect scenes. Another indication of rapid movement is the fact that many phrases begin with the conjunction "and", although this is not normally translated into English. The colloquial character of language and style matches the types of people who join Jesus in this story: they are mainly ordinary persons such as fishermen, women (who in those days were seen as inferior to men), and outcasts like lepers, tax collectors, and other sinners.

The narrator in this record is external to the events and never appears in the story itself. At the outset he reveals who Jesus is in his opinion, the Christ (Messiah) and the Son of God (1:1, 11). The book's leading question is if the characters in the story will agree with the narrator. As presented by Mark, Jesus' public life is characterised by conflicts with his relatives and fellow inhabitants of Nazareth (3:21,30-35; 6:1-5), his followers (8:14-21), the Jewish authorities (eg 3:1-6; 8:11-13; 12:1-44) and the powers of evil (1:12,13,21-27; 5:1-13; 9:14-29). They all somehow fail to recognise or to acknowledge Jesus for who he is. The powers of evil do recognise Jesus as "the Holy one of God" (1:24, cf. 1:34; 5:7) but the value of that recognition is limited because they do not submit to him voluntarily. However, it does show us that true insight is supernaturally given.

Pedestrian crossing, Japan. Mark tells us that the good news of God's kingdom is here and the door to it is open to everyone

Luke
THE GOSPEL FOR ALL

OVERVIEW
Based on Mark but expanded through careful research (1:1-4), Luke is the only Gospel with a sequel (Acts), taking Jesus' message from Jerusalem to Rome, underlining it is for all people everywhere.

SUMMARY
Luke's ordered account of Jesus' life takes us on a journey:

From heaven to Bethlehem
Against the background of the coming of Messiah's forerunner (1:5-25,39-80), Luke shows that Jesus was no mere man but "Son of the Most High" (1:32), God himself miraculously coming to us (1:26-38). Born in David's city of Bethlehem (2:1-7), Jesus was welcomed by ordinary people (2:8-20) and acknowledged by the spiritually faithful (2:21-38).

From Bethlehem to Galilee
The family returned home to Galilee where Jesus grew up (2:39-40). Revealing nothing about these years other than a visit to Jerusalem (2:41-52), Luke jumps ahead to John the Baptist's ministry of preparation and to Jesus' baptism (3:1-20) and temptations (4:1-13). Back in Nazareth, through a reading from Isaiah, Jesus proclaimed the sort of ministry he was beginning, one of freedom for captives (4:14-21). But Nazareth rejected him, so he relocated to Capernaum (4:22-31) from where he taught, healed, did miracles and trained his disciples (4:31–9:50). Peter at last grasped that Jesus was the Messiah and it was from this point onwards that Jesus began to tell his disciples about the death that awaited him and the challenges that faced them (9:18-26).

From Galilee to Jerusalem
Jesus then began a long journey to Jerusalem (9:51ff), teaching all who would listen, but also encountering increasing opposition (11:14-23,37-54; 20:1-26). The journey climaxed with his triumphal entry into Jerusalem and its temple (19:28-44), which made the religious leaders even more determined to get rid of him (19:47-48). They succeeded by falsifying charges and having him crucified (22:1–23:56). While this seemed the end of the story, it wasn't: Jesus rose again and appeared to his disciples (24:1-49).

From Jerusalem to heaven
The journey was completed as Jesus returned to heaven (24:50-53). But the story wasn't over, as Luke goes on to show us in Acts.

Author
Luke, a doctor (Colossians 4:14) and travelling companion of Paul (2 Timothy 4:11) wrote Luke and Acts, both books being dedicated to the same wealthy patron, Theophilus (Luke 1:3; Acts 1:1).

Date
It is likely that Luke was written after Mark, since he quotes so much of his material. It is hard to be more exact; whereas some date the Gospel to the 60s of the first century AD, others think of a date towards 80. This suggests a date somewhere between AD 60 and 70.

OUTLINE – LUKE

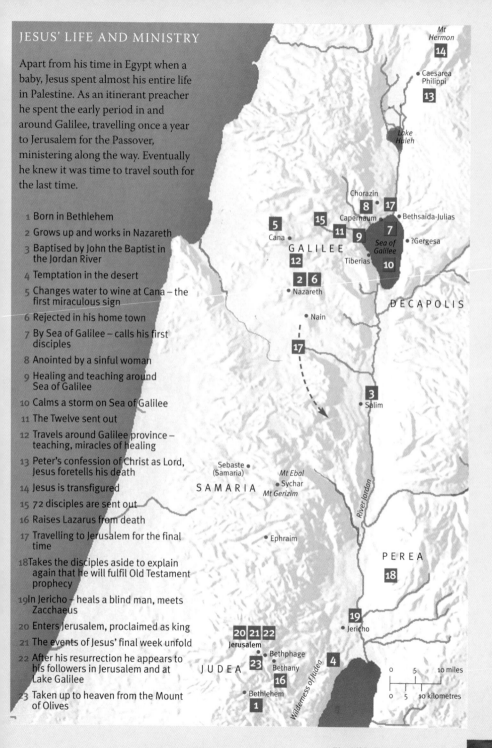

JESUS' LIFE AND MINISTRY

Apart from his time in Egypt when a baby, Jesus spent almost his entire life in Palestine. As an itinerant preacher he spent the early period in and around Galilee, travelling once a year to Jerusalem for the Passover, ministering along the way. Eventually he knew it was time to travel south for the last time.

1 Born in Bethlehem
2 Grows up and works in Nazareth
3 Baptised by John the Baptist in the Jordan River
4 Temptation in the desert
5 Changes water to wine at Cana – the first miraculous sign
6 Rejected in his home town
7 By Sea of Galilee – calls his first disciples
8 Anointed by a sinful woman
9 Healing and teaching around Sea of Galilee
10 Calms a storm on Sea of Galilee
11 The Twelve sent out
12 Travels around Galilee province – teaching, miracles of healing
13 Peter's confession of Christ as Lord, Jesus foretells his death
14 Jesus is transfigured
15 72 disciples are sent out
16 Raises Lazarus from death
17 Travelling to Jerusalem for the final time
18 Takes the disciples aside to explain again that he will fulfil Old Testament prophecy
19 In Jericho – heals a blind man, meets Zacchaeus
20 Enters Jerusalem, proclaimed as king
21 The events of Jesus' final week unfold
22 After his resurrection he appears to his followers in Jerusalem and at Lake Galilee
23 Taken up to heaven from the Mount of Olives

JESUS' LAST WEEK

1 SUNDAY

Jesus enters the city through the Golden Gate, riding on a donkey. Hailed by the people as Messiah

Matthew 21:1-11
Mark 11:1-11
Luke 19:28-44
John 12:12-19

2 MONDAY

Jesus drives out the money-changers and stall holders from the temple precinct

Matthew 21:12-17
Mark 11:12-19
Luke 19:45-48

3 TUESDAY

Teaching in the temple. At Bethany a woman anoints him "in preparation for burial"

Judas agrees to hand Jesus over to the priests

Matthew 26:6-16
Mark 14:1-11
Luke 22:1-6
John 12:1-8

4 WEDNESDAY

A quiet day with friends in Bethany

5 THURSDAY

The Last Supper: Jesus shares a final passover meal with his disciples

Matthew 26:17-30
Mark 14:12-26
Luke 22:7-38

Jesus struggles in prayer to accept the ordeal he faces

Matthew 26:36-46
Mark 14:32-46
Luke 22:39-46

Betrayed by Judas, taken captive by soldiers

Matthew 26:47-56
Mark 14:43-52
Luke 22:47-53
John 18:1-4

The last days of Jesus' life were spent in Jerusalem at Passover week. He travelled to Jerusalem knowing he would die.

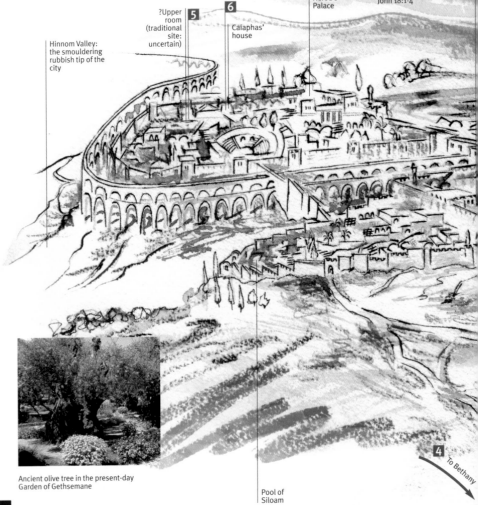

Hinnom Valley: the smouldering rubbish tip of the city

?Upper room (traditional site: uncertain)

Caiaphas' house

Herod's Palace

Ancient olive tree in the present-day Garden of Gethsemane

Pool of Siloam

6
FRIDAY

Peter denies knowing
Jesus

Matthew 26:69-75
Mark 14:66-72
Luke 22:54-62
John 18:15-18,25-27

Jesus is tried by the
Jewish Council, accused
of blasphemy

Matthew 26:57-58
Mark 14:53-65
Luke 22:63-71
John 18:19-24

Taken to Pilate, the
Roman Governor, tried
and condemned to death

Matthew 27:11-26
Mark 15:1-15
Luke 23:1-25
John 18:28–19:16

Jesus is tortured, taken
to Golgotha, crucified
and dies

Matthew 27:27-56
Mark 15:16-41
Luke 23:26-49
John 19:17-37

Jesus' body is buried and
sealed in a new tomb

Matthew 27:57-66
Mark 15:42-47
Luke 23:50-56
John 19:38-42

7
SATURDAY

The Sabbath – the Jewish
day of rest

8
SUNDAY

The risen Christ is seen
by Mary Magdalene, then
the disciples

Matthew 28:1-20
Mark 16:1-18
Luke 24:1-49
John 20:1-23

Mount of
Olives

Fort
Antonia

Golden
Gate

1

Pool of
Bethesda

5

Gethsemane

The
temple

6

site of
olgotha

Kidron
Valley

KEY THEMES – LUKE

A Gospel of truth

Luke tells us that he "carefully investigated" his facts so that the reader could know "the certainty of the things you have been taught" (1:1-4). Wherever we can check his details (historical, political, social or geographical), they are always amazingly accurate, which gives us confidence to believe the rest of his story. In particular, Luke emphasises both the incarnation and resurrection in his Gospel, wanting us to know the truth of these two events as the firm foundation for our faith.

A Gospel of inclusion

From beginning to end, Luke shows that Jesus' message was for everyone. Early in his Gospel he traces Jesus' genealogy right back, not to Abraham as in Matthew, but to Adam (3:23-38), showing he had come for the whole human race. Jews found this hard to grasp; so while Nazareth was happy with Jesus' claim that he had come to bring God's promised freedom (4:14-22), they quickly turned against him when he suggested this included non-Jews (4:24-30). In one of his parables (10:29-37) Jesus dared suggest that there could be such a thing as a good Samaritan (a hated people as far as Jews were concerned). However, Luke also includes rich and influential people, such as Joanna in 8:3. At the end of the Gospel, Jesus is still underlining that his message was for "all nations" (24:47).

A Gospel of compassion

Luke's background as a doctor is reflected in his recording many healing miracles of Jesus and his compassion for those in need, reflected for example in his tender words to the leper (5:12-13). In the miracles he shows a tenderness for the healed and a deep respect for the power of the healer, with Jesus saying that he can drive out demons by the mere touch of his "finger" (11:20)!

Luke has a strong emphasis on Jesus reaching out to everybody, especially those whom society excluded: the poor (16:19-31; 21:1-4), the outcasts (17:11-19; 18:9-14), women (7:36-50; 10:38-42) and children (9:46-48; 18:15-17). Not even the religious were excluded by him, even though many of them excluded him, and he would often eat with them (7:36-50; 11:37-54; 14:1-24).

A Gospel of the Spirit

There is a strong emphasis in Luke (and in Acts) on the work of the Holy Spirit. The Spirit was active, after centuries of silence, even before Jesus' birth (1:15,17,35,41,67; 2:25-27); but once filled with God's Spirit at his baptism (3:21-23), Jesus could begin Isaiah's prophesied Spirit-anointed ministry (4:18,19). Jesus is marked out as a man of the Spirit (10:21) who said God wanted to show his extraordinary generosity and goodness and give this same Spirit to all his children (11:13).

RELEVANCE FOR TODAY – LUKE

A passion for growth

Jesus was a well-rounded man who "grew in wisdom and stature, and in favour with God and men" (2:52) – that is, intellectually, spiritually and socially. God wants us to grow in each of these dimensions too and not be imbalanced, as the Pharisees were.

A passion for the Spirit

If Jesus needed God's Spirit to live and minister, how much more do we. Jesus said that God is a good Father who gives the Spirit to those who ask him (11:13) to help them in their need (12:11,12). Blasphemy against the Spirit – resisting his work – is dangerous (12:10).

> "Do not be afraid.
> I bring you good news
> of great joy that will be
> for all the people."
>
> **Luke 2:10**

A passion for prayer

Prayer had a central place in Jesus' life, especially at key times (3:21; 5:16; 6:12; 9:28,29; 11:1; 22:39-46). He taught his disciples to pray (11:1-4) and underlined the importance of never giving up in prayer (11:5-13; 18:1-5). We need the same passion today, knowing we can do nothing without our Father's help.

A passion for the lost

While the Pharisees liked spending time with "the found", Jesus "came to seek and to save what was lost" (19:10), for finding the lost brings great joy, as the parables of the lost sheep, lost coin and lost son remind us (15:1-32). Jesus calls us, not to spend all our time with "the found", but to go and find "the lost", just as he sent his disciples to do (9:1-6; 10:1,2).

A passion for the unloved

Jesus modelled the importance of loving the unlovely, deliberately reaching out to those that the Pharisees avoided – sinners, tax collectors, prostitutes – and telling his followers to do the same (14:12-14). God's love is for everyone, and so must ours be. If we find ourselves only spending time with "nice" people, we are not being true to Jesus' call.

A passion for learning

Luke wrote his Gospel so that Theophilus, and others, "may know the certainty of the things you have been taught" (1:4). Simply believing in Jesus isn't enough; we need firm foundations of his truth in our lives, letting that challenge and change us (6:46-49). Luke particularly draws attention to the areas of religious ritual (5:33–6:5; 11:37-53) and money (12:13-34; 16:19-31; 18:18-30), both important to the Pharisees, as areas of important change for Jesus' followers.

AN INCLUSIVE GOSPEL

Luke writes an inclusive Gospel – including men and women, rich and poor, Jew and Gentile.

A Gospel for the curious

In an era where we are caught between scepticism on the one hand and curiosity on the other, Luke's serious piece of commissioned research is a powerful tool for introducing the curious to Jesus. Luke includes many well-known parables such as that of the prodigal son (15:11-32). These apparently simple stories contain deep truths about Jesus, God and humanity.

Nepali girls, high in the Himalayas

A Gospel for the cautious

Today many believe that Christianity has little room for those who do not fit in. Luke's Gospel, peopled with corrupt tax collectors, hesitant lepers, uncertain disciples and strong-minded women provides the ideal reading material for them. Its pages will not put them off, but rather extend an invitation to them to find out more. Not only that, but there is another book to follow on with the story of the inclusiveness of the early church: see Acts.

A Gospel for children

In former times, children were valued very little. Greeks and Romans controlled the size of their families by abandoning children. Out of all the evangelists, Luke pays most attention to children (1:41,44; 2:40-52; 9:46-48; 15:11-32; 18:15-17); 9:47 would suggest that there was one wherever Jesus was.

A Gospel for the critical

Luke's frankness makes him appealing to the sceptical and the critical. His picture of Jesus stands out against a dark background of shabby and shallow religion. He shows how our faith should influence our handling of money and possessions. Like the characters in several parables we are all managers, servants who look after our master's property (12:42; 16:1,3,8).

A comprehensive Gospel

No single description of Jesus stands out in this Gospel. Luke emphasises Jesus' humanity (eg his frequent praying) but also describes him as Son of God (1:32,35; 4:41; 10:22). Jesus is the *saviour*, a word used for kings, gods, doctors and philosophers. He is king in the line of David (1–2), a prophet but also the suffering servant of Isaiah 53.

John

FINDING LIFE

OVERVIEW

Different in approach to the other three Gospels, John selected some key incidents and teachings from Jesus' life to explore and explain them in more depth so that people might understand more of Jesus and the life they had through him (20:31).

SUMMARY

John begins his Gospel, not with the Christmas story, but in eternity (1:1-18). Seeing Jesus as the fulfilment of both ancient hopes and contemporary thought, he calls him "the Word" (a term understandable to both Jews and Gentiles) who had been with God for ever (1:1,2) but who at a moment in history "became flesh" (1:14), the most succinct summary of the incarnation in the Bible. John then divides his account of Jesus' life into two halves: his public ministry (1:19–12:50) and his private ministry (13:1–20:31).

In the first half he alternates *seven signs* (John's word for Jesus' miracles) with *seven sayings* (lengthy teachings or "discourses" explaining those signs to his disciples or others) backed up by *seven statements* about who he claimed to be (the "I am" sayings), building towards the conclusion that "Jesus is the Christ, the Son of God" (20:31). From Jesus' three Passover visits to Jerusalem, it is possible to work out that this ministry covered just over three years.

The second half records Jesus' private ministry (13:1–20:31), covering the final week of his life and his preparing his disciples for his death, including washing their feet (13:1-17), predicting his betrayal (13:18-30) and Peter's denial (13:31-38), telling them of his departure and the Spirit's coming in his place (14:1–16:33) and praying for them (17:1-26). Like the other Gospels, John then records Jesus' arrest in Gethsemane (18:1-11), his trials (18:12–19:16) and his crucifixion and burial (19:17-42), followed by the empty tomb and

Jesus' resurrection appearances (20:1-31).

In an epilogue he records two later resurrection appearances, and Jesus' recommissioning of Peter after his disastrous denial of Jesus (21:15-19).

Author

Strictly speaking, the text is anonymous. The name John in this Gospel always refers to John the Baptist. Yet the tradition of the church unanimously ascribes it to John, James' brother and one of the sons of Zebedee. The author probably introduces himself in 1:37-40 and 18:15-17 as an unnamed disciple. He may also be the "disciple whom Jesus loved" mentioned in 13:23, 19:25-27, 20:2 and 21:20-23. This is more a statement at his wonder that Jesus loved him than a measure of his own importance. The Gospel is more about its subject than its writer. A comparison between the style of this Gospel and the letters of John the apostle certainly suggests that they were written by the same person.

Date

The tradition of the church tells us that John's Gospel was written last of the four. The great sophistication of John's Gospel also made many scholars ascribe a late date to it. However, the discovery of an early papyrus fragment dating from the first quarter of the second century AD means that it cannot have been written after AD 100. The author does not allude to the destruction of the temple in AD 70 so that some even date the book during the AD 60s. The majority still think it was written at the end of the first century AD.

OUTLINE – JOHN

KEY THEMES – JOHN

Who Jesus was

While the other Gospels gradually reveal Jesus' identity, John reveals immediately that he is the Lamb of God (1:29,36), Messiah (1:41,45), Son of God (1:34,49), indeed no one less than God himself (1:1-3). Jesus makes open claims about his relationship with the Father, leading to many debates and conflicts with religious leaders and even attempts to kill him for his blasphemy (5:17-18; 8:58-59; 10:33). But Jesus was clear that to reject him was to reject the Father (8:19; 14:6).

What Jesus did

John knew many of Jesus' miracles (20:30) but chose just seven, for Jews the perfect number. John calls these "signs": not just demonstrations of power but pointers to who Jesus is. The *seven signs* are: turning water into wine (2:1-11), healing an official's son (4:43-54), healing a cripple (5:1-15), feeding the 5,000 (6:1-15), walking on water (6:16-21), healing the man born blind (9:1-41), and raising Lazarus (11:1-44).

What Jesus said

From Jesus' many public teachings, John again selected just seven: discussing new birth with Nicodemus (3:1-21), talking with the Samaritan woman (4:1-42), his relationship with the Father (5:19-47), Jesus as the Bread of Life (6:22-70), teaching at the Feast of Tabernacles (7:1-52), true relationship with God (8:12-59), and Jesus as the Good Shepherd (10:1-42).

What Jesus claimed

Another "seven" is found in Jesus' "I am" sayings. This was God's name, revealed to Moses (Exodus 3:14); so in using this and linking it to Old Testament symbols, Jesus was making huge claims. He said, I am the bread of life (6:35); the light of the world (8:12); the gate for the sheep (10:7); the good shepherd (10:11); the resurrection and the life (11:25); the way, truth and life (14:6); the true vine (15:1). His final use was absolute, with no qualification or description, which caused enormous reaction (8:58).

Why Jesus died

Right at the beginning John the Baptist recognised Jesus as "the Lamb of God who takes away the sin of the world" (1:29) and Jesus told Nicodemus that "the Son of Man must be lifted up" (3:14). Caiaphas, prophesying more than he knew, said "it is better for you that one man die for the people than that the whole nation perish" (11:50). For John, it was his death and resurrection that made it clear that "Jesus is the Christ the Son of God" (20:31).

I am the bread of life (6:35-51)
Do we draw on his resources – "the inexhaustible riches of Christ" (Ephesians 3:8)?

I am the light of the world (8:12)
As we follow Jesus Christ, may our light be seen in the world (Matthew 5:14-16).

I am the gate for the sheep (10:7,9)
We are to remember that the only way to become part of God's family is through Jesus Christ (14:6).

I am the good shepherd (10:11)
We are to listen to Christ and follow him; we can feel secure in his loving care. We may enjoy his provision. We are to stay close to, not wander away from, him.

I am the resurrection and the life (11:25)
We can bring "impossible" situations, people and relationships to Jesus; we are to ask him to bring life, new life, to show his power in healing and other miracles. Do we believe this (11:26)?

I am the way, the truth and the life (14:6)
We are to focus on him, trusting that he has our future safe in his hands. He is the way through all the twists and turns of life.

I am the true vine (15:1-8)
We are to receive Christ's life — his resources — into our lives. We are to obey the command to remain in Christ: keep communication channels open.

God's presence

The one who was with God and was God from the beginning (1:1,2) "became flesh and *made his dwelling* among us" (1:14), literally "pitched his tent". Just as God's tabernacle was pitched among his people during the exodus, so God "pitched his tent" among us through Jesus. Our challenge is to now "pitch" that presence where he is not known.

God's love

God sent his Son into the world because he loves it so much (3:16). He calls us to respond, not just by loving him but also by loving one another (13:34,35), reflecting the unity and love within the Trinity itself, not in theory but in reality, so that the world may believe (17:20-26).

God's action

Knowing that miracles need *explanation* and words need *demonstration*, John interwove Jesus' teaching and miracles. Still today, God's word needs demonstrating in action, and our actions need explaining in words so people will understand the gospel.

God's message

The life Jesus offers is available to all, as the contrasting stories of Nicodemus and the woman at the well demonstrate. Whether religious or sinner, enquirer or excuser, male or female, Jew or non-Jew, Jesus can make a difference. We should never doubt that anyone is beyond his reach.

God's truth

In a world of many viewpoints, John proclaims the importance of absolute truth, seeing Jesus as the true light (1:9), true bread from heaven (6:32), true vine (15:1), even truth itself (14:6). Jesus' followers need not be ashamed of claiming they have the truth, but they must also ensure there is no place for un-truth or half-truth in their lives.

God's Spirit

The Holy Spirit is needed not only to begin the Christian life (3:5) but also to live it (14:15-27). In the chapters that cover Jesus' last evening with the disciples, there is a great deal recorded about the role of the Holy Spirit in the disciples' ongoing lives. They are told that he will act as their illuminator, shining a new light on the truths which Jesus has taught them (14:26). He will act as their Counsellor, coming alongside with his help and expressing the presence of Jesus to them (14:16). When they move out into the world to spread the gospel, he will bring spiritual conviction on those who

> **"These are written that you may believe that Jesus is the Christ, the Son of God, and that by believing you may have life in his name."**
>
> John 20:31

listen (16:8-10). Jesus wants every believer to experience his Spirit like streams of living water flowing from within (7:38,39).

God's restoration

Peter was devastated by his denial of Jesus (18:15-18,25-27), at last seeing how his big words weren't matched by big actions. His return to fishing (21:3) reflected his discouragement, but Jesus kindly restored him, letting him cancel his three denials with three affirmations of love (21:15-19). Peter had to learn that failure did not disqualify him, providing he handled it properly.

Acts

ADVENTURES OF THE EARLY CHURCH

OVERVIEW
With Jesus ascended and the Spirit now given, the gospel began to spread, just as Jesus promised. Acts describes the church's birth and its rapid progress across the known world.

SUMMARY

Pentecost
After the ascension, Jesus' disciples returned to Jerusalem to pray and await the promised Holy Spirit (1:1-26). Coming at Pentecost (2:1-4), he transformed the previously fearful followers and produced 3,000 conversions that first day (2:41) and a new way of living (2:42-47). Acts then records the church's subsequent advance "in Jerusalem, and in all Judea and Samaria, and to the ends of the earth" (1:8).

Jerusalem (chapters 1–7)
The apostles' ministry (3:1-26) brought not only conversions (4:4; 5:12-16) but also persecution (4:1-22; 5:17-42; 6:8–7:60). However nothing could stop them, though Ananias and Sapphira's deception almost destroyed the very thing the church was becoming known for and was ruthlessly dealt with (5:1-11). The persecution climaxed in Stephen's martyrdom (7:54-60).

Judea and Samaria (chapter 8)
The church got stuck in Jerusalem and Judea, enjoying success but failing to push out further; so God used the persecution to drive them out of their comfort zone (8:1). Philip preached so successfully in Samaria (8:4-13) that the apostles had to go and see what was happening and pray for the new believers to receive the Spirit (8:14-25). At last, the gospel had escaped its Jewish confines. An African eunuch's conversion was another step in the church reaching out to everybody (8:26-40).

The ends of the earth (chapters 9–28)
A huge turning-point was Saul's conversion (9:1-18), leading to the gospel reaching Damascus and Tarsus (9:20-31). Meanwhile Peter's vision prepared him for God giving his Spirit to Gentiles (10:1–11:18). Another breakthrough came when Saul (now Paul) made Antioch his base, from which his missionary travels stretched ever-deeper into the Roman empire, with churches planted in Asia Minor, Greece and even Rome itself (chapters 13–28). Acts has an open-ending, underlining that the work of the gospel still continues.

Author
1:1 links this book to the Gospel, also written by Luke for Theophilus. Luke's use of the first person plural in 16:10 reveals that from this point onwards he was largely writing on the basis of his personal recollections of the events. Subsequent passages containing the word "we" may well indicate events of which he had particularly vivid memories. These include the departure from Philippi in 20:5 and the journey by sea from Caesarea to Rome in 27:1.

By the time Luke tells about Paul's arrival in Rome in the final chapter, he has probably brought the story to the point where his wealthy sponsor Theophilus knows the details for himself.

Date
The events described in the book last for some thirty years, up to Paul's arrival and stay in Rome in AD 60–62, so it must have been

written after that date. Scholars are divided over the exact time of writing, some placing it around AD 70–80. Yet the fact that Acts makes no mention of the Jewish revolt in AD 66–70 or Nero's campaign of persecution in AD 64 makes it likely that it was written earlier, immediately after Luke's Gospel. Whilst Paul was awaiting his trial in Rome, Luke, his travelling companion, probably used the time to write down the remarkable events that had happened.

The key to Paul's letters
The book of Acts represents vital background reading for the letters of Paul and the other apostles. All the churches to whom Paul wrote letters appear in the book of Acts. From this book we can learn about the circumstances in which those particular churches were founded, the kind of opposition they faced and their initial response to the gospel. This makes our reading of those letters easier and richer. All the theology in Paul's letters is applied theology. In other words, it represents the principles of the gospel as applied to particular settings. Understanding those settings can help us to read his theology, and then apply it to our own particular circumstances.

OUTLINE – ACTS

Peter and the church in Jerusalem

1:1-14	The ascension of Jesus Christ
1:15-26	The election of Matthias to replace Judas
2:1-47	The day of Pentecost
3:1–4:31	Peter and John heal in the name of Jesus Christ
4:32–5:11	The early Christian fellowship
5:12-42	The authorities fail to suppress the church

The expansion of the church to Samaria and the Gentiles

6:1-7	The appointment of helpers ("deacons")
6:8–8:1	The witness and death of Stephen
8:2-40	Ministry in Samaria
9:1-31	The conversion of Paul
9:32–11:18	Peter's ministry to the Gentiles
11:19-30	The gospel established in Antioch
12:1-25	The opposition of Herod

Paul's missionary outreach to the Gentiles

13:1–14:28	The first missionary journey
15:1-35	The Council of Jerusalem
15:36–18:22	The second missionary journey
18:23–21:16	The third missionary journey
21:17–22:29	Paul's arrest in Jerusalem
22:30–23:11	The trial before the Sanhedrin
23:12-35	The transfer to Caesarea
24:1-27	Paul appears before Felix
25:1-12	Paul appeals to Caesar
25:13–26:32	Paul appears before Festus and others
27:1–28:10	The voyage to Rome; shipwreck
28:11-31	Two years under house arrest in Rome

KEY THEMES – ACTS

Spirit and effort

Acts underlines the importance of cooperation between God's Spirit and human effort. The church couldn't be launched until the Spirit came (2:1-4,42-47), but it was only as Christians responded to him that it grew. Believers took huge risks and endured real hardship to spread the gospel, but it was the Spirit alone who empowered them (4:8) and convicted their hearers (2:37). Luke stresses the importance of receiving the Spirit as the hallmark of real faith (2:1-4; 8:14-17; 9:17; 10:44-48; 19:1-7).

Jew and Gentile

Although the Jesus movement started within Judaism, Jesus' heart had always been for it to spread to all nations (eg 1:8). It wasn't until after Stephen's martyrdom that it began to spread more widely, initially to Samaritans as persecution forced the believers out from Jerusalem (8:1-3). However, Peter needed a divine vision to take the step of visiting a Roman household and was shocked when they too received the Spirit (10:44-46), leaving him with no choice but to baptise them (10:47,48). The church had to grapple with the implications of this (11:1-18), discussing it at special council in Jerusalem (15:1-29) where it was decided that Gentiles didn't need to become Jews and be circumcised to be saved.

Empire and kingdom

Paul often clashed with the Roman authorities. In 16:35-40 he insisted that the authorities in the city of Philippi treat him properly under Roman law. In Corinth a landmark ruling was issued by the Roman proconsul which regarded Christianity as an offshoot of Judaism and therefore protected it under Roman law (18:14,15). When threatened with flogging in Jerusalem, he claimed his legal rights as a Roman citizen to prevent it (22:25) and he later insisted on his right to stand trial before the emperor himself (25:10,11). Chapters 22–26 show that Christianity is harmless to a proper civil government.

Obstacle and opportunity

Each time the church encountered an obstacle, it was turned into an opportunity. So, the persecution in Jerusalem led to a spreading of the gospel (8:4-8); a night in jail for Paul brought the jailer and his family to faith (16:25-34); a disagreement between Paul and Barnabas led to a multiplication of missionary endeavour (15:36-41); and Paul's shipwreck gave an opportunity to witness to Malta's governor (28:1-10).

Peter and Paul

Acts focuses largely on Peter and Paul rather than all the apostles, drawing several parallels between them, perhaps to underline they were both foundational in the development of the church and to emphasise the unity of the Jewish and Gentile missions. While we learn much about Paul's movements in Acts (after all, Luke accompanied him at times), Peter disappears by chapter 15, although the New Testament contains other clues of what he did. He started to travel further, developing links with Christians in "Pontus, Galatia, Cappadocia, Asia and Bithynia" (1 Peter 1:1) and, according to tradition, ending up in Rome where he became a significant figure in the church and where both Peter and Paul were martyred.

RELEVANCE FOR TODAY – ACTS

The need for prayer
Acts not only starts with prayer (1:14); it also
continues with prayer. Prayer characterised
the church's meetings (2:42), was their first
response to every situation (4:23-31) and
guided their decisions (6:6; 13:1-3) and
ministry (9:40). God doesn't need our prayers,
but he loves to respond to them as he draws us
into establishing his will in the world. In our
age of instant communication, let's not forget
that prayer takes us right to the throne room of
heaven itself.

The need for the Spirit
Acts, like Luke, is a book of the Spirit. Nothing
could happen for the disciples until the Spirit
came, and nothing happened without the
Spirit thereafter. Luke shows how different
people groups all received the Spirit; none
were excluded. Still today the church needs the
Holy Spirit if it is to be as effective as the
church in Acts.

The need for courage
The early church was born out of the courage
of the first Christians. They crossed oceans
and mountains, faced beatings, stoning,
imprisonments, shipwreck and worse, driven
on by their love for Jesus and a passion to share
his gospel. Acts challenges us: are we ready to
share the gospel, wherever God puts us and
whatever the cost?

The need for wisdom
Acts reveals the challenge of accommodating
people from different religious backgrounds,
who speak different languages and come from
different social strata. It wasn't always easy, but
God gave them wisdom, as when they solved
the tensions between the widows from
Palestinian and Greek backgrounds
concerning food distributions (6:1-7). In
today's multicultural world, the church still
needs wisdom to live genuinely as one,

A pastor, Nicaragua. The gospel is good news for all
peoples and cultures

knowing it cannot accept divisions and still be
the church.

The need for sharing
Luke describes with apparent approval the
sharing by the earliest Christians of their
goods as need arose (2:44-45; 4:31-37) and
mentions the well-known Barnabas as an
example of this generosity. In the church today
those who can afford it should support those
who are in need, at home and abroad.

The need for mission

Antioch, 300 miles north of Jerusalem, lay on a major trade route. It was a cosmopolitan city where many races met – Jews, Romans, Greeks, Persians, Central Asians, Indians – and so was an ideal location for a mission-minded church. While Jerusalem stayed entrenched in its Jewish roots, Antioch's cosmopolitan mix and missionary outlook made it far more significant in the Christian mission. God is still looking for churches that will be constantly ready to look beyond themselves.

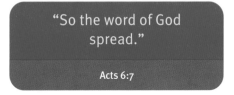

> "So the word of God spread."
>
> Acts 6:7

The need for strategy

Much of the church's success came down to Paul's missionary strategy, targeting key regional cities (eg Ephesus and Corinth) as bases for new church plants from which future evangelistic effort could develop. Still today the best missionary and evangelistic strategy is thought out rather than ad hoc, as Antioch discovered.

PAUL'S TRAVELS

PAUL'S 1st JOURNEY

Antioch
Iconium
Lystra
Derbe
Colossae
CILICIA
Tarsus
PISIDIA
Perga
Antioch
Attalia
SYRIA
CYPRUS
Salamis
Paphos

CORSICA
Rome
Three Taverns
Sea
Adri
ITALY
Puteoli
SARDINIA
Tyrrhenean
Sea
Messana
Rhegium
SICILY
Catana
Carthage
Syracuse

MALTA

AFRICA

PAUL'S FINAL VOYAGE TO ROME

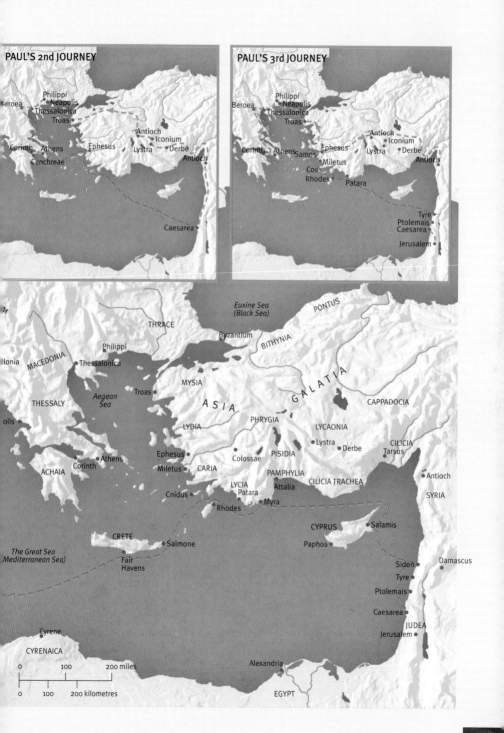

PAUL'S 2nd JOURNEY

Beroea
Philippi
Neapolis
Thessalonica
Troas

Corinth Athens
Cenchreae
Ephesus
Lystra
Iconium
Derbe
Antioch

Antioch

Caesarea

PAUL'S 3rd JOURNEY

Beroea
Philippi
Neapolis
Thessalonica
Troas

Corinth Athens
Samos
Ephesus
Miletus
Antioch
Iconium
Lystra
Derbe

Antioch

Cos
Rhodes
Patara

Tyre
Ptolemais
Caesarea

Jerusalem

Euxine Sea
(Black Sea)
PONTUS

THRACE
Byzantium
BITHYNIA

Philippi
MACEDONIA
Thessalonica

Ionia

MYSIA
GALATIA

Troas

THESSALY
Aegean
Sea
ASIA
CAPPADOCIA

olis
LYDIA
PHRYGIA
LYCAONIA

Ephesus
Lystra
Derbe
CILICIA
Tarsus

Athens
Corinth
Miletus
Colossae
PISIDIA

ACHAIA
CARIA
PAMPHYLIA
CILICIA TRACHEA

Cnidus
LYCIA
Patara
Attalia
Antioch

Rhodes
Myra
SYRIA

CRETE
Salmone
CYPRUS
Salamis

The Great Sea
(Mediterranean Sea)
Fair
Havens
Paphos

Sidon
Damascus

Tyre

Ptolemais

Caesarea

Cyrene
JUDEA
Jerusalem

CYRENAICA

Alexandria

0   100   200 miles

0   100   200 kilometres

EGYPT

Romans

THE HEART OF THE GOSPEL

OVERVIEW

In this letter Paul sets out important truths about the Christian gospel in a detailed and systematic form. Romans focuses on how sinful people can be restored to a right relationship with a holy God through the atoning death of Jesus Christ. Paul then explains how this gospel can be expressed in daily life.

SUMMARY

See handbook, p.416.

Author and date

Paul had long wanted to visit Rome (1:10-12). He planned a mission trip to Spain and intended to stop in Rome en route (15:23,24,28). Not all the Christians in Rome would have heard of him, so this is a letter of introduction setting out the insights (a spiritual gift, 1:11), that he hopes to share. Paul knew a lot about the church in Rome (1:8; 16:1-20) and expected them to encourage him too (1:12).

He probably wrote this letter while working in Corinth during his third missionary journey. He refers to Phoebe, a deacon at Cenchrea (a port for Corinth) in 16:1, and also Timothy (16:21) who we know accompanied him from Corinth to Jerusalem (15:25; Acts 20:4). This dates the letter to about AD 57. There has never been any doubt that Paul wrote it.

Background

Paul did visit Rome, but not in the way he expected. During his stay in Jerusalem he was rescued by Roman soldiers from a riot, and then arrested. He used his Roman citizenship to appeal for a fair trial before the Emperor (or Caesar) in Rome, and he was eventually taken there and kept under house arrest. This is recorded in Acts 21–28.

Rome, in Italy, was the capital of the Roman Empire which stretched across most of Europe, North Africa and the Near East. Rome was a prosperous city, housing about a million people, many of them in multi-storey apartment blocks. It had spectacular public administrative, religious, cultural and sporting buildings, some of which survive as tourist attractions today.

Rome had a large Jewish community. Visitors from Rome heard Peter preach in Jerusalem on the Day of Pentecost (Acts 2:10) and they may have been converted and formed the first church back home. Other Christians travelling to Rome would have joined and supported them later.

The Jews were expelled from Rome in about AD 50 (referred to in Acts 18:2). The historian Suetonius says this was because of riots relating to "Chrestus" – probably the Jewish community had been split by teaching about Christ. In later traditions the apostle Peter is often associated with Rome, but his precise relationship and possible visits are unrecorded in the New Testament.

OUTLINE – ROMANS

Introduction

Human sinfulness and God's judgement

Salvation by grace through faith

The new life

Questions about the people of Israel

The application of the gospel to daily life

Concluding messages

KEY THEMES – ROMANS

Human sinfulness

The letter opens with a powerful exposure of human corruption. People have an instinctive awareness of God's existence (1:19,20) and of his requirements (2:14,15). Yet everyone has chosen to go their own way ("all have sinned", 3:23). Jews (who had received God's detailed law) and non-Jews are equally guilty before God (chapter 2). As a result, the human race has gone from bad to worse and is under the judgement of God (1:21-32).

Christ's sacrifice

God has provided a wonderful answer to this impossible situation. The death of Jesus Christ is "a sacrifice of atonement" (3:24-25). Because he, a perfect man, "died for the ungodly" (5:6) he reconciled us to God (5:10). Jesus is the "second Adam". The first Adam introduced sin into the world and was the author of spiritual death. Jesus has brought forgiveness and renewal into the world and is the source of eternal life (5:12-19).

Faith's submission

This letter is about God's offer of salvation by grace, which we appropriate through faith – that is, trust in God – and not by our failed attempts to keep God's law (3:21-31). So even Abraham, the founder of the Jewish nation, was justified by faith (chapter 4) and not by his works. But the submission of faith doesn't end there. It continues through discipleship, which includes personal sacrifice to God's purposes (12:1,2) and generous and loving conduct towards both Christians and non-Christians (chapters 12–14).

God's supremacy

No one deserves God's forgiveness and salvation. We can't earn it by what we do. But God is gracious enough to offer forgiveness and eternal life as a free gift. Grace (5:15-16) is sometimes spelt out today as "God's Riches At Christ's Expense". Grace does not mean that God overlooks sin. Because of Christ's sacrifice, God remains just (punishing sin which was laid on Christ) while at the same time justifying (putting right with God) sinners who put their faith in him (3:25,26).

Israel's status

Paul was a Jew but he had become the apostle to the Gentiles (non-Jews, 1:5). Naturally, people were puzzled by the relationship of Jews to God now that the church was equally open to all races and cultures. Christianity was not a sect of Judaism but a branch that had grown from it. In chapters 9–11 Paul emphasises God's faithfulness and says that God will indeed save a remnant of Jews (9:27-29). Many will join Gentiles in God's kingdom (11:1-6,25-27).

River baptism, Portugal. Paul teaches that salvation is ours through faith in God alone. The act of baptism signals that we have been put right with God and intend to follow his way

GOD SPOKE TO THEM THROUGH ROMANS

Paul's letter to the Romans has had a profound effect on individuals and through them the church and the whole world.

Martin Luther: one of the founding fathers of the Reformation

Augustine

In the summer of 386, Augustine sat in a friend's garden. He was in tears because he lacked the will to break with the old life and begin the new. On his lap he had the book of Romans, and having read a passage, he said: "A clear light flooded my heart, and all the darkness of doubt vanished away." He became a great leader of the church and one of its most influential thinkers.

Martin Luther

In 1513, Martin Luther, an Augustinian monk and a professor at Wittenberg University, became deeply concerned about his own salvation. He thought deeply about Romans: "Night and day I studied until I grasped the truth – what being right with God really means. It is when in his loving kindness and great mercy, God makes us right with himself through our faith," he said. "From that moment I felt reborn – as if I had gone through an open door into heaven." Luther was one of the great architects of the Reformation.

St Augustine, from a medieval illuminated manuscript

John Wesley travelled around the country by horse to take the gospel to the people

John Wesley

One day in 1738, Luther's introduction to Romans was being read at a meeting in London. It was May 24 and about 8.45 in the evening. A young man in the audience, John Wesley, was very interested. The words from Luther were describing how God changes our hearts when we put our trust in Jesus Christ. John found his heart "strangely warmed". He wrote, "I felt I did trust in Christ, Christ alone for salvation. An assurance was given me that he had taken *my* sins and saved *me* from the law of sin and death." John Wesley was able to speak to many and bring many to faith in Jesus Christ.

RELEVANCE FOR TODAY – ROMANS

Powerful influence

Romans has a great influence on church history and is worth studying for that reason. Augustine (4–5th century) Martin Luther (16th century) John Wesley (18th century) and Karl Barth (20th century) all rediscovered the truths of Romans and their teaching remains powerful and relevant today.

Profound teaching

Romans is like a systematic theology. It sets out the doctrine of salvation in careful detail, explaining the relationships between Christ's death, Jewish law, God's grace and human faith. However, it has virtually nothing about the resurrection or the return of Christ, both of which are also key doctrines. Therefore, profound as it is, Romans needs to be read alongside other Bible books if we are to have a complete understanding of Christian beliefs.

Pressing questions

The question of how theology impacts on behaviour is important. Paul knew that his teaching could be misunderstood. So having explained justification by grace through faith, he asked, if God's grace is revealed because of human sin, shall we go on sinning so we can experience more divine grace? No! he says. When you trusted Christ, you died to sin so your behaviour should change (6:5-7,23).

Positive assurance

But that raises another question: I do sin, however hard I try not to! Yes, says Paul – and so do I. In chapter 7 he explains the inner battle and failure he (and everyone) experiences. The reason, he says, is that while we are being renewed by God's Spirit, we're still fallible people, so our old and new natures

> "Therefore, since we have been justified through faith, we have peace with God through our Lord Jesus Christ."
>
> **Romans 5:1**

struggle with each other. But God is great and saves us in our struggle (7:24,25). Our salvation is secure despite our failings (5:1-5) and once we are in Christ no one can condemn us (8:1,2) nor separate us from God's love (8:38,39). Indeed, God is working positively for his own purposes in all our circumstances (8:28,29).

Practical discipleship

12:1 launches one of Paul's most searching passages about personal and community conduct. Among his challenges are these:

- Stick to God's standards, not the world's (12:1,2).
- Be humble; don't pretend you're super-spiritual (12:3-8).
- Love each other sacrificially and express it by helping people (12:9-13).
- Act lovingly to people outside the church who mock or attack you (12:14-21).
- Be a good citizen, obey the law and pay your taxes (13:1-7).
- Be consistent and don't backslide into your old ways (13:8-14).
- Be gentle and considerate; don't bully or boss each other (14:1– 15:13).

1 Corinthians
ADVICE TO A DIVIDED CHURCH

OVERVIEW
The church in Corinth suffered from many problems as people who had been used to a carefree self-centred lifestyle came to terms with the demands of Christian discipleship. In this letter Paul deals with such urgent matters as personal morality, public worship, and splits in the church.

SUMMARY
Despite the difficult issues Paul needed to discuss, he opened the letter with positive greetings and thanksgiving. The first issue he tackles is that of the party strife within the church (1:10–4:21). This is followed by matters relating to sexuality and marriage (chapters 5–7), legal disputes between Christians (6:1-11), the attitude towards idolatry (chapters 8–10), women in Christian worship, the Lord's Supper (chapter 11), the use of spiritual gifts in particular in worship (chapters 12–14), and the resurrection of Jesus Christ (chapter 15). The final chapter contains brief notes on the collection for the church in Jerusalem, personal plans, and greetings.

Author and date
The New Testament contains two letters of Paul to the Corinthians. From these, it appears that he also wrote at least two others which no longer exist. Tracing the sequence of these letters helps us to understand what was going on, and to date the existing letters accurately. It seems to go like this:

- Corinthians A (now lost) written because Paul heard of serious problems. See 1 Corinthians 5:9.
- Corinthians B (our 1 Corinthians) written partly in response to questions sent to Paul by the church (1 Corinthians 7:1).
- Corinthians C (now lost), which was a sharp telling-off because the church hadn't changed (see 2 Corinthians 7:5-12).

- Corinthians D (our 2 Corinthians) written to encourage them after news came that the church had reformed. See the introduction to 2 Corinthians for more detail about this.

Between these letters a number of visits to Corinth were made by apostolic delegates who were also Paul's sources of information (for example, 1 Corinthians 16:17). From all the available evidence, it seems that 1 Corinthians was written by Paul while he was working in Ephesus, about AD 55 (16:8).

Background
Corinth was a large cosmopolitan city in southern Greece. It was well known for the loose morality of its occupants and visitors, and for the ready availability of prostitutes, most of whom were associated with religious cults. There was also great social mobility and the church was apparently quite mixed.

Corinth owed its prosperity to two ports nearby, making it a trading centre. The city that Paul visited had been built by Julius Caesar in 46 BC, after a previous city had been destroyed a century earlier.

Paul had founded the church there in about AD 51–52, and stayed there for about two years (Acts 18:11,18). This makes the Christians' behaviour even more surprising: they had received a long spell of good teaching. Paul visited them at least once again (2 Corinthians 2:1; 13:1-2) but this is not recorded in Acts.

OUTLINE – 1 CORINTHIANS

Introduction

A divided church

Matters of morality and law

Christian freedom and responsibility

Order in public worship

Christian hope and resurrection

Final comments

KEY THEMES – 1 CORINTHIANS

Church unity

The church had divided into factions each "following" a leader (1:12; 3:4). Paul says that as Christ is not divided (1:10,13), Christians should be united. Leaders are servants of God, each contributing to church development, but ultimately God alone makes the church flourish, and he is its focus of unity (3:5-9; 4:9-17).

The diversity of human talents and spiritual gifts demonstrates our interdependence in one "body of Christ". This should strengthen, rather than weaken, unity (12:12-31). In his famous description of Christian love, Paul provides a recipe for self-sacrificing unity (chapter 13).

Personal morality

Corinth was notorious for its loose sexual culture. New Christians may not change their habits overnight, but to Paul's dismay some still showed little evidence of change. This was not a matter of occasional sexual lapses, but of gross immorality. He said the church had to disassociate itself from such members (5:1-13).

Paul explained that sex unites two people in body and soul, and the body is a "temple of the Holy Spirit", so sexual relations outside marriage are wrong (6:12-20). Sex has a rightful place in marriage, and while Paul advocated celibacy for the sake of the gospel he recognised that marriage was better than burning sexual frustration (chapter 7).

Freedom and responsibility

In Corinth, most meat sold in butchers' shops had been slaughtered in cult rituals. Some Christians believed eating it was sinful. Paul disagreed, because an idol is nothing and God is supreme (8:4; 10:25,26). However, for the sake of Christians with sensitive consciences believers like him should respect their views and if necessary refrain from eating such meat. It is wrong to encourage someone with a weaker conscience to do something they feel is sinful. Paul says we should put the spiritual well-being of others first, and not insist on everyone adopting our views (10:24,31-33). This is especially relevant today where Christians disagree over cultural details.

Public worship

Paul insists that public worship events should be orderly, reflecting the orderly nature of God (14:33). In Corinth, there were two major problems:

- The Lord's Supper had degenerated into a party. At this time, the communion service recalling Christ's death on our behalf was part of a shared fellowship meal. But the rich refused to share their food with the poor, and others started before everyone had arrived. Having scolded them for disorderly conduct (11:17-22), Paul explains the origins and meaning of communion (11:23-26). Light-hearted participation is spiritually dangerous (11:27-30)
- The use of spiritual gifts such as tongues and prophecy had become self-indulgent displays. Paul provides detailed guidance for the church's worship meetings (chapter 14).

Resurrection hope

Some people could not understand the resurrection, perhaps because they were so fixated on the material elements of this life. In chapter 15 Paul explains that:

- There's no doubt Christ rose from the dead.
- Therefore people can rise from the dead, and we all shall when Christ returns at the end of time.
- Indeed, if we have nothing to look forward to in the next life, our faith is a waste of time.
- We will have a different resurrection body which won't be perishable.
- This is great news: death, our greatest "enemy", is defeated for ever!

RELEVANCE FOR TODAY – 1 CORINTHIANS

Most of the key themes of 1 Corinthians are directly relevant to major issues faced by Christians in all cultures today. They can be summed up like this:

Don't split your church over secondary matters

Such secondary matters could include the particular emphasis or method of a leader, or the way in which worship is conducted and spiritual gifts manifest. The important thing is that the basic truths of the Gospel – Christ's death and resurrection – are taught, believed and applied.

> "I did not come with eloquence or superior wisdom ... so that your faith might not rest on men's wisdom, but on God's power."
>
> 1 Corinthians 2:1, 5

Recognise God-given boundaries to sex

There are boundaries to human sexual conduct which are for the good of individuals and society as a whole. Ignoring the boundaries can lead to the disintegration of relationships and families. Christians are called to model God's standards, not to mimic the world's standards.

Put other people's interests first

This is the cardinal principle of Christian love. If you are a leader, or have a specific spiritual gift or ministry, don't use your authority or influence for personal gain. Even when you don't agree with someone's view on a secondary or cultural matter, respect it and don't rubbish the person.

Think about the impact of public worship

We are to think about the impact of our public worship on other people – both committed Christians and interested visitors. Make the most of people's special gifts but make sure everything is well conducted and honouring to God. Worship should witness to the reality and presence of God, and be intelligible to all those present.

2 Corinthians
COMFORT IN SUFFERING

OVERVIEW

The problems that Paul had dealt with in his first letter to the Corinthians had improved, so he wrote to express his relief. However, another more personal issue had arisen: Paul's integrity was being questioned. So he set out his track record of faithful discipleship and intense suffering for the Gospel.

SUMMARY

Although initially Paul received good news (chapters 1–9), it appears that one of the factions he had encountered in the church (1 Corinthians 1:10-12; 3:1-4) developed into a rival church which rejected Paul as an apostle. They were doing what people often do: they asserted their presumed superiority by rubbishing someone else (chapters 10–13). Paul was hurt. The criticism was unjustified. In response he detailed all that he had endured for Christ.

Author and date

Paul had written to the Corinthians at least three times before this letter (see the introduction to 1 Corinthians for details). This letter was probably written about AD 56, a year or so after 1 Corinthians, from northern Greece (Macedonia), which is implied in 2:12,13. In between he had paid them an unsuccessful visit (12:14; 13:1,2).

However, many scholars believe that 2 Corinthians contains two separate letters, which were probably united for convenience into a single scroll early in the history of the church. The first letter, full of encouragement and relief, is chapters 1-9. The second letter, much more downbeat, is chapters 10–13. The reason for believing this is the sharp change of tone in chapter 10. In the earlier chapters Paul had expressed his joy that his advice had been taken, an offender disciplined, and that Titus had returned from Corinth greatly encouraged (7:5-16). Paul was so delighted that he wrote "I can have complete confidence in you" (7:16)!

Sadly, his confidence was misplaced. He had heard that the Corinthians consider him weak (10:10) and foolish (11:16). His authority was being challenged by people he called "false apostles" who are agents of Satan (11:13-15). In response, he renewed his warning to unrepentant sinners (13:2-3) and challenged his readers to consider if they had left the faith (13:5).

This additional letter (Paul's fifth to Corinth) was probably sent after chapters 1–9 and the unsuccessful second visit, before Paul made his planned third visit to Corinth (13:1) which is probably implied in Acts 20:1-3.

Background

For information about the city and the church, see handbook at 1 Corinthians, p.261.

OUTLINE – 2 CORINTHIANS

A. THE LETTER OF ENCOURAGEMENT

Ministry update

1:1-2	Greetings
1:3-14	Paul's sufferings and God's consolation
1:15–2:4	Paul's travel plans after his visit to Corinth
2:5-13	Forgiveness offered to a sinner

Ministry of the new covenant

2:14–3:6	Adequacy for ministry
3:7-18	The glory of the new covenant
4:1-15	The splendour of the gospel in the midst of suffering
4:16–5:10	The inner realities and the promise of the future
5:11-21	The gospel of reconciliation

Ministry methods

6:1-13	The open style of Paul's ministry
6:14–7:1	The danger of compromise with unbelievers
7:2-16	Joy over Titus' positive report

Ministry with money

8:1-15	An encouragement to keep giving
8:16–9:5	An endorsement of Paul's helpers and the collection
9:6-15	An exhortation to generosity

B. THE LETTER OF EXHORTATION

Ministry involves suffering

10:1-18	Paul's refutations of his critics
11:1-15	An attack on the false apostles
11:16–12:10	Paul's "foolish'" boasting in weakness

Ministry fears and hopes

12:11–13:10	The third visit to Corinth
13:11-14	Concluding greetings

KEY THEMES – 2 CORINTHIANS

Paul's consistency

- **He was consistent in his plans.** Some people accused him of changing his mind about visiting them, throwing doubt on his authority. Paul explained why he changed his plans (1:12– 2:4). During the delay he continued to be anxious about them, and sent Titus to gather information (7:2-16). Later he set out his revised plans for the third visit (13:1-10).

- **He was consistent in his preaching.** Paul rarely defended or justified himself but the Corinthians' jibes forced him to. He protested that he never gained financially from his preaching (2:17; 11:8,9). He claimed that his was a God-inspired consistency and competence (3:1-6) and he never changed his message or his methods (4:1-6). In chapters 10–11 he denounced as false apostles those who spread lies about him (such as his alleged timidity in person and boldness in writing). They were preaching another gospel. He may not have been a trained preacher (11:6) but he did have the Spirit of God (3:17-18).

- **He was consistent in his patience.** Paul had been on the brink of death (1:8-9) and it was never far from him (4:7-12). He listed his troubles in 6:8-10 and expanded on them in 11:23-29. He suffered from a "thorn in the flesh" (12:1-10) which may have been a sight impediment or other physical disability. Was he bitter? No way! He knew God's help, maintained his hope, and so bore it patiently as the cost of discipleship (1:10; 4:8; 12:10).

God's comfort and glory

This letter has lots of teaching about God. It opens with praise for God's comfort (1:3-11). Paul, unselfish as ever, adds that such an experience isn't for his personal benefit alone but is meant to be shared. So too is God's glory, which shines on us and which we reflect to others around us (4:16-18). That thought leads Paul into a joyful section on the hope of heaven (5:1-10) before he later praises God again for his support in the most amazing and horrific situations (12:7-10).

Churches' charity

Giving money is often a touchy subject, but Paul wasn't afraid to broach it. He commended the Macedonian churches which were a great example to everyone for their sacrificial giving to mission and the relief of suffering. And then he says that the Corinthians, who some while before had also proved very generous, should continue to give as evidence of their genuine love for the Lord (chapters 8–9).

RELEVANCE FOR TODAY – 2 CORINTHIANS

Submit gently

Paul's robust defence of his ministry has a subtle undercurrent. All the time, he is urging people to be humble and not self-assertive, to be gentle with each other rather than boasting about their achievements. You see this especially in 10:12-18 where he refuses to compare himself with others. Making comparisons can either depress us (because we can't match their achievement) or make us feel proud because we think we're better than they are. What's important, he says in 10:18, is God's commendation. Our aim is to please God, not gain a human reputation. That means submitting to him and fulfilling our calling.

Start again

Paul's teaching about reconciliation in 5:1–6:2 is often used in evangelistic talks, but it applies equally to believers as to unbelievers. The answer to disunity in society or the church is to seek reconciliation. God is the great reconciler: through Christ's death sinful people have been brought into fellowship with a holy God, and Christians now share in his work of reconciliation. "We are ... Christ's ambassadors" (5:20). Amazing: each Christian is a valued diplomat in God's service with the special task of bringing peace where there is dissension. We can start again after a row; and so can others, with Christ's help.

> ## "We live by faith, not by sight."
>
> 2 Corinthians 5:7

Share generously

How we hate to part with our worldly wealth and goods! But it isn't ours, it's God's. He gives us all we have, and all we need; we won't suffer if we give some away (9:8-11). Paul's memorable phrases are easy to repeat and hard to apply: "God loves a cheerful giver" (9:7); though Jesus "was rich, yet for your sakes he became poor" (8:9) – thus giving us an example to follow. You can't be expected to give what you haven't got, Paul adds (8:12). And he challenges the attitude which applauds the accumulation of wealth at others' expense, suggesting that God's will is equality and "enough" for all (8:13-15). He is surely angry at the inequality in the world today.

Suffer graciously

Christianity does not bring a prosperity gospel but realism. Paul knits his persecution for the gospel with his "thorn in the flesh" into a single thought: we all suffer. His positive attitude refuses to allow his faith to be rocked by personal discomfort. It is a great example in our age that expects quick fixes for all ills. God is bigger than our pain. And yes, Paul prayed to be free of it. But when he wasn't, he accepted the verdict and carried on serving, expecting a better life in the future.

Galatians
THE GOSPEL OF FREEDOM

OVERVIEW
The churches to which this letter is addressed had caved in to teachers who said that you cannot be a Christian unless you also observe the Jewish ceremonial law. Paul wrote to correct this "false gospel". He said it led to spiritual slavery, in contrast to the freedom brought by the death of Jesus Christ and the indwelling presence of the Holy Spirit.

SUMMARY
Whereas most of Paul's letters begin with praise to God and thanksgiving for the readers and their faith, Galatians has only a short introduction (1:1-5) after which Paul immediately goes on the attack and states his point: what others after him have preached in Galatia is not the true Gospel (1:6-9). He takes much time to establish his credentials as an apostle, the credentials of the Gospel that he received from Jesus Christ himself (1:10–2:10). He recalls an earlier controversy over the issue of the law, an incident in Syrian Antioch which brought him head to head with his fellow apostle Peter (2:11-14), and he rounds off the first part of the letter with a statement of the Gospel (2:15-21).

A second round of polemics begins with the blunt address "you foolish Galatians" and continues to remind them of the work of the Holy Spirit among them as evidence for the truth of the Gospel as preached by Paul (3:1-5). Twice Abraham is introduced as an example of true faith (3:6-14,15-18). Paul explains that the role of the law was to prepare the Jewish people for the Gospel (3:19-29) so that Christians by definition are not subject to it (4:1-7). A series of personal utterances of concern for the readers follows in 4:8-20, underscored once more with reference to Abraham, this time in relation to his wives Hagar and Sarah (4:21-31). 5:2-6 applies the entire argument to the specific issue of circumcision and 5:7-12 is one more personal appeal. A discussion of the relation between the law and the freedom in the Spirit follows in 5:13-26, with 6:1-10 offering practical suggestions for mutual relations within the fellowship. A final time Paul sums up his appeal (6:11-15) before he closes with a few words of blessing (6:16,18).

Author and date
This letter includes the themes and emphases that are a common feature of Paul's ministry and writings. What is less certain is to whom it was addressed and when it was written.

In Paul's time, two areas were called "Galatia", both within modern Turkey.

The most likely view is that Paul wrote to churches in the Roman administrative area called Galatia, in the south. Here were the cities of Antioch, Iconium, Lystra and Derbe which Paul visited and where he started churches (Acts 13–14). That makes Galatians the earliest of Paul's letters, probably written about AD 47–48 soon after his visit (1:6). He doesn't mention the Council of Jerusalem (Acts 15) which was about AD 48–49, and which he would have referred to had it happened because it strongly supported his position. Alternatively, Paul may have written to people in the north of the region at a later date (c. AD 55).

Background
The Jewish people had been given laws in the Old Testament, to which their leaders had added still more detailed legislation. Now that

non-Jews came to faith in the God of Israel, it was logical to assume that they too should abide by these rules. Yet God had revealed to Paul that he accepts believers in Jesus Christ without observance of the law. This was the gospel Paul preached but his adversaries wanted to make all Christians subject to the law. They had arrived in the new churches soon after Paul had departed (1:6-9).

OUTLINE – GALATIANS

The problem stated

Paul's credentials

Theological arguments against legalism

Theological arguments for Christian freedom

The joy and responsibility of Christian freedom

KEY THEMES – GALATIANS

Paul's personal experience

What we know about Paul's life from Acts 8–14 is supplemented in Galatians. He describes what happened after his conversion: his visits to Arabia and Damascus (1:14-17; Acts 9:19-25), then Jerusalem (1:18; Acts 9:26-30). His time in Syria (1:21) probably refers to Tarsus, which is where Barnabas found him and drew him into a wider ministry (Acts 11:22-26).

The visit to Jerusalem in 2:1 is probably that of Acts 11:27. There, the other apostles accepted Paul's ministry to the Gentiles without imposing Jewish regulations (2:1-10), a decision later reinforced by the Council of Jerusalem (Acts 15). His argument with Peter (2:11-21) is unrecorded in Acts and is ironic because it was Peter who was first convinced of God's acceptance of Gentiles (Acts 10:1–11:18). It's a complex jigsaw, but it does fit together!

The promise of salvation

Paul stresses that God's approval and our eternal salvation is mediated only by Jesus Christ and depends on faith in Christ, not on fulfilment of religious regulations (eg 2:15-16,20-21). No one kept all the Old Testament rules anyway so that all were under God's curse (3:10). Jesus took this curse on himself so that by trusting in his atoning death and resurrection we can be saved (3:11-14). As a result, all racial and cultural distinctions are swept aside and all believers are on an equal footing (3:26-29).

The purpose of the law

By "the law" Paul means the Jewish ceremonial law, not the moral law summed up in the Ten Commandments. The rules about food, methods of worship, and certain cultural matters are no longer compulsory. He uses the shorthand "circumcision" (5:6) to mean the whole ceremonial law, because that aspect of it was a key part of the false apostles' teaching.

However, Old Testament people weren't misguided. The law gave them a framework for understanding and relating to God while faith was in its infancy, like a guardian protecting them until the full revelation of Christ (3:19–4:7). The law points forward to Christ and is fulfilled by him.

God's power for living

We're free to be the people God intended us to be, without being enslaved to the burden of having to fulfil meticulous religious rituals! Such freedom is also what Jesus taught (John 8:31-36). We have been adopted into God's family. We're no longer domestic servants; we're heirs of the Father (4:4-11; 5:1). We have a new dynamic, God's Holy Spirit, and a new responsibility – to live in harmony with and obedience to our loving God (5:13-26).

RELEVANCE FOR TODAY – GALATIANS

Avoid legalism

An important part of biblical interpretation is to look for the principles behind the teachings. In Galatians, the principle is "legalism": the insistence that every Christian should conform to certain rituals or practices.

Such practices vary hugely from culture to culture, however! For some Christians, not drinking alcohol is almost an article of faith; for others, it is a natural thing to do, provided it isn't taken to excess. The problem is that such regulations can become "primary" issues that define a Christian. The only primary issues that Scripture allows are those which Paul emphasises in Galatians: the life, death and resurrection of Christ. If our faith is firmly in those, then issues not directly associated with the moral law are "secondary" matters over which we may disagree, but should not divide.

Argue carefully

Paul's arguments in 3:15-19 and 4:21-31 can be puzzling. Paul was a Jewish rabbi, and in this letter was combating people from a Jewish background. Therefore he uses the allegories and accepted Jewish beliefs of his day to show that his teaching isn't contrary to God's word.

This is a good example to follow. In our discussions with people from many backgrounds, it is important to start where they are in their understanding and background knowledge. We may be able to find points of contact, as Paul did, which lead people towards a fresh and more complete understanding of the gospel. Indeed, this is the main principle of cross-cultural mission.

Act consistently

The argument with Peter (2:11-21) illustrates a common problem. We believe we should act in a certain way, but cave in under pressure and don't act consistently. That Peter could fall this way may be some comfort; everyone is vulnerable. That is why at the end of the letter Paul stresses the need to "live by the Spirit" (5:16). The Holy Spirit can give us the courage to be consistent when our human hearts fail us.

THE GOSPEL SPREADS

One effect of persecution – driving Christians away – plus missionary work by the apostles and others combined to spread the gospel throughout the Roman world and eventually beyond.

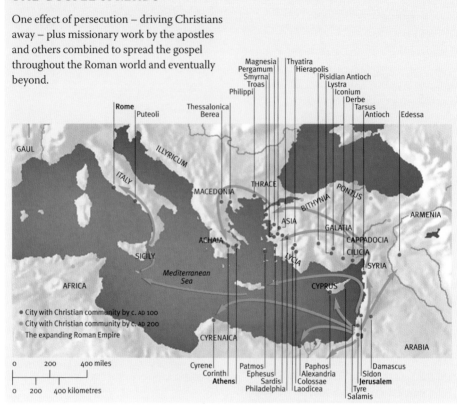

Magnesia | Thyatira
Pergamum | Hierapolis
Smyrna | Pisidian Antioch
Troas | Lystra
Philippi | Iconium
| Derbe
Rome | Thessalonica | Tarsus
Puteoli | Berea | Antioch | Edessa

GAUL
ILLYRICUM
ITALY
MACEDONIA
THRACE
PONTUS
ASIA
BITHYNIA
ARMENIA
GALATIA
ACHAIA
CAPPADOCIA
SICILY
LYCIA
CILICIA
SYRIA
Mediterranean Sea
AFRICA
CYPRUS

- City with Christian community by c. AD 100
- City with Christian community by c. AD 200
- The expanding Roman Empire

CYRENAICA
ARABIA

0   200   400 miles

0   200   400 kilometres

Cyrene | Patmos | Paphos | Damascus
Corinth | Ephesus | Alexandria | Sidon
Athens | Sardis | Colossae | Jerusalem
Philadelphia | Laodicea | Tyre
| Salamis

Apply the gospel

Christianity is a framework for living. Paul sets out the difference between "the acts of the sinful nature" (what human beings tend towards) and "the fruit of the Spirit" which is a list of virtues reflecting God's character being formed in us (5:19-26). It's a challenging list. Jealousy, rage and envy afflict all of us even if immorality and idolatry don't. None of us can read Galatians 5 lightly. The world around us expects us to demonstrate the fruit of the Spirit – and so does God.

> "I have been crucified with Christ and I no longer live, but Christ lives in me."
>
> Galatians 2:20

Ephesians
INSPIRED BY GOD'S ETERNAL PURPOSES

OVERVIEW

Ephesians is full of inspiring language. It describes God's eternal purposes for the rescue of humanity from the clutches of sin and death through the death and resurrection of Jesus Christ. Punctuated by prayers and praises, it urges readers to live out in practice the changed life that God has graciously given them.

SUMMARY

Ephesians falls neatly into two equal parts: chapters 1–3 have a doctrinal content whereas chapters 4–6 are ethical. The letter includes many topics which would have been covered in an introduction to the Christian faith but at quite a high level.

After a brief introduction and greetings (1:1-2) Paul praises the grace of God in Jesus Christ, then he mentions the Holy Spirit (1:13,14). The second half of chapter 1 addresses God directly in prayer, asking for the work of the Holy Spirit and for certainty of the believers' hope of the future. In chapter 2 attention shifts further to the position of the believers, with verses 1-10 spelling out how they were saved and verses 11-22 explaining that they belong to God's holy people, the church which consists of believers from Jewish and Gentile backgrounds. Paul then discusses the contribution of his own ministry to the church (3:1-13) and prays once more for it (3:14-21).

The second half of the letter addresses the unity, growth and development of the church (4:1-16) before it moves on to the individual believer. Here Paul considers the consequences of being a Christian. Specific topics include the roles of husband and wife (5:21-33) and other groups (6:9). The letter ends with a discussion of spiritual armour (6:10-20) and the usual personal notes and blessings (6:21-24).

Author

Ephesians is unlike any of Paul's other letters. It contains few personal reflections or greetings, apart from identifying the author as Paul (1:1, 3:1) and the final mention of Paul's messenger Tychicus (6:21,22). The subject matter is typically that of Paul, but the language is not. The original Greek contains over 40 words not used anywhere else in the New Testament, and a similar number of other words used in the New Testament but never in Paul's other letters. However, the early church accepted Paul's authorship without question. The language differences could be due to a different scribe taking Paul's dictation, and no real alternative to Paul has ever been suggested.

Date

The lack of personal data makes it difficult to date Ephesians, but it was clearly written while Paul was in prison (3:1,13; 4:1; 6:20). Ephesians has a number of similarities to Colossians, although the ideas are more developed in Ephesians and were therefore probably written after Colossians. But it probably wasn't long after, as it is usually grouped with Colossians, Philippians and Philemon as the four "prison epistles" written by Paul when he was under house arrest in Rome (see Acts 28:16,30,31), about AD 60.

Background

This "letter" is more like a sermon, an inspirational talk at a conference, or even an essay, rather than a personal letter. Paul doesn't deal with any specific issues in the local church, as he does in his other letters. The destination of Ephesus (1:1) is missing from some important early copies which has led scholars to suggest that 'Ephesians' was a circular letter (with perhaps several copies being sent at the same time) which was taken around the churches of Asia Minor (modern Turkey). Ephesus was the chief city in the area at that time. Paul wrote the letter to encourage Christians to persevere in their faith and to remind them of some basic truths and responsibilities of being a Christian.

OUTLINE – EPHESIANS

KEY THEMES – EPHESIANS

Chosen people

Paul focuses on the idea of adoption (1:5) to stress the privilege of belonging to God. Roman citizens adopted sons not because they were orphaned but because they had potential as servants. Jews went further: they gave adopted children the full rights and benefits of natural children. Christians are chosen by God because he recognises our worth, and gives us full rights in his worldwide family.

The benefits are huge:

- sharing in the limitless riches of heaven (1:3,4)
- enjoying the freedom and forgiveness of grace (1:7,8)
- receiving insight into God's purposes (1:9,10)
- being integrated into God's plans and family (1:11,12)
- receiving the Holy Spirit as a sign of God's faithfulness (1:13,14).

And that's just the start! This is more than a theological principle; it's a living experience. Paul prays that we will feel and know this dynamic love and living presence of God (3:16-19).

Changed lives

Becoming a Christian is a wholesale change of life. It starts on the inside – a complete re-orientation of heart and mind – and is expressed in a radically new lifestyle. Paul describes the inner change in stark terms in 2:1-10. However "alive" we felt in our pre-Christian state, we were in fact dead to God and alienated from his heavenly riches. But out of his grace, through no merit or effort of our own, he made us alive: a spiritual resurrection. There is no greater contrast than life and death: that is the magnitude of the change.

With the privilege comes responsibility. We are not saved *through* our good deeds but we are saved *in order to do* good deeds and express God's life to others in the world (2:9,10). Paul describes the duties of the Christian in 4:17–6:23. The old self has been put off (4:22-24), and so our speech, work, and relationships are all to be transformed (4:25-32). Out goes impurity and immorality (5:3-7) and in comes the renewal of the Spirit (5:15-20), with the requirement to be considerate rather than selfish in relationships (5:22–6:9).

Church unity

How can people from different cultures work and worship together? In God's purposes there is no longer a distinction between Jew and Gentile: racism and cultural superiority of one group over another is banished for ever (2:11-18). We are all part of the same "temple" (2:19-22), and God has given the church gifted people to help maintain the unity of the Spirit (4:1-16).

RELEVANCE FOR TODAY – EPHESIANS

> "For it is by grace you have been saved through faith – and this not from yourselves, it is the gift of God – not by works, so that no-one can boast."
>
> Ephesians 2:8-9

How to pray for others

Ephesians contains two of Paul's prayers which are a great example to follow when we pray for other people. In 1:15-19 he:

- Thanks God for them
- Asks that they may have wisdom
- Prays they will know God better
- Prays that they will know real hope and experience God's power.

In the second, 3:14-19 (it concludes in 3:20,21 with a doxology that is often used at the end of worship services), Paul:

- Expresses adoration of God
- Prays for the inner spiritual strengthening of his readers
- Prays that they will be totally loving
- Asks that their understanding of Christ's love will be complete
- Prays that they will be filled with the fullness of God.

How to live in harmony

Conflicts easily arise through "personality clashes". These are not really any different from the racial and cultural clashes that Paul refers to. The secret of dealing with them is for both sides to recognise their unity in Christ. Through him we have been reconciled to each other as well as to God (2:14-22).

The key to putting unity into practice is love. If we love God, we should be able to deal lovingly with other members of the body of Christ. In 4:25–6:9 Paul notes some principles:

- Share your possessions (4:28)
- Talk positively, not negatively (4:29)
- Control your temper and learn to forgive (4:31,32)
- Be humble and submit to each other (5:21)
- Let mutual love rule in the home (5:33)
- Treat workers well and don't antagonise employers (6:5-9).

How to witness in the world

The world watches to see if we reflect the life of God that we speak about. So honest work (4:28), being kind rather than nasty to or about people (4:31,32), avoiding immorality and impurity (5:3-7) and drunkenness (5:18) are vital components of effective witness.

How to deal with the devil

There is a malignant spiritual power seeking to destroy the work of God. But the power of God is much stronger, and in God's armoury Christians have all they need to resist attack and defeat the enemy. The passage about the armour of God (6:10-18) draws on the image of a Roman soldier (to whom, perhaps, Paul was chained in prison) and he repeats his confident assertions to stand firm and keep praying!

Philippians
JOY IN CHRIST

OVERVIEW

Paul wrote this letter for two reasons. He wanted to thank the Christians in Philippi for a gift they had sent him (4:10), and to commend to them Timothy (2:19-24) and Epaphroditus (2:25-30), whom he was sending to Philippi. Paul also updates his readers on his current news. He includes a poem about the divinity of Christ which is one of the most famous New Testament passages.

SUMMARY

After the usual greetings, Paul begins with a warm thanksgiving to God for the church and its faith, which leads to a prayer that their love will increase even further (1:1-11). He then gives ample attention to his personal circumstances (1:12-26). It is unclear to him if he will be released or convicted, but he is open to both possibilities. Paul next encourages the readers to lead worthy lives, despite the fact that they also have to cope with some form of persecution (1:30). His appeal becomes more specific when he sets Jesus Christ as an example of humility and readiness to serve (2:1-18). The letter seems to be coming to a close with Paul's announcement that he will send Timothy to Philippi and also hopes to come in person (2:19-24). First, however, Paul will send Epaphroditus back to his home town, presumably with the letter (2:25-30). Both missionaries are warmly commended. The phrase beginning with "Finally" (3:1) could be the letter's final line, but for some reason Paul continues with some warnings against unspecified troublemakers mixed with testimonies about his own faith (3:1–4:1). Whereas they are proud of their achievements, Paul refuses to boast; he puts all his trust in Jesus Christ. A few specific exhortations follow (4:2-9) before Paul discusses the relation between the church and himself (4:10-20) and concludes the letter with warm greetings.

Author and date

There has never been any doubt that the apostle Paul wrote this letter. It contains a number of personal references which tie it in with other New Testament writings and with what we already know of Paul.

However, the date at which he wrote it is unclear, because scholars are divided over where he wrote it from. Clearly, Paul was in prison (see 1:7,13,14). Many believe that this refers to his house arrest in Rome (Acts 28:16), which dates the letter at about AD 61. This would link Philippians with Ephesians, Colossians and Philemon as the four "prison epistles" written by Paul from Rome.

But there are also some good reasons for suggesting that he wrote it when he was in prison in Caesarea before being transported to Rome. That would date the letter about AD 58–59. A third view is that he was imprisoned in Ephesus about AD 53–55, but this is deduced from inferences in the New Testament; there is no direct evidence that such an imprisonment actually happened.

Background

There was a strong bond of friendship and love between the Philippian Christians and Paul, which comes across in the letter. He had not spent a long time with them, but they had taken him to their hearts and continued to support his ministry.

Philippi was a prosperous city in

>>> Macedonia (modern north-eastern Greece). A Roman colony, it was organised by the Romans as if it was a city on Italian soil. Paul went there, having seen a vision of "a man of Macedonia" begging him to preach the Gospel (Acts 16:9-12). Some scholars believe this man to have been Luke, the author of Acts, who then began to accompany Paul on his travels as can be seen from the "we" form in Acts 16:10,11.

Paul had started preaching to the strong Jewish community in Philippi when he arrived (Acts 16:13). The conversion to Christ of a fortune teller stirred up opposition and Paul and Silas (his companion) were jailed. Released by an earthquake, they were pardoned by the authorities who had not realised that the apostles were also Roman citizens (Acts 16:35-40).

OUTLINE – PHILIPPIANS

Personal reflections

Follow the example of Christ

Keep the faith

Thank you for your fellowship

KEY THEMES – PHILIPPIANS

Delight in fellowship

Paul was a pioneer church planter who was always on the move, but he also had a deep pastoral heart for the churches he had started. This short letter is full of pastoral concern for, and encouragement to, people he clearly loves:

"I long for all of you with the affection of Jesus Christ" (1:8).

He recalls his joy at their response to the gospel and their work with him (1:3-8) and prays for their continued spiritual growth (1:9-11). He urges them to remain united in

fellowship, caring for one another (2:1-4; 4:2,3), not complaining (2:14-18).

Above all, he is delighted at the gift of money they sent to help him survive. He thanks them for it and for what it represents: a loving act of fellowship to a fellow Christian who is in trouble far away (4:10-20).

Determination to keep going

When Paul had been imprisoned in Philippi he had praised God, rather than cursing his luck (Acts 16:25). Now suffering a longer sentence, he continues that example. He has witnessed to soldiers and visitors, and encouraged local Christians to be bold (1:12-18).

Always optimistic, he hopes to carry on serving Christ, and expects to visit Philippi again (1:19-30). In a memorable passage, he announces his determination never to rest on his achievements. His Jewish background had prepared him for Christ, but is now superseded (3:1-11). Paul has a great passion for Christ: he longs to know him more and more (3:8-10). He realises that he still has more to learn, do, and discover: so he presses on (3:12-15).

Coming out of church, Burkina Faso. Paul was a great believer in the importance of the local church

Divinity of Christ

In a great hymn, Paul sets out the uniqueness of Christ's divinity (2:5-11). He shows that Jesus gave up the glory of heaven in order to live as a human being. Jesus obeyed God by accepting a humiliating death, and is now exalted to the highest place in heaven as ruler of all. The context of the hymn shows that Paul sets Christ as an example for all believers.

Desire for news

Paul was never "parochial" nor was he a "hit and run" preacher! He was always keen to exchange news with other churches. So here, he tells the Philippians his news, to encourage them (1:12-26). Then he prepares them to receive his assistants Timothy and Epaphroditus (2:19-30), clearly expecting Timothy to bring back to him news of how the Philippians are faring (2:19).

RELEVANCE FOR TODAY – PHILIPPIANS

Coping with pressure

Paul's positive outlook while physically chained to a Roman guard is an example and inspiration to anyone who is facing pressure or feeling "chained" to a situation they would prefer not to be in. The whole letter revolves around this. Paul sees every situation as an opportunity to witness for Christ (1:12). He is clearly aware that God is present with him always to support and inspire him. He knows Christ will give him strength in everything (4:13) and provide for all their needs (4:19).

Living purely

The Philippians were under pressure as well (1:29,30). We can be tempted to compromise our faith and act in ways that do not honour Christ. Paul urged his readers to maintain the highest standards always (1:27). Among the risks he warns against are lapsing into selfishness (2:3), giving up (2:12), arguing among ourselves (2:14,15), and letting our minds be dragged down to the world's level (4:8,9).

Maintaining priorities

Christians have two key priorities. We are to maintain our relationship with, and worship of, God. A person under pressure can become depressed and self-pitying. So Paul tells us to rejoice in who God is and what Christ has done and is doing (1:18; 3:1; 4:4) because praise liberates the spirit if not the body.

He urges the Philippians to pray for and about everything, knowing that they will receive peace of mind as a result (4:6,7). He values their intercession and believes that such prayer will be answered positively (1:19).

> "I press on towards the goal to win the prize for which God has called me heavenwards in Christ Jesus."
>
> **Philippians 3:14**

A second priority is to maintain good relationships with other Christians. Divisions can easily occur but they hinder the gospel (2:14,15). Paul identifies a running feud in the church, asking not only that the people involved will be reconciled but also that others will actively help them (4:2,3). Real unity means giving practical support as well as enjoying spiritual fellowship (2:1-4).

Keeping perspectives

Life on earth is important: everyone has work to do for God. But Paul also knows that life with God after death will be even better. At times, he would rather welcome death, but he recognises that it's not yet God's time – so he decides to carrying on working (1:20-26), and thus sets an example for all. This is further emphasised in 3:12-15. Knowing that there is more to do and discover, looking forward to the end, helps us see today's pressures in God's eternal perspective.

Colossians and Philemon

JESUS CHRIST IS LORD OF ALL

OVERVIEW

The thriving church in Colossae was being diverted from the Gospel by some "superspiritual" teachers who claimed insight into additional "mysteries". Paul sought to correct that error in Colossians, and at the same time wrote separately to a friend (Philemon) in that church concerning a runaway slave who had become a Christian.
Note: references are to Colossians, except where stated.

Author and date
Paul's authorship of these two letters has rarely been questioned, and most scholars continue to agree that they are genuinely from him.

Both letters were written from prison (4:10,18; Philemon 9,10,23). This was almost certainly Paul's house arrest in Rome (Acts 28:16,20), which dates the letters from about AD 60. This was the same period as for the other "prison epistles", Ephesians and Philippians.

Background
Paul had not visited Colossae as far as we know. The church there began as a result of Paul's ministry in Ephesus (Acts 19:1-12). One of the converts there was Epaphras, who took the Gospel back to his home city of Colossae (1:7; 4:12,13; Philemon 23).

Colossae was about 110 miles east of Ephesus. It had once been a prosperous city on an important trade route. But by this time it was declining because the trade route had shifted north to nearby Laodicea which was becoming richer as a result (see Revelation 3:17). Laodicea is mentioned in 4:13,16 as having had a letter from Paul which is now lost.

Philemon, an inhabitant of Colossae and a church member, like many people at the time owned a slave called Onesimus. He had run away, found his way to Rome, and in prison there had heard Paul preach and had become a Christian. The letter contains Paul's plea for Philemon to be merciful to the returning and repentant slave. (It would have been customary to torture or execute him.)

SUMMARY

Colossians
After the formal opening salutation (1:1-2), Paul gives his attention to the faith of the church, indicating that he both thanks and prays for it. His reference to salvation by Christ in 1:14 brings him to a hymn in praise of Christ (1:15-20), which he subsequently applies to the readers. In 1:24–2:7 he discusses his own efforts as messenger of the good news

about Christ; the final two verses of this passage are transitional as Paul moves on to the issues at stake in the church which he discusses in 2:8-23, the central passage of the letter. The second half of the letter is the practical application. In 3:1-17 we find general guidance for the life in Christ in contrast to the readers' old lifestyle, followed in 3:18–4:6 by specific guidance for different groups of people. Finally, 4:7-18 consists of greetings and personal notes.

Philemon

In his letter, Paul plays on the meaning of the name Onesimus, which means "useful" (Philemon verse 11): "Formerly he was useless to you, but now he has become useful both to you and to me."

It is possible that this Onesimus is the same Onesimus who was bishop of Ephesus, whom Ignatius, the bishop of Antioch early in the second century AD, mentioned in a letter, even referring to the same pun on the meaning of his name "Useful" ... so it may be that the runaway slave became a bishop!

OUTLINES

COLOSSIANS

Introduction

1:1,2	Greetings
1:3-8	Thanksgiving for their faith
1:9-14	A prayer for the Colossians

Jesus Christ is Lord

1:15-20	A hymn of praise about Christ's greatness
1:21-23	Practical applications
1:24–2:5	Paul's work for the church

False teachers refuted

2:6-19	Warnings against false teachings
2:20-23	An analysis of the false teaching at Colossae

Live out your faith

3:1-17	The old self and the new
3:18–4:1	Rules for Christian households
4:2-6	Further instructions for Christian living
4:7-18	Final greetings

PHILEMON

1-3	Introduction and greeting
4-7	Thanksgiving and prayer
8-21	Paul's plea for Onesimus
23-25	Final greetings and blessing

KEY THEMES

Christ's supremacy

Colossians 1:15-20 contains one of Paul's two great hymn summaries of the person and work of Christ (the other is in Philippians 2:6-11). His precise language lifts readers into worship and praise and stresses truths of cosmic dimensions:

- Christ is the exact human representation of the eternal God (1:15) and is himself fully God (1:19)
- He is the creator of everything (1:16)
- He sustains the whole universe (1:17)
- He rose from the dead and is Lord of the church (1:18)
- His redemption embraces the whole of creation (1:20).

Paul also teaches about Christ's rescue of us from sin and death in 1:13 and God's sovereign choice of Gentiles as well as Jews to share in his riches (1:27). Some of these truths are repeated in 2:9-15.

Colossians' heresy

This is not identical with any heresy known by name but we learn a lot about it by the way Paul refutes it. It suggested (2:2-4) there were deep spiritual mysteries to which the teachers had access (perhaps like some eastern mysticism today). It advocated harsh personal discipline or asceticism with restrictions on food and sex (2:21-23). There were detailed rules about worship ceremonies and an unhealthy interest in angels (2:16,18). Paul said it was deceptive (2:8); it sounds like a "pick and mix" religion of works intended to influence spiritual powers.

Christian holiness

Paul never teaches theology without also encouraging its application in daily life. So he gives the whole of chapter 3 to the marks of Christian living. In 3:12-17 he lists virtues we are to embrace, from compassion to forgiveness. They are in stark contrast to the vices we are to avoid (3:5-9). Note there that greed is identified with idolatry (3:5), something which people in western countries especially tend to overlook.

Charity for a slave

In a fascinating insight into Christian ethics, Paul urges Philemon to be merciful to the runaway slave Onesimus who had become a Christian (Philemon 10). Paul was doing the right thing in sending Onesimus back, even though Paul could make use of him (Philemon 11-14) and Philemon might punish him. So Paul calls on Philemon's sense of Christian forgiveness to welcome Onesimus back as a brother (Philemon 15-16). Paul then offers to pay personally any compensation for the slave's absence which Philemon might require (Philemon 18). That's Christian charity. The fact that the letter was preserved suggests that Philemon accepted it!

RELEVANCE FOR TODAY

Focus on the big picture

Paul's treatment of the Colossian heresy is very instructive. He focuses first on Jesus Christ and shows us exactly who he is. Then he deals with the heresy in some detail. This method reminds us that it is very easy to lose sight of the big picture – the main truths about God and Jesus – by becoming side-tracked by speculations, traditions, and debates about secondary issues. Human ideas won't last (2:22), but Jesus is eternal (1:18). So we focus on the main truths about Jesus (3:1,2) in order to keep everything else in perspective. That makes it much easier to assess the truth or otherwise of fresh ideas.

Fulfil your calling

If we set our minds on Jesus (3:1,2) we will begin to see how we are to live in the world. Notice in ch. 3 that Paul shows an act of will is involved in changing our behaviour. The supernatural inner change brought by the Holy Spirit is ongoing: our nature is being renewed (3:10). It's not fully renewed yet. Therefore Paul urges deliberate actions: put to death (3:5), rid yourself (3:8), don't lie (3:9), clothe yourselves (3:12). Discipleship is a partnership; God changes us only as far as we will allow him to.

Find purpose in your work

For some Christians, work in the secular world is a necessary drudge, but not the "real" work of the gospel. Paul would disagree. In 3:17, 23 he restores to human work the dignity and purpose with which God originally endowed it (see also Genesis 2:15). All work can be done for the Lord, he says. It follows that slaves (employees) should do their best for their

> "[Jesus Christ] is the image of the invisible God, the firstborn over all creation."
>
> **Colossians 1:15**

masters (employers) and staff should be treated by their bosses with respect and fairness (3:22–4:1). Being a good worker or boss is part of Christian witness in the world (4:5).

Friends are to be valued

Paul was very mobile – unusual in his day, but common in ours. He moved around a lot, made friends and moved on. But he kept in touch with them, and prayed for them. Tychicus had a special role as a messenger, keeping everyone in touch (4:7-9). The list of greetings and comments in 4:10-15 is not one to gloss over. These were valued people. Their mention tells us they were valued by God as well as Paul. God values those we no longer see, too; remembering them in prayer draws us closer together in the body of Christ.

Early-morning commuters, Paris. Paul taught that all work can be done for the Lord so should be done with all our heart

1 Thessalonians
KEEP UP THE GOOD WORK

OVERVIEW
The church in Thessalonica was a joy to Paul. He wrote to encourage the Christians to continue to be a shining witness to Christ despite their suffering. The letter contains many personal comments and deals with issues about Christ's return which were confusing some people.

SUMMARY
After the usual greetings, Paul brings thanks to God for the change in the readers from pagans to followers of Jesus Christ. The example of their conversion and Christian lifestyle has become known in other places and they eagerly await Christ's return (chapter 1). Paul then rehearses his time in the city, emphasises his friendly relationship with the readers, and lays his personal behavior down as an example (2:1-16). He tells how, unable to travel himself (2:18), he sent his co-worker Timothy back to Thessalonica and how he rejoiced when Timothy came back with positive information about the faith of the congregation (2:17–3:13). A section with mixed practical instructions introduces the second half of the letter (4:1-12). Subsequently Paul addresses a particular concern of the congregation about the death of some their members (4:13-18) and adds more general instructions about how to prepare for the return of Jesus (5:1-11). The final teaching is again more general (5:12-22). Good wishes and a blessing bring the letter to a close (5:23-28).

Author and date
Paul's authorship has been accepted throughout church history. The letter has all the hallmarks of Paul's ministry and teaching. It was probably written in AD 50–51, making it one of the earliest of Paul's letters. (Galatians was probably the first.) Paul wrote it while he was staying in Corinth (Acts 18). It is possible to be precise about the date and place because Paul's movements at this time are easy to pinpoint by comparing various New Testament passages (see below).

Background
Paul visited Thessalonica after fleeing Philippi on his second missionary journey. His time there is described in Acts 17:1-10. There was a good response to his preaching, especially among the majority Gentile population (Acts 17:4). However, he had begun preaching to Jews (as was his custom) and jealous Jews stirred up trouble and he had to flee (Acts 17:5-10). Acts 17:2 may imply he was only there for three weeks, but the time gap between verses 4 and 5 in that chapter could be longer than that.

From Thessalonica Paul went to Berea (Acts 17:10-15) then Athens (Acts 17:16-24) and finally Corinth (Acts 18:1). During this time Timothy was sent back to Thessalonica (3:2,6; Acts 17:15; 18:5). Timothy's report prompted Paul to write this letter.

We know that Paul was in Corinth AD 50–51 because Acts 18:12 mentions Gallio as being the proconsul there at the time. An inscription found at the site of the city confirms that Gallio was indeed there for that year.

Unlike many New Testament cities, Thessalonica still exists and flourishes today. It is in north-eastern Greece. In Paul's time it was home to about 200,000 people. It was set at the junction of two major trade routes and had a fine harbour. It provides a good example of how Paul chose strategic locations for his ministry. Thessalonica drew many visitors and travellers from a wide area; those who responded to the gospel there would take it wherever they travelled (see 1:8)

OUTLINE – 1 THESSALONIANS

The church as it is

Paul's concern for the church

How to live for Jesus Christ: part one

Issues about Jesus Christ's return

How to live for Jesus Christ: part two

KEY THEMES – 1 THESSALONIANS

Paul's example

The apostle reminds his readers of how he operated in order to encourage them to continue following his example (1:6). This isn't pride; it's a way of saying, God's power is sufficient for us if we keep faithful (1:5; 3:12,13; 5:23).

Paul had suffered in Philippi (Acts 16:22-24) before visiting Thessalonica, and had continued to suffer afterwards (Acts 17:5,13). Suffering, he says, is part of discipleship (3:3,4). The fact that he endured it showed that his motives for preaching were pure; he didn't preach for personal gain, power over people, or prestige (2:3-5). He even took a job in order not to depend on their gifts (2:6-9). His concern for them (2:17–3:2) reveals Paul as a pastor as well as an evangelist. He cared greatly about the spiritual welfare of people who had come to faith through his ministry.

The church's model

What Paul praises them for here is enough to tell us that they were Christians who, like Paul, took their responsibilities seriously whatever the cost. So they became a shining example to others (1:7). This what they were like:
- They worked for God (1:3)
- They endured hardship (1:3)

- They rejoiced in the gospel (1:6)
- They spread the message (1:8)
- They were wholehearted in their commitment (1:9).

Christ's return

This was clearly puzzling some in Thessalonica. Paul ends every chapter with a reference to it (1:10; 2:19; 3:13; 5:23) and gives detailed teaching from 4:13 to 5:11. There were two big issues:

Assurance about the dead

Some Christians thought that if you died before Jesus Christ returned you would miss out on the new creation. So they were grieving not only the human loss of people they loved, but also what they thought was an eternal loss too. Paul corrects this view in 4:13-18. Dead

Listening to the gospel over the airwaves in Swaziland. The good news of Jesus brings real hope

Christians have "fallen asleep". When Christ returns, they will rise from the dead before anything else happens (4:15,16).

Challenge for the living

We will never know when Christ is about to return. Paul repeats here what Jesus himself taught (Matthew 24:36-44). We have two options, he says. We can please ourselves, assuming that Christ won't come for ages, or we can live as if he was coming tonight. He urged the latter, because we are called to keep spiritually awake, alert to the work of God in and around us (5:5-7), and therefore living pure and holy lives (4:1-12; 5:12-22).

RELEVANCE FOR TODAY – 1 THESSALONIANS

1 Thessalonians is an intensely practical letter and all the key themes are relevant in every age and culture. So let's take those themes another way, asking ourselves some searching questions.

Set an example to others

The challenge is both personal and corporate. Paul was leading from the front, showing by his personal dedication and his willingness to suffer that God isn't defeated by human opposition or difficult circumstances. But the church as a whole was also setting an example through its faithfulness and witness. It is often the joint activity of a group of Christians that makes the biggest impact on others. So: Is my personal life setting an example to encourage fellow-Christians and to show Jesus to the world? Is our church life harmonious and dedicated to serving Christ in word and deed?

Stay focused on Jesus

It isn't very fashionable today to think about the return of Christ – or even the journey through death which each of us must make. Yet it provided a focus for Paul's ministry and the lives of many persecuted or deprived Christians. But Paul did not simply offer a promise of future blessing just to help people cope with present stress. It was much more than that.

By focusing on the return of Jesus we have a goal, an aim. We have a task to do – help build the kingdom of God – in a limited (and unknown) time-frame. Jesus will hold us

> "We believe that Jesus died and rose again and so we believe that God will bring with Jesus those who have fallen asleep in him."
>
> 1 Thessalonians 4:14

accountable for what we've done when he returns. So Paul is really saying get on with the job while we've got time! So:

Am I so focused on serving Jesus in thought, word and deed that I would be ready for him if he came back tonight?

Show your faith by your life

Christian witness is in deed as well as word. Non-Christians look at us and ask if we are consistently applying what we say we believe. Paul knew this, and so included his two sections on practical Christian living. They include sexual morality (4:3-8), love for one another (4:9-10) and being a good citizen (4:11,12). The many brief commands in 5:12-22 provide a good checklist for Christian discipleship, and include supporting full-time Christian workers, being patient and kind and keeping joyful and balanced in worship. So: When I read these instructions, am I keeping all of them fully in all circumstances?

2 Thessalonians
WAIT PATIENTLY FOR CHRIST'S RETURN

OVERVIEW
The Christians in Thessalonica continued to be confused about the promised return of Jesus Christ to earth. Paul told them that Jesus would return after a period of lawlessness. Meanwhile, Christians should not opt out of their social and family responsibilities while waiting for Jesus to come.

SUMMARY
After the formal opening words (1:1,2), Paul adds prayers for the church. There is thanksgiving in 1:3,4 but only in 1:11,12 is it specified what Paul is praying for; in between he assures them of God's judgement over their enemies, which is a comfort to them. The main topic is the return of Jesus Christ and Paul emphatically explains that this has not yet happened (2:1,2); on the contrary, before it takes place "the man of lawlessness" (2:3,8,9) must come and draw people away from God (2:3-12). However, despite the prospect of hard times the readers are safe in the protection of the God they are worshipping (2:13-15) and Paul blesses them (2:16,17). The practical section begins with a request for prayer for Paul and assurances of God's faithfulness (3:1-5). Paul then addresses those in the church who have left their occupations in eager anticipation of the return of Jesus Christ, and urges them to resume normal life (3:6-13). Some notes on disobedient members are appended (3:14,15) before Paul brings the letter to a close with a prayer for peace in his own hand (3:16-18).

Author and date
There was no doubt in the early church that Paul wrote this letter. In modern times, doubts have been expressed because there are a number of unusual words in the letter that Paul does not use elsewhere, and some of the subject matter (such as the "man of

lawlessness") is rare in both Paul and the rest of the New Testament. Some have also suggested that this letter was written before what we know as 1 Thessalonians.

However, the teaching does not contradict the rest of the New Testament, and in many respects complements it. And 2:15 implies that Paul has indeed already written to the Thessalonians. It is therefore likely that Paul wrote this up to six months after 1 Thessalonians, perhaps when Timothy and Silas returned from having delivered it. Paul would still have been in Corinth at the time.

Background
See handbook at 1 Thessalonians, p.285 for details of Paul's visit to the city and subsequent travels.

We know from Acts, and from Galatians assuming that was the first of Paul's letters, that false teachers arose in the early church only a decade or so after the death of Jesus. In 2 Thessalonians Paul reveals a related disturbing problem: people were forging letters supposed to come from Paul, and others were spreading false rumours that Jesus had already returned to earth (2.2). Today's scams and false news stories had their counterparts 2,000 years ago!

Paul was anxious about the impact of these rumours and forgeries on the very young Christians in Thessalonica. So he wrote 2 Thessalonians to counter the false teaching. In so doing he has provided us with some clear teaching about the return of Christ, which helps us to interpret Christ's teaching and parts of the book of Revelation. And, practical as ever, Paul suggests how his important theology should be applied in difficult daily life.

OUTLINE – 2 THESSALONIANS

The church that is suffering
1:1,2   Greetings
1:3,4   Thanksgiving for the Thessalonian church
1:5-10   God will vindicate his people
1:11,12   A prayer for the Thessalonians

The truth about Jesus' return
2:1-12   Teaching about the "man of lawlessness"
2:13-17   Encouragement to stand firm in the faith

The responsibility of Christians to work
3:1-5   A request for prayer
3:6-15   An exhortation to discipline the lazy
3:16-18   Concluding prayer, greetings and blessing

KEY THEMES – 2 THESSALONIANS

Jesus' return
Paul's teaching about the second coming resembles that of Jesus in Matthew 24:26-31 and 25:31-46. Jesus will come to judge the earth (1:8,9) with the great rejoicing of the saints (1:10). The time of his coming is unknown (2:2) but will be after a period of confusion and suffering (2:4,9-12).

God's justice
When life seems unfair, people ask how a just God can allow it. They may have been doing that in Thessalonica, where Christians were persecuted for their faith. Paul reassures them that God is indeed just. While his justice may not be obvious in this life, it will be seen when Jesus Christ returns. Then, God will punish evil people and save those who suffer (1:5-10).

Satan's attack
Paul's description of the deceptive "man of lawlessness" (2:1-12) has no parallel elsewhere in the New Testament. However, it ties in with Jesus' prediction of great evil to come, and of false prophets demonstrating deceptive signs and wonders (Matthew 24:15-25). It also reminds us of passages about the antichrist such as Revelation 13.

It is pointless trying to identify this figure with any single person in history. People who combine despotic political power with false religious appeal arise at various times, and Christians always have to be ready to battle against evil. Paul assured his readers that there is a restraining power at work (2:7). God keeps Satan on a long lead but never lets him off it. Paul does not specify what the restraining power was; he may mean the *Pax Romana*, the peace and order of the Roman Empire. Despite the excesses of some emperors, the Romans generally restricted the widespread abuse of power.

The Spirit's power

Christians can cope with intense suffering and persecution because the Holy Spirit makes us more like Jesus ("sanctifies us", 2:13). We are to share in Jesus' kingdom (2:14) and he will support and encourage us until that day (2:16,17; 3:5).

Christians' responsibility

Whether Jesus returns sooner or later, we are not to be idle. Paul stresses the need for honest work (3:6-15). People were created to work, and God calls us to play a full part in the development of his world. Paul set an example by working while he preached; he didn't sponge off others, and neither should any other Christian.

RELEVANCE FOR TODAY – 2 THESSALONIANS

Be patient when suffering

This is easy to say and hard to apply. The Thessalonians' endurance is a sign of the genuineness of their faith (1:4,5). Their suffering itself was a calling from God, not (as some might suggest) a curse from God. Because of their endurance, their faith and love was growing (1:3). Difficult circumstances can nourish faith, rather than destroy it. God loves us dearly, but he may not always smooth our path through life.

Be confident when tempted

As Paul was to tell the Corinthians later (from his own experience and, perhaps, from having observed the Thessalonians), God will never allow us to be tested (or "tempted") beyond our endurance (1 Corinthians 10:13). He is still in control and will protect us from Satan (3:3). He does that by focusing our minds on his love and imparting to us the same strength that Jesus had (3:5). Our part is to keep trusting him, so that we can draw on his strength when we need it.

Be careful in what you believe

All Christians can be misled. Sadly, we are more likely to be convinced that others are wrong than entertain the possibility that we are mistaken! Paul warned the Thessalonians not to believe the false letters and rumours (2:2). Evil can appear good (2:9). But how could they know they were false? Paul's teaching at the

time was incomplete – this letter fills out what he had taught in person. Paul implies here what he later said explicitly to the Corinthians: think carefully about prophecies before accepting them as true (1 Corinthians 14:29). We have the benefit of the whole of Scripture against which to test fresh ideas. Searching the Scriptures with others, prayerfully and thoughtfully, will enlarge our understanding and protect us from error.

> "As for you, brothers, never tire of doing what is right."
>
> 2 Thessalonians 3:13

Be tireless in doing right

Paul's first readers were very excited about their new-found faith – as "young" Christians often are. Their excitement led them into lifestyles that didn't reflect God's will, and which were a poor witness to the world. Some had given up work to prepare for Christ's return. Idleness and dependence on others isn't right (3:6-13). God doesn't usually call us to give up our day jobs; rather, he sends us back into the world to "do right" (3:13) by honouring him in all our work and relationships.

1 Timothy
INSTRUCTIONS FOR CHURCH LIFE

OVERVIEW

Timothy had been left in charge of a church in Ephesus. Paul reminded him of some basic principles governing church life which Timothy was to enforce. These include matters relating to the conduct of worship and social welfare, the behaviour of church leaders and handling false teachers.

SUMMARY

Chapter 1 is an introduction, containing greetings typical of any letter of the time (1:1,2). The purpose of the letter is to lay down ground rules for Timothy to use in the church at Ephesus. Such rules are a type of law which Timothy must use with authority against false teachers who also claim to be teaching the law.

The main body of the letter (2:1–6:2) sets out rules for dealing with the various pastoral problems outlined in the introduction. Thus, false teachers, mentioned in the first chapter, probably because that seemed the most urgent problem, are spoken of again in 4:1-4. Marks of good leaders are listed in 3:1-13, and are more personally applied to Timothy himself in 4:6–5:3. The falling away of converts is addressed in 4:1 but more in the conclusion. Matters of church discipline are set out in 5:17-22 and elsewhere, as these various problems do not form neat boundaries but overlap. Other problems concern church prayer meetings (2:1-8); women (2:9-15); widows (5:3-16); and slaves (6:1,2).

The conclusion (6:3-20) is a mixture of last-minute advice about problems, especially the falling away of converts, personal exhortation to live a godly and exemplary life, doxology (praise to God), and a real farewell.

Author

There was little doubt in the early church that Paul was the author. Serious doubts have been raised in the last 200 years. These rest partly on the differences in language used here compared with that used in Paul's undisputed letters. However, Paul was well educated and would have had a wide vocabulary, and this is not itself a conclusive argument. Another argument concerns the nature of the heresy which Paul counters and the structure of church life which he outlines. Both are said to reflect situations known later than the first century. However, Paul's descriptions suggest the early beginnings, rather than settled beliefs and practices. There is also an issue about personal allusions (see below). Paul's authorship is still highly likely.

Date and background

1 Timothy has to be considered alongside 2 Timothy and Titus, and together they are called the three "Pastoral Epistles", because they deal largely with matters of church order and leadership. They were probably all written after Paul's imprisonment in Rome (Acts 28:16,30).

It would seem that after his initial house arrest, Paul was freed for a while and went on a journey not recorded in Acts, visiting some of the churches he had previously planted. It is clear from 1:3 that he had been to Ephesus again (his first visit is recorded in Acts 19:1-41 and he met again with the church leaders in Acts 20:13-39). In 3:14 he says he hopes to return there but we cannot be sure that he did. See the introductions to 2 Timothy and Titus for possible visits to other churches he made at this time.

Timothy was not an apostle and is best

described as an apostolic delegate, or Paul's friend and assistant. Paul endorsed Timothy's authority over the church in Ephesus, so that in effect when Timothy spoke, it was Paul speaking. Perhaps Timothy used the letter itself to reinforce his authority (see 3:14,15). You will find more about Timothy in the introduction to 2 Timothy.

OUTLINE – 1 TIMOTHY

The gospel true and false

Matters of public worship

Matters relating to church leaders

Instructions to Timothy

Responsibilities towards various groups

Various additional instructions

KEY THEMES – 1 TIMOTHY

Instructions for Timothy

There are several explicit passages of instructions to the young assistant. Especially he is to:

Oppose false teachers (1:3-11; 4:1-10)

These were people obsessed with speculations and controversies that distracted others from the true gospel. They were legalistic, imposing heavy disciplines on people, and taught that the material world is evil. This may be an early form of what developed into Gnosticism in the second century AD. Paul counters it by saying that the law of God is to rebuke sinners, not restrict saints (1:8-11). He also says that the material world is part of God's good creation and is therefore to be received gratefully rather than treated with scorn (4:3-5).

Fight the good fight (1:12-20; 4:11-16; 6:11-21)

Paul reminds Timothy of the gospel of God's grace and urges him to keep it by recalling the prophecies about his ministry (1:18; see also 6:12). This would also help Timothy overcome his natural shyness (2 Timothy 1:7) and so deal with people who looked down on him because he was young (4:12). He was simply to get on with study and ensure that he set a good example (4:12,13).

Instructions about church life

Church worship had not taken on a widely accepted liturgical pattern at this time, but here (and in 1 Corinthians 12–14) Paul indicates that certain disciplines are to be observed:

- Prayer for authorities (2:1-7). Paul often urged good citizenship (eg Romans 13:1-7) and here he urges intercessions for secular leaders. Prayers for peace help everyone; peace promotes human welfare and enables the unhindered spread of the gospel.

- Observation of cultural boundaries (2:8-15). The New Testament church existed within a patriarchal society in which men were the dominant leaders. Although Paul appreciated the ministry of women (eg Romans 16:1-4,12) he did not encourage them to take on traditional male roles; that would have been too radical for the infant church. Today, some Christians say such male dominance was a reflection of a passing culture and is not mandatory. Others suggest it is part of God's creation order and remains mandatory for the church.

Instructions about church ministers

Again, the pattern of ministry was not finally established. Today some regard the elders referred to by Paul as the equivalent of priests or presbyters – ministers in charge of a church. However, the principles Paul lays down for them and for deacons apply to all who exercise responsibility in the church. They are personal qualities, not precise definitions of roles (3:1-12).

RELEVANCE FOR TODAY – 1 TIMOTHY

How to serve

Paul's advice to Timothy and his instructions to church leaders gives us principles we can apply to any form of Christian activity.

- Our lives should be exemplary (3:2-4,7; 4:12). Leaders cannot exempt themselves from the standards they encourage in others; they must practise what they preach.
- Leaders are responsible for pointing out error (1:3; 4:6,11); they cannot stand by if the faith is compromised or false teaching is given.
- Leaders should not be domineering or throw their weight about, but treat others with respect (5:1,2; 6:1,2).

How to share

Christians in Ephesus seem to have been as naturally lazy and selfish as people anywhere! We all like to take the easy option. Paul has some strong words to say about sharing, in different contexts.

- In Paul's day widows might become destitute without help from the church as women generally couldn't work outside the home (5:3). Supporting fellow-Christians less well-off than we are is an important part of discipleship.
- Families should look after their needy relatives (5:8,16). This is taken for granted in many developing countries, but not necessarily in the west where families break down and the elderly are put into care homes.
- Paul is scathing of those who become "ladies of leisure" instead of accepting greater responsibility for their lives (5:13). We can apply this to anyone who can, but doesn't,

work (for whatever reason); our time and resources are to be used for others and for the church if we do not need to work in order to survive.

- People who are better off than others should find ways of using their money for the good of others and not make a god of it (6:9,17-19).

How to stand

Timothy was clearly vulnerable in Ephesus because he was an outsider, and young. It would have been easy for him to fail in his responsibilities because of the pressure he felt. Paul showed him (and us) how to stand firm in difficult situations where we are not fully accepted by others, by:

- Remembering his call which God had confirmed (1:18; 4:14)
- Holding onto the faith he had received and not swerving from it (1:19; 4:16; 6:20)
- Living consistently in a way that pleases God (6:11-14)
- Above all, holding onto God himself (4:9,10).

> "Godliness with contentment is great gain. For we brought nothing into this world, and we can take nothing out of it."
>
> 1 Timothy 6:6-7

2 Timothy
PAUL'S FAREWELL ENCOURAGEMENTS

OVERVIEW
Paul was in prison with little hope of release. He had left Timothy to look after the church in Ephesus and wrote to encourage his young helper to stand firm in the face of opposition, false teaching and suffering. This is an intensely personal letter from a Christian leader who knows that his days are numbered.

SUMMARY
The letter begins with a standard greeting (1:1,2), which already sets the warm relational tone of the letter. Timothy is his child (Greek *teknon*), a word used both for masters to disciples and as a term of endearment to an adult (rather like "dear boy"). The main body of the letter can be divided into four heads, following the chapter divisions. 1:3-18 asks Timothy not to distance himself from Paul's suffering in prison. Chapter 2 exhorts Timothy to teach others and warn them, suggesting a continuing public ministry for Timothy, but at the same time, he needs to teach and warn himself. The issue of sound teaching as opposed to false is the one continuing concern from the first to the second letter. Chapter 3 sees this more in terms of a battle between truth and falsehood, teaching and deceiving, where practically, Timothy needs to live in the truth and resist falsehood. The final chapter (4:1-8) urges him to live in the light of Jesus Christ's second coming. The farewell greetings paint a picture both of Paul's loneliness in prison and yet the ability he still had to direct a number of people in the affairs of the young church. The bottom line of the letter is that he wants Timothy's presence, and before winter, when all travelling by sea stops (4:9,21). As in many of his other letters, he sends greetings to friends and forwards greetings from fellow-Christians in Rome.

Author and date
It is likely that Paul wrote this letter, and the serious doubts that have been raised by some scholars are dealt with in the introduction to 1 Timothy.

Some time elapsed between the writing of 1 and 2 Timothy. Paul had been travelling but was now a prisoner again in Rome, this time in a common gaol (1:8; 2:9) rather than under house arrest (Acts 28:16). His location may have been hard to find (1:17), which could account for the loneliness reflected in the letter. Paul refers to a number of friends, and asks for visitors and items to make him more comfortable (4:9-13,16). He clearly expected to be executed (4:6-8).

This probably dates the letter about AD 66 during the crackdown on Christians by the Roman Emperor Nero who – according to later traditions – executed both Peter and Paul. As he saw the end coming, Paul wrote to Timothy to urge him to keep going; he wanted to ensure that the work he had given his life for would continue.

Background
We cannot work out Paul's movements after he was released from house arrest in Rome. We know from 1 Timothy 1:3 that he had been to Ephesus. In 2 Timothy 4:13,20 he refers to recent visits to Troas, Miletus and Corinth. Other visits are referred to in Titus 1:5; 3:12.

Timothy was one of Paul's converts in Lystra (Paul visited it and other places in Acts 13:14–14:23, which he refers to here in 3:11). Timothy's father was Greek but his mother and grandmother Jews who became Christians (1:5; Acts 16:1). He joined Paul on missionary journeys, having first been circumcised in order not to offend Jews (Acts 16:2-4). From then on he is frequently cited as a close companion of Paul (eg 1 Thessalonians 1:1) and was sent as Paul's delegate to Corinth (1 Corinthians 4:17) and then Ephesus (1 Timothy 1:3).

Paul was very fond of Timothy ("my dear son", 1:2; 2:1) who had been set apart for ministry (1:6), despite being timid (1:7) and young (1 Timothy 4:12).

OUTLINE – 2 TIMOTHY

Loyalty expressed and encouraged

Personal instructions for Timothy

Paul's appeal for help

KEY THEMES – 2 TIMOTHY

Persevere through suffering

Paul's prison was clearly uncomfortable (1:8; 2:9). But suffering had been predicted for him at his conversion (Acts 9:15,16) and had become a way of life. He concluded that it was part of discipleship for many Christians (3:12). So in 2:3-7 he encouraged Timothy to endure suffering, using two common images. A soldier on active duty would have to face hardship and possible death; an athlete going for gold would have to break through the pain barrier and keep the rules. Whenever he wrote about suffering, Paul also wrote about God's faithful help and support (3:11; 4:17); he never lost his faith.

Preserve God's truth

False teachers and godless people were everywhere in the early church, just as they are today (3:1-9; 4:3,4). Here, Paul took the unusual step of naming some false teachers and Christians who had betrayed him or deserted the faith (1:15; 2:17,18; 4:10,14,15). In the face of this varied opposition, Timothy's task was to guard the gospel (1:13,14). Paul suggested four ways he might do this, by:

- Reminding people of it (2:14)
- Keeping his own life exemplary (2:22)
- Avoiding needless petty disputes over minor details and controversies (2:14,16,23)
- Teaching Christians gently in order not to inflame opposition (2:24-26).

Preach the word

Several times Paul urged Timothy to preach the word of God (2:2,25; 4:2) but he could only do that if he was himself a careful student of it (2:15). Paul returns to the theme in 3:14-16, and 3:16 is a key verse for our understanding of the nature and purpose of Scripture. Paul says it is "God breathed" (sometimes translated "inspired" but the word is literally "ex-spired"). It means that the Holy Spirit led the writers to write down eternal truths in their own words through which future generations would be able to hear God speaking. The writers' unique personalities were not taken over. The resulting Scripture not only tells us about God and his mighty works, but also challenges our behaviour and attitudes.

Paul's hope

Nearing the end of his life, Paul faced what lay beyond the grave. He was not now concerned about the end of the world and the second coming of Christ; but about the individual's hope. He was assured of being kept safe (1:12), confident of salvation (2:10), and looked forward to "the crown of righteousness" (4:8). Above all, he had fulfilled his calling; he had no regrets (4:7).

Discipleship group, Bulgaria. Paul urged Timothy to guard against false teaching by concentrating on and teaching the basic truths of the gospel

RELEVANCE FOR TODAY – 2 TIMOTHY

Stay focused

There were many distractions, temptations and problems for Timothy to deal with, as there are for us. Throughout this letter Paul urges him to stay focused on:

- His preparation and calling (eg 1:5-6; 3:14). Looking back to those who taught us the faith, and at our conversion, spiritual growth and calling to service, can help us to face difficulties with determination and faith.
- The gospel (eg 1:13,14; 2:10-13). Twice Paul urges Timothy to have nothing to do with pointless debates (2:16,17,23). Instead he is to focus on, and teach, the basic truths of the gospel, such as the life, death, resurrection and atonement of Jesus. It is easy, but wrong, to let secondary matters take on the status of primary matters.
- The Scriptures (2:15; 3:15-17). Timothy had our Old Testament and some of Paul's writings to keep him focused on God's purposes and in tune with God's will. Bible study is important even when we know Scripture well; God speaks through it into our current circumstances.
- The power of God. Timothy was quiet and sensitive, easily discouraged. Paul urged him to draw on the power of the Spirit to keep going (1:7), just as God had assisted Paul (3:11).
- His task in the church. In 4:5 Paul tells him in effect: "Just get on with it, and leave the problems to God!"

Support your friends

We will never know why so many people deserted Paul (1:15; 4:10,16). It must have been partly because some had departed from the faith, and others were afraid of "guilt by association" – of incurring the anger of the authorities and getting arrested themselves. Paul longed for his friends as he became aware of his vulnerability and mortality in prison. He even feared that Timothy might be ashamed of him (1:8).

> "All Scripture is God-breathed and is useful for teaching, rebuking, correcting and training in righteousness."
>
> 2 Timothy 3:16

Like Jesus, deserted in the Garden of Gethsemane (Matthew 26:56) and crying in utter loneliness on the cross, "My God, why have you forsaken me?" (Matthew 27:46) Paul knew the reality of divine support (4:17) but desperately needed human comfort. He was grateful for visits from Onesiphorus (1:16) and Luke (4:9), and longed to see Timothy and Mark (4:11). Such support can be costly for those who give it, but which is more important: showing practical love for someone, or abandoning them out of fear or laziness? One day, we might be the person who needs support.

Titus
CONTROL THOSE PASSIONS!

OVERVIEW
The new church on the island of Crete was presenting a poor witness to the gospel. Its members hadn't brought their passionately selfish lives into line with the demands of love and kindness. Paul had sent Titus there to sort them out (1:5). In this letter Paul directs him, using blunt language, concerning the standards of behaviour he expects from leaders and church members.

SUMMARY
The letter sets out greetings in 1:1-4. Titus, like Timothy, is Paul's child (Greek *teknon*), his faithful disciple. Chapter 1 deals with the appointing of elders, Titus' first priority in the new churches set up in Crete. The problem of divisive people in the church is addressed. They are mainly Jewish "converts," if they have truly been converted, but seem to be guilty of those vices the Cretans were renowned for especially lying. Chapter 2 deals with what Titus should say to whom: young and old, men and women, and slaves. There is a simple statement of the message of salvation that is to be delivered to all. Chapter 3 contains a list of the practical and behavioural virtues Titus should teach the church as a whole, and he touches briefly on church discipline. The final few verses (3:12-15) are the farewells, personal and administrative instructions and greetings.

Author and date
There is little doubt that Paul wrote this letter which is grouped with 1 and 2 Timothy as the "Pastoral Epistles". What doubts have been raised are dealt with in the introduction to 1 Timothy.

It was written after Paul's release from house arrest in Rome (Acts 28:16), when the apostle embarked on further journeys. These are not recorded in Acts, and we cannot put together a clear itinerary. The introductions to 1 and 2 Timothy both indicate some places he

visited, and Titus adds two others. One was Crete (1:5) where Paul and Titus had recently planted a church. Paul had previously visited Crete while on his way to Rome as a prisoner (Acts 27:7-12), but the ship appears to have stayed only a short while not leaving enough time for a mission then. The other was Nicopolis in Greece (3:12) to which Paul appeared to be heading when he wrote this letter.

Paul probably wrote Titus between 1 and 2 Timothy, from Corinth which is mentioned in 2 Timothy 4:20. The date would be about AD 65.

Background
Titus, like Timothy, was converted through Paul's ministry ("my true son in our common faith", 1:4) and became a trusted assistant. Like Timothy, he was a Gentile although unlike Timothy Paul never saw the need to have him circumcised so as not to offend the Jews to whom they often ministered (Galatians 2:1-3). And unlike Timothy, he was probably a robust character not easily frightened by difficult people.

Although Titus is never mentioned in Acts, his name does appear in Paul's letters. These may not provide an exhaustive list of his postings, but clearly he was Paul's choice for trouble spots:
• Jerusalem, to explain the Gentile mission (Galatians 2:1)

- Corinth, several times including acting as Paul's messenger (2 Corinthians 7:6,14,15; 8:6,16-21)
- Crete, to sort things out (1:5)
- Dalmatia, to churches otherwise unknown (2 Timothy 4:10).

OUTLINE – TITUS

Introduction: the task to be done
1:1-4   Greetings
1:5-9   Regulations concerning the appointment of elders
1:10-16   A warning against false teachings

The teaching to be given
2:1-10   Instructions to groups of believers
2:11-15   The theological basis of Christian living
3:1-8   Directions for Christian living
3:9-11   Final exhortations and warnings

Conclusion: the travel to be undertaken
3:12-15   Personal requests and greetings

KEY THEMES – TITUS

Summaries of the gospel
The church in Crete appears to have been new (see "Author and date" above). Part of Titus' task there was to remind the Christians of the heart of the Gospel. The letter contains three classic summaries of the gospel which remain useful reminders of the most important Christian truths.

- **God's eternal plans** (1:1-3). Paul always began letters with some acclamation of God's greatness and this is no exception. Here, he tells us that God planned from the beginning of time the full revelation of his purposes through Christ.
- **The purpose of Christ's death** (2:13,14). Paul stresses the divinity of Christ ("our great God and Saviour, Jesus Christ"), which some false teachers may have been questioning. His death was to redeem us from sin and to form a community of God-centred people.

- **The nature of renewal** (3:4-7). We did not deserve God's forgiveness, Paul says, but in his generosity he saved us and renewed us so that we could live a completely new life now, and inherit eternal life after death.

Standards for leaders
Church structures had not been put in place when Paul left Crete, so Titus was to set them up (1:5). Paul's lifestyle requirements for church leaders given in 1:6-9 are briefer than but similar to the lists in 1 Timothy 3:1-13. They cover not only an understanding of Christian doctrine (v.9) but especially an exemplary personal and home life.

What is different here is that Paul uses the word "overseer" (from which our word "bishop" comes) as well as "elder". However, he is clearly writing about the same role. This tells us that the threefold structure of ministry (deacon, elder/presbyter, bishop) which characterised the church in later times was not yet in existence.

Standards for church members

Six times Paul uses what for him is an unusual phrase and emphasis on personal conduct: Christians are "to do what is good" (1:16; 2:7,14; 3:1,8,14), and teach what is good (2:3). This is partly so that our witness is consistent – we practise what we preach (2:5,8) and to make the faith attractive to others (2:10). Among the ethical standards Paul stresses are:

- Self-control (2:2,5,6,12)
- Careful and moderate speech (2:3,8,9; 3:2)
- Honesty and integrity (2:12; 3:1; see also 1:11-12 for the opposite vice).

RELEVANCE FOR TODAY – TITUS

Be controlled

Self-control isn't easy, and some people are naturally more hot-headed than others. Many Cretans had short tempers and found it hard to turn off their passionate natures. Paul says we can change because of God's grace (2:11-14). We can infer from the letter three ways to help us:

- Jesus saved us in order that we might reflect God's character and purpose (2:14). Therefore, it is right that for every action we should ask, what would Jesus do?
- The Holy Spirit has given us a fresh start (3:5,6). The images of being "washed", "born again" and "renewed" all show us that God can and does change us for the better.
- However, changing our behaviour also involves an act of will. God doesn't do it all for us; his grace "teaches us to say 'no'" (2:12).

Be good

The Christian faith is not just a matter of believing certain doctrines. For Paul, right belief was important, but so too was faith in action. Paul is sometimes compared unfavourably with James who stressed that "faith without works is dead" (James 2:17). This is unfair on Paul because even in his most theological letters, he stresses that we are saved by faith for good works (see Ephesians 2:8-10).

In Titus, Paul stresses this more than in any of his other letters because the gospel hadn't made a noticeable difference to Cretans' lives. Doing good is not always attractive. It takes time and resources that you could otherwise spend on enjoying yourself. People can take advantage of you and presume on your kindness. Paul wants the Cretans to know that this isn't the issue. God is good, and his goodness cost him the life of his Son. Christians are to be good and do good, whatever the personal cost.

> "When the kindness and love of God our Saviour appeared, he saved us, not because of righteous things we had done, but because of his mercy."
>
> **Titus 3:4-5**

Be an example

If people see us behave in bad ways, when we claim that God is good, or if they see us being hateful when we say that God loves us, they will conclude that Christianity is a delusion and doesn't work. Paul urges the Cretans to show the gospel as well as tell it. This will silence critics (2:8) and draw others in (2:10). It also ensures that we are productive – we achieve something worthwhile (3:14). The key is humility (3:2), a virtue that was lacking in Crete and is rarely in abundant supply in any church.

Hebrews
CHRIST IS GREATER

OVERVIEW
When life gets tough, it is tempting to want to give up on Christianity. Hebrews is an encouragement to persevere with faith – it is pointless to return to an old way of life because only Jesus Christ can bring God's forgiveness and great promises of hope.

SUMMARY
Hebrews begins with a powerful statement of the greatness of Christ as God's Son and bringer of salvation (1:1-4). He is greater than the angels (1:5–2:4), but he became a human being, who has shared in suffering and death (2:5-18).

Christ is next seen to be greater than Moses, who led the Israelites out of slavery (3:1-6). Many Israelites, however, did not enter into God's Promised Land because of their disobedience, and Christians must not be like them (3:7–4:11).

In the next long section (4:14-10:18), the author shows that Christ is greater than the Jewish sacrificial system and its regulations. Jesus was called by God (5:1-10) to be the great high priest (4:14-16). Readers must not fall away from faith (5:11–6:8) because Christ is the high priest who enables us to inherit God's promised blessing (6:9-20). Christ is not like the other priests, but like Melchizedek, is a priest for ever (6:20–7:22). Because Jesus lives for ever, he is able to offer complete salvation to all who come to God through him (7:23-28). Jesus therefore brings a new covenant between God and his people (8:1-13). In this covenant, Jesus sacrifices his own life to bring about God's forgiveness and blessing (9:11-15). In this single sacrifice, Jesus fulfilled the old covenant (9:1-10; 9:16–10:18).

In the light of this, the readers of Hebrews must persevere with their faith in Jesus Christ (10:19-39). The Old Testament contains countless examples of faith (11:1-38). They, however, looked forward to the time when Christ would come (11:39) – so Christians have even greater reason to persevere (11:40–12:3). Readers are encouraged to resist sin (12:4) and to submit to God's fatherly discipline (12:5-13).

Hebrews closes with instructions and encouragements for the Christian community, to hold fast to true faith in Jesus Christ (12:14–13:25).

Author
Unknown. The apostle Paul, Barnabas (Acts 4:36; 9:27; 11:25-30; 13–14) and Apollos (Acts 18:24-28) are commonly proposed, but no suggestion is entirely convincing.

Date
Difficult to specify as we have no information; possibly late AD 60s.

Background
The readers were well acquainted with Jewish Scriptures and practices. Many were probably Jewish Christians who were being tempted to return to the Jewish faith because of threat of persecution. The readers may have been in Rome (see 13:24).

OUTLINE – HEBREWS

KEY THEMES – HEBREWS

The Old and the New

Throughout Hebrews, the author makes a contrast between the covenant God made with his people in the Old Testament and the new covenant that has been established by Jesus Christ. At every point, the new covenant based on Jesus Christ is greater and better (7:22; 8:6,13):

- The messengers of the old covenant were prophets (1:1), including Moses (3:2-5), and angels (2:2); the messenger of the new covenant is Jesus Christ, the Son of God (1:2-4; 3:6).
- The priests of the old covenant could only serve until they died (7:23); Jesus, the great high priest, lives for ever (7:24, see 6:20–7:21). Other priests were weak and sinful; Christ is perfect and sinless (7:28).
- The old sacrifices for sin had to be repeated regularly, first for the priest and then for the people (7:27; see also 10:1-3,11); Jesus offered his own life (9:11-14) once for all as a sacrifice for the sins of others (7:27; 9:28; 10:10,12).

- The old covenant could not transform human lives (7:18-19); the new covenant is able to bring forgiveness and make believers holy (10:14-18; see also 8:8-12 and 12:24).
- The old covenant brought people to Mount Sinai, where they received a terrifying revelation (12:18-21); the new covenant brings believers to God's heavenly kingdom, which is full of life and joy (12:22-24).

God's promises

Although there is a contrast between the old covenant and the new, the two covenants are held together by God's promises. In the old covenant, God promised rest to his people if they obeyed him (3:7-19). Many did not enter this rest because of their disobedience, but God still promises to bring rest to those who come to him through the new covenant of Jesus Christ (4:1-11). God's promise to bless Abraham's descendants (6:13-14) is now being accomplished through the ministry of Jesus (6:18-20). The new covenant is God's way of bringing the promised forgiveness and transformation (8:7-12). If Christians hold onto their faith in Christ, they will receive what God has promised (9:15; 10:36; 11:39-40). The final promise of God is to give his people an unshakeable kingdom (12:26-29).

Christ's obedience

Hebrews sees Christ as the obedient Son of God (1:2,3). Christ accepted the call of God to become a priest (5:5-6) to serve God and provide a way of salvation (2:17). Christ's obedience is more astounding because it led him through intense suffering and death in order to be a sacrifice for sin (eg 2:14-18; 5:7; 9:26; 12:2,3; 13:12). Christ's obedience through suffering makes him the perfect Son of God (2:10; 5:8; 7:28), who is able to save others (2:18, 5:9) and be an example for Christian perseverance (12:2,3).

RELEVANCE FOR TODAY – HEBREWS

Turn to Christ as our only hope

The readers of Hebrews were in danger of giving up on their faith in Jesus Christ (2:1-3; 3:12-14; 10:35-39). They were experiencing persecution (10:32-34), and some were tempted to go back to the familiar old covenant. Hebrews is a reminder that the Christian faith is much better than the angels (1:4), prophets (1:1,2; 3:1-6), priests (4:14,15; 7:23-28), sacrifices (9:11-14; 10:4,11-14) and law (7:19; 12:18-24) of the old covenant. Unlike these other things, Christ is able to bring believers to God and purify them (9:14; 10:22; 13:12).

We may not be tempted by the same Jewish customs today, but there are many other distractions to our faith. It can be easy to look for salvation by following self-help books or motivational therapists, rather than by looking to Jesus Christ. We must trust in Christ's unique position as the only one who can truly bring us to God.

Take in the Old Testament imagery

Many of the images from Hebrews sound strange to us. However, it is important for us to understand the person and work of Jesus against the background of the old covenant.
• As a high priest, Christ knows what we are going through (4:14,15), and is at God's right hand, praying for us (7:25), which is a source of great encouragement.

> "So do not throw away your confidence; it will be richly rewarded. You need to persevere so that when you have done the will of God, you will receive what he has promised."
>
> Hebrews 10:35-36

• As a sacrifice, Christ makes atonement for sin, removing the stain of sin from our lives and making us pure (eg 9:13,14; 13:11,12). In the light of Christ's suffering and sacrifice, we should be ready to make our own sacrifice of praise (13:15) and good works (13:16).

Trust in God continually

Hebrews has a lot to say about faith. The Israelites wandering in the wilderness were an example of unbelief (3:7-12,19). By contrast, Hebrews 11 gives a long list of people who lived by faith. They had faith in God's ability to fulfil his promises, even though they couldn't see how this would happen (11:1,39). Their trust in God remained strong, even though they experienced hardship and persecution (eg 11:32-38). These Old Testament characters should be an encouragement to readers who are thinking about giving up their Christian faith (12:1).

Hebrews warns that those who turn away from Christ will not receive salvation (2:2,3; 6:4-6). Christians must persevere with their faith (4:11; 6:11), avoiding deliberate sin (10:26-31; 12:14-17), and drawing strength from other Christians (10:24,25) and from the example of Jesus Christ (12:3).

WHAT IS HOLINESS?

Commenting on Hebrews 12:14, J C Ryle wrote:

Holiness is the habit of being of one mind with God. A holy person will:

- endeavour to shun every known sin and to keep every known commandment
- strive to be like our Lord Jesus Christ
- pursue long-suffering, gentleness, patience, kind temper, control of the tongue, moderation and self-denial
- seek to mortify the desires of the body
- follow after love and brotherly kindness, after a spirit of mercy and benevolence towards others
- seek purity of heart
- follow after the fear of God, like the fear of a child, who wishes to live and move as if he was always before his father's face, because he loves him
- seek humility
- pursue faithfulness in all the duties and relations in life
- strive for spiritual-mindedness.
  (updated from J C Ryle, Holiness)

OLD TESTAMENT ALLUSIONS

Hebrews uses Old Testament concepts to explain Christ's work. There are references to:

- a Sabbath rest. According to Hebrew tradition, God "rested" on the seventh day of creation, and expected his people to keep the seventh day holy by not doing any work. Hebrews uses this as a picture of the salvation which Christ brings.
- the covenant. The contract or agreement that God gives to his people. For the Jews, this agreement was expressed in the law of Moses. But now God has given a better agreement to his people through Christ.
- Christ as a high priest. Under the law of Moses, the high priest represented the people to God ... and sacrificed animals to secure forgiveness of their sins. God has provided a perfect high priest who offered, not animals, but himself.
- the Most Holy Place. A room within the tent of meeting (or tabernacle) which contained the ark of the covenant. Only the high priest was allowed to enter it, once a year, to offer sacrifices. Hebrews sees it as a picture of heaven, where Christ enters into God's presence.

James
PRACTICAL FAITH

OVERVIEW
What does the Christian life look like? James answers this question by giving a collection of clear instructions on some important issues. His letter is packed full of practical wisdom for living a godly life.

SUMMARY
After a short introduction and greeting (1:1), James launches into a call to his readers to persevere in the face of trials (1:2-4), reminding them to trust in God's ability to provide help (1:4-8) rather than in their own resources (1:9-11). God will reward those who stand firm (1:12), but those who give in to temptation will be trapped by sin and led to death (1:13-15).

James is particularly concerned about the way his readers speak. He wants them to avoid talk that is angry (1:19), uncontrolled (1:26), slanderous (4:11) or boastful (4:13-17). Instead they should learn to be controlled in their conversation (3:1-12), and to speak the truth without resorting to swearing (5:12).

A central message of the letter is that Christians must do the word of God, and not just hear it (1:22-25). James says that "faith without deeds is dead" (2:14-26).

A couple of passages deal with wealth in the church: wealthy people are not to be treated with more respect than poorer people (2:1-13), and rich business-owners are warned not to oppress their workers, because they will face God's judgement (5:1-6).

All of James' readers are warned against greed (4:1-10), encouraged to be patient in suffering (5:7-11) and reminded to pray together for forgiveness and healing (5:13-18).

Unlike other New Testament letters, there is no closing greeting. Instead, James urges his readers to look out for wayward Christians, and bring them back to the truth (5:19,20).

Author
James, the brother of Jesus. James met the risen Jesus (1 Corinthians 15:7), was with the other disciples at Pentecost (Acts 1:14) and became the recognised leader of the Jerusalem church (see Acts 15:13-21, Galatians 2:9,12).

Date
This is uncertain but could be as early as AD mid 40s, in which case this is one of the earliest New Testament writings.

Background
James wrote with many congregations in mind and intended the letter to be passed around the churches. The introduction (1:1) and various Old Testament allusions (eg 2:21-24,25; 5:11,17,18) suggest the readers were mainly Jewish Christians. Some were facing pressure to give up on their faith (eg 1:2-4), while others were struggling to live out the commandments of Jesus (eg 2:8).

OUTLINE – JAMES

KEY THEMES – JAMES

James is often described as "wisdom literature", similar to Proverbs and Ecclesiastes. Like these, James uses short examples from history (eg 2:21-24,25; 5:10,11,17,18) or from the observable world (eg 1:11,23-25; 3:3-8) to highlight God's eternal truth. Yet James has the directness of prophets like Jeremiah and Amos, and there is also much that reminds us of Jesus' Sermon on the Mount (Matthew 5–7). Unlike other New Testament letters, James does not follow a clear argument from beginning to end, but reads more like a series of short stories – or even sermons – that indicate the type of life that pleases God (1:12).

Wisdom

Wisdom is the main theme of James. If we lack wisdom, we can ask God to give it to us (1:5). Wisdom is not measured by the amount of knowledge a person has, but by their ability to live a good life (3:13) – a life that shows the fruit of a relationship with God (3:17,18). A wise person will match words with actions, but an unwise person is a hypocrite who says one thing but does another (3:14-16; see also 2:1-11).

This "heavenly wisdom" (3:17) is behind James' appeal to put into practice what the word of God says, and not simply to listen to it (1:22). The wise person actually obeys God's commands, and so doesn't forget them (1:25). Faith without deeds is not only dead (2:17,26) but also foolish (2:20); wise people will become mature by accompanying faith with action (2:22).

God as Lawgiver and Judge

Like other wisdom literature, James focuses on God's character as the just judge. God has given numerous instructions to show us how to live in the way he wants (1:20, 27; 4:12). Christians who have experienced the grace of God in conversion (1:18) must not forget that their works will still be judged by God (2:12,13). As judge, God hears the complaints of those who are oppressed (5:4), as well as the slander (4:11) or grumbling (5:9) of Christians. God is ready to give generously to all who ask in faith (1:5,17; 5:15,16). He will ultimately reward those who have lived for him (1:12; 2:21-24; 4:10).

The pressures of life

James is fully aware of the difficulties of living for God in an unbelieving world. He mentions many pressured situations his readers would be facing: trials (1:2,12), temptation (1:13-15), poverty (1:9; 2:15,16), quarrels and slander within the church (4:1-12), oppression by the rich (2:6,7; 5:1-8), illness (5:13-16) and apostasy (5:19,20).

RELEVANCE FOR TODAY – JAMES

James is an excellent example of applying Jesus' teaching to the challenges of day-to-day Christian life. Although James does not often quote Jesus, much of what he writes has roots in Jesus' own teaching (eg 5:12 is similar to Jesus' words in Matthew 5:34-37). Like James, we should reflect on Jesus' teaching to help us live wise and godly lives. This is how Christians should make a real difference to the world.

Believing and praying

James wants his readers to believe in the goodness of God, and not to doubt that God will give good gifts to them if they ask in faith (1:5-8,17). Elijah is an example of someone who prayed in faith (5:17,18), and James encourages his readers to pray in times of trouble, joy, sickness and sin (5:13-16). If we have faith in God, we should always be praying.

Doing

"Faith without deeds is dead" (2:26). True faith must be practical. If we have received God's grace, we must make sure we provide for the needs of others (1:27; 2:15,16) and keep ourselves away from sin (1:21,27; 4:8). True faith is obedience to God's "royal law" (2:8) and an eagerness to do God's will (2:21-25). We should take every opportunity to put our faith into practice.

Money

James has strong words about equal treatment of rich and poor (2:1-9) and for rich people who think their possessions are not subject to God (5:1-6). Much social injustice would be avoided by listening to James!

Speaking

James is very concerned about the way Christians speak. Although the tongue is so small (3:3-5), it can ruin the testimony of a Christian if it is not kept under control (3:6-8). However, if it is used carefully to praise God and bless other people, God is honoured and the Christian is considered mature (3:2,9-12). We should not curse (3:10), quarrel (4:1,2), slander (4:11), boast (4:16) or swear (5:12). Instead, we should use our tongues to pray for each other and sing songs of praise (5:13).

Persevering

Some of James' readers were in danger of giving up because of the pressures they were facing. James encourages them to trust in God's generous provision (1:5), to seek him for forgiveness and renewal when they fail (4:8-10; 5:16) and to be patient in their trials because God the Judge will come soon to deal with evildoers (5:8,9) and reward the righteous (1:12). Whatever our circumstances, God will help us to persevere, if we ask him in faith.

> "Who is wise and understanding among you? Let him show it by his good life, by deeds done in the humility that comes from wisdom."
>
> James 3:13

1 Peter

GOD'S GRACE IN DIFFICULT DAYS

OVERVIEW

Living a Christian life can lead to difficulties and suffering. Peter wants his readers to be ready for these challenges, so he writes to remind them about the grace of God which they have already received in Jesus Christ. This grace will give them the strength and hope they need.

SUMMARY

The letter begins with a short introduction and greeting (1:1,2). Peter is aware of the difficulties his readers are facing (1:6), but knows that God is keeping them safe by his power (1:5) and will bring them through their trials to full salvation (1:4,5,9).

Even though they are suffering, Peter's readers must remember that they are in fact very blessed: Jesus has redeemed them (1:18-21) and now they have been born into God's living kingdom (1:3,4,23). This salvation is so great that prophets looked forward to it (1:10-12) and the angels long to look into it (1:12)!

Those who have been born into God's kingdom must live holy lives as children of God (1:13-16), and become mature in faith (2:2,3). As this happens, Christians grow together into a people who honour God (2:4-10).

Peter is particularly concerned that Christians live good lives in every area of society (2:11–3:7). They are to be careful how they live, so that if they suffer, it is because they are doing good and not because they are evildoers (3:8-17; 4:12-16).

Christ's death and resurrection have declared God's victory over sin and death, making salvation and cleansing possible

(3:18-22). Christ is the example for Christian living (4:1,2) and the standard of judgement for the world (4:5,17).

Peter reminds the church to live in harmony, and to serve one another in the strength God gives (4:7-11). Leaders, in particular, are to serve the church (5:1-4).

Peter closes with a reminder to resist the devil (5:8,9) and to trust in God, who will give grace and strength to help in times of suffering (5:10,11).

Author

Peter, one of Jesus' closest disciples. Peter is probably writing from Rome (called "Babylon" in 5:13).

Date

Probably in the early AD 60s – just before the Roman Emperor Nero's persecution of Christians, which broke out in AD 64.

Background

Peter wrote to a number of congregations in Asia Minor (1:1 – modern-day Turkey). Many were suffering insults and difficulties for their faith in Jesus Christ (eg 1:6; 4:12-15; 5:9). The letter could also have been for new Christians at their baptism (3:21, and language of "new birth" throughout).

OUTLINE – 1 PETER

KEY THEMES – 1 PETER

Suffering

Throughout the letter, Peter refers to the suffering of his readers. They have been facing all kinds of difficulties (1:6), from physical harm (2:19) to slander (3:16) and insults (4:14). Some of Peter's readers were surprised that the Christian life had led to suffering (4:12), but Peter reminds them that Jesus himself had suffered the same things and more (eg 2:21-23; 4:1). Other Christians throughout the world were also facing the same difficulties (5:9).

Christians must make sure that they are suffering for doing good, and not because they are evildoers (2:20; 4:15,16). God will bless them (3:14; 4:14) and give them strength (5:10), and suffering will make their faith stronger and purer (1:7; 4:1).

Full salvation

Christians have already received salvation through the death and resurrection of Jesus (1:3-5; 2:24; 3:18). They have entered into God's kingdom (1:3,23). Christ has saved them from their empty way of life (1:18). This salvation was predicted by the prophets (1:10,11), and was part of God's plan from the very beginning (1:20).

Christians can also look forward to future salvation (1:5). When Jesus is revealed, the whole world will see that the Christian life pleases God (1:7; 2:12). Those who suffer for their faith now will receive God's reward (5:4), and will inherit the blessings of his kingdom (1:4).

In the present, Christians can count on the grace and strength of God (1:9; 4:11; 5:10,12).

The church as God's family

Peter reminds his hearers that they have been chosen by God (1:1-2) to be obedient children of their heavenly Father (1:14). Together with all Christians, they have become living stones in God's house (2:4,5). As God's special people, they have inherited the blessings of Israel (2:9,10) – they belong to "the family of God" (4:17). They must learn to live together with love, and to use their gifts to serve one another (4:8-11). The leaders of the church are to be caring shepherds (5:1-3, see John 21:15-17).

The life of Christ

Jesus is the centre of Peter's thoughts. Peter often refers to events in Jesus' life and ministry, which Peter knew about as a first-hand witness (5:1). He speaks of Christ's suffering and death (eg 2:21-24; 4:1), his resurrection (1:3,21; 3:21) and his ascension (3:22). Christ is now the foundation (2:4-8) and Chief Shepherd (2:25; 5:4) of the church. He will come again (1:7,13; 5:4) to be judge of the world (4:5).

Old Testament Scriptures

For its length, 1 Peter has more quotes and allusions from the Old Testament than other books in the New Testament. The Scriptures are particularly relevant because both Peter's readers and ancient Israel lived in hostile environments and struggled to behave as God's people.

RELEVANCE FOR TODAY – 1 PETER

Imitating Christ

When Peter's hearers are suffering for their faith, they must remember that they are simply following in the steps of Christ (2:21). He is an example of patience under persecution and trust in God (2:23, see also 3:9). When faced with suffering, we should have the same attitude as Christ (4:1) and live entirely for God (4:2).

Being good citizens

Christians should be model citizens in society, by showing respect to the civil authorities (2:13,14) and their neighbours (2:17). They are resident foreigners and should not withdraw into ghettos (1:17; 2:11). Peter calls for humility and submission in the household from slaves (2:18), wives (3:1-6), and husbands (3:7). Within the church, leaders should be servants rather than lords (5:1-3) and young people should submit to them (5:5). All Christians should serve each other (4:10) and show mutual love, humility, hospitality and respect (4:8,9; 5:5). We should behave like this so that no one outside the church can accuse us of doing wrong (2:12,15). Most of all, humility and service please God, who will bless us for it (5:6).

Living in hope

Peter encourages his readers to be hopeful. Even though they are suffering in the present, their future is secure because of the resurrection of Jesus (1:3,21). Christ has already redeemed us from our sins (1:18), and is now enthroned as Lord in heaven (3:22). We wait for him to be revealed (1:7), when he will reward his faithful people (5:4) and bring them their full inheritance as God's children (1:4,5).

Because of this hope, we must make sure we do not get caught up in the sins of the world (1:13, 4:4) or the tricks of the devil (5:8). We should use every opportunity to explain our hope to other people (3:15).

Being joyful

Throughout the letter, Peter reminds his readers that they have good reason to be joyful. Even though we may have difficulties in the present, we can rejoice that God will use our sufferings to complete his work of salvation in us (1:6-9). We will be overjoyed when Christ is revealed (4:13)!

> **"Dear friends, I urge you, as aliens and strangers in the world, to abstain from sinful desires, which war against your soul."**
>
> 1 Peter 2:11

2 Peter

GROWING IN GRACE

OVERVIEW

False teachers were trying to lead Peter's readers away from Christian truth. Peter's letter warns them that false teaching leads to destruction, and he urges them to remember the true promises of God. By doing so, the readers will become stronger Christians.

SUMMARY

In the short greeting (1:1,2), Peter notes that his readers have received a precious gift of faith (1:1). God gives rich resources to his people (1:3-4) so that their faith will grow (1:5-9). If they work at their faith (1:10), they will be welcomed into God's eternal kingdom (1:11).

Peter wants to make sure that his readers will remember the truth of Christianity after he has died (1:12-15; 3:1-2). They can be sure he has told them the truth because he was an eyewitness of Jesus' life, even the transfiguration (1:16-18; see also Matthew 17:1-8). The prophecies of the Old Testament (1:19-21) also show that Peter was not making up stories about Jesus (1:16).

In contrast to Peter, false teachers invent stories and doctrines that can lead Christians astray. These false teachers will be destroyed in the judgement of God while those who hold on to the truth will be saved (chapter 2).

Christians should not be surprised that there are false teachers (3:3). These people laugh at God's promise, because they think that God will never come to create a new, righteous world (3:4-7,13). However, God works to his own timescale (3:8). He is patiently waiting for the right moment to fulfil his promise (3:9-13,15). Peter notes that the apostle Paul says the same thing in his letters (3:15-16).

In the light of all this, Peter's readers should be careful to lead holy lives, so that when God fulfils his promise he will be pleased with them (3:11,12,14). They must avoid the errors of the false teachers (3:17) and grow in the grace and knowledge of Christ (3:18).

Author

The apostle Peter (1:1) at the end of his life. 1:14 could refer to the conversation between Jesus and Peter in John 21:18,19. The author was present at the transfiguration (1:18) and mentions a first letter in 3:1.

Date

Mid AD 60s, shortly before Peter's death.

Background

The letter was written to a wide group, including the recipients of the first letter (3:1, see section at 1 Peter). The readers are facing challenges from false teachers. Among the first readers was probably Jude who used chapter 2 as a basis for his own letter.

OUTLINE – 2 PETER

KEY THEMES – 2 PETER

The danger of false teaching

Peter's main reason for writing was the threat of false teaching in the church (3:17). False teachers were deceiving the believers (2:1). Their teaching may have seemed appealing and persuasive (2:9-19), but Peter shows his readers how to identify the false teachers:

- They invent stories (2:1,3), unlike Peter, who has told them the truth (1:16-21).
- Their lifestyle does not match the gospel, but is full of shameful practices (2:2,13,14,19).
- Their motivation for teaching is greed (2:3,14; and the example of Balaam in 2:15, see Numbers 22).
- They despise authority (2:10) and are proud and arrogant (2:10,11).
- They especially try to trap weak or young Christians (2:18).
- Their teaching contradicts Scripture (2:21; 3:5,16).

The certainty of salvation

Unlike the false teachers, Peter bases his teaching on the truth about Jesus (1:16-18; 3:1), the prophecies of the Old Testament (1:19-21; 3:1) and the promises of God (1:4; 3:9,13). God's promise is to give salvation to those who believe in Christ, by rescuing them from the evil of the world and giving them life in his kingdom (1:4,11). Peter points to examples from Old Testament history to show that God is able to keep his promises. In particular, he mentions Noah (2:5) and Lot (2:6-8) to show that God is able to save the godly. This should give Peter's readers confidence that God can also act on their behalf (2:9).

The Day of the Lord

Peter tells the believers to expect the "Day of the Lord" to come at any moment (3:10). This was the day promised in the Old Testament and spoken of by Jesus (3:2). It will be the day of final judgement for the ungodly, when all that is unholy will be consumed by fire (3:7,10,12). But it will also bring God's new heaven and new earth, which will be filled with righteousness (3:13).

The false teachers denied that God would ever intervene (3:4). But for Peter, it is a certain promise (3:9,13), and the hope of believers (3:12,14; 1:11).

RELEVANCE FOR TODAY – 2 PETER

Watch out for false teachers

Peter reminds us that there will always be false teachers around (3:3) who teach their own invented stories rather than the truth of the gospel (2:1). In order to be able to recognise error, Peter's readers must study the true teachings about Jesus Christ (1:12-15,19; 3:1,2). By growing in the knowledge of Christ (3:18) and the Scriptures (3:2), Christians can be on their guard against false teachers (3:17) and will not be led away from true faith.

Be ready for Christ's coming

Peter's readers must look forward to the future God has promised (3:12). We may have been waiting a long time (3:4,8), but the delay is because God is patient and wants more people to be saved (3:9,14). When the Day of the Lord comes, it will be sudden and surprising, like a thief in the night (3:10). God's people will have a new home in the new heaven and new earth (3:7,13). Because we do not know when it will happen, we must always be ready. This means we should get rid of all sin from our lives, and make every effort to be holy and right with God (3:11,14).

> "Therefore, dear friends, since you already know this, be on your guard so that you may not be carried away by the error of lawless men and fall from your secure position. But grow in the grace and knowledge of our Lord and Saviour Jesus Christ."
>
> 2 Peter 3:17-18

Grow as a Christian

Peter begins the letter by reminding his readers that their faith is a precious gift from God (1:1). God has given Christians all the resources they need (1:3), along with the promise and hope of salvation (1:4). If God has given us such great gifts, we must make every effort to nurture our Christian lives (3:18). We must grow in Christian qualities like goodness, knowledge, self-control, perseverance, godliness, kindness and love (1:5-7), so that we will be productive servants in God's kingdom (1:8). If we keep growing like this, we are unlikely to be led astray by false teaching (1:10; 3:17).

1 John
LIVING IN LIGHT AND IN LOVE

OVERVIEW

The message of 1 John is easy to understand: God is light and God is love. However, it is much more difficult to put this understanding into practice. John's letter shows us what it means to live in the light and love of God.

SUMMARY

Unlike other New Testament letters, 1 John does not begin with a greeting. Instead, John tells his readers that they can trust his message about Jesus because he himself saw, heard and was with Jesus (1:1-3). John is now passing on what Jesus had taught him (1:4-5).

God is light (1:5), so everyone who wants to be in fellowship with God must also live in the light (1:6,7). This means we must not hide our sin, but confess it to God and receive his forgiveness (1:8–2:2). To live in the light, we must obey God's commands (2:3-8), especially to love our fellow Christians (2:9-11).

John's readers already live in fellowship with God (2:12-14), but John reminds them that they cannot also love the world (2:15-17). Some people have left the church and are trying to lead others astray (2:18,19,26), but John encourages his readers to keep hold of the truth they already know (2:21-27).

In God's great love, he has made us his children (3:1), so we must become like Jesus Christ (2:29; 3:2,3). God's children will get rid of sin from their lives (3:4-10). They should also love one another (3:11-18) so that they will please God (3:19-24). John urges his readers to learn to recognise truth from error (4:1-6).

God is love (4:16), so everyone who wants to be in fellowship with God must also live in love (4:7-21) and obey God's commands (5:1-5).

John's readers know their faith is real because God lives in them by his Spirit (5:6-15). John ends by encouraging his readers to keep away from sin and hold on to true faith (5:16-21).

Author

Strictly speaking, this letter is anonymous. As it has much in common with the fourth Gospel, the church has always accepted it as being written by the same author, the apostle John. The author clearly has a position of authority in the group of churches he addresses and they will have known him well.

Date

There are no hard facts about this but most people think of a date towards the end of the first century AD.

Background

The readers of the letter were well known to the apostle John. Some of the congregation had recently left them (2:19), perhaps to follow false teaching (2:26). John writes to reassure them that their faith in Jesus Christ is true (5:13). As tradition tells us that John spent his later life in Ephesus, the readers probably lived in the same area, the west of modern Turkey.

OUTLINE – 1 JOHN

KEY THEMES – 1 JOHN

God is light

John uses the contrast between light and darkness to speak about the difference between holiness and sin. Just as there is no darkness in light, so there is no sin in God (see 3:5): he is light (1:5). Christians must therefore walk in the light and avoid the darkness of sin (1:7). If we do not walk in the light, we are hypocrites, who say that we are in fellowship with God, but do not act as if we are (1:6). The test for living in the light is loving other Christians (2:9-11).

Those who live in the darkness do not know the truth, either about God (1:10; 2:4-5) or themselves (2:11). However, God is able to rescue us from darkness and sin through the work of Jesus Christ (2:1,2; see also eg 3:5). If we follow Jesus (2:6) then he will shine his light into our lives (2:8) and purify us from sin (1:7,9).

God is love

God is love (4:16), and he has showed that love to us by sending Jesus to give us new life (3:16; 4:10). God's love is generous (3:1), dependable (4:6) and universal (see 2:2; 4:14).

God's love for us is the reason (4:11,19) and pattern (3:16) for our love for one another. Those who belong to God must live a life shaped by love, just as God does (4:16, 21).

God's children

1 John is full of terms of family relationship. John calls his readers "dear children" (eg 2:1, 12, 13,18,28; 3:7,18; 4:4; 5:21) and "dear friends" (eg 2:7; 3:21; 4:1,7,11). The warmth of their relationship is because both John and his readers are God's children (5:19).

God has made them his children because of his great love (3:1). They have been born again into God's family (3:9; 4:7; 5:1) and God's Spirit now lives in them (3:24; 4:4,13). God's children are given the gift of eternal life (5:11,12). One day, they will become like their heavenly Father (3:2). Unlike the children of the devil, God's children do what is right (3:10).

God's truth

John is concerned that his readers continue to believe the truth that they already know (2:20,21,24). They must especially keep hold of the truth about Jesus Christ (2:22; 5:5) – that he came as a real human being to bring God's salvation to the world (4:2,3; 5:6).

RELEVANCE FOR TODAY – 1 JOHN

Living with God

Christians live in fellowship with God – with the Father and the Son (1:3; 2:24) and the Spirit, who lives in them (eg 3:24; 4:13). They are God's dearly loved children (3:1), and God listens to their prayers (5:14-15). God lives with them and gives them eternal life (2:24,25; 5:11).

We must nurture this valuable relationship with God by avoiding all sin (1:6; 2:1) and following his commands (1:7; 2:6; 5:3). If we do sin, we must not hide it, but confess it to God, who will forgive and cleanse (1:8,9). It is a great privilege to live in fellowship with God. But it is also a great responsibility: we need to take sin seriously, so that we can be pure like our loving Father (3:3).

Living with others

Christians are born into God's family, so they now have brothers and sisters in the faith (see 5:19). John's readers must make sure they are in fellowship with other Christians (1:3, 7). Christians will know that their faith is real because of their love for their brothers and sisters (3:14). They cannot claim to love God if they do not also love his children (eg 4:20,21; 5:1)!

Love for one another is a central part of the Christian message (3:11). Jesus commanded his followers to love one another (3:23). Love is not a warm feeling, though. John wants us to love one another in practical ways (3:17,18). If we want to follow Christ, we must serve our fellow Christians with love.

> "If we walk in the light, as he is in the light, we have fellowship with one another, and the blood of Jesus, his Son, purifies us from all sin."
>
> 1 John 1:7

Living in the world

John contrasts the life of God's children with life in the world (2:15). For John, the world is a place of darkness (see 1:5,6; 2:11) and sin (2:16). People in the world follow their own desires rather than God's will (2:17). The world is under the control of the devil (5:19): his children do evil (3:10) and refuse to acknowledge Jesus Christ (4:3). The world hates God's children (3:13).

John reminds us that the evil desires of the world will not last (2:17). Jesus came into the world to be its Saviour (4:14), by defeating the devil (3:8) and by revealing God's love (4:9). No one can love both the world and God, so we should not love the world (2:15). Instead, our faith in Jesus will set us free from the evil desires of the world (5:4,5). If we truly desire this, God will help us (5:18).

2 John and 3 John
LOYALTY TO THE TRUTH

OVERVIEW
These two letters are very short, but their message is clear and direct: Christians must be loyal to the truth they have received in the good news of Jesus Christ.

SUMMARY
2 John was written to a local church (2 John 1). John is pleased that some members of the church are still walking in the truth (2 John 4) and he reminds them that this means they should love one another (2 John 5,6). John warns them about false teachers in the church (2 John 7-9). They should be careful not to welcome people who follow this teaching (2 John 10,11). Once again, John notes that he will deal with particular issues in the church personally when he visits them (2 John 12).

3 John is addressed to Gaius, a personal friend of the apostle John (3 John 1,2). Some travelling missionaries have recently visited John and told him many good things about Gaius (3 John 3,4). These missionaries had resolved to stay only in the houses of Christians on their journeys (3 John 7), and Gaius had made them very welcome and given them his support, even though he did not know them at first (3 John 5). The visitors have returned to Gaius from John, carrying this letter, and John asks Gaius to look after them again (3 John 6,8). In contrast to Gaius, another member of the church called Diotrephes did not welcome the visitors

(3 John 10). John tells Gaius that he is aware of the trouble Diotrephes is causing in the church (3 John 9,10). Gaius should follow the example of good people like Demetrius (3 John 12) rather than evil people like Diotrephes. John notes that he will deal with the problem personally when he visits the church in the near future (3 John 10,13,14).

Author
"The Elder" (2 John 1; 3 John 1) who does not give his name. Traditionally seen as the apostle John, who also wrote 1 John and the fourth Gospel.

Date
Uncertain; possibly in the AD 80s or 90s.

Background
As John's ministry took place in Asia Minor (present Turkey), the readers probably lived in that area. 2 John was written to "the chosen lady and her children" (2 John 1). This was a way of referring to a congregation of Christians.

3 John was written to Gaius, a member of an otherwise unknown congregation, and a personal friend of the apostle John (3 John 1).

OUTLINE

2 JOHN

1-4 Greetings and commendation
5,6 Love one another
7-11 Warning about false teaching
12,13 Closing greetings and promise of visit

3 JOHN

1,2 Greetings
3-6 Commendation of Gaius
7,8 Showing hospitality to Christian workers
9,10 Condemnation of Diotrephes
11,12 Encouragement to do good
13,14 Closing greetings and a promise of a visit

KEY THEMES

Truth

John is delighted that members of the church fellowship are still living in the truth (2 John 4; 3 John 3,4). This truth is the message about Jesus Christ (2 John 9) and his human life (2 John 7), which they have known from the beginning of their faith (2 John 5).

Truth holds the Christian community together (2 John 1). Truth is not, however, just an intellectual understanding of the teaching of Jesus. For John, truth means a commitment to staying close to Jesus and obeying the Father's commands (2 John 4). Truth here is almost a personification of Jesus. This is why John can say that truth lives within the Christian (2 John 1) and lasts for ever. As his readers continue to walk in the truth, they will know the grace, mercy and peace of God (2 John 3).

Love

Christians cannot claim to live in the truth if they do not love one another. This message, which was central to 1 John, is repeated in 2 John. Loving one another is the defining mark of the Christian community. John's readers have heard this command from the beginning of their faith (2 John 5,6), so they should put it into practice.

Hospitality

Hospitality is a particular example of Christian love for one another, and an illustration of the way Christians are brought together by the truth. In 3 John, Gaius is commended because he showed hospitality to some travelling missionaries (3 John 5). Hospitality was especially important for Christian missionaries in the first century, who could suffer much hardship on their travels. It was not just a nice thing to do, but, more importantly, it showed a love for the truth and a commitment to helping the kingdom of God to grow (3 John 8). In contrast to Gaius, Diotrephes had refused to show hospitality to the visitors, and had gone further by trying to stop others from doing so too (3 John 10). This was not just bad manners, but showed that Diotrephes was also refusing their message. Since the visitors were connected to the apostle John, Diotrephes was therefore refusing John's teaching (3 John 9).

In 2 John, John reminds the church that they must be careful to whom they show hospitality. While they should welcome everyone who shares the truth with them, they should refuse to welcome false teachers (2 John 10). Showing hospitality to false teachers is as bad as the false teaching itself (2 John 11).

RELEVANCE FOR TODAY

Be discerning

Christians have to discern between true and false teaching. This was and is especially important when travelling teachers arrive, who are not known by the community. Only teachers who follow the truth can be received and given an open platform (2 John 10,11; 3 John 8).

In order to discern the difference, Christians need to know the truth themselves. It is not wise to simply accept every teaching that we hear. Rather, we must be discerning and make sure that the teaching we receive is consistent with the teaching of Christ (2 John 9).

> **"I have no greater joy than to hear that my children are walking in the truth."**
>
> 3 John 4

Be hospitable

If teachers are bringing the truth, then John insists they should be welcomed with open arms (3 John 8). Hospitality is, in fact, a Christian duty. Christian workers should be treated in "a manner worthy of God" (3 John 6). By helping Christian workers, John's readers and we are in fact becoming part of their work too (3 John 8; see as a contrast 2 John 11). The care, love and acceptance we show to our leaders and other Christian workers and missionaries is an indication of our attitude towards God and his good news.

The personal touch

It is obvious that there were significant problems in the communities to which John wrote these letters. There appears to have been a rival group within Gaius' church, perhaps led by Diotrephes, which was refusing John's teaching (3 John 9,10). The other church was under threat from false teachers (2 John 7). John, however, does not deal directly with these situations in these letters. He gives general instructions to the church to continue in the truth and to watch out for error (2 John 8; 3 John 11). However, he promises that he will deal with the specific situations personally, when he comes to visit (2 John 12; 3 John 13,14). He apparently did not want to deal with them by letter.

This is good advice for dealing with pastoral problems in the church today. In an age of many different methods of communication, meeting face to face remains a wise, Christian way of resolving conflict. It helps to avoid many misunderstandings.

Jude
GOD'S JUDGEMENT

OVERVIEW

Jude's letter is a solemn warning of God's judgement on those who claim to be Christians but who do not live in a godly way. However, God will show mercy to those who trust in Jesus Christ and make every effort to keep themselves spiritually healthy.

SUMMARY

Jude had originally intended to write a general letter about the Christian faith (verse 3); however, the appearance of "godless men" in the Christian community (verse 4) made him change his plans and write about the danger of turning away from true faith instead.

After a short introduction (verses 1,2), Jude warns his readers that godless people have managed to slip unnoticed into their fellowship. These people claimed that God's grace allowed them to sin, and so made no effort to live under Christ's lordship (verse 4). They ignored the warnings of God's judgement from the Old Testament (verses 5-7) and the example of the archangel Michael (verse 9). Instead, they continued to do evil (verses 8,10) and follow the way of Cain, Balaam and Korah (verse 11). Jude describes the spiritual emptiness of their lives (verses 12,13,16) and notes that they will receive the judgement that they deserve (verses 14,15).

Jude's readers should remember that ungodly people will always be around the church (verses 17-19). They must therefore concentrate on their own spiritual healthiness (verses 20,21). They should make every effort to save those who are in error and encourage those who doubt (verses 22,23).

Jude ends with an outburst of praise to God the Father and to Jesus Christ (verses 24,25).

Author

Jude, brother of Jesus (named Judas in the Greek and in Matthew 13:55 and Mark 6:3), who was with the disciples in Jerusalem after the resurrection (Acts 1:14). He was also brother of James (verse 1), the author of the New Testament letter by this name.

Date

Possibly late AD 60s.

Background

Jude knew his readers well (verse 3, see also "beloved" in verses 17 and 20), which suggests he was writing to particular congregations with whom he had a special relationship, rather than more generally. His readers had heard at least a couple of apostles in person (verses 17,18).

OUTLINE – JUDE

KEY THEMES – JUDE

False Christianity

The main section of the letter (verses 4-19) describes the sin of godless people in the congregation to whom Jude was writing. The list of their characteristics is unpleasant:

- They are immoral (verse 8), acting like wild animals (verse 10).
- They reject God's authority (verses 4,8) and so slander his angels (verse 8).
- They are abusive (verse 10).
- They grumble and find fault with others, while doing whatever they themselves want (verse 16).
- They boast about being spiritual (verse 16).
- They flatter other people to gain their support (verse 16).
- They are divisive (verse 19).

Jude compares them to three Old Testament examples: Cain, who was jealous of his brother (Genesis 4); Balaam, who was greedy for money (Numbers 22–24); and Korah, who rejected God's authority (Numbers 16).

The worst part of their sin was that they still claimed to be true Christians, and so had deceived the rest of the church (verse 4). They were living as members of the Christian community, taking part in the fellowship meals and possibly even having some authority in the church (they are called "shepherds", verse 12). They claimed God's grace, but refused to live under the lordship of Christ (verse 4) and did not have God's Spirit (verse 19). Jude exposes these people as false Christians. They do not produce the good fruit they should (verse 12) and so are only fit for shame and judgement (verse 13).

Certainty of judgement

Although the false Christians had managed to slip into the church unnoticed (verse 4), Jude wants his readers to know that God did not overlook their sin. Jude uses examples from the Old Testament and other Jewish writings to illustrate this:

- The unbelieving Israelites were destroyed in the wilderness, even after being saved from Egypt (verse 5; see Numbers 14).
- God judged the rebellious angels (verse 6).
- Sodom and Gomorrah were destroyed (verse 7; see Genesis 19).
- Enoch's prophecy spoke of the certainty of God's judgement (verses 14-15, referring to a non-biblical Jewish writing, *The Book of Enoch*).

The false Christians will be destroyed by their sins (verse 10) and be cast out of God's presence into woe (verse 11) and darkness (verse 13).

God's keeping power

In contrast to the false Christians, Jude's readers can celebrate that they are being kept safe by Jesus Christ (verse 1). If they keep themselves in his love (verse 21), then he will bring them safely to his glorious future kingdom, purified of all their sin (verse 24). This is a cause for great joy for both God and us (verses 24,25)!

RELEVANCE FOR TODAY – JUDE

Hypocrisy in the church

The false Christians who are described in this letter had managed to become part of the church family without being challenged about their behaviour (verse 4). They had no problem with being fully involved in the church's life (verse 12), even though they did not really live under Christ's lordship. Jude's letter was a wake-up call to the church to be aware that false Christians were among them (verses 17,18).

This letter shows that heresy (false teaching) was not the only danger for the early church. Here in Jude, the danger is hypocrisy (claiming to be Christians but not living a holy life). Jude's letter urges his readers to fight for the true faith which they had received (verse 3) and not to allow the hypocrites to divide the church (verse 19) by leading others astray.

We too should be alert to the danger of hypocrisy in our own lives and in our church fellowships. God's amazing grace does not mean we can continue in sin (verse 4; see also Romans 6:1,2).

Staying healthy

Jude encourages his readers to stay spiritually healthy, which will help them to avoid the errors of the godless people. He gives a series of instructions (verses 20,21):
- Learn more about the true faith
- Pray in the Holy Spirit
- Stay within God's love
- Wait for the return of Jesus Christ.

In addition to these things, which focus on a personal relationship with God, Christians also have a responsibility for others (verses 22,23):

> "Keep yourselves in God's love as you wait for the mercy of our Lord Jesus Christ to bring you to eternal life."
>
> **Jude 21**

- Help those who have doubts about their faith
- Save those who do not know the danger they are getting into
- Warn those who are deliberately going their own way.

While Jude celebrates God's power to keep Christians in his care, he also notes the responsibility of Christians to keep themselves healthy and ready to serve God. The best way for us to avoid the error of godlessness is to keep ourselves spiritually healthy and active in mission.

Using stories

Jude uses a wide range of examples from both the Old Testament (verses 5,7,11) and from other Jewish writings (verses 6,9,14,15) to illustrate his teaching. He also uses examples from nature (verses 12,13) and reminds his readers of what they have already heard from the apostles (verses 17,18).

Good Christian teaching will use a variety of illustrations from many different sources to add clarity to the points being made.

Revelation
THE VICTORY OF CHRIST

OVERVIEW

Is God able to triumph over evil? The book of Revelation answers "yes", by giving its readers a view of what is going on behind the scenes of world history: the risen Christ is on the throne and is at work to bring his glorious kingdom to earth.

SUMMARY

Revelation begins with a declaration of God's greatness (1:4-8) and a description of the vision that the author John received (1:1-3,9-18). The risen Christ instructs John to write the vision down, and to send letters to seven churches, giving specific messages of warning and encouragement (1:19–3:22).

John is next given a picture of the worship of heaven (4:1-11). At the centre of this worship is the Christ the Lamb (5:6), who is praised because his sacrificial death has given him authority to open the scroll which holds God's purposes for the future (5:1-5,7-14). As the seals of the scroll are opened, terrible events take place which act as warnings of God's coming judgement (6:1-17). God's people, however, are marked out to preserve them through these troubles (7:1-8; 9:4) so that they will give praise to God (7:9-17). When the final seal is broken (8:1), another series of terrible events occur as seven angels blow seven trumpets (8:2–11:19).

John's vision continues with a scene of conflict between God's people and Satan (12:1-18). John sees two beasts which represent Satan's evil power (13:1-18), while the people of God are kept safe (14:1-5). Three angels (14:6-11) bring God's message of judgement (14:14-20). Seven final plagues are brought by seven more angels (15:1–16:21), before the kingdom of Satan, called Babylon, is brought to judgement (17:1–18:24).

This brings a great shout of praise from heaven (19:1-10) before a final great battle between heaven and Satan (19:11-21). At last, both the righteous and the wicked receive their judgement (20:1-15). In a final scene, John glimpses the glory of the new heaven and the new earth (21:1–22:5). Revelation ends with an encouragement to be ready for the coming of Jesus (22:7-21).

Author

The author calls himself John (1:1; 22:8) and is in exile on the island of Patmos (1:9). Many believe he is the apostle John, author of the Gospel and three letters, although in these writings his name does not occur.

Date

Most scholars think about AD 95, during the Roman emperor Domitian's persecution of Christians. Others think of AD 69, just after the reign of Nero.

Background

Revelation was written to seven churches in Asia Minor (now western Turkey, 1:4). Some were suffering persecution for their faith in Jesus Christ (eg 2:3,10,13), others dealing with false teaching (eg 2:2,14,15,20-25), others with lukewarm Christianity (eg 3:1-3,15-18).

OUTLINE – REVELATION

KEY THEMES – REVELATION

The Lamb's victory and sovereignty

Christ is the one who has secured God's victory over the powers of Satan and now sits on the throne with God (5:13, 11:15). In the first scene of John's vision, he appears as an awesome figure (1:10-16) who has authority over death and Hades, the realm of the dead (1:18). Later, he appears as a Lamb in the centre of God's throne, who is able to open the seals on the scroll which contains God's purposes for the world (5:5-10). Then he is a mighty warrior, leading God's army to victory (19:11-21). The source of Christ's power and authority is his sacrificial death and resurrection (1:5; 18; 5:9,10,12).

Satan's schemes

John shows his readers that the evil they were facing was not simply human, but demonic. The evil in the world is an attack on God and his people by Satan. Satan is the source of the false teachings and persecutions that threaten the life of the church (2:9,13,24; 3:9) and is responsible for deceiving the nations (20:3,7-10). He is represented as a dragon (12:3-9; 20:2) who seeks to frustrate God's purposes by leading people astray (12:9). His forces are described in terrifying ways: terrible beasts (13:1-18), a huge army (20:8,9), and a city drunk on the blood of Christian martyrs (17:3-6).

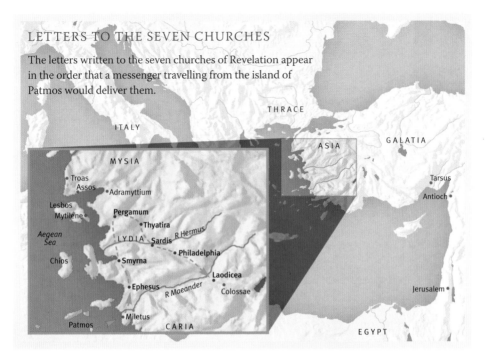

LETTERS TO THE SEVEN CHURCHES

The letters written to the seven churches of Revelation appear in the order that a messenger travelling from the island of Patmos would deliver them.

God's judgement

Much of the imagery of Revelation points to God's judgement of Satan's evil schemes. In the main part of John's vision, a series of terrible disasters occur as the seven seals on God's scroll are opened (6:1–8:1), seven angels blow seven trumpets (8:6–11:19), and seven bowls of God's wrath are poured out as plagues on the earth (15:1–16:21). These events appear to be warnings of God's final judgement, which happens with the seventh of each series (8:1-5; 11:15-19; 16:17-21). Yet John explicitly adds that humanity did not repent of its sins (9:20; 16:9,11). In the final judgement, Satan is captured and thrown into a lake of fire (19:20; 20:10). All who had followed him are also destroyed (14:6-11, 19-20; 19:21; 20:11-15). This final destruction is called the second death (2:11; 20:6), but is also seen as a lake of fire (14:10; 19:20; 20:10,14). Once destroyed, Satan and his forces can no longer threaten God's kingdom.

The faithful's reward

Revelation gives a picture of the reward God will give to his faithful people:

- Safety from the worst tribulation (3:10; 7:14)
- Eternal life with God in his new creation (eg 2:7,10; 7:15-17; 21:1–22:5)
- Clean robes, symbolising purity (3:5; 7:14)
- Authority within God's kingdom (2:26,27; 3:21; 20:4).

God's faithful church is seen as the bride of Christ (19:7-9; 21:9) who will live for ever in God's new world, in which heaven and earth are joined together (21:1-3)!

RELEVANCE FOR TODAY – REVELATION

Revelation is full of rich symbolism and strange images. Many people have tried to use the book to produce a timeline for the future of the world. However, John's vision does not follow a chronological order, and many of the images are simply different ways of talking about the same reality. The purpose of Revelation is not to give a schedule for God's plans, but to encourage Christians who are experiencing hardship and persecution.

> "We give thanks to you, Lord God Almighty, the One who is and who was, because you have taken your great power and have begun to reign."
>
> **Revelation 11:17**

God's power

Revelation's central message is the certainty of the power of God to defeat the forces of evil and bring about his new creation. John's readers were facing difficult times, and they may have begun to wonder if God was really able to save them. Revelation shows that by his death and resurrection, Jesus Christ has power and authority over all other forces in the world (see 1:5,17,18; 3:21; 5:9; 19:13). While Satan may seem powerful, he has already been defeated by Jesus, and will soon be utterly destroyed. In difficult and confusing times, it is vital to remember that the throne of the universe is occupied by God and by the Lamb, Jesus Christ (4:1–5:6; 11:15).

Christian patience

Until God's power is finally revealed, Christians must have patience. In the letters to the churches, Jesus encourages his people to remain faithful to him and to persevere through trials (2:3,10,25,26; 3:2,3). Christians are to patiently endure the disasters and judgements that are brought upon the world (13:10; 14:12), so that they will be part of the great multitude worshipping around the throne of God (7:9-17; 14:1-5; 15:2-4). We are reminded that Christ will bring his kingdom soon, so we must always be ready (22:7-20). When persecution, hardship or confusion comes to us, we should remember that God has promised to bring us to his glorious kingdom, if we patiently persevere.

Eternal praise

The book of Revelation is punctuated with outbursts of praise. Praise is given to God by the angels, creatures and elders in heaven (3:8-11; 5:9-12,14; 7:11-17; 11:15-18; 16:5-7; 19:1-8), the multitudes of faithful Christians (7:9,10; 14:1-3; 15:2-4) and even the whole of creation (5:13). God is praised for his glorious character (4:8,11; 7:12) and the Lamb is worshipped for the salvation he has accomplished (5:9,10,12; 7:15-17). These outbursts are declarations of who God is (16:5-7) and what he has done (11:15,17-18; 19:1-8), and are filled with joy, love and thankfulness. As Christians, we join in this great symphony of praise to our great God!

Bible Teaching

The material is arranged under ten major subject headings: the Bible, God, Jesus Christ, the Holy Spirit, Humanity, God's Messengers, Salvation, the Christian, the Church and the Last Things. Each major subject is divided into six sections and each section contains up to six separate studies.

This teaching material can be used for personal study or as a resource to aid Bible teaching in a group or in a church programme.

Bible Teaching

CONTENTS

THE BIBLE

GOD

JESUS CHRIST

THE HOLY SPIRIT

SALVATION

THE CHRISTIAN

THE CHURCH

THE LAST THINGS

MAKING THE MOST OF THIS STUDY MATERIAL

Personal study

This Bible Teaching study material can be used as a companion to the Bible: as a resource to aid Bible teaching and for personal, regular study of the Scriptures.

The material is arranged under ten major doctrinal headings. Each doctrine is divided into six sections. Each section consists of up to six studies. If the whole series is completed, studying one section each week, all the material will be covered in just over one year. Each study is contained in two pages.

- **The main text** gives the theological overview. The Key Truth text summarises the subject. The Postscript text draws out a significant conclusion.
- **The Bible Study section**, while having a multiple use, is ideal for home study groups. This gives a passage of the Bible, selected to convey the main emphasis of the main study, with questions that are purposely designed to open up discussion.
- **The Reflection section** is a futher aid to meditation and personal response.

This whole section concludes with a thought for each day (pages 454-463).

Group study

Study groups of all ages will benefit from the teaching they discover as they follow the guidelines within the course. Group leaders should prepare by: becoming familiar with the passages provided, being ready to support them with cross references; carefully reading the study material; being prepared to ask questions as a basis for discussion, and preparing further questions of their own.

Church programme

Ministers, pastors and teachers will find this material an invaluable reference source when preparing programmes for the church. The headings have been phrased so that the truth of the Bible is contained within the words of the headings themselves.

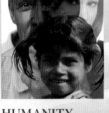

1. Its Main Sections

THE OLD TESTAMENT

History
The historical books of the Old Testament (from Genesis to Esther) show how God is involved in human history. He created the world, he chose a people to carry out his plan for saving all humanity and he provided them with laws for correct living.

These books of the law and the story of the nation of Israel provide the foundation for New Testament Christianity.

Poetry and Wisdom
Proverbs, riddles, songs, parables and allegories all occur in the wisdom and poetry books (from Job to the Song of Solomon). These books mirror the human response to God and to life. Despair, love and joy; the emptiness of life without God; bitterness, anger and triumphant faith – every emotion and situation has purpose when God is in the picture.

Prophecy
The prophets were men whom God called to speak for him to his people. They explained the past, reminding the people of God's law and his promises; they challenged the evils of the present; they also declared the future acts of God. Although these 17 books often speak of judgement and doom, they also tell of a future hope – the coming of a Messiah and of a new relationship with God.

THE NEW TESTAMENT

History
The four Gospels are based on the accounts of eyewitnesses who heard and saw Jesus of Nazareth, and they identify him as the Messiah, in fulfilment of the Old Testament.

The book of Acts goes on to show what took place after the death and resurrection of Jesus, and how the Christian church grew within the Jewish and Gentile worlds.

Letters
The New Testament letters were addressed to individuals, churches or groups of churches. They give the reader a vivid impression of the life of the first Christians, and the problems they faced.

These letters often show us the mistakes that Christians made, alongside the teaching of the apostles that gave correction and guidance in Christian living. Because Christians still have similar needs and weaknesses, the 21 New Testament letters have relevance for the church in every age.

Prophecy
The final book in the Bible consists of a series of visions seen by the apostle John, which reveal the situation affecting believers, unbelievers and the whole created order.

The book of Revelation is written in the language of symbolism and prophecy. It has inspired Christians down the ages with its message of the God who controls history, and who finally defeats all the powers of evil.

BIBLE CHECK

Old Testament
History: Genesis 12:1-3; Joshua 24:14,15
Poetry: Psalm 127; Ecclesiastes 3:1-9
Prophecy: Amos 5:21-24; Isaiah 53
New Testament
History: Mark 1:14,15; John 20:30,31; Acts 1:1-3
Letters: Romans 12:1,2; Titus 3:3-8; 1 Peter 2:9
Prophecy: Revelation 1:8-11; 12:7-12; 22:12,13

KEY TRUTH

There are 66 books, collected in two "libraries". They were written over a period of some 1,500 years. These books can be placed into the six sections in the following pages.

POSTSCRIPT

One of the remarkable things about the Bible is that although it is a very old book, written to guide people in their lives centuries ago, it is still able to answer the needs of people today.

BIBLE STUDY Psalm 119:1-32

Whether in a home group, student circle or simply on your own, use these questions to help you in the study of this passage.

1 The great Baptist preacher, C.H. Spurgeon, described Psalm 119 as "an ocean of fire". As you read these verses, ask yourself what there is in them that caused this reaction.

2 Already you will have noticed that every verse has some reference to the word of God: laws, statutes, precepts, decrees, etc. What can be learnt about the character of God's word from these different terms?

3 Although Psalm 119 has no title, its style suggests that it originated with David, the shepherd boy who became Israel's king. Can you identify sentences in this passage which would have had relevance to episodes in David's life? Look, for example, at verses 9,14,19,23,24,28.

4 What does verse 18 have to teach us about our attitude, on coming to God's law? Why do we need our eyes to be "opened" in any case?

5 "Meditate" (verse 23). 250 years ago a Yorkshire preacher, William Grimshaw, defined meditation as "the soul's chewing". How is this to be done with God's word?

6 When the Psalms were written there was no New Testament. Look up Galatians 3:29. What may we learn there about the relationship of the Old Testament to the New?

7 Identify the four personal resolves of the psalmist in verses 30-32. All of them are active. How can these become your own? Spend, now, some time in prayer and personal application of this great psalm.

REFLECTION

A Read Luke 24:13-35. What does this tell us about the Bible's power to banish fear and aid understanding? Notice the number of sections in the Old Testament referred to in verses 27 and 44.

B While all Scripture is inspired by God, some books may be of more importance than others. Which do you think these are, from both the Old and New Testaments?

C Look at 2 Timothy 3:16,17. Why has God given us the Bible?

D Look at Galatians 3:29. What does this teach us about the relationship of the Old Testament to the New?

2. Its Inspiration

The identity of its divine author

The Bible claims that God is its ultimate author. The conviction that God was speaking through the messages of the Old Testament is expressed many hundreds of times.

Both the Jewish people and the New Testament writers accepted that the Old Testament was inspired by God. Jesus himself upheld this view.

He believed the Scriptures, and by the way he quoted them showed that they were more important than human opinions and traditions.

The New Testament writers, for their part, were also aware that they were not teaching human wisdom, but rather God's message to humanity.

The diversity of its human writers

The biblical writers came from many different cultures and eras and represented a very wide range of intellects and abilities.

There was a diversity of circumstance. Some wrote as prisoners in exile, while others ruled kingdoms. There was a diversity of employment. Some were ordinary bakers, shepherds or tent-makers, while others enjoyed high positions in society. There was a diversity of character – from the despairing to the joyful.

The unity of its many themes

This unique library of books confronts the reader with its unity, although written over some 1,500 years. It is ancient, yet modern in its relevance to human needs. It is diverse, yet one – held together by its common theme of God's people and their desire and need of a coming Saviour. The Old Testament finds its fulfilment in the New Testament. The New Testament has its roots in the Old Testament. The library is one.

The authority of its inspired truth

From early times the value of these books so impressed itself on God's people that they acknowledged their authority and received them into the category of inspired Scripture. They recognised that it was God who was speaking.

It was not the act of binding the books into the Bible that gave them their inspiration. This they already possessed. The authority of the Old Testament was recognised by the Jews, by Jesus himself, and also by the New Testament writers, who frequently quoted the Old Testament. The New Testament writings were also accepted by the church from its early days as having the final say in everything that Christians believe and do.

The reality of its moral impact

The Bible is not afraid to portray evil honestly, even when some of its finest characters are involved in it. But in contrast, it also shows us the highest moral standard in history – the life of Jesus Christ.

This is the book that consistently challenges evil, transforms lives and exalts Christ.

BIBLE CHECK

Identity: Jeremiah 1:9; 2 Peter 1:21; 2 Timothy 3:16,17

Diversity: Amos 7:14,15; 1 Kings 4:29-32; Acts 18:3

Unity: Matthew 5:17,18; Luke 24:25-27,44

Authority: Joshua 1:7,8; Matthew 22:29; Psalm 19:7-11

Reality: Deuteronomy 32:45-47; Hebrews 4:12

KEY TRUTH

When we say that the Bible is "inspired" we mean that God spoke his message through the people that he chose. These people did not become like robots under God's control, but kept their own identities, while being guided by God.

POSTSCRIPT

Like any other book, the Bible was written by human authors. But, unlike any other book, it was guided and planned by God from beginning to end. It is because God stands behind the Bible that all Christians owe it their loyalty and their obedience to its demands.

BIBLE STUDY 2 Timothy 3:10–4:8

Here is the apostle Paul, encouraging his junior fellow-worker Timothy to be confident of God's word in all his ministry, whatever the difficulties and opposition. These questions will help in the study of this passage:

1 Reflect on the opposition that the faithful teaching of the word of God invites (verses 10-13). Why is this so? What does this have to do with Scripture's central focus (John 5:39,40)?

2 Look at verses 14 and 15. How and when were you first introduced to the Scriptures? Compare experiences.

3 What are the Scriptures uniquely qualified to do for us? Look at verses 15-17.

4 "God-breathed", "inspired by God" (verse 16). How is the "inspiration" of the Bible different from the 'inspiration' of, say, the works of Shakespeare? Compare Luke 24:27 and 2 Peter 1:21.

5 Consider the solemn responsibility of communicating "the word" to others (4:1,2). What should be our true motivation? What should be our attitude?

6 What are we up against in the proclaiming of God's revelation (4:3,4)? In what ways do you see these tendencies at work today?

7 Four direct commands are given to Timothy in 4:5. How do they apply to modern representatives of God's truth? What are our encouragements from Paul's words in verses 6-8? Finish the study by praying for people you know, world-wide, engaged in spreading the message of the Bible.

REFLECTION

A Read Exodus 3:1-14 and 4:1-17. Why was Moses reluctant to speak for God? What reasons did God give for trusting him?

B When the prophets spoke God's message they were often attacked or even killed by the people. Why? Does this still happen today?

C How did Jesus regard the Scriptures? See Matthew 5:17-19. How can we best learn from his example?

D God spoke through the writers of the Bible without robbing them of their individuality. Consider some of these writers. What do we learn from this about the way in which God uses people?

THE BIBLE

3. Its Interpretation

THE BIBLE MUST BE:

Seen in its historical setting

One of the ways in which we can understand the meaning of a Bible passage is to gain an understanding of its original meaning to the earliest readers. The more we know about the customs and politics of Bible times, the clearer its meaning will be.

For example, the New Testament commands that slaves should obey their masters. We must understand this in the light of the fact that slavery was generally accepted at that time (even though it was seen as part of the order that was passing away because of Christ).

Similarly, a knowledge of customs at that time helps the modern reader to understand the meaning of Jesus' command to his disciples to wash one another's feet – which might otherwise seem irrelevant today.

Consistent with its surrounding passage

We can better understand the meaning of a Bible word when we examine the sentence in which it occurs. In the same way, we can only truly understand a sentence when we look at the surrounding paragraph.

The leaders of many false cults and sects often twist the truth of the Bible by taking a sentence out of its context. In this way they use the Bible to support their own beliefs. Christians must be careful to find out what the Bible is really saying – even when it hurts.

In harmony with the rest of Scripture

Individual passages of Scripture are to be interpreted in the light of the whole Bible. When this is done, no one part of Scripture will be found to conflict with another. When we are confronted with apparent contradictions in the Bible, it is probably because we do not know the consistent teaching of the Bible as a whole.

The challenge to the reader of the Bible is to develop a truly biblical way of thinking.

Consistent with the purpose of God's revelation

The Bible tells us all that we need to know about God's plan for his creation and for humanity. There are many questions which we might want answered, about which the Bible says very little or nothing. But God's word tells us all we need to know about him and his plans.

We must recognise that the Bible is first of all a book of salvation. Therefore, we should avoid making clever interpretations on matters outside its main purpose.

Understood in changing cultures

The Bible has a living message, with power to transform lives and characters. Although it was given in cultures far removed from those of modern times, its relevance to life is undiminished today.

As we interpret the Bible, however, we must be prepared to wrestle with the words and terms used by the biblical writers, and to translate them in ways that the modern reader can understand.

KEY TRUTH

Interpretation means the discovery of the true meaning of the Bible. Several things are important to remember as we try to understand the Bible's teaching.

POSTSCRIPT

The Bible is not a scientific textbook, nor a history book. Yet it will not conflict with scientific findings nor with historical facts. Its purpose is different – that of portraying God's plan for humanity, in Christ.

BIBLE STUDY Nehemiah 8:1-12

Here is a passage that describes God's ancient people, the Jews, in the 5th century BC. They have been restored from the terrible days of exile in Babylon. Although now under Persian domination, they have an opportunity, not only to restore Jerusalem's shattered walls, but to rebuild their life – around the Book of God. Focus now on these questions:

1 "The Book of the Law of Moses" (verse 1). This was probably Deuteronomy. What are the advantages of studying the Scriptures together?

2 Picture the scene described in verses 1-6. This was a national occasion. How far has the Bible's message given a foundation to modern-day civilisations?

3 Study the key to the whole chapter (verse 8) and discuss the importance of such words as "clear", "meaning" and "understand".

4 Why is it unsatisfactory when numerous different "meanings" are forced onto a passage? (Compare 2 Corinthians 4:2). What was the result when the one true interpretation was made known to Ezra's listeners (verses 9,12)?

5 In the light of this passage, consider the reaction of others when God's message became clear to them (eg Jeremiah 15:16; 1 Thessalonians 1:6).

6 Scripture elsewhere gives warnings against false teachers who use the Scriptures wrongly (eg 2 Timothy 3:6-8; 2 Peter 2:1-3). To what extent is this a problem in your society?

7 Look at verse 5: Ezra opened the book. What resolves will you make for yourself, as you take the lessons of this passage to heart? Pray about them now. Make 2 Timothy 2:15 your motto.

REFLECTION

A Read John 13:1-15. In the time of Jesus, to wash someone's feet was an act of humility and kindness. In what ways can we obey Jesus' command in verse 14 today?
B Some words used in Bible translations are not a part of everyday speech. Find out what words like "salvation" or "repentance" mean, and put them in your own words.
C What should our reaction be when we find Christian people equally divided over the correct interpretation of a Bible passage?
D What is the strength of knowing individual verses of the Bible by heart? What is the limitation?

4. Its Application

Read prayerfully

The Bible is not simply an interesting book to read: it is a book to get involved in. It deals with issues that vitally concern the reader's life, character and destiny.

To read the Bible with prayerful dependence on the Holy Spirit is a safeguard against hardness or pride – it also shows that the reader is willing to submit to God's moral direction.

Listen personally

The Bible is not a book of abstract philosophy – it is a book about life and about people in real situations. Isaiah spoke specifically to the people of Jerusalem. The apostle Paul often greeted friends by name in his letters. The book of Revelation was written to Christians who were suffering persecution.

But we must go on to say that the Bible's rewards and promises are for every reader, of whatever century. As we open our lives to the Bible's message, we can expect God to communicate with us.

Look expectantly

As we read the Bible, we will be surprised and even shocked by some of the events that act as warnings within its pages. There will be other passages that challenge or puzzle us. We must expect to be stretched to the limit of our capacity by this book.

Apply regularly

When we read and apply the Bible regularly, one of the great benefits is that we start to see the world in a Christian way. We also see the Bible as a whole, and not as unconnected fragments.

As young children need a regular diet for proper growth, so the Christian needs to feed spiritually upon the Scriptures, applying their truths to daily living. As a result, our characters are transformed.

Act obediently

The Christian will repeatedly be confronted with the Bible's commands. The Bible challenges us to obey God's word, and not only to listen to it.

Jesus said that it is not enough merely to hear his words. It is only when we hear and obey that our lives are like a house built on rock – safe and secure.

Read totally

The Bible reader should aim at a full and balanced appreciation of all that the Bible may teach on any given topic. To rely on individual verses or on favourite selected passages (valuable though these are) will not lead us to spiritual maturity.

As we persist in reading the Bible thoroughly, worship becomes a living force, our work for God becomes a vital activity, and Christ becomes a daily companion.

BIBLE CHECK

Read: Psalm 119:33-40;
Matthew 7:7,8

Listen: 1 Samuel 3:10;
Revelation 1:3

Look: Jeremiah 23:29;
1 John 5:13

Apply: Psalm 1:1,2; 1 Peter
2:2,3

Act: James 1:22-25; Matthew
7:24-27

Read: 2 Corinthians 4:2;
Colossians 3:16

KEY TRUTH

The Bible is meant to change
the way in which we live.
As we apply the Bible, God
instructs, supports, cleanses
and directs us in our daily
lives.

POSTSCRIPT

God gave us the Bible, not just
for us to enjoy its stories or
learn about him. He gave us
the Bible so that we
may live in the way that he
wants. Applying the Bible
can be challenging and
uncomfortable – but it must
be done.

BIBLE STUDY James 1:19-27

It is all very well to understand the Bible's message, but is it
being put into practice? This is a great theme of James, the half-
brother of Jesus Christ (Matthew 13:55). It is a letter addressed
to believers in general; this passage has a relevance for all time.
The following questions will help in its understanding:

1 What sentence in this passage most clearly sums it up?

2 What is the best attitude with which we should come to the
word of God?

3 Why is mere listening the way of self-deception (verse 22)?
Compare your findings with Matthew 7:26,27.

4 Reflect on the phrase "the word planted in you" (verse 21).
What does this mean? How does it happen? Think of the
parable of the sower (Luke 8, eg verse 15).

5 What is the point of the illustration in verses 23-25? How
would you apply this to your own actions?

6 Verses 26 and 27 raise an obvious question regarding our
intake of God's word; how has it changed our lives? This
applies to the words we are speaking, and the things we are
doing. From these verses, describe a religion that is real in
today's world.

7 Is it time to learn a sentence of the Scriptures by heart, as a
result of reading this passage? Before you turn to prayer, look
up, and start to learn Joshua 1:8 ... the reference, the words,
and then the reference again, to make it stick!

REFLECTION

A Read Psalm 119:97-112. Try
to list some of the benefits
that result from meditating on
the Scriptures.

B Christ once told a parable
about the different kinds of
soil into which the good seed
fell (Mark 4:1-20). Try to
describe the kind of life that is
"good soil", in which the seed
of God's word can grow.

C Discuss with your friends in
practical terms the times of
day when you find it best to
read the Bible.

D Hebrews 4:12 describes the
power of the Scriptures. Try
to enumerate some of the
instances in the Bible where
this power is demonstrated.

5. Its Central Theme

The continual conflict

The conflict in the Bible began when Adam and Eve questioned God's authority. From this simple beginning stemmed the entrance of sin into the world, and the revolt of humanity against God's rule.

The Bible traces the spread of this conflict between humanity and God.

It shows how people soon became hostile to each other, as well as to God. The need of humanity to be reconciled to God becomes the central theme of the Bible.

The promised Saviour

The Old Testament speaks clearly about the longing for a future deliverer from sin and guilt. However, this is more than a mere hope. The prophets, particularly, speak of God's promise of a Saviour, who will establish a new agreement with God's people – with forgiveness and liberated service at its heart.

The New Testament points unmistakably to Jesus Christ as being this promised Saviour.

The work of Christ

The coming of Jesus Christ in history fulfils all the hopes of the Old Testament, and provides the basis for the New. In Jesus, God himself entered human history, and opened the way for forgiveness and holy living. This was done through Christ's death, his resurrection and his gift of the Spirit. Death is defeated, the power of Satan is broken, and the ascended Christ rules.

The new community

The New Testament portrays the followers of Christ as the society of the saved – called to be members of his world-wide church. Wherever the rule of Christ operates in people's lives, there his church is found.

This new community worships its reigning Lord, and is called upon to fulfil its mission of evangelism and practical service to the whole world. Jesus Christ personally upholds it in every experience. When he comes again, its membership and task will be complete.

The ultimate victory

The whole of creation will be involved in the final triumph of God. His love and justice will be upheld for everyone to see, and the whole empire of evil will be overthrown.

The great landmark of the future is the return of Jesus Christ, personally, historically, visibly and triumphantly. He will come as Judge of the whole world as well as Saviour of his people. The date of his coming cannot be predicted, although calamities, wars and the appearance of false Christs confirm the approach of this final event of history.

Christian believers look forward to a new heaven and a new earth. They look forward to a day when they will receive new bodies which will never age or die. Then sin and sorrow will be banished for ever, and their salvation will be complete.

BIBLE CHECK

Conflict: Genesis 3; Titus 3:3
Saviour: Isaiah 53; Jeremiah 31:31-34; Luke 24:44,45
Work: Mark 1:15; Luke 2:28-32; Titus 3:4-7
Community: Matthew 16:18; 28:19,20; Ephesians 2:18-22
Victory: 1 Thessalonians 4:13-18; Revelation 21:1-4

KEY TRUTH

Although humanity has rebelled against God and ignored his laws, God has a plan for rescuing us. This plan is centred around Jesus Christ, and concludes in God's ultimate victory over sin, Satan and death.

POSTSCRIPT

It is important for the Bible reader to understand, by consistently reading the whole Bible, that God is at the centre of all things, and is in ultimate control of the universe.

BIBLE STUDY Revelation 5:1-14

Written around AD 95, towards the end of the reign of the emperor Domitian, the book of Revelation presents the oppressed believers of every generation with a series of visions, first given to the exiled apostle, John. In this passage the theme of all the ages is opened for us. Use these questions to help in the study:

1 The "scroll" of John's vision contains not Scripture as such, but rather the secrets, the explanation of all history and its meaning. Can you think of some of the candidates who have stepped forward in their claim to be a universal teacher?

2 "I wept and wept" (verse 4). Why this failure on the part of great leaders and movements to unravel the meaning of life? Compare your findings with Daniel 2:27,28.

3 The one successful candidate is then announced (verse 5). What is special about his title? See Isaiah 9:6,7; 11:1,2. Who is this figure?

4 What is significant about this royal leader turning out to be a Lamb that has been slain (verses 6,7)? Genesis 22:8, Exodus 12:21-23 and 1 Corinthians 5:7,8 will help.

5 Discuss, from verses 8-10, this central theme of the universality of Christ's redemption of the world. When were you first caught up in this?

6 It is now the turn of the angels to sing (verses 11,12). What do we learn here about the position of Jesus Christ?

7 Verses 13,14. Is this universal song your song? What does this passage do for your own world-view? Turn now to prayer.

REFLECTION

A Consider Titus 3:3-7. How far are the major themes of the Bible summed up in this passage? Are Paul's words true of your own experience?

B A Chinese person once said of the Bible, "Whoever made this book made me." Do you agree with this? What lies behind such a sentence?

C What is the most important reason for having a biblical way of looking at life? Because the Bible brings comfort and hope? Because society needs belief of some kind? Because the Bible is true? Try to give your reasons.

D How does a biblical view of life help a person to grapple with the issues of wrongdoing, strife and injustice?

THE BIBLE

6. Its Contents

THE OLD TESTAMENT

Genesis The start of God's plan for his people.

Exodus God's people are freed from slavery.

Leviticus Preparing God's people for worship.

Numbers God's people wander in the wilderness.

Deuteronomy God's people called to obedience.

Joshua Success in the Promised Land.

Judges Failure in the Promised Land.

Ruth The story of a faithful daughter-in-law.

1 Samuel The emergence of Israel as a kingdom.

2 Samuel Israel's greatest King – David.

1 Kings Solomon – the temple – the division.

2 Kings The divided kingdom, and the prophets.

1 Chronicles God's faithfulness to his people.

2 Chronicles The fall of Israel as a nation.

Ezra The return from exile, and the new start.

Nehemiah Danger as Jerusalem is rebuilt.

Esther Esther's courage saves the exiled Jews.

Job Dialogues on the sufferings of a godly man.

Psalms Humanity's honest response to God.

Proverbs Wisdom for living.

Ecclesiastes The world's philosophy exposed.

Song of Songs A poem of love.

Isaiah The prophet of hope.

Jeremiah The prophet of tragedy.

Lamentations The prophet of sorrow.

Ezekiel The prophet of God's glory.

Daniel The prophet of confidence in God.

Hosea The prophet of love.

Joel The prophet of the Day of the LORD.

Amos The prophet of justice.

Obadiah The prophet of doom.

Jonah The prophet of repentance.

Micah The prophet of restitution.

Nahum The prophet of retribution.

Habakkuk The prophet of doubt and faith.

Zephaniah The prophet of judgement.

Haggai The prophet of dedication.

Zechariah The prophet of restoration.

Malachi The prophet of expectation.

THE NEW TESTAMENT

Matthew The teaching of the promised Messiah.

Mark The work of a powerful Saviour.

Luke The concern of a loving Saviour.

John The belief in a personal Saviour.

Acts The witness to a risen Saviour.

Romans God's righteousness upheld and applied.

1 Corinthians A church's problems corrected.

2 Corinthians The ministry of the church.

Galatians The gospel and Jewish law contrasted.

Ephesians Christ's relationship with the church.

Philippians The love and loyalty of a church.

Colossians The person of Jesus exalted.

1 Thessalonians New converts encouraged.

2 Thessalonians The second coming of Christ.

1 Timothy Instructions for church behaviour.

2 Timothy The pastor of a church encouraged.

Titus Christian self-control.

Philemon To the owner of a runaway slave.

Hebrews The greatness of Christ exalted.

James Practical instructions for a living faith.

1 Peter The suffering of the church explained.

2 Peter The perils of the church foretold.

1 John The reality of divine fellowship.

2 John Walking in the truth exhorted.

3 John Living in the truth practised.

Jude Apostasy in the church condemned.

Revelation The triumph of God over all evil.

Please note The themes opposite are only a guide. Each theme should not be seen as the only theme of any particular book, but as a distinct emphasis of that book.

BIBLE STUDY Deuteronomy 4:32-40

The children of Israel are poised at the border of their Promised Land. The 40 years of wandering come to an end. Our passage is part of a great address in which Moses is summarising the adventure with God – which is really the story of the Bible. Use these questions for your study:

1 The sweep of God's dealings with the human race goes back to Creation itself (verse 32). What is the value of reviewing the road by which we have come?

2 "... the voice of God speaking" (verse 33). What is the great truth behind these words? Compare them with Hebrews 1:1,2.

3 How far does the overall message of the Bible's 66 books tie in with what you read in verse 34?

4 Try to itemise, in this passage, the different actions of God that have led to his people knowing and acknowledging him (verse 35,39).

5 Verse 40 concerns the keeping of God's commands. Discuss those books of the Scriptures that have so far helped you significantly.

6 Reading the Bible may seem a formidable prospect. Examine and think through the best way of arranging a programme of regular Bible reading.

KEY TRUTH

Each book of the Bible has its own distinctive central themes. The list here is a sample of some of these themes.

POSTSCRIPT

Each book of the Bible should be read as a whole, so that an overall view is gained of its contribution to God's message to humanity.

REFLECTION

A Look at Matthew 4:1-11. Consider each of the temptations that confronted Jesus. Why did he make use of the Old Testament so much to resist the devil? What may we learn from this?

B Discuss with your friends which biblical book has helped you most, so far. How has it helped? Which book do you look forward to reading next? Why?

C Why is it important to read the Bible? Look up 1 John 5:13 and John 20:31.

D Perhaps you feel daunted by the thought of getting to know the books of the Bible. What is the best way of arranging your Bible reading programme?

GOD

1. The Trinity

Revealed in the Old Testament

The Old Testament stresses that God is one. The prophet Isaiah, in particular, says that there is only one God, and that all other "gods" are false. And yet at the same time, the opening sentence of the Bible uses a plural form for God's name (Elohim) and does so hundreds of times subsequently. Thus, at no point is it right to think of God in a unitarian way.

There are enough indications in the Old Testament for us to recognise the idea of three persons within the Godhead. For example, God sometimes refers to himself as "us", and there are appearances and visions of him which suggest different members of the Trinity.

Asserted in the New Testament

In the New Testament Jesus gives us some very clear teaching about the Father and the Spirit. Jesus shows us the wonderful truth that there is one God, and the Father, the Son and the Holy Spirit are all together this one God.

The New Testament does not give us a formula about the Trinity but the evidence is unavoidable. In the unity of the one God there is a Trinity of persons achieving man's salvation, and in whose name we baptise.

Known by faith

Proof texts are not enough for a clear understanding of the Trinity. We must study all the teaching of Jesus and of his apostles, and observe the threads of truth that run through the Bible which relate to the will of the Father, the work of the Son and the inner working and witness of the Holy Spirit.

God the Father

The first person of the Trinity is called Father, not primarily because of his relationship to his creatures, but because of his relationship to the eternal Son.

Because of our union with Christ, the Eternal Son, we are brought to share in that dynamic relationship between the Father and the Son.

God the Son

The second person of the Trinity is called the Son. He became a man, Jesus Christ, in order to rescue humanity from the domination of sin. As Son of God he was involved with the Father in the creation of all things and shared in his eternal glory.

Within the Trinity the Son is obedient to the Father in all that he does. Thus the Son was sent by the Father and only acted under his Father's authority.

God the Holy Spirit

The third person of the Trinity was sent from the Father in Christ's name, to make personal in the lives of Christians all that Christ had made available through the cross. Just as Jesus once lived among us, so the Spirit now lives in us.

Although he was active in the Old Testament, a distinctive task of the Spirit began after the ascension of Jesus. He is the one who points attention to Christ, who speaks to the church in every age and who equips Christians with abilities to serve God.

BIBLE CHECK

Revealed: Isaiah 44:6-8; Genesis 1:26; 18:1-15

Asserted: John 14:15-26; 16:5-15; Matthew 28:18-20

Known: John 16:12,13; 2 Corinthians 13:14; 1 Peter 1:2

The Father: Matthew 11:27; Luke 10:21; Acts 2:32-36

The Son: John 1:1-18; Colossians 1:15-20; Hebrews 1:8

The Holy Spirit: Romans 8:9-11; 1 Corinthians 2:10,11

KEY TRUTH

There is only one God. But God consists of three persons, the Father, the Son and the Spirit, who are all equally God.

POSTSCRIPT

The Trinity must not be a truth that has no relevance to our lives. We will understand the truth of the Trinity best as we experience the work of the Father, Son and Holy Spirit in our lives.

BIBLE STUDY John 14:8-21

The teaching of the Bible that relates to the three Persons within the Godhead is never presented as a formula, a neat doctrine or as a philosophical system. The Trinity is always alluded to in the most natural way. Study these verses now, and allow the following questions to help:

1 What do we learn from Jesus' dramatic reply to Philip's question (verses 8-10)?

2 In verse 12 Jesus declares that in the future, his followers will accomplish things greater in dimension than what was possible when Jesus was here on earth. How could this be so, and why? For an illustration look at Acts 2:38,39. Look too at the context of Christ's words (verses 16 and 17.)

3 Notice in verses 16-18 how the three Persons of the Trinity all feature; at some points the titles seem interchangeable. Try to think through the different roles or activities of the Father, Son and Holy Spirit. For further clarification, see Romans 8:3,4,11.

4 A Christian convert once wrote, "It became quite obvious to me that by the Trinity, 'Father, Son and Holy Spirit,' Christians meant one God in three Persons, and not three separate deities." Discuss this in the light of John 17:11.

5 It is probably through Christian experience that the truth of the Trinity is most easily understood (verse 21). How should that affect the way in which we speak to inquirers about the Trinity?

6 In your prayer time, use Ephesians 3:14-19 as an example of a thoroughly Trinitarian prayer. Then end with "the grace" of 2 Corinthians 13:14.

REFLECTION

A Read John 14:8-21. Go through this passage carefully and try to see how the different persons of the Trinity relate to one another, both in who they are and what they do.

B Why did God not reveal the truth of the Trinity as clearly in the Old Testament as he did in the New? What does this tell us about the way God reveals himself?

C Read Exodus 3:1-6. What can we learn from Moses' response to God as we think about the Trinity?

D The teaching of the Trinity is much more than mere discussion over certain words. How can people make sure of benefiting practically from the teaching?

GOD

2. The Creator

God the creator

The universe has not always existed. The consistent teaching of Scripture is that the cosmos had a beginning. It was not formed from any matter that already existed. God, the one and only creator of the universe, brought the world into being by the unaided power of his word.

God did not need to create the universe, for he is self-sufficient. He decided to bring all things into being for his own glory. The creation involved all three persons of the Godhead. The opening chapter of the Bible records our beginnings in majestic and timeless language that communicates to every culture and era.

God the sustainer

The Bible teaches that God the creator is also the provider and sustainer of all that he has brought into being. He is not an absentee God who made the world and then left it to run itself.

Far from remaining aloof and remote from his creation, God continues to work in it. He is intimately involved in the running of the universe and the forces of nature, and he is in overall control of governments and communities. Christ also taught of the Father's concern for the least of his creatures.

God is achieving his purpose

God is in ultimate control of all that he has created. This does not mean that we are unable to decide things freely for ourselves. God has given us that freedom, even though we chose to rebel against him. But it does mean that God is active, and is bringing about the things he wants to happen.

He is achieving his purpose.

God's purpose may be stated very simply. It is to restore fallen humanity and the creation itself to the freedom and perfection that have been lost because of humanity's rebellion. God the creator is also God the redeemer.

Earth as a focal point

The earth is a very small planet in a vast universe, and it could not be argued that our world occupies any central position in creation. But it is apparent from the Bible that the creator of the cosmos has set his loving concern upon this earth.

As human beings we are physically dwarfed by the immensity of our surroundings, but the universe should hold no terrors for us, because of the place the world has in God's purpose. Ours is the visited planet, the part of creation where a special relationship has been planned between God and ourselves, who have been formed in his image. Human beings are central to God's plan for the whole universe.

BIBLE CHECK

Creator: Nehemiah 9:6;
Hebrews 11:3; Genesis 1
Sustainer: Acts 14:17;
Hebrews 1:3
Achieving: Daniel 2:20-22;
Romans 8:18-25
Earth: Psalm 8:3-9; Revelation
21:1-3

KEY TRUTH

God has brought into
existence the whole of
creation, which he sustains
and upholds by his power. He
created the universe out of
nothing, and did this for his
own purpose and glory.

POSTSCRIPT

A person who is in rebellion
against the creator will
inevitably have a human-
centred view of God and
creation. The Christian learns
to see creation as it really is,
with God at the centre and in
control.

BIBLE STUDY Genesis 1 and 2

Here is the grand "overture" to the Bible. It lays the first mighty
plank of the biblical revelation, and we must remember Christ's
words of Matthew 19:4,5 that by implication confirm these
chapters, along with all Scripture, as coming from the mouth of
God himself. Although it is hardly possible to do justice to these
two chapters in a single study, the following questions may help
to identify the main teaching:

1 What can you learn from these chapters about the God of
creativity? Why is there no place in them for Pantheism (in
which God and Nature are understood as identical)?

2 Someone has once said, "God's first rule is order." What are
the indications here of a God of regularity?

3 What can be understood from chapter 1 about the God of
variety? Concentrate on the occurrences of the word
"separate". Note also the separation of the human race from
the animal kingdom in 1:26, and the separating of ourselves
into the two sexes (1:27 and 2:21-24).

4 Notice the establishing of the foundational one-day-in-seven
principle in 2:2. How can this pattern of creation be
preserved?

5 "The image of God", 1:27. How are we to understand this
separation of ourselves from animals? Look on at verse 28,
and 2:7. Compare with Psalm 8:3-9. Reflect on the personality
of God, and how it is that we are not described as "which" but
as "who".

6 There is much to be learnt here about the God of
responsibility and our appropriate care of the environment.
Read 2:8-17 and discuss.

REFLECTION

A Read Genesis 1, and think
about its description of the
world's beginnings. Where
does this chapter place you, as
a person, in the universe? See
Psalm 8:3-8.

B The Bible gives us reasons
to feel happy with ourselves as
human beings, but also
reasons to feel unhappy. Why
is this?

C What features in our world
do you most appreciate, and
give thanks for?

D Why is the truth of creation
important today? Is it enough
to say that God is the creator,
or should we regard the details
of how he created important
as well?

3. God's Being

God is everywhere (omnipresent)

God is the creator of nature and is therefore not to be confused with it (the mistake of the Pantheists). At the same time we should not separate God from his creation and think of him as absent (the mistake of the Deists).

The Bible teaches us that there is no place in creation to which we can go that will put us at a distance from God. He is present everywhere in the universe. We must be careful not to limit God in the way that he is present among us. He is present creatively in his works; he is present morally in the area of human behaviour; he is present spiritually among his people; he is present sovereignly in nations, governments and systems.

God is all-powerful (omnipotent)

The Bible gives us many examples of God's power. He brings the designs of powerful nations to nothing. He is in control of nature – and this comes out especially in the miracles Jesus performed.

However, all these instances might suggest to us that God is just a lot more powerful that we are. The fact that he is all-powerful is shown by his role as the creator of all things, the judge of all humanity, and the one who will subdue all the forces of evil. The Bible tells us he is the only God, and all power belongs to him.

God knows everything (omniscient)

God's knowledge follows from his universal presence. Because he fills heaven and earth, all things are open to his view and knowledge. He is completely aware of the past, present and future. He knows about all events, thoughts, feelings and actions.

The knowledge gained by other beings must be built up and learned. God's knowledge is eternal and is entirely his own – he has learned it from nobody.

This teaching is vital to our understanding of God. If God did not know everything, it would not be possible to believe in the justice of his judgements in history and at the end of time. This is also true in the realm of worship. The Christian prays to a God who fully understands our state and our needs, who hears and perceives not only our words but our secret thoughts and desires, and who knows the end from the beginning.

God is eternal and unchanging

The Bible describes God as the first and the last. He always has existed, and he owes his existence to no one. In contrast to the ever-changing and decaying world, the Scriptures teach us that God is unchanging in his person and purposes.

He neither increases nor decreases. He can never be wiser, holier or more merciful than he has ever been or ever will be.

For the believer, limited by a temporary body and a changing environment, the eternal God provides a permanent foundation and a secure home and resting place.

BIBLE CHECK

Everywhere: Psalm 139:7-12; Jeremiah 23:23,24
All-powerful: Genesis 17:1; Job 42:1,2; Jeremiah 32:17
Knows: Psalm 139:1-6; Hebrews 4:12,13
Eternal: Isaiah 44:6; Malachi 3:6; James 1:17

KEY TRUTH

There are certain aspects of God's being that are unique to him, and can never be shared with any other being.

POSTSCRIPT

These descriptions of God only give us half of the biblical picture of him. It is the moral aspect of God which completes the picture and shows us that goodness is at the heart of the universe.

BIBLE STUDY Psalm 139

"In its essential burden," wrote Dr Campbell Morgan, "this is the greatest song in literature." Read the passage prayerfully, and then try to take in something of the nature of the God we follow, with the help of these questions:

1 The passage seems to be divided into four sections; verses 1-6,7-12,13-18 and 19-24. Try to establish the dominant thought of each section. All of them point to some aspect of God.

2 "I", "me", "my". These words that run through the psalm tell us that God, in his different attributes, may be experienced personally. How did this happen for David? Compare, for example, verse 11 with 2 Samuel 12, especially verses 12,13.

3 We learn from verses 7-12 that there is no hiding place from God. Think first of a biblical example of this fact (eg Jonah 1:3), then of some modern instances. Have you known of this experience?

4 Some modern theories about humanness maintain that person-hood does not belong to infants, either in the womb or newly-born. How does this psalm run counter to these theories?

5 Look at verse 19 onwards. Although we note that there is nothing actually personal about the psalmist's condemnation of the ungodly, there is evidently a challenge that he is obliged to face up to. What is it?

6 Look at the beginning and end of the psalm (verses 1-4,23,24). Why is it such a tremendous discovery to learn of God's intimate knowledge of our lives?

REFLECTION

A Read Psalm 139:1-18. What major truths about God are expressed in verses 1-6, 7-12 and 13-18? How does the writer see his relationship to God? Try to list all that God has done for him.
B How should our understanding of God's being affect the way that we pray? After thinking about this, turn to Psalm 139:23,24.
C Look at Deuteronomy 29:29. How do these words of Moses help us in matters where our knowledge (eg of the future) is limited?
D Try and make the praises of the apostle Paul your own, as you worship God in the words of Romans 11:33-36.

4. God's Character

God's truth is inseparable from his character

The truth of God is the foundation of all knowledge. Truth is unalterable.

It will not change or accommodate itself to varying cultures and standards. Truth is essential to God himself – it always has existed and always will exist.

Thus our existence is not a delusion, as some people claim, and the laws of the universe will not shift. Truth comes from God and is consistent with his character. We see this supremely in the person of Jesus, who as Son of God claimed to be the centre of all truth.

God's holiness reacts against all impurity

God is holy. There is no statement in the Bible which is more demanding than this. God's holiness means he is totally committed to goodness and is at war with evil.

The Bible teaches that God alone is completely pure and free from evil. As a result it is impossible for wrongdoers to live in God's presence until they have been made clean.

God's love extends to all humanity

The Scriptures are full of the love, mercy, grace and faithfulness of God. Human love is seen as an imperfect reflection of the love that characterises God.

This is the love that longs to pardon the evildoer while yet satisfying the demands of divine justice. Its highest expression is seen at the cross.

God's mercy holds back what we deserve

God's holiness and moral purity demand that those who revolt against his authority should face judgement and be overthrown. However,

the Bible is full of examples of the restraining hand of God's mercy.

Thus the Bible shows us that God is slow to punish sin. He prefers to give people the opportunity to turn from wrong.

God's grace gives us what we do not deserve

The word "grace" means that "God is generous towards us even though we deserve his anger." There are two kinds of grace. On one level there is common grace where God's gifts in nature (the seasons, our natural abilities and human relationships) are given to the human race, regardless of the attitude of those who receive.

On a spiritual level we receive God's saving grace. He has given his assurances and promises to the human race throughout history, sending his messengers to raise the standards of societies and to free them from slavery to evil. Supremely, he has given his Son to the world so that the gift of eternal life might be freely available – to those who respond.

God's faithfulness provides for daily life

The writers of the Psalms constantly refer to the faithfulness of God, illustrated in the ceaseless cycle of nature and in the return of the morning each day. It is God's world and his resources are around us.

Humanity has to face danger and hardship in a world which is imperfect because of the intrusion of sin – and the Christian is as liable to face illness and testing as the non-Christian. But those with a trust in God are assured of his overall care and control of events.

Truth: Jeremiah 14:14;
Numbers 23:19; John 14:6
Holiness: Isaiah 6:1-5;
Habakkuk 1:13; Revelation
15:4
Love: Psalm 103:13; John 3:16;
1 John 4:7-11
Mercy: Nehemiah 9:16,17;
Hosea 11:8,9; 2 Peter 3:9
Grace: Matthew 5:43-45;
1 Corinthians 1:4-8;
Ephesians 2:8-10
Faithfulness: Psalm 89:1,2;
1 Thessalonians 5:23,24

KEY TRUTH

The truth, holiness and
goodness of God find
expression in his works and
actions, extending even to
those in rebellion against his
rule.

POSTSCRIPT

It is important to see all the
aspects of God's character.
If we only see God as holy,
he will appear harsh and
demanding. If we only see him
as loving, he will seem to be
unjust and powerless.

BIBLE STUDY Hosea 11:1-11

Here is the character of God, displayed within the great
romance of the Old Testament; his relationship with Israel.
The context is the broken marriage of the prophet Hosea.
Told by God to take back his wayward and now enslaved wife
Gomer, the whole prophecy revolves around the theme of love
that agonises between righteous judgement and free
forgiveness. It is, ultimately, God's dilemma with his people.

1 Begin with verses 1-4. How is God pictured here? What was
the response to his attitude? Has the situation changed down
the ages?

2 How would you summarise the result of turning from God, in
verses 5-7? What is the challenge to modern-day Christians?

3 We come to the heart of Hosea's entire prophecy in verses 8
and 9. (Admah and Zeboiim were two cities coupled with the
immoral Sodom and Gomorrah. For their fate, look up
Deuteronomy 29:23.) What is the dilemma that causes God
such agony? Note, at the end of verse 8, that it is in the
character of God himself that the solution is found, where
righteous justice and forgiving love can meet. Look up Psalm
85:10; Romans 3:25,26; 1 John 3:1.

4 Like the faithless Gomer, Israel's sin would lead to slavery, but
there was a way of restoration. Look at verses 10 and 11. Can
you think of examples in Christian history when similar
restorations and times of revival have taken place? What were
the secrets of these revivals?

5 Reflect on the remark that God is the greatest sufferer in the
universe.

REFLECTION

A Consider the teaching of
Psalm 103, and try to list some
of the qualities of God's
character that are featured
there. Which of these qualities
have you felt to be at work in
your own life?

B What is the biblical answer
to those of us who carry on
sinning, taking it for granted
that God will forgive us?
Consider your reply in the
light of Romans 2:4,5.

C What is the difference
between God's common grace
and his saving grace? Who are
the receivers of God's gifts in
each case?

D How can we best express
our gratitude to God for the
goodness that we have
received from him?

5. The Fatherhood of God

GOD IS FATHER:

By creation – of all things

Although the Bible never designates God directly as "Father of the creation", nevertheless his creativity is frequently linked with his character as Father. The universe is under his care and fatherly authority.

In the Scriptures God is portrayed as Father of human beings only in a general sense – because he created us. The close and intimate relationship that could exist between God and the individual believer was not fully revealed until it was taught and made possible by Jesus Christ. God is the Father of all people but only in a very limited sense. This is because of the universal rebellion against God's authority that has characterised the human race throughout history.

By covenant – of Israel

In the Old Testament, God initiated a solemn agreement with Israel by which he would be their God, the people of Israel would be his people and would submit to his rule and authority.

It was in this national sense that God became the Father of Israel, giving to his people guidance, protection – and discipline on the many occasions when he was disobeyed.

By adoption – of Christian believers

It was Jesus Christ who revealed the fatherhood of God towards believers in an intimate sense unknown in any other faith. He taught his followers to speak to God as their heavenly Father.

As the New Testament teaching develops we learn that salvation firstly includes giving the new believer forgiveness and the right to stand before God. But secondly, we are adopted into the circle of God's family with all the privileges that follow. Thirdly, and better still, we are given the spirit of sonship and a change of heart that encourages us to speak to God as a child would to its own father.

Such a relationship knows no human parallel. Those who have entered into such a relationship can truly be said to have been born of God. They are his children.

From eternity – of Jesus Christ

It is true that Jesus addressed God in his prayers as Father, but he never joined in prayer with his friends, nor spoke to them about 'our' Father.

The exception was the Lord's Prayer, but even then it was made clear that the prayer was for them to pray, not for himself.

Evidently, Jesus was God's Son in a way that the disciples were not. It is in the Gospel of John that the eternal relationship between the Father and the Son is most clearly seen.

BIBLE CHECK

Creation: Acts 17:24-29; Ephesians 4:6

Covenant: Isaiah 63:16; Malachi 2:10

Adoption: Romans 8:14-17; Galatians 4:4-6

Eternity: Luke 11:1-3; John 20:17; John 17:5,24

KEY TRUTH

God is Father, generally, of the creation he has made. He is also Father to all Christians, whom he has adopted into his family. But uniquely, he is the Father of Jesus Christ.

POSTSCRIPT

Because of human weakness, we must distinguish between the standards set by our own father and God's perfect fatherhood. The fatherhood we have known, at its best, can only faintly mirror God's care and concern.

BIBLE STUDY Luke 11:1-13

This passage is one of the reasons why "Father" is the name by which Christian believers know God the best. It was Jesus, above all, who taught his followers to understand their relationship with God in a close and intimate sense that had never been understood before, and that knows no parallel in any other faith.

Use these questions to highlight this truth:

1 What was different about Jesus' praying that provoked the request of verse 1? Compare Matthew 6:5-8.

2 Father (verse 2). There was a Father term used of God in the Old Testament, but it was more of a national title. This new use of "Father" no longer puts us at a distance. It is a learnt truth. When did members of the group first begin to discover it?

3 The Lord's Prayer of verses 2-4 gives us a model or pattern for prayer, rather than a rigid formula. Try to identify the areas of faith and life covered by these petitions.

4 Look now at verses 5-8. Here is a cameo of life that demonstrates one massive point – that our heavenly Father is utterly unlike the man in bed. In what respects? What then should be our encouragements?

5 From verses 9 and 10, what main attitude should characterise our praying?

6 Verses 11-13 give us a yardstick from which to define true fatherhood. What does this say to a generation whose image of fatherhood has often become twisted in today's fallen world? Compare your findings with Ephesians 3:15. Then have some prayer together.

REFLECTION

A Study Galatians 4:1-7, which shows the contrast between slaves and sons (see verse 7). Trace, from verse 4, the processes by which the Christian has been made a child of God. What are the privileges that the Father gives to his children.

B How should our view of God as our Father affect the way that we pray? After thinking, check your reply with Matthew 7:9-11.

C How should you answer a person who wasn't a Christian who claimed that God was the Father of all, and that there was no need to worry about prayer, the Bible, or church?

D What do you think pleases God the Father most of all? What grieves him most? Compare your findings with Luke 15:11-24.

GOD

6. God's Revelation

GOD REVEALS HIMSELF:

Supremely in Jesus

Throughout history God has been communicating to humanity. In the Old Testament God sent messengers and prophets to speak his messages, but it is in Jesus Christ that his revelation is complete and perfect. This is why Jesus is called "the Word". He is the fullest way in which God has revealed himself to us. Jesus' life, his teaching and his character portrayed God perfectly for he was God living as a man.

Through the Bible

Through a unique collection of writings brought together over a period of about 1,500 years, God has made plain his plan for humanity, using people he guided to convey his message.

Some men were chosen to write selected history, others to communicate wisdom and worship, yet others to unfold the future, or to give instruction for belief and conduct. Every book has its individual way of showing us God, within the unity of the Bible.

Through creation

The whole creation proclaims the glory of God. The universe holds together and finds its logic in the Eternal Logos (the Word – God the Son). He is the Light that lights every person in the whole world. On Judgement Day nobody will be wondering who their judge is, because he has confronted us in everything around us all our lives.

In history

The Bible shows us how to understand history. God has revealed himself in a powerful way through history. God's plan is revealed in the rise and fall of great empires, Egyptian, Babylonian or Roman. Jewish history is seen in the Bible as the means by which the Messiah would finally come.

Furthermore, it cannot be a coincidence that the beginning of the Christian faith took place at a historically stable time, when communications were excellent in the Roman Empire, and when there was one common language – Greek.

In humanity

God also reveals himself in the very way in which we are made up. Human beings are made in God's image, and this image, although distorted through deliberate rebellion, is not obliterated. As a result, human nature can point to the work of the creator.

Human complexity and creativity is a signpost of God's revelation, as also is the power of the human conscience, instincts and emotions. It is evident that people were made to enjoy relationships and these very relationships show the character of the God who made us.

Through human experience

God continues to speak to us in the present. His voice is heard in many ways: through human friendship, through the arts and through our appreciation of all that is beautiful.

Christ's followers are also given the Holy Spirit, who speaks both to individuals and churches, and who progressively transforms those who listen to him. In these ways God continues to reveal himself to us in the present.

Hebrews 1:1-4;
John 1:1-18; 14:8-10
Bible: 2 Peter 1:19-21;
Romans 16:25-27
Creation: Psalm 19:1-4;
Romans 1:18-20; John 1:9
History: Psalm 75:6,7; Daniel
2:44
Humanity: Genesis 1:26,27;
Psalm 139:13-16; Romans
2:14,15
Experience: 2 Corinthians
3:17,18; Revelation 2:29

KEY TRUTH

"Revelation" means that God
has spoken to us so that we
can understand him and
respond to his love.

POSTSCRIPT

The creation proclaims the
glory of God – but it is only
through the written and
spoken gospel that God shows
his power to save.

BIBLE STUDY Psalm 19:1-14

This psalm of David is concerned with God's revelation, or
declaration, of himself. It is impossible for our fallen race to
discover God unless he does declare himself to us. Study this
passage, with the help of the following questions:

1 From the first section (verses 1-6), we may learn about God's
general revelation of himself. How would you describe this
revelation to someone else? What is its power? What is its
limitation? For a New Testament parallel, look up Romans
1:20.

2 From God's general revelation, the psalmist turns to his
verbal and special revelation (verses 7-11). In what does it
consist? List the terms by which it is described.

3 In what ways is this special revelation superior to the voice of
nature? From these verses, try to itemise its effects upon us.

4 What is the psalmist's response to what he has learnt from
God's revelation? Verses 12-14 give the answer. Apply what
you find to yourself.

5 Look up the New Testament quotation of verse 4 in Romans
10:18. There the apostle Paul clearly sets the verse within the
context of the New Testament gospel of Christ. What are the
great implications of this?

6 How do the words of God's writers and the wonders of the
universe relate to Christ, God's personal revelation? Look up
Hebrews 1:1-3. Now spend some time in prayerful
application of these truths.

REFLECTION

A Consider carefully 2 Peter
1:16-21. What were the two
ways in which Peter witnessed
the truth of Christ? What
encouraging features can you
find in this passage about
God's revelation? Compare
verse 19 with Psalm 119:105.
B According to Romans
16:25-27, what is the purpose
of God's revelation?
C Why does not everybody
accept God's revelation in the
various forms in which it
comes? What does his

revelation mean to you?
See 2 Corinthians 4:3-6.
D How do you explain
kindness and bravery in
people who have no belief in
God at all?

1. His Incarnation

Christ was Son of God before time and space

The Bible teaches that Jesus did not come into being when he was born, but that he has always existed as the Son of God. It was through him that God created the universe, and in him all things hold together.

It was by a supernatural conception

The circumstances of Jesus Christ's birth help us to understand that he was born without sin. The human bias to sin is inherited from our parents. Because of the unique conception of Jesus he was born without this bias.

While Christ's birth was as normal as that of any human, his conception occurred through the intervention of the Holy Spirit. Because of this Jesus was both God and man.

It upholds Christ's full deity

As the New Testament unfolds, the fact that Christ is God is increasingly revealed. The hints turn to signposts and the signposts turn to bold acclamation.

The signposts are: Christ's character (his sinlessness and purity), his claims (to be the centre of all truth, to be the world's judge, and to have a unique relationship to the Father), and his conduct (in performing miracles, forgiving sins and accepting worship).

It establishes Christ's full humanity

The New Testament shows that Christ was fully human born into a Hebrew family and subject to the Hebrew law.

He experienced all the problems that people have to face. He was exposed to hunger and thirst, fatigue and sorrow, and he faced the full force of temptation – yet without ever giving way. Although he was still fully God, Jesus (as a man) shared completely all human weaknesses. Because of this he was perfectly qualified to be the unique go-between, bringing humanity and God together.

It explains Christ's unique personality

Jesus Christ is without parallel, for he is both God and man, in two distinct natures, and one person for ever. It was the same Jesus who declared that he was thirsty, who also referred in a prayer to the glory which he shared eternally with the Father.

The New Testament writers do not try to explain as a philosophy how one personality could be both human and divine. But the portrait they give us identifies him both with human beings and with God.

It validates Christ's saving ministry

There are aspects of the incarnation that are beyond our understanding. But one thing is clear. We know enough to realise that in Jesus Christ, truly God and truly human, is found the one Saviour that the human race needs.

By laying aside his eternal splendour, and involving himself in humanity's burdens – even to the point of death on the cross for our sins – he becomes the reconciler between God and humanity, and by his resurrection he brings our humanity to heaven.

BIBLE CHECK

Before time: John 1:1-3;
Colossians 1:15-17

Supernatural: Matthew
1:18-25; 1 Peter 2:22;
Hebrews 4:15

Upholds: John 8:46,50-58;
Luke 5:20,21;
John 20:26-29

Establishes: Galatians 4:4,5;
Hebrews 2:14-18; 5:7

Explains: Matthew 8:24-27;
John 19:28; 17:5

Validates: 1 Timothy 2:5;
Philippians 2:5-11

KEY TRUTH

The word "incarnation" means
"to become human". The New
Testament tells us that God
became a human being. This
person, Jesus Christ, was fully
God and fully human.

POSTSCRIPT

Errors have arisen in Christian
history when either Christ's
deity or his humanity has been
neglected. It must be
understood that in every way
he is fully God and fully
human.

BIBLE STUDY Colossians 1:15-20

The apostle Paul is writing, around the year AD 55,
to Christian believers in Colossae, a city situated in present-day
western Turkey. He writes from prison,
to counteract false teaching that threw doubt upon the divinity
of Jesus Christ. The following questions will help in the
understanding of this passage, and in a stronger grasp of the
nature of Christ.

1 This passage has been called the "Creed of Christ's Pre-
eminence" (Handley Moule). As you scan these sentences
what particular phrases in them point to such a description?

2 Try to understand Christ's relationship to creation. Why is it
that the term "firstborn" (or "heir", verse 15) does not imply
that Christ is a created being? Look carefully at verses 15-17
and compare with Hebrews 1:2,3.

3 A university student once asked, "Is Jesus Christ the ultimate
– or is there something yet bigger than him that I must seek?"
This passage gave him his answer and he became a Christian.
What is there in these verses that would have helped him?

4 In what sense may we say that Christ is the explanation and
the goal of the whole universe?

5 There are those who will say, "Let us try to find the best from
all traditions and reconcile them into a final, ultimate
synthesis." How should we reply to this theory? Verses 19 and
20 will help.

6 Establish from verse 18 the relationship of Jesus Christ to the
church. Where is the one and only place that God will meet
with us, and where we can find peace with him? What does
this say to the message that we communicate to the world?

REFLECTION

A Consider Colossians
1:15-20. How does this
passage portray Christ in his
relationship to creation, to the
church, to God and to the
cross?

B People have argued over
almost every aspect of Christ's
incarnation. His full deity and
full humanity have come in for
particular attack. Why do you
think this is, and what are the
reasons for the limit to our
understanding of this
teaching?

C In what ways should we
follow the example of Jesus'
life as a man? See Hebrews
12:2-4 for one possibility.

D What do we gain from the
fact that Jesus is, like us, a
man? And what do we gain
from the fact that, unlike us,
he is God?

2. Main Events in the Gospels

His humble birth

Jesus was born, during the reign of the Roman emperor Caesar Augustus, into an extremely poor family. He was born in alien surroundings during a Roman census, and he was born into immediate danger – as King Herod searched to kill him.

These two elements, the humility and insecurity of Jesus' birth, were to set the pattern of his whole life.

His sinless baptism

The baptism of Jesus marks the beginning of his ministry. John the Baptist was calling his hearers to a baptism of repentance. Jesus, however, had no sin of which he could repent. But by his submission to John's baptism, he showed his identification with sinful humanity. The descent of the Spirit like a dove and the Father's words of acceptance which accompanied the baptism came as God's approval of the ministry that was to follow.

His prolonged temptation

Immediately following his baptism Jesus went into the desert for a period of forty days during which he fasted, and was tempted by the devil.

The temptations that are recorded for us took the form of challenging Jesus to bypass his mission. Jesus successfully resisted these and all the other temptations that occurred throughout his life.

His revealing transfiguration

Towards the end of his public ministry Jesus took three of his disciples to a mountain-top where he became brilliantly irradiated before them. Moses and Elijah appeared and spoke with Jesus about his coming ordeal in Jerusalem. The disciples also heard a voice of divine approval as at Christ's baptism. The event was clearly a preview in miniature of Christ's glory that lay ahead.

His obedient death

The tide of events turned against Jesus after his triumphant entry into Jerusalem. The Passover meal that he celebrated with his friends was swiftly followed by his betrayal, by a series of unjust trials, by death on a cross and by burial.

It was a dark hour but it was the hour for which Jesus had come into the world. He made it clear that he had come, not only to teach and heal, but also to suffer and die for all humanity.

His victorious resurrection

36 hours after the burial, Jesus' tomb was found empty, except for the discarded graveclothes. It was sufficient for John who "saw and believed".

Then Jesus began to appear to his friends over a period of 40 days. This was not an illusion, for he took food, could be touched, and was seen alive by hundreds of people. And yet he was uniquely and powerfully different – the victor over death.

His glorious ascension

The last time the disciples were to see Jesus was on the Mount of Olives. He commanded them to make disciples everywhere and he promised them the gift of the Spirit who would give them the power to do this.

He was then taken from them visibly. He would not be seen again until his return.

BIBLE CHECK

Birth: Luke 2:1-7; Matthew 2:1-18; Luke 9:57,58

Baptism: Matthew 3:13-17

Temptation: Matthew 4:1-11

Transfiguration: Luke 9:28-36

Death: Matthew 26 and 27; Luke 22:53

Resurrection: John 20 and 21; Luke 24:36-43

Ascension: Matthew 28:16-20; Luke 24:44-53

KEY TRUTH

The four Gospels present the reader with selected significant events in Christ's life. The events listed here are of particular importance.

POSTSCRIPT

It is rewarding to compare the accounts of Christ's life in the four Gospels and to see how the writers, from their differing viewpoints, complement one another.

BIBLE STUDY John 2:1-11

This passage follows the great first chapter of John, with its majestic teaching about the coming of Christ as the Word, as the life, as the light and as the Son. The chapter ends with Jesus' prediction of heaven being opened and the angels of God ascending and descending upon the Son of Man. We would expect chapter 2 to take us into the realms of glory and the spectacular! But read on:

1 A tiny village in a very minor Roman province – together with a small crisis in a wedding reception. How can this be John's first "sign" of Christ's incarnate glory? Discuss this point.

2 If Mary, the mother of Jesus, had heard the ringing testimonies of chapter 1 (eg verse 49), it is possible that she spoke here, in verse 3, expecting Jesus to indicate that the hour of his emergence as Messiah had come. How then are we to understand Jesus' reply in verse 4? Compare John 17:1 and Mark 14:41,42.

3 Look at verses 5-10. How do these verses illustrate the truth that, through the Incarnation, Jesus takes hold of the ordinary, the ordinary becomes better – and the best is yet to come? What signal was being given to the disciples?

4 Can we learn something here about miracles and their purpose – from one who refused to turn stones into bread for himself. Who refused to perform miracles for Herod's benefit? Verse 11 gives a clue.

5 Not everybody got the point. The toastmaster can only joke with the bridegroom. "Fancy keeping the best wine until the end!" Why should this happen?

6 Look again at verse 11. Reflect on all that was to follow: the travels, the miracles, the transfiguration and the cross. What was this first revelation of Christ's "glory" hoping to achieve?

REFLECTION

A Read John 17:1-5. What exactly was the 'work' that Christ was given to do? How did the main events in his life contribute towards it?

B From what we know, how did Jesus prepare himself for his main work? How did he prepare his disciples?

C Jesus Christ had no home of his own, never travelled outside Palestine and never wrote a book. To what, then, do you attribute the impact that he has made upon the world?

D "If only Christ were on earth today." How do you react to this wish when it is expressed? Look at John 16:5-7.

3. Main Aspects of His Ministry

Authority that convinced

The authority with which Jesus taught amazed the people who heard him. The prophets of old repeatedly declared "The Lord says ..." But Christ's frequent phrase was "But I say to you ..." He directed his hearers towards himself.

The Jewish leaders of Jesus' day took their authority from the great teachers of the past, but Christ taught in his own name and authority.

Parables that provoked

The teaching of Jesus Christ was given in terms and images understood in daily life, and this is particularly true of his unforgettable parables which both concealed and revealed truth.

People would often be captivated by the story of the Runaway Son or the Rich Fool, only to discover that the parable had been about themselves.

Miracles that confirmed

Christ's authority was further demonstrated by his miracles. The wind and the waves were obedient to his command, and even the dead were brought back to life.

But most of his miracles were acts of healing that were part of his mission of love. They also pointed to his identity as the Son of God and to the coming of God's kingdom.

Compassion that attracted

Christ's deep concern for people was born from his understanding that humanity is created in God's own image, but that we are also fallen and live in a fallen world.

Because of this Christ showed care and concern for the individual.

This can be seen in his many encounters with the bereaved, the sick and the demon-possessed. The crowds were quick to recognise the high value that Jesus placed on the individual, and they came to him in large numbers.

Training that prepared

Towards the beginning of the second year of Jesus' public ministry, the twelve disciples were chosen to share in his work of teaching, preaching and healing. These men learnt from Christ's example and from the private instruction he gave them. He also trained them for their future work as they (and some 70 others) were sent out two by two to do his work.

The Twelve did not understand all that was being taught them at the time, but their training was to be vitally important in the future development of the church.

Controversy that challenged

From the outset the words and actions of Jesus had a controversial cutting edge that finally provoked a collision between himself and the Jewish authorities.

Jesus clashed with the Jewish leaders over the following issues: that he mixed with sinners, challenged traditions, liberated the Sabbath, and that he claimed to be God.

BIBLE CHECK

Authority: Matthew 5:21,22,27,28,31-34; 7:24-29

Parables: Mark 4:2; Matthew 13:10-17; Luke 15:11-32

Miracles: Mark 1:23-28; John 10:31-33

Compassion: Matthew 9:35-38; 15:32-39; John 11:30-44

Training: Matthew 10:1-15; 16:13-21; 1 John 1:1-4

Controversy: Mark 2:5-7,15,16; Matthew 23:13-36; 26:62-66

KEY TRUTH

Christ was unlike any prophet or religious teacher that ever lived. By his authority and deeds and by the power of his teaching and his example, he challenged his hearers to believe in him as the unique Son of God.

POSTSCRIPT

It is a remarkable fact that while Jesus directed his hearers towards himself, he never at any time gave the impression of being conceited, arrogant or selfish.

BIBLE STUDY Matthew 5:1-16

There were crowds around Jesus, but it was basically to the "disciples" that he addressed the Sermon on the Mount, as it has come to be called. Jesus is preaching a sermon, but he is also painting a portrait of the ideal believer. He is further planning a mission, as he goes on to teach in terms of "salt" and "light". The following questions will help in the understanding of the challenging radicalism of Christ.

1 Scan verses 1-12 to understand a little of how the values of Christ's kingdom directly collide with those of society.

2 Some have criticised the Sermon on the Mount as being beyond the average person. Now ask yourself whether it was ever intended for an "average" person! How different is the member of Christ's new society to be?

3 In verses 3-10, are these the differing qualities of eight separate people, or do they form a photo-fit of one person? Compare your findings with Galatians 5:22,23.

4 The qualities we are looking at are all inward in nature. Why?

5 If you are in a group, let each member "adopt" one of the virtues listed, and try to say, from what they already know of the Scriptures, what is meant by it, and how we would recognise its expression today.

6 What can be learnt from verses 11 and 12 about persecution of the believer; its cause, its history and our right reaction?

7 Verses 13-16 feature two illustrations of the outward and visible difference that Christians should make in society. Apply them to your own fellowship and church, and pray around them.

REFLECTION

A Consider Jesus' teaching in Matthew 5:1-12. In what way did his words overturn the world's values? Try to list the blessings that belong to the members of Christ's kingdom.

B How can a Christian best put into practice that attitude of Jesus to individuals? How can this be done in your own area?

C The true Christian cannot avoid controversy. What issues need to be faced at present in the name of Christ?

D What parable of Jesus has spoken to you recently? Discuss this with some of your friends.

4. His Names

Son of God

As no one else, Jesus taught his disciples to think of God as their Father in a particularly intimate way. But because of his use of the terms "my Father'" and "your Father" it is clear that he saw his own relationship to the Father in a quite different way from that of his followers.

The Jewish authorities recognised this and accused Jesus of making himself equal with God. The term "Son of God" occurs most frequently in John's Gospel.

The Word

The Old Testament tells us that God created all things by his word. He spoke and it came to be. The apostle John shows that this word was in fact God's Son, without whom nothing would exist.

The Word is also involved in God's creation in another important way. He is the perfect expression of God to humanity. Because Christ is the Word, he did not merely bring us God's good news, but he is himself that good news.

High Priest

This title, given to Christ in the book of Hebrews, is drawn from the Old Testament system of sacrifices. A sacrifice had to be made every year by the High Priest on behalf of God's people to atone for their sins.

Christ, by his sacrificial death (never to be repeated) is the perfect mediator and High Priest.

Messiah

For centuries the Jews had looked for a future King who would be a descendant of David. This person was called the "Messiah" by the Jews (which in the Greek language is *Christos*, from which we get "Christ").

He would have God's authority and power to bring in the end of the age and establish the kingdom of God.

It was Simon Peter who made the first clear declaration that Jesus was the Christ, but it is important to note that Jesus totally rejected the popular idea of the Messiah as being a political deliverer from the Roman Empire. He saw his messianic role as one of suffering and death for the salvation of humanity.

Son of Man

Jesus used this name more than any other to describe himself. Although it seems to speak of his humanity, in reality it is a pointer to his deity, for the term is drawn from the book of Daniel, where the Son of Man rules an everlasting kingdom.

Jesus used the title in three ways – when speaking of his earthly ministry, his death and his coming glory. It is suggested that he favoured this title because it carried no nationalistic associations, it implied an identification with humanity, and it had both 'overtones of divinity and undertones of humanity.'

Lord

To call Jesus "Lord" was, in the New Testament church, the mark of a true Christian. To use this name invited opposition – from the Jewish authorities on the grounds of blasphemy, and from the Romans on the grounds of treason against the Emperor. This was the name that ascribed all authority to Jesus.

BIBLE CHECK

Son of God: John 20:17; 5:18,25; 20:31

Word: Psalm 33:6-9; John 1:1-4,14; Revelation 19:11-13

High Priest: Leviticus 9:7,8; Hebrews 7:23-28

Messiah: Matthew 16:16,21; John 4:25,26

Son of Man: Daniel 7:9-14; Matthew 8:19,20; 20:17-19; 24:30

Lord: 1 Corinthians 12:1-3; John 13:13; Philippians 2:9-11

KEY TRUTH

The many different names of Jesus Christ reveal the distinctive characteristics of his person and the work that he came to do.

POSTSCRIPT

The very fullness of Christ defies human imagery and thought. The six titles described here are not the only ones the Bible gives to him. It is encouraging to list the numerous other titles given to Jesus.

BIBLE STUDY Revelation 19:6-16

This book. written in about the year AD 96, at a time when the emperor Domitian tyrannised the Roman empire, has encouraged believers, "the saints of God" down the ages, and particularly at times of stress and opposition. It portrays the victory of Christ, despite the terrifying ordeals that confront his people. In this piece of futuristic writing, the apostle John, alone in exile, has just described the end-time collapse of the world of evil. Here Christ is identified through vivid imagery and by a variety of titles. Be encouraged!

1 In verses 6-10, the rule of God is portrayed as supreme amid the acclaim of his people. What is the significance of the form of the celebration described?

2 The "Lamb" is also the bridegroom of his bride the church. What is so special about the Lamb? Compare Revelation 12:11.

3 "Jesus" (verse 10). When did that name first begin to become important and treasured within your group? Reflect upon the world-wide family of believers who "hold to the testimony of Jesus".

4 The vision changes at verse 11. "White" consistently stands for purity and heaven in the book of Revelation. Think through the implications of following the Rider on the white horse (eg verse 14; see also verse 8)

5 Come now to the specific "names" of verses 11-16. There are four of them (verses 11,12,13,16). What can be learnt about Christ himself from these four "names"? What caution should we be aware of. In what way should the unknown name of verse 12 caution us?

6 Spend some time in worship and intercession, applying the lessons of these and other names of Christ, as you pray.

REFLECTION

A Read Matthew 16:13-28. Jesus praises Peter for recognising him as Messiah, but then forbids that the identification be made public. Why? In what other ways is Jesus described in this passage, and how does he see his role?

B In what ways is Christ superior to the Old Testament priesthood? Look at Hebrews 7:23-28.

C Why do we bother about a title for Jesus Christ? What is the danger today in simply referring to him as "Jesus"? Compare your answer with Mark 13:5,6.

D Which, of Jesus Christ's many titles, has meant a lot to you? What new aspect of his person has come to light through this study?

5. His Atoning Death

CHRIST'S DEATH ...

Initiated a new relationship

The Bible teaches that human sin has created a barrier of guilt between him and his creator. However, Jesus accepted the responsibility for human sin and willingly took its penalty on the cross. The Bible calls this propitiation – Jesus became a sacrifice to turn away the anger of God. A new relationship is now available for those who respond to the good news that their sins can be forgiven.

Hostility has been replaced by friendship. Those who become united to Christ are viewed by God as though they had never been rebels at all. Indeed the Christian is seen as a new person altogether.

Fulfilled Old Testament Scripture

The Old Testament showed that God and humanity could not be reconciled unless a sacrifice was made. Only then could the guilt of sin be removed.

The Old Testament animal sacrifices could not in themselves take away sin nor could they be a final solution to the problem of sin. The New Testament sees them as illustrations of the perfect sacrifice Jesus was to make.

Destroyed Satan's kingdom

The power of Satan's kingdom was broken through the death and resurrection of Jesus Christ. The final destruction of the devil is yet to be. The Christian is aware of his activity and influence – but is confident of victory and protection through the power of the cross.

Reversed sin's dominion

In the Bible, the idea of redeeming (or "buying back") a person who is enslaved is very strong. Christ is presented as the one who, by his death, redeems his people from the penalty of God's moral law.

Because Christ has taken our guilt upon himself, sin no longer has the power to dominate the life of the Christian.

Provided a way of victory

With the power of the devil limited (and ultimately doomed) and with the guilt of sin removed, the cross of Jesus Christ has set the Christian free.

The Christian is not set free from the fight for moral purity – rather he is set free for the fight. The 'tenses' of salvation are as follows: we have been saved from the penalty of sin by a crucified Saviour; we are being saved from the power of sin by a living Saviour; we shall be saved from the presence of sin by a coming Saviour. From the cross onwards, the message is one of victory.

Guaranteed an eternity with God

The cross is the guarantee that God has set his eternal love upon his people; there could be no stronger demonstration than the death of his Son.

Death is still an enemy, but it is an enemy that is defeated because of the death and resurrection of Christ. Like the devil, death will face ultimate annihilation. The cross assures the Christian of a promised inheritance in God's eternal kingdom.

BIBLE CHECK

Initiated: 2 Corinthians 5:15-19; Romans 5:8-11
Fulfilled: Hebrews 10:1-12; Isaiah 53:4-12
Destroyed: Colossians 2:15; 1 John 3:8
Reversed: Galatians 3:13; Romans 6:6-11
Provided: 1 John 1:7-9; Titus 2:14
Guaranteed: Romans 8:31-39; Hebrews 2:14,15

KEY TRUTH

The word "atone" was coined by bringing the two words "at one" together. This expresses its meaning. By dying for the sins of the world, Jesus Christ has made it possible for all humanity to be made "at one" with God.

POSTSCRIPT

A great proportion of the four Gospels is taken up with the events surrounding Christ's death. The cross was not a tragic accident – it was the event to which Christ's whole life was directed.

BIBLE STUDY Matthew 27:32-56

Here is a passage, obviously the work of an eyewitness, stripped of all embroidery, yet notable for its sometimes ironic fulfilling of Old Testament prophecy. It was a very public death, watched by the soldiers (verse 36), visible to the passers-by (verse 39), to the religious hierarchy (verse 41), and witnessed by the centurion and many women (verses 54 and 55). As the passage is read, let the old spiritual raise the very personal question. Were you there, when they crucified my Lord?

1 Let each member of the group try and establish the central or key thought of the passage, and then compare notes. What is the biggest thing this passage is saying?

2 "Simon" (verse 32) was father of Alexander and Rufus, according to Mark 15:21. Does this mean that by the time of writing these two were already known Christians? Romans 16:13 gives us a further hint that this may be so. Ponder the effect that the cross would have had on Simon.

3 Let a member of the group read Psalm 22:1,7,8, 14-18, and then discuss the bearing that this psalm has upon Matthew 27.

4 "If you are the Son of God" (verses 40,43). When had Jesus heard those words before? Look up Matthew 4:5 – was that a similar challenge to by-pass the ordeal of the cross? What was the irony of verse 42? Compare verse 40 with verse 54.

5 Read on about the death of Jesus and then reflect on verses 51-53, "when a shudder ran through nature" (Alfred Edersheim). What confidence do these events give us (compare Exodus 26:33 with Hebrews 10:19-22)? What did the cross do to death itself? See 2 Timothy 1:10. Now spend time in prayer and worship.

REFLECTION

A Read Matthew 27:32-54. Consider Christ's death in terms of its fulfilment of the Old Testament (for example Psalm 22).

B Just before he died, Jesus cried out, "It is finished!" (or "accomplished") – John 19:30. What was the significance of this saying? After thinking about this, read John 12:27 and 17:4.

C What is the best response that a Christian can make to the sacrificial death of Jesus Christ?

D In 1 Corinthians 1:18-25 we learn that the message of the cross is an offence to many. Why should this be so?

6. His Triumphant Resurrection

The foundation of the Christian faith

The resurrection of Jesus Christ lifts Christianity from the level of philosophy, or a mere code of conduct, to the supreme stature of God's good news for the human race.

In the resurrection God set his seal of approval upon Christ as Son of God, and underlined the value of his death. It was the resurrection that transformed the followers of Jesus, and sent them out into the world to preach the good news. The resurrection is the pivot of the Christian faith.

An event supported by evidence

If we enquire into the evidence for the resurrection, we are confronted first by the factual evidence. There is the empty tomb, containing only the abandoned grave clothes, and the persistent failure of all explanations other than that Christ had risen. Also to be faced are the numerous reported appearances of the risen Jesus, at different times and before different people.

There is also the psychological evidence. For example, there are the transformed disciples, the conviction of the early church in the face of persecution, and the change from Saturday to Sunday as the Christian day of worship (after centuries of Sabbath worship).

A promise of ultimate victory

If Christ had not been raised from the tomb, his death would have been evidence enough of the failure of his mission.

Thus the resurrection gives positive assurance that the Christian believer has not believed in vain. The mission of Jesus did not end in failure but in triumph. Ultimately all things, even the 'last enemy', death itself, must submit to the victory and rule of Jesus.

The power of Christian experience

To the Christian, the resurrection of Christ is far more than a past event of history. It plays a vital part in Christian living in the present and colours the outlook, hopes and motives of every believer.

The New Testament teaches us that Christians must be ready to be like Jesus Christ in his life and death. This means that since we have died to self-interest (as Jesus died), it follows that we live a new life (as Jesus rose to new life). The Christian lives and works in the very power by which God raised Jesus from the dead.

The assurance of eternal security

Christ's victory over death has made immense changes in the area of sorrow and bereavement. The finality has been taken out of death.

All those who die can know that Christ has been through this experience before them, and will bring them through it to be with him.

Furthermore, because Christ's body was raised from death, the Christian has the guarantee that he too will receive in eternity a resurrection body of beauty and strength. This new body will be related to the old but without weakness or decay.

BIBLE CHECK

Foundation: 1 Corinthians 15:12-19; Romans 1:4
Event: John 20:1-29; 1 Corinthians 15:1-8
Promise: 1 Corinthians 15:24-28; Acts 17:30,31
Power: Philippians 3:10,11; Romans 6:5-14
Assurance: John 11:25,26; 1 Corinthians 15:20,42-57

KEY TRUTH

The Bible says that God raised Christ from the dead. By doing this God declared that his Son was the Saviour of the world. The historical event of the resurrection is also the foundation of Christianity.

POSTSCRIPT

It is worth remembering that Jesus would never have risen from the dead so triumphantly if he had not first been willing to give up his life. We only receive God's new life when we give up the control of our own lives.

BIBLE STUDY 1 Corinthians 15:1-11

The Christian faith welcomes every attempt to investigate, and even "disprove" the resurrection of Jesus Christ; in many instances, the attempt has resulted in the convincing of the critic that the story is true. In this chapter, Paul expands upon this key-stone of the apostolic gospel. The following questions will help in an understanding of the passage selected.

1 From verses 1 and 2, how important are the truths that Paul is writing about?

2 In verses 3-5, Paul is establishing the common ground of belief throughout the church. Identify the four events listed in these verses. What is significant about the fact that all four events occur in a single sentence?

3 Stay with verses 3-5. How do they answer the theory that Christ was only raised spiritually? What is the significance of such phrases as "he was buried", "on the third day" and "according to the Scriptures"?

4 How do verses 5-8 meet the hypothesis that perhaps the early Christians were suffering from hallucinations?

5 Paul writes of his own change of heart and subsequent work in the gospel (verses 9-11). What is the significance of the four pronouns of verse 11 – "I", "they", "we", "you"? Why should we not be satisfied with Scripture interpretations that are out of harmony with each other – or even in collision? What does belief in the bodily resurrection of Jesus Christ do: (a) to your view about your own future, and (b) to your present lifestyle?

REFLECTION

A Consider 1 Corinthians 15:1-11. What are the main points of emphasis in the gospel proclaimed by Paul? Try to list the evidences for the resurrection put forward by Paul, including the change in himself.

B How has the message of Christ's resurrection affected your own view of death and the future?

C On the evidence available, what kind of body did Jesus possess when he appeared to his disciples after his resurrection? Read Luke 24:39-43.

D Look at Galatians 2:20. What does this mean, in practical terms?

THE HOLY SPIRIT

1. His Person

He is the third person of the Trinity

The Holy Spirit is presented in the Bible as a person fully worthy of worship. Not only is he included in the Christian formula of baptism and in the apostolic blessing, but his works are described as the works of God.

He was associated with the work of creation; he gives the Christian new life; he is the source of all knowledge, the guide and helper of the church in all ages; and he makes salvation a real experience to individuals. Also, the apostle Peter equated lying to the Holy Spirit with lying to God (Acts 5:3,4).

When Christ had left the world, the Spirit was given his most specific work. The book of Acts (which is the account of the early church) portrays the Spirit as directing and controlling the new Christian movement.

He knows as a person (mind)

The Holy Spirit is more than a force; he is a person, with a character of his own. The Bible teaches that it is through the Holy Spirit that God knows us completely. It is the mind of the Spirit that helps to shape the life of the Christian.

Jesus declared that the Holy Spirit would remind the apostles of his words and teaching. The Spirit speaks (as in the letters to the seven churches of Revelation), intercedes and assures Christians that they belong to Christ.

He feels as a person (emotion)

Because the Holy Spirit is a person, it is no surprise to discover that he can feel emotion, as we understand the term, for human beings have been made in God's image.

As a result, it is possible to make the Holy Spirit sad. He can also be insulted – and therefore we must be careful, in what we say and do, not to insult the Spirit who lives in us. The Bible challenges us to bring glory to God by the quality of our lives and characters. In this way we will please the Holy Spirit.

He acts as a person (will)

The same Spirit who was involved in the creation, who equipped God's leaders in the past and inspired the prophets, is the Spirit who came in power upon the early church, and acted in it and through it. Throughout the Bible we can see his active personality.

For example, the New Testament shows us that he convicts people of their sins (as happened on the day of Pentecost). He leads and instructs Christ's followers. At other points in the New Testament he forbids certain courses of action and appoints leaders for the church. In such ways we see that the Spirit is a person who acts decisively in executing God's plans.

BIBLE CHECK

Third person: Matthew 28:19; 2 Corinthians 13:14; John 15:26

Mind: 1 Corinthians 2:10-12; John 14:26; Revelation 3:6

Emotion: Ephesians 4:30,31; Hebrews 10:29

Will: John 16:8,13; Acts 8:29; 16:6; 20:28

KEY TRUTH

The Holy Spirit is the third person of the Trinity. He comes from the Father and the Son, and is equal with them. He is the one who actively carries out God's will and who works in the lives of Christians.

POSTSCRIPT

The ascension of Jesus and the coming of the Spirit at Pentecost meant that although Jesus was no longer visibly and physically present, the Spirit would be invisibly present with God's people everywhere. Christ now comes to every believer through the Holy Spirit. In having the Holy Spirit, we have Christ.

BIBLE STUDY John 14:15-27

Jesus is comforting his disciples and preparing them for the time when, after his death, resurrection and ascension, he would be bodily absent from this world. The disciples were apprehensive, but Jesus has good news for them in his reassuring teaching about the coming of the Holy Spirit. Use the following questions to pinpoint the great truths he was giving to them – and to us!

1 Look at verses 15-17 and reflect on the fact of all three Persons of the Trinity being identified within a single sentence. Where else in the passage do all three Persons feature together?

2 What can we learn from the titles given to the Holy Spirit in this passage? Counsellor, Spirit of Truth, Holy Spirit? Why is it not correct to speak of the Holy Spirit as "It"?

3 Jesus has already spoken of his impending bodily departure. How then are we to understand his words in verse 18? What is the great encouragement that we may draw from these words?

4 Who can receive the Holy Spirit? The answer is in verses 15,17,21,23 and 24. What is the state of the disobedient and the unbelieving? Look up 1 Corinthians 2:14.

5 What reassurance was given to the apostles in verses 25 and 26 for their future responsibility in proclaiming and writing the truth as it has come to us today?

6 Acts 2 reminds us of the historical fulfilment of Jesus' teaching here. From Pentecost onwards forgiveness and the gift of the Spirit would be granted to all who repented and turned in faith to Christ. When did this first occur for members of the group? See Acts 2:38,39.

7 John 14:27 is worth learning by heart. Learn it, with the correct reference.

REFLECTION

A Turn to John 16:5-15. It might have been imagined that Jesus' departure would be a disadvantage for his people. Why is this not true? From this passage, try to list the advantages of Christ's physical absence.

B When were you aware, for the first time, that God the Holy Spirit was acting in your life? Compare your experience with others.

C Why do we find that so many Christian people focus on Christ rather than the Spirit? How do you react to this? See John 16:14.

D How far is it possible for a Christian to know when the Holy Spirit has been pleased or displeased by certain acts or deeds?

2. His Names and Descriptions

HIS NAMES

The Holy Spirit

The third person of the Trinity is best known by this name. It was the name used by Jesus in his final words of promise to his disciples, and by Peter in his sermon on the day of Pentecost. The name conveys the Spirit's holiness and opposition to sin.

The Spirit of God

This title is used many times in both Old and New Testaments. It signifies both that the Spirit is God, and that he has God's power. Jesus claimed it was by the Spirit of God that he confronted the demonic world of his day.

The Spirit of Christ

This title brings great comfort and assurance to Christians, because it shows us that Christ was true to his word by not leaving his followers desolate when he ascended to heaven. The Spirit was sent in fulfilment of Christ's promise: "I will come to you."

The Spirit of Truth

The apostles were assured that the Holy Spirit would enable them to remember Christ's teaching and lead them into all the truth. The reader of the Bible may be thankful for its trustworthy, divine authorship.

The Counsellor or Helper

The literal meaning of the term "Counsellor" is one who comes alongside. This name is reassuring for Christians facing temptation, doubt, demanding service or opposition.

HIS DESCRIPTIONS

Wind

This vivid description of the Spirit's activity is used often in the Bible. There is Ezekiel's vision of the dry bones being given new life; there are Christ's words to Nicodemus in John 3, and the sound of rushing wind at Pentecost. The key ideas conveyed are mystery, sovereignty and energy.

Water

The chief reference to the Spirit's work as water comes from some words Christ spoke. Jesus talked about streams of life-giving water flowing from those who believe in him. He was clearly talking about the life-giving activity of the Holy Spirit.

Fire

Malachi predicts the coming of God's messenger in terms of refining fire, and this picture is picked up in the New Testament. John the Baptist said Jesus would baptise with the Holy Spirit and with fire. It is possible that the tongues of flame at Pentecost were to show the Spirit's refining activity.

Oil

In the Old Testament, anointing with oil was a sign that God had chosen someone for a particular task, so priests or kings were set apart for God's service. The Bible tells us that Jesus was "anointed" by the Spirit, and this is also true of his followers.

Dove

The Spirit, in the form of a dove, descended on Jesus at his baptism. While Jesus undoubtedly possessed the Spirit already, this event pictures the gentleness associated with the dove. This gentleness would characterise Christ's work.

BIBLE CHECK

Holy Spirit: Acts 2:32,33
Spirit of God: Matthew 12:28
Spirit of Christ: Romans 8:9
Spirit of Truth: John 16:13,14
Counsellor: John 16:5-7
Wind: Ezekiel 37:1-14; John 3:8
Water: John 7:37-39
Fire: Malachi 3:1-3; Matthew 3:10-12
Oil: Exodus 30:30; Acts 10:37,38; 2 Corinthians 1:21,22
Dove: Mark 1:9-11; John 1:32,33

KEY TRUTH

The character and activities of the Holy Spirit are emphasised through the various names and descriptions by which he is known.

POSTSCRIPT

We must be careful not to press these images of the Spirit's work into being anything more than helpful pictures.

BIBLE STUDY Acts 2:1-21

"Pentecost" has had a new meaning ever since this passage was written by Luke. Until then it represented the Jewish "Harvest Festival", which took place just 50 days after the start of the Passover (Greek *penteconta* – fifty). But for New Testament believers "Pentecost" is the day associated with the giving of the Holy Spirit in full to all who repent and turn in faith to Christ. Use these questions in the exploration of this truth.

1 Try to picture the scene described in verses 1-4. To what degree was this experience foreseen? Let different members of the group look up Joel 2:28-32; Ezekiel 36:26,27; John 16:7-10; Acts 1:5.

2 What attributes and activity of the Holy Spirit are conveyed to us by the symbols of "wind" and "fire"?

3 Pentecost has been described as a unique event, a saving event, a universal event and an evangelistic event. How would you understand this from the passage?

4 What is the significance of the miracle described in verses 5-12? What can be learnt by comparing this event with that described in Genesis 11:8,9?

5 What has Pentecost achieved for you, in your relationship to Christ's disciples across the world?

6 Evidently, we are to understand "the last days" (verse 17) as referring to the period immediately following Christ's earthly ministry. How should this realisation affect (a) our priorities, (b) our prayers?

REFLECTION

A Read Acts 2:1-13. What impressions do you gain from this account? What three signs indicated that the era of the Holy Spirit had begun for the church? In what ways was Pentecost unique? What makes it the secret of the church's life?

B Which of the names of the Holy Spirit do you warm to most in your experience? Why?

C Single out one or more of the Holy Spirit's qualities, suggested by his description, and turn your discovery into prayer or thanksgiving.

D At Pentecost, the apostle Peter links the gift of the Spirit to the gift of forgiveness (Acts 2:38,39). What may we learn from this about Christian communication?

THE HOLY SPIRIT

3. His Work

He convinces of sin

Because the Holy Spirit knows as a person, it follows that the lives of individuals are open to his scrutiny. Our needs can be fully met by him, for he is God.

As Spirit of truth, his work is to convince the unbeliever of being wrong. This is not achieved by human means – it only takes place as the Holy Spirit makes the message of the Bible a living force in a person's heart and conscience. In this way, the Holy Spirit opens the eyes of men and women to their true spiritual condition.

He illuminates truth

As it was the Holy Spirit who inspired the writing of God's word, so it is he who shows us what the Bible means. He makes the words of the Bible understandable and relevant to our lives.

Without the enlightening work of the Holy Spirit, the truth of God's message remains misty, and can even appear nonsensical or offensive.

He reveals Christ

The apostles were taught that when the Spirit came in power upon them, his task would be to focus the spotlight, not on himself, but on Christ.

This is the pattern of Christian experience. From Pentecost, the disciples became aware, not so much of the Spirit who was now controlling their lives, but of Christ and his love. It was indeed the Spirit of Christ who now ruled them.

He lives in believers

The Old Testament recognises that the Spirit works in a selective way, limiting his activity to certain individuals and tasks. But the prophets predicted a coming time when God would put his Spirit permanently within the lives of all his people. This prediction was finally fulfilled on the day of Pentecost.

The apostle Paul writes of Christ making his home in the hearts of his disciples, for it is the Spirit's work to make Christ real to the Christian. No one who belongs to Christ is without the Spirit. He empowers and equips us for the whole of life.

He inspires prayer

Because the Spirit is the Counsellor or Helper, we may look to him for assistance in all forms of Christian service and spiritual warfare.

In particular, the Spirit helps us to pray, because he understands our weaknesses. He prevents prayer from degenerating into mere mechanical drudgery or powerless routine.

He prepares for heaven

The entire Christian life is a life that is directed by the Spirit. The Christian has been set free from the control of sin, and God no longer judges him for it. However, although sin no longer controls, the disciple of Christ faces a life-long battle to develop a holy character.

It is the Spirit who helps a Christian in this battle and prepares him for the glory of heaven.

BIBLE CHECK

Convinces: John 16:8-11; Ephesians 6:17; Hebrews 4:12

Illuminates: John 14:25,26; 16:13; 1 Corinthians 2:12-14

Reveals: John 15:26; 16:14; Acts 7:55

Lives: Ezekiel 36:26,27; Ephesians 3:16,17; Romans 8:9-11

Inspires: Romans 8:26; Ephesians 6:18

Prepares: Romans 8:1-4, 16,17; 2 Corinthians 3:18

KEY TRUTH

The Holy Spirit is mainly featured in the Bible for his work in the lives of men and women.

He is responsible for all the activities listed here.

POSTSCRIPT

It is vital that we do not underestimate what takes place when the Holy Spirit enters a person's life and personality. All Christian growth happens because of him.

BIBLE STUDY Romans 8:1-17

The eighth chapter of Paul's letter to the Romans is loved by believers everywhere. One ancient writer observed, "If Holy Scripture was a ring, and the epistle to the Romans a precious stone, chapter 8 would be the sparkling point of the jewel." Chapter 8 is a reassurance for the Christian who, having read in the earlier chapters of all that God has done for us, is faced with the unhappy realisation that we still sin, and we still die. Has anything really changed, then? Paul makes the point that there is a change.

1 In verses 1-4, how would you describe the new situation that makes life "livable" for the believer?

2 Try to identify some themes that run through this chapter: Life and Death, Spirit and Flesh, Sinful Nature, Past and Future.

3 How do you make sense of these themes? We love Romans 8, but we are not always quite sure why! Try to see from these verses how the whole sweep of our lives and our discipleship is taken into account and provided for by the work of God.

4 The work of God – through all three Persons of the Trinity. Where, in this passage, do we learn that: (a) through the saving act of Christ we can face death, (b) through the indwelling work of the Spirit we can face evil, and (c) through the accepting love of the Father we can face the future? What is so special about verse 11?

5 The Spirit is at work in the believer – but what is our responsibility? See, for example, verses 5,12,13.

6 When were you first aware of experiencing the truth of verse 16?

REFLECTION

A Look at Romans 8:1-17, which gives teaching on life in the Spirit. List what is accomplished by the Holy Spirit. What is our duty (verses 12-17)? And what are our privileges?

B If Christian discipleship is governed by the Spirit, what is there left for us to do? Is Christianity an active or a passive affair? Check your answer with Philippians 2:12,13.

C What attitude should we have towards those who do not appreciate, or respond to, God's love? What is likely to bring a change in their outlook?

D How may our resources for living be described? Compare your answer with 2 Corinthians 4:16.

4. His Activity in the Christian

Life – new birth by the Spirit

Without the power of God, an individual is considered to be 'dead' spiritually. He shows no signs of life as far as God is concerned. The Bible teaches that the gift of new life is available because of the death of Christ on the cross.

This new birth is brought about by the Holy Spirit in the life of a person who responds to the good news of Christ. According to the Bible, that person can be described as a new being and an inheritor of God's kingdom. The new birth is not earned by personal achievement – it is God's free gift.

Assurance – the witness of the Spirit

The Holy Spirit comes to assure the Christian of the reality of his new relationship with Christ. He confirms that Christ's death will always be sufficient to provide complete forgiveness for sins.

He also confirms that the new believer is a child of God, and that the Bible's promise of eternal life is to be believed. The changing life and desires of the new Christian are a part of this inner witness by the Holy Spirit.

Unity – fellowship in the Spirit

Every Christian has received the Holy Spirit, and is said to have been "baptised in the Spirit". "Baptism" includes the ideas of entrance and membership. The Christian is brought into the life of the Spirit at conversion and is united to all other Christians in the body of Christ's church.

Ownership – the seal of the Spirit

The presence of the Holy Spirit in a person's life is the invisible yet permanent stamp of God's ownership upon that life.

Two ideas are present here. First, we belong to God and therefore cannot be separated from his love. Second, we are given the guarantee that God will keep us securely. Eventually, God will claim his own people finally and completely.

Power – the fullness of the Spirit

Christians are commanded to be filled with the Spirit, as a continuous and regular experience. This is not something that only happens once. We are filled with the Spirit so that our lives may be holy and our work for Christ effective. To be filled, we must obey God and submit to his rule; we must turn from evil daily and depend upon God's power; we must give ourselves in the service of other people.

Confidence – the pledge of the Spirit

The Bible teaches that the Holy Spirit is given to the Christian as a foretaste of all that God has prepared for his people in the future.

As we experience a small part of the fullness of life that God will one day give us, the Holy Spirit encourages us to press on. He makes us more confident about the future God has planned for us.

BIBLE CHECK

Life: John 3:3-8; 2 Corinthians 5:17; Titus 3:4-7

Assurance: Romans 8:15,16

Unity: Mark 1:8; 1 Corinthians 12:13; Ephesians 4:3-6

Ownership: Ephesians 1:13,14; 4:30; Romans 8:38,39

Power: Ephesians 5:18; Acts 4:31

Confidence: 2 Corinthians 5:5; 1 Corinthians 2:9,10

KEY TRUTH

From the beginning of our Christian discipleship, the Holy Spirit lives within us. He gives us the power to follow Christ, confidence in believing, and unity with other Christians.

POSTSCRIPT

A great deal of our life in the Spirit consists in living out and developing what God has already given us.

BIBLE STUDY Ephesians 3:14-21

Until now, in this letter to the Ephesian Christians, the apostle Paul has been explaining how salvation through Jesus Christ has been extended to non-Jews – Gentile believers. They have been adopted into God's family and have received from him an eternal inheritance. They have been made alive in Christ (chapter 2), and now, with all God's people are no longer treated as "foreigners", but as fellow citizens in God's household. Now follow his prayer for these Gentile Christians. These questions will help in understanding it.

1 Here is a prayer that simply pours out of Paul's spirit. What are the give-away phrases and words that reveal Paul's deepest desires for his Christian friends?

2 What parts of this prayer indicate its "Trinitarian" content?

3 Where does the prayer imply that to have the Holy Spirit in our lives is the same as having Christ in our lives? Why is this so? Compare John 14:17,18 and Romans 8:9.

4 Do all these phrases amount to no more than a hot-air balloon? Try and tie some of them down. For example, if by 'his glorious riches' Paul means what God has already bought for his people through Christ, then what is this? Look back a little in this letter to 1:5,7,9,11,13,14.

5 Notice the word "power" (three times). In many non-Christian philosophies, this is regarded as something to do with the tangible or sensational. What are the indications in this letter that Paul is referring to a moral and character-transforming power, a power for effective service of others? Look at 4:11,12,22,32.

6 Study the "doxology" (verses 20,21) and allow your expectation to rise, as you now turn to prayer for the Christian fellowship.

REFLECTION

A Read Paul's prayer in Ephesians 3:14-21. What is the 'power' that he desires for his friends? Where does this power come from, and what will it do for us?

B Look at verse 20 of the same chapter. What instances can you recall in Christian history, or from your own experience, that illustrate these words of Paul?

C Which of the different blessings of the Holy Spirit has meant the most to you?

D Why is there no instance in the Bible of any individual claiming publicly to be filled with the Spirit – although this was sometimes stated about an individual by those who knew him? Read Acts 6:1-6.

5. His Fruit

Love

Christ said that his "new" commandment was that we should love one another. It was new because the love he had in mind was modelled on his own – a selfless, sacrificial and practical love that is revolutionary in any age.

Joy

The person who is reading the Bible for the first time will be surprised to find that joy and persecution go hand in hand in numerous instances (eg Matthew 5:11,12; Acts 5:41; James 1:2,3; 1 Peter 4:12-14).

This kind of New Testament joy is totally independent of circumstances. It is the joy of Christ's reign in our lives, inspired by the Spirit.

Peace

The peace which "passes all understanding" was described by Jesus to his disciples as "'my' peace". It does not mean the absence of trouble, but the deep peace that protects the life that is hidden in Christ.

Patience

The apostle Paul longed for the readers of his letters to be tolerant and patient in the face of each other's faults. Peter pointed to the example of Christ's endurance and patience under suffering. The strongest kind of patience comes only from Christ.

Kindness

Wherever the Spirit of Christ is involved in a situation or person, kindness will be seen in action. We can see Christ's unique brand of kindness in his parables, in his breaking of conventions to help the outcast, and in the value he placed on the individual.

Goodness

It was the transparent goodness of Jesus that drew people to him long before his true identity was known. Goodness is love in action. It expects no rewards, and it stems from a heart of purity and openness. It points other people to God.

Faithfulness

God delights to give his servants responsibilities. As we are faithful in the small tasks God gives us, he will trust us to do greater things. The Bible reminds the Christian servant of the final day when the faithfulness of his service will be assessed.

Gentleness

Once again, the Bible shows us that true gentleness was seen in Jesus Christ. In the face of extreme provocation he never lost control and never flaunted his immense power. His disciples needed to learn this quality – notably James and John (Luke 9:51-56).

Self-control

Excess and a lack of discipline result from moral weakness, while self-control is a sign of strength and growth in character. Paul said that we should be like athletes, who go into strict training before a sporting event. Thus, when the Spirit is in control, we experience the difference he makes.

BIBLE CHECK

Love: 1 Corinthians 13
Joy: 1 Peter 1:3-9
Peace: John 14:27
Patience: 1 Peter 2:23
Kindness: Titus 3:1-5,8
Goodness: 1 Peter 2:11,12
Faithfulness: Matthew 25:14-30
Gentleness: Matthew 11:28-30
Self-control: 1 Corinthians 9:24-27

KEY TRUTH

It is the work of the Holy Spirit to transform our characters. The qualities listed here are developed in us by the Spirit and are taken from Galatians 5:22,23.

POSTSCRIPT

We should recognise that natural gifts in the Christian are enhanced, rather than diminished, by the work of the Holy Spirit.

BIBLE STUDY Galatians 5:13-26

Paul the apostle is writing to the Christians in what was probably the south of present-day Turkey, around the year AD 48. He is aware that because of false teaching, his readers are in danger of slipping back into a sub-Christian gospel that is no gospel at all (Galatians 1:6,7). This would also affect the character and behaviour of the church. Read the passage and try, with the use of these questions, to understand more of how the Holy Spirit produces Christ-like living.

1 Having read the passage, identify the two "combatants" at war in the life of the believer. They are named some five times. How aware are you of this conflict? When did you first become aware of it?

2 In what way does this passage contradict the theory that when someone becomes a believer and receives the Spirit, the fallen nature that they were born with is killed off or "eradicated"?

3 Is it a good sign, then, or a bad sign, when a new Christian is aware of temptation and conflict?

4 Now identify the two opposing lifestyles in this passage. The "acts" of verse 19 affect what realms of behaviour? And the "fruit" of verse 22 affect what areas of relationship?

5 Now identify the two contrasting daily attitudes that should characterise the believer in regard to the sinful nature and the Spirit. See verses 24 and 25.

6 How does this affect the discipline of the Christian?

7 Discuss how the fruit of the Spirit is produced in our lives – naturally (John 15:4,5), willingly (John 15:3-7), painfully (John 15:2).

REFLECTION

A Read and think about 1 Corinthians 13. Why is love of this kind so vital, and so revolutionary? How may it be developed in an individual – and in a fellowship?

B Go through Galatians 5:22,23 and discover whether these qualities can be grouped under different categories. For example, fruit relating to God, to others, etc.

C Try to list some people in the Bible who had obviously developed one or more of the fruit of the Spirit.

D Why do the Bible translations that mention "fruit" in Galatians 5:22, not make the word plural – "fruits"? How does the Christian develop these qualities – one by one, all together, instantaneously, painfully?

6. His Gifts

The gifts exalt Christ

While the "fruit" of the Spirit is concerned with character, the gifts of the Spirit relate to abilities and functions distributed among believers. All the fruit should be exhibited in every Christian but the gifts differ widely from person to person.

The hallmark of spiritual gifts is that they glorify Christ. The Holy Spirit was sent for this very purpose – to illuminate the Lordship of Jesus.

The gifts involve all

Four passages of Scripture list some of the gifts: Romans 12:6-8; 1 Corinthians 12:8-10; Ephesians 4:11,12; 1 Peter 4:10,11.

It is significant that the gifts of the Spirit are not restricted to outstanding individuals, or leaders in the church. Each believer has at least one gift, and these gifts are to be discovered and developed, for all God's people are to be involved in Christian ministry and service of some kind.

The gifts should unite all

The church of Christ is likened to a body, composed of many limbs and parts, each part relating to the whole.

The individual believers, then, should see the abilities and functions that God has given them as gifts available for the whole body. In this respect, Paul had to correct the divided Corinthian church.

Gifts lay foundations

The church of Christ is also likened to a building, built upon the unique and powerful ministry of the apostle and prophets, Christ himself being the stone that holds the whole building together.

The gifts which characterised the apostles may not be in evidence today in the highest sense of those callings, but there are Christians who in a secondary sense have been sent (as were the apostles) to establish the church across new frontiers, or who speak to the church in relevant terms (as were the prophets) to encourage and build it up.

Gifts build up the fellowship

There is a great variety of spiritual gifts featured in the New Testament. The Christian is to make careful use of every gift received, to build up harmony and unity in the fellowship.

It is important that individual believers are not jealous of the gifts of others, nor insist on the superiority of their own. As we use God's gifts, we should be humble and look for ways in which we can serve others.

Gifts promote mission

The gifts of the Spirit are given for more than building up the church – they are given to widen its boundaries.

However corrupt and challenging their environment, Christ's followers are called – individually and collectively – to use their gifts in proclaiming the good news, vigorously co-operating with the Spirit of God, making mature disciples.

BIBLE CHECK

Exalt: 1 Peter 4:10,11; John 16:14
Involve: 1 Corinthians 12:7-11
Unite: 1 Corinthians 12:12-26; Romans 12:4,5
Lay: Ephesians 2:19-22
Build up: Ephesians 4:11-13
Promote: Colossians 1:27-29; 1 Corinthians 14:24,25

KEY TRUTH

The Holy Spirit distributes among Christians a variety of spiritual gifts, which are to be used for the building up of Christ's body, the church. No believer is without a gift.

POSTSCRIPT

Everyone has "natural" gifts from birth, which are given by God. By giving these back to him, these can be enhanced and made use of by Christ as we learn to follow him.

BIBLE STUDY 1 Corinthians 12:4-20

Paul again! Here he is writing to the Corinthian Christians who, of all the New Testament churches, were the most unruly and confused; worldly (3:1), immoral (5:1) and divided (11:17,18). They were confused over virtually every aspect of Christian living. Now the apostle is trying to correct their thinking about the gifts of the Spirit. We have, then, to read between the lines a little in this passage, as we try to understand the main emphasis that the apostle is making.

1 What point is being made by the three-fold use of the words "same", "all" and "one" in verses 4-6,8,9,11?

2 What is the overall purpose of gifts, imparted by the indwelling Spirit of God, in the life of the church? Verse 7 gives the clue. How far is this recognised as the purpose of gifts among the believers in your church or fellowship?

3 It is obvious that the Corinthians were familiar with certain gifts of a miraculous nature. What does Paul say about the origin of these gifts? Where are they in evidence? How does he regulate their use in public, particularly their speaking in tongues? (14:26-28).

4 Look on at verses 12 and 13. "Many" ... "one". How should a church apply the idea of the "body" of Christ to itself?

5 In verses 14-20, what is the great lesson that believers across the ages need to take to heart?

6 Encourage group members each to look up other lists of 'gifts' in the New Testament; Romans 12:6-8, Ephesians 4:11-13, 1 Peter 4:10,11. Speaking gifts, prophetic gifts, serving gifts, administrative gifts; now spend time in prayer, giving thanks for the gifts and dedicating them back to the Giver.

REFLECTION

A Look at Romans 12. What does Paul teach us about the way in which we use our gifts, and our attitude to other Christians? What difference should this make to your local church?

B What is the best way of discovering what your gifts are, as a Christian? How can other Christians help you to do this?

C How far is your own fellowship using the gifts of everyone to promote Christ's mission in the world? Identify any gifts that are being neglected in this respect, and that can be encouraged.

D Why do certain abilities or gifts sometimes cause problems for a church, as they seem to have done at Corinth?

1. Our Uniqueness

HUMANITY IS:

A whole being, physical and spiritual

The Bible teaches that all humanity has a common origin and nature.

We were created as intelligent beings and we are recognised as the head of all living things. As such, humanity is to govern the earth and to use its resources responsibly.

Because of humanity's place in creation, God made us as physical beings, completely involved in God's world. But humanity is not merely physical. We also have a spiritual dimension – we can be fully aware of God and all that he demands. These two dimensions, physical and spiritual, make up the whole person.

This description of humanity is given in the biblical account of creation, which, in its scope, simplicity and dignity is without parallel anywhere in literature.

A spiritual being, made in God's image

What characterises humanity as unique is our creation in the image and likeness of God. We possess a similar nature to God and we are therefore capable of a relationship with our Maker.

Because humanity is made in God's image, this does not mean that we are God, or even that we are a part of God. The Bible clearly teaches that humanity is distinctly different from God. Therefore humanity is not God in disguise, nor are we an 'incarnation' of God. But there is in us a key element that sets us apart from, and above, the rest of creation. We have been made to love God, to worship him and to enjoy his company.

A personal being, with mind, emotion and will

Humanity is not only made for God. We are also made for a variety of personal and loving relationships within the human family – this shows how human life is to be the image of the loving relationship between the Father, Son and Spirit. The human spirit reveals qualities of tenderness, loyalty and self-sacrifice. We are capable of original thought and of intelligent choice. We are aware of ourselves, capable of humour, sorrow, or hatred. We appreciate beauty and enjoy recreation.

These qualities of humanity show that we are not mere animals or machines. Our instincts, affections and aspirations prove that we are far removed from being a mere collection of chemical reactions. The Bible recognises that we have the dignity of personality and freedom.

A moral being, responsible for our actions

The Bible assumes and teaches that humanity has a moral aspect, which relates us to our Creator. This may be seen in the laws which govern even the most primitive societies. Humanity recognises the difference between right and wrong.

The animal kingdom behaves according to the drive of mere instinct. Humanity possesses a drive that makes us morally aware – a drive which says "I ought".

As a result, it is basic to the teaching of the Bible that we are not victims of our upbringing or circumstances. Rather, we are responsible for our actions and must answer for them. If we remove this concept from our understanding of our nature, we also remove any true content from such words as reward, merit, justice and even forgiveness.

BIBLE CHECK

Whole: Acts 17:26; Genesis 2:15,19,20; Matthew 4:4

Spiritual: Genesis 1:26,27; Psalm 8:3-6

Personal: Genesis 2:18; Luke 10:25-37

Moral: Romans 2:14,15; Psalm 51:1-3

KEY TRUTH

The Bible tells us that humanity is the summit of God's creation. We are the only beings who may enter into a personal relationship with the creator.

POSTSCRIPT

It is the dimension of God in human beings that raises us above the level of an animal, a machine or an accident.

BIBLE STUDY Genesis 1:27,28; 2:7-24

It would be hard to imagine that the vast creation existed for our sake, without the Bible's emphasis, first, of God-centredness in the creation; secondly, that creation is not the home of the human species so much as the home of a race of God-like beings; thirdly, that all creation centres in a Man who is heir to it all, and in whom everything holds together (Colossians 1:15-17). The Bible takes only two pages over the creation – "a week's work"! It requires over a thousand pages to tell our story.

1 Is it the creation that defines our size and identity? Reflect on the truth of 1:27 and 2:7.

2 "Image" but only an image. How can we counteract modern theorists who tell us that we are God and there is nothing we cannot do?

3 By contrast, we are told that we are no different from other living creatures; that a new-born child is simply an animal. How would we answer this, from 2:28 and from Psalm 139:13-16?

4 Look at 2:8-17. What do we learn here about human responsibility?

5 2:18-25 gives us our creation charter of sexuality, marriage and community. Discuss the point that it isn't singleness that isn't 'good' but solitude.

6 "Helper" (2:18-21) – does that imply a second-class being? Discuss the fact that the Hebrew word *ezer* elsewhere describes the kind of "help" that only God can give – eg Psalm 121:2; Hosea 13:9.

7 Think through the creation principle (2:24) of a one-man/one-woman, publicly recognised contract for life, within which is expressed the God-given intimacy of physical union.

REFLECTION

A Read Psalm 8. What gives significance to humanity in the vastness of the surrounding universe? What do we learn of our status and of our responsibilities? In what way does this Psalm correct current errors of thinking?

B A famous film star once said, "I am just a piece of meat." From the Bible, how may we comment on and correct such a statement?

C Look at Genesis 1:26,27. In what ways do you think we are like God? In what ways are we unlike him?

D How do you react to the belief that wrong-doing is a kind of disease, for which there is, somewhere, a proper form of treatment? May this sometimes be true?

2. Our Diversity

Natural dimensions

God has given us the earth as a home to live in and to look after. It is a home that is teeming with life and overflowing with variety and colour. Its seasons are regulated and its resources are immense.

The world and matter are not evil (as various non-Christian teachings have maintained) but are part of God's good creation. Food and bodily health are the gifts of God and are to be received with thanks. Through agriculture, industry and creativity, humanity is to be productive in the home that God has given us.

Creative dimensions

In general it is true that when the Scriptures have been taken seriously, technology and science have flourished in a productive way. This is because the Bible encourages us to explore and develop the wonderful works of God. Mining, trade, manufacture and construction, performed responsibly, are all part of our task.

Cultural dimensions

Humanity possesses what the animal kingdom can never know – a capacity for the appreciation of what is beautiful for intellectual development, for literature and the arts, and for sport and recreation.

Life on earth is meant to be enjoyable, but cultural activity calls for as much discipline as any other part of life. Nevertheless, rest and recreation are a vital part of the programme of human life.

Social dimensions

Humanity was placed on the earth to live, not in isolation from our neighbour, but in the pattern of community and family that stems from God's own nature. God has made us for relationships.

The Bible points out the enormous value of friendship, and above all, marriage. The relationship between a husband and wife is seen as a gift from God. Through shared problems and pleasures, companionship and the joy of sexual intimacy, married partners are able to strengthen each other throughout life.

We have been created to show compassion and justice in the way we treat others. Only when humanity uses these qualities do our relationships in the family, in social care, in government and in work become what God meant them to be. God's desire for all people is that they should love one another.

Religious dimensions

Humanity was made by God and we have a spiritual capacity. As humans are far from God, we constantly search for our spiritual home. The search takes many forms which are seen in the great religions of the world, in the quest for oneness with God, and for an experience which materialism is unable to give.

Jesus confirmed both an Old Testament saying and the findings of the human heart when he declared that "Man does not live on bread alone" (Matthew 4:4). We need more than the physical essentials of life. It is the Bible that gives to searching humanity the answers that philosophers and sages of religion have always been unable even to guess at: that God was on a search himself – for humanity whom he loves.

BIBLE CHECK

Natural: Genesis 8:22; Psalm 104:5-30; 1 Timothy 4:3,4

Creative: Genesis 1:26-28; 9:1-3; Psalm 8:6-8

Cultural: Exodus 35:30-35; Daniel 1:3,4

Social: Genesis 2:18-24; Romans 13:8-10

Religious: Psalm 90:1; Ecclesiastes 3:11

KEY TRUTH

The many different sides of humanity show positively that we are created by God, and for God.

POSTSCRIPT

Humanity's immense powers should inspire us to develop to the full our potential for creative service in our world.

BIBLE STUDY Psalm 139

The "brightness" of this psalm was described by the Baptist preacher C.H. Spurgeon as being like that of a sapphire stone – "It flames out with such flashes of light as to turn night into day."As you read the psalm, ask yourself whether there is anywhere in literature that such a vivid and moving portrait of God has been given to us – by a man who found himself and knew himself only in relationship to his creator.

1 Look at verses 1-6. List the areas of life that the psalmist David recognises as coming under God's complete knowledge. What is David's reaction to this insight?

2 Move on to verses 7-10. Can you think of others who experienced God in this way? Compare Genesis 3:9; Jonah 1:3. What is the most encouraging discovery of these verses?

3 As you read verses 11 and 12, try to identify those aspects of life that plunge human beings into "darkness". A journalist once wrote, "I am frightened like a child in a dark room; I look for a window, and Christ is the window." What has been your experience?

4 How do verses 13-16 speak to the anxieties and dilemmas of every generation – to the present generation? When did we become human? What does God's "book" speak to you of?

5 Should we feel threatened ... or outraged ... at God's sovereignty and control of our lives? How far can you identify with David's reaction?

6 Verses 19–24: suddenly David is back to being king again, and to the conflicts of daily life. But note the humility with which he concludes his remarkable reflections.

REFLECTION

A Read 2 Corinthians 5:1-10. How does the apostle Paul view his physical existence; his heavenly future; and the experience of being linked to both?

B What natural abilities has God given you? How have they enriched you as a person? What is the danger of having many natural abilities?

C How do you see your role in a society that is often corrupt? As one of involvement, separation, compromise, condemnation? Check your answer with John 17:15,16 and Matthew 5:13-16.

D At times in history, Christians have looked distrustfully at the arts. Why is this so? What principle should govern us in our attitude to music, painting, films and literature?

3. Our Rebellion and Fall

Humanity's innocence gave us fellowship with God

"Innocence" is the correct word to use of our original moral state.

Adam and Eve were not righteous, in the sense of possessing a developed uprightness of character; rather they were child-like in the trusting and open simplicity of their walk with God.

However this innocence was not an in-built and unalterable characteristic. We were not programmed to obey our maker, in the way that a computer must function, for humanity was not like a machine. Adam and Eve were real people, living in a free relationship with God.

Unlike their descendants, that first human couple originally had no inward urge to sin. But whether or not they were to remain in a relationship with God depended upon the choices that they could freely make.

Humanity's freedom gave us the power of choice

The Bible reveals that humanity had real choices in regard to our relationship with God. We were not compelled to go God's way. In any true relationship, the people concerned must have the freedom of choice that raises them above the level of being robots or puppets.

God did not hide from humanity that we had the power of choice. The instructions given were clear enough and easy to do. The human race was free to choose.

Humanity's choice gave us true responsibility

Although we are influenced by other people in what we do, ultimately, we must take the responsibility for the decisions we make. To have the ability to choose between right and wrong means that we also have the responsibility to choose what is right.

In the story of humanity's fall, we see how people try to avoid their responsibility. Adam blames Eve, who in turn blames the serpent. In the way that God deals with each of them, he shows that they were all guilty for the sins that they had committed.

Humanity's decision led us into moral rebellion

Humanity's revolt against our Creator cannot be described as an accidental slip. Our first parents questioned God's authority by disobeying him, and they doubted whether God really knew what was best for them. As a result, the human race deliberately rebelled against God and followed their own way.

What humanity thus became – sinful and fallen – we still are today. Estranged from the Creator, the human race as a whole must be described biblically as a fallen race. It is not that the image of God in humanity has been completely destroyed. It is still there, although distorted and marred. But there is no area of our mind and personality that does not exhibit a degree of "fallenness".

The sin principle has become universal. Men and women today, from their actions and choices, underline their involvement with the fallen race.

BIBLE CHECK

Innocence: Genesis 2

Freedom: Genesis 2:16,17; 3:6,7

Choice: Genesis 3:8-19; Matthew 12:36,37

Decision: Genesis 3; Psalm 51:5; Jeremiah 17:9

KEY TRUTH

God in creation gave humanity the gifts and privileges that allowed us individuality and freedom. The wilful misuse of these led humanity into rebellion and his subsequent fall.

POSTSCRIPT

The fallenness of humanity means that for the whole of our lives we have a tendency to rebel against God. All humanity is on the same level of need.

BIBLE STUDY Psalm 51

This is perhaps the best known of what are called the Penitential Psalms. Written by David, after committing both adultery and murder (2 Samuel 11 and 12), it portrays more vividly than anywhere in Scripture the heartfelt plea for mercy on the part of the fallen sinner. David's sin had begun with a look, then continued with a message, a meeting, adultery, deceit and finally murder. These questions may help in getting to the heart of our rebellion, fall and reinstatement.

1 Notice in verses 1-3 how wrong-doing is described: "transgression" (rebellion), "iniquity" (pollution, corruption) and "sin" (failing the standard). What does this tell us about our problem? Compare Jeremiah 17:9.

2 Look at verses 3 and 4. Why is it that we can never say that what someone does in private is their own affair?

3 Verse 5 expresses the truth of what is called "original sin". Read Romans 5:12 for further amplification. Reflect in your study on what this means for society, in the need for locks on doors, receipts on payments, tickets, passes, police, etc.

4 Verses 6 and 7 indicate that the cleansing has to be from inside out. What is the ground by which we can be put right? Look back at verse 1. Compare Romans 3:23-25.

5 In verses 2 and 7, David has asked to be made clean. Now in verses 10-12 three further prayers follow. What area of his life do they apply to? The clue lies in the word that is common to all three prayers.

6 "Willing", verse 12. How is their motivation to be strengthened, so that God's follower wants to live purely?

7 Can you make David's vow of service (verses 13-19) your own?

REFLECTION

A Read and study the Ten Commandments (Exodus 20:3-17). Why did we need the Law to be given at all? What areas of life do these commandments deal with? Why are they still relevant today? Do you know them by heart?

B Whose fault is it, when we do wrong? The devil's? God's – for having given us free choice? Our "fallen" nature?

Compare your findings with Genesis 3:11-13; Romans 1:20; 3:19,20.

C How can Christ's followers strengthen their desire to choose the good and not the evil?

D We are responsible for everything that we choose to do. Describe, in your own words, what responsibility means. What does this tell us about the God who made us?

4. Our Rebellion and Condemnation

Rebellion and guilt

God made us to live in relationship with all of humanity on a collective basis. Therefore it is not surprising that Scripture teaches that the whole race is involved in the original fall, although no one is condemned for the sin of any other person.

Because we have rejected goodness and follow our own way rather than God's, we are guilty before him. Guilt is both a feeling and a fact. It is a feeling because our consciences tell us when we have done wrong. We feel ashamed and guilty for what we have done. It is a fact because God knows that we have rebelled against him.

We are guilty in the same way that a criminal has been proven guilty.

We deserve God's judgement.

Guilt and condemnation

The effects of our revolt against the authority of God are inescapable. In Genesis chapter 3 Adam and Eve are sent away from Eden and are told that they will only be able to live off the earth by hard work.

God had no choice but to condemn humanity. Because of his justice and holiness he cannot tolerate evil. Therefore, when God condemns us he shows that he is taking our sin seriously. To be condemned is to experience the anger of God.

Condemnation and separation

Although humanity must face physical death and hardship as a result of our rebellion, the Bible emphasises that our main loss is spiritual. Our most precious privilege, that of free access to God and fellowship with him, has been forfeited.

Throughout human history, and that of God's people, it is sin that has created barriers between us and the holy God. We find ourselves confused by our own capacity for evil and out of place in the world because we are separated from God.

Estranged from God, we are ignorant of our Maker and of his ways and we are unable to fulfil our destiny. We cannot enter into peace with God, and we cannot undo the past.

Separation and death

"The Tree of Life" in Genesis 2 conveys the idea of the eternal life of God. When humanity fell out of fellowship with God we were deprived of such life. The Bible teaches that sin and death are linked to each other.

The apostle Paul declares that death is the payment we receive for sinning. The difference between death as a spiritual state, and death as the end of physical existence is not always clearly drawn in Scripture. Spiritually and physically, death is an outrage in the teaching of the Bible, because it is God's judgement upon sin. As such it could never be abolished but by the action of God.

The physical conquest of death by Jesus Christ overshadows all else in our understanding of this issue.

BIBLE CHECK

Rebellion: Romans 5:12-17; Ephesians 2:1-3

Guilt: Psalm 14:2,3; 143:2

Condemnation: Genesis 3:23,24; Isaiah 59:1,2

Separation: Genesis 2:15-17; Ezekiel 18:4; Romans 6:23

KEY TRUTH

It is disastrous that humanity has rebelled against the Creator, for God in his absolute holiness will not tolerate sin, but must condemn the sinner. As a result, humanity is guilty, confused, and separated from God.

POSTSCRIPT

Because of the universality of sin, it is all too easy to become used to locks, keys and tickets, and other daily reminders that fallen humanity is not to be trusted.

BIBLE STUDY Romans 3:9-20

In this passage we are coming in at the tail end of a careful argument by the apostle Paul. Before the good news can come into focus, it is essential that the news can be faced.

1 Theologians sometimes speak of our need in terms of "total depravity" – it is not that we are necessarily as bad as we can be, but rather that there is no part of our lives that is untouched by sin. How far do the various quotations from the Old Testament bear this out, in 3:10-18?

2 In the face of God's law, every mouth is to be silenced (verse 19). What argument does Paul use earlier against the universal moralist? See Romans 2:1. Who are such people today?

3 Next it's the turn of the "naturalist" – those who may not know the commandments, but nevertheless have within them a moral sense. What speaks to them? See Romans 2:14,15 and 1:20.

4 Move on to the Jewish legalist – Romans 2:25-29 (especially verse 23). What is the problem here? What is its modern counterpart?

5 Then there is the ritualist. See Romans 2:25-29 (especially verse 29). Was this a problem for Paul's day only or do we see it today? What is the flaw at the heart of this thinking?

6 To cap it all we have the hedonist – the lover of self-pleasing, who hopes to take advantage of God's mercy (3:7,8). How recognisable is this figure? How does Paul react?

7 Which of these different categories have members of the group come from? Meditate and pray together around 3:9.

REFLECTION

A Read and examine Psalm 51, written by David after an incident in 2 Samuel 11 and 12. How does David understand God's attitude to sin; the nature of sin; the remedy (both short-term and long-term – see Ezekiel 36:25-27); and his own right attitude for the future?

B Why are terms such as sin, guilt and the fall of humanity not fashionable in some circles today? Were they ever fashionable?

C Christians are people with joy in their hearts. How is it possible to live with the biblical concept of our fallenness and yet to avoid dwelling constantly on our own failures?

D What are the practital indications from our surroundings that this world, while still a good place to live in, has lost its initial perfection?

5. Our Quest and Dilemma

Our religious search

Humanity is continually torn between the revelation of God, culminating in the person of Christ, and the numerous attempts to make a path to God.

These attempts have taken many forms in history, ranging from primitive superstition and magic to powerful and sophisticated religious systems.

In Bible times, God's leaders were continually challenging their hearers to forsake the man-made ways to God, and to accept the revelation of the one and only Lord. Many of the New Testament letters highlight the issue of false teachers and religious trails that lead to idolatry and error.

Our philosophical wanderings

The way of philosophy is the age-old search for the elusive wisdom and knowledge about the ultimate reality of the universe. Most attempts arrive at different conclusions, and some arrive at none.

The conclusions of philosophy (when God's revelation had been left out of the picture) are perfectly mirrored in the Old Testament book of Ecclesiastes. The writer shows that the human mind, without the help of God, is unable to come up with convincing answers to the meaning of life.

Our psychological contradictions

Our true nature constantly comes into collision with our fallen and sinful state. Because we were created in the image of God, humanity was designed to enjoy the company of our Maker. Our instincts will not easily allow us to forget our origin and our capacity for rational and satisfying relationships.

However, our fallenness and state of enmity with God make us a mass of contradictions. For humanity is not only at war with God. History all too frequently has shown us to be at war with our neighbour, with our environment, within our family and with ourselves.

Our problems do not stem so much from our outward circumstances, as from our own inner state. Jesus taught this and so did his apostles.

True identity and significance continue to elude all those who do not know God. Hence the symptoms of disorder. Hence the need of a Redeemer.

Our physical drive

Besides the loss of harmony in our emotions, will and relationships, the Bible points to the abnormal predominance of our physical and sensual appetite as being a result of the fall.

Thus, history's periods of spiritual poverty have tended to coincide with a marked increase in society's dependence upon money, alcohol, promiscuity and dehumanised pleasure.

Humanity has great potential for creativity and technical advance, but when this is not controlled by a God-centred view of the world, indiscipline and slavery are the inevitable result.

BIBLE CHECK

Religious: Acts 17:22,23;
2 Timothy 4:3,4
Philosophical: Ecclesiastes
1:16-18; 1 Corinthians
1:20,21
Psychological: Mark 7:21-23;
James 4:1-4; Romans 7:18-24
Physical: Ephesians 4:17-19;
Titus 3:3

KEY TRUTH

The history of the human race tells us about our quest for the meaning of our existence. People will remain in confusion, unless they experience the light and life of God. This confusion is seen in the areas listed here.

POSTSCRIPT

The Christian who fails to grow spiritually is liable to be caught up in the very dilemmas that ensnare the world, losing our assurance of peace with God.

BIBLE STUDY Ecclesiastes 2:1-16

The book of Ecclesiastes paints a superb picture of what human life is really like when God is taken out of the frame. It stems from the time of King Solomon of the 10th century BC; indeed it may be based upon his own critique of life. It is presented as the experiences of the Philosopher or "Teacher", who deliberately places himself in the shoes of a godless person. The resulting world-view is one of empty meaninglessness (1:2). Put yourself in these shoes now, as you come to this selected passage.

1 "… during the few days of their lives" (verse 3) – describe the mindset that the writer is adopting in verses 1-3.

2 Read verses 4-6; what was the driving force behind the expenditure of effort? Can you think of any of Jesus' teaching that has a bearing upon it? eg Luke 12:16-21.

3 Who or what is at the centre of the programme mapped out in verses 7-11? What is the great lesson to be learnt? How well is it being learnt among group members?

4 The writer seems to wonder whether anyone in the line after him can do better (verse 12). Try to understand the cynicism of the sentences that follow. What is it that gives rise to such apathy? Verse 16 gives the clue.

5 The writer is both teasing and tantalising at the same time – leading his readers along the line of their own godless logic. What is there to be said for the believer following his example, in the face of alien beliefs and outlooks?

6 Two ways to live! Which is it to be? Take a final glance at Ecclesiastes 12:1,2 and prayerfully encourage each other now.

REFLECTION

A Look at James 4:1-10, for a picture of people who are in open rebellion against God. What characterises their actions, and what explains them? What is the road to spiritual recovery, and what encouragements are there in this passage?

B What examples are there, in your own area, of people searching for religious answers to life? How can your church best contribute to their search? Compare your findings with 1 Thessalonians 1:5.

C As a Christian, can you recall what it was still to be in ignorance of God's friendship? How far did Revelation 3:17 describe you?

D List the ways in which people are at war with themselves, their neighbours, nature and God.

6. Our Enemies

Satan

The devil is not all-powerful or present everywhere at once, as God is. He is a created spirit or angel, who chose to rebel against the authority of God.

He is the enemy of humanity (the word Satan means "opponent" or "enemy"). His aim is to humiliate humanity, to separate us from God, and to destroy us. His power is immense, but limited. He is a deceiver, a liar, a tempter and a murderer. He is described in Scripture as a roaring lion and as a dragon.

His defeat was achieved through the death and resurrection of Jesus, and will be completed when he is finally judged and destroyed by Christ. Meanwhile, the devil is to be resisted (James 4:7).

Sin

Sin came into the world through the devil's temptation, and became universal in the life of humanity through the fall. Sin is defined in the Bible as breaking the law of God, as enmity with God, as rebellion, and as falling short of God's standard.

The outbreak of sin reveals itself in a great variety of ways, sometimes in gross acts, but equally powerfully in the subtle undermining of will, motivation and character. As a Christian focuses on Christ, so our determination to fight against sin is strengthened. With Christ's help sin is to be rejected (Hebrews 12:1,2).

The world

By the "world" the Bible frequently means the society, system and outlook which is hostile to God and limits life to earthly existence only. Those who live in this way limit their desires to gaining possessions and position, and exclude God altogether.

The results of living by this philosophy are all too evident in human life and Christians can be powerfully tempted by the things we see in the world. However, we can take courage in the defeat of the world by Jesus. Meanwhile we are to shine as lights in the world (Philippians 2:15).

The flesh

Apart from its usual meaning, "flesh", often termed "sinful nature" or "human nature" in modern Bible translations, refers to the sinful bias which every individual has. This sinfulness is found in both obvious and hidden selfish indulgence.

We all possess this fallen nature throughout life. As the Christian also possesses Christ's Spirit, but is still in the flesh as well, he becomes something of a battleground between flesh and spirit. However, we learn to live according to the Spirit and not the flesh (Romans 8:9).

Death

Death is our great enemy, pursuing us from infancy, disturbing our peace and haunting our hopes. However, the Christian recognises that Christ is the great destroyer of death and of the very fear of death. Like others, the Christian faces life's problems and trials, but we give thanks to God who gives us victory through Jesus Christ (1 Corinthians 15:57).

BIBLE CHECK

Satan: 1 John 3:8; 1 Peter 5:8,9; Revelation 12:7-12

Sin: 1 John 3:4; Romans 3:23; 8:10

World: 1 John 2:15,16; James 4:4; John 16:33

Flesh: check Romans 7:18; Galatians 5:17

Death: 2 Timothy 1:10; Hebrews 2:14,15; Revelation 21:4

KEY TRUTH

As a result of our fall, we find ourselves faced by real and powerful enemies that can only be overcome by the greater power of God.

POSTSCRIPT

A subtle temptation for the Christian is to blame personal failures on the devil or on the pull of the world. When we sin, it is because we have chosen to do so.

BIBLE STUDY James 4:1-12

James, the earthly brother of Jesus Christ (Matthew 13:55), is writing a general letter to Christians everywhere. We are to be a credit to Christ in the consistency of our behaviour, despite the severity of the trials and temptations that confront the believer (James 1:2,3). Here we are urged to choose sides:

1 James addresses himself in verse 1 to the conflicts that have characterised all human history – both on the public and the private level. Why is it too shallow an explanation to say that such conflicts are the result of poverty, class distinction or tribalism?

2 At least seven symptoms of human disorder feature in verses 2 and 3. Try to list them, and ask yourselves to what extent our human race has advanced, morally combating these evils.

3 Why must we choose between "the world" and "God" (verse 4)? What is meant by 'the world'? For further help, see 1 John 2:15,16.

4 The issue condenses into a starker choice still, in verses 5-7, where James seems to be alluding to Proverbs 3:24 and Matthew 23:12. What is this choice now? What should encourage us in choosing rightly?

5 So far we have looked at the many projections of our inner turbulence, and at the two alternatives that demand our loyalty. What evidence is there today among God's people of the repentance described in verses 8 and 9; and of the mutual love that slander denies (verse 11)?

6 Verse 11 points to the only single ultimate authority. Commit yourself to God afresh in prayer now.

REFLECTION

A Read Ephesians 6:10-18, and think about the Christian's defences against spiritual opposition. List the commands in that passage – "Put on", etc. How do you interpret the various pieces of armour? Why may we expect to win?

B Whose world is it – the devil's – or God's? Compare your findings with 1 John 5:19; Matthew 4:8,9; 1 Samuel 2:8; Psalm 24:1 and Revelation 11:15.

C Specify different situations when the Christian should run from evil, meet it head-on, undermine it, or stand firm.

D In what ways is humanity always changing? In what ways do we remain the same?

GOD'S MESSENGERS

1. Angels

Angels are worshippers around God's throne

Angels are part of the life of heaven, and in certain respects are superior to human beings; yet they are separate from God. They are not to be worshipped; their essential role is that of attending upon God, acclaiming his holiness and praising his Son.

At such limited times when angels have become visible (as in special visitations of God or in prophetic visions), they reflect the awesome holiness and harmony of heaven.

Angels are executors of God's will

They are numerous and may be known by different terms: "holy ones", "messengers" or "sons of God". The "cherubim" (plural of "cherub") are presented in the Scriptures as winged creatures flying to fulfil God's commands, guarding the way to his presence and acting as conveyors of his throned presence.

Angels are witnesses to God's saving acts

Angels are in evidence at the birth of Jesus; on the eve of his crucifixion; on the morning of his resurrection and on the occasion of his ascension. They will be Christ's heralds at his final return in glory.

They are said by Jesus to rejoice at the repentance of a sinner, and he speaks of them as gathering in his redeemed people at the end of the world.

Angels are messengers at times of revelation

At the beginning of certain great eras in God's redemption, angels have featured as announcers. Instances of this occur with the call of Moses the great lawgiver, with the commissioning of prophets, at the outset of the gospel story and with the momentous extension of Christ's salvation to the Gentiles.

These announcements were variously received with reactions of awe, fear, astonishment and holy joy.

Angels are protagonists at times of conflict

We learn from the Bible of an angelic rebellion and fall under the leadership of Satan, "the serpent", "the devil", "the father of lies", "the Accuser". Although his defeat was assured by the victory of Christ's death, the conflict with evil will not be fully over until Satan's final destruction.

Witness and prayer, then, are conducted on the part of God's saints in the light of a continuing angelic conflict with the demon world. Biblically, Michael is understood as heading the angel hosts.

Angels are ministers at times of crisis

At many points in God's dealings with his people – patriarchs, prophets, apostles and indeed Jesus himself received ministry and help from angels at particular moments of stress, temptation or danger.

But all inheritors of salvation are assured of the protection and support of God's angels. While we may be grateful for their presence, they are not to be reverenced as intermediaries between us and God. An undue attention to the angels can lead to distortions of the faith.

BIBLE CHECK

Worshippers: Psalm 8:5; Daniel 7:9,10; Revelation 5:11,12

Executors: Psalm 89:5; Genesis 3:24; Exodus 25:18-22; Ezekiel 1:4-24

Witnesses: Luke 2:8-15; 22:43; 24:4-8; Acts 1:10,11; 1 Thessalonians 4:16; Luke 15:10; Matthew 24:30,31

Messengers: Exodus 3:2; Isaiah 6:1-7; Luke 1:28-38; Acts 10:1-8

Protagonists: Luke 10:18; Joshua 5:13-15; 2 Kings 6:17; Daniel 10:13; 12:1; Revelation 12:7-9

Ministers: Genesis 19:15; 22:11,12; 1 Kings 19:5-7; 2 Kings 6:15-17; Matthew 4:11; Acts 12:7-10; Hebrews 1:14; Colossians 2:18

KEY TRUTH

Angels belong to a heavenly order of spiritual, though created, beings.
In their ceaseless worship, they act as messengers of God and as ministers to God's people.

POSTSCRIPT

Certain errors are corrected by the Bible truth that our future human destiny is higher than that of the angels, for our final fulfilment will be in the glorified Christ (Hebrews 2:5-9).

BIBLE STUDY Isaiah 6:1-8

Here is a vision of awesome holiness, given in 740 BC to the young Isaiah, at the start of a long prophetic ministry that was to span the reign of five kings. At that time, the average Hebrew of the world, over which the sovereign Lord ruled, was limited to an area no bigger than New Jersey or Wales. All that changed with the rise in the east of the mighty Assyrian empire that trampled down everything in sight in the name of its ferocious gods. Suddenly, Israel and Judah looked tiny. Had their God also become provincial? Not according to the prophets! Let us learn from Isaiah's call:

1 Isaiah's world-view is shaped here in verses 1-4. What does it centre in? Who, more precisely, is "the Lord"? See John 12:39-41.

2 If Isaiah's attention is riveted on the throne, what is the apparent purpose of the angelic figures (verses 2-4)? What do their appearance and their utterances point to?

3 To what extent should Isaiah's reaction of verse 5 be the norm? Is our view of the Lord's glory and holiness greater or lesser than his? Compare 2 Corinthians 4:6. Compare also Isaiah's words with those of Peter the apostle in Luke 5:8.

4 Why should we be grateful for the ministry of angels? See verse 6 and 7 and compare Luke 2:10-12.

5 Although angels feature many times in the Scriptures, why is there no one major passage about them?

6 From verse 8, what was it that would "hold" Isaiah through all his future trials? What holds any of us?

REFLECTION

A Turn to Hebrews 1 and 2:5-9. While there are numerous references in Scripture to the angels, why is it that there is no classical "passage" that gives specific detailed teaching on the the topic? Why is it that angels seem to feature as ancillaries to the main story line?

B As humans, we were made "a little lower" than the angels (Hebrews 2:7; see Psalm 8:5).

But the implication of Hebrews 1:13,14 and 2:5-9,16 is that our destiny lies higher than the angels. How do you explain this apparent contradiction – a little lower ... eventually higher?

C Consider the nature and status of angels in comparison to Christ, to human beings and to the Holy Spirit.

D In the light of these studies, how would you summarise the chief activities of angels?

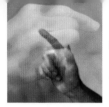

GOD'S MESSENGERS

2. Patriarchs

Forerunners of a new beginning

The patriarchal age began with God's call to Abraham to leave his home in Haran and go to the land of Canaan. Abraham and his immediate descendants, Isaac and Jacob, represent a new start in God's dealings with the human race.

The first 11 chapters of the Bible end in the confusion of the Tower of Babel, with humanity scattered and sin spreading across the world. What hope remained? The call of the Patriarchs is the beginning of the divine answer.

Inheritors of a promised land

To the patriarchs and their descendants is given the promise of a land that they are to possess and occupy. In their own lifetime they were not to see it; even so, the Old Testament develops this theme of God leading his people into a land of their own. The New Testament shows how the patriarchs had their hope set, not just on the land of Israel, but more importantly on the coming new creation.

We must also recognise that the New Testament language of inheriting a land, ties in with the blessing of knowing Christ and the new creation hope that we have in him.

Ancestors of a universal family

The patriarchs are foundational people for the whole faith of the Bible. Their descendants would be the world-wide family of believers, and would be numbered like the stars of heaven.

It is as we come to the New Testament that we learn that the "seed" promised to Abraham is Christ himself, for all God's promises are fulfilled in him. Today all who belong to Christ, both Jews and Gentiles, can be said to be the descendants of Abraham and the patriarchs.

Their message of the covenant

At several points, the divine contract – or covenant – between God and Abraham was confirmed and strengthened. By it, God pledged himself to Abraham and his posterity. His people, for their part, were to separate themselves to God, as symbolised by the outward rite of circumcision.

The "new covenant", inaugurated by Christ, is not a new way of salvation; its basic message was unchanged from patriarchal times – the people of God must put their faith only in Christ.

Their message of election

There was nothing about the patriarchs that merited God's singling out of them for blessing; Abraham came from a family of idol-worshippers in Mesopotamia. Equally it must be insisted that God did not choose this one family for reasons of favouritism.

They were selected for a theological, moral and missionary purpose – for the benefit of all humankind. To the patriarchs were revealed the distinctive names and character of God, for the blessing of every nation.

Their message of obedient faith

Abraham, Isaac and Jacob (and their descendants, known later as Israel) bequeathed to their successors a model of how to walk with Christ. In spite of their various failings, they learnt the ways of prayer and sacrifice in a life of nomadic travel.

Their trust in the faithfulness of God was highlighted supremely in Abraham's willingness to sacrifice his son Isaac. Their God became defined as "the God of Abraham, Isaac and Jacob".

Genesis 11:26–
12:1; 11:1-9; Acts 7:8

Inheritors: Genesis 12:1-7;
15:7-16; Hebrews 11:13-16;
1 Corinthians 3:21,22

Ancestors: Genesis 15:1-5;
Galatians 3:16,29; 2
Corinthians 1:20

Covenant: Genesis 17:1-14;
Jeremiah 31:31-34; 1
Corinthians 11:23-25

Election: Genesis 18:18,19;
Deuteronomy 4:35-40;
Romans 4:16-25

Obedient faith: Genesis
28:10-22; 22:1-18; 1 Kings
18:36

KEY TRUTH

The patriarchs were the
earliest heads of the representative family selected by God
to receive his covenanted
blessings, on behalf of
believers in all generations.

POSTSCRIPT

In regard to the land promised
to the patriarchs, chapters
9–11 of the letter to the
Romans provide a full
overview of the past, present
and future, affecting this
important topic.

BIBLE STUDY Hebrews 11:8-19

This chapter is God's "Hall of Fame". The apostolic writer is
aware of a tendency among some to slip back into their old,
pre-Christian way of thinking, and he points them to the
"better" way provided now in the new covenant, centred in
Christ. Here are some outstanding examples of those who have
gone ahead of us. Among them, none was more prominent
than the patriarch Abraham:

1 As you scan the passage, identify the main episodes that the
writer emphasises as requiring the faith of Abraham.

2 What was the motivation, the mind set, that kept Abraham
on track? (Verses 9, 11 and 19 give clues.)

3 Although Abraham received the promise of a "land" (verse 8)
and of descendants as numerous as the stars and the sand
(verse 12), in his actual lifetime he possessed no more than a
single cave (Genesis 23:17-20) and one son, Isaac. One cave
and one son. How does this bear out the truth of verse 13?
What then does it mean to "see", in the language of verse 13?

4 The "city" (verse 10), the "better country" (verse 16). Try and
understand salvation in terms of the original promise, the
partial fulfilment, the universal extension in the gospel, and
finally the eternal completion. Discuss these different facets
of the one glorious truth.

5 Notice the New Testament commentary (verse 19) on
Abraham's sacrifice of Isaac, narrated in Genesis 22. How was
Abraham a true pioneer of faith in this respect?

6 Is it worth all the aggravation, being a believer in God?

REFLECTION

A Reflect on Hebrews 11:8-19
and the life of Abraham. Here
is the beginning of the worldwide family of believers. Try
and identify from the passage
the various episodes that
required the "faith" of
Abraham.

B What was the motivation,
the mindset, that kept
Abraham on track? Verses
9,10,19 give clues. How does a
right view of the future help us
in the tensions of the present?

C Abraham's descendants are
said to have "seen" something
(verse 13). What have they
seen? What does such a
"seeing" mean for today's
Christian?

D In what senses could it be
argued that the hazardous life
of faith is a blessing?

GOD'S MESSENGERS

3. Priests

Although the principles of sacrifice and priesthood are laid down from the beginning of the Bible (eg Genesis 4:3-5; 8:20; 14:18-20), the truth that all people everywhere need a God-given mediator began to be taught in earnest when Israel was becoming a nation under Moses and Aaron. Through the priestly tribe of the Levites, and Israel's sacrificial system, spiritual lessons of everlasting importance are to be learnt:

We cannot come to God lightly

Washings, cereal offerings, sin offerings, burnt offerings, the Day of Atonement – the rituals associated with the worship tent of the tabernacle (and the temple that was to follow), fall strangely on the modern ear.

But the education was vital; access to God is impossible unless sin is dealt with.

We cannot come to God directly

A representative, a go-between, is necessary. The Levites were to act as priests on behalf of the people. They themselves underwent thorough ceremonial cleansing before they were counted fit for their task. Of all the priests, only Aaron the high priest could enter God's "Most Holy Place" – and then only once a year. The principle of mediation was basic for Israel.

We cannot come to God cheaply

The lesson sank in supremely through the feast of the Passover, instituted on the eve of Israel's deliverance from Egypt. The feast commemorated the application of the blood of a lamb to every Hebrew doorpost on the night that death took its toll of Egypt's firstborn sons. Where blood was visible, life was spared. It was for the priests to continue this principle until the coming of Christ. Without the shedding of blood there is no deliverance.

Christ, the perfect Mediator

The Old Testament priesthood pointed to Jesus Christ and his atoning sacrifice for the sins of the world. Being both human and God, he is the ideal and unique go-between on behalf of sinful people. He is both sacrifice and High Priest. While Aaron had to offer repeated sacrifices both for himself and his people, Christ in his moral perfection offered a single sacrifice for sins, once and for all. Now as heavenly High Priest he provides open access to God the Father, interceding on behalf of all believers.

The cross, the final sacrifice

Until the time of Jesus' death, a heavy curtain in Jerusalem's temple separated the inner "Most Holy Place" (representing God's inaccessibility) from the rest of the building.

As Christ uttered his dying cry on the cross, an earthquake took place; simultaneously the temple curtain was ripped from top to bottom.

It showed that the death of Jesus, like the disintegrated curtain, had opened the way into God's presence for all believers. Never again would a sacrifice for sin be required.

Believers, the new priesthood

All this means that the whole Old Testament system of sacrifice and priesthood has been superseded and swept away by the one valid sacrifice of Jesus, described as "Christ our Passover lamb". A new priesthood has come into being; it is that of all believers everywhere. They offer, not a sacrifice for sins, rather sacrifices of praise and thankful service to God, and intercessory prayer on behalf of others. The temple now is spiritual, formed of "living stones". Christ's followers.

BIBLE CHECK

Not lightly: Leviticus 1:1-9; 16:20-22; Numbers 3:5-13

Not directly: Numbers 8:19-22; Leviticus 16:32-34; Isaiah 53:6,12

Not cheaply: Exodus 12:7-14; Leviticus 17:11; Exodus 24:8

Christ: 1 Timothy 2:5,6; Hebrews 7:23-27; 4:14-16

The cross: Hebrews 9:1-4; Matthew 27:50,51; Hebrews 10:19-22

Believers: Hebrews 9:11-15; 1 Corinthians 5:7; 1 Peter 2:4,5

KEY TRUTH

The priests of the Old Testament nation of Israel were the agents of mediation through whom God was to be approached. As such, they foreshadowed Jesus Christ, God's final and perfect Mediator for all time.

POSTSCRIPT

Christian elders and leaders are required to set a Christ-like example to the members of the church, in the fulfilling of their priestly duties.

BIBLE STUDY Hebrews 10:1-18

"In your beliefs, how do you get forgiven?" The speaker was a Christian.

"Forgiven?" echoed the member of another faith. "Why … God just forgives. He is merciful."

"Really? Just like that? You mean that six million people can be put through the gas chambers, and God says to the perpetrators, 'All right, I'll forgive you, that's fine; we'll say no more about it.' How can God do that without undermining his own morality?"

"You've made me think," came the reply.

1 The story of the Bible is about this issue. Sin cannot be lightly forgiven by the perfect and moral ruler of the universe. Read the key of this passage, in verse 12, and reflect on the wonder of what this one "priest" has achieved.

2 Shadows and realities (verse 1). Two systems are being contrasted in this passage. Identify the various contrasts between the many priests and their duties of the Old Covenant, and the unique high priest of the New. What is the special facet of the new covenant (verse 16)?

3 What is the greatest contrast of all? Verses 2 and 10 use the same phrase.

4 The sacrifice of animals, though not representing God's ultimate desire, nevertheless had a purpose. How would you describe it, from verses 3 and 9?

5 "Never make perfect" (verse 1) … "made perfect" (verse 14) – had you noticed that contrast? If Christ's sacrifice of himself has removed everything that blocked our approach to God, how does this affect our life of prayer?

REFLECTION

A Study Hebrews 10:11-18. Why can't God simply "forgive" sins? And why the need of a priest to be go-between?

B Two systems are here being contrasted: the old and the new. List as many contrasts as you can find in this passage. What is the major thing that stands out about them?

C "Made perfect" (verse 14) – the meaning is that everything that hindered our approach to God has been removed by Christ's sacrifice of himself. What does that say to us about the life of prayer?

D If every believer today is a priest (1 Peter 2:5), what form should our "spiritual sacrifices" take? How does this affect daily living?

4. Prophets

They received God's summons

From the beginning there were prophetic stirrings among God's people. Abraham himself was termed a "prophet" (Genesis 20:7). But it was supremely through Moses that the true nature and task of a prophet became established.

With many of the prophets we read of a direct "call", frequently from youth, sometimes dramatic. Some accepted reluctantly, in their recognition that they were being sent to uncaring listeners. It was, however, their awareness of having been in God's presence that stamped their ministry with authority. From Samuel's time there were "schools" of prophets; from Joel's period stemmed the great writing prophets. These were "men of God", "seers", "watchmen" and intercessors, standing in the breach on behalf of people under judgement.

They challenged God's people

The prophets were no mere product of Jewish life; they came into direct collision with Jewish ways, notably the repeated tendency to compromise the unique faith of Israel with that of other nations. It was Elijah's fearless stand against the prophets of Baal that placed him, in Jewish estimation, for ever on a level with Moses.

The issues were many: idolatry, syncretism, social injustice and spiritual apathy. These sins were confronted by prophets of God's kingdom of righteousness, peace, universality and permanence. Their moral authority exceeded that of even priests and kings. The exception was King David who, as the inspired psalmist, became classed as a prophet himself.

They revealed God's mind

The true prophets, as contrasted with the false, were concerned to speak out, however unpopular their message. They held firmly to five mighty concepts; that God is one with no rivals; that, as "the living God", he is active in redeeming and sustaining his people; that he is faithful to his covenant with Israel; that he is righteous and must judge evil; and that he is merciful and provides a blood-bought way by which sin can be forgiven.

They addressed God's world

The horizons of the prophets extended far beyond Israel's borders, taking in the time-span of world history. They were commentators on the past.

By their ministry, history became revelation. They were interpreters of the present, seeing current events as indications that God was executing his judgements on Israel and the nations alike. They were visionaries of the future. The prophecies of Daniel, like those of the book of Revelation, were given to comfort God's people at a time of great stress. Their ultimate fulfilment would only be realised in the era of the gospel, and even beyond at the end of the age.

They foretold God's Messiah

It was John the Baptist, the last prophet of the old era, who heralded the arrival of Jesus as the fulfilment of the long-awaited promise of a coming ruler whose kingdom would last for ever. Christ, as God's final "Word" to this world, is recognised as fulfilling the age-old expectation of a Moses-like "prophet" who must be listened to. Although there were New Testament prophets – a gift of the Spirit to the church – with the emergence of the New Testament Scriptures, their importance stays largely foundational, like that of the apostles.

BIBLE CHECK

Received: Exodus 3;
1 Samuel 3; Isaiah 6;
Jeremiah 1; Habakkuk 2:1

Challenged: Deuteronomy
34:10-12; 1 Kings 18:16-40;
Amos 5:21-24; Acts 2:29,30

Revealed: Jeremiah 20:9;
2 Peter 1:20; Deuteronomy
4:32-40

Addressed: Isaiah 5:1-7;
Daniel 2:36-46; 7:13-18;
Revelation 1:12-20

Foretold: John 1:19-34;
Isaiah 9:2-7; 53:1-12;
Deuteronomy 18:15; Acts
3:17-22; Ephesians 2:20

KEY TRUTH

The prophets of the Bible,
in their speaking and writing,
stood before their people
as those who had first been
called to stand in the presence
of God. As such, their inspired
utterances have been bound
up for ever in the Scriptures.

POSTSCRIPT

It is a loyalty to the Scriptures
and the gospel, and the ability
to make them relevant in
today's world that stamp a
church or a Christian leader as
"prophetic".

BIBLE STUDY Jeremiah 1:1-19

This most heroic of all the Old Testament prophets had a
remarkable and turbulent career that stretched from 626 BC to
the fall of Jerusalem in 587 BC, a ministry of 40 years.

At no time did he gain favour with his listeners.
A true patriot who loved his people, he was nevertheless called
to pronounce against them in God's name, and he suffered
throughout his career. Use these questions as you study this
passage:

1 Take time to read the whole of the first chapter. How is it that
the message of the prophets, worldwide, have a far greater
readership than that of Plato or other highly advanced ancient
philosophers?

2 How common to God's servants of any generation is the
hesitation expressed by the prophet in verse 6? Let different
group members look up Exodus 4:10; Isaiah 6:5; Jonah 1:1-3;
How did God compensate for the weaknesses of his servants?
(See verses 7-9.)

3 Jeremiah was sent to prophesy to the southern kingdom of
Judah. But his commission was wider. How wide? What does
this tell us about God's word throughout the ages?

4 Two visions come to Jeremiah (verses 11-15), one positive
with its message of blossom, spring and fulfilment; the other
negative, with its message of disaster pouring upon Judah.
What does this tell us about the "bitter-sweet" nature of
service for God? Compare Revelation 10:9-11.

5 Can you think of others of God's servants who, despite their
frailties, have mirrored the protection described in verses
18,19?

REFLECTION

A Take time to read Jeremiah
1. Jeremiah was called to be a
prophet for God in the year
626 BC. Why is it that the
message of the prophets has a
wider readership today than
that of Plato or other ancient
philosophers?

B How typical is the hesitation
expressed by the prophet
(verse 6)? Compare Exodus
4:10; Isaiah 6:5; Jonah 1:1-3.

How did God compensate
for the weaknesses of his
servants?

C Jeremiah was sent to
prophecy to the southern
kingdom of Judah. But his
commission was wider. How
wide? What does this tell us
about God's word throughout
the ages?

D What lessons can we learn
from the prophets as we face
God's call to service today?

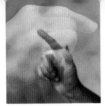

5. Apostles

An apostle is one "sent" or "commissioned". In this sense Christ was the supreme Apostle, sent from his Father. The term is also applied to "representatives" of the gospel, sent by the churches. But in general, "apostles" describe the unique group, invested with Christ's authority in the early church.

Personally appointed by Christ

Originally twelve in number, they were chosen by Jesus to be with him, to go out preaching and exercising spiritual authority in his name. Outside of the twelve, certain others became recognised as apostles, either directly or by association, Paul being outstanding.

Historically acquainted with Christ

The great qualification was a first-hand knowledge of Jesus' earthly ministry, from the time of John the Baptist until the Ascension. In this way the apostles could "witness" to the fact that the resurrected Christ was the same individual that they had worked and travelled with. The apostle Paul had not been with Jesus from the beginning, but the revelation he received was direct, not second-hand, and his later encounter with the risen Christ was unique to him alone.

Supernaturally accredited by Christ

The work of a true apostle was to be authenticated by miracles. These stamped the apostle as a messenger of Christ. The future reliability of the apostles' teaching for the whole church was also guaranteed by Jesus' pledge of the Holy Spirit's promptings and inspiration in all their future work.

As far as the Christian fellowship was concerned, the calling of an apostle was a gift of the Holy Spirit to the church. But in this instance there would be no renewal of the gift in subsequent generations. Yet the entire church has benefited from Christ's apostles.

They provided the church's foundations

Here was a "foundational" gift to the church at its very beginning, and the growth and progress of the church ever since has been the superstructure. Across the ages, "twelve" and its multiple would be taken as a symbol of the people of God – standing both for the Old Testament tribes of Israel and the New Testament apostles of Christ.

They defined the church's teaching

Jesus assured the apostles that after his bodily departure the Holy Spirit would guide them into all truth. This meant that the apostles' teaching became definitive for the church, and was placed on a level with the rest of Scripture. It follows that the strongest warnings are given in the New Testament about the presence of false apostles. Indeed the greatest threat to the early church came from false teaching.

They inspired the church's mission

All the other ministries of the church flowed out of that of the apostles, the "pillars" who gave the new missionary movement its leadership and impetus. The call to minister to a dying world stems from the momentous commission given by Jesus to the apostles.

BIBLE CHECK

Personally: Mark 3:13-19; Galatians 1:19; 2:9; 1 Corinthians 15:7-9

Historically: Acts 1:21,22; Galatians 1:11,12; 1 Corinthians 9:1,2; 15:8-11

Supernaturally: 2 Corinthians 12:12; John 14:25,26; 1 Corinthians 2:6-16

Provided: Ephesians 2:19-22; Revelation 21:14

Defined: John 16:12-15; Acts 2:42; 2 Peter 3:16; 2 Corinthians 11:13

Inspired: Galatians 2:9; John 20:19-22

KEY TRUTH

The apostles, a group limited to those who had been originally selected by Jesus Christ to act in his name, have provided the church for ever with its unchangeable standard for belief and practice.

POSTSCRIPT

Although the apostles have no successors today, it is possible to speak of a church or ministry being "apostolic" provided it is proclaiming the apostles' teaching.

BIBLE STUDY Galatians 1:6-24

Sometimes goods have to be taken off the shelves of stores and supermarkets, because of malicious tampering. Even if only a little of the product has been affected, the remedy has to be swift and radical – for people's welfare is at stake.

So with the gospel. In this instance the gospel has been tampered with by false teachers, and the letter to the Galatians, written around AD 48, represents a strong defence of two things; God's pure gospel and Paul's true apostleship.

1 Paul has often been criticised for his strong condemnation of those who preach falsely. But is he any harsher than other apostles – or indeed than Jesus himself? Different group members can look up 2 Peter 2:17; Jude 12; Revelation 22:18 and Luke 17:1,2.

2 Paul has been attacked throughout history for preaching an invented gospel different from Christ's. The apostle makes two points in verses 11 and 12. What are they?

3 Look at verses 13-24, especially verse 20. Why this insistence that the gospel was revealed to him in independence from the other apostles; that he had not "consulted" anyone; that he had been in isolation in Arabia? The clue lies in 1:1.

4 Consider the fact that the apostles were all preaching the same truths (eg Galatians 2:6-8; 1 Corinthians 15:11). What does this say to those today who are content with a diversity of interpretations of the Scriptures?

5 How "apostolic" is your fellowship? Look up Acts 2:42; 1 Corinthians 15:3-5; Jude 3.

REFLECTION

A Turn to Galatians 1, and especially verses 11-24, where Paul takes up one of the major themes of his book – the genuineness of his apostleship. What main point is he making? The clues are in verses 11,12,15-20, and relate to the fact that in the early days of his call to be an apostle, his contact with the other apostles was minimal.

B Consider the fact that the apostles were all proclaiming the same truths (Galatians 2:6-8; 1 Corinthians 15:11). What does this tell us about disharmony in some modern-day preaching? Where should churches see their priorities?

C "And they praised God because of me" (verse 24). Not everybody did in Paul's day, nor does everybody do so today. Why?

6. Evangelists

Their work is God's gospel

The term "evangelist" comes from a word that means gospel or good news. The evangelist is the announcer of such news. But it must be emphasised that the work of evangelism is primarily the work of God himself. It was God who first "evangelised" Abraham, and Jesus who was to be found "evangelising" in Jerusalem's temple.

It is therefore God's mission before it can ever be that of the evangelist. The evangelist is simply one who is caught up in the wonder and joy created by the gospel and who cannot remain silent.

Their home is God's church

The true evangelist is drawn from within the local church membership, for it is there that the Holy Spirit distributed his gifts. The believer who has been given the gift of evangelism is to work in harmony and unity with those of other callings in the church.

Thus the work of evangelism is one of those gifts of the Spirit by which the body of Christ, the church, may be built up. Whether they are evangelists at large, such as Philip, or those settled in the oversight of a church, such as Timothy, they are called, not to create their own following, but to serve the churches that send them.

Their message is God's salvation

The evangelist is called to proclaim that what sinful men and women under divine judgement cannot do for themselves, God has done for them in Jesus Christ. Christ has died for the sins of the world and is now raised and ascended as universal Lord and Saviour.

The work of the evangelist is to call people to repent of their sins and personally to accept Christ, for the forgiveness of their sins and the gift of the Holy Spirit.

Their confidence is God's word

A characteristic that has always marked out the true evangelist is a distrust of self or of natural gifts, and a reliance upon "the testimony about God". The New Testament evangelists were aware that their message was based upon the inspired word of God; they encouraged each other to preach and learn from the Scriptures that make people wise for salvation and equip them to serve God.

It was the work of the evangelist to take the words of Scripture and to apply them with urgency and relevance to people without Christ.

Their power is God's Spirit

Jesus had left his friends with the apparently impossible task of bringing his witness to the whole world. It was the promise of the coming Holy Spirit that made the difference. As the early followers of Christ were filled with the Holy Spirit they found the boldness to speak in his name.

Human oratory and tricks of persuasion can never be the power behind God's evangelists. Evangelism is to be a demonstration, through changed lives, of the power of God.

Their goal is God's glory

The need of unforgiven sinners facing the judgement of God will always weigh heavily upon the evangelist. But the highest motivation for evangelism is a passion for the glory of God.

The conversion of sinners is a grace of God alone.

The evangelists of the New Testament were sent out by the churches to proclaim Christ as Lord to all the world. When this is faithfully done, they are a glory to his name.

Work: Galatians 3:8; Luke
20:1; Acts 4:18-20; Romans
10:14,15

Home: Ephesians 4:11,12;
Acts 21:8; 2 Timothy 4:5

Message: 2 Corinthians
5:17-21; 1 Corinthians
15:3-5; Acts 4:12

Confidence: 1 Corinthians
2:1,13; 2 Timothy 3:14–4:2;
Acts 8:26-35

Power: Acts 1:8; 1 Corinthians
2:4,5

Goal: Galatians 1:23,24;
2 Corinthians 4:15; 8:23;
1 Corinthians 9:11-18

KEY TRUTH

While all Christians are
to share their faith, some
individuals are called to be
evangelists, with a special gift
from the Holy Spirit, to
announce the good news of
the gospel.

POSTSCRIPT

Although there is a place for
the evangelist to receive a
living for the service that is
given, a modest lifestyle and a
restrained discipline should
characterise the whole
ministry.

BIBLE STUDY 2 Corinthians 4:1-18

Both letters of Paul to the Corinthians are taken up with a
single theme, that of power through weakness. Of all the New
Testament churches, the Corinthian was the most confused
and the least mature. The false teachers had made a bid for the
soul of the church, and power-hungry bogus apostles were
promoting their own status and discrediting Paul.

When the thrilling work of proclaiming the gospel is
dishonoured by the power-grabbers, the peace-breakers and
the sheep-stealers; by self-promoting triumphalism and by the
wrenching of Scripture to bolster a dubious message ... the
Corinthian correspondence is the result.

1 This passage is full of fascinating paradoxes or contrasts. Try
   to follow them through: weakness and power, mortality and
   life, affliction and glory, etc. What does this teach us about
   the ministry of making Christ known?

2 Why is it necessary to apply to ourselves the standards of
   openness and integrity followed by Paul in verse 2?

3 Look at the discouragements! (eg verses 4,8,9). Why is it then
   that "we do not lose heart" (verses 1 and 16)? What has the
   answer got to do with the glory of Christ and the message of
   the cross?

4 "Treasure ... jars of clay" (verse 7). Why this contrast between
   the message and the messenger? If this is evangelism as it
   should be, where do we see it at its best today?

5 Can you think of evangelists in the New Testament who
   worked in the spirit and lifestyle of this passage? See Acts
   8:26-40; 7:54-60. Spend time now in prayer for evangelists
   you know.

REFLECTION

A Read 2 Corinthians 4. This
passage is full of paradoxes or
contrasts. Try to follow them
through: weakness and power,
mortality and life, affliction
and glory, etc. What does this
teach us about the ministry of
evangelism?

B Meditate on verse 5, and
identify evangelists and
missionaries who deserve our
support and our prayers in the
way they proclaim the gospel.

C Verses 1 and 2 give
important guidelines to the
evangelist. What are they?

1. God's Plan for Humanity

God's plan – his will is sovereign

The Bible teaches that God is above everything, and he uses the most unlikely people to carry out his purposes .

Thus, Jacob and not Esau (who was the older of the two) was chosen to be head of the family which God would use to rescue humanity. Similarly David, the youngest of his family, was chosen as the one through whose descendants the Messiah would come. In the New Testament, those who were called to be God's people in Christ were called purely on the basis of God's own purpose and generosity.

God's plan – his work is eternal

The Bible teaches us that God's work of salvation, centred in Christ, has been planned from eternity.

The death of Jesus in Jerusalem at a fixed point in time was the result of the wilful act of angry sinners, but it must also be seen as an event planned by God from before the beginning of the world.

God's plan – his choice is specific

While the Bible is against the idea of "fatalism" (that is, whatever God decides for us, we are fated to do), it does teach that God's plan is more than simply a general call to all humanity. Those who freely respond to his call learn that God had chosen them from among many, according to his own purpose and will.

God's people – separated for holy living

Properly understood, the biblical teaching of predestination will never generate complacency in those who are chosen by God. For the people of God are called to be holy.

In the Old Testament, something that was specially set apart for the service of God was called "holy". So it is with the Christian. On freely responding to God's call, we learn that we have been predestined, from eternity, for a life of obedience and Christ-likeness.

God's people – called to good works

God's call of Abraham, of Isaac and Jacob, was for the specific purpose of bringing benefit to the world.

God's people, in the New Testament, are called to a life of good deeds and energetic mission. It is not for them to determine who are among the called. Their responsibility is to proclaim and reflect the goodness of God to all of humanity.

God's people – preparing for future glory

God's eternal plan for his people has a glorious future in view. From the beginning, the Christian has been chosen for salvation; this includes the future life of glory with Christ.

It is Christ who provides the key to God's plan. Without him, there is no salvation, and the Christian is nothing. It is only as we are identified with him that we can hope to share in his victory over death, and in the eternal home he has planned for us. The future glory begins now – in faithful service and obedience.

BIBLE CHECK

Will: 1 Corinthians 1:26-29; Romans 9:10-18

Work: Acts 2:23; 1 Peter 1:18-20; Revelation 13:8

Choice: Matthew 22:14; Romans 9:20,21,27

Separated: Romans 8:29; Ephesians 1:4; 1 Peter 1:1,2

Called: Philippians 2:12,13; Acts 9:15; 1 Peter 2:9-12

Preparing: 2 Thessalonians 2:13,14; Revelation 17:14

KEY TRUTH

God has always had a plan for rescuing those who are in rebellion against him. The Bible tells us that although we are free to respond to God, he has already chosen us to be his people. The word "predestination" means that God has selected and separated a people for himself.

POSTSCRIPT

The biblical emphasis regarding God's sovereignty and human free-will is not found somewhere between the two, but in both extremes. If we over-emphasise man's free will, then God will seem to be powerless. If we over-emphasise God's sovereignty, then human beings will seem to be denied any choice.

BIBLE STUDY Ephesians 1:3-12

Under the guidance of the Holy Spirit, the apostle Paul had targeted Ephesus as a strategic growth point for the church of Jesus Christ. He spent longer in Ephesus than in any other church. The likelihood is that this was a "circular" intended for all the churches on the Ephesus postal route, on the seaboard of what is modern-day Turkey. Our passage before us is, in the Greek original, a single unbroken sentence! Try to take in the sweep of Paul's thought as he writes about God's plan of salvation:

1 How impossible would the plan, as it is described in verse 10, have looked to those inhabitants of a teeming pagan city? What is the keystone of God's eternal plan? It features in every single verse.

2 What can you learn from verse 3-6 about God's eternal plan, on which we are to rest our confidence? Paul is working back from salvation to ... what?

3 What can be learnt in this passage about the central work of Christ – a second ground for our confidence? How does verse 7 anchor the high-flown language in a concrete, earth-bound way?

4 What can you trace here about the personal working of the Holy Spirit – as a third ground on which the Christian's confidence rests? The "seal" (verse 13) seems to stand for the mark of genuineness, the stamp of ownership (Ephesians 4:30) and the guarantee of security (compare Matthew 27:66, same Greek word). Work out how this applies to the Christian.

5 "Mystery" (verse 9) refers in this context, not to something impenetrable, but to a secret, once hidden, but now blown open – for everyone! When did this happen for you?

REFLECTION

A Read Ephesians 1:3-12. What should be the reaction of those who are called? What is the immediate purpose of this call, the future purpose and the ultimate purpose?

B Meditate on John 6:37,44; 2 Peter 1:10,11, where God's sovereignty and human free-will are combined.

C Why should a true understanding of predestination not stop us from urging those we know to choose to become Christians?

D Some may argue that they are not called. Where does Scripture teach that God's redemption is offered to all? Compare your findings with, for example, 1 Timothy 2:4,6; Titus 2:11.

2. Humanity's Need of Salvation

Humanity's need of a new direction

Although created by God, and for him, human beings have left the path of obedience to God. We are out of touch with God and all that he has planned for us, and without him life does not make sense to us.

Humanity is also under judgement. Jesus Christ's analysis was that the majority of humanity is treading the path of ruin and destruction. People are condemned for their rejection of God's truth.

Humanity's need of a new nature

Humanity is in bondage because of our refusal to follow God's commands. On our own, we are unable to change our nature as the sin principle dominates us, and our actions and habits show that we are in slavery.

We live our lives under the shadow of death, and over the ages no amount of philosophy, guesswork or moral endeavour has been able to remove the spectre of ageing and dying.

Humanity's need of a new motivation

The brevity and purposelessness of life without God are reflected in art and literature throughout history, particularly in times when society openly rejects God's standards.

The Bible indicates that we need the dimension of God if life is to be lived with dynamism and purpose. Without God we find no satisfying, alternative way of life.

Humanity's need of personal fulfilment

We are in urgent need of a sense of destiny and achievement in this world. Our aspirations will sometimes take the form of extreme materialistic ambitions; at other times they will shrivel into despair and aimlessness.

Jesus warned his hearers that a person's life should never be totally taken up with the accumulation of possessions. He taught that whoever spent his life and energies upon the material world would have made a bad bargain.

Humanity's need of social acceptance

From earliest times, as illustrated by the story of the Tower of Babel, human beings have been aware of the need for the friendship and acceptance of others. History illustrates our search for true fellowship, mutual trust and companionship.

But ideals, agreements and political arrangements all fall short of what we are searching for. The cynicism expressed in the book of Ecclesiastes shows us this clearly. Human beings are lonely.

Humanity's need of a spiritual dimension

As fallen people we cannot appreciate the spiritual side of life, left to ourselves. But because God made us, we feel incomplete without a Godward dimension.

Furthermore, we are unable to explore this dimension unaided, because we are described as being poor, weak, blind, and even dead. In the absence of spiritual awareness, our prospects appear to make a mockery of our once high position.

BIBLE CHECK

New direction: Hebrews 9:27; Matthew 7:13; John 3:19

New nature: Jeremiah 13:23; 17:9,10; John 8:34; Ecclesiastes 8:8

Motivation: Ecclesiastes 6:12; John 6:66-68

Fulfilment: Ecclesiastes 2:10,11; Luke 12:15; Mark 8:34-37

Social: Genesis 11:4; Ecclesiastes 5:8

Spiritual: 1 Corinthians 2:14; 2 Corinthians 4:4

KEY TRUTH

The human race is estranged and cut off from God. Humanity needs a new direction and nature, if we are to avoid permanent ruin and eternal judgement. We cannot bring about this change for ourselves.

POSTSCRIPT

Although we all need God's salvation, many people are unaware of their own need. A person may become so used to living in separation from God that conscience becomes dead. Such complacency is only further proof of our ruined nature.

BIBLE STUDY Ephesians 2:1-10

Paul outlines to his Christian readers in Ephesus the hopelessness of their case before the arrival of the gospel among them. Ephesus was a centre of idolatry, given over to the worship of Artemis (or Diana), whose temple was four times the size of the Parthenon at Athens. When salvation in Christ's name was preached at Ephesus for the first time, it rocked commercial interests and provoked a riot (Acts 19:23-41). This was the world out of which the new believers had been drawn:

1 "Dead" (verse 1). Dead in what way? Dead to what? Usually the doctor's work ceases at death. What then is the state of those without Christ? See end of verse 12.

2 "Transgressions and sins" (verse 1) – how popular would this description have been with a worshipper at the temple of Artemis? How are we to help those who say they have no needs at all?

3 In verses 2 and 3, identify those phrases that refer to the world, the flesh and the devil. Why is it wise to keep all three adversaries in view rather than transfer all the categories into a single camp – that of, say, the devil?

4 "Objects of wrath" (verse 3). How do phrases like this square with the teaching of Jesus? See Matthew 13:41, 42; Matthew 18:6. Were members of the group ever aware that verse 3 once described them? If not, this serves as a useful reminder.

5 "But" (verse 4). This is the word that opens the door and lets in the light. As you read the remaining verses, think of the idolatrous Ephesians, raised in an instant to the situation of verse 6.

6 All this speaks to us of grace (verses 5,7,8). Discuss the meaning of this wonderful word. See Romans 3:24.

REFLECTION

A Study Ecclesiastes 2:1-11. Try to analyse this profile of a person without God. What drives him? What is his programme? What are his achievements and what does he get? Has verse 11 found an echo in other generations?

B How far are people in your own fellowship beginning to experience the answers of God to all these human needs?

C What makes Ecclesiastes so relevant to much of present-day society?

D How far have you experienced these needs in your own life? How far do you still experience them?

3. The Way of Salvation

The basis – the death of Jesus

The apostles proclaimed the death of Jesus Christ as the means by which God has dealt with the sins of humanity. They declared that without his death there could be no basis for salvation. On the cross, Christ accepted the judgement and separation from God brought about by the sins of the world.

This message directly fulfilled Old Testament prophecy, and the words of Christ himself. It was also taught in the New Testament letters.

The basis – the resurrection of Jesus

If the cross was seen as the means by which God had dealt with sin, the resurrection was proclaimed by the early church as the evidence and proof that Christ's death had been truly effective, and had been recognised by God the Father.

The message of Christ's resurrection was not taught merely as a point of academic discussion. The early witnesses announced it as a living reality.

The call – to repentance

The good news was recognised to have a distinctive moral challenge at its heart. The sinner who hears the gospel is called upon to "repent", which means to turn from the old life. This turning is more than a mere regret for the past. It is a change of attitude, leading to a change of direction.

The call – to faith

If repentance is seen as a turning from the old life, faith is to be understood in similarly active terms. It is turning towards the saving power of Jesus Christ.

There are three aspects to faith. There is belief in a fact, for true faith must start by believing with the mind. There is also belief in a word, or promise particularly as given by God. But, vitally, there is belief in a person – Jesus Christ. This requires a living relationship of love and trust with Christ. Without these three aspects faith is incomplete.

The promise – forgiveness

There is a finality and a completeness about the forgiveness of sins that is promised to all who respond to the good news of Christ.

Forgiveness is made available only at the price of Christ's death, and God gives it freely and permanently. To be forgiven does not merely mean the wiping away of our past sins – it means the beginning of a new way of life. Because God forgives us, we are able to enjoy his friendship and acceptance.

The promise – the gift of the Spirit

The forgiveness of sins and the gift of the Spirit go together as the promise of New Testament Christianity. God freely gives us the Holy Spirit when we repent and believe in him.

The gift of the Spirit makes the blessings of the gospel and the presence of Christ personal to the Christian. He gives us power for service and reassures us of the promise of eternal life. The Holy Spirit makes actual all that Christ's death made available.

BIBLE CHECK

Death: Acts 4:10-12; Isaiah 53:4-6; 1 Peter 3:18

Resurrection: Acts 2:32-36; Romans 8:11

Repentance: Acts 3:19; Luke 15:10; 24:46,47

Faith: Acts 13:38,39; 26:18; John 3:16; Revelation 3:20

Forgiveness: Acts 3:19; Psalm 103:11,12; Ephesians 1:7,8

Gift of the Spirit: Acts 2:38; Ephesians 1:13,14

KEY TRUTH

In all the preaching of the early church, as documented in the book of Acts, the way of salvation follows a distinctive pattern. First there is the basis of salvation – Christ's death and resurrection – followed by God's call; and then there is the promise to all who respond.

POSTSCRIPT

In becoming a Christian there is a part that only we can play and a part that only God can play. We repent and abandon our old way of life. God forgives us and empowers us through the Holy Spirit.

BIBLE STUDY Titus 3:3-8

Crete is the setting of this small but powerful letter from the apostle Paul to his trusted lieutenant Titus, around the year AD 62 or 63. Crete had become a part of the Roman Empire in 67 BC; it was a sizeable island, dominating the south of the Aegean Sea – mountainous, superstitious and tough to handle! Here Paul is concerned to hold his retan friends to the unchanging fundamentals of salvation's message. What was this message?

1 Somebody once said, "I didn't know I was lost until I was found." Why is it important to revisit our past, as Paul invited his readers to do in verse 3?

2 "Disobedient, deceived and enslaved" (verse 3) – how far do members of the group recognise these terms as describing their pre-Christian situation?

3 Now, in verses 4-8, the apostle reviews the process and wonder of salvation. What is the key word (verse 5)? What do you learn from the coupling of "God" (verse 4) and "Jesus Christ" (verse 6) as "Saviour"?

4 What are the phrases in this passage that speak of the new birth, participation in the out-pouring of the Holy Spirit at Pentecost, justification, and eternal life? Notice the word "washing" (verse 5). To what does this refer? For a clue, look up Ezekiel 36:25,26.

5 Think about the ground of our salvation. What is it, and what is it not?

6 The "appearing" of verse 4 can only refer, as in 2:11, to the coming of Christ and his self-giving at the cross (2:14). In the light of this, how do you define "grace" (verse 7)?

7 We know what we are saved from. What are we saved for? See verse 8.

REFLECTION

A Start reading half-way through Paul's sermon in Acts 13:22-41. What are the main elements in Paul's message? What is said about Jesus, and how is it said?

B Try to isolate one or more New Testament passages that helpfully sum up the message of salvation. Compare your findings with others. For instance, look at John 3, Romans 3, Ephesians 2, Titus 3.

C What is the relative importance of the mind, the emotions and the will in the response of the individual to the good news?

D What is the main goal in proclaiming salvation in Christ? Check your thoughts against Colossians 1:28, and Matthew 28:19,20.

4. Acceptance

God regenerates the believer as a new being

So radical is the renewing work of the Spirit that it is spoken of in terms of new birth, or "regeneration". It is described as birth "from above". As an individual repents and believes in Christ, so the Holy Spirit enters his life and personality and joins him to the family of God. The Spirit also gives him a new nature characterised by the hallmarks of a new moral outlook, love for the family of God, and faith in Christ.

God reconciles the believer in a new relationship

Until the good news is received and acted upon, a state of hostility exists between God and the individual. It is the death of Christ that specifically alters the situation. On the cross, Christ himself accepted the guilt and penalty for the sins of humanity. The way is opened for a repentant sinner to receive the reconciliation thus made available by God in Christ.

It is the cross that satisfies God's justice – for there God's anger against sin was fully poured out. This is why the cross is called a propitiation.

God redeems the believer through a new covenant

The old covenant was an agreement entered into by God with the Jews, primarily on the basis of the law of Moses. It established a way of life for them after their deliverance from Egypt. This old covenant was a shadow of the new covenant, pointing to the new covenant in all its details.

The new covenant (foretold by Jeremiah) was to achieve through the cross what the old could never do. The deliverance was of another kind, personal and internal, on the basis of Christ's shed blood, for the forgiveness of sins and the redeeming (or "buying back") of the sinner. This was a costly price indeed.

God justifies the believer for a new position

To "justify" is a legal term, which means to declare that a person is righteous. God has done this for the person who has responded to Christ, on the basis of the death of Jesus.

Justification is said to be by "grace" (which means God's undeserved favour), for it is a free gift. It is also by blood, for Christ's death is the means by which God could legally forgive the sinner. It is also by faith, for there is nothing the sinner can contribute to his new position of righteousness – nothing beyond accepting the gift in grateful faith.

God glorifies the believer for a new life

In the New Testament letters, it is noticeable that salvation is repeatedly expressed in three stages. First, there is the free grace of God as the initial act and base. Second, there is the growth of godliness in the Christian as a progressive experience. Third, glory is seen as the future goal and pinnacle. The Christian's great confidence is in the certain return of Christ, the promise of a resurrection body and a share in God's eternal glory.

BIBLE CHECK

Regenerates: Ezekiel 36:25-27; John 3:3-8; Titus 3:4,5
Reconciles: 2 Corinthians 5:18-21; Romans 5:10
Redeems: Jeremiah 31:31-34; Mark 14:24; 1 Peter 1:18,19
Justifies: Romans 3:23-26; 5:1; Titus 3:7
Glorifies: Romans 8:28-30; Philippians 3:20,21

KEY TRUTH

The sinner is accepted by God in Christ, and made a new person. The benefits this position and relationship bring should make the Christian eternally grateful.

POSTSCRIPT

New believers may be confident that God has accepted them because of the promises in the word of God, the finished work of Christ, and the inward witness of the Holy Spirit.

BIBLE STUDY **Romans 5:1-11**

The apostle Paul has been developing a logical argument as he sets out God's way of salvation. He had argued for universal guilt across the human race; he has outlined the way by which people can be justified and placed in a right standing before God, on the basis of Christ's death for us all (Romans 3:24-26). He moves on now to the wonderful consequences of what it means to be justified.

1 Think through what is meant by peace with God, the first stated result of being justified. For Paul did not apparently have much "peace" in his turbulent career. However, as a preacher once said, "A dull bovine contentment is the stagnancy of life and not peace with God." What is this peace?

2 Linked with peace is a further benefit. How would you put verse 2 into your own words? Try and give a definition of "grace". Can one fall in and out of grace? See John 6:37.

3 In verses 2 and 3 there are two reasons given for rejoicing. How surprised are you that these two reasons are so close to one another? Why are they linked like this? (Compare 1 Peter 1:11; 4:13; 5:1; 5:10.)

4 The unbelieving world does not think about trials in the way outlined in verse 3 and 4. How is it that the Christian can see affliction and adversity as productive?

5 Meditate on the sense of God's love, that he puts into the lives of all those who are justified (verses 5-8). Meanwhile what four words described us? (See verses 6,8,10).

6 Is the best yet to be? Give reasons for such thinking, from the rest of this passage.

REFLECTION

A Read Romans 5:1-11, with its portrayal of the Christian's new position in Christ. Look for the key terms. List the ways in which God has been generous to us, and give thanks to him for them.
B In what sense can we say that we have been "justified by grace / blood / faith"?
C Write down the qualities you have enjoyed in a relationship with one of your friends. Write down the demands such a relationship makes. How is your relationship with God the same, and how is it different?
D Do the Christian's troubles end, upon entering into peace with God? What does Romans 5:1-5 teach us?

5. Sanctification

A separation to God

While justification is the work of a moment – that of declaring the sinner righteous – sanctification is the process of a lifetime – that of making the sinner righteous in life and character.

Holiness means separateness. In the Old Testament, houses and animals were sometimes set apart for the special use of God. Christ's followers have been called by God to be set apart – so that they may become more like Christ and holy in character.

A separation from the world

The Christian is called to co-operate with the sanctifying purposes and power of God. There must be a willingness to abandon evil and impure ways; to be separate from all that could impede the development of Christ-like living.

Sanctification is not the separation of a hermit or recluse, because Jesus mixed with sinners and yet in his standards and character was "set apart" from sinners (Hebrews 7:26). His desire for his followers is that they remain involved in the world, while remaining free from its evil.

A separation for holy living

Success in Christian living is, to a great degree, dependent on our readiness to be given to God in total self-sacrifice and surrender.

The Christian who takes holiness seriously is viewed as a "slave" of righteousness; as a "living sacrifice" to God; as a clean household utensil.

A separation by the Holy Spirit

Although the Christian's co-operation is vital in the process of sanctification, the power comes from the Holy Spirit.

Throughout the Old Testament, the prophets challenge Israel to have circumcised hearts, hearts that have the law of God written upon them. The prophets called the people to not just know the law in their heads, but to love it from their hearts. This is what the Holy Spirit does in us. He gives us right desires and begins to change our characters so that we act in a way that pleases God.

A separation through the word of God

The Bible has a cleansing effect in the Christian's life. The Holy Spirit uses the Bible to enlarge the Christian's vision of Christ and strengthen his desire for holy living.

The Bible is also a guide to the way of life God wants us to live. It shows us what our priorities and attitudes should be. The Bible tells us that the words of God can be planted in our personalities. The Holy Spirit does this.

A separation that progresses throughout life

Sanctification is a process in which encouragement and challenge go side by side. The believer understands that we have been saved from the penalty of sin; that we are being saved from the power of sin that we shall be saved from the presence of sin.

BIBLE CHECK

To God: Leviticus 27:14;
2 Thessalonians 2:13
The world: 2 Corinthians
6:17–7:1; John 17:15
Holy living: Romans 6:19;
12:1; 2 Timothy 2:20,21
Holy Spirit: Ezekiel 36:27;
Galatians 5:16-18
Word of God: John 15:3;
17:17; Psalm 119:9;
James 1:21
Progresses: 2 Corinthians
1:10; 3:18; 1 Thessalonians
5:23

KEY TRUTH

The word "sanctification"
describes the process that God
wants every Christian to
experience. God wants us to
be sanctified, increasingly to
become more like him in all
that we think and do.
Sanctification means to grow
in holiness.

POSTSCRIPT

The fact that Christians
become awake to their sins
and failures is a sign of
progress. We must go further,
however, bringing our sins to
God for his forgiveness, and
enlarging our vision of Christ.
In this way we shall
increasingly want to be more
like him. It is in the area of
motives that the battle for
holiness rages the strongest.

BIBLE STUDY 2 Peter 1:3-11

The apostle Peter was an old man when he wrote this, the
second of two letters. This was written, mainly to non-Jewish
readers, to encourage Christian people to keep on in their faith,
and to resist the false teachers of the day who menaced them in
their "precious" faith (1:1).

It is not just the start, but the continuing of the life of faith
that is the mark of the genuine believer. Is there a good platform
of knowledge for our growth as Christians? Are we holding
onto the fact that we have been separated as a different, a holy
people for God? These are the issues that this passage takes up:

1 Look at verses 3 and 4. How would you answer the fears of
  new believers who imagine that, having made a beginning
  with Christ, they are now out on their own and expected to
  manage?
2 We may "participate in the divine nature" (verse 4). This
  cannot mean that human Christians have become part of
  God. What then does it mean? Scripture interprets Scripture
  – John 1:12,13; 15:4,5 will help.
3 In verses 5-7 we are presented with a kind of "ladder of
  progress". If the power and resources come from God, what is
  required of us? In practical terms, how do you do this?
4 Go through these qualities that are looked for in the believer.
  Somehow they are all linked to knowledge (verses 2,3,5,8).
  How are you going to attend to this programme, and to fulfil
  Paul's prayer in Philippians 3:10?
5 "Short-sighted and blind ... forgotten ..." (verse 9). The remedy
  for this condition is in verses 10 and 11. Can you do that for
  yourself? Can you do it for each other in the fellowship?

REFLECTION

A Read 2 Peter 1:3-11. How
are the Christian readers of
this letter described, as
regards their past state, their
present responsibilities and
their future goals?
B Forgiveness is always free.
But to presume on God's
mercy, in order to continue in
sin, has no place in the
Christian life. Why? See Titus
2:11-14.

C What are the tensions of
staying involved in the world,
and yet being separate from its
evil (John 17:15)?
D Effort seems to be required
of Christians who desire to
grow (2 Peter 1:5-7,10). What
kind of effort is needed? What
are the rewards for such
effort, as mentioned in the
passage?

6. In the Letter to the Romans

It features the following themes:

Condemnation – Romans 1:1–3:20

Paul tells us that the theme of his letter is "the righteousness of God".

He then shows that the righteousness of the Gentile and Jewish world falls far short of God's standard and is therefore under his condemnation. All the world is guilty.

Justification – Romans 3:20–4:25

God's way of declaring the sinner to be righteous is independent of Old Testament law (although the Old Testament witnesses to it). It is provided freely, through the death of Christ, for all who have faith of the kind illustrated in Abraham.

Reconciliation – Romans 5:1-21

From the firm base of being put right with God, Paul amplifies the blessings and security of justification for the believer. He contrasts Adam with Christ – the new representative and Head of the human race, whose one righteous act is capable of setting free all humanity.

Identification – Romans 6:1-23

Paul defends the truth of justification against the charge that it encourages deliberate continuation in sin and in lawlessness. Paul argues that the believer has now been identified with Christ in his death and resurrection, and indeed has become a "slave" of righteousness.

Liberation – Romans 7:1-25

From justification and identification with Christ, Paul moves to a third privilege of the believer – freedom from slavery to the law. The Christian's slavery is now to Christ in the new way of the Spirit (verses 1-6). It is not the law, of course, that is to be blamed for man's sin, but fallen human nature (verses 7-13). In his internal conflict, the Christian may know liberation and power (verses 14-25).

Sanctification – Romans 8:1-39

Now that the old legal slavery belongs to the past those who belong to Christ live by a stronger principle and power – the life of the Spirit.

Those whose life is controlled by the Holy Spirit fulfil God's laws from the heart. They are assured by the Spirit's presence in their lives that they are God's children. Nothing can now separate them from the love of Christ.

Election – Romans 9:1–11:36

Paul now faces the problem of the Jew's rejection of their own Messiah. He interprets this in the light of election – the truth that God chooses a people for himself. God is supremely sovereign, and uses even the disobedience of the Jews to divert his blessing to the rest of the world. Meanwhile God has not completely abandoned the Jews.

Transformation – Romans 12:1–15:13

Paul applies himself to the practical duties of Christian living. The life of the believer is to be a transformed life of service, sharing with other Christians, duty to the government, and respect for others' convictions.

BIBLE CHECK

KEY TRUTH

The letter to the Romans is the apostle Paul's "manifesto" of Christian truth, in which the way of salvation is clearly proclaimed and applied.

POSTSCRIPT

All who have encountered salvation will want to know more about the truth of their experience. Although the book of Romans may tax the reader's concentration, it is rewarding to read through it slowly and understand the truth of salvation at a deeper level.

BIBLE STUDY Romans 8:28-39

Running through all the first eight chapters of the letter to the Romans has been the unfolding plan of God. This great section now ends with one of the most inspiring passages of the New Testament, in which adversity is cut down to its true size, every accusation against the believer is destroyed, and God's love becomes a platform of confidence for time and eternity.

Read these verses, and use the following questions to help in the study of them:

1 Begin at the much-loved verse 28. It may be worth going round the group, and inquiring about the different circumstances in which the strength of this statement has so far been proved.

2 What is the ultimate "good" that God works for in us? Verse 29 gives the answer. How far do you recognise that this is the goal of all Christian living? Compare 2 Corinthians 3:18.

3 Predestination (verses 29 and 30) is not a topic for dry academic dispute; it is a comforting family secret for those who have responded to the claims of Christ. From these verses, what precisely is the comfort?

4 What great themes of the letter to the Romans can you trace in this passage? They are virtually all there.

5 Examine the five "unanswerable" questions of verses 31-36. Why is the word "if" so important in verse 31? What human predicaments do these questions relate to?

6 Is the language of verses 37 and 38 just a burst of purple oratory? On what reality is this based? Look back to verse 32. Compare 1 Corinthians 3:21 and 22.

REFLECTION

A Read Romans 8:28-39. In what way is God's purpose working on behalf of his people? What great themes of the letter to the Romans can you trace in this passage?

B In verses 31-39, what reasons does the apostle give for his triumphant confidence – in terms of the believer's relationship to God, to Christ, and to circumstances?

C Look at the question of verse 31. What do the themes of Romans mean to you, or what are they beginning to mean to you?

D A review question: in what way are justification and sanctification different from each other?

THE CHRISTIAN

1. Described

A sinner saved by grace

It was at Antioch that believers in Christ were first called Christians – probably as a term of abuse. However, Christians have always valued this identification, because of the immensity of the debt they owe to Christ, after whom they are called.

It is God's grace that has brought the sinner into union with Christ. Grace is the free, unearned favour of God towards the sinner. This grace is only possible because of the cross, and it is made real to us by the Holy Spirit. Salvation cannot be earned. It is a free gift to be received by faith.

A member of God's family

In his letter to the Roman Christians, the apostle Paul teaches that the people who did not belong to God at all are now, by his grace, called sons of the living God.

Such a title is not naturally ours. It is only given to those who receive Jesus Christ. It is by the power of God's love that this "adoption" into his family takes place. Being part of the church means to learn the discipline and joy of being in the family.

A disciple of Jesus Christ

A "disciple" in Jesus' day was a person who followed both his master's teaching and his way of life. Christ said that those who were willing to love him and obey him first above all else were his disciples. A Christian is a person who has responded to his call, "Follow me".

A temple of the Holy Spirit

In the Old Testament, the Jews were given special instructions on how to build the temple – and on it they lavished all their riches, craftsmanship and care, so that God should be glorified in every possible way. In his letter to the Corinthians, Paul tells us that our bodies are the temple of the Holy Spirit. This means that all our abilities and powers should be devoted towards glorifying God.

A pilgrim in an alien environment

Many of the Old Testament's great figures are described as people who had no permanent home of their own. Abraham, for example, left the security of his family home to live in tents in a foreign land. The writer to the Hebrews describes such people as those who saw that the earth was not their home. Similarly, the New Testament urges us not to put our trust in material possessions, and to guard against indiscipline. For we too must realise that this earth is not our true home. Christians are like foreigners and strangers, with their permanent home elsewhere.

A citizen of heaven

The Christian will not find permanence in this passing age – our permanent home still lies in the future. But the full membership and many of the privileges of that future home are with every Christian now.

As a result, the Christian is described as a citizen of heaven. We see ourselves as people who belong to another country and we are ambassadors of that country even in this present age.

BIBLE CHECK

Sinner: Acts 11:26; Ephesians 2:8,9; 1 Timothy 1:15

Member: Romans 9:25,26; John 1:12,13; Ephesians 3:14,15

Disciple: Luke 14:26,27; Matthew 9:9

Temple: 1 Kings 6; Acts 7:48,49; 1 Corinthians 6:19,20

Pilgrim: Exodus 22:21; Hebrews 11:8-16; 1 Peter 2:11,12

Citizen: Ephesians 2:19; Hebrews 13:14; Revelation 22:14

KEY TRUTH

A Christian is a person who has received Jesus Christ as Saviour and Lord, and has submitted to the rule of God's kingdom.

POSTSCRIPT

It is unwise, and untrue to the Bible, to believe that a person can receive Jesus Christ as Saviour without receiving him as Lord.

BIBLE STUDY Luke 5:1-11

Here is a story of utter simplicity. It occurred one fine summer's day on a small lake, $12^1/2$ miles long by $6^1/2$ miles wide – one of a string of lakes that stretches from Israel right down into Africa and along the great Rift Valley, a scar on the earth's face that is observable from the moon. In nearly all those lakes tilapia fish are to be found, and Lake Gennesaret (or Galilee) was no exception.

Read the story carefully, because it is your story, the beginning of the greatest movement and family of faith that the world has ever seen, and which will never have an end.

1 What was the draw that day? What is always the draw? Is it a draw for you?

2 Jesus had met and called Simon and his colleagues before (Matthew 4:18-22). But it seemed to have been little more than a limited discipleship, a foot in the door? For what were the "disciples" doing, while the preaching was going on (verse 2)?

3 How common to you is the phenomenon that the real business often begins when the preaching has come to an end (verse 4)?

4 Reflect on the fact that the acknowledged lifetime fishing expert accepts advice on his trade from someone whose noted speciality was woodwork. What does this tell you about Christ? What is the key phrase of verses 5 and 6 – indeed of the whole passage?

5 Here in verse 6 is a catch that is going to get itself into the record books – better still, into the Bible. A whole new life is opening up for Peter (verses 8-11). Define it.

6 Could you have done what Peter and his companions did? After half a lifetime? Discuss this together, then pray.

REFLECTION

A Study Ephesians 2:1-10,19. Reflect on the "but" of verse 4. In what way is it the shaft of light that illuminates the passage? If you were going to speak on verses 8 and 9, what major points would you make?

B Two descriptions of the Christian are given in Ephesians 2:19. To what extent have you experienced the privileges implied by these terms?

C What are the insecure aspects of being a Christian? What are the secure aspects?

D Try to think of some less prominent biblical illustrations of the Christian, and of what they imply. (Clue: look at 2 Timothy 2.)

2. The Christian and the Bible

THE BIBLE ...

Directs the Christian for life

Biblically, a disciple of Jesus is recognised by unashamed loyalty to Christ's person and unquestioning obedience to his commands. The Master cannot accept disciples who want to establish their own method of instruction or set their own course.

Jesus taught that those obedient to his words would be characterised by stability; the disobedient would be overthrown. This is a principle throughout Scripture. The Bible is like a lamp, guiding the Christian.

Equips the Christian for battle

The believer must learn from Christ, who resisted the devil's temptations in the wilderness with his knowledge of the Old Testament. A working knowledge of the Bible is a weapon of spiritual power.

Equally, in defending the Christian faith, the Christian who enters the arena having thought through the issues beforehand is at an immense advantage. A biblically-trained mind is a weapon of priceless value. The Bible is like a sword, protecting the Christian.

Energises the Christian for service

The disciple is called to be fruitful in service, bringing both the compassion and challenge of Christ's message to bear upon a needy world.

It is the inexhaustible supply found in God's living word that gives Christian service its vitality and freshness. The Bible's depths can never be plumbed. The Bible is like water, renewing the Christian.

Corrects the Christian from error

The Bible exposes and corrects many errors and distortions of true belief. There is the legalist – the victim of convention; the empty ritualist – the victim of superstition; the traditionalist – the victim of pride; the rationalist – the victim of unbelief; and the mere theorist – the victim of laziness.

The Bible is God's message to us. Because of this, we should always be open to it to correct our own wrong ideas, and to replace them with God's truth. The Bible is like a mirror, reforming the Christian.

Develops the Christian in the faith

The Bible is food for every Christian. We are called upon to grow up from spiritual childhood, strengthened by God's word.

As we advance towards maturity, we should be able to see the great themes of Scripture as a connected whole, rather than as a collection of scattered thoughts. The Bible is like milk, nourishing the Christian.

Informs the Christian of God's mind

The Bible is God's written revelation. It is impossible to arrive at a knowledge of his plan and will on the strength of our own guesswork.

God has given us the Bible so that we should not be in the dark about who he is, and what he is doing.

The true wisdom that leads to salvation is arrived at by a humble and careful study of God's Bord. The Bible is like treasure, enriching the Christian.

BIBLE CHECK

Directs: John 8:31,32; Matthew 7:24-27; Psalm 119:105

Equips: Matthew 4:1-11; 1 Timothy 1:18,19; Ephesians 6:17

Energises: John 15:16; Isaiah 55:10,11; Psalm 1

Corrects: Isaiah 29:13; Mark 7:9-13; James 1:23-25

Develops: 2 Timothy 2:15; 1 Corinthians 14:20; 1 Peter 2:2,3

Informs: Romans 11:33-36; 2 Timothy 3:14,15; Psalm 119:162

KEY TRUTH

Through the Bible, the Christian comes to an understanding of God's plan, and receives nourishment for Christian living.

POSTSCRIPT

To develop a balanced faith, the Christian should read the Bible regularly and thoroughly. Unless we read all of the Bible, we may distort or over-emphasise some aspect of its message.

BIBLE STUDY Matthew 4:1-11

Jesus has been baptised by the river Jordan, and in doing so has identified himself with sinful humanity whom he had come to save and redeem. In that moment he had also received, with the Spirit's sign, God's endorsement of his mission to the world.

This early landmark of his ministry was followed immediately by a period of temptation in the solitude of the wilderness. The testing was severe but Jesus was ready, prepared – and armed with his knowledge of Scripture.

1 In the invitation to turn stones into bread – held out to one whose kingdom was not of this world, yet who would one day feed 5,000 people in the wilderness – what was the power of this temptation? What was the significance of Jesus' quotation from Deuteronomy 8:3 – given in the context of God's miraculous sustaining of the Israelites in their wilderness journeys?

2 Next comes the temptation, in the form of an offer of round-the-clock protection. So the devil is not hesitant about quoting the Scripture himself. But he has not quoted it accurately. What was the significance of the omission? See Psalm 91:11,12. Notice Jesus' answering quotation (Deuteronomy 6:16) – again in the context of Israel in the wilderness. Why was Jesus determined that he would not win the world to himself by a spectacular deed?

3 The third temptation is in the form of a deal – a carve-up of power. This time the answer comes in the form of Deuteronomy 6:13. What was the principle at stake here?

4 Practically, how are you to be equipped to fulfil the requirement of the 2 Corinthians 10:3-5?

REFLECTION

A Read 2 Timothy 3:14–4:5. What is the nature of the Bible's power, and what does it achieve? What can regular readers expect it to do in their lives? What are the dangers which may be avoided through the Bible's message? **B** What would be a good plan and schedule for the reading of the Bible? What plans have your friends found helpful?

C Why is it vital to become mature in the truth of the Bible? Compare your findings with Acts 20:29-32. **D** Read Psalm 19:7-11. Try to list the ways in which the writer of this psalm delights in God's word, and make this passage a subject for praising God.

3. The Christian and Prayer

For communion with God

Christian prayer is not a technique. To try to manipulate God for our own purposes is the way of magic, and of the old cultic religions – when people are at the centre. With Christian prayer God is at the centre.

On the human level, we do not like to "use" those whom we love – and the same is true of those who have entered into a relationship with God of trust and acceptance. Jesus taught his friends to talk to God as to their heavenly Father, and not to use meaningless incantations characteristic of heathen worship. For prayer involves a relationship. We should learn from the example of Jesus, who would regularly go away and spend time alone with his Father.

For growth in God

Prayer is like breathing, in the life of a Christian. When we pray regularly, there takes place in our lives a steady growth in character and inner resources. Contrary to popular opinion, prayer is not a sign of weakness, but of strength and progress.

Prayer is an education. The disciples needed to be taught by Jesus, and he gave them a pattern of prayer that the church has never forgotten. The Christian of every age faces the same lessons, disciplines and privileges of growing in God.

For the service of God

God does not need our prayers. Prayer does not affect his will and overall purpose for us. But the Bible teaches, and our Christian experience confirms, that prayer does affect his specific actions in fulfilling his will.

The reason is that God has appointed prayer as a key way of involving his people in the carrying out of his will and service in this world. The Christian learns to pray in the name of Jesus – that is, with his interests at heart. He also learns to pray with the help of the Holy Spirit. Prayer is the most important form of service we can ever employ.

For the praise of God

The Christian is a temple of the Holy Spirit, and is therefore to glorify God in everything. Thanksgiving, joy and praise are key aspects in a Christian's attitude, according to the New Testament.

To praise God is to make great affirmations about him. This is evident in the book of Psalms, in which we repeatedly read of God's greatness and of what he has done for his people. As we meditate on the great themes of the Bible, so our praise of God becomes a vital part of prayer.

For the experience of God

Prayer can bring God into the heart of every human emotion and experience. The writers of the Psalms were able to look to God for guidance in times of uncertainty. The apostles were able to turn to him in praise and prayer when in prison. Paul was strengthened by God, even though his prayer for relief from affliction was not granted. Prayer allows God to mould and develop the new man in Jesus Christ.

BIBLE CHECK

Communion: Matthew 6:5-8; Mark 1:35; Luke 5:15,16

Growth: Ephesians 3:14-19; Matthew 6:9-13

Service: James 5:16-18; Ephesians 6:18

Praise: 1 Thessalonians 5:16-18; Psalm 34:1-3; Psalm 150

Experience: Psalm 57:1-3; Acts 16:22-25; 2 Corinthians 12:7-10

KEY TRUTH

Prayer is God's chosen way of communication and fellowship between the Christian and himself. It is the secret of spiritual growth and effective service.

POSTSCRIPT

There is a particular power and the promised presence of Christ when believers meet together to pray in his name, according to the promise of Matthew 18:19,20.

BIBLE STUDY Nehemiah 1:1-11

Nehemiah was a Jew, a child of the Babylonian captivity, now ended. Judah, however, was still under the overall rule of Persia. Certain stages of national reconstruction had been begun, but Jerusalem's city walls still remained to be rebuilt. It was 445 BC, and Nehemiah was still in Persia, as cup-bearer to the king. He feels the pull of Jerusalem, which he has never seen, and in frustration turns to prayer:

1 In the face of the grim news from Jerusalem, Nehemiah's is an example of prayer that weeps (verses 4 and 5). This was the prayer that settled a life's work – but there is no obvious request in it. What, then, is the strength of this prayer? (verses 5-11)

2 Despite Nehemiah's grief, note the absence of hysteria in the prayer. What do these words express about the character, the promises, and the redemption of God? Can we find a corrective here, in some of our modern praying, from this prayer that worships?

3 Nehemiah is praying far from the scene of Jerusalem. Yet what can be learnt here about prayer that watches and is vigilant? What can we learn about the hard work of intercessory prayer? Compare Ephesians 6:18.

4 Here, too, is prayer that waits. Notice the word "today" in verse 11. Yet how long did Nehemiah have to wait until his request was granted? The answer comes in 2:1-4 – four months later.

5 How does prayer help us in getting a right perspective on problems and people around us? Notice how prayer reduces the mighty king to the level of "this man" (verse 11).

6 "It is prayer and prayer alone that can make history" (James Ellul). Discuss.

REFLECTION

A Think about the Lord's Prayer as recorded in Matthew 6:9-13. What pattern does it set out for us in our prayer life? What similar patterns have you established in your own praying?

B Why bother to pray? Try to list some convincing reasons.

C Why do most people find prayer not the easiest of activities? How can we help one another in this?

D A Scots preacher has said, "We have actually got it all wrong when we speak about 'praying for the work,' because prayer is the work." How do you react to this statement?

4. The Christian and Witness

Proclaiming a person

Because Christianity is concerned with a person rather than with a philosophy or religious system, the early disciples of Christ found little difficulty in witnessing. Whatever their education or background, they had all experienced the transforming power of the risen Christ.

Their witness was about him – and so Philip on the desert road spoke of Jesus to the Ethiopian official. This means that all who obey Jesus as Lord have something to share. Every Christian is a witness.

Explaining the truth

While it is Christ we proclaim, there are however, important facts in the Christian message which must be explained and understood if individuals are to become more than mere converts. The apostle Paul's aim was that men and women should grow to become spiritually mature in Christ.

In societies where there is little awareness of God or the Bible, it is vital that the truth should be taught, argued and explained.

Sharing a love

Behind the message of reconciliation is the motivating power of Christ's love. Christ sends us out into the world, not merely to talk about him, but to share his love and our love with others. Paul said that he preached because he was compelled by the love of Christ.

Witnessing consistently

Jesus said that the mark of his disciples was to be the presence of love in their fellowship. Their lives were to shine as lights in the world, through their words, their deeds and their life-style.

Such a witness is not a burdened, strained obligation. It springs naturally out of the life lived in union with Christ. Such witness is ready to seize and buy up the opportunities as they come; to give answers to those who are seeking, with humility and love.

Witnessing personally

When the early church experienced its first persecution, the believers were scattered throughout Judea and Samaria – except for the apostles. Although these Christians were without the leadership of the apostles, we learn that they went everywhere, witnessing of Christ.

It was a matter of standing out in unashamed and personal testimony. Earlier the apostles had declared that it was impossible for them to keep silent about Christ. When we are living close to the love of God, we find that we cannot keep the good news to ourselves.

Witnessing collectively

There is great strength and encouragement for all who join in combined witness. Jesus recognised the need to send his disciples out two by two.

On the day of Pentecost, as Peter rose to proclaim Christ, his eleven companions stood with him. The book of Acts repeatedly tells us that the first Christians worked together. Here was a unity in proclamation – a characteristic of any church which is working with Christ.

BIBLE CHECK

Proclaiming: Acts 1:8; 8:35; Luke 24:46-48

Explaining: Colossians 1:28,29; Acts 18:4; 2 Timothy 2:2

Sharing: 2 Corinthians 5:14; 1 Thessalonians 2:7-13

Consistently: John 13:34,35; Philippians 2:14-16; 1 Peter 3:15

Personally: Acts 8:1,4; Acts 4:18-20; Psalm 40:10

Collectively: Acts 2:14,42-47; Philippians 1:27

KEY TRUTH

Christian witness is the means by which God, through his servants, continues the work of his Son, in bringing the message of salvation to the world.

POSTSCRIPT

Witnessing should never be a burdensome Christian duty, but the grateful privilege of those who have an experience of Jesus Christ.

BIBLE STUDY Luke 10:1-16

This account of the sending of the 72 disciples only occurs in Luke. It is different from the sending of the twelve apostles in 9:1. They formed a permanent group – parallel in idea to the twelve tribes of Israel. Those called in Luke 10, by contrast are called "others". While Christians today can never be apostles in the strict sense, we can say that we are the obvious successors to the "others".

1 Jesus was sending his representatives ahead of him, like couriers of his kingdom (verse 1). What were they to announce concerning his kingdom?

2 The kingdom is the rule of God, through Christ the King, in the lives of his followers everywhere. But what is its impact? Look at the definition in Romans 14:17. Is this any different from the message of salvation? When did the kingdom of God first touch you?

3 Couriers ... but there is a second piece of imagery that describes Christ's witnesses. It is in verse 2. How should this description of us affect our priorities and plans? On the strength of this, how would you answer those critics who say that Christians live such narrow lives? (Compare Matthew 13:38.)

4 A third piece of imagery is in verse 3. What aspect of Christian service and witness does this highlight? Have you modern examples?

5 While we cannot press pre-Pentecost situations into our own era, we can learn a great deal from the style of verses 4-16. What can we learn in our witness about travelling light; with earnestness and modesty; with urgency and confidence?

REFLECTION

A Read the story of Philip and the Ethiopian official in Acts 8:26-40. What can we learn from Philip about bringing others to Jesus Christ? What qualities do we see in Philip? How prepared was the official for this encounter?

B Which is easier – to speak to a stranger or to an acquaintance about Christ? Which seems to be the more effective, and why?

C Read 1 Thessalonians 2:7-13. List the qualities of Paul in this passage – his motive, his efforts, his persistence. How should these verses affect our way of spreading the good news?

D Bearing in mind your gifts, what is there that you can do, naturally and freely, to help make Christ better known?

5. The Christian and the World

THE CHRISTIAN IS ...

Called out of the world

"The world" means both this present, temporary age and the hostile system of thought and action that operates on this planet. This is our environment.

But the Christian's true home is not here. Whatever our physical situation – good or bad – all that we value most strongly (our heavenly Father, Jesus Christ, our inheritance, our hope) is elsewhere. The New Testament urges Christ's followers to set their hearts on the eternal and heavenly dimension.

Separated from the world

This thread runs through most of the New Testament letters. Christians, because of their heavenward calling, are to avoid the trends and evil associations of fallen society. Their ethical standards are to be the highest of all.

Separation, however, does not mean that the Christian is called to withdraw from society, but to be kept committed to Christ within it.

Sent into the world

The appeal of the New Testament is not simply that Christ's disciples should avoid being polluted by the world; rather they are to purify it.

The Christian's attitude to the world should never be one of contempt. It is God's world, and we are to be involved in its redemption.

To overcome the world

We must avoid judgemental views that simply dismiss the world as beyond the reach and care of God. But on the other hand, we should not fall into the trap of believing that the world is morally, socially or politically perfectible, however much may be done by Christians and others of good will to alleviate its problems. The true redemption of the world cannot be completed until the future glory of Christ is revealed.

Thus, the Christian is called upon to overcome the evil tendencies and pressures that the world brings to bear upon him. We are caught in a spiritual battle that involves every Christian in this dark age, and therefore we must be armed with spiritual weapons. Christ himself has given us the assurance of his strength for the fight, and of the ultimate victory of God over all evil.

To journey through the world

The Christian is a citizen of heaven, with relationships and privileges that are outside this world. We are like the Old Testament Jews, journeying towards a promised land, confident in the assurance of God's presence and guidance.

The pilgrim is required to exercise obedience and discipline. At times we are likened to a soldier who cannot afford to get entangled in civilian pursuits – or to an athlete who must observe the necessary rules.

Our Christian life is the story of a pilgrimage through a world that is staggering under its problems. But we travel on with faith as our lamp.

BIBLE CHECK

Called out: 1 Corinthians 7:29-31; Hebrews 10:33,34; Colossians 3:1,2

Separated: James 4:4,5; Ephesians 5:3-11; John 17:15,16

Sent into: John 20:21; Matthew 5:13-16; John 3:16,17

Overcome: Romans 8:19-21; Ephesians 6:10-18; Romans 8:37

Journey: Philippians 3:20; Joshua 1:9; Hebrews 11:16

KEY TRUTH

Christian witness is the means by which God, through his servants, continues the work of his Son, in bringing the message of salvation to the world.

POSTSCRIPT

A true understanding of the world that God loves will strengthen the Christian's calling to go into all the world and proclaim Christ to every person.

BIBLE STUDY Ephesians 6:10-20

The apostle Paul is writing from prison to the Christians of a city which is already a thousand years old; sophisticated, worldly and promiscuous. The believers must have felt the challenge of being Christ's ambassadors in a hostile environment, as they walked along the 70-foot wide boulevard, running from the harbour of Ephesus to its great theatre. And then there was the heathen temple of Artemis which gave the 300,000-strong population its chief industry.

1 As you look at this passage, try to assimilate the strength of the spiritual opposition that faced Paul's contemporaries. Then think of your own setting. Who had the harder task?

2 Study the active verbs of this passage. What were the Christians told to do? What do these verbs speak to you of? How do they challenge us today?

3 How should we be encouraged when we think of the spiritual powers that oppose the work of God? Look at Colossians 2:15; 1 John 4:4; Revelation 12:11.

4 Let different members of the group "adopt" a piece of the Christian's armour, described in verses 14-17, and then compare notes as to the value and purpose of each piece, and what they signify today.

5 Our problem is that we are not to isolate ourselves from the world and it's affairs and standards. How does a Christian prepare to "stand firm," while still being involved?

6 Verses 18 and 19 – the prayer life! What are your resolves, jointly and privately, as a result of studying this passage?

REFLECTION

A Read and study 2 Timothy 4:1-22. Paul is in prison, nearing the end of his pilgrimage, in Rome. How does he view the current scene, his own situation and the future, and his acquaintances? Contast the careers of Demas and Mark (compare with Acts 15:37-39).

B The Christian does not regard the present world system as perfectible. How can we avoid adopting either a judgemental attitude that writes the world off, or an extreme optimism that ends in disillusionment?

C Read John 16:33. Why did Jesus encourage his disciples by saying these words? What do they mean for them – and us?

D How can we keep our eternal goals clearly in view?

6. The Christian Life

A vocation to be fulfilled

The New Testament overflows with phrases that speak of goals, aims and ambitions. The apostle Paul alone is an example. He wants to finish his course; he desires to win the approval of God; he longs to proclaim Christ to those who have never heard of him. All his ambitions were centred in Christ himself, who was to have first place in everything.

All Christians have a calling – to be God's own people. Such a vocation overrides all other callings in life and, indeed, enhances them.

A character to be developed

God's purpose for his people is that they should become like his Son Jesus Christ in the holiness of their living. To be a Christian does not mean only to believe in certain facts about Christ. Rather, it means to develop a Christ-like character. The Christian is to co-operate in this process, combatting sinful habits and attitudes through the power of the Holy Spirit.

A fellowship to be maintained

The Christian is given ways and means by which the relationship with Christ may be maintained. Two examples of this are prayer and the Lord's Supper.

The apostle John's first letter has much to say about the fellowship of the Christian life. It is a fellowship of life, for it centres in Christ, the Word of life. It is a fellowship of love, for all who are connected to Christ are connected also to each other. It is a fellowship of light, for there can be no darkness or hidden impurity where God is involved.

Energies to be harnessed

God has given us many natural gifts. When we become Christians we are not to give up these abilities. Instead, motivated by the truths of our faith, we are to devote them to God's use, that they may reach their full potential and power.

The quality of daily work, our relationships and service will be heightened by the dynamic of Christ's resurrection power. We should recognise that we are not placed on this earth simply for ourselves. We are to be used.

Minds to be developed

A Christian framework of thinking enables an individual to establish his relationship to the universe simply because Christianity is true.

By opening our intellects to the truth of God, we can be convinced about the deepest issues of life.

Each Christian must see to it that his mind is stretched to the limits of its capacity. Paul described those who were swept about with every shifting belief as "babies". His prayer was that the minds of younger Christians might be illuminated fully by the light of Christ. They were to be adult in their understanding.

A hope to be realised

It is the historic nature of the Christian faith – culminating in the resurrection of Jesus – that gives to God's people the eager expectation of their final inheritance in glory. The one who was raised will surely return; the past is forgiven; the present is covered, and tomorrow belongs to us.

BIBLE CHECK

Vocation: Philippians 3:14; Romans 15:20; Colossians 1:18

Character: Romans 8:29; 2 Peter 1:5-8; Ephesians 5:1,2

Fellowship: 1 John 1:1-7; Ephesians 4:3-6; John 15:4

Energies: 1 Corinthians 15:58; Ephesians 2:10; Colossians 3:23,24

Minds: 1 John 5:20; Ephesians 4:13,14; Ephesians 1:18

Hope: 1 Peter 1:3-9; Titus 2:13; Revelation 22:20

KEY TRUTH

A Christian is reaching full potential as progress in life and faith is made. The Christian life is seen in the ways listed here.

POSTSCRIPT

It is vital that Christ's followers should make, not merely converts, but disciples, men and women of mature character and sound judgement.

BIBLE STUDY Philippians 3:7-14

Paul had a special bond with the Christians at Philippi, for this was the first church ever founded on European soil. We read of its beginnings in Acts 16. This letter was written around the year AD 61, and it forms another of Paul's prison letters. In this passage, Paul is confiding his own testimony of Christ, and outlining his goals and values for all of life. These are among the most powerful and moving personal resolves ever recorded in Scripture. The following questions may help in the study of the passage:

1 In verses 7-9, the writer is doing his mathematics. He is weighing up the best of what this world can offer against the "hardest" aspects of Christian discipleship. Which outweighs the other? What tips the balance? Who else made a similar calculation? See Hebrews 11:25, 26.

2 Look at verses 10 and 11. Can one have the "positive" aspects of Christian experience, without the "negative"? What is it about the death of Christ that exerts such a magnetic pull upon the believer?

3 Verses 12-14 convey the idea of a race. Discuss the tensions that Paul faced, between the start and the finish, between the past and the future, between immaturity and perfection. How do these tensions affect us today? How should we deal with them?

4 "One thing I do"– verse 13. In fact Paul did many things; he made tents, he lectured, he travelled, he founded churches, he wrote letters. What did he mean by the "one thing"? Why is it so vital to be a person of one main objective?

5 What is "the prize" of verse 14? The clues are in this passage, and in 1:21.

REFLECTION

A Read John 15:1-17. Reflect on what it means to be united with Christ. How is this achieved? What are Christ's expectations of his people? What are the privileges and challenges of this relationship?

B Bertrand Russell (who was an atheist) once said of Christianity: "There is nothing to be said against it, except that it is too difficult for most of us to practise sincerely." How accurate is this assessment? Give your reasons.

C How does your Christian faith affect your daily work? Discuss this with your friends.

D How would you describe your relationship with Jesus Christ?

1. Its Characteristics

It is the church of Jesus Christ (historical)

Through the centuries it is only the church that has experienced the presence of Jesus Christ within its membership. This is because it is Christ's church, purchased for himself by his own blood, and cared for as a husband cares for his wife. Jesus declared that where two or three individuals meet in his name there his promised presence would be experienced. No matter how small the group – there is the church.

It is the company of all believers (universal)

This is the church of different eras: past, present and future – together, they form the church. It is the church of different cultures, found in countries scattered over the earth, but united by its common Lord. It is a church of different characteristics, abilities and temperaments, and it is a church featuring different levels of experience, from elderly Christians to the newest disciples – yet one church.

It is a unity of the Spirit (spiritual)

The unity of the Spirit, of which the apostle Paul wrote, is more important than the differences of groups and denominations. The church can only truly be one, because of the one Spirit who unites it.

Although all Christians are to work for unity and mend divisions, it is not uniformity nor unanimity that they are to seek. Rather, it is a recognition of all who exhibit the family likeness.

Its authority is God's word (scriptural)

Down the ages the church has had a vital relationship with the Scriptures; it is the scriptural revelation that is the basis of the church's belief and stability.

The church has been commissioned to defend this revelation, to proclaim it, and to submit to its authority. The Bible is the church's authority and tells us all that we need to know about salvation and Christian conduct. On these, the Bible has the final say. On other matters, however, such as church government, there is no clear blueprint – and this no doubt helps to explain the differences existing between churches even in New Testament times.

Its programme is worldwide (international)

The programme of the church is the programme of Christ. Jesus said that his task was to bring good news to the poor and liberation to the oppressed.

When Christ's earthly ministry had finished, he commanded the church to carry out his mission to the world. The book of Acts shows us the way in which the church's mission expanded from Jerusalem to Judea and Samaria, and then to the whole earth. Our task is one of evangelism and service and to do this, we are empowered by the Holy Spirit.

Its destiny is heaven (eternal)

The church on earth is living between two comings. It looks back to the birth and ministry of Jesus Christ, and it looks forward to his glorious return.

Meanwhile it works in the knowledge that Christ is preparing a future home. On a certain day, known only to God, the trumpet will sound and the church will be united to Christ.

BIBLE CHECK

Of Jesus Christ: Matthew 16:18; Matthew 18:20
Company: Colossians 3:11; Revelation 7:9,10
Unity: Ephesians 4:4-6; John 17:20-23
Authority: Jude 3; 2 Timothy 1:13,14
Programme: Luke 4:16-21; John 20:21; Acts 1:8
Destiny: Matthew 24:30,31; John 14:1-3

KEY TRUTH

The church of Christ is the whole company of redeemed people. Christ is present and active in the church, and uses it for his work in the world.

POSTSCRIPT

The biblical picture of the church, as described above, helps the church to keep the right priorities in its mission and worship. It also serves as an accurate test to show whether movements and sects which claim to be part of the church are true or false.

BIBLE STUDY Ephesians 2:11-22

Paul the apostle recognised Ephesus as a strategic centre for reaching out with the message of Christ into the whole Roman province of "Asia", now western Turkey. Ephesus was important as a cultural, commercial, political and religious centre. While in essence it was Gentile and heathen, it also had a sizable Jewish population.

It was this letter to the Ephesian Christians that the New Testament's teaching about the church as God's new society reached perhaps its richest form – in a society that provided as hostile an environment for church growth as possible.

1 In verses 11-13, take up each of the terms that described the spiritual status of the Gentiles. How great was the gulf between them and the Jewish covenant? And what was the one factor that could possibly bring unity between the two alien groupings?

2 Did you notice the "but" of verse 13? (Compare 2:4.) Continue now with the "for" of verse 14. What was Christ's purpose? What were his achievements (verse 14-18)?

3 "One new man" (verse 15 ... "a single new humanity"). Notice that Jews do not become Gentiles, or Gentiles Jews. Here is an altogether new being. What conclusions do you draw from this passage as you view the world church scene? What corrections may we need to make?

4 Here, in verses 19-22 is described something to rival Ephesus' great temple of Artemis – but with many differences! Describe them.

5 Come back to the cross (verses 13 and 16), and rediscover your unity with the followers of Jesus everywhere.

REFLECTION

A Read Ephesians 4:1-16. What gives the church its essential unity (verses 4-6)? How is this preserved? How does this compare with the kind of unity that Christians should seek (verses 11-16). How is this achieved?

B A church leader once said, "The church is the only institution in the world which exists primarily for the benefit of non-members." How far do you agree with this statement?

C Some Christians strongly emphasise their own church tradition. Others treat denominations as unhealthy. Yet others are indifferent. What is your view?

D Read 1 Timothy 3:15. What can your own circle of Christian friends do to further the truth of God more?

2. Its Main Description

A firm building

The New Testament letters take up Christ's theme of "building" his church – although this idea is not to be confused in any way with literal buildings for Christian worship.

The apostles Paul and Peter, in particular, saw the church as a spiritual building, composed of "living stones" – Christians. This picture shows us how Christians depend upon each other and upon Christ as the building's cornerstone.

A virgin bride

A relationship of deep intimacy is suggested by the New Testament idea of the church "married" to Christ. We are told that Christ loves the church, and has made it pure and faultless by his death.

The apostle John's vision of the new heaven and the new earth describes the church as Christ's bride, prepared and ready to meet her husband.

A functioning body

The picture of the church as a body, with Christ as its head, emphasises that the church is a living organism and not an organisation.

As in the picture of the church as a building, the dependence of the church upon Christ is stressed, but we also learn the important truth that no member of the body is disposable – or of overriding importance.

A permanent city

The theme of the city of God is usually seen in the Bible as a future hope. God's people live as strangers in the world, and are looking for the city which is to come.

The city of God is mentioned a number of times in the book of Revelation, where the writer is speaking of the church. When God's chosen people are finally brought to completion, the city will be a vast community of purpose, life, activity and permanent security.

A stable family

The terms "family" or "household" of God point again to the relationship that exists in the church between the members and the head. And God's very fatherhood provides a pattern for family life now.

Great encouragement – particularly to Gentile converts in the early church – was found in the fact that all shared equally in the privileges of God's household, Jews and Gentiles alike. No longer was the Gentile an outsider or foreigner. This should also be true of the church today – because barriers spoil the family life God wants the church to have.

An active army

The references to the church as an army are not heavily pronounced in Scripture. However, the New Testament teaches that the church is involved in a spiritual warfare.

Intensity, activity and victory are the main ideas conveyed to us by this imagery; the weapons and the victory itself being God's.

BIBLE CHECK

Building: 1 Peter 2:4,5;
Ephesians 2:20-22
Bride: Ephesians 5:25-27;
Revelation 21:2
Body: 1 Corinthians 12:12-31;
Ephesians 1:22,23; 4:15,16
City: Hebrews 13:14;
Revelation 21:10-27
Family: Ephesians 2:19;
3:14,15; 1 Timothy 3:14,15
Army: Ephesians 6:12;
Revelation 12:11

KEY TRUTH

There are a number of different pictures of the church in the New Testament. Looked at together, these pictures give us a full idea of the nature and character of the church and its mission.

POSTSCRIPT

It must be emphasised that the church is an organism rather than an organisation, a living fellowship rather than mere buildings, a close family rather than a collection of individuals.

BIBLE STUDY 1 Peter 2:1-10

This wonderful letter, written by the apostle Peter in AD 63 or 64, came out just in time to prepare the harrassed and scattered Christians of Asia Minor for the great persecution that erupted under the emperor Nero in the summer of 64. Its message is one of hope and confidence despite "all kinds of trials" (1:6).

Like Paul to the Ephesians, Peter in this passage uses vivid terminology to describe the new society that God has brought into existence through Christ. Use these questions to assist the study:

1 Read verses 1-3. This was no time for believers to turn on each other, but rather develop a healthy spiritual appetite. How much are you praying for yourself and for each other in this respect? "Make us hungry!"

2 In verses 4 and 5 the metaphor changes from babies to ... what?

3 In the spiritual and "invisible" temple of the church, what place and function does Christ have in verses 4-8? Notice from the Old Testament quotations how Christ is both a source of confidence and a disaster. Why is this so?

4 Four descriptions of the Christian community follow in verse 9. How are we to see ourselves in a largely unbelieving society? What are our functions, in verses 9-12?

5 "The people of God" (verse 10). If no other group is classed in this way, what is this saying to us in the church?

6 Animal sacrifices belonged to the past. What is a "spiritual sacrifice" (verse 5)?

REFLECTION

A Read and think about 1 Peter 2:1-10. A number of figurative expressions are used of Christians in this passage. Try to list them, and consider their implications.

B Which of the various descriptions of the church have you found most helpful? Why?

C Reflect on how much Christ has done for his church, as you consider each picture of the church in turn.

D Look at 1 Corinthians 12:12-31. What do these verses tell us about the jealousy and pride in the church? How do you regard those in your fellowship who seem more gifted, and those who seem less gifted than yourself?

3. Its Relationship to Christ

Christ died for the church

Christ's death is related not simply to individuals, but to the people of God, the church. The announcement to Mary about the impending birth of Jesus was that he would save his people from their sins.

It was clear, when Jesus took the cup and gave it to his disciples at the last supper, that he saw his death as bringing a new "Israel" or people of God into being. Ever since that time, the church has remembered in the Lord's Supper the cost Christ paid to found the church.

Christ builds the church

Jesus came to found, not a philosophy, but a community. It was basic to the early Christians' thought that new converts were immediately added to the fellowship; that all who had fellowship with the Father and the Son would be related to one another.

It was more than addition, however. Christ is the very source of the church's life, and so to be in the church is to experience Christ's life in a unique way. By his Spirit he directs the church, gives spiritual gifts to its members and creates unity and love.

Christ protects the church

In the Old Testament God's people were often protected by God, for example, in the story of the blazing furnace in the book of Daniel.

In the New Testament, we are told that Christ protects his people, the church. He defends the church from the attacks of Satan, and preserves it in adversity. More than this, he provides the power for the church to launch its own attacks against Satan. The church is not on the defensive – it is on the offensive.

Christ purifies the church

In the Old Testament, some of the prophets pictured Israel as a wife who had been unfaithful to her husband. God's people had been unfaithful to the promises they had made in their covenant with him.

The church is only seen as faithful and pure in the New Testament because of Christ. He has cleansed the church by his death, and continues to keep her holy. We are told that finally Christ will receive the church as a perfect bride: faithful and pure.

Christ intercedes for the church

The word "intercede" means to act on someone else's behalf as a peacemaker. It is encouraging to know that because of Christ's death on our behalf, he is now in heaven as a man, representing us before the Father.

Because Christ intercedes for us, we are assured of at least three guarantees. First, we are forgiven because of his death. Second, we have free access to God because of his presence in heaven. Third, we are protected against condemnation for our sins by his words spoken in our defence.

Christ prepares for the church

Jesus reassured his friends when he warned them of his departure that they need not be anxious about the future, as he would be preparing a home for them. This shows us that Christ loves the church, and longs to enjoy the company of those who believe in him. His work will not be complete until the church is in the place he has prepared for it.

BIBLE CHECK

Died for: Matthew 1:21; 26:26-29; Acts 20:28

Builds: Ephesians 4:11-16; Acts 2:46,47

Protects: Daniel 3:19-27; Matthew 16:18,19

Purifies: Jeremiah 3:6,14; Ephesians 5:25-27

Intercedes: Hebrews 7:25-27; 1 John 2:1; Romans 8:34

Prepares: John 14:1-4; 1 Thessalonians 4:16,17

KEY TRUTH

The life, witness and continuance of the church is totally dependent upon its relationship to Jesus Christ, its builder and protector.

POSTSCRIPT

Christ's love for his church led him to give up his own life for her. The church is called to do the same – to submit to the interests of her Lord and to fulfil his will.

BIBLE STUDY Ephesians 4:1-16

Paul is far from his friends, under house arrest in Rome, awaiting trial under Nero. Yet he is able to remind his readers of the soaring heights to which Christ has lifted the members of God's New Society in Ephesus; men and women who have been chosen in him, predestined, made alive with Christ, reconciled through the cross, given access to the Father, made fellow-citizens and built into a holy temple.

1 In view of the Ephesian Christians' high calling, how are they now to live (verses 1-3)?

2 When it comes to unity, notice the frequency of the word "one" (verses 3-6). What does this tell us about certain unchangeable facets of the world-wide Christian church?

3 Move on to verse 13. If, in verse 3, there is already in existence a spiritual unity to be maintained, there seems to be a second unity that is yet to be attained. Try to establish from verses 13 and 14 the nature of this unity and goal that still lies ahead.

4 If the church at large – indeed any local fellowship – is travelling from a unity that already exists towards a unity that lies ahead, what lies between? What makes it possible to negotiate this journey? The clue lies in verses 7-12.

5 If oneness was the earlier theme, now the diversity of the gifts given by the incarnate and now ascended Christ (verses 9,10) comes into prominence. What are the gifts for?

6 The Head … the body (verse 15,16). How do we practise this unique relationship?

REFLECTION

A Consider the message of Revelation 3:1-6. John is conveying Christ's message to the church in Sardis (in present-day Turkey). How is this passage relevant to the church in general, and to your fellowship today? List the accusations, the challenges, and the promises of these verses.

B "The Bible knows nothing of solitary religion" (John Wesley). Why should a Christian bother about the church of Jesus Christ?

C Look at Revelation 1:5,6. What has Jesus done for his church?

D Read Daniel 3:13-28. What message is there in this story for today's church?

4. Its Authority and Mission

Guarding the truth

The church is not to create truth, but guard it. It is described as the pillar of the truth; as contender for the faith that has been entrusted to God's people.

Thus the church must follow the apostles both in its standard of teaching and quality of mission. It must do more than guard the truth – it must proclaim it. Equally, it must do more than speak – it must speak the truth. The church is to be scripturally-minded and missionary-hearted.

Correcting the unruly

The Bible teaches that the authority of church leaders must be held in high regard if there is to be healthy discipline in the fellowship. On the other hand, leaders are to be held accountable for their standard of teaching and personal morality.

Indiscipline, immorality and division in the church are not to be condoned. However, all disciplinary measures are to be tempered by the desire to build up the offender and by the forgiveness that surrounds the family of Christ.

Challenging evil

Morally, spiritually and doctrinally, the church of God has always been surrounded by evil. The Bible teaches that evil can be overcome by the power of good. The church must challenge evil by its vigilance and by its determination to live and preach the truth.

Evangelising the world

Before he ascended, Jesus gave his disciples a specific command that is to be obeyed by the church in every age. They were to make disciples everywhere, spreading the good news of Christ throughout the world.

We are to announce that Jesus Christ, once crucified for the sins of the world, is alive, and that he is Lord; that forgiveness and the gift of his Spirit are for all who belong to him through repentance and faith. The message is to be proclaimed universally, obediently, relevantly, joyfully and yet urgently. We do it at his command.

Serving the world

Jesus never expected the church to be a proclaimer of words without being a performer of deeds. Christian service is a partner of evangelism, both activities being a necessary part of the mission of God.

Christ is the example for the service that his church is commanded to bring to the world. He fed the hungry, he healed the sick and he brought hope to the despairing. He identified with humanity in all its needs.

The same should be true of the fellowship he came to create.

Glorifying God

The church lives for the glory of God. In all that it does, it should direct attention and praise to God. It fulfils this purpose as it bears fruit in faithful service, and mirrors his love.

More particularly, it glorifies God as, following in the steps of Christ, it suffers with him. Jesus said that the hour of his death was the hour of greatest glory. So the suffering and the glory of God's kingdom are combined in Jesus.

BIBLE CHECK

Guarding: 1 Timothy 3:15; Jude 3; 1 Timothy 6:20

Correcting: Hebrews 13:17; 1 Corinthians 5:9-13

Challenging: Romans 12:17-21; Jude 19-21

Evangelising: Matthew 28:18-20; 1 Thessalonians 1:5-10

Serving: 1 John 3:17,18; Titus 3:8; Philippians 2:5-7

Glorifying: John 12:27,28; 1 Peter 4:12-14; Revelation 1:9

KEY TRUTH

The church is not a passive society in the world. It receives its power and direction from Jesus Christ, who has given it his authority to fulfil his mission.

POSTSCRIPT

It is repeatedly in the very weakness of the church that its greatest power is seen.

BIBLE STUDY 1 Thessalonians 1:1-10

Thessalonica lay right across the Via Egnatia, a great Roman trunk road which ran from western Greece right through to Constantinople and the east. East and west met at Thessalonica. As early as AD 49 Paul came to the city, and had a three-week mission there, before Jewish opposition forced out the evangelists. The account is written up for us in Acts 17:1-9.

But those three weeks were enough; a church had been started! Some months later Paul wrote to the new church. Had his mission failed? Evidently not, for good news had been brought to him by Timothy (3:2). Paul writes this opening passage with joy:

1 Thessalonica was a test case in heathen Europe. What are the evidences that the mission had not failed? Look at verse 2-5, and list the graces. How typical are these of Christian disciples?

2 Now analyse the experience in verses 6 and 7. To what extent was this new church a model of New Testament patterns? Compare Acts 14:22. In the world today where do we see these same characteristics?

3 Now absorb the impact of this church, in verses 8-10. To what extent had the Via Egnatia played a part? What was the reputation of this young energetic church?

4 Your church could touch the world. The Roman roads have given way to other communication aids, including the Internet. But there are other resources open to Christians across the centuries, chief of which is intercessory prayer. What is your church or fellowship doing to make your faith "known everywhere"?

5 Look back to the report of Thessalonica's mission in Acts 17. What was the power that explained it all? See Acts 17:7.

REFLECTION

A Read Acts 12:1-19. Consider the church's situation. What were its problems? Its mood? Its influence? Its surprises?

B Where does the balance lie in practice, for you, between spreading the good news and giving practical service? What adjustments do you need to make?

C How do you react to disagreememts in your fellowship? How far do the words of 2 Timothy 2:23-26 apply?

D To what extent are you able to take a positive initiative where you are, in being the "salt" that improves society (Matthew 5:13)?

5. Its Ordinances

BAPTISM

Admission to membership
Ever since Christ's command to make disciples and to baptise them in the name of the Trinity, baptism with water has been the outward distinguishing mark of the Christian.

More than a symbol
When an Ethiopian official was baptised by Philip the evangelist, he was full of joy, although his knowledge of Jesus was limited. Baptism is a powerful event. Received rightly, it becomes a means of God's grace to the Christian.

Death to the old life
Baptism is a farewell to the old life – it is a baptism into the death of Christ. It signifies that the one baptised has been crucified with him, and that the life of sin and self belongs to the past.

Rising to the new life
Baptism is the emergence to the new life; it speaks powerfully to Christians of being raised with Christ, of walking in the light, of peace with God.

Identification with Christ
In his own baptism, Jesus identified with sinful humanity. In our baptism we are privileged to identify with him, unashamed to be known by his name.

THE LORD'S SUPPER

We commemorate
Christ left us no monument or memorial; he never even wrote a book. What he left us was a fellowship "meal" by which we could draw close to him and remember the sacrifice of his body and his blood given for us in death. This is the *backward* look.

We communicate
It is not a dead Christ who is worshipped in the holy communion, but a risen Saviour. As his people share in the bread and wine, they give thanks and praise, and use the opportunity to renew their fellowship with the risen Lord. This is the *upward* look.

We appropriate
Jesus told his disciples to "take" the bread, as he sat with them. Here is no one-man drama. We are not spectators, but deeply involved; if we come to the Lord's Supper with a right attitude, we receive God's grace and strength for Christian living. This is the *inward* look.

We participate
The disciples all drank from the cup, as it was passed from one to another. It is, indeed, a sharing occasion. Believers do not come together in this way merely as individuals, but as a family. This is the *outward* look.

We anticipate
Christ told his disciples that the Lord's Supper should be observed regularly – until his return. Then our communion with him will be direct, face to face. Thus the service is a pointer ahead. This is the *forward* look.

BIBLE CHECK

Admission: Acts 2:41
More than: Acts 8:38,39
Death: Romans 6:3,4
Rising: Colossians 2:12
Identification: Galatians 3:27
Commemorate: Luke 22:19,20
Communicate: John 6:56
Appropriate: Mark 14:22
Participate: 1 Corinthians 10:16,17
Anticipate: 1 Corinthians 11:26

KEY TRUTH

Baptism and the Lord's Supper were both instituted by Jesus Christ as dynamic symbols of the gospel. The water of baptism signifies cleansing and entry into God's church. The bread and wine of the holy communion signify the receiving of Christ's body and blood, given for us in death.

POSTSCRIPT

It is important not to under-emphasise the value of these two ordinances, given by Jesus Christ. Through them we come to a deeper awareness of Christ's death and living presence.

BIBLE STUDY Luke 22:14-27

Jerusalem was the crossroads for all Judaism. People had flocked to the Holy City to celebrate the event that had propelled their nation into being – the passing-over of the angel of death and the dramatic deliverance from Egypt. This particular year it was more than routine that brought the extra crowds in. The minds of thousands were occupied with stories of a young Galilean preacher. Would this be the year when political deliverance from Rome would come from him?

1 Jesus himself was wishing the moment nearer. Why? Compare verse 15 with Matthew 26:18.

2 Why did Jesus choose the Passover meal as the occasion to institute what we know now as the Lord's Supper? The clues are all in the passage. Don't miss out on the word covenant. Look up 1 Corinthians 5:7 as a key verse.

3 It sounds strange to modern ears to speak of "eating the flesh" and "drinking the blood" of someone. For the meaning of these very Jewish terms take time to look up 1 Chronicles 11:1 and Psalm 27:2 – and we will see that these phrases refer to taking advantage of the life of someone else. Apply this now to the Lord's Supper for a very clear answer as to what we are doing in the eating and drinking.

4 Discuss the power of "remembrance" (verse 19) for a believer. What difference would it make to the church if there was no such event as the Lord's Supper?

5 Is it surprising that in history wrangles and controversy have arisen, even over this holy occasion? What evidence is there of wrong attitudes, even on the founding night?

REFLECTION

A Read Luke 22:14-27. Why did Jesus connect this event with the Old Testament Passover (see Exodus 12:25-27), and with the new covenant, prophesied by Jeremiah (Jeremiah 31:31-34)?

B Read Acts 16:29-33. In these verses, baptism is shown to be an important event in the Christian's life. Why do you think that baptism is important?

C As you attend the Lord's Supper or holy communion, in what frame of mind should you come – towards Christ himself, yourself, and your neighbour?

D Pick out the encouraging factors about that evening, and also the discouraging elements. What do they tell us about the gospel and ourselves?

THE CHURCH

6. Its Ministry and Order

Preaching and teaching

The acceptance of Christianity's revealed truth has never been an optional extra in the church. We read in the New Testament of the standard or form of teaching required for growth and discipleship.

The issue of false teaching is dealt with on page after page of the New Testament letters. What protected the infant church was its anchorage in the apostolic teaching, received not merely on an intellectual level, but practised in daily life.

Prayer and intercession

Prayer was the power-house of the early church. It was the unseen weapon that established bridgeheads for the gospel in areas dominated by idolatry and moral darkness.

Prayer is the way in which God's power becomes effective, unhindered by considerations of space, time, culture, or even the prison bars that people have erected.

Fellowship and caring

It has been pointed out that the early church was revolutionary. This was not because it roused slaves against their masters, but because it was more revolutionary still – it demolished the old distinctions altogether. The true liberation was freedom in Christ.

People divided by social status, religious background and language now became brothers and sisters in God's household. The apostles taught that widows are of importance in God's family; the sick are to be prayed for, and the hungry fed.

Worship and praise

Worship is the main purpose of the church. Jesus promised that even where only two or three met in his name, there he would be present with them. Praise and thanksgiving are the distinctive marks of the living church.

The worship of the Christian fellowship is not tied to a building or a structured order, although it is possible that "liturgies" (forms of worship) were developing by the time the New Testament letters were written.

However the New Testament clearly states that it is not only the leaders who worship God, but all God's people. There is a "priesthood of all believers", offering spiritual sacrifices.

Leadership and government

In the early church even the precise patterns and titles of ministry differed a little from church to church. Ephesus had "elders", while Philippi had "bishops" (both presumably describing the same function of pastoral oversight). There were also "deacons" who served in a helping capacity, while the apostles were in a class of their own.

Those in the pastoral ministry belong to the church; the church does not belong to them. They are God's gift to the church. They are to feed the flock, they are to be blameless in their beliefs and in their conduct and their ministry is to resemble that of Christ, who came to be a servant of all.

BIBLE CHECK

Preaching: Romans 6:17;
1 Timothy 1:3-7; Acts 2:42
Prayer: Acts 4:31; Romans
15:30; 1 Timothy 2:1,2
Fellowship: Colossians 3:11;
1 Timothy 5:1,2; James 1:27
Worship: Colossians 3:16;
Hebrews 13:15,16; 1 Peter
2:5-9
Leadership: Philippians 1:1;
1 Corinthians 3:5;
Titus 1:5-9

KEY TRUTH

The church is to maintain a
presence for God in the world,
proclaiming his message and
uplifting his name, under the
guidance of appointed leaders.

POSTSCRIPT

It is important neither to
create a hierarchy, through
undue elevation of the
leadership, nor to endanger
truth and order in the church,
through devaluation of those
with oversight.

BIBLE STUDY Titus 1:1-16

Crete was the destination of this short but powerful letter,
written about AD 62, from Paul to Titus, his trusted colleague.
Crete had become a part of the Roman empire in 67 BC; it was a
sizeable island, dominating the south Aegean Sea,
mountainous, superstitious and tough to handle. The Greek
poet Homer said that it had 100 cities. The shaky and
inexperienced church needed a reliable leader, and Paul's letter
has much to say about true leadership and service:

1 "I left you in Crete" (verse 5). How many of the group know
  what it is to be left in charge? What were Titus' first tasks?
2 "Straighten out" (verse 5) – the same Greek word is used
  elsewhere for setting a broken bone. How disordered was the
  church in Crete? Scan the letter briefly for the give-away
  clues.
3 The appointed elders are to be "blameless", though as
  commentator John Stott states, "not flawless" – that is,
  without public blame in a public office. Discuss this insistence
  on high standards (compare 1 Timothy 3:1-7).
4 Examine both the vices and virtues listed here. How should
  we take similar precautions in public church appointments?
5 Notice too the doctrinal purity that is insisted upon (verse 9).
  The message is "trustworthy", for God does not lie (verse 2).
  What are the two duties required of the faithful teacher (verse
  9)?
6 What are the chief characteristics of false teachers (verses 10-
  16)? How are they to be blocked?
7 What is the main lesson that you can take from this study for
  your own fellowship?

REFLECTION

A Study 1 Peter 5:1-11. List
the qualities to be found in
one who shepherds God's
flock. What was the
association in Peter's mind
that prompted these terms?
Check your answer with John
21:15-17.
B What are the tensions that
the church of Christ inevitably
experiences (verses 5-9)?

C Look at 1 Timothy 4:11-16.
These are Paul's words to a
young church leader, Timothy.
What are the responsibilities
and rewards of church
leadership? In what ways
should we pray for our
leaders?
D Why is the church not a
"democracy"? And yet, why is
it not a hierarchy?

1. The Hope of the Christian

The promises to God's people

God is working in history. The Christian is confident in the righteousness of God, which is working through the events of this world towards the final glory that must eventually follow the ministry and sufferings of Christ. It is his personal return that will usher in the new age.

Resting on the predictions of the Old Testament, the promises of Christ and the conviction of the apostles, the Christian is assured of the sovereign control of God to the end of time.

The fulfilment of God's purposes

The preaching of the apostles demonstrated the Christian belief that the return of Jesus, to make all things new, would be the ultimate fulfilment of his work of salvation.

For the believer, the appearance of Christ will come as the longed-for conclusion and perfection of the salvation already won through the sacrifice of the cross.

The defeat of God's enemies

The outcome of the conflict between good and evil is already settled. The death and sub-sequent resurrection of Jesus has ensured the defeat of sin, death, and all the powers of evil.

But it will not be until Christ's public and powerful return in glory that God's righteousness will be finally upheld. God's victory will then be evident to all.

A living hope

It is Christ who fills the Christian with the confident expectation the Bible calls "hope". All the New Testament passages which describe the last things focus their attention on him.

It is in the resurrection of Jesus that we find particular encouragement. Our living hope is that like him we too shall rise from death to enjoy the new heaven and the new earth from which death and decay are banished. Christ's followers await a new body, incorruptible and powerful. This body will relate to the old existence, but Paul tells us that it will be significantly different.

A steadfast hope

The quality of Christian hope is that it imparts courage and patience for the present. It is not a vague desire for better times, nor is it a resigned and passive submission to life's problems while we wait for a new tomorrow.

The hope that is centred in Christ has kept the church through the ages during persecution and hardship. It is the hope that demolishes fear, and transforms pessimism into godly and practical optimism.

A purifying hope

Our hope in the return of Christ in the future should have a deep effect on the way we live now. Ours is not the hope of the curious who look only for the details of signs and dates while remaining detached and unaffected.

To the Christian, Christ's return is a reality. As a result, priorities, decisions and life-style will inevitably be shaped by the thought of his coming.

BIBLE CHECK

Promises: 1 Peter 1:10-12; Isaiah 11:1-9

Fulfilment: Acts 3:17-21 Romans 8:18-23

Defeat: Philippians 2:9-11; 1 Corinthians 15:24-26

Living: 1 Peter 1:3-5; 1 Corinthians 15:20-23,51-55

Steadfast: 1 Thessalonians 1:3; Romans 8:24,25

Purifying: 1 John 3:2,3; Hebrews 10:23-25; Jude 24,25

KEY TRUTH

The Christian's hope is a confidence in the rule and purposes of God, which find their goal in the return of Jesus Christ at the end of the age.

POSTSCRIPT

Christian history indicates that those who have their eyes on the age to come are the ones who are most effective in this passing age.

BIBLE STUDY 1 Peter 1:1-12

It does not matter which country or century you are from – the description of the Christians to whom the apostle Peter's letter is addressed is all-embracing: "God's elect, strangers in the world, scattered ..." These scattered – and soon to be persecuted – believers had no New Testament; so the opening greeting (verse 2) is packed with helpful reminders that their conversion was no accident. Planned by the Father, achieved by the Son in the sprinkling of his blood and applied by the Spirit in sanctifying power – theirs was a Trinitarian faith.

1 Note the key words in this opening burst of praise (verses 3-8) ... hope ... inheritance ... salvation ... faith. What two great events is this confidence based on – and we must remember that Peter was a first-hand witness!

2 What are the phrases here that point to the believer's eternal security – regardless of the impending suffering mentioned in verses 6 and 7?

3 Identify the words of strong expectation for the future. How does Peter refer to the final culminating point of all our work and witness? How far is this mind set your own?

4 Why do joy and testing go so frequently together in the New Testament? Look up James 1:2; 1 Peter 4:12,13. What should we be teaching new believers about the trials they face?

5 Discuss the wonder of loving someone whom you have never seen with your eyes (verse 8). When did this first begin to happen to you?

6 Why is ours such a privileged era in which to live? Verses 10-12 give us the answer.

REFLECTION

A Read 1 Peter 1:1-12. What were the circumstances of the readers of this letter? How can a Christian rejoice (verse 8) in the midst of adversity (verse 6)? What is the nature of the Christian hope, and how is it created?

B Christians love someone they have never seen (1 Peter 1:8). How is such love generated and made a reality?

Check your answer with Romans 15:4.

C In what ways do you look forward to the future, and to what extent do you fear it?

D How can the Christian's view of the future make a serious contribution to society as it attempts to grapple with the problems of tomorrow?

2. The Prelude to Christ's Return

In the natural realm

It is extremely important that as we read in the Bible about the famines, earthquakes and plagues that will feature before Christ's return, we should not be too quick to identify such an era with our own.

The Bible's repeated use of the phrase "the last times" refers to the entire period between Christ's first and second comings. Therefore, before Christ's return we should not be surprised to see natural and even cosmic disasters.

In the social realm

Stress and social disorder are characteristics of the period before Christ's second coming. We are told that people will be arrogant and proud, materialistic and immoral. The Bible says that these will be terrible times when human sin is unchecked.

There will also be those who make a mockery of religion and of any talk of a return by Jesus Christ.

In the international realm

Jesus made it plain, as he taught his disciples, that wars, revolutions and political disturbances would characterise the coming age. These events would not mean that the end had come – they would be signs of the presence and advance of the kingdom. They would be the labour pains heralding the birth of the new order.

In the family realm

Hatred and division, even within families, were predicted by Jesus Christ as being features of the last times.

The family relationship would be endangered, and loyalties would be strained – in certain circumstances to the point of betrayal.

In the personal realm

During the last times, those who have no relationship with God will experience an increase in fear and insecurity.

Jesus predicted that the situation would be similar to that of Noah's generation. There would be aimlessness, with men and women eating and drinking, getting married and going about their daily business, yet estranged from God and with no real purpose for living.

In the spiritual realm

From descriptions in the book of Revelation we can see that the spiritual realm will be unrestricted in its rebellion. Paul describes the coming of "the man of lawlessness," who will declare himself to be God, and will demand worship. Also there will be numerous "false christs" who will attempt to lead people away from the truth.

The church, while exercising great influence through its proclamation of the gospel, will nevertheless face considerable pressure and persecution during the last times.

BIBLE CHECK

Natural: Luke 21:11,25; Romans 8:22

Social: 2 Timothy 3:1-5; Jude 18; 2 Peter 3:3,4

International: Mark 13:7,8; Luke 21:9,10

Family: Mark 13:12; Matthew 10:34-36

Personal: Luke 21:26; Matthew 24:37-39

Spiritual: Matthew 24:4-14; 2 Thessalonians 2:3-10

KEY TRUTH

Before Christ returns, Christians may expect to see varying degrees of disorder in the world. This gives them an opportunity to evangelise and offer hope.

POSTSCRIPT

In the Gospels, Jesus' prediction of the destruction of the Jerusalem temple merges with his description of the last times. Whatever our interpretation, Christ's prediction about the temple is a prefigure of his further prediction of the end.

BIBLE STUDY Matthew 24:1-35

Jesus is predicting the End – something that could never be rehearsed – and he needs no rehearsal. But we do, if its reality is ever to sink in. One such rehearsal of future glory occurred in miniature at the Transfiguration (17). Here in this passage Christ starts by telling his disciples about the "end" of something they would be very familiar with – the temple.

1 Verses 1-3: It is vital to observe the nature of the disciples' questions – two questions in one! What were they assuming?

2 Now scan verses 4-21, as Jesus gives two answers in one. One is on the global and futuristic scale, the other on the local and immediate – with the division occurring at verse 15. Broadly, what are these two predictions about? Why does Jesus telescope them?

3 Rome's destruction of Jerusalem, and the temple, in AD 70 (verses 15-21) was itself prefigured and "rehearsed" in 169 BC by the desecration of Jerusalem's temple by the Seleucid king Antiochus Epiphanes – the "abomination that causes desolation" predicted in Daniel 11:31. What is Jesus emphasising by alluding to this familiar and terrible episode of Jewish history?

4 The teaching is of an approaching catastrophe, the bitter memory of the past – both pointing to the march of history, referred to in verses 4-14 and 22-28. What is the general pattern of events in our own history that believers should be prepared for? Try and list them from these verses.

5 Jesus then speaks of the final end itself (verses 29-35) – of the whole chain of events that would begin to have happened in the lifetime of those present (verse 34). How should Christ's words affect our lives today?

REFLECTION

A Read Matthew 24:3-14. Try to list the events and patterns foreseen by the Lord as taking place between his departure from earth and his return. In what way do you think they apply to this generation?

B Why was Jesus not more specific? Compare your findings with Matthew 12:38-42 and Matthew 24:36.

C Reflect on the attitude that we should have regarding Jesus' warnings of world events. How do his words affect our lives today?

D What is faulty in the desire to know the precise details about the Lord's coming? Compare your answer to Matthew 24:42 and Deuteronomy 29:29.

3. The Return of Christ

CHRIST WILL RETURN ...

Prophetically

There are numerous Old Testament passages that refer to the kingly rule of Christ – predictions that plainly will not be fulfilled until his return.

The New Testament prophecies are found throughout the Gospels, Acts, the letters and the book of Revelation. They refer to Christ's return as a Coming, as a Revealing, as the Day of the Lord and as his Appearing.

Personally

We are not, of course, to think of Jesus as absent from the world and from his people at the present time, for he promised to be with his followers until the end.

But while he is with the church invisibly at present, by his Spirit, Christ's coming at the end will be visible and personal. The assurance was given to the apostles, at the time of the ascension, that it would be the very same Jesus who returned.

Visibly

The return of Jesus Christ will be no secret, hidden affair. The Bible teaches that earth's entire population will see the event.

To some, the appearing of Jesus will be a glorious and wonderful sight, but we also learn from the Scriptures that many will be dismayed.

Suddenly

The Lord spoke of life in this world at the time of his coming as being very similar to life in Noah's day at the time of the flood. Marriage, eating and drinking – life would be continuing as usual.

But then, at a single stroke, everything would be interrupted. The Bible describes Jesus Christ's return as being like a lightning flash, like a thief in the night and like a master paying an unexpected visit on his servants. It is clear that people will be taken unawares, in spite of the many warnings of Scripture. All Jesus' parables relating to his coming include this aspect of suddenness.

Triumphantly

This second coming of Christ will be utterly different from the squalid obscurity in which he first came. The return will be accompanied by great power and splendour. In the face of the victorious majesty and power of Jesus Christ's appearing, every person will be forced to acknowledge that he is truly Lord.

Conclusively

The appearing of Jesus Christ will be the final chapter in the human story. His coming will bring governments, nations, authorities and every kind of enemy of God under his rule and judgement.

Death will be destroyed. Satan, and the whole empire of evil will be overthrown for ever. And Christ's people will be united to their Lord in the new creation that he has prepared for them.

Prophetically: Daniel 7:13,14; 1 Thessalonians 4:16-18

Personally: Matthew 28:20; Acts 1:11

Visibly: Matthew 24:30; Revelation 1:7

Suddenly: Matthew 24:27,36-51; 1 Thessalonians 5:2,3

Triumphantly: Luke 21:27,28; Philippians 2:9-11

Conclusively: 1 Corinthians 15:24; 1 Thessalonians 4:17

KEY TRUTH

All Christians look forward to the personal return of Christ at the end of the age, as predicted by the Bible.

POSTSCRIPT

History is full of examples of false predictions relating to the time of Christ's return. The Christian is best prepared for this event by being involved in active, obedient service.

BIBLE STUDY 1 Thessalonians 4:13–5:11

This was the church that had begun under the preaching of Paul in a mission of only three weeks (Acts 17:1,2). In that time they had been well taught, before Jewish opposition drove the evangelists out. Now however, that Paul is writing to the Thessalonians some months later, he is aware of a question that is puzzling the young Christians. If one of their members died before the second coming of Christ had taken place, would that person be at a disadvantage, in contrast to those who were still alive? This is the starting point of the passage. Read it now, and use these questions to help you:

1 How are we to understand the second coming in relation to the faithful departed (verses 13-18)? Would those who were "still alive" (verse 15) have precedence over them? How could the Thessalonians "encourage" (verse 18) the recently bereaved?

2 Scan the same verses again and establish the position of the church on earth, at the time of the Coming. Observe that Paul, naturally, classes himself among such.

3 Look more closely at verses 15-17, and consider the Coming in relation to the Lord himself. Paul's teaching is only "in accordance to the Lord's own word". Compare these verses with, say, John 14:1-3.

4 Consider 5:1-3 and the teaching about the Coming in relation to time. Compare Matthew 24:42-44.

5 Look at the same verses now, in relation to the unbelieving world. Compare these verses with 2 Thessalonians 1:7-9 and Matthew 24:37,38.

6 Lastly, consider the Return in relation to the Christian's present activities (5:4-11).

REFLECTION

A Study 1 Thessalonians 4:13–5:11. Why was this passage written? From these words, how may we understand the coming of Christ, in relation to Christians who have died, the Day itself, its timing and our right preparation for it?

B Compare John 14:3 with 1 Thessalonians 4:16-18. How does Paul's teaching relate to Christ's?

C What should be your attitude to readers of the Bible who, while believing in the main fact of Christ's coming, may not agree with you on every point of interpretation?

D What do your non-Christian friends think about the future of the world? How does their view differ from yours?

4. The Judgement

God will be declared as just

The final judgement is a definite future event that will take place at the second coming of Christ. The Bible says that it is unavoidable – as unavoidable as death itself.

At the judgement the balances of true justice will be set right for ever. There will be no excuse left to any who come under judgement – for it will be seen by everybody that the dealings of God are completely just and righteous.

Christ will be acknowledged as Lord

The judgement will signify the end of world history and the struggle between good and evil. Every power that has stood in opposition to God will be put under Christ's feet, and every tongue will confess that he is Lord.

At the judgement, Jesus Christ will receive the glory and worship that is due to him from his people, for he will have gathered them to himself from the whole earth. Their sins will not be counted against them, for by his death on the cross he has already taken their judgement upon himself.

Christians will be accountable for their service

While no Christian will be judged on the basis of the sins he has committed, it is taught in the Bible that Christ's people will be assessed for the quality of their service.

No Christian will ever be lost, but the coming Day will expose our work, which will be rewarded according to its worth. The faithful Christian is thus challenged to please his returning master throughout life's present opportunity.

The disobedient will be rejected for their unbelief

The basis of the judgement will be the response that individuals have made to the light that God has given them. The great sin of the New Testament consists in rejecting the light of Christ. When asked what the vital priority of life was, Jesus replied that it was to believe in himself.

The separation from God to which unbelievers are condemned is therefore no more than an underlining of their own choices regarding God's revelation to them.

Satan will be destroyed for ever

Satan is not all-powerful. The book of Revelation shows that he is very active in many different ways but he does not occupy the centre – for God never leaves his throne.

Thus, the judgement will bring the victory of the cross to completion. Satan and his allies will be overthrown and destroyed by God.

BIBLE CHECK

God: Hebrews 9:27; Psalm 96:13; Acts 17:31

Christ: 1 Corinthians 15:24-26; John 5:24; Philippians 2:11

Christians: Romans 14:12; 2 Corinthians 5:9,10; 1 Corinthians 3:10-15

Disobedient: John 3:19; 6:28,29; 2 Thessalonians 1:7-9

Satan: Revelation 20:10

KEY TRUTH

The final judgement will be the climax of this world's events. It will set right the injustices of history, underline the choices of individuals, and demonstrate the righteousness of God and the victory of Jesus Christ.

POSTSCRIPT

Judgement is not a popular theme in societies which have become soft and indulgent. However, we must recognise that by the choices individuals make, they sentence themselves.

BIBLE STUDY 2 Peter 3:1-18

The apostle Peter is nearing the end of his life and he knows it (1:14). His concern is that the next generation of believers would hold on firmly to the apostolic truth.

These were difficult days for the Christian church, faced as it was by spiritual and cultural pressures that threatened to swallow it up. Use these questions to prompt your study of this passage:

1 What main event is the apostle emphasising in this chapter? Verses 7, 10 and 12 allude to it. Where did Peter get this concept from? Look up Matthew 24:29-31. Observe its finality (verses 10,12).

2 What authority does Peter want his readers to rely upon for his teaching? Look at verse 2, and compare Ephesians 2:20.

3 Verses 3-5 highlight the viewpoint of the critics with regard to the last times. How similar is their argument to that of every generation? Compare Jeremiah 17:15.

4 How does the believer resist the propaganda that we are just part of a closed system and that nothing outside the life of this world can affect it? The answer lies in 1:12,13,15 and in 3:1,2,8.

5 Answering the scoffers, the writer points to three "outside' and unforeseen events affecting this world, two of which had already happened. What are they (verses 5-7)?

6 How can we practically prepare for the final day? Look for the references to patience, to godliness, to focusing and to "growing".

REFLECTION

A Read Matthew 25:1-13. What is the main thrust of this parable of Jesus? Contrast the two groups of girls. What does this passage teach us about the end times, and about our choices in life?

B At the end, there will be a separation between evil and good. Is the world getting better or worse? Compare your thoughts with Matthew 13:24-30.

C What does 1 Corinthians 3:12-15 teach people about their responsibilities and opportunities?

D What does Christ's teaching about judgement tell us about the nature of humanity?

5. The Resurrection

Christ its guarantee

Christianity presents the resurrection of the body as the final goal of our salvation – a supernatural event coinciding with the return of Jesus Christ.

This resurrection, which is the inheritance of every Christian, derives its pattern from Christ. The Bible says that Christ's resurrection is like the first sheaf of a large harvest, in which all Christians will be gathered. This is what the Bible means when it uses the word "firstfruits". Christ's resurrection is the guarantee of this event.

Nature its illustration

This expectation of a bodily resurrection is illustrated by Paul in his first letter to the Christians in Corinth.

Paul answers the objection that the resurrection is impossible, by referring to the miracle of sowing and reaping, in which a small seed is transformed into a plant. The resurrection does not mean a mere shadowy existence of the soul, but a glorious and transformed body.

Eternal life its outcome

The resurrection body is designed for a totally different environment from this passing, mortal age. When it is raised, it is a spiritual body, suited for life in the presence of God. There, believers will know an existence unlimited by the effects of the fall.

From humiliation to glory

Christians are assured in the Bible that when they finally see Christ, they will have a body like his. We are not given many details about the nature of the resurrection body, beyond that the believer's body is weak and ugly at death, but that when raised, it possesses marvellous beauty and strength.

Probably, the reason why we are only given a limited understanding of the resurrection body is that in this new life the focus will be on Christ himself and not on details of secondary importance. He will be at the centre, and that is what really matters.

From the natural to the spiritual

At death, the believer's body is physical; at the resurrection it is spiritual.

If Christ's resurrection body is the pattern, then we can understand that this body will be perfect in every way.

It will be a body that has continuity with the old body (and we will recognize one another in the new creation), and yet a body that is suited to that immortal, redeemed creation.

From mortality to immortality

All reminders of death, decay and disease will be banished from the new bodies of Christ's people. The apostle Paul seems to indicate that those believers who have died before Christ's return still await their resurrection bodies and for the present are without a body, although truly with Christ. They, like those who are still alive at Christ's return, will be raised to live for ever.

BIBLE CHECK

Christ: 1 Corinthians 15:20-23; Philippians 3:20,21
Nature: 1 Corinthians 15:35-38
Eternal life: 1 Thessalonians 4:16,17; John 5:24-26; 6:40
Humiliation: 1 Corinthians 15:43; 1 John 3:2
Natural: John 20:19; 1 Corinthians 15:44; Luke 24:36-43
Mortality: 1 Corinthians 15:42,50-55; Philippians 1:21-24

KEY TRUTH

The Bible teaches that Christians will be raised from death to enjoy eternal life with God.

POSTSCRIPT

The Christian's hope is not to escape from the body, but to be raised as a new body to live the quality of life God has always intended for us.

BIBLE STUDY 1 Corinthians 15:50-58

"The resurrection of Christ has altered the face of the universe," writes David Gooding. "Not only is death not an irreversible process; it is not even a permanent institution" (*True to the Faith*, Hodder). Here in this passage the apostle Paul has arrived at the stirring climax to his classic chapter on the Resurrection. He has covered various difficulties and objections; now he concludes with a ringing declaration:

1 In verse 50, Paul demolishes any idea of a crude return of a dead corpse to what it was before. How does he do this, with his use of terms? What was the difference between the raising of Lazarus and the resurrection of Christ? Compare John 11:44 with John 21:6,7.

2 Look on at verses 51-53. Discuss the nature of the "changed" bodies of Christ's followers. What clues do we have? Look back to verses 42,43 and Philipians 3:21.

3 "The last trumpet" (verse 52). To what does this refer? A parallel is found in Matthew 24:31 and 1 Thessalonians 4:16. How much does this expectation make sense of the present for you?

4 Turn to verses 55-57. "The sting is not in death but in sin," wrote Leon Morris (*1 Corinthians*, Tyndale Press). Relate this to the achievements of Christ on our behalf.

5 Apply verse 58 to the various callings and pieces of service represented in the study group.

6 How confident are you that your own body will one day be resurrected?

REFLECTION

A Read 1 Corinthians 15:20-28. How does Christ's resurrection affect the future? In what sense do we understand the defeat of death? How is this confidence reflected in Christian living today?

B What difference, in practice, does a Christian faith seem to make to people in the face of death?

C Turn to the Old Testament passage of Ezekiel 37:1-14, which relates to the message of resurrection. Think and pray about situations that need this kind of transformation.

D Because Christ is risen, we too shall be raised from death. In what ways does this give the Easter story extra meaning for you?

6. The New Order

The triumph of the Lamb

The Bible ends, in the book of Revelation, with an undisguised theme of victory, centred in Christ. Christ is described as the "Lamb" (which links him with the Old Testament sacrifices in which lambs were killed to take away sin). He is the Lamb who was killed, but is now worthy of receiving the praise of all creation.

It is through the shedding of his blood that complete victory over evil has been achieved.

The new creation

Revelation chapter 21 describes a new heaven and a new earth. The word "heaven" here means the rest of the universe, with all the stars and planets.

The old universe, with its weakness and decay, is radically redeemed. There are no more heartaches, pains or sicknesses. This new creation is made for God and his people to live in. There is a note of finality and triumph in the words of verse 6 "It is done."

The new Jerusalem

This chapter also describes the final home of those whom God has raised to eternal life. This walled city, the new Jerusalem, has been prepared by God for his people – for it comes from him.

The evil are excluded from the city, and inside it there will be perfect fellowship and worship of God. We are told that there will be no temple in the city, because God is the temple. The sun and moon will not be needed, because God's splendour will illuminate the city. This is the city of God.

Paradise restored

In the opening chapters of the Bible, Adam and Eve were placed in the Garden of Eden. At the centre of this garden was the tree of life. However, after the fall, Adam and Eve were driven out of paradise by God, and barred from the tree of life.

The last chapter of the Bible shows that God will restore humanity to paradise, and that we will have free access to the tree of life. Thus, at the very end of the story of God's redemption, humanity is back in fellowship again, in touch at last with the very life of God.

Jesus is coming

As John concludes with his portrayal of Christ as the returning bridegroom, the prophecy of the book of Revelation is witnessed to be true by the angel, by John himself and by Jesus. It is to remain unsealed, for the message is to be obeyed. It is not to be hidden, and it is not to be meddled with.

The concluding message is simple: "I am coming soon." The offer is free – that of the water of life for all who will come and accept it.

The final sentences of the Bible include a prayer for strength, offered on behalf of all God's people who are not yet within the security of the walled city. There is also a prayer of joyful hope and anticipation: "Come, Lord Jesus."

Triumph: Revelation 5:12,13; 7:17; 12:11; 17:14

New creation: Revelation 21:1-8; 2 Peter 3:10-13; Romans 8:18-23

New Jerusalem: Revelation 21:2,3,9-27

Paradise: Genesis 2:8-10; 3:22-24; Revelation 22:1-5,14

Coming: Revelation 22:6-21; Isaiah 40:9,10

KEY TRUTH

Christian people look forward to a new heaven and a new earth, where the dwelling place of God and his Christ are to be found.

POSTSCRIPT

In the new order, Christians will have new bodies, there will be a new Jerusalem and a new heaven and earth. All these things marred by sin, have to be changed. But we have the confident assurance that God himself, with his love and faithfulness, will not change.

BIBLE STUDY Revelation 21:1-14

Imagine that there was no book of Revelation. The impression then gained, at the close of the Bible would be of an unresolved conclusion, with God's saints contending valiantly for the faith, but with no apparent final verdict on the conflict between good and evil.

The verdict of this book is inescapable. You cannot read the last pages of this wonderful prophecy and stay in the camp of the pessimists! Let this final vision of the glory of God's kingdom inspire you in everything you are doing.

1 Verse 5 seems to be the key thought. What is its link with verses 1,2 and 4?

2 We are visualising a scene of glory (verses 10-14). How does this vision of the future make sense of the present turbulence, frailties and evils, mentioned in this passage?

3 How does our vision of the centre give shape to the whole? For the centre, see verses 3 and 5. How can we best transfer this thought into our own world-view?

4 "It is done" (verse 6) This is the tense of the "prophetic past" – it is as good as done already! How does this vision of the certain triumph of God add strength to the task in hand?

5 In the light of verses 7 and 8, discuss the statement, "God's judgement is the proof of his goodness."

6 What do the many "gates" of verses 12-14 speak to us of?

7 Why does God not achieve all this now, at a stroke?

REFLECTION

A Read Revelation 21. Try to put into your own words something of what this pasage is telling us about God and his people. Would any kind of person feel at home in the new creation?

B "I am coming soon." What does this concept do to your priorities at present? What should you do about it?

C Read Revelation 22:17. What are the different thoughts in this verse? What effect should they have on your praying and witnessing?

D What are the suggestions and hints of a likeness between your own Christian fellowship and the perfection of the new Jerusalem? How can such a likeness be developed?

Focus on The Bible

ITS MAIN SECTIONS

A God who loves to bless
■ Genesis 12:1-3

A God who demands our allegiance
■ Joshua 24:14,15

A God for all the seasons of life
■ Ecclesiastes 3:1-8

A God who hates injustice
■ Amos 5:21-24

Time to receive the good news
■ Mark 1:14,15

Don't conform, be transformed
■ Romans 12:1,2

Jesus said, "I am the Alpha and the Omega"
■ Revelation 1:8-11

ITS INSPIRATION

The identity of its divine author
■ 1 Peter 1:20,21

The diversity of its human writers
■ Acts 18:3

The unity of its many themes
■ Matthew 5:17,18

The reality of its moral impact
■ Hebrews 4:12

It is ideal to meditate on
■ Joshua 1:7,8

All the Bible is inspired
■ 2 Timothy 3:16

Jesus said, "Come, follow me"
■ Matthew 4:19

ITS INTERPRETATION

Each part must be seen in its historical setting
■ John 13:14

Each part must be consistent with its surrounding passage
■ 2 Corinthians 4:2

Each part must be in harmony with the rest of Scripture
■ Matthew 22:29

Each part must be consistent with the purpose of God's revelation
■ Deuteronomy 29:29

Each part must be understood in changing cultures
■ Acts 8:34-38

Faithfulness in interpretation
■ Revelation 22:18,19

Jesus said, "Do not be afraid"
■ Matthew 28:10

ITS APPLICATION

Read prayerfully
■ Psalm 119:33-40

Listen personally
■ 1 Samuel 3:10

Look expectantly
■ 1 John 5:13

Apply regularly
■ Psalm 1:1,2

Act obediently
■ James 1:22-25

Read totally
■ 2 Corinthians 4:2

Jesus said, "Have faith in God"
■ Mark 11:22

ITS CENTRAL THEME

The continual conflict
■ Genesis 3

The promised Saviour
■ Jeremiah 31:31-34

The work of Christ
■ Luke 2:28-32

The new community
■ Ephesians 2:18-22

The ultimate victory
■ 1 Thessalonians 4:13-18

A useful summary
■ Titus 3:3-7

Jesus said, "Your sins are forgiven"
■ Luke 7:48

ITS CONTENTS

God's plan for his people
■ Genesis 1:26-28

The promise of freedom
■ John 8:36

A God of faithfulness
■ Psalm 36:5

A God of justice
■ Deuteronomy 32:4

A God of love
■ 1 John 4:10

Jesus is coming back for his own
■ 1 Thessalonians 4:16,17

Jesus said, "The Scriptures speak of me"
■ John 5:39

Focus on God

THE TRINITY

In the Old Testament
- Genesis 1:26,27

Asserted in the New Testament
- John 14:15-26

Blessing the church
- 2 Corinthians 13:14

The Father commits his works to the Son
- Matthew 11:27

The Son revealed through the Holy Spirit
- John 15:16

God in the believer
- Romans 8:9

Jesus said, "We will come to him and make our home with him"
- John 14:23

THE CREATOR

In the beginning
- Genesis 1

God the creator
- Nehemiah 9:6

God the sustainer
- Acts 14:17

God is achieving his purpose
- Romans 8:18-25

Earth as a focal point
- Revelation 21:1-3

What is man?
- Psalm 8:3-8

Jesus said, "I will be with you always"
- Matthew 28:20

GOD'S BEING

God is everywhere
- Jeremiah 23:23,24

God is all-powerful
- Genesis 17:1

God knows everything
- Hebrews 4:12,13

God is eternal
- Isaiah 44:6

God is unchanging
- James 1:17

Truths about God
- Psalm 138:1-18

Jesus said, "Come to me"
- Matthew 11:28

GOD'S CHARACTER

God's truth is inseparable from his character
- John 14:6

God's holiness reacts against all impurity
- Habakkuk 1:13

God's love extends to all humanity
- 1 John 4:7-11

God's mercy holds back what we deserve
- Hosea 11:8,9

God's grace gives us what we do not deserve
- 1 Corinthians 1:4-8

God's faithfulness provides for daily life
- Psalm 89:1,2

Jesus said, "I will give you rest"
- Matthew 11:28

THE FATHERHOOD OF GOD

By creation – of all things
- Acts 17:24-29

By covenant – of Israel
- Isaiah 63:16

By adoption – of Christian believers
- Romans 8:14-17

From eternity – of Jesus Christ
- John 17:5

The Father's gifts
- Galatians 4:4-7

The Father's delight
- Luke 15:11-24

Jesus said, "Learn from me"
- Matthew 11:29

GOD'S REVELATION

Seen supremely in Jesus
- John 14:8-10

Seen through the Bible
- Romans 16:25-27

Seen through creation
- Psalm 19:1-4

Seen in history
- Psalm 75:6,7

Seen in humanity
- Romans 2:14,15

Seen through human experience
- Revelation 2:29

Jesus said, "Father, forgive them"
- Luke 23:34

Focus on Jesus Christ

HIS INCARNATION

Christ was Son of God before time and space
■ John 1:1-3

It was by a supernatural conception
■ Matthew 1:18-25

It shows Christ as fully God
■ John 8:46

It establishes Christ as fully human
■ Galatians 4:4,5

It explains Christ's unique personality
■ Matthew 8:24-27

It validates Christ's saving ministry
■ 1 Timothy 2:5

Jesus said, "Today you will be with me in paradise"
■ Luke 23:43

MAIN EVENTS IN THE GOSPELS

His humble birth
■ Luke 2:1-7

His sinless baptism
■ Matthew 3:13-17

His revealing transfiguration
■ Luke 9:28-36

His obedient death
■ Luke 23:26-43

His victorious resurrection
■ Luke 24:1-8

His glorious ascension
■ Luke 24:44-53

Jesus said, "Trust in God"
■ John 14:1

MAIN ASPECTS OF HIS MINISTRY

Authority that convinced
■ Matthew 5:21,22,27,28

Parables that provoked
■ Mark 4:2

Miracles that confirmed
■ Mark 1:23-28

Compassion that attracted
■ Matthew 9:35-38

Training that prepared
■ Matthew 10:1-15

Controversy that challenged
■ Mark 2:5-7

Jesus said, "Trust also in me"
■ John 14:1

HIS NAMES

Son of God
■ John 20:17

The Word
■ Revelation 19:11-13

High Priest
■ Hebrews 7:23-28

Messiah
■ John 4:25,26

Son of Man
■ Matthew 8:19,20

Lord
■ 1 Corinthians 12:1-3

Jesus said, "You are the salt of the earth"
■ Matthew 5:13

HIS ATONING DEATH

... initiated a new relationship
■ 2 Corinthians 5:15-19

... fulfilled Old Testament Scripture
■ Isaiah 53:4-12

... destroyed Satan's kingdom
■ 1 John 3:8

... reversed sin's dominion
■ Galatians 3:13

... provided a way of forgiveness
■ 1 John 1:7

... guaranteed an eternity with God
■ Romans 8:31-39

Jesus said, "I am the bread of life"
■ John 6:35

HIS TRIUMPHANT RESURRECTION

The foundation of the Christian faith
■ Romans 1:4

An event supported by evidence
■ John 20:1-29

A promise of ultimate victory
■ 1 Corinthians 15:24-28

The power of Christian experience
■ Romans 6:5-14

The assurance of eternal security
■ John 11:25,26

More evidence!
■ 1 Corinthians 15:1-11

Jesus said, "I am the light of the world"
■ John 8:12

Focus on The Holy Spirit

HIS PERSON

Part of the Godhead
▪ Matthew 28:19

The very character of God
▪ 2 Corinthians 13:14

He knows us through and through
▪ 1 Corinthians 2:10,11

He feels
▪ Ephesians 4:30

He hurts
▪ Hebrews 10:29

He guides
▪ Acts 8:29

Jesus said, "… the Holy Spirit … will teach you all things …"
▪ John 14:26

HIS NAMES AND DESCRIPTIONS

The Holy Spirit
▪ Acts 2:32,33

The Spirit of God
▪ Matthew 3:16

The Spirit of Christ
▪ Philippians 1:19

Wind
▪ Acts 2:2

Water
▪ John 7:38

Fire
▪ Matthew 3:11

Jesus said, "I am the gate for the sheep"
▪ John 10:7

HIS WORK

He convinces of sin
▪ John 16:8-11

He illuminates truth
▪ John 14:25,26

He reveals Christ
▪ John 15:26

He lives in believers
▪ Romans 8:9-11

He inspires prayer
▪ Romans 8:26

He prepares for heaven
▪ Romans 8:1-4

Jesus said, "I am the good shepherd"
▪ John 10:11

HIS ACTIVITY IN THE CHRISTIAN

Life – new birth by the Spirit
▪ John 3:3-8

Assurance – the witness of the Spirit
▪ Romans 8:15,16

Unity – fellowship in the Spirit
▪ 1 Corinthians 12:13

Ownership – the seal of the Spirit
▪ Ephesians 1:13,14

Power – the fullness of the Spirit
▪ Ephesians 5:18

Confidence – the pledge of the Spirit
▪ 2 Corinthians 5:5

Jesus said, "I am the resurrection and the life"
▪ John 11:25

HIS FRUIT

Love never fails
▪ 1 Corinthians 13:8

Let God's peace rule
▪ Colossians 3:15

Devote yourself to what is good
▪ Titus 3:8

God loves faithfulness!
▪ Matthew 25:23

Gentle, like Jesus
▪ Matthew 11:29

Personal discipline
▪ 1 Corinthians 9:25-27

Jesus said, "… the Holy Spirit … will teach you all things"
▪ John 14:26

HIS GIFTS

The gifts exalt Christ
▪ 1 Peter 4:10,11

The gifts involve all
▪ 1 Corinthians 12:7-11

The gifts should unite all
▪ Romans 12:4,5

Gifts lay foundations
▪ Ephesians 2:19-22

Gifts build up the fellowship
▪ Ephesians 4:11-13

Gifts promote mission
▪ Colossians 1:27-29

Jesus said, "I am the way"
▪ John 14:6

Focus on Humanity

OUR UNIQUENESS

I am a whole being, physical and spiritual
■ Deuteronomy 8:3

I am a spiritual being, made in God's image
■ Genesis 1:26,27

I am a moral being, responsible for my actions
■ Romans 2:14,15

I have natural dimensions
■ Psalm 104:5-30

I have creative dimensions
■ Psalm 8:6-8

I have religious dimensions
■ Psalm 90:1

Jesus said, "I am the truth"
■ John 14:6

OUR DIVERSITY

Created by God
■ Psalm 100:3

Created for God
■ Psalm 100:3

Created to glorify God
■ Psalm 100:4

Family is God's way
■ Genesis 2:18

Searching for God
■ Ecclesiastes 3:11

More than bread alone
■ Matthew 4:4

Jesus said, "I have come that they may have life, and have it to the full"
■ John 10:10

OUR REBELLION AND FALL

Humanity's innocence gave us fellowship with God
■ Genesis 2

Humanity's freedom gave us the power of choice
■ Genesis 2:16,17

Humanity's decision led us into moral rebellion
■ Genesis 3:8-19

Humanity's rebellion and guilt
■ Romans 5:12-17

Humanity's condemnation and separation
■ Isaiah 59:1,2

Humanity's separation and death
■ Romans 6:23

Jesus said, "I am the life"
■ John 14:6

OUR REBELLION AND CONDEMNATION

All have fallen short of the mark
■ Romans 5:12

The soul who sins will die
■ Ezekiel 18:4

All are guilty
■ Romans 5:18,19

All have turned away
■ Psalm 14:3

All are awaiting judgement
■ Romans 2:16

But thanks to God
■ Romans 8:1,2

Jesus said, "Whoever does not believe [in me] stands condemned already"
■ John 3:18

OUR QUEST AND DILEMMA

Looking for truth
■ Acts 17:22,23

Philosophy can be a blind alley
■ Ecclesiastes 1:17,18

Full of contradiction
■ Mark 7:21-23

God's workmanship, created in Christ Jesus to do good works
■ Ephesians 2:10

A spirit at war with God
■ James 4:5

Slaves to our emotions
■ Titus 3:3

Jesus said, "If the Son sets you free, you will be free indeed"
■ John 8:36

OUR ENEMIES

Satan
■ 1 Peter 5:8,9

Sin
■ Romans 8:10

The world
■ 1 John 2:15,16

The flesh
■ Romans 7:18

Death
■ 2 Timothy 1:10

Defence against enemies
■ Ephesians 6:10-18

Jesus said, "I am the true vine"
■ John 15:1

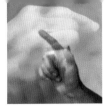

Focus on God's Messengers

ANGELS

Heavenly beings
■ Psalm 8:5

God's messengers
■ Luke 24:4-7

Rejoicing when a sinner
repents
■ Luke 15:10

Revealing God's will
■ Exodus 3:2

Protecting God's own
■ 2 Kings 6:17

Attending Jesus
■ Matthew 4:11

Jesus said, "… their angels in
heaven always see the face of
my Father in heaven"
■ Matthew 18:10

PATRIARCHS

By faith Abraham obeyed
■ Hebrews 11:8

By faith Abraham offered
Isaac
■ Genesis 22:7-9

By faith Isaac blessed Jacob
and Esau
■ Genesis 27:27-29,39,40

By faith Jacob worshipped
■ Hebrews 11:21

God's promise to Abraham
■ Genesis 15:5

The promise fulfilled
■ Matthew 1:1-17

Jesus said, "Before Abraham
was born, I am"
■ John 8:58

PRIESTS

Set apart
■ Exodus 28:1-5

The go-between
■ Leviticus 1:1-9

Past imperfect
■ Hebrews 7:11

Present perfect in Christ
■ Hebrews 7:26-28

The priesthood of believers
■ 1 Peter 2:4,5,9

Living stones
■ 1 Peter 1:5

Jesus said, "This is my blood
of the covenant … poured out
for many"
■ Matthew 26:28

PROPHETS

Called by God
■ Isaiah 6:8-10

Challenging falsehood
■ 1 Kings 18:21

Revealing injustice
■ Amos 5:21-24

Revealing God's mind
■ 2 Peter 1:21

Showing the way forward
■ Daniel 2:36-46

Heralding the Messiah
■ John 1:29

Jesus said, "Watch out for false
prophets"
■ Matthew 7:15

APOSTLES

Christ's authority
■ Matthew 16:18

Appointed by God
■ John 20:21-23

Witnesses to the resurrection
■ Acts 1:21,22

Evidence
■ 2 Corinthians 12:12

Foundation of the church
■ Ephesians 2:19,20

Teaching the truth
■ John 16:12-15

Jesus said, "You will be my
witnesses"
■ Acts 1:8

EVANGELISTS

Good news to tell
■ Acts 8:5

Chosen by God
■ Ephesians 4:11

Proclaiming Christ
■ 1 Corinthians 15:3-5

Confident in God's word
■ Acts 8:35

God's power
■ Acts 1:8

Showing a changed life
■ Galatians 1:23,24

Jesus said, "He who receives
you receives me"
■ Matthew 10:40

Focus on Salvation

GOD'S PLAN FOR HUMANITY

God's plan – his will is sovereign
■ Romans 9:10-18

God's plan – his work is eternal
■ Acts 2:23

God's plan – his choice is specific
■ Matthew 22:14

God's people – separated for holy living
■ Romans 8:29

God's people – called to good works
■ Philippians 2:12,13

God's people – preparing for future glory
■ Revelation 17:14

Jesus said, "Peace be with you!"
■ John 20:21

HUMANITY'S NEED OF SALVATION

Humanity's need of:
a new direction
■ Hebrews 9:27

a new nature
■ Jeremiah 13:23

a new motivation
■ John 6:66-68

personal fulfilment
■ Luke 12:15

social acceptance
■ Genesis 11:4

a spiritual dimension
■ 1 Corinthians 2:14

Jesus said, "Remain in my love"
■ John 15:9

THE WAY OF SALVATION

The basis – the death of Jesus
■ Acts 4:10-12

The basis – the resurrection of Jesus
■ Acts 2:32-36

The call – to repentance
■ Acts 3:19

The call – to faith
■ Acts 13:38,39

The promise – forgiveness
■ Psalm 103:11,12

The promise – the gift of the Spirit
■ Acts 2:38

Jesus said, "I chose you to go and bear much fruit"
■ John 15:16

ACCEPTANCE

God regenerates the believer as a new being
■ Ezekiel 36:25-27

God reconciles the believer in a new relationship
■ 2 Corinthians 5:18-21

God redeems the believer through a new covenant
■ Jeremiah 31:31-34

God justifies the believer for a new position
■ Titus 3:7

God glorifies the believer for a new life
■ Romans 8:28-30

The Christian's new position
■ Romans 5:1-8

Jesus said, "I did not come to bring peace, but a sword"
■ Matthew 10:34

SANCTIFICATION

A separation to God
■ 2 Thessalonians 2:13

A separation from the world
■ 2 Corinthians 6:17–7:1

A separation for holy living
■ 2 Timothy 2:20,21

A separation by the Holy Spirit
■ Galatians 5:16-18

A separation through the word of God
■ John 15:3

A separation that progresses throughout life
■ 2 Corinthians 1:10

Jesus said, "The Son of Man came to serve"
■ Mark 10:45

IN THE LETTER TO THE ROMANS

Election
■ Romans 9:21-24

Transformation
■ Romans 12:1,2

God's working on behalf of his people
■ Romans 8:28-30

Reasons for having confidence in God
■ Romans 8:31-34

No separation from God
■ Romans 8:35-37

The love of God
■ Romans 8:38,39

Jesus said, "Give to God what is God's"
■ Mark 12:17

Focus on The Christian

DESCRIBED

A sinner saved by grace
■ Ephesians 2:8,9

A member of God's family
■ John 1:12,13

A disciple of Jesus Christ
■ Luke 14:26,27

A temple of the Holy Spirit
■ 1 Corinthians 3:16

A pilgrim in an alien environment
■ Hebrews 11:8-16

A citizen of heaven
■ Hebrews 13:14

Jesus said, "My words will never pass away"
■ Mark 13:31

THE CHRISTIAN AND THE BIBLE

The Bible:
equips the Christian for life
■ John 8:31,32

equips the Christian for battle
■ Matthew 4:1-11

energises the Christian for service
■ Psalm 1

corrects the Christian from error
■ James 1:23-25

develops the Christian in the faith
■ 1 Peter 2:2,3

informs the Christian of God's mind
■ Romans 11:33-36

Jesus said, "Do not worry"
■ Matthew 6:25

THE CHRISTIAN AND PRAYER

Prayer is:
essential for communion with God
■ Mark 1:35

essential for growth in God
■ Matthew 6:9-13

essential for the service of God
■ James 5:16-18

essential for the praise of God
■ Psalm 150

essential for the experience of God
■ Psalm 57:1-3

God's special way of communication
■ Romans 8:15

Jesus said, "Seek and you will find"
■ Matthew 7:7

THE CHRISTIAN AND WITNESS

Proclaiming a person
■ Acts 1:8

Explaining the truth
■ Colossians 1:28,29

Sharing a love
■ 2 Corinthians 5:14

Witnessing consistently
■ John 13:34,35

Witnessing personally
■ Acts 4:18-20

Witnessing collectively
■ Philippians 1:27

Jesus said, "Whoever will lose his life for my sake will find it"
■ Matthew 10:39

THE CHRISTIAN AND THE WORLD

Called out of the world
■ 1 Corinthians 7:29-31

Separated from the world
■ Ephesians 5:3-11

Sent into the world
■ John 20:21

Sent into the world
■ Matthew 5:13-16

Sent to overcome the world
■ Romans 8:37

Journeying through the world
■ Hebrews 11:16

Jesus said, "Love the Lord your God"
■ Mark 12:30

THE CHRISTIAN LIFE

A vocation to be fulfilled
■ Philippians 3:14

A character to be developed
■ 2 Peter 1:5-8

A fellowship to be maintained
■ Ephesians 5:1,2

Energies to be harnessed
■ 1 Corinthians 15:58

Minds to be developed
■ Ephesians 1:18

A hope to be realised
■ Titus 2:13

Jesus said, "Love your neighbour as yourself"
■ Mark 12:31

Focus on The Church

ITS CHARACTERISTICS

It is the church of Jesus Christ (historical)
■ Matthew 16:18

It is the company of all believers (universal)
■ Colossians 3:11

It is a unity of the Spirit (spiritual)
■ Ephesians 4:4-6

Its authority is God's word (scriptural)
■ 2 Timothy 1:13,14

Its programme is worldwide (international)
■ Luke 4:16-21

The unity the church should have
■ Ephesians 4:1-16

Jesus said, "You must be born again"
■ John 3:7

ITS MAIN DESCRIPTION

A firm building
■ 1 Peter 2:4,5

A virgin bride
■ Revelation 21:2

A functioning body
■ 1 Corinthians 12:12-31

A permanent city
■ Hebrews 13:14

A stable family
■ 1 Timothy 3:14,15

An active army
■ Ephesians 6:12

Jesus said, "Love your enemies"
■ Luke 6:35

ITS RELATIONSHIP TO CHRIST

Christ died for the church
■ Acts 20:28

Christ builds the church
■ Ephesians 4:11-16

Christ protects the church
■ Daniel 3:19-27

Christ purifies the church
■ Jeremiah 3:6,14

Christ intercedes for the church
■ 1 John 2:1

Christ prepares for the church
■ John 14:1-4

Jesus said, "Be merciful"
■ Luke 6:36

AUTHORITY AND MISSION

Guarding the truth
■ 1 Timothy 6:20

Correcting the unruly
■ 1 Corinthians 5:9-13

Challenging evil
■ Romans 12:17-21

Evangelising the world
■ Matthew 28:18-20

Serving the world
■ Titus 3:8

Glorifying God
■ 1 Peter 4:12-14

Jesus said, "What can a man give in exchange for his soul?"
■ Matthew 16:26

ITS ORDINANCES

Baptism – admission to membership
■ Acts 2:41

Baptism – more than a symbol
■ Acts 8:38,39

Baptism – death to the old life
■ Romans 6:3,4

Baptism – rising to the new life
■ Colossians 2:12

The Lord's Supper – we commemorate
■ Luke 22:19,20

The Lord's Supper – we anticipate
■ 1 Corinthians 11:26

Jesus said, "God so loved the world that he gave his one and only Son"
■ John 3:16

ITS MINISTRY AND ORDER

Preaching and teaching
■ Romans 6:17

Prayer and intercession
■ Romans 15:30

Fellowship and caring
■ Colossians 3:11

Worship and praise
■ Colossians 3:16

Leadership and government
■ Philippians 1:1

Qualities for shepherds of God's flock
■ 1 Peter 5:1-11

Jesus said, "You will be my witnesses"
■ Acts 1:8

Focus on The Last Things

THE HOPE OF THE CHRISTIAN

Promises to God's people
■ 1 Peter 1:10-12

Fulfilment of God's purposes
■ Acts 3:17-21

Defeat of God's enemies
■ Philippians 2:9-11

A living hope
■ 1 Corinthians 15:20-23, 51-55

A steadfast hope
■ 1 Thessalonians 1:3

A purifying hope
■ Jude 24,25

Jesus said, "You will receive power when the Holy Spirit comes on you"
■ Acts 1:8

THE PRELUDE TO CHRIST'S RETURN

Before the return:

Disorder in the natural realm
■ Luke 21:11,25

Disorder in the social realm
■ 2 Timothy 3:1-5

Disorder in the international realm
■ Mark 13:7,8

Disorder in the family realm
■ Mark 13:12

Disorder in the personal realm
■ Luke 21:26

Disorder in the spiritual realm
■ 2 Thesssalonians 2:3-10

Jesus said, "My sheep listen to my voice"
■ John 10:27

THE RETURN OF CHRIST

Christ will return prophetically
■ Daniel 7:13,14

Christ will return personally
■ Matthew 26:64

Christ will return visibly
■ Matthew 24:30

Christ will return suddenly
■ Matthew 24:27,36-51

Christ will return triumphantly
■ Luke 21:27,28

Christ will return conclusively
■ 1 Corinthians 15:24

Jesus said, "I give eternal life"
■ John 10:28

THE JUDGEMENT

God will judge everyone
■ Hebrews 9:27

Christians will not be condemned
■ John 5:24

Christians will be accountable for their service
■ Romans 14:12

The disobedient will be rejected for their unbelief
■ John 3:18-20

Satan will be destroyed for ever
■ Revelation 20:10

Separation between good and evil
■ Matthew 13:24-30

Jesus said, "I know my sheep"
■ John 10:14

THE RESURRECTION

Christ, its guarantee
■ 1 Corinthians 15:20-23

Nature, its illustration
■ 1 Corinthians 15:35-38

Eternal life, its outcome
■ 1 Thessalonians 4:16,17

From humiliation to glory
■ 1 John 3:1,2

From the natural to the spiritual
■ 1 Corinthians 15:44

From mortality to immortality
■ Philippians 1:21-24

Jesus said, "My sheep know me"
■ John 10:14

THE NEW ORDER

The triumph of the Lamb
■ Revelation 5:12,13

The new creation
■ Revelation 21:1-8

The new creation
■ 2 Peter 3:10-13

The new Jerusalem
■ Revelation 21:9-27

Paradise restored
■ Revelation 22:1-5

Jesus is coming
■ Revelation 22:6-21

Jesus said, "Let the little children come to me"
■ Matthew 19:14

Living the Christian Life

This part of the book is for those who not only want to "understand" but also to "live" the Christian life to their fullest capacity. It is for participants, for those who really want to be involved and make progress in the Christian life.

To be a participant we have to start, and the best place to start is at the beginning! But starting at the beginning does not mean stopping there. We must move on if we are going to know the real thrill of participating in this adventure with God.

We shall make many mistakes as we progress. Indeed, the mistakes we make will in themselves encourage us to depend more on God, realising that he is only too willing to help us. Real, lasting progress is always the result of this partnership with God.

Each section is like a journey. Starting with the first section, we move on through a further eight areas of practical Christian living until we come to the final section: "Arriving".

These nine sections each have six complete studies, giving to the individual or group 54 studies in all.

Living the Christian Life

CONTENTS

GROWING p.496

The need for growth
Growing into Christ
Growing in faith
Growing in knowledge
Growing in love
Bible summary: Becoming like Jesus

The source of growth
The Spirit lives in us
The Spirit sanctifies us
The Spirit empowers us
The Spirit unites us
Bible summary: The fruit of the Spirit

The evidence of growth
A growing experience
A growing confidence
A growing usefulness
A growing battle
Bible summary: The battle for the mind

The secret of growth
In touch with God's purposes
Aware of God's presence
A source of God's power
Taking time to pray
Bible summary: What is prayer?

A pattern for growth
Love prayers
Sorry prayers
Thank-you prayers
Asking prayers
Bible summary: Jesus' pattern for prayer

The problems of growth
Exercising faith
Waiting for answers
Keeping alert
When God seems silent
Bible summary: God's mysterious ways

DISCOVERING p.508

Discovering a new life
Journey into life
A constant companion
New every morning
I know where I'm going
Bible summary: Becoming a disciple

Discovering God's way
Shown through conscience
Shown through God's law
Shown through Jesus
Shown through the Bible
Bible summary: The Ten Commandments

Discovering God's will
Praying it through
Searching the Scriptures
Talking it over
Making up your mind
Bible summary: Living through faith

Discovering God's word
A book of truth
A book of example
A book of warning
A book of challenge
Bible summary: All we need to know

Applying God's word
Equipment for the journey
A light for dark paths
A sword for hard battles
Strength to keep going
Bible summary: Jesus' view of the Bible

Handling God's word
Reading it regularly
Soaking it up
Studying its teachings
Discovering its characters
Bible summary: Understanding God's word

BELONGING p.520

**Belonging to
God's family**
One Father
One Lord
One Spirit
One faith
Bible summary:
   All one in Christ

**Belonging to
each other**
Baptised into Christ
A club for sinners
A new set of friends
En route for heaven
Bible summary:
   A universal church

**Worshipping
together**
The reason for
   worship
The object of worship
The source of
   worship
The value of worship
Bible summary:
   Make a joyful
   noise!

Sharing together
Praying together
Learning together
Giving together
Eating together
Bible summary:
   One in fellowship

**Ministries for
each other**
The need for leaders
The need for pastors
   and teachers
The need for
   organisers
The need for
   submission
Bible summary:
   Ministry in the
   New Testament

Working together
The local church
A caring church
A witnessing church
A growing church
Bible summary:
   The church across
   the world

TESTING p.532

**The reality
of testing**
It happens to everyone
It may not seem fair
It is allowed by God
It can teach us more
   about God
Bible summary:
   The patience of Job

**Testing
through doubt**
A touch of humility
A touch of opposition
A touch of faith
A touch of confidence
Bible summary:
   The nature of faith

**Testing through
temptation**
An ever-present
   danger
Sometimes our own
   fault
Often subtle and
   cunning
Always a way out
Bible summary:
   Jesus' temptations

**Testing
through failure**
The gospel for failures
The weakness of
   human nature
God's promise of
   success
The gospel of new
   beginnings
Bible summary:
   The disciple who
   failed Jesus

**Testing
through pain**
Pain in the world
Coping with suffering
Healing is possible
The end of all suffering
Bible summary: Paul's
   "thorn in the flesh"

**Testing through
persecution**
The gospel offends
   people
The ways they attack
The call to be faithful
Resisting, even to
   death
Bible summary: The
   promise of peace

WINNING p.544

Jesus is king
He conquered sin
He conquered death
He conquered evil
He will conquer the
world
Bible summary:
Jesus' cosmic plan

Victory is certain
No need to sin
No need to fear
No need to doubt
No need to falter
Bible summary:
He is able

Right in the heart
Jesus comes first
Thinking straight
Pure motives
Love determines
action
Bible summary:
Not I, but Christ

Overcoming evil
Be sure of your
ground
Depend on God's
power
Learn to say no
Tell Satan to go
Bible summary: The
armour of God

Resisting pressure
The pressure to
conform
The pressure to
compromise
The pressure to
complain
The pressure of
complacency
Bible summary:
United we stand

Onward Christian soldiers
Building the kingdom
Salt in the world
Light for the world
Winning enemy
territory
Bible summary:
What is the
kingdom of God?

SERVING p.556

Called to serve
Called by God
Compelled by love
Committed through
faith
Concerned for others
Bible summary:
Pictures of service

Power to serve
Sharing God's work
Filled with his Spirit
Controlled by his
word
Equipped with his
gifts
Bible summary:
Doing what comes
naturally

Serving in the church
The first shall be last
Lending a hand
Caring for the needy
Speaking God's word
Bible summary:
Building
community

Into the world
A life that is different
Lips that are pure
Little things count
Loving our enemies
Bible summary:
Pilgrims in a
strange land

Sharing good news
A message for
everyone
Talking about Jesus
Letting God work
Telling the
neighbourhood
Bible summary: All
things to all people

Service for life
Ready for change
Giving everything to
Jesus
Supporting his
workers
Praying for God's
servants
Bible summary:
Paul, a servant of
God

HOW TO USE THIS MATERIAL

The material has been arranged for maximum flexibility of use, and for a wide range of situations and readers.

Use it in personal study

This material may be used as a companion to the Bible. It may be used as a reference to the teachings of the Bible, but it may also be used for personal, regular study of the Scriptures. It is made up of 54 studies, and if one main section is studied each week, the total material will be covered in the course of just over a year.

By using a reference Bible or concordance, each study may be extended. The passages given in the "Bible Check" can serve as a starting point for readers' own discovery of the Bible. In this way a comprehensive view of each theme can be built up. It would be useful for you to keep your own notebook handy.

Use it in a group

The material in this section will be of particular value wherever Christian people meet together. Study groups of all ages will greatly profit from the teaching they will discover for themselves as they follow the guidelines given here. It will also prove beneficial where newcomers to the Christian faith are eager to learn the practical implications of their belief.

Group leaders are encouraged to make the following preparations before using this material in any discussion. First, they should become familiar with the Bible passages provided, and be prepared to support these with cross references. Second, they should carefully read through the study material itself. Third, they should be prepared to use the questions as a basis for discussion, and to prepare further questions of their own.

Use it in a church programme

Ministers, pastors and teachers will find this material an invaluable reference source for subject material when preparing programmes for the church. For example, the six studies could be used as the basis for a six-week course of Sunday sermons or midweek meetings.

The headings are designed to capture the truth of the Bible. It is hoped that this will be helpful to preachers and teachers alike.

Use it in schools and colleges

The teaching material, Scripture passages and questions will help to stimulate those involved in religious education, as well as members of informal religious discussion groups and forums. The material has been planned as a comprehensive aid so that students from many different backgrounds of worship and tradition may learn together from the Bible's teaching in a way that prepares them for life.

Some extra features about this material:

1. Each study has four divisions which help in retaining the key truths presented.

2. Key Bible passages and references are provided with every study so that you can see what God's word actually says about it.

3. Included in each study are questions ("To think about..."). We trust this will be a real help, especially for group discussion.

4. Each main study is introduced with a "Key truth" and concludes with a "Postscript". Again, this is provided to help you to retain important truths.

5. Beside the 54 main studies there are "Bible summaries". Each summary follows a main study and is complete in itself. We encourage you to supplement the main study by looking up the references and Bible passages in the "Bible summary".

There is one thing that we have not provided and that is the help of the Spirit of God to all those who seek to live for him. We do with confidence, however, commend to you a dependence on him as you seek to live and make progress as a Christian.

The Christian life is for all of us a matter of progress, and each day brings new opportunities for growth. It is our sincere prayer that you will find this section a useful guide in living the Christian life.

What it's all about

KEY TRUTH

Being a Christian consists of a close personal relationship with God, and not just of following a certain code of behaviour.

A life lived with God

Many people think that being a Christian is a matter of living in a certain way: being kind to others, giving to charities, going to church services, and not committing crime or fraud.

The Bible sees it differently, however. While all these things are part of living a Christian life, the essence is called "faith". That means trusting God personally, as well as believing certain truths.

Jesus complained that some of the religious people of his day had become so tied up by rules and regulations that they were neglecting their relationship with God. The gospel, or good news, is that ordinary people can once again know God personally and live in harmony with him.

A life given by God

Since the world began, people have tried to find God and have invented all kinds of ways to please him. But the whole Bible shows how futile these attempts are. Because people have refused to obey God's commands, the whole world is now cut off from him.

The only way people can make lasting contact with God is to welcome Jesus into their lives. He was God's perfect Son, who became a man in order to explain God's purposes to the world. And when he died, he took on himself the punishment for human rebellion, and opened up the way for us to God.

No one can create a new relationship with God for themselves. He has already done everything necessary; his way can only be accepted – or rejected.

A life dependent on God

Trusting Jesus is not like wearing a lucky charm. It is not simply a way of getting on the right side of God and making sure of a place in heaven.

Being a Christian is a matter of trusting God all the time. It involves staying in touch with him so that we receive his instructions and do what he asks each day.

It can bring a whole new dimension to our lives. But the Christian life will not always be easy. Saying "no" to wrong things is often difficult. Facing unexpected problems can be shattering. But he promises to help all who follow him.

A life lived for God

Most important of all, being a Christian means living for God. Some people throw everything into work, family life or special interests. Christians are called to put all their energy into serving and pleasing God.

TO THINK ABOUT ...

Make a list of the different attitudes and activities that are often associated with being a Christian.

- Which of these are really important, if being a Christian is about having a close personal relationship with God?
- Are there any that are simply human rules and regulations? Why are these dangerous?
- Think about which is easier: to follow a set of rules, or to develop a friendship. Now think about which is more *worthwhile*. Why do we sometimes try to turn Christianity into a set of rules?

That does not mean that they are expected to stop what they are doing and become preachers or missionaries! Each person has talents and abilities which God wants to be fully used, with love and care. He wants each person's faith to influence all their relationships and activities.

BIBLE CHECK
A life lived with God John 17:3; 2 Timothy 1:12
A life given by God John 14:6; Acts 4:12
A life dependent on God Luke 9:23-25; John 15:1-5
A life lived for God Matthew 6:24; James 2:14-18

POSTSCRIPT
The Bible never separates "believing" from "doing". Faith and work go together. If you emphasise one more than the other you may have a philosophy or a lifestyle, but you will not have true Christianity.

Our friends often have an important influence on our lives.
- How important is your relationship with God? Is he just another friend, or does a relationship with him come before everything else?
- How does your relationship with God shape your life?

Thank God that your relationship with him is based purely on his love for you, and not on your own attempt to reach him. Ask God to forgive you for the times when you have let other things become more important. Pray that he will help you to grow in your relationship with him.

BIBLE SUMMARY
WHAT GOD HAS DONE

The Bible describes how the first people who knew God refused to do what he asked. Ever since, humanity has been disobeying God's laws. So people are out of touch with God in this life, and prevented by death from enjoying eternal life in heaven (Ephesians 2:1-3).

A picture of hope
The Old Testament tells how God showed people how they could get in touch with him again. He told them to obey his laws. And he said that their sin was so serious that the only remedy for it was an innocent victim – an animal in those days – who would carry the death penalty on their behalf (Leviticus 16:6-10).

But that was only a picture of God's greatest act of love. Animals could not provide a permanent solution. The New Testament says: "God so loved the world that he gave his one and only Son, that whoever believes in him shall not perish but have eternal life" (John 3:16).

An act of love
Jesus Christ was the only person who has ever lived who was sinless. Even his enemies could not fault him. And he saw his death as "a ransom for many" (Mark 10:45); the innocent suffered the sentence passed on the guilty. John the Baptist called him, "The Lamb of God, who takes away the sin of the world" (John 1:29).

But because he was God as well as man he conquered death by rising to life again and promised that all who welcomed him would receive eternal life (John 3:36). That life was to begin at once. Eternal life is knowing God for oneself and enjoying his presence for ever (Romans 8:38,39).

Making a new start

KEY TRUTH

Becoming a Christian is like starting life all over again, by handing over the control of our lives to Jesus Christ.

Seeing the need

God is a person almost beyond our imagination. He is the powerful creator of everything which exists, yet he also knows just how each individual thinks and feels. He is holy, too – he can do nothing wrong.

By contrast none of us is perfect. We have not always kept God's laws. We have done things which even our conscience knows are wrong. And above all, we have left God out of our thinking.

As a result, we are separated from God by a barrier largely of our own construction: self-will, self-indulgence and self-confidence. The Bible calls this barrier sin: it prevents us from knowing God personally.

Saying sorry to God

None of us likes to admit that we have been wrong. It is even harder if we have to admit that the whole direction of our life so far has been off course – going our way instead of God's.

But we cannot get to know God for ourselves without first telling him we are sorry for having neglected him and for the wrong things we have done. And that includes thoughts and words as well as actions.

Perhaps we also need to say sorry to other people whom we have hurt along the way.

Saying no to sin

We often teach children to say sorry when they do wrong, but watch them blunder on in the same way moments afterwards! Saying sorry is not enough; we have to show we mean it, too.

God knows what we are really like, and words never fool him. We must put all our sin behind us, and promise him not to go wilfully our own way again. This is what the Bible calls "repentance".

For some people this may involve a very radical change in the way they live. For others the change will be more inward, in the way they think and speak. God promises to help us, whatever is involved.

Saying yes to Jesus

Jesus has already done everything necessary to restore our relationship with God by dying on the cross and rising from the dead. He offers the gift of eternal life to any who will accept it.

But we cannot be half-hearted about it. We cannot ask God for his forgiveness if we are not also prepared to let him take charge of our life from then on.

If you have never made a fresh start with Jesus,

TO THINK ABOUT...

Take some time to think about the direction of your life.

- Do you think the direction of your life pleases God?
- What does "repentance" mean? What effect should repentance have on the direction of your life?
- Have you ever made a new start by confessing your sin to God and receiving his forgiveness? If you haven't, are you ready to do so now?

When we make a new start, we come into God's family for the first time. The Bible gives us three pictures of this: birth, adoption and coming home.

or if your Christian life has become stuck in a rut, you can use a simple prayer like this: "Dear God, I am sorry I have left you out of my life, and sinned against you in thought, word and deed. Thank you for sending Jesus to die on the cross so that I could know you for myself. Forgive my sin, and give me the power of your Spirit to live for you every day until you bring me to be with you for ever in heaven. For Jesus' sake, Amen."

BIBLE CHECK
Seeing the need 1 John 1:5-8; Romans 6:23
Saying sorry to God 1 John 1:9,10; Psalm 51:1-4,10-12
Saying no to sin Matthew 4:17; Ephesians 4:22-24
Saying yes to Jesus Revelation 3:20; Matthew 11:28-30

POSTSCRIPT
Jesus called people to follow him just as they were, without trying to reform themselves first. But he also said that once they had begun to follow him, he himself would change them.

- How do these pictures relate to your own relationship with God?
- What is new about your life now that you have made a fresh start? Have you let Jesus take control of the direction of your life?

Thank God that he has made it possible for you to belong to his family. Confess to him all the sin that you want to put behind you, and ask him to fill you with his Spirit so you can live a brand new life.

BIBLE SUMMARY
WHAT HAPPENS WHEN YOU START

There are a number of pictures in the Bible which illustrate what happens when a person welcomes Jesus into their life. Three of them have one thing in common: they refer to a family (see Ephesians 2:19).

A happy event
The first picture is of a baby born into the family. When a person accepts Jesus as the one who has cleared away their sin and opened up the way to God, they are "born again" (John 3:3). They have become a true child of God, because God's Spirit has given them a new, eternal life (John 1:12,13). Like a human baby, the new Christian has a lot of learning to do and they can easily make mistakes or even be led astray (1 Peter 2:1,2).

A new status
The next picture is that of adoption, when a child of one family is accepted as a true son or daughter of another. No one has the right to belong to God's family. Everyone is by nature shut out of it; they belong in the devil's domain. But God adopts those who trust Jesus into his family, welcoming them as his own children (Romans 8:15,16).

Where we belong
Finally, there is the well-known picture of "coming home". In Jesus' parable of the lost son, a rebellious child decides to come home, sorry for having run away, wasted his life and brought shame on the family (Luke 15:11-32). His father (God) sees him from a distance, goes out to meet him and welcomes him home. His sin is forgiven, and the family celebrates his return.

A new way of living

KEY TRUTH

Living as a Christian means enjoying and experiencing life in a totally new way.

A new life

Before Jesus Christ enters our lives we are spiritually dead – unable to know God and draw on his help. But once we have committed ourselves to him, he promises to make everything fresh and new.

He gives a new quality of life which is open to God and lasts for ever. It includes new hope, peace and joy, and power and patience to cope with difficulties.

It has new standards of conduct, and new attitudes, too. But all these things are given to us by God, and cannot be created by our own efforts.

A new relationship

To the Christian, God is no longer a distant, shadowy figure. He is a real person who can be known, loved and worshipped.

He is like a new friend, always ready to help and strengthen us. But the Bible usually calls him "Father", because like the best of human fathers he promises to provide all we need to carry out his purposes.

Sometimes he will tell us off. But he never bullies his children. And for our part, it will take time to get to know him better.

A new family

If the Christian were an only child of our heavenly Father, life would be very lonely. But in fact we are born into the worldwide family of God. In every town and district we have "brothers" and "sisters" who love the Father.

This family is generally known as the church. It may be large or small in a local situation, and like human families it is not always perfect. But it has important functions.

It exists to help each Christian grow in the faith. God has provided it so that we can find the support and encouragement we need.

A new friend

When Jesus was on earth, his followers were upset when he spoke of leaving them. But he promised to send "The Comforter" (the Holy Spirit) to be with them.

The Holy Spirit is God active in the Christian's life. He points us to Jesus and helps us understand the Bible and speak to God in prayer. He shows up what is wrong in our lives, and gives power to put it right.

And he promises to give us abilities to help other Christians, using God's strength, not our own.

TO THINK ABOUT...

The Christian life is a new way of living because God now lives in relationship with us as Father, Son and Holy Spirit.

- What does it mean to call God "Father"? How are human fathers like our Father God? How are they unlike him?
- What role does Jesus have in your life?
- Do you think the Spirit is essential for your Christian life? Why should he be?
- Why does our new relationship with God change everything?

Many other people across the world also share this relationship with God through Jesus Christ and the Holy Spirit.

BIBLE CHECK

A **new life** 2 Corinthians 5:17,18; Colossians 3:12-17

A **new relationship** John 14:23; 1 Peter 5:7

A **new family** 1 Peter 2:9,10; Ephesians 2:19-22

A **new friend** John 14:26; 1 Corinthians 12:4-11

POSTSCRIPT

The new life is a gift from God. Some people only allow him to make superficial changes to their lives, but Jesus wants to change us right through.

- How should we think about these other people? Are they just friends, or do we have a closer connection with them?
- Why is it important that we belong to a worldwide family of believers?

Thank God for the excitement of a new way of living with him and with other believers. Pray that you will be filled with his Spirit to equip you for this new life.

BIBLE SUMMARY

THE FULLNESS OF GOD

When we describe what God does for us, we use different names for him: Father, Son (Jesus), and Holy Spirit. Sometimes people mistakenly think they are different gods, or that only one has any relevance to us today.

In fact, God reveals himself as three "persons". Each is fully God, but has a different function. But when we talk about God being "in" a Christian's life, all three persons are involved (John 14:23).

Christ in you

Jesus, the Son of God, lives in us from the moment we receive him as the one who takes away our sin and gives us eternal life (Colossians 1:27). He promises never to leave us (Hebrews 13:5).

Filled with the Spirit

The Holy Spirit also enters our life at the same time (Ephesians 1:13,14). But the Bible also speaks of other times during the Christian life when he "fills" a person, usually when they face a special task (eg Acts 4:31). However, we should always be filled with the Spirit, his life flowing into and out of us to others (Ephesians 5:18).

When we specially need the Spirit's blessing to help us worship or serve God, Jesus tells us to ask the Father and we will be given the power of the Holy Spirit (Luke 11:13).

But he never gives his power in advance of its being used. And there are times when he cannot fill us, because sin has crowded him out (Ephesians 4:30).

God's unbreakable promises

KEY TRUTH

God promises to help us in many ways, and he never breaks his word.

The promise of security

We do not know what will happen tomorrow. We may face entirely new circumstances: poverty or wealth; illness or tragedy; hard decisions; unexpected opportunities; changes in relationships.

Because life is to some extent uncertain, we are often tempted to find a sense of security in familiar objects or people. But they can change too. Only God offers perfect security.

He promises never to let go of his children. He will never abandon us even if we forget him. He holds us secure in his love all through this life, and into the next.

The promise of support

We are most conscious of the need for God's help when we face difficulty or temptation. But if we are to do everything God wants, we need to draw on his power all the time.

In fact, we need his support just as much when life is running smoothly. Then it is easy to forget him, and so to fail him by something we do or say.

God promises his help at all times. But he never promises to brush aside our problems. In fact, problems often become opportunities to experience and demonstrate his power.

The promise of guidance

For many people, the journey through life is rather like stumbling through a dark forest. It is hard to find the way which will be most rewarding.

God, because he knows both us and the circumstances of our life in every detail, promises to show us the right thing to do at each step along the way.

He also has a special purpose for each person, and he promises to lead us to it. So as we go in the direction he has prepared, we experience a new harmony with him.

The promise of his presence

Sometimes Christians complain that life for the very first followers of Jesus must have been much easier than it is now, because they could see and touch their master.

But in fact it was harder. Jesus could only be in one place at a time. Now he promises to be

TO THINK ABOUT ...

Make a list of some of God's promises as you find them in the Bible.

- Does God keep his promises? Are there reasons why you can believe that he does? Are there promises he has already kept in your life?
- Do you find it easier to believe God's promises when times are difficult or when times are easy?
- What stops you from depending upon God? Do you think he will fail you, or do you prefer to control your own life?
- How should you respond to God's promises?

with everyone everywhere who loves and serves him.

We may not always feel him near us, but the Bible is never in any doubt. Jesus said, "I will be with you always, to the very end of the age" (Matthew 28:20).

He stays on hand to help, teach and guide us.

BIBLE CHECK

The promise of security John 6:37-39; Romans 8:38,39

The promise of support Matthew 11:28 30; Philippians 4:11-13

The promise of guidance Psalm 32:8; Isaiah 30:21

The promise of his presence Psalm 139:7-12; Matthew 28:19,20

POSTSCRIPT

Human beings will often break their promises because they are weak and imperfect; God can never break his promises because he is all-powerful and perfect.

Think of the situations you are facing in life at the moment.

- Can you think of any of God's promises that are especially relevant?
- How will trusting God to keep these promises change the way you live? How will it change the way you pray?

Thank God that he always keeps his promises, even when it is difficult for you to see how he will do so! Thank him that he is always with you. Tell God that you are willing to depend on his promises today.

BIBLE SUMMARY
GOD KEEPS HIS WORD

Some people will promise anything but never do what they say. God is not like that. He cannot change his mind and let us down. In the Old Testament he was specially known as a God who made solemn promises (or "covenants") and kept his word (Deuteronomy 7:9).

Two-edged promises

But as the nation of Israel soon found out, God's promises are two-edged. We can only enjoy all that he offers if we continue to obey him (Deuteronomy 7:10,11). Some of his promises, of course, are unaffected by our sin. He does not rob Christians of eternal life when they do not obey him (John 6:39).

That truth is, however, intended to inspire us to loving devotion, not to encourage us to be careless. God is so gracious that he loves us even when we ignore him (Romans 6:1-4).

Three special promises

The Bible stresses three special promises of God:

- He promised Noah that he would never again destroy the earth by flood in his anger at human sin (Genesis 9:15).
- He promised that Abraham would be the father of many nations, and have a special close relationship with God. And in believing that promise Abraham demonstrated what faith really is (Genesis 17:7,8).
- And he made a "new covenant" with the Christian church through the death of Jesus: that he would be our God and we would be his people for ever (Hebrews 8:6-13).

The help which God gives

KEY TRUTH

God has provided four special ways in which we can receive his help.

Help through prayer

We often have lots of questions to ask God. Prayer is the way in which we can tell him how we feel, what our needs are, and share with him the problems and opportunities we face.

The Bible tells us that God is always ready to listen to our prayers, and loves to answer them. But sometimes we ask for things which will take us away from his purposes, so he will not give us these. We may be so full of requests that we never stop to ask what he really wants.

And he frequently waits for us to ask before giving us what we need, because only when we ask humbly are we ready to receive gratefully.

Help through the Bible

Our relationship with God is always two-way. We talk to him in prayer, and one of his ways of speaking to us is through the Bible (sometimes referred to as his "word").

The Bible authors were guided by God as they wrote down their experiences of him and the truths he revealed. All God wants us to know about himself and how to live for him are contained in its pages.

And the Holy Spirit will make it come alive to us and apply it to our circumstances, if we seek his insight.

Help from God's people

We have already seen that God has made us members of his family. Our "brothers" and "sisters" in Christ have special gifts and insights which God uses to help us. In fact, he intends that we should be almost as dependent on each other as on him, for we all lack wisdom.

Some people will be able to help us understand God's truth and the Bible better. Others will be able to advise us about our problems. We can talk and pray with them, and learn together from the Bible, sharing with all what God shows to each.

And it is always a good idea to talk to other Christians before making important decisions, to receive both advice and support.

Help through worship

Worship happens when a group of Christians meet together to express love and gratitude to God for all that he is and all he has done. They may sing and even shout; they may be quiet and thoughtful. And, of course, we can worship God on our own, as we think about his love to us.

Praising God helps us in two ways. First, it reminds us of how great he is. The things which concern us then seem smaller, and our

TO THINK ABOUT...

We need God's help at all times, so these four ways of receiving his help are not just for special occasions! Think about how you can build them into your daily life.

- How much time do you spend in prayer? Do you make sufficient time and space away from distractions so that you can be open with God? How does prayer help?
- How does the Bible bring God's help? Should that affect the way you read the Bible?
- Do you acknowledge the help that other Christians can give you? Why is it wrong to try to be a Christian on your own?

confidence grows in God's ability to deal with them. Secondly, it opens us to the Holy Spirit, making us more able to hear and obey him, and to receive his power.

BIBLE CHECK
Help through prayer John 16:24; Matthew 7:7-11

Help through the Bible 2 Timothy 3:16,17; John 16:12-15

Help from God's people Ephesians 4:11-14; Romans 12:4-8

Help through worship Acts 4:31; Psalm 29:1-4,10,11

POSTSCRIPT
Make a list of all the things you could praise God for, then praise him!

- Why is worship important? Do you allow yourself to genuinely worship God, or are you always thinking about the problems you need help with?

Take time to bring your own life before God in prayer. Ask him to speak to you through the Bible, and through other Christians. Worship him for his kindness and care.

BIBLE SUMMARY
EVERYONE HAS NEEDS

Even Jesus himself, his closest followers and all the great characters of the Bible, needed to use prayer, the Scriptures, "fellowship" with God's people and worship, to keep themselves in harmony with God.

Prayer often preceded important events. Jesus prayed all night before choosing his twelve apostles (Luke 6:12,13). And they and their close friends "devoted themselves" to prayer after Jesus left the earth, before the Holy Spirit filled them with power on the Day of Pentecost (Acts 1:14).

A weapon for battle
Jesus used the Scriptures as a weapon to fight off the subtle and powerful temptations he received in the desert before he began his public ministry (Matthew 4:3-11). The Psalmist said that the way to lead a pure life was to store God's word in his memory so that he could draw on it at a moment's notice (Psalm 119:11).

Caring for each other
Paul often writes appreciatively of the help he was given by other Christians (eg Colossians 4:7-11). The Bible records the ways in which God's people cared for each other. It was a care which sometimes meant rebuking and challenging, as well as encouraging, each other.

As for worship, it seems to have been such a natural desire and thing to do (eg Acts 20:7) that only in extreme cases is it actually commanded (Hebrews 10:24,25).

A permanent life

KEY TRUTH

The Christian life never stops; there is always more to learn, and heaven to look forward to.

A joyful life

Jesus promised his followers the two things which everyone wants but few ever find: inner peace and joy. Neither depends on an easy life. Rather, they stem from the confidence that our loving Father is in control of it, whatever happens.

Christian joy is a sense of thankfulness for God's care and love. We are no longer tied down by our sin but are free to be the people he intended us to be. We really have something to celebrate!

Joy is a gift from God, however, and not something we can just turn on or manufacture by a certain technique. And it always focuses on him, and is not a feeling to be enjoyed for its own sake.

A growing life

The Christian life has only just begun when a person becomes a member of God's new family. Just as a human child has many things to learn, and takes a long time over it, so too does a child of God.

There is always something new to learn about God and his ways. And Scripture tells us to go on to perfection – which is a long way ahead! Growing in faith can be an exciting, as well as an exacting, adventure.

Sometimes we will only grow more like Jesus when we face difficulty and apply our faith to it, just as he did. But he also promises to renew our old, sinful nature, so that we steadily move forward in our Christian life.

A giving life

Christian faith is not meant to be kept to ourselves. The first followers of Jesus couldn't stop telling others of what God had done for them.

We have something to give to others – a "gospel", or "good news" – which transforms people's lives, attitudes and relationships.

And we have something to share with each other, too: love and concern, some new gift or ability, a possession – anything which will help build up others' faith and minister to their needs. Only as we give in faith will we grow in it.

An everlasting life

Some Christians are laughed at as being "too heavenly-minded to be of any earthly use". We are not meant to be useless. Our ultimate home is heaven, but our feet are to be firmly on the ground.

TO THINK ABOUT...

Think about the eternal life that God promises to give his people.

- Does "eternal life" refer to the future? Or the present? Or both? How does your present Christian life relate to the future God has promised?
- Do the things you do now have eternal significance?
- What aspects of your life today will also be part of life in God's future kingdom? What aspects will not?
- Do you think a Christian should strive to be perfect, like Jesus?

But, in fact, sometimes we may not be heavenly-minded enough. We have been promised eternal life in heaven with Jesus for ever. That is meant to inspire and encourage us in our life now.

We know that death is not the end for us. We have nothing to fear for the future. We have hope, and we shall not be disappointed in the wonderful place God has waiting for us.

BIBLE CHECK

A joyful life John 15:11; Psalm 95:1-7

A growing life Philippians 3:12-16; Ephesians 4:13,14

A giving life John 13:34,35; Luke 6:38

An everlasting life Revelation 22:1-5; Philippians 1:21-24

POSTSCRIPT

Jesus said that the Christian life is a narrow path, compared to the broad road of self-indulgence followed by many other people. But his way leads to abundant life now and for ever.

- In which areas of life do you know you need to grow?
- Which Christian characteristics do you need to develop? Do you need to be more joyful? Or more giving?

Thank God that his love for you will never fail – and that your relationship with him will continue in God's new creation. Ask for the Spirit's help to become more like Jesus, so that you will already live the type of life that God wants you to have in his eternal kingdom!

BIBLE SUMMARY

HOW PERFECT CAN YOU GET?

Jesus told his followers that they should be "perfect" (or mature) Christians (Matthew 5:48). Although God's word promises forgiveness for the sins Christians commit, it does not expect them unconcernedly to commit them (1 John 2:1,2). Jesus himself was perfect, and we are to follow his example (1 Peter 2:21-23).

But we are not instantly made perfect when we receive Jesus, even though our sin is swept away and is no longer a barrier between us and God. His life enters us, his power is available to us, and we have to learn to make use of it. This takes time, and we will make mistakes (James 3:1,2).

Becoming perfect

The Bible tells us to become perfect by obeying God's will (1 Peter 1:14-16). As we do so, we become more skilled in understanding and knowing what God wants us to do (Hebrews 5:12-14).

Sometimes we will get frustrated, because our own human nature, which still retains its imperfections and limitations, never quite manages to be as good or do as well as God's Spirit within us is urging us to. There is a battle going on inside us between the old and the new (Romans 7:15-25).

Battling against evil

And there is a battle against evil, too, as we are tempted, mocked and unsettled by evil forces which come sometimes from the most surprising quarters (Ephesians 6:12,13). But Jesus' people are promised victory over them (1 John 5:4,5).

Know yourself

KEY TRUTH

We can only fully appreciate all that Jesus has done for us when we see ourselves as he sees us.

A spiritual person

God has made every human being a unique person. But we all have certain things in common, such as a similar physical shape, and abilities like speech, thought and emotion.

We also have a natural desire to seek God. Unlike other creatures, we can know him in a personal way, although many people have a substitute "god" to which they devote their lives.

God gave us this ability so that we would live in harmony with him. Lives which include worship and love of God through Jesus Christ start to become what God intended they should be.

A sinful person

Nobody except Jesus himself has lived a fully perfect life. It was because of people's failure to obey God's laws (our "sinfulness") that Jesus had to die on the cross.

But even Christians, who have accepted Jesus' death on their behalf as the way to knowing God, remain sinful. Every part of us is still less than perfect – our thoughts, knowledge and actions.

That is why sometimes we fail to live the Christian life as fully as we intend. It is still easy to fall into the old ways of living. But Jesus always gives us his power to avoid sinning if we ask for it.

A saved person

Christians often talk about being "saved from their sins". To some people that sounds like the language of another culture. But everyone knows people are saved from burning houses, or from drowning in rivers.

So a Christian is a person who has been saved from a terrible fate – living without God for ever. And we are "saved" the moment we receive Jesus into our lives, just as a drowning person is saved the moment they are grabbed by their rescuer.

But being saved is not just a past experience. Having been saved is a constant fact and a continuous experience; we have been given a new life.

A separated person

Jesus has called us to set aside the ways of the world. This does not mean going into seclusion, but abandoning the attitudes to life and other people which are common in our society when these conflict with Jesus' love and purposes.

TO THINK ABOUT ...

Make a list of what you think makes human beings different from the rest of God's creation.

- What aspects of being human does society around you usually think are most important?
- Does God see things differently? What aspect of human life do you think he sees as most important?

Christianity is about becoming the true human being God intended you to be.

- What does the life of Jesus teach you about being human?
- In what ways do you fall short of this (sin)?

Sometimes that will mean saying "no" to things we once liked or enjoyed, because they would hinder our relationship with him.

But more important, it means saying "yes" to what he wants. When the Bible uses the word "holy", it means being dedicated to doing God's will. It involves caring for others, sharing Jesus' love and avoiding sin.

BIBLE CHECK
A spiritual person Acts 17:26,27;
   Philippians 2:9-11
A sinful person Romans 3:23; 1 John 2:1,2
A saved person 1 Timothy 1:15;
   Matthew 1:21
A separated person Matthew 6:24;
   Ephesians 2:8-10

POSTSCRIPT
While we all have certain characteristics in common, God made us with quite different personalities. We are not meant to look or feel the same, nor to do the same things as others, and he deals with us just as we are.

- What does "salvation" mean? How is it related to your whole life – body, mind, heart, soul and spirit?
- How do you think the Christian life is more truly human than other ways of living?

Thank God that he has made you as you are. Ask him to forgive you for the times when you don't live as he intended, and pray he will help you by his Spirit to live a properly human life – just like Jesus.

BIBLE SUMMARY
A WHOLE PERSON

Sometimes people talk about parts of the human personality as if they were all quite separate. They speak as if the body had a mind of its own! Although the Bible does distinguish between different parts, it never regards them as separate. When it refers to one part, it intends us to see the whole person from that angle.

The mind or heart
"Mind" and "heart" often mean the same in Scripture. They refer to a person as a thinking, feeling being. Emotion is part of the Christian's life (Romans 12:15). Even Jesus wept (John 11:35,36). But God gave us minds so that our reactions would always be based on an understanding of God's truth (Romans 12:2).

The body
The Bible never regards the body or its functions as sinful, even though sinful things are done with it (Romans 12:1). It is to be cared for (1 Corinthians 6:19,20). After death we will be raised to life by God who will then give us a new body which will never decay or grow old (1 Corinthians 15:42-44).

Soul and spirit
The "soul" refers to the whole living person. The word is often translated as "life" (Mark 8:35,36). Often soul and spirit are used interchangeably. Spirit, however, sometimes has a more precise meaning. It can refer to our inner motives. So the Egyptian king who refused to let Moses leave his country was hardened in spirit (Exodus 7:14). And when Paul prayed with his spirit (1 Corinthians 14:14) as well as with his mind, his whole being was involved in that prayer.

Knowing God

KEY TRUTH

God is a person with whom we can have a lasting, growing relationship of love and trust.

A personal God

All through the Bible, God is thought of as a person. He is never regarded merely as a force or power, like for example electricity, which only works in set ways.

Of course, he is not entirely like a human person. He does not forget his promises, he never stops loving, and he does not lose his temper!

But he is personal. The Bible has many accounts of how he spoke to people, showed them his plans, and taught them how to respond to him. Its central message is that he can be known by anyone at any time and in any place.

A holy God

Although God loves and cares, there is another side to his character. He can do nothing wrong himself, and he cannot accept wrong-doing by others.

He is often described as holy. That means he is perfect in himself, and separated from all that is imperfect. That is why Jesus had to die on the cross: the perfect man suffered the just punishment for our sins so that we could know this holy God.

Each time a Christian does something which is against God's holiness, the relationship with God is hurt, although not destroyed – just as when a close friend lets down the person he loves.

A loving God

God's love is so much greater than human love because it continues when it is not deserved, or even when it is rejected. And because it is a pure, holy love, it does not depend on what we are like, nor does it spring from favouritism.

The Christian encounters God's love first at the cross. In his love for us, God sent his Son to live and die in the world. But we can experience it every day, too, as we ask for and receive his help and guidance, as we discover his power, and as we see all he has done. Even in the darkest times, his love still shines through.

A purposeful God

The world is very old, and there have been many generations of people living in it. God, who created it, has long-term plans which he has worked out over many centuries.

The best example is the long time he took

TO THINK ABOUT ...

Note down the ways people normally describe who (or what) God is.

- How are these ways different from the revelation in the Bible that God is personal?
- Do you ever think of God as an impersonal force or power rather than as a personal friend and Saviour? Why?
- If God is personal, how can you get to know him better? What sort of attitude towards him should you have?

preparing the Jewish nation for the birth of Jesus. For us, it means we live at a point in history when what we do for God, however small it seems, contributes to the fulfilment of his purposes in the future.

And that also means that he has specific things for us to do: perhaps a career to follow, a person to help, or a spiritual gift to use.

BIBLE CHECK

A personal God John 17:3; 2 Timothy 1:12
A holy God 1 Peter 1:14-16; Leviticus 11:44,45; Isaiah 6:1-5
A loving God John 3:16; 2 Thessalonians 2:16,17; 1 John 4:10-12
A purposeful God Ephesians 1:9-12; 3:3

POSTSCRIPT

Knowing God personally involves learning about him from the Bible as well as experiencing him in our lives.

We have seen that God is holy, loving and purposeful.
- What other characteristics could be used to describe the God of the Bible?
- Now think of stories from the Bible to illustrate each of these characteristics.
- Do you have any experiences of these aspects of God's nature from your own life?

Thank God that he has made himself known to you, and to the whole world, in Jesus Christ. Pray that the Spirit will enable you to know him more and more – not as a distant object, but personally.

BIBLE SUMMARY
WALKING WITH GOD

"Enoch walked with God" (Genesis 5:22). "Walking with God" means keeping him always in mind, aware of his purposes and reflecting his character. It implies patience too, in not running ahead to do something which might seem right but is wrong in God's timing.

Walking in faith

Abraham is a good example of a faithful relationship to God. He believed God when he was told his wife would have a son, even though it was many years before the boy was born (Hebrews 11:8-12).

Then, later on, he obeyed God even at extreme times of testing, for example when God told him to prepare to sacrifice his son Isaac. God saved the boy at the last minute and praised Abraham for his faith (Hebrews 11:17-19; Genesis 22:1-19).

Walking in light

John, one of Jesus' closest followers, said we should "walk in the light, as he [Jesus] is in the light" (1 John 1:7). "Light" means "God's truth and holiness".

As we allow his "light" to expose our sinfulness and make clear how we should live, we begin to enjoy deep Christian friendship (or "fellowship") with others and experience the forgiveness and help of God.

Walking by the Spirit

Paul said that a Christian could either "gratify the desires of the sinful nature" or walk "by the Spirit" (Galatians 5:16). Our natural tendency towards self-centred living is not God's way, he said. So in order to overcome it, he told his readers to live in daily dependence on the Holy Spirit who dwells in their lives (Galatians 5:25).

Know your enemy

KEY TRUTH

Christians are confronted by forces which threaten to hinder or destroy their relationship with God.

The world

The physical universe was created by God, and although it shares in the effects of human sinfulness, it is not itself an evil place as some people have thought.

However, the world which people have created, the world of social, business and political life, is often organised without any concern for God and his laws.

The Bible warns us that this "world" has attitudes and beliefs contrary to Christianity. It is frequently more concerned with getting than giving. It may regard as right what God says is wrong. Jesus said that although we do not belong to this world but to his kingdom, we are nevertheless called to serve him in it.

The flesh

Whenever the New Testament refers to "flesh" as something sinful, it does not mean the physical body, but our natural selfishness. It is often translated "sinful nature". This is the "old nature" which Jesus seeks to replace with his love.

Sometimes, when there is an opportunity to do something positive for God, we feel lazy or tired, or try to get it done easily by not doing it properly. That feeling is the "flesh" resisting the Holy Spirit within us.

And sometimes we will feel a strong urge just to indulge ourselves no matter what the cost is to us or to others. That, too, is a fleshly desire which God wants us to resist.

The adversary

The Bible is in no doubt about the existence of a personal evil spirit called the devil (see Bible Summary). Some forms of opposition to the Christian life are especially associated with him.

First, there is temptation to do wrong, or perhaps to use wrong means to achieve God's purposes. Then there are doubt and lack of faith, which hinder our effectiveness for God. And finally there is personal conflict in the church which ruins our witness of love.

Sometimes, other people do the devil's work for him by ridiculing our faith, opposing the work of the church, and even persecuting Christians.

The last enemy

Death is described in Scripture as "the last enemy". It is a barrier through which we have to pass before we can enter eternal life in God's presence.

TO THINK ABOUT ...

The enemies of the Christian life are the world, the flesh, the devil and death.

- What does "the world" mean for you? What systems of thought or behaviour try to influence you and distract you from the Christian life? What are the main influences in the wider world today?
- How does "the flesh" affect your life with God? What are your particular temptations and sins? Why are they dangerous?
- Why is it important that we acknowledge the existence of the devil as a personal evil spirit?
- How is death an enemy of the Christian life?

Jesus has already passed through death and come back to life again – he has defeated this enemy so that it cannot prevent us entering heaven.

But we must still die. The Christian has nothing to fear from death itself, although the act of dying is often a sad and sometimes a frightening occasion. It reminds us of the weakness of human life which will only be restored in heaven.

BIBLE CHECK

The world John 17:15-18; 1 John 2:15-17
The flesh Matthew 26:41; Galatians 5:15-25
The adversary Mark 8:31-33; 1 Peter 5:8,9; Ephesians 6:11,12
The last enemy 1 Corinthians 15:53-58; Philippians 1:21-24

POSTSCRIPT

Although Christians face opposition from many directions, they need never be defeated because the power of God is greater than all their enemies.

Christ has already defeated all these enemies by his death and resurrection.

- How does this knowledge help you to face the world? the flesh? the devil? and death?

Pray that God will help you to see the areas of your life and the society around you that are influenced by these enemies. Ask for his strength to stand up to evil, defeat temptation, fight against the devil and face death with confidence in Christ's resurrection life.

BIBLE SUMMARY
THE DEVIL STILL ROARS

The devil, sometimes called Satan or the adversary, appears right at the start of the Bible narrative, when he tricks Adam and Eve into disobeying God (Genesis 3:1-7). He is always around, prompting people into wrong courses of action (eg 1 Chronicles 21:1,7), until he will be finally destroyed at the end of time by God (Revelation 20:10).

The spiritual being

The Bible does not speculate about the origin of Satan. The main clues are in Isaiah 14:12-17, Luke 10:18 and 2 Peter 2:4, which imply that he is a spiritual being (or angel) who rebelled against God. Sometimes he is shown as being in God's presence, opposing his plans (Job 1:6,7; Zechariah 3:1,2).

An evil being

His sole purpose is to destroy or hinder God's work (1 Peter 5:8,9). So he tried to make Jesus stray from God's path (Matthew 4:1-10).

Sometimes he tempts people in subtle ways, disguising his real motives and character by plausible-sounding ideas (2 Corinthians 11:14). At other times his opposition is clear and his attack direct, as when he takes total control of people as in Mark 5:1-13.

A dying being

He cannot possess those who are already indwelt by God's Spirit, although he can tempt them and if they are not careful, defeat them. But Jesus' death on the cross has already sealed his fate. His power is limited – like that of a wild animal tied to a rope – and he will never get what he wants. He is no match for God.

Knowing where you stand

KEY TRUTH

God wants us to be sure about the permanence of his love.

Saved for ever

A person who saves someone from drowning does not let go of them if they struggle in fear. Neither will God let go of us, even if at times we struggle to get away from him.

Because we have been "born again" or adopted into God's family, we have become new people. We will never be the same again. We were "saved" when we received Jesus, and all who receive him have been given the unbreakable promise of eternal life.

We cannot lose that life; it cannot be taken from us. It depends, not on us living perfectly, but on God who cannot lie.

Kept from falling

God's promise does not refer only to life after death. He does not keep us safe just for heaven. He wants to keep us close to him all through our lives, too.

He promises to protect us in situations which we could otherwise not cope with, although he will often allow us to be stretched beyond what we believe our limits to be. And when we are tempted, he offers the strength to say "no".

The Bible often refers to God as a fortress. Those who trust him are safe and will not be defeated, however hard the battle around them.

Equipped for victory

All we have thought about may make the Christian life sound negative and passive. Certainly, we do need to be realistic about the strength of the opposition we face and the impossibility of our withstanding it unless we depend entirely on God.

However, being a Christian is in fact a very positive way of living. It is actually an assault on the enemies of God. Having got our defences in order, we can go on the attack.

Jesus promises victory – over temptation, difficulty, and all opposition. We can work for these victories through prayer, by applying the truth of the Bible, telling others about Jesus, and by careful avoidance of sin.

Constantly forgiven

It was hot and dusty where Jesus lived and people would wash the feet of visitors when they entered the house. Once, when Jesus did this to his closest followers, he said, "A person who has had a bath needs only to wash his feet; his whole body is clean."

Christians have "had a bath" in the forgiving love of God before setting out on the Christian

TO THINK ABOUT ...

Think about a time when you sinned and failed God after you became a Christian.

- How did the sin affect your relationship with God? How did you respond?
- What does the Bible say about sin in the life of a Christian? Can it be forgiven?

God assures you of his love and care for you, even when you sin. Your salvation depends entirely upon him, not your own efforts.

- How does this assurance affect the way you live your life? Does it give you more strength to do what God wants you to do?
- What will you do next time you face temptation?

life. But like the travellers, they can pick up "dust and dirt" – sin along the way – which needs to be forgiven and regularly washed out of their lives.

God promises to keep on forgiving and renewing us throughout our lives. But he also expects us to avoid sin as if it were a horrifying disease.

BIBLE CHECK

Saved for ever John 6:38-40;
Romans 8:1,2,38,39
Kept from falling Matthew 6:13; Jude 24;
Psalm 59:9,16,17
Equipped for victory Psalm 98:1,2;
1 Timothy 6:11,12; 1 John 5:4,5
Constantly forgiven John 13:8-11; 1 John
2:1,2; Matthew 6:14,15

POSTSCRIPT

Because we can be confident about our relationship with God, we can serve him boldly and confidently, too.

Thank God for his constant love for you, and for his forgiveness available in Jesus Christ. Tell him that you want to have victory over temptation, difficulty and opposition, and ask for his Spirit to give you the strength to remain faithful to him in these times.

THE UNFORGIVABLE SIN

Occasionally some Christians become convinced that they have committed such a bad sin that they can never be forgiven. However, their very concern shows they can still be forgiven, because they know they have done wrong and are concerned about it. The only person whom God cannot forgive is the one who will not admit his need of that forgiveness (1 John 1:6).

Blasphemy against the Spirit

Jesus did say that there was one unforgivable sin (Matthew 12:31). He called it "blasphemy against the Spirit".

Blasphemy against the Holy Spirit is deliberately (not just mistakenly) attributing to Satan the work of God. Only a person totally opposed to God can say that. They will never want forgiveness, and so will not receive it.

Apostasy

Hebrews 6:4-8 says that a person who has experienced Jesus' new life cannot be forgiven if they commit "apostasy". This is much more than, say, Peter's denial of Jesus (Mark 14:66-72). Peter was forgiven.

Apostasy describes the action of a person who leaves the family of God (of which they were not true members) and then seeks to destroy it. Such a person is unable to receive anything God offers.

Not guilty

Sometimes, Christians become depressed because their feelings of guilt are so strong and they feel they cannot be forgiven. Jesus not only forgives, but washes away our guilt. We need to forgive ourselves, and not sink under a weight of guilt. (See Psalm 103:1-14.)

Knowing the truth

KEY TRUTH

The Christian life is based on the truth God has shown to us, and he wants us to put that truth into practice.

Set free by truth

Jesus once said, "You will know the truth, and the truth will set you free" (John 8:32). When we have accepted God's truth about ourselves, our needs, and Jesus' death, we are set free from the prison of sin: it cannot separate us any longer from God's love.

We are also set free from ourselves. Jesus offers us the help we need to overcome the faults and failings which hurt others but which we have been powerless to change.

And he sets us free from Satan's clutches, too. The powers of evil may attack us, but they can no longer harm us.

Surrounded by truth

Everyone knows that there are right and wrong ways of doing certain things, like building a house. If the rules are not followed, the house will fall down.

God created people to live according to certain rules. They are summarised in the Ten Commandments. They are like a moral and spiritual guidebook. They tell us to love God, care for others, and look after the things he has given us.

Far from being restrictive, preventing us from doing what we would like, God's truthful laws are like the fence at the top of a steep cliff. They prevent us from harming ourselves and each other.

Taught by the truth

The best way to find out the truth about someone is to question them personally and compare their answers with what others say about them.

God promised that because Christians know him personally, they will also understand and know the truth about him, his world and his purposes. But we do not suddenly receive a whole library of knowledge when we become Christians.

As God teaches us in our experience, we have to check that experience against what the Bible says. God's word always reflects God's truth, whereas our experience – or our understanding of it – may be imperfect.

Inspired by truth

Jesus often found himself in difficult situations. So, too, did his first followers. But they never tried to get out of them by telling lies.

When Peter lied about his relationship with Jesus (he denied he knew him just when Jesus needed his support), he deeply regretted it.

TO THINK ABOUT ...

Write down some of the things about God, the world, and yourself that you have learned as a Christian.

- How did you learn these things? Think about the different ways God uses to teach you the truth about himself, his world and yourself.
- Do you find some aspects of the truth uncomfortable? Do you find other aspects encouraging?
- How does the truth set you free?

King David in the Old Testament used trickery and murder to get what he wanted, and he was punished by God.

The whole Christian life is based on truth. God never does wrong, nor does he lead his people to do wrong. He expects us to think, speak and act honestly, even if others around us do not.

BIBLE CHECK
Set free by truth John 8:31-36; John 14:6; Galatians 5:1
Surrounded by truth Exodus 20:1-17; Matthew 5:17-20
Taught by the truth Psalm 119:9-16; John 17:17; 1 John 2:20-22
Inspired by truth Ephesians 4:25; 1 Peter 2:22

POSTSCRIPT
It is easier to be truthful in practice if we are also thinking truthfully in our minds.

Truth is not just about knowledge; Christians must live truthfully as well.
- How does God's law help you to live truthfully? Is it simply a list of rules and regulations?
- Are there any situations in which you find it difficult to speak or live truthfully? Why do you find them difficult? What can you do to be more truthful?

Thank God for his truth which sets you free. Ask him to forgive you for the times when you try to avoid the implications of his truth. Pray that his Spirit of truth will help you today.

LAW AND GRACE

Paul's letter to the Galatians, like most of the New Testament letters, was written to meet a special need. The Christians in Galatia had started to make fresh rules for new converts to follow (Galatians 1:6-9). So Paul explains the uses and limits of rules in the Christian life.

Faith is the key
The Christian life begins by trusting (or having faith) in Jesus Christ and in all he has done. We cannot have a right relationship with God just by keeping his rules, because in fact we have broken at least some of them already (2:16; 3:6).

Jesus has saved us from the law which demanded that we pay in full the punishment for our sins (3:10-14).

The law came first
God's law was given centuries before Christ came to earth. It was meant to help people understand God's nature and how they should live (3:19,23-26). It was a temporary measure until Jesus came to deal with it and give God's final teaching to humanity (4:4-7).

Rules out; obedience in
The Christian life is not the product of detailed human rules about behaviour, or of superstitious ritual (4:8-10). However, that does not mean that Christians can do anything they like; the Holy Spirit helps us to live in obedience to God's will (5:1,13-24).

Knowing your privileges

KEY TRUTH

God has given us many privileges to inspire and encourage us in our Christian lives.

Belonging to God's family

The "family" of God – all those who love and serve him – is not restricted to one place. It extends across the whole world. And it stretches right back into history.

Belonging to such a well-established group is a privilege because we know that as members of it we are right at the centre of God's purposes for the world.

And it is an encouragement because we can look back on how other Christians have triumphed over temptation and conquered evil. From their example we can learn how to live Christian lives, and know that what we face has been faced before – and God's power seen in it.

Being an ambassador

An ambassador is a person chosen to represent their country's interests in a foreign land. They tell people what their country believes, and they help their compatriots when they visit that land.

Every Christian is an ambassador for Christ, representing his kingdom in a "foreign" land – a society which does not care much for him.

That means our first loyalty is to Jesus. Christians will always try to live as he wants, rather than follow the standards of the world around them. And their duties never stop; they are ambassadors wherever they go. People will judge our Lord by what we do and say.

Bearing good news

The Christian is a messenger as well as an ambassador. We have been given a message to pass on to other people; the message, or good news, of Jesus' life, death and resurrection.

The Christian faith is not something to be kept secret. Jesus told us to proclaim it to all who will listen. God is concerned for everyone, everywhere.

Not all Christians have a special gift for preaching or teaching. But everyone can tell others the simple facts that God cares for them and can be known by them. It is a message the world badly needs to hear, because so many people feel lost or anxious, and do not have the joy of knowing God.

Becoming a saint

People often think of saints as very holy men and women who did miracles and who have statues or pictures made of them.

TO THINK ABOUT ...

Many companies and organisations give special privileges to their valued customers or employees.

- What kinds of privileges are available in the society around you? Do you belong to any clubs or groups that give you special benefits?
- Now make a list of the privileges you have because you are a child of God (eg you can pray to your heavenly Father). How do these privileges compare with those that the world offers?

Privileges are closely connected with responsibilities.

- Do you have any new responsibilities now that you belong to God? What are they?

494 Living the Christian Life: Knowing

But the Bible calls every Christian believer a saint. One of our privileges is being regarded so highly by God. The trouble is, we are not always very saintly people!

So we are called to live as saints – to grow in our faith and understanding so that we shall actually be what God has intended we should be. It is not a matter of whether or not we feel saintly, nor of adopting an artificial air of other-worldliness. Rather, we are simply to reflect the love of Jesus through our daily lives.

BIBLE CHECK

Belonging to God's family Romans 8:15,16; Hebrews 11:32–12:2

Being an ambassador 2 Corinthians 5:20; Ephesians 6:18-20

Bearing good news Acts 8:4; 2 Kings 7:3-10; Luke 8:38,39

Becoming a saint Colossians 1:1-4; Philippians 2:1-13

POSTSCRIPT

It is easy to take our privileges for granted, so it helps if we thank God for them regularly.

- Ambassadors receive all they need to live on from the country they represent. Why are Christians called ambassadors for Christ?
- How will you tell someone the good news about Jesus this week?

Thank God for the privilege of being his child. He provides all you need to be a holy, faithful ambassador for Christ. Tell him that you don't want to take these privileges for granted, and pray for opportunities to serve him.

BIBLE SUMMARY

WHO IS ON THE LORD'S SIDE?

Joshua had what seemed to be an impossible task ahead. Moses, the man who led Israel out of slavery in Egypt, was dead. And Joshua had the job of helping a vast number of people settle into a new country (Joshua 1:1-5).

But he was promised the power of God, who had not failed Moses (1:5). His own courage was to be strengthened by reading the Scriptures (1:8,9).

Promises, promises

As God's people moved into the new land, they were told to keep God's commands and do things his way. At first they promised to do so (1:16-18), but they soon forgot what they had said (7:10-15).

But not Joshua. At the end of his life, having gone through many difficulties and suffered many disappointments, his faith remained as strong as ever. "Choose for yourselves this day whom you will serve," he said – either the false gods or the real God. "But as for me and my household," he added, "we will serve the Lord" (24:15). The privilege of serving God dominated his whole life.

The need for growth

KEY TRUTH

However long a person has been a Christian, they still have more to learn and experience of God's love and purposes.

Growing into Christ

If anyone wants to know exactly what living a Christian life involves, they need only read the accounts of Jesus' life. Neither his enemies nor his closest friends could point to any wrong actions or words.

He is the example we are to follow, the standard by which our words and deeds can be measured. When faced with a difficult decision, it is often helpful to ask, "What would Jesus have done if he was here?"

But we are not only to grow more like him. The Bible reminds us of the need to grow closer to him personally: to love him more dearly and serve him more faithfully.

Growing in faith

As a friendship develops between two people, so too does trust. Christians learn steadily how to trust Jesus and so their faith grows stronger.

God has given us many promises: to help, provide, lead, teach and protect his followers. Most Christians find it helpful to take God at his word in one or two small things. Then, as they learn to trust him and apply his truth, they can move on to bigger things.

But God is not like an automatic machine giving us whatever we ask. His promises relate to his purposes for us, so growing in faith also involves discovering his will.

Growing in knowledge

"Knowledge" in the Bible often means "understanding" or even "experience", rather than simply "knowing facts". Knowing God involves growing not only in Bible knowledge, but also in understanding his will.

In a human friendship a person may know instinctively how the other feels or what they want. The aim of the Christian life is to develop a deep awareness of God's general purposes, so that we can discover more easily what he specifically wants in each situation.

This understanding grows through prayer, Bible reading, worship, and the willingness to put Jesus first in everything.

Growing in love

One of the hardest parts of the Christian life is allowing Jesus to change our habits and attitudes, and especially our relationships with other people. The selfishness which prefers to dominate others, rather than submit to them, dies hard.

So every Christian has to grow in love, by learning how to say sorry, how to care for

TO THINK ABOUT …

Think about a family member or friend who is very close to you.

- Has your relationship with that person developed over time? Why is it important that friendships and relationships grow?
- How is your relationship with God similar? Does it need to grow in some of the same ways?

others, and how to be kind even to those who hate or despise in return.

The rule for Christian living is God first, others second, and self last. And to apply that, we need the help of the Holy Spirit. The standard is too high to achieve on our own.

BIBLE CHECK

Growing into Christ Ephesians 4:15; 1 Peter 2:21-23

Growing in faith Luke 17:5; 2 Corinthians 10:15; 2 Thessalonians 1:3

Growing in knowledge Colossians 1:9,10; 2 Peter 3:18

Growing in love 1 Thessalonians 3:12,13; 4:9-12

POSTSCRIPT

A growing person does not have to wait until they reach a certain stage before they can be useful to God; serving him is in fact an important aid to growth.

Make a list of the areas of your life with God that have already grown since you became a Christian.

- Has your relationship with God stopped growing? If so, why?
- Are there particular areas of your Christian life that you need to grow in right now?
- What practical steps will you take to grow in these areas?

Thank God that he is so immense that you will never stop growing in your relationship with him – there will always be more of his love and will to discover. Pray that he will challenge you to grow in your Christian life.

BIBLE SUMMARY

BECOMING LIKE JESUS

Christians are sometimes – and usually wrongly – accused of being a closed group of people who conform to certain customs. Like the rest of God's creation, there is enormous variety among Christians. As we grow in our faith, we begin to conform not to each other but to the character of Jesus.

Our nature renewed

The Bible teaches that every human being is created in the image of God (Genesis 1:26). But human sinfulness has damaged and distorted our likeness to God.

During the Christian life the damage is slowly repaired by the Holy Spirit (Colossians 3:9,10), and our whole self is finally and completely renewed in heaven (1 John 3:2).

God's will for us

Every Christian aims to be like Jesus – and every non-Christian expects us to be like him. The process of becoming like him – honouring God in all that we do – is sometimes called "sanctification", or growth in holiness (1 Thessalonians 4:3). The Holy Spirit will point out things in our lives which need correcting (John 16:8). And, like growing children, there are certain things we can do to aid this process.

The Bible is called "food" or "milk", and so we can draw spiritual nourishment from it (1 Peter 2:2). Using the gifts which God has given us is like exercising our bodies (1 Corinthians 9:26,27; Ephesians 4:11-16). And keeping in touch with God through prayer is like breathing fresh air (Ephesians 6:18).

The source of growth

KEY TRUTH

The Holy Spirit is the source and inspiration of all Christian growth.

The Spirit lives in us

The Christian is like a house with many "rooms" – he or she is a person with many interests, relationships and talents. When we become a Christian, the Holy Spirit enters our house – our life. Slowly he moves from part to part clearing away the dust of sin, opening up the windows of the mind so that God's light can shine in, filling us with new life.

But he does not always break down locked doors. He dwells within us, but may not have access to every part, unless we invite him in to do his work, and help us grow as Christians.

The Spirit sanctifies us

The Holy Spirit wants to make us "holy" – people reflecting the love and goodness of God. He does this in three ways.

- First, he points out what is wrong in our life, perhaps through our conscience, some Bible passage, or even through another person.
- Then he gives his help and strength to overcome that sin or habit.
- And thirdly, he replaces sinful words and actions with what the Bible calls the "fruit of the Spirit". These are positive attitudes like love and patience which are expressed in practical service to God and other people.

The Spirit empowers us

The New Testament word for the power the Holy Spirit gives us is *dunamis*, from which comes the word for dynamite. His power can be explosive!

Sometimes he will blast away things that stand in the way of God. He will break down barriers which other people set up in order to protect themselves from the gospel of Jesus Christ.

But often, his power is also experienced when he gives us patience to endure suffering, or strength of character and wisdom to do a difficult task. He can be powerful as dynamite; he can also be gentle as a dove.

The Spirit unites us

Each Christian is a member of God's family, but like an ordinary human family, the members do not always get on well with each other. In fact, the family is made up of many differences of opinion.

But the Holy Spirit is concerned to help us show our faith by working together despite our differences. That is why he gives special abilities or "gifts" to Christians, so that we can both give to and receive from each other some spiritual truth.

TO THINK ABOUT ...

God gave you his Holy Spirit when you became a Christian.

- What does the Bible say about the Spirit's role in the Christian life?
- Are you aware of the Spirit's work in your life, or do you find him too mysterious and so ignore him?
- Are there any areas of your life that you try to keep away from God's Spirit? Perhaps you don't want these areas to change, or perhaps you would like to change them in your own strength.

The Spirit also "reconciles" people: he helps to heal broken relationships, and brings love and peace to situations where before there was hate and discord.

BIBLE CHECK
The Spirit lives in us Revelation 3:20; John 14:16,17
The Spirit sanctifies us Ephesians 4:30; 1 Peter 1:14-16
The Spirit empowers us Romans 15:13,17-19; Ephesians 3:20; 2 Timothy 1:7
The Spirit unites us Ephesians 4:3; 1 Corinthians 1:10-13

POSTSCRIPT
Growing in the Christian life involves submission to the Holy Spirit, and also willingness to learn from other Christians.

The Spirit's work is not just to clean up our lives; he is also the source of positive growth.
• Which part of the fruit of the Spirit is most needed in your life right now?
• Why is it important that the Spirit unites you with other believers?

Thank God that he has given you the gift of his Spirit. Allow the Spirit to flow through your life and transform you. Ask for his power and strength to cultivate every part of the fruit of the Spirit.

BIBLE SUMMARY
THE FRUIT OF THE SPIRIT

One of the simplest, most beautiful but also most demanding descriptions of the Christian is found in Paul's letter to the Galatians (5:22,23). He lists nine virtues, which he calls "the fruit of the Spirit", which cannot be produced merely by our own effort but are the result of God's work in our lives (compare John 15:18). This is what they mean:

Love towards God
"Love" means self-sacrificing devotion to God. "Joy" refers to our thankfulness for all that he has done for us through Jesus, and "peace" reminds us of our healed relationship with him. As the fruit grows in us, we are likely to become more loving, joyful and peaceable people, bringing a sense of God's presence to others.

Patience towards people
"Patience" is the virtue of keeping calm with people who are aggressive or thoughtless in their attitude towards us. "Kindness" means being thoughtful and sensitive about people's needs. And "goodness" is the willingness to help people practically with no thought about the cost to ourselves.

At peace with ourselves
The Christian becomes "faithful" in the sense of being someone others can trust not to let them down. They are "gentle" too, which implies being humble, reasonable, considerate and unselfish. And finally, the Christian is "self-controlled", experiencing the power of God's Spirit in every area of human weakness.

The evidence of growth

KEY TRUTH

Christian growth can be measured by the steady changes which take place in a person's life.

A growing experience

Jesus is alive! That has been the cry of Christians in every generation. They believe it for two reasons. One is that they can point to the historical certainty that Jesus rose from the dead. And the other is that they can see evidence of his influence in their lives. Looking back, they can see how he has helped them overcome sin and temptation. But above all, they can recall times when God has acted in some way in their lives: answering prayers, using their words or actions to encourage other Christians or to bring people to Christ, and showing he is in control in some difficulty or problem.

A growing confidence

As we begin to see God at work in our own lives and in the lives of others around us, our confidence in God's promises and power will increase and our fears will decrease. As that happens, we will be encouraged to ask him to do greater things.

The New Testament often speaks of boldness in approaching God and in attempting things for him.

But of course, Christian confidence is always in what God is both able and willing to do. There is no place in the Christian life for the kind of over-confidence which is not humbly depending on God at all times.

A growing usefulness

God has something for each Christian to do. It may be a specific job within the church – for example preaching, or counselling others. It may be showing his love in appropriate ways in our day-to-day life.

The Holy Spirit has showered all kinds of "gifts" on the church, which those who receive them are to use for the benefit of everyone else. Teachers and preachers, artists and administrators, people who can organise and others who can help.

One of the Bible's most touching stories of usefulness is that of John Mark. He found the going too hard while travelling with Paul, who later refused to take him back, even though others trusted him. But at the end of his life Paul called for Mark, saying how useful he was.

A growing battle

Shortly after Jesus was baptised by John the Baptist at the start of his public ministry, he experienced severe temptation. It is a common experience: great blessing is sometimes followed by tough spiritual warfare and

---

TO THINK ABOUT ...

Your Christian life is living evidence of the power of God.

- What experiences or characteristics could you point to in your own life to show that Jesus is alive and is now your Saviour and Lord?
- Do you have more "evidence" now than when you first became a Christian? Should you?
- How does this evidence affect your confidence in God?

testing. It has been said that the devil only concerns himself with those who threaten his temporary hold on the world. A Christian determined to serve Jesus is just such a threat.

So growing Christians may also find themselves fighting Christians; the battle gets hotter as faith grows stronger.

BIBLE CHECK

A growing experience 1 Corinthians 15:3-8; Acts 12:5-11

A growing confidence Ephesians 3:12; 6:19,20

A growing usefulness Acts 13:13; 15:37-40; 2 Timothy 4:11; Romans 12:4-8

A growing battle 2 Corinthians 2:10,11; 1 Thessalonians 2:17,18

POSTSCRIPT

The Christian will be encouraged by becoming aware of growth, but the person who spends time looking for growth is likely to become self-centred.

Sometimes you may not even notice that you are growing until you look back over a period of your life and see what God has done. At other times, the changes will be clearer.

- Are there new ways you could serve within your local church?
- Are you aware of any spiritual battles in your life? Are these the result of your growing faith?

Thank God that your faith in him brings real changes in your life. Pray that his Spirit will help you to become more like Jesus, so that everyone will be able to see that he is your living Saviour and Lord.

THE BATTLE FOR THE MIND

A verse in the Old Testament book of Proverbs is translated in one Bible version as: "As he thinketh in his heart, so is he" (Proverbs 23:7, KJV). Throughout the Bible the mind – our inner attitude and real beliefs – is seen as the key to spiritual growth. If our thoughts are wrong, our actions can never be right (Matthew 7:17-20).

Become a non-conformist

Every group of people tends to have its own agreed standards and way of looking at things. In some cases these are quite opposite to Jesus' teaching. The world around may say, "Take all you can get." But Jesus said, "Give all you have." So if we are to lead a Christian life, we cannot always think in the same way as others (Romans 12:2). Jesus said that our old, sinful approach to life was to be finished with for ever (Mark 8:34-37).

Let your mind be renewed

The Bible never says "don't" without also saying "do". So God remoulds our minds from the inside (Romans 12:2), putting in them his love and laws (Hebrews 10:15,16). At the same time, he tells us to concentrate on what is good, holy and of God (Philippians 4:8), and thus to develop renewed minds (Ephesians 4:22-24).

Our new way of thinking is characterised by the humility and concern which Jesus himself showed (Philippians 2:3-9). In fact, the Christian has the privilege of being given insight into Jesus' own mind (1 Corinthians 2:15,16).

The secret of growth

KEY TRUTH

Prayer is the chief means by which Christians maintain and develop their relationship with God.

In touch with God's purposes

A person taking part in a major activity involving many others needs to keep in touch with the organiser. The participant needs to know exactly what job the organiser wants them to do.

Prayer is a way of keeping in touch with what God wants us to do. If we pray in accordance with his purposes, then he promises to give what we ask at the right time. But if we neglect prayer, it is easy to stray from his plan.

Prayer is nothing more or less than conversation with God. It is a natural and important part of our relationship with him. What is more, he really wants to hear us!

Aware of God's presence

If you are talking to a person, it is impossible not to be aware of their presence! But when we pray, it is sometimes helpful to repeat Jesus' promise, "I am with you always"; he is present, although we cannot see him.

Sometimes, when we pray, we will feel him near us, perhaps almost with a physical sensation, or by a deep awareness inside. But what we feel is less important than what prayer actually does. It brings us close to God. Jesus, through his death, has broken down the invisible barrier of sin which once had barred us from God's presence. Now, the simplest prayer is like having a personal audience with a king, who cares for us and longs to help us.

A source of God's power

Some remarkable things happened when Jesus' early followers prayed. Many people became Christians through their preaching. Others were healed of their diseases. Peter and Paul were both released from prison by God's powerful intervention as a result of prayer.

Even Jesus prayed, sometimes all night, and he told his followers that some works of God could only be achieved by concentrated periods of prayer which were not stopped even for food.

It is often true that the prayerless Christian is a powerless Christian. God sometimes chooses to channel his power to us and others when we pray.

Taking time to pray

Jesus sometimes looked for a quiet place away from all disturbances so that he could pray to his heavenly Father. His example is a good one to follow.

There is so much to talk to God about. And human nature (and the devil's tempting) can

TO THINK ABOUT ...

Keep a note of the amount of time you spend in prayer over one week, and what you pray for.

- Do you find prayer exciting, boring, invigorating, difficult, or something else? Do you think this relates to your understanding of what prayer is?
- If prayer is the secret of Christian growth, why do we sometimes think we can get by without praying?
- Can you identify common themes in your prayers? Are there aspects you are missing?

find all sorts of excuses for avoiding it. So it is often helpful to set aside a convenient time on most days to pray, just as you set aside time to eat. And keeping a list of things to pray about will help you to forget nothing.

Paul also reminded his readers to pray at all times. A brief prayer in the middle of the day, when we are especially conscious of our need for God's help, or when we are thinking of someone else, is important and effective.

BIBLE CHECK
In touch with God's purposes 1 John 5:14,15;
 1 Timothy 2:1-6
Aware of God's presence Ephesians 3:11,12;
 Hebrews 10:19-22
A source of God's power Mark 9:28,29;
 Acts 4:31-33
Taking time to pray Psalm 5:1-3; Luke 6:12

POSTSCRIPT
Every decision we take, every situation we are in, is a legitimate subject for prayer. But we are also told to pray for others, that they too may know God's power.

Consider how you can establish a regular time of prayer in your life. If you have never done this before, start by setting a realistic goal – perhaps 10 minutes every day. In time, you will want to increase this!
• How can you be aware of God's presence in your prayer times? What distractions do you need to deal with?
• How does prayer bring change and growth?

Thank God that he is listening to you now. Bring him your concerns for yourself and for the world around you.

BIBLE SUMMARY
WHAT IS PRAYER?

Prayer is often hard to understand, as well as to practise. But there are two important facts on which it depends.

Open to God
People sometimes ask why God wants us to pray for things when Jesus has said that he already knows our needs (Matthew 6:8). The main reason is that the act of asking implies a humble dependence on God, which is the basis of the Christian life (Matthew 6:8). God delights to give good gifts to those who ask him.

If we are able to receive his gifts humbly, we will be more likely to use them properly. Besides, while we pray we may realise we are asking for the wrong thing, so our prayers can be modified (James 4:3-10).

Deeply concerned
Prayer is, in a sense, very easy: just telling God, aloud or silently, how we feel or what we need. We don't even have to use special words. But in other ways it is hard; the prayer which God answers is often hard work, because it is part of our spiritual battle (Ephesians 6:18).

Also, in our praying it is important to mean what we say, sincerely asking for what we believe is his will for us – and to trust that God is actually able to do what we ask (Mark 11:22-25; James 1:6).

Some prayers consist of deep longing and groaning inside our hearts and minds, and cannot be fully expressed in words. But God still understands and answers them, because they are inspired by his Spirit (Romans 8:26,27).

A pattern for growth

KEY TRUTH

Prayer consists of praising and thanking God, and being sorry for our wrongdoing, as well as asking for things.

Love prayers

The friendship between God and the Christian is marked by love. Love grows between two people as they learn to express their feelings for each other. So Christians grow as they experience God's loving care and learn to express their love for him.

Our love prayers, or "adoration" and worship, tell God we love him for all that he is and for all that he has done for us through Jesus Christ.

Such prayers help us to grow closer to him, deepen our appreciation of him, and keep us open to receiving his help and his gifts. The Psalms are full of love prayers, and many Christians find them helpful as a basis for their own.

Sorry prayers

The wrong things we do can grieve God, and make our relationship with him more difficult.

Each time we pray it is a good idea to start by telling God we are sorry for the sins we have committed. We can then experience his forgiveness in a fresh way, and can clear away the blockages which prevent us knowing his power.

We also need to be willing to say sorry to other people whom we have offended, and to forgive those who have wronged us. We can hardly be open to God's forgiveness if we are bitter and resentful towards other people.

Thank-you prayers

These are like love prayers, but they are a response to specific things that God has done for us or others.

We can thank him for answering our prayers, for providing for our needs, including things we take for granted yet still depend on him for, like a meal we are about to enjoy. We can also thank him for helping or guiding us, and for intervening in some situation.

Saying thank you before we ask for other things can help to increase our faith. It is a reminder of how much God has done already.

Asking prayers

These are the easiest and most common of all prayers but they should really come at the bottom of the list. It is a limited relationship which is expressed only in a series of requests or demands.

The Bible tells us to ask for three things. One is the spiritual resources and blessings God wants to share with us: deeper faith, knowledge of his will, the ability to obey him. Another is our daily needs – food, drink,

TO THINK ABOUT ...

Think about the four elements of prayer mentioned here.

- Does your prayer time usually include all these elements? Are there any that are often missing?
- Why is it important to express praise and adoration to God? Why do we tell God how great he is?
- Do Christians still need to say sorry to God?
- What things can you thank God for today?
- How can you stop your asking prayer from becoming simply reciting a list of demands?

clothes and shelter – because in many parts of the world people do not think of them as God's provision but as an automatic right.

And finally we are to ask for specific things: that someone we love will come to Jesus; that God will act in a situation, and for whatever he knows is good for us to have and enjoy.

BIBLE CHECK
Love prayers Psalm 31:23; 95:17; 113:1-9
Sorry prayers Matthew 6:14,15; Psalm 51
Thank-you prayers Psalm 116; Philippians 1:3-11
Asking prayers Luke 11:9-13; James 1:5-7

POSTSCRIPT
As we grow in the Christian life, prayer becomes more natural and spontaneous. It may sometimes grow stale unless we give each element its proper place.

• Why is it important to have a balance of these four elements of prayer?

The Lord's Prayer that Jesus taught his disciples can be used as a prayer itself, as well as a pattern for praying in our own words.
• Do you use the Lord's Prayer on a regular basis? Should you?

Think about what the words of the Lord's Prayer mean. Then turn it into your own prayer, thanking God for this way to grow in your life with him.

BIBLE SUMMARY
JESUS' PATTERN FOR PRAYER

Jesus did not in fact teach a great deal about prayer; he told his followers to get on with it, because it is natural to talk to our heavenly Father. However, in the "Lord's Prayer" (Matthew 6:7-15) he gave a summary of how to pray and for what: not just a prayer to be recited.

Children and servants
First, we approach God as his children, remembering his greatness – "Our Father in heaven ..." and his holiness – "hallowed be your name". Then we ask that people all over the world will come to love, honour and serve him – "your kingdom come", and that we ourselves may serve him faithfully – "your will be done".

Beggars and debtors
The next phrase reminds us to ask God to provide for our daily needs – nothing is too small for him – and to pray for the hungry and homeless – "Give us today our daily bread". Then we ask his forgiveness, and tell him we forgive those who have wronged us, just as Jesus forgave his murderers before his death – "Forgive us our debts, as we also have forgiven our debtors."

Guarded and kept
Finally, there is a reminder of our weakness: a prayer that God will protect us from the trials which will crush our faith – "lead us not into temptation", and that he will release us from the power of Satan – "deliver us from the evil one".

The problems of growth

KEY TRUTH
The Christian life is not an escape route from difficulty, but a way through difficulty.

Exercising faith
Jesus said that even a tiny amount of faith was all that was needed for God to work powerfully. But he also made it clear that he would not do great things if people did not believe he could.

Faith is not certainty, but trust. Growing as a Christian through prayer depends on our trusting God entirely to do what will most honour him, in his way and in his time.

Actually believing he will answer our prayers is not easy, but if we are too timid to ask, we may not see him work powerfully.

Waiting for answers
God is not always in a rush to do things, for he stands beyond time and is working out his purposes over many centuries. Sometimes we will have to wait a while before he answers our prayers.

This in itself can be a test of our faith: do we really want what we are asking for, and do we really believe Jesus can give it? He told us to keep on asking until we receive.

There are two things to do while we wait. One is to keep looking for an answer, which may be different from the one we expect. The other is to make sure that all our prayers, and our whole life, are lined up with his will.

Keeping alert
The person who wants to do things for Jesus Christ will always find opportunities – a word of explanation about their faith, an act of kindness, a job within the church. There will be challenges, too, and unexpected problems to face.

The Christian who is constantly in touch with God through prayer will be able to make the most of these opportunities and challenges. A short silent prayer at the time will keep our mind focused on him and help prevent us from relying on our own lesser abilities.

The example of Nehemiah in the Old Testament is a good one to follow. He and his helpers prayed quickly about their needs, then worked hard and sensibly at their jobs.

When God seems silent
Many Christians experience times when God seems very far away, when their prayers seem to be unanswered, and when living the Christian life becomes hard and laborious.

It might be that they have sinned against God. Maybe something in their life – a personal relationship, for example – needs resolving. Or they may just be tired, or unwell.

TO THINK ABOUT ...

Think about some of the difficulties that children face as they grow up.

- Does this help you to understand why growing as a Christian can sometimes be difficult or frustrating?
- Are there any aspects of the Christian life that you are finding challenging at the moment? Can you think why?
- What does it mean if God doesn't seem to be answering your prayer?
- How can you learn to be patient?

But it might also be that God himself is leading them through what some have called "the dark night of the soul" – a time when their longing for God deepens and their faith is eventually strengthened, through being tested. Growing up in the Christian life, just like growing as a human person, is not all fun and games.

BIBLE CHECK

Exercising faith Luke 17:5,6; Matthew 13:57,58

Waiting for answers Luke 18:1-8; James 5:7-11

Keeping alert Nehemiah 2:4,5; 4:7-15; Proverbs 3:5-8

When God seems silent Psalm 38:9-22; 42:1-11

POSTSCRIPT

The Bible says Jesus was made perfect (or complete) through suffering. Those who obey him and follow him may find that he calls them to suffering, too, and through it to discover more of his love.

When you face difficulties in your Christian life, God doesn't ask you to pretend there are no problems. If you are sure there is no sin in your relationship with him, then sometimes you must simply wait and trust.

• Is it possible to praise God and trust him, even when you don't understand what he's doing? Why?

Thank God that he knows the problems you face. Tell him that you are trusting him to help you, and ask him to give you enough strength for each day.

GOD'S MYSTERIOUS WAYS

When something unexpected occurs, people often ask, "Why has God allowed this to happen?" Usually it is a sort of complaint; they regard the event as undeserved punishment. But for the Christian, whatever happens can provide an opportunity to move forward in the Christian life, though the question "Why?" may remain.

God's ways are different

Everyone knows that God is greater than any human being, so it is hardly surprising to read in the Bible that his ways and thoughts are beyond human understanding (Isaiah 55:8,9). They are too complex for us to work out (Ecclesiastes 3:11). That is why the Bible encourages us to pray carefully before making major decisions (see Jesus' example in Luke 6:12-16).

Human wisdom is limited

People usually do what they believe is right, but human wisdom can be very far from God's truth because it is not always informed by his law and will (1 Corinthians 2:3-10). Even Christians can be misled and mistaken (1 Corinthians 1:10-13; Galatians 1:6-9).

Despite this, God promises to give us wisdom to know how to act correctly in each situation (James 1:5,6).

A new set of values

In fact, Jesus' teaching is often opposite to the accepted wisdom of the people around us. They usually say it is a sign of God's blessing to be rich; Jesus said it was a sign of his gracious love to be able to give to those in need at whatever cost to oneself (Matthew 5:42). We are so used to our godless ways, that the Christian life can seem very strange and different.

Discovering a new life

KEY TRUTH
The Christian life is like a journey in which there are many things to be discovered.

Journey into life
When Jesus first called a group of twelve men (known as the apostles) to follow him, they literally set off on a journey. Together they travelled around the land, teaching God's truth to all who would listen.

Jesus used the picture of a journey to illustrate the Christian life. He said it is like turning off the broad, easy road of self-indulgence that leads away from God.

Instead, the Christian way is a narrow, steep path. It has many obstacles and is sometimes hard going. But it leads to new life: a life lived in harmony with God, full of new joys and discoveries, which goes beyond death.

A constant companion
The Christian never walks alone. Even when we feel very lonely – perhaps when we are the only Christian in a place where others are hostile to our faith – God is always there.

He promises never to leave us. He will show us what he wants us to do, and how to do it.

He is like an expert guide. He knows the way through the difficulties which lie ahead. And he has many new things to show and teach us as we follow him into the sort of life he wants us to lead.

New every morning
From time to time, ever since the days of the early church, people have claimed that God has given them a completely new teaching. They offer a new, improved version of Christianity. They either allow something which was previously forbidden in the Bible, or they insist on some custom being added to the gospel before a person can be fully recognised as a Christian.

But they are always wrong. God's purposes for his people, and his teaching, never change. Neither do his laws, nor the simple way of faith in Jesus through which we come to him.

His truths are always fresh, however. They never grow stale, and come to us "new every morning". Because Jesus is alive, he is always doing new things in us and for us.

I know where I'm going
Some people who rightly recognise how great God is find it hard to understand that he is concerned with the details of their lives.

But he is – just how great he is! He not only forgives our sins and gives us eternal life, but he also has a special purpose for us in this life too.

That means the path we follow on our "journey into life" has already been prepared

---

TO THINK ABOUT ...
Think of a time when you went on a journey to a new place.
- Were you excited about going somewhere new? How did you feel about leaving familiar places behind?

The Christian life is rather like that. Although Christians leave many things behind, they have an exciting journey ahead of them.
- How does it make a difference to understand faith as a journey, rather than as having already arrived at a destination?
- How can you be sure that you are travelling in the right direction? Where do you look for guidance?

by God. Life is not just a series of accidents; there is a plan to it. That plan is always good, although not always easy.

BIBLE CHECK
Journey into life Matthew 7:13,14; John 10:9,10

A constant companion Psalm 23; Ephesians 3:14-21

New every morning Ecclesiastes 1:9; Lamentations 3:22,23; Galatians 1:6-9

I know where I'm going Ephesians 2:10; Romans 12:2; Hebrews 13:20,21

POSTSCRIPT
Although there are many things to discover in the Christian life, the end is never in doubt. Jesus has prepared a place for us in heaven.

- Is it significant that Christians follow Jesus? What does it mean for you that Jesus has gone ahead of you on the road of life?
- What are the costs in following Jesus?

Thank God for the excitement of the journey of faith. Thank him for your companions on the journey – Jesus ahead of you, the Spirit with you, and fellow Christians around you. Ask for his help to follow faithfully.

BECOMING A DISCIPLE

The word "disciple" means a follower, one who learns from their teacher. Jesus does not want passive converts, but active disciples, people who will go on to discover the richness of the Christian life.

Jesus comes first
Jesus said that nothing should come between him and the Christian. Even family relationships would weaken our discipleship if they interfered with it (Luke 14:26).

However, he made it clear that families were not to be neglected (Mark 7:9-13; John 19:26,27).

A rich person once asked what he had to do to become a follower of Jesus. Jesus told him to sell all his possessions and give the money to the poor. In his particular case, he would have done anything for Jesus except that. But Jesus made it clear that there can be no exceptions; love for Jesus is the Christian's priority. He wants us to put all that we have and are at his disposal (Luke 18:18-30; compare 9:23-25).

A willing sacrifice
Jesus does not require his followers to make sacrifices or give to the church in order to gain acceptance by God. Jesus' death was the ultimate sacrifice which brings God and people into harmony with each other (Hebrews 10:11-18).

But God does call us to offer ourselves as living sacrifices (Romans 12:1,2). That does not mean committing suicide, but being willing to do whatever Jesus wants, in the sure knowledge that his way is always best.

Discovering God's way

KEY TRUTH

God has shown us his unchanging purposes in several ways, so that we may be sure of what he wants.

Shown through conscience

One aspect of being made "in the image of God", as the Bible describes us, is that we know there are such things as right and wrong.

Unfortunately, the human conscience can be mistaken in what actually is right or wrong. It can be influenced by local custom and what we have been taught to believe.

But the Holy Spirit renews and revitalises the Christian's conscience. God's law slowly becomes more perfectly "written on our hearts" so that we learn to tell instinctively what we should or should not do.

Shown through God's law

God has not laid down many rules and regulations for the Christian life. He wants us to love, serve and honour him freely, because we wish to and not because we feel we have to.

However, he has given a basic moral code, not just to Christians, but to all humanity. It is set out in the Ten Commandments (see Bible Summary).

These reflect the way God has made the world. They are the "Maker's instructions" on how human life is designed to operate. We cannot expect to find peace and happiness if we break these laws, because we are destroying the very structure of peace and happiness itself.

Shown through Jesus

Jesus Christ was God's final and most complete revelation of who he is and what he wants. In Jesus' life we find an example of how everyone should live, and in his teaching we discover God's principles for daily life.

Jesus showed that God's way has two vital elements:

- The first is loving and serving God at all times, and never compromising our faith.
- The second is to love other people with the same kind of self-giving love which Jesus showed in his life, and particularly on the cross. That means putting their interests before our own.

Shown through the Bible

In the past, God revealed his will through people, often called prophets, and through Jesus' closest friends, the apostles. Their words are written in the Bible, through which God speaks today.

In the Bible we see how God's people in the past discovered his will, which never changes

TO THINK ABOUT ...

It is easy to say that you want to do what is right. It is often much more difficult to discover what is right in some situations.

- Can you think of an occasion when you were unsure what was the "right" way? How did you decide? Do you think you made the right choice?
- How effective is your conscience? Is it always wise to be led by your conscience?
- Do you think the Ten Commandments are still relevant today? Why?
- How did Jesus show God's way?
- How can the Bible help you to know the difference between right and wrong?

in principle, even if today's circumstances seem different.

The Bible is a permanent record of what God has said and done. Through it we can find out how he wants us to live, and what he wants us to avoid.

BIBLE CHECK
Shown through conscience Romans 2:14-16; Hebrews 9:13,14; 10:19-22
Shown through God's law Exodus 20:1-17; Matthew 5:17-20
Shown through Jesus John 13:15-17,34,35
Shown through the Bible Romans 15:4; 2 Peter 3:1,2

POSTSCRIPT
God has promised to help us keep to his ways. If we trust our own abilities, we will fail, but if we draw on his power we can succeed.

Jesus showed the world that it is always right to love God first and then love others.
• How can you put this into practice? Are there any situations you are facing at the moment where this would affect your actions?

Thank God for the ways in which he shows his purposes to the world. Thank him especially for Jesus, and ask for the help of the Holy Spirit to live more and more in line with Jesus' life.

BIBLE SUMMARY
THE TEN COMMANDMENTS

These ten brief instructions in Exodus 20:1-17 are the core of the Bible's teaching about our relationship with God and with one another. They fall into two sections:

Duty to God
The first four concern our approach to God. He is a God who saves his people (v.2; compare Jesus' work on the cross, Matthew 1:21). He cannot have any rival (v.3).

Because God is the mighty creator of the earth and is Lord over all creation (vs.5,6) people cannot, and should not, try to show what he looks like. Nor should we treat the power which belongs only to God as if it came from a lesser source (vs. 4,5). An "idol" is anything we put in the place which God alone should have.

God is holy, and therefore is to be respected in word and deed (v.7). He has created people in such a way that they need to take one day in seven off work to relax and enjoy their God (vs.8-11).

Duty to others
Family life is something precious and to be preserved (v. 12), because it is the basis of a stable society. That is why casual sexual relations are forbidden (v.14); they weaken the family bond and deny the deep unity created between a married couple who share everything.

Human life is sacred and not to be taken (v.13), and the same applies to property belonging to others (v.15). We are not to lie for the sake of personal comfort or gain (v.16). And, as Jesus pointed out, inner attitude is as important as outward act (eg Matthew 5:21-30). So wrong desires which could lead to theft, murder or adultery must be shunned.

Discovering God's will

KEY TRUTH

God promises to guide us in every situation, so that we can do his will.

Praying it through

When we want to find out God's specific purpose for us – whether it concerns the job we are to follow, a task to take on in church, or a problem we have to face – the first thing to do is pray specifically about it.

Jesus did this shortly before his crucifixion. Knowing he was about to be betrayed, and that death as a sacrifice for our sin would certainly follow, he prayed that God would spare him.

But he was determined to do only what God wanted, so he submitted to the Father's will. Through prayer, our will can be guided so that it matches God's will, and we can be strengthened to do it.

Searching the Scriptures

The Bible is often the means God uses to guide us. Our reading of it will make us familiar with his general purposes.

But there will be times when a particular passage "speaks" to us in a very clear way. It seems to fit exactly our situation. It may be a word of challenge to change something, or a word of encouragement to go ahead with a decision we are about to make.

It should not be used like a horoscope or magic oracle, however. People who dip into it at random can sometimes get a shock. One person who is supposed to have done that hit on the verses "Judas went … and hanged himself" (Matthew 27:5) and "Go and do likewise" (Luke 10:37)!

Talking it over

Big decisions are often made more easily after we have discussed them with an experienced Christian friend – perhaps a church leader.

Some people have a special insight into God's plans and our circumstances. Others are able to help us think through a situation, on the basis of their deeper experience of God. Sometimes their invitation to us to do something might in itself be sufficient guidance for us.

Even a casual remark, or perhaps a talk given at a church service or meeting, can be used by God to challenge and guide us.

Making up your mind

When the time comes to make a decision, some doubt may still remain in our minds. This might be for various reasons: our incomplete knowledge of the situation or even because God is testing our faith and our love for him.

There is no infallible rule. If the doubt persists, however, it is usually best not to act in

TO THINK ABOUT …

Think of a few situations for which you need the specific guidance of God – they may be major life changes or seemingly insignificant decisions.

- How do you find out what God wants in each of these situations? Is there only one way to find God's will, or does it differ according to the specific circumstances?
- If God can show you his will in different ways, what should you be looking out for? Where should you be looking?
- Do you think God's guidance is always clear? If it is not, is that because you are not listening properly, or because God is not giving a complete answer?

the way proposed. Christians frequently – but not always – experience a sense of inner "peace" when they reach a right decision. God's Spirit gives them the assurance that they are on the right track.

But such feelings should not be accepted on their own, because they can be wrong. And even with them, we still have to act "in faith", trusting God to take us through to the next stage.

BIBLE CHECK

Praying it through Luke 22:39-46;
Acts 10:9-16,27-29
Searching the Scriptures Romans 15:4;
2 Peter 3:15,16
Talking it over Acts 15:6-23;
Galatians 2:11-16
Making up your mind Acts 15:23-28;
Romans 1:9-15

POSTSCRIPT

Sometimes our sin or self-will makes us unable to receive God's guidance. Then we need to ask him to make us willing to do whatever he says.

- Can you think of other Christians who can help you to discover God's will? Are you willing to listen to them?
- Are there times when we have to act without being sure of God's will?

Ask God to help you to be alert for his direction. Thank him that he will always go with you, and is ready to forgive you even if you go astray.

LIVING THROUGH FAITH

The Bible reminds us that Christians live by faith in Jesus rather than with certain, clear knowledge about the future (2 Corinthians 5:7). This means some decisions are made when we believe that they are what God desires, even if they seem unusual at the time (Hebrews 11:8). But faith is not folly; it is confidence that God has led us so far and will lead us on in the future (Hebrews 11:1,2). It does not mean we should stop using our minds!

God's common sense

One of the most obvious ways God guides us is through the circumstances we are in. The Good Samaritan did not need to ask for guidance in Jesus' parable. He saw a man who had been beaten up and knew that, because of his need, God wanted him to stop and help (Luke 10:33,34).

Similarly, Paul was often hindered from visiting Rome because of pressures to work in other places, although he longed to go there. In addition, the gospel had been preached in Rome already, so it would have been wrong to duplicate the effort (Romans 15:22-29).

Using our gifts

Jesus once told a parable about the use of gifts (or talents) given to those who follow him (Matthew 25:14-30). It was clear that whether his servants had many or few gifts, they all had the ability to use them in the events of daily living.

He looks to us, also, to use the gifts and abilities we have. Even if they seem insignificant to us, they are important to him (Matthew 10:40-42).

Discovering God's word

KEY TRUTH

The Bible is the permanent record of God's revelation to humanity, and contains all we need to know for our new life in Jesus.

A book of truth

The Bible is a unique book. Although it tells the stories of ordinary people and their experiences of God, it is much more than a religious biography.

It is uniquely "inspired" by God. That means he guided the people who wrote it so that what they put down was a true record of God's nature and purposes.

Although the Bible contains 66 books written over some 1,500 years by more than 40 authors, it does not contradict itself. It contains different emphases, of course, and we see how God's revelation grew clearer through the years, but the truth it teaches is consistent.

A book of example

Although the Bible contains passages of pure teaching – some of Paul's letters, for example – mostly it is about people.

Their surroundings were different from ours, but our feelings and problems are much the same as theirs were. So we can read stories of men and women who knew God well, and discover how they coped and remained faithful to him. They will challenge, excite and encourage us.

There are also examples of how not to live, and what mistakes to avoid. The people in the Bible were really human, ordinary people – warts and all!

A book of warning

The Bible includes books of "prophecy" including Isaiah, Jeremiah, Ezekiel, Daniel and Amos in the Old Testament, and Revelation in the New Testament.

Occasionally, they foretell the future. Some of these prophecies have been fulfilled, some have yet to take place, and many apply to more than one period of history.

But the prophets were also God's messengers who warned his people that God was holy and just. They reminded them that they could not lead sinful lives and still receive God's help and favour, and they often spoke of God's judgement or punishment given even to those who claimed to serve him but who, in fact, were evil.

A book of challenge

The Bible presents us with two kinds of challenge. One is through great men and

---

TO THINK ABOUT ...

Note down the parts of the Bible you have studied recently, or heard talks about.

• Are there any sections of the Bible that you have not looked at recently?

It is often easy to fall into the habit of only reading the same passages.

• Is it important to read from the whole of the Bible – both Old and New Testaments? Why?

• What practical steps can you take to make sure you are reading the whole of the Bible, and not just your favourite parts?

• If the Bible is God's word, how should that affect the way you read it?

women of God, who challenge us by their total devotion to him.

The other is more direct. We are challenged by some of the writers to believe the truth which they have written down and to live lives which are worthy of God.

We are also challenged to take his message out into the world which prefers to ignore it. The Bible contains the truth which has brought us to faith in Jesus Christ, and it challenges us to take that message to others.

BIBLE CHECK
A book of truth John 17:17; 2 Timothy 3:14-17
A book of example Hebrews 11:29-40; 12:14
A book of warning Jeremiah 17:1-10; Revelation 2:1-7
A book of challenge Mark 8:34-38; Luke 24:45-49

POSTSCRIPT
The Bible is not a book to be read like any other. To hear God speaking to us through it, we will need to pray for the help of his Holy Spirit.

- Is it possible to understand the Bible's message without the help of the Holy Spirit?

Thank God that he speaks to make himself known. Thank him for the richness and diversity of the Bible. Pray for the help of his Spirit to understand what the Lord is saying to you today.

BIBLE SUMMARY
ALL WE NEED TO KNOW

The Bible contains all we need to know about God, Jesus, ourselves, and the world, in order to live Christian lives (2 Timothy 3:16,17). But it has often been ridiculed or questioned, even by Christian scholars.

Entirely trustworthy
The phrase "inspired by God" in 2 Timothy 3:16 means "breathed out by God" (NIV "God-breathed"). God did not dictate his Bible to its authors, but guided their thoughts so that what they wrote was true and would encourage us to know, love and serve him.

The Bible contains all that we need to know in all matters of belief and behaviour (2 Timothy 3:15). If we follow what it says we can discover the reality of Jesus. It is also "useful for teaching"; we do not need to add any human laws to it. The Holy Spirit who inspired it will interpret it to us (John 16:13-15; 2 Peter 1:20,21).

Not an encyclopaedia
The Bible does not contain all that there is to be known; about science, sport or sociology, for example. It does not even tell us everything about God; the universe would be too small to contain such knowledge!

Paul was dismayed that people were speculating about details which the Bible did not refer to (Colossians 2:8). The Bible speaks with authority about being a Christian and the content of Christian belief. Where it is silent, we are encouraged to trust God's wisdom in not revealing everything to us (1 Peter 1:10-12).

Applying God's word

KEY TRUTH

The Bible is a basic tool for the Christian life; by using it carefully we will keep close to God.

Equipment for the journey

Just as no explorer would dream of leaving home without food, maps and a survival kit, so God does not expect us to go through life without some basic equipment which we will need on the way.

Our chief piece of equipment is the Bible. It provides wisdom for dealing with difficult situations, insight into the real needs of the world, and understanding of both God and his ways.

Above all, it provides us with spiritual "food". Our relationship with Jesus is nourished and enriched when we read and apply his word. It draws us closer to our Guide.

A light for dark paths

The Christian life takes most of us into situations where God's way is far from obvious. Besides, we are travelling through a world which the Bible says is "in darkness" because its affairs are not illuminated by the life and light of Jesus.

So the Bible helps to shed light on things. It explains why people are awkward, why evil exists and how it can be overcome or avoided.

Through our regular reading of it, God will often provide us with just the illumination we need to cope with a situation or to answer a difficult question.

A sword for hard battles

Paul the apostle called God's word the "sword of the Spirit" (Ephesians 6:17). This is because it has a sharp, powerful action. It penetrates beneath the protective layers of pride, selfishness and deceit which people sometimes use to keep God's truth out of their lives.

Sometimes we need to use the Bible like a sword, to cut down opposition to Jesus. When arguments with non-Christian friends fail, the Bible will sometimes succeed in convincing them – but we have to learn to use it carefully, not clumsily.

And when we face temptation, the words of Scripture read, spoken and applied can help us to victory over Satan.

Strength to keep going

The Christian life is like a long expedition through different kinds of country. Sometimes the going is quite easy, like walking on level ground.

At other times it is hard, like climbing a steep rocky hill or struggling through a fast-flowing river or dense forest. It is then that Christians can become disheartened.

TO THINK ABOUT ...

God's word is relevant to all situations and seasons of life.

- When do you turn to the Bible most often? Is it when times are good, or when times are difficult? Why?
- How do you feel your life is going at the moment? What do you think the Bible's message is for you just now?
- How have you used the Bible recently to fight temptation? To discover guidance? To gain strength? To help you worship God?

The Bible provides encouragement and strength to keep going. Sometimes the hardest thing to do is actually to open the Bible; the devil does all he can to make us doubt its power and so stop us using it.

BIBLE CHECK

Equipment for the journey
Psalm 119:97-104; 1 Peter 2:1-3

A light for dark paths
Psalm 119:105-112,130; 1 John 1:5-7

A sword for hard battles
Psalm 119:9-11,113-115; Ephesians 6:17; Hebrews 4:12,13

Strength to keep going
Psalm 119:25-40,73-80; 2 Timothy 2:15

POSTSCRIPT

The Bible does not group together all its teaching about specific issues. To find out what it says, we need to get to know it well.

God gives the Bible to help you in your Christian life. He also gives it to you so that you can help others.

- Can you think of a situation involving other people in which you could use the Bible to offer guidance, comfort or even rebuke?

Thank God for the ways in which his word is relevant and useful for your life. Ask the Holy Spirit to apply God's word to you more and more.

BIBLE SUMMARY

JESUS' VIEW OF THE BIBLE

Although Jesus was the Son of God who came to reveal God's truth to humanity (Hebrews 1:1-4), he used the Bible of his day, the Old Testament, a great deal.

A weapon to fight with

When he was confronted by the devil in the desert before the start of his public ministry, Jesus answered his temptations by quoting the Bible (Matthew 4:1-11). He found in Scripture a perfect and simple answer to his temptations. He did not argue; he just showed what God's word said and stood by it.

Evidence of God's work

Frequently Jesus, and the apostles, quoted the Old Testament to show how events in their experience had been foretold, and to prove that God was still at work. For example, he said John the Baptist was the prophet foretold several centuries earlier by Malachi (Matthew 11:10). And he applied the Bible to those who refused to listen to what he said. As the prophets had warned, they had refused to listen just when God was trying to speak to them in a new way (Matthew 13:14,15).

Support for his actions

Jesus was often challenged by people to justify what he was doing, especially when it conflicted with their customs. So, when he was accused of breaking the Old Testament law about observing the Sabbath, he quoted a precedent – the action of King David – for what he was doing (Matthew 12:1-8).

DISCOVERING

Handling God's word

KEY TRUTH
To discover the truth of God's word, we need to approach it in several different ways.

Reading it regularly

Most Christians find it helpful to spend some time each day reading the Bible, usually just before their prayer time, perhaps first thing in the morning or last thing at night.

This helps to focus our thoughts on God and gives us subjects to pray about. Some lesson from the Bible can be used as a basis for prayer for ourselves or others, or for worship and praise.

Using the Bible in this way, we can read steadily right through it. It is easiest to start with one of the Gospels, say Mark, then move on to some of Paul's letters (Ephesians is a good one to begin with), before turning to the Psalms in the Old Testament. That way, we get a broad taste of the different parts of the Bible.

Soaking it up

In countries where there are few books, or where many people are unable to read, God's word has always been memorised. The habit of learning passages by heart is a good one, even for those who have a Bible readily available.

There are two reasons for this:
- One is that, like Jesus, we then have an instant reply to the devil's temptations. We can answer him back quickly and decisively.
- The other is that we will know exactly what we believe at any time of need. A few basic verses such as John 3:16 will remind us of the basic gospel, and promises such as Matthew 11:28 will help us when we are under pressure.

Studying its teachings

There is much to learn from the Bible about God, the world, ourselves, and what Jesus has done and will do for us.

So in reading the Bible, we also need to fit together the teachings we get from its different parts. Then we can build up a picture of God's truth and will not be prey to false teachers who try to unsettle our faith.

If you have a Bible with cross references in the margin, or if you have a concordance, you can follow through a subject more easily. If not, make some notes as you go along and build up your own index of subjects. There are also some helpful books on Bible teaching available.

Discovering its characters

The Bible has many rich descriptions and accounts of people who learned the hard way to do God's will.

It is thrilling to read about some of them, like the young shepherd who became King

TO THINK ABOUT ...

Make a list of the different ways you can learn (eg listening to a lecture, discussing in a group).
- Which ways of learning do you find most helpful?
- Can you think of ways of studying the Bible that correspond to your different methods of learning?
- How can you put these together into a regular pattern of Bible reading and study?

David. Others are tragic figures, like Samson: physically strong and courageous but morally weak. Yet all of them have both achievements and failures.

They have much to teach us, because we see ourselves and others in them. Time spent gathering stories about such people from the different Bible books in which they appear can be rewarding and enjoyable.

BIBLE CHECK
Reading it regularly Joshua 1:8; Psalm 119:97; 1 Peter 2:2; 2 Timothy 3:16,17
Soaking it up Psalm 119:11; James 1:22-25
Studying its teachings Matthew 7:15-23; 1 Timothy 4:6-10; 6:3-5
Discovering its characters Hebrews 11:24-28; 12:1-3

POSTSCRIPT
When you come to a "difficult" passage in God's word, try to interpret it in the light of other related statements in the Bible in which the meaning is clear. Usually the obvious, most simple explanation is the right one.

Getting to know the Bible is not just about having the right methods. In fact, it is more important to have the right attitude!
- What is the right "heart condition" for reading the Bible? Are there other conditions that might affect this, like location or time of day?
- How can you prepare yourself to read the Bible and receive God's message through it?

Pray that the Holy Spirit would prepare your heart to hear God's word. Tell God that you want to handle the Bible wisely and truthfully, and that you are ready to respond to him.

BIBLE SUMMARY
UNDERSTANDING GOD'S WORD

Some people have claimed that you can make the Bible say what you want it to. That is true, if you take statements or sentences out of their context. There are three things to ask about any passage which will help you understand it. Take as an example the parable of the Good Samaritan in Luke 10:25-37.

What sort of passage?
This is clearly not an historical event, nor is it a closely argued piece of Christian doctrine. It is a parable, a story designed to teach one point. Jesus shows this at the end (vs.36,37). It is a story which was, of course, quite plausible. Something like it probably had happened.

What does it say?
The main elements are that first and foremost we must love God (vs.25-28) but that loving our neighbour goes hand in hand with it as an expression of that love. And our neighbour can be anyone in need, not just someone we happen to like – Jews did not like Samaritans.

What does it mean for me?
Jesus' command to the lawyer (v.37) is always applicable. This is not a nice story to be enjoyed, but an example to be applied.

Belonging to God's family

KEY TRUTH

All Christians are members of God's international family, the church, because of their shared faith in Christ.

One Father

There is only one God. Despite all the different religions and different ideas about him, only one God truly exists. And he, says the Bible, so loved the world that he sent his Son Jesus Christ into it so that we could be reunited with him.

God becomes our "Father" in a special way when we receive the risen, living Lord Jesus into our heart and home, giving them over to his control.

And he is "Father" to all Christians, everywhere. Because we belong to him, we also belong to one great "family", his church.

One Lord

Christians are not only worshippers of the one true God – they are servants of Jesus Christ, too.

Jesus was unique. While being fully human, though sinless – his physical needs and emotional feelings were like ours – he was also fully God. Through him, God took on the limitations of human life in order to reveal himself to us and to bring us back to himself.

That is why the Bible calls Jesus "Lord", a title it usually reserves for God. Jesus is king over the whole world, and he becomes our king, or Lord, when we first trust him. All Christians share this relationship with him.

One Spirit

The Christian church was "born" when God sent his Holy Spirit on the first followers of Jesus. It was six weeks after Jesus' final resurrection appearance (his "ascension"), on the Jewish festival of Pentecost.

The Holy Spirit is active in every Christian: we could not even have come to trust Jesus without the Holy Spirit first showing us our need of him.

So he binds us together in one family. He is the invisible bond who creates unity and friendship between Christians. He gives us "gifts" or talents, to equip us to help each other grow in faith.

One faith

Christians differ widely from one another not only in personality but also in the aspects of the faith they emphasise, and in the ways they express it. But there is really only one Christian faith. It is summed up in the basic truths which all members of God's family share, and which centre on what Jesus did for us.

TO THINK ABOUT ...

Make a list of as many different Christian denominations or movements as you can. Find out about the way Christians worship in another part of the world.

- When you look at all these forms of Christianity, is it easier to note the similarities or the differences? Do Christians often stress their differences from each other? Why do they do this?
- How is it possible that all Christians belong to the same family?
- Think of a time when God's Spirit created unity between you and another Christian. Why is it important that the Spirit does this?

He became a man, died so that our sins could be forgiven, rose from the dead, and now promises eternal life to all who trust him. And those who teach differently, says the Bible, do not belong to the family.

BIBLE CHECK

One Father Acts 17:22-31; Romans 1:18-23; 1 John 3:1
One Lord John 8:51-59; Philippians 2:5-11
One Spirit Acts 1:1-5; 2:1-4; Ephesians 4:1-7
One faith 1 Corinthians 15:1-8; Galatians 1:3-9

POSTSCRIPT

It is important to distinguish between those truths which are essential to genuine Christian faith, and those which, while important, can be interpreted and applied in different ways. Christian unity is based on the former, not the latter.

- What do you think are the essentials of the Christian faith? Compare these with the things you often emphasise in your own faith and church.
- How can you show that you belong to a worldwide Christian family this week?

Thank your Father God that he has called Christians together from all parts of society and everywhere in the world. Pray for the Spirit's help to serve, love and believe together.

BIBLE SUMMARY

ALL ONE IN CHRIST

Christianity is the only faith or ideal which has consistently achieved what all others seek: genuine unity and equality of people while continuing to respect and value their different abilities.

Rich and poor

The first Christians came from a variety of backgrounds. Many were poor and uneducated, working as slaves (1 Corinthians 1:26-29). But some came from the rich and ruling families (Philippians 4:22), and others were evidently well-off householders who gladly opened their homes as meeting places for the church (Romans 16:3-5).

Jew and Gentile

Perhaps the greatest miracle in the early church was the discovery by the first believers, who were Jews, that God's purposes in Jesus included non-Jews (Gentiles) as well (Acts 10:9-16,34-38).

They met to discuss this, and decided that no Jewish customs should be imposed on others (Acts 15:12-21). Later, Paul was to describe how God had broken down the wall of hostility between the groups, something people, not God, had erected (Ephesians 2:11-22).

No distinction

The church knows no sexual, social, racial or cultural barriers (Galatians 3:28). But such distinctions have not been destroyed; so everyone retains their personal identity. Our differences have been put into perspective by something greater: the love of Jesus for all who know they are sinful and need his forgiveness and new life (Colossians 1:15-23).

Belonging to each other

KEY TRUTH

Because Christians all belong to God's family, there is a special bond of love between them.

Baptised into Christ

The one thing above all others which binds Christians together is the fact that we all have to start the Christian life at the same place – the cross of Jesus Christ.

For there, humanity and God were reconciled. From the cross comes the possibility of new, eternal life. Jesus' death shows that we all have the same basic need: we are all sinful, and we need his "salvation".

Baptism, in whatever form it takes, is a symbol of our submission to Jesus Christ through faith in him as our personal Saviour. Being put under, or sprinkled with, water, symbolises death to our old self; rising from the water signifies the new life the risen Jesus gives; the water itself is a sign of the washing away of our sins. By entering God's family in the same way through faith – we are united to each other.

A club for sinners

Sometimes the church is made out to be an exclusive club for good people. In fact, it is just the opposite. It is where people meet who know they are not good, and who need the help of Jesus.

Every Christian already belongs to the family of God, so it is a natural thing to join with others to share our faith, encourage and help each other, and worship God together.

Each person will find some churches more helpful than others. Try to find one where the Bible is clearly taught and believed, and where the people are wanting to learn and grow together.

A new set of friends

When some people become Christians, their old friends (or even relatives) do not want to know them any more. And even if they do, they may not understand their new approach to life.

Within the church, however, will be people whom we can learn to love and trust. They will be able to help us – and we may be able to help them.

Making new friends takes time. It calls for openness and tact by all concerned. But because you already have the bond of faith, do not wait for others to approach you first!

En route for heaven

There is a good answer to those who say it does not matter if Christians don't get on with each other. We will have to get on with each other – in heaven!

Jesus has promised us eternal life. In

TO THINK ABOUT …

Think of which group of people in your life you feel you belong to the most.

- Is this the church? Why or why not? Should it be the church?
- Most clubs or societies gather around a common interest or goal. What should be the basis of the church's fellowship?
- Why has baptism been so important for the church all through its history?

heaven, which is the visible presence of God, the whole church is gathered together to worship and praise Jesus.

Therefore he wants us to make every effort to express and enjoy our oneness on earth. Besides, if the world sees our love for each other, it will be encouraged to take our message seriously.

BIBLE CHECK

Baptised into Christ Romans 3:21-26; Galatians 3:23-28

A club for sinners Ephesians 2:1-7; Hebrews 10:23-25

A new set of friends Romans 16:1-16; 2 Timothy 4:11-22

En route for heaven Revelation 7:9-14; John 13:35

POSTSCRIPT

We should never expect a local church to be perfect – because no single member of it is perfect. And we should expect to find needy people in it, who find only in Jesus the answer to their needs.

Just like any human group, belonging to the church can sometimes be frustrating!

• Have you ever been frustrated with your church? What did you do? What should you do?

• If the church today is a glimpse of life in God's new creation, what things are you looking forward to?

Pray for the group of Christians that make up your church. Thank God for bringing you together, and ask for his Spirit's help to become more open to each other and to new Christians.

BIBLE SUMMARY
A UNIVERSAL CHURCH

The church of Jesus Christ does not consist of human structures or "denominations", so far as God is concerned. So no single group can claim to be "the one true church". The real church is made up of people throughout the world who have submitted their lives to Jesus' control. Jesus cares for and develops their relationship with one another (Ephesians 5:25-27).

Different in emphasis

The differences in human personality are not eliminated by faith in Jesus. They are not meant to be. But they have led to churches which cater for a certain kind of person, which emphasise certain doctrines more than others, or which worship in a certain kind of way.

Paul condemned divisions in the church at Corinth (1 Corinthians 1:10-13), but he did not insist that the separate groups always met together or did everything in the same way. Differences are allowed in the Bible, divisions are not.

United in truth

The New Testament knows nothing of close-knit international "churches". It only knows of a loose federation of local churches, which are joined together by mutual love and concern, and kept in touch with each other by the apostles and other teachers.

What united them was their concern for the truth of the gospel (Philippians 1:3-11). Christians who are agreed on the basic truths of the gospel are able to witness powerfully together in their community, even if they worship in different buildings.

Worshipping together

KEY TRUTH

Worship is a natural expression of a Christian's love for God; sharing with others in worship can stimulate our faith.

The reason for worship

"God is worthy to be praised!" That is what the writers of the Psalms – which are like hymns – conclude.

There are many aspects of God's character which inspire worship. He made, and continues to uphold, the physical universe. He loves, cares and provides for his people. He sent Jesus to die on the cross for our sins. He promises to bring justice and peace to the new world he will make when Jesus returns to earth.

These things give the Christian a sense of thankfulness for his goodness, and wonder at his greatness. They are the basis for Christian worship.

The object of worship

Every human being needs to worship someone or something outside themselves. That is part of being made in the image of God: he has built into human nature the need to worship him.

Worship is simply concentrating our whole mind, heart and life on something in which we find satisfaction. So in some places people build statues to please the spirits which they believe will help or hinder their life.

Elsewhere, people devote themselves to jobs, political ideals, pastimes, and so on. But for the Christian, Jesus, the Father and the Holy Spirit alone are worthy of worship. They alone hold everything together and give meaning and purpose to life.

The source of worship

There are times when we feel more like worshipping God than at others. We may be conscious of some special help he has given us, or, by contrast, we may be anxious about something.

But Christian worship is not dependent on our feelings. It focuses on God who never changes.

And it is inspired at all times by the Holy Spirit within us. He alone can lift our hearts to God. Otherwise we could easily become self-satisfied or depressed.

The value of worship

Worship has three important effects. The first is that it reminds us of how great God is. We need that reminder because daily events can blind us to him, just as a small object in front of our eyes blocks out the sun.

TO THINK ABOUT ...

Make a list of the common elements of your worship with other Christians.

- What does your worship say about who God is and what he has done?
- How is Christian worship different from people's "worship" of other things in their lives?
- Do you find it easier to worship with other Christians, or on your own? Why is it important that you do both?

Secondly, it lifts our spirits. It can restore to us the joy of knowing Jesus, even when we find life difficult. Worship with other people can be very stirring.

And finally, it can open us to the power of God. He loves a cheerful giver, the Bible says; if we give ourselves in wholehearted worship, we are more ready to receive his gifts of love.

BIBLE CHECK
The reason for worship Psalm 147:1-11; 150:1-6
The object of worship Romans 1:20-23; Revelation 4:8-11
The source of worship Ephesians 5:18-20; Philippians 3:3
The value of worship Psalm 96; Acts 16:25-34

POSTSCRIPT
There are many styles of worship. We need to find a church whose worship style suits our personality, and where we can feel part of God's family.

Hymns, songs, prayers and liturgies were all written to express a living, loving relationship with God.

- Are there any elements in your worship that have simply become a routine? Is this good or bad?
- Is it a good thing to worship in different forms, even if some may not be natural to you? How could this be helpful, or unhelpful?
- What practical steps can you take to ensure that your worship is always genuine and fresh?

Worship God now!

MAKE A JOYFUL NOISE!

There are many elements in Christian worship. It is helpful to use all of them, in private as well as in church.

The need for order
Most churches have a structure for their worship. People often find this helpful, because they know what is happening all the time. Paul stressed the need for order, but he also allowed for spontaneous contributions as the Holy Spirit prompted them.

God, he said, is "not a God of disorder but of peace" and people should be helped (or "edified") in worship, not confused. (1 Corinthians 14:26,33,40.)

Songs and silence
Music has always been a vital ingredient in worship (see Psalm 150). A catchy tune and stirring words can unite people in praise, perhaps with hand-clapping (Psalm 47:1; James 5:13), and a quieter, moving hymn can strike a note of wonder.

But silence is helpful, too, when we can sit and remember God's presence with us, think about a passage from the Bible or something which has just been said, and "listen" for God to teach us through it (Psalm 62:1; Ecclesiastes 3:7; Zechariah 2:13).

Body, mind and spirit
Every part of our personality can be used in worship of God. He looks for wholehearted love and service, rather than outward ceremonies which can sometimes be meaningless (Amos 5:21-24; Romans 12:1,2).

In Bible times, people would stand up to pray, sometimes lifting their arms into the air (Psalm 141:2; Luke 18:10-14). It does not matter what position we take up, so long as God is really worshipped.

BELONGING

Sharing together

KEY TRUTH

Worship in church meetings is a time not only for meeting with God, but also for sharing with each other in fellowship.

Praying together

When we meet with other Christians to worship God, it is easy to treat the meeting as if it were our own personal time of worship or prayer which we have when other people happen to be having theirs.

Worship together, however, is really a time when the whole family of God brings its joint praises and requests to the Father.

Coming to the Father with things we are all agreed about can be a powerful way of drawing still closer to each other in love and unity. And God has made a special promise to answer our prayers when we are united in our requests.

Learning together

The Bible is, under the guidance of the Holy Spirit, an open book. Anyone can read and understand it. At least, they can up to a point. But God has appointed some members of his family to be teachers so that we can understand its truth more adequately.

Such people have a special gift of understanding, explaining and applying God's word. Through their ministry the rest of us can grow closer to God and serve him more effectively.

It is therefore helpful to listen to, or read, their teaching. But it is also helpful to meet in groups to discuss each other's insights into the Bible and how we can apply it locally.

Giving together

Part of our worship of God is giving gifts of money or goods to those who work in the church full-time to teach us and to win others

for Jesus. Gifts for other members of the family of God who may be in special need are important, too.

In some churches, the collection of gifts (or the "offertory") becomes part of the worship. In others, a container for gifts is placed by the door. And some people prefer to give directly to people or church agencies of their choice.

There are no set rules about how much to give. But many Christians find that the Old Testament standard of one tenth of their income is a helpful one to follow.

Eating together

The night before he was crucified, Jesus had a meal with his closest friends. During that meal he took a loaf of bread, broke it into pieces and passed it round. Then he passed round a cup of wine for all to drink.

He said that those two staple food items symbolised his broken body and shed blood on

TO THINK ABOUT ...

God did not only give his new life to you; he gives it to all who follow him.
- How should this change your attitude towards other Christians?
- How important to you is your fellowship with others? Why?
- Can you be a Christian on your own?

Make a list of the ways you already share together with other Christians.
- Are there other things you should or could be doing together?
- Is there a prayer concern you have which you could share with someone else or a group?

the cross, through which we can be reconciled to God.

Ever since, the "breaking of bread", "Holy Communion" or "Eucharist", has been central in the worship of Christians. By eating bread and drinking wine together, we recall all that Jesus has done for us. That physical act is a powerful reminder of our unity with him.

BIBLE CHECK

Praying together Matthew 18:18-20; Acts 4:31; 12:6-12

Learning together Acts 2:42; 1 Timothy 4:13

Giving together Malachi 3:8-12; Acts 4:32-37; 1 Corinthians 16:1,2

Eating together Matthew 26:26-29; 1 Corinthians 11:23-32

POSTSCRIPT

Sharing together also includes sharing our joys and sadnesses with those who can appreciate them and who will pray or rejoice with us.

- Why is it important to listen to other people's understanding of the Bible?
- What happens when the church gathers around the Lord's Table to eat bread and drink wine together? Do you think this is a shared experience or a private experience? Or both?

Thank God for the Christians you share with on a regular basis. Pray for them now, and ask the Spirit to make your fellowship more joyful and meaningful.

BIBLE SUMMARY

ONE IN FELLOWSHIP

"Fellowship" is a biblical word which means "sharing together". The original word, *koinonia*, is sometimes used because it is well known. It sums up the love and concern we are encouraged to show to each other.

Centred in Jesus

If we trust him and live as he wants us to, said Jesus' closest friend, John, we have fellowship with him (1 John 1:2-7). This is the basis for fellowship with other Christians. It reminds us of the incredible fact that we are Jesus' friends, and not just servants (John 15:14,15).

Sharing together in Jesus

Our fellowship with each other is therefore a loving expression of gratitude that God has drawn us to himself (1 Corinthians 1:9,10). It is shown in our caring for one another's needs (1 John 3:14-18), by being sensitive to and sharing in one another's joys and sorrows (Romans 12:15), and loving in the same self-giving way as Jesus loved us (John 13:34).

Ministries for each other

KEY TRUTH

God has provided a number of different functions or "ministries" within the church so that it can grow and work smoothly.

The need for leaders

Jesus once looked at the crowds of people who followed him everywhere, and felt sorry for them. He said that they reminded him of sheep without a shepherd. They appeared aimless and confused.

Throughout history, God has always provided leaders who can see where God wants his people to go, and who are able to encourage and inspire them to follow.

That does not mean they have the authority to push people around, however. But there is both a human and spiritual need for people with genuine vision and God-given enthusiasm and confidence who will act as responsible leaders. Otherwise, we might do nothing at all for him.

The need for pastors and teachers

A pastor is one who is able to help people in a personal way; a teacher is one who can explain the truths of Christianity clearly. Sometimes, but not always, the same person has both gifts.

We need people who are able to help or "counsel" us because everyone faces problems or difficult situations from time to time. The pastor's advice should be based on the Bible, and coupled with deep human and spiritual insight.

The need for teachers is that we may grow in the faith and avoid errors of belief, which will weaken our effectiveness for God. We can never learn enough about him, but such knowledge will strengthen our faith.

The need for organisers

During the first exciting months of the Christian church, after the Day of Pentecost, the twelve apostles found they were doing everything: preaching, teaching, counselling, organising meetings and distributing gifts.

They felt this was wrong, so they appointed some "deacons". These were strong Christians and had a gift for organising things and handling money. They took over the practical work, leaving the apostles to do their own work unhindered.

There will always be people to do this today, to save the church minister from becoming overworked.

The need for submission

The leader, the pastor, the teacher, and others with different gifts, such as prophets and evangelists, can only exercise their ministries if the rest of the church allows them.

Paul said that when people claim to speak God's word, we should test what they say by the Scriptures, and think it over. But if we have

---

TO THINK ABOUT ...

Make a list of as many different tasks within the church as you can – they can be very visible (eg preaching) or seemingly small (eg tidying chairs).

- Do you think they are all "ministries"?
- What makes something a "ministry" rather than simply a job to do?
- Does God use people because of their natural talents, abilities and personalities, or despite them?

already acknowledged their gifts, then it is natural for us to submit to their judgement. Otherwise, chaos will ensue. God told the prophet Ezekiel that people would praise his words but not apply them. They refused to follow God's leading through the prophet, and so their witness became weak and ineffective.

BIBLE CHECK
The need for leaders Matthew 9:35-38; Joshua 1:1-6
The need for pastors and teachers 1 Timothy 4:11-16; 2 Timothy 4:1-5
The need for organisers Acts 6:1-7; Romans 12:6-8
The need for submission Ezekiel 33:30-33; 1 Corinthians 14:29; Hebrews 13:17

POSTSCRIPT
The church is neither a dictatorship, with one person making all the decisions, nor a democracy, where everyone takes part in decision-making. Rather, it is a fellowship, with all sharing as God enables them.

Think about the person you are, and the special gifts God has given you.
- Why does God give talents and gifts to his people?
- How are you serving in the church? Are there ministries you should be offering to help with? Are there ministries you should be letting other people share, or even stepping away from yourself?

Thank God for who you are, with your personality, abilities and gifts! Pray for opportunities to use them to serve in his kingdom, and for wisdom and strength to take the opportunities!

BIBLE SUMMARY
MINISTRY IN THE NEW TESTAMENT

The main emphasis in the early church was that every Christian had some ministry from which others could benefit (Romans 12:4-6). There is no such thing as a one-person ministry in the New Testament, with a single person trying to do everything. But there are certain leadership functions outlined.

Apostles and prophets
The apostles had unique authority from God to establish churches and teach the truth (Romans 1:1; 1 Timothy 2:7). Prophets were often used to bring a direct word from God to the people (Acts 11:27-30). Christians today are not agreed on exactly how, or even if, the equivalent of the first apostles and prophets exists.

Elders or bishops
It would seem as if each church had several elders (the Greek word is sometimes translated "bishop") – the "shepherds" or "overseers" of the church. They were the local leaders, who encouraged the church, and probably often acted as teachers as well. They are described in 1 Timothy 3:1-7.

Deacons and other organisers
Paul also describes deacons, in 1 Timothy 3:8-13. It is clear that he expected those who took any responsibility to be people that others respect (compare Jesus' statement in Luke 12:48).

Other ministries in the church included helpers, who assisted in practical tasks (Romans 12:7); people with the gift of healing (1 Corinthians 12:9); some who could speak or interpret other languages inspired by God in worship or prayer (1 Corinthians 12:10); and those who performed acts of mercy or kindness (Romans 12:8).

Working together

KEY TRUTH

The church is often called "the body of Christ", because like a body it consists of many parts all working together for the good of the whole.

The local church

The church of Jesus Christ exists on three levels:

- There is the worldwide church of all true believers, which does not have a single, recognisable structure.
- Then there is the regional or national church, which may have its own customs.
- And there is the local church, to which we belong. That local expression of "the body of Christ" is truly Jesus' hands, feet and voice in the local community, taking his love and message to those who need it.

Most local churches function to an extent independently, although many are also linked to other churches in a "denomination", which have a similar outlook.

A caring church

The church is more like a hospital than a hotel. Rather than offering shelter to the spiritually rich, it offers help to the spiritually poor and sick.

A church which is being faithful to Jesus will attract all kinds of people, some of whom no one else cares for. They may have personal problems, or be difficult to get on with. But Christians are told in the Bible to welcome one another in the Lord. Such care is not always easy, but it is an expression of, and response to, God's love to us.

A witnessing church

The good news about Jesus is too good to be kept to ourselves. Indeed, there is no other hope for human beings to find God except through Jesus.

So we also have a duty to tell others about him. That is partly an individual matter. We can share our faith, however difficult we find it to put into words, with our families and friends.

But the church as a whole also proclaims the gospel. Often it can do so more effectively than the individual because we can pool all our resources to make a united impact with our message and new life.

A growing church

The church, like a human family, is always growing. New members are being born into it. Some members may leave the area and set up a new branch of the family where none existed before.

There are two sorts of growth we can expect to see:

TO THINK ABOUT ...

Think about the ways in which the parts of the human body all work together.

- What does this tell you about the way the church lives and works?
- Does "the body of Christ" refer to the worldwide church, the regional church, the local church, or the church throughout all the ages? Or is it all or some of these?

Make a list of the things Christians can do together.

- Is cooperation more or less effective for each of these activities?

- One is growth in numbers, as people become Christians and join in the life of the family.
- The other is growth in holiness. Together we can look for ways in which we can come closer to Jesus as a group, and discover how we can be more effective in our witness for him. He always has something fresh for us to do and learn.

BIBLE CHECK

The local church Matthew 5:14-16; Revelation 2:12-17

A caring church Matthew 5:46-48; Colossians 1:3-8

A witnessing church Matthew 28:18-20; 1 Thessalonians 1:8-10

A growing church Acts 2:46,47; Ephesians 4:15,16

POSTSCRIPT

Because the church consists of more than just our local group of Christians, the Bible encourages us to learn about others and to help them whenever possible.

- What barriers often prevent Christians from working together? Are these good reasons?
- What could you or your local church do to work with other Christians in your area to spread the good news of God's kingdom? What could you do in the wider world?

Christ is the head of the church. Pray that the Holy Spirit will keep you and your church close to him, so that he can direct you to work together with others to do his will.

BIBLE SUMMARY

THE CHURCH ACROSS THE WORLD

From its spectacular beginning in Jerusalem around the year ad 33, the Christian church spread right across the Roman Empire, westwards into Europe and eastwards towards India, by the end of the first century. Indeed, it was an international church from the beginning, because many turned to Christ from the wide variety of nationalities present in Jerusalem on the Day of Pentecost (Acts 2:7-13).

Sharing our riches

The church soon learned to share its blessings. For example, when there was a famine in Jerusalem, the churches of Asia Minor, hundreds of miles away, organised a collection and sent money, so that their brothers and sisters in Christ would not go hungry (Acts 11:29,30; 1 Corinthians 16:1-4). Through Paul and the other apostles, news about various churches spread, so that all were encouraged (Colossians 1:3-8).

A missionary church

But above all, the church has a message for the world. Jesus has called us to go to every race, tribe and language with the gospel, so that all have an opportunity to hear it before Jesus returns to earth (Matthew 24:14; Revelation 7:9,10).

For Peter, Paul and their friends no distance was too great, no hardship too severe, to prevent them going to strange lands with the only message which can unite, save and renew men and women everywhere. Paul's example remains a challenge to this day (2 Corinthians 11:23-33).

The reality of testing

KEY TRUTH

Every Christian's faith is tested so that we may grow stronger.

It happens to everyone

Think of the most famous people in the Bible: Abraham, Moses, David, Jesus, Paul. They all went through times of testing, when living for God seemed especially hard.

Sometimes they faced opposition when people tried to stop them doing God's work. Sometimes they had to battle with strong personal desires to leave God's way.

And at times it seemed that everything was against them as problems and difficulties mounted up. But they became famous, partly because they showed how to overcome the difficulties everyone faces.

It may not seem fair

When people suffer in some way, they sometimes complain that they do not deserve such an experience. They feel that God is wrongly punishing them by inflicting trouble on them.

But suffering is not usually a matter of deserved or undeserved punishment. We simply live in an imperfect world – one which has been made imperfect by generations of human sinfulness – and everyone inevitably faces problems.

Sometimes it seems that bad people get away with their sin while Christians find the going very hard. That is not always true, and God promises that all sin will be punished eventually. But as Christians are opposed to evil, we can expect the devil to try hard to upset us.

It is allowed by God

The things which test our faith most are often those we least expect to happen. So it is easy to assume that they have taken God by surprise, too.

In fact, they have not. Nothing which happens to us is outside of God's purposes. He does not, however, always stop unpleasant things happening. To do that he would have to be constantly interfering in the natural processes he has created, for example, to stop fire hurting someone.

This does not mean that God deliberately plans to hurt us. He wants us to let his love shine through to us always, and he never lets us be tested beyond the ability he gives us to cope.

It can teach us more about God

Everything in the Christian life can be used to draw us closer to God, and teach us more about him.

TO THINK ABOUT ...

Christians are not sheltered from problems or opposition. In fact, sometimes the Christian life might seem to bring more problems!

- How do you react to difficulties? Do you try to ignore them, explain them, or something else?
- Do you think your life would be better or worse without difficulties? Why?
- How does God use these times to strengthen your faith?

In fact, Christians sometimes find that in a time of testing they are made to realise just how far they have wandered from God, or just how great and loving he is.

Above all, it reminds us of just how weak and inadequate we are, and how much we need his help and power. We appreciate his help most when we most need it.

BIBLE CHECK

It happens to everyone 1 Peter 4:12-16; 5:8-11
It may not seem fair John 16:32,33;
   Revelation 21:5-8
It is allowed by God Romans 8:28-30;
   1 Corinthians 10:13
It can teach us more about God
   1 Thessalonians 1:4-8; 1 Peter 1:6-9

POSTSCRIPT

Although everyone desires a comfortable, trouble-free life, such an existence is not always as good for us as we imagine: it can lead to self-satisfaction and spiritual laziness.

Think of a difficulty that you have faced recently or are facing at the moment.
- How is this difficulty a test of your faith? Do you think all difficulties test your faith?
- What particular thing are you learning about God through this situation?
- Do you think God wants you to be tested? Why, or why not?

Tell God about the situations and circumstances you find hard, and how they test your faith. Pray that he will give you the strength he promised, so that your relationship with him will grow stronger.

BIBLE SUMMARY
THE PATIENCE OF JOB

Job is an Old Testament character who was rich and well-respected. He was a godly man, too, who tried to pass on his faith to his children (Job 1:1-5). But then his world fell to pieces.

The role of Satan
The book of Job reveals that Satan sometimes has access to God (1:6). He told God that Job worshipped him only because life was easy (1:10,11). So God gave Satan permission to test Job's faith by attacking his possessions and family (1:12), and then, later, by making him ill (2:5-9).

Job's faith stayed firm
Job's faith had two aspects. There was his faith in God, which remained unshaken. He still trusted God even when people around him said he was mad to do so (1:20-22; 2:9,10). But he was also very upset (3:1-26), cursing the day he was born.

His friends told him he must have sinned, to bring such awful things on himself (eg 11:1-6). But his faith in his own integrity before God also remained firm; he knew he was not being punished, so his suffering remained a mystery to him.

Job's faith was deepened
But good as he was, and undeserved as his sufferings were, Job still had something to learn. God later revealed his true greatness to him (38:1-21, etc), and Job realised that even his strong faith had still been rather shallow (42:1-6). The story had a happy ending – Job became wealthy again – but he was wiser after his experience.

Testing through doubt

KEY TRUTH

Doubt can be a means God uses to draw us nearer to him, but it can also paralyse the Christian's life if it is not dealt with.

A touch of humility

There are two kinds of doubt:

- One is usually called "scepticism" – the harsh unbelief of someone who does not wish to know and trust Jesus.
- The other is the uncertainty which sometimes hits a Christian. It may be a lack of confidence about whether we truly belong to God's family, or about God's willingness to do something in our life.

Such doubt can arise from genuine humility: we know ourselves to be sinful and do not expect God to be lenient. But such an attitude forgets the enormous love and power of the one who came not "to call the righteous, but sinners to repentance" (Luke 5:32).

A touch of opposition

Doubt is one of the chief causes of inaction among Christians. If we doubt whether something is right, or whether God wants us to act in a particular way, we are unlikely to go ahead. If a doubt is an instinctive reaction prompted by the Holy Spirit to something which is wrong or unwise, that can be good. But if the proposed action would honour God and help others, doubt is bad.

So the devil often sows doubts in people's minds to stop them doing God's work, and to cause confusion in the church. Doubts, like weeds, stop the fruit of the Spirit from developing properly.

A touch of faith

Doubt and faith are closer to each other than many people think. After all, faith, although firmly based on what God has said in the Bible, is not total knowledge.

Therefore faith can easily slip into doubt: the kind of uncertainty which the devil sowed in Eve's mind in the garden of Eden – "Did God say …?" – grows worryingly larger.

When that happens, it is helpful to do two things. One is to recall the ways in which God has helped us or others in the past. The other is to remember the unchanging facts on which our faith is based: the total revelation of God's word. His plan will never be inconsistent with this.

A touch of confidence

God does not always clear away our doubts as soon as we ask him. He may want us to think through our doubts, and return to faith much stronger as a result.

That process can be lonely and painful. We need the support of friends with whom we can talk things through – or to offer them our

TO THINK ABOUT …

Make a list of things you have doubts about from your daily life (eg that it won't rain!).

- Is doubt always bad? How can it be helpful in some situations?

Now think about doubt in the Christian life. Note something you have doubted about the faith or your own Christian life.

- Is it wrong for a Christian to doubt?
- Can you think of a situation where doubt might be helpful? On the other hand, can doubt be sinful? When?

support, and try to understand them, when they have this experience.

But in the end, doubt, if it persists for a long time and grossly hinders our Christian life, may have to be labelled sin: it could be a refusal to take God at his word. If that is the case, then we need to confess the sin and accept, in faith, his forgiveness. That act of confidence will lead to many more!

BIBLE CHECK

A touch of humility Luke 18:9-17; 1 Timothy 1:12-17

A touch of opposition Matthew 13:24-30,36-43; James 1:6-8

A touch of faith Genesis 2:15-17; 3:1-22; John 20:24-29

A touch of confidence 1 Timothy 1:3-7; 2 Timothy 1:11-14

POSTSCRIPT

Doubt can lead to faith, but it can also become an excuse for not pressing on in the Christian life, and accepting a comfortable existence in which God is unable to work powerfully.

- How can you move through doubt to a clearer faith and stronger trust in God? What practical steps would you need to take to do this?
- Are there any doubts you need to let go of at the moment? Are there any aspects of your faith that God is prompting you to consider more carefully?

Thank God that you can be utterly confident in his love for you. Pray that the Spirit would help you to discern God's will and ways more clearly.

BIBLE SUMMARY

THE NATURE OF FAITH

Jesus' friends once asked him to increase their faith. His reply was unexpected. If they had faith as small as a grain of mustard seed, he said, they could move mountains (Luke 17:5,6; Matthew 17:20).

It depends on God

The disciples had in fact asked the wrong question. Faith is not something which grows in quantity. It is not something we can possess more or less of; that would make it dependent on ourselves. Rather, our faith is in what God can do. So what seems "a little" faith can achieve much, because it knows that nothing is too great for God (Genesis 18:14).

The disciples should have asked, "Improve our faith". We need to learn how to trust God simply, without reservation. See Matthew 8:5-13, where a soldier recognised that Jesus needed only to utter a word of command and his request would be granted.

It submits to his will

Jesus taught his followers to pray, "Your will be done" (Matthew 6:10). God's will is always good (Romans 12:2), but he will often only work through people who trust him (Mark 6:5,6; 9:23,24). So faith requires boldness which expects God to work, and humility to ask only for that which will fit in with his purposes.

While it is often right to qualify our requests with "If it is your will" (Matthew 26:39), such a prayer can be a veiled form of unbelief. There are many occasions when we can be sure that what we ask is God's will, and so we can pray with conviction and confidence (John 14:14)!

Testing through temptation

KEY TRUTH

Every Christian faces temptations to disobey God, but the power of God is always greater than the temptation.

An ever-present danger

Because many people do not acknowledge Jesus as their king, the world is full of temptations for the unwary Christian. The Christian life is like walking along a jungle path where there are dangers everywhere.

Some people will deliberately try to make us disobey God, saying he won't notice or that no harm can come from, say, a petty theft or lie.

The lifestyle of others will itself be a source of temptation, because it may blind us to God's better way of living. Plus of course, Satan will try to trip us, and our own human nature will want to take the easy way out of a situation without asking what God wants.

Sometimes our own fault

Jesus taught us to pray, "Lead us not into temptation." Another way of putting it would be, "Do not let us stray into tempting situations."

While we cannot avoid temptation altogether, we can often avoid people and places which are likely to provide a strong source of temptation to us personally.

Everyone is different, so there cannot be a set of rules covering every situation. But, for example, a person who gets drunk easily should obviously avoid situations where they will be able or expected to drink a lot of alcohol. While God promises to help and protect us, we should not expose our weaknesses unnecessarily.

Often subtle and cunning

Some temptations are very obvious – to disobey God, to lie, to steal – but others are more subtle.

Instead of being tempted to do something which is clearly wrong, we may be tempted to do something which is only wrong because it is not God's will for us, or because we are doing it from wrong motives. King David learned that when he tried to count the people of Israel – an act which stemmed from his pride.

And other temptations show up Satan's cunning even more; they may be half right. He simply tries to steer us gently off course, and so reduce our effectiveness for God.

Always a way out

Facing temptation is never easy; often it is a test of whether we really want to do what is right and experience God's power, or to be self-indulgent.

Sometimes, as we battle with temptation, the pressure to give in increases. Normally, however, each refusal to give in makes victory over the temptation easier.

TO THINK ABOUT ...

Make a list of things you have doubts about from your daily life (eg that it won't rain!).
• Is doubt always bad? How can it be helpful in some situations?

Now think about doubt in the Christian life. Note something you have doubted about the faith or your own Christian life.
• Is it wrong for a Christian to doubt?
• Can you think of a situation where doubt might be helpful? On the other hand, can doubt be sinful? When?

There are times, too, when Satan seems to leave us alone after we have resisted him, only to come back with a renewed attack when he gets an opportunity.

Although God has promised always to give us the ability to overcome temptation, we have to admit that sometimes we prefer the "pleasures of sin". Without our cooperation God's help is limited.

BIBLE CHECK

An ever-present danger Luke 17:1-4; 1 John 2:15-17

Sometimes our fault Matthew 6:13; 18:7-9; James 1:12-15

Often subtle and cunning 1 Corinthians 6:1-6; 2 Corinthians 11:12-15

Always a way out 1 Corinthians 10:12,13; James 4:7; 2 Peter 2:9

POSTSCRIPT

Human will-power is not enough to overcome temptation. We need the Holy Spirit to strengthen our will so that we can resist temptations to sin.

- How can you move through doubt to a clearer faith and stronger trust in God? What practical steps would you need to take to do this?
- Are there any doubts you need to let go of at the moment? Are there any aspects of your faith that God is prompting you to consider more carefully?

Thank God that you can be utterly confident in his love for you. Pray that the Spirit would help you to discern God's will and ways more clearly.

BIBLE SUMMARY

JESUS' TEMPTATIONS

Jesus was often tempted, so he understands and can help us when we are tempted (Hebrews 2:17,18). Few of his temptations are recorded, but those he experienced before he began his three-year teaching ministry are given in detail in Matthew 4:1-11.

Jesus was feeling weak

Jesus' temptations came when he was very tired and hungry, and so least able to resist (v.2). That is how Satan often attacks us; his only thought is to overthrow God's people by any means. Jesus became the object of Satan's attack because he knew the importance of Jesus; he tries to crush all who represent even the smallest threat to his evil ways.

Satan twisted the Bible

Satan began by trying to make Jesus doubt his calling: "If you are the Son of God ..." (v.3). Then he twisted the Bible, quoting it at Jesus and telling him to apply its promises for the wrong reason – for the sake of a spectacular stunt, rather than out of obedience to God (v.6). Then he made Jesus a promise he had absolutely no power to fulfil (vs.8,9).

Jesus stood firm

Jesus responded in two ways. First, he quoted the Bible at Satan (vs.4,7,10). He did not argue: he simply faced Satan with the real truth. But he also trusted himself entirely to God at the same time. He was hungry, but he knew that God would provide bread for him without his having to misuse his own powers in a selfish way. He really did want to serve God only (v.10), and when Satan saw that, he left him alone for a while (v.11).

Testing through failure

KEY TRUTH

Sometimes God allows us to make mistakes, so that we may learn to let him guide us in the way we should use our freedom.

The gospel for failures

Jesus once told his followers that he did not come to call righteous people, but that he came to call sinners to turn back to God. That is why some people find the Christian faith unpleasant: they have to admit they have been wrong.

We begin the Christian life by admitting that in God's sight we are failures. We have not obeyed and loved him with all our heart.

God deals with us as we really are, not as we would prefer other people to imagine us. And that is true all through the Christian life: he wants us to be honest with him – and with each other.

The weakness of human nature

Despite all our good intentions and our prayers, we sometimes fail God. We give in to temptation. We fail to do something we know we should have done.

Sometimes we are just plain wrong. We are lazy or uncaring. Sometimes we are blind to the opportunity to experience God's power or show his love until it is too late.

That is because we are still weak even though God's Spirit dwells in our lives. Our human nature can still stray from God's path.

God's promise of success

When Nehemiah, an important official in the government of Babylon, went to see the king with an important request, he prayed for success. Later, when he was back in his native Jerusalem, helping to build up the ruined city, he kept praying that God's work would get done despite the opposition.

His is one of many examples in the Bible of people who faced difficult tasks, who prayed that God would help them overcome, and who eventually achieved what they set out to do.

Sometimes, however, God does ensure that despite our mistakes we still do what he wants. That reminds us of just how great he is!

The gospel of new beginnings

When we do fail God, our faith in his love can be severely tested. We may feel very guilty or depressed because we know we have let him down.

While it is right that we should not take our failure lightly, we should not let it cripple our Christian life.

The promise of forgiveness with which we began the Christian life still holds true. God

TO THINK ABOUT ...

Think about a time when you fell short of God's standard for your life.

- How did you react? Was it easy to be honest with God about your sin, or did you want to make excuses for yourself?
- How did it make you feel about God? What does God feel about you? Does God accept you back completely after you have failed?
- What counts as a "failure" in the Christian life? Is it worse to do something wrong, or not do something that is right?

sets us on our way again, as we tell him that we are sorry for our failures. And he continues to give us the power of his Spirit with which to love and serve him.

BIBLE CHECK
The gospel for failures Luke 5:29-32; 1 John 1:5-10
The weakness of human nature Romans 7:15-20; James 3:2-10
God's promise of success Nehemiah 1:4-11; 4:9,15-20
The gospel of new beginnings Romans 6:1-11; 1 John 2:1-6

POSTSCRIPT
While God understands and forgives our failures, we cannot excuse them. He is always ready to help us do what is right.

Make a list of some well-known characters of faith from the Bible (eg Abraham, Jonah).
• Can you think of a time when each of them fell short of God's standard or failed in fulfilling God's purpose for them? What happened next? Did God stop using them?
• Can failure help you to grow in your faith?

Thank God for his grace and forgiveness. Tell God that you want to do what is right, and ask for his help each day.

BIBLE SUMMARY
THE DISCIPLE WHO FAILED JESUS

The Bible is not full of success stories which seem entirely beyond our abilities. It has many accounts of ordinary people's failures, too, which help us to see that their successes were very much the result of God's work, and not their own special ability.

Full of promise
Peter, one of Jesus' closest followers, who was also called Simon, was always full of big promises. He boasted that he would never let Jesus down (Matthew 26:33-35). He was convinced that Jesus held all the answers to his need (John 6:67-69) and was the first to recognise Jesus as being the Son of God (Matthew 16:13-16).

A total let-down
Peter even tried to protect Jesus from going to the cross, not realising that it was part of Jesus' work to do so (Matthew 16:21-23; John 18:10,11). But when Jesus was put on trial, Peter was frightened. The servants of the high priest were talking over the day's events by a fire when one of them recognised Peter as a follower of Jesus. Peter panicked and denied he had known Jesus (Mark 14:66-72). He soon realised his mistake, and broke down in tears of regret.

Back to normal
After his resurrection, Jesus made a point of talking specially to Peter, to encourage him and give him a new job to do (John 21:15-19). There was no word of rebuke; he understood, and knew that Peter was deeply sorry. From then on, Peter became a pioneer preacher introducing many people to Jesus (Acts 11:1-18).

Testing through pain

KEY TRUTH

Suffering is a universal experience from which Christians are not always free, but through which they can still experience God's love.

Pain in the world

In one sense, pain is a good thing: it is a warning that something is wrong in our body, or that danger, such as fire, is near.

But there is much suffering which in itself has no virtue: suffering from illnesses, accidents and natural disasters which everyone can experience.

Some suffering stems directly from human sinfulness: murder, war, theft. Other forms of suffering occur because the whole world is imperfect. The Bible says everything has been affected by the sin of the human race.

Coping with suffering

It is natural to complain when we suffer: no one likes the experience, and we may feel it is unfair of God to allow it. But the first thing we have to learn is to accept that for the time being this is the state in which we have to serve God.

However, during our suffering, God may seem far away. It may be hard to pray; we may not be able to concentrate on the Bible.

Therefore Christians have a great responsibility to visit and help in every possible way all those who suffer.

What is more, we have the unfailing promise that Jesus is always with us even in our sufferings – and that his love never dries up. He knows from personal experience what suffering is about.

Healing is possible

Both Jesus and the apostles not only preached the gospel, they also healed the sick. There is no record that they healed everyone, and Paul, for example, appears to have had a long-standing problem which God did not remove (see Bible Summary).

There are two ways in which God heals people today. One is through normal medical treatment – because he is still the Lord of our bodies and their functions. And the other is as an answer to special prayer on our behalf, with or without medical treatment.

We are told to pray for healing. But healing may not always be sudden; God may have a lot to teach us as we slowly get better. The inner healing of mind and spirit is as vital as that of the body.

The end of all suffering

The Bible paints a beautiful picture of heaven, the place where all Christians will spend their lives after death in the close presence of Jesus. In heaven, it says, there will be no more death,

TO THINK ABOUT ...

Think about a Christian you know who is suffering pain at the moment.

- Why is there pain in the world? Why are Christians not exempt from experiencing pain?

Many of the people who were healed by Jesus had been excluded from worshipping God in the temple because of their illnesses. After they were healed, they could worship God again.

- What does this tell you about the nature of healing? Do you think God heals people for the same reasons today?

disease, hatred, war or any other suffering. Everything will be made new and perfect.

It is a picture which is meant to encourage and inspire us in this life. We know that one day all that we long for will happen. Meanwhile, we are not to stop our efforts to ease or remove suffering. Part of being a Christian is to bring a touch of heaven to earth.

BIBLE CHECK
Pain in the world Luke 13:1-5;
  Romans 8:18-23
Coping with suffering 2 Corinthians 1:3-11;
  Hebrews 12:7-11
Healing is possible Mark 1:32-34; Acts
  5:14-16; James 5:14,15
The end of all suffering Romans 8:18;
  Revelation 21:1-4

POSTSCRIPT
Sometimes, it is only through suffering that the deep things of God become clear to us, and the work which God has given us to do is completed – just as Jesus had to suffer in order to do his work.

- Why do you think Jesus heals some people and not others?
- How can you help other Christians who are suffering? What encouragement can you give to them? What is the best thing to pray for in times of pain?

Thank Jesus that he has experienced intense suffering, so he knows the pain you and others go through. Pray that pain will bring new experiences of God's love.

PAUL'S "THORN IN THE FLESH"

Paul was a remarkable person. He, above all others, spelt out Jesus' teaching in detail for the benefit of the church. He travelled thousands of miles in sailing ships, on horseback and on foot to take the message of Jesus to new countries or districts.

A life of suffering
In doing that task Paul suffered a great deal. He lists some of his sufferings in 2 Corinthians 11:23-33 as he uses his experience to prove his genuineness. No one would be shipwrecked, beaten up, robbed, starved and overworked unless he believed in his calling!

Paul also wrote that he was prepared to suffer for Jesus, because Jesus had suffered much for him. He remembered, too, how he made Jesus' followers suffer before he became a Christian (Philippians 3:7-11).

Weakness becomes strength
There was, however, one particular pain from which Paul wanted to escape. He had what he called a "thorn in the flesh" (2 Corinthians 12:7-10). No one is sure what this was. It may have been a physical deformity or very poor eyesight.

Paul felt that it hindered his work, so he prayed for healing. But God answered, "My grace is sufficient for you, for my power is made perfect in weakness."

Three times Paul prayed for healing, and each time God gave him the same answer. After that, he accepted his disability. He was more open than ever to receiving God's strength for his work and he proved that God could use weak people to do his will (1 Corinthians 1:25).

Testing through persecution

KEY TRUTH

In every generation some Christians are ridiculed, hurt or even killed by other people simply because they love and serve Jesus Christ.

The gospel offends people

The message of Jesus brings truth to light, but some people prefer their world of lies and wrongdoing. They therefore try to stop the spread of the Christian faith or hinder Christians from living it out.

Others will ridicule the faith because its simple message seems nonsense to them. They do not believe there is a God, or if there is, they claim he has not revealed himself finally and completely through Jesus Christ.

In some countries, people regard Christianity as a threat to their political ideals, so they pass laws limiting its activities, or banning it altogether.

The ways they attack

Sometimes, the pressure on us will come from those closest to us – our families or special friends. They may have a different faith, or simply not understand what has happened to us. They may accuse us of being disloyal to them; some Christians have been thrown out of their families as a result.

Persecution can be violent. Christians have been imprisoned and tortured for their faith. They have been banned from certain jobs, or banished to special hospitals.

But often the pressure is less obvious. People may pick arguments, or try to make us sin. They may exclude us from their social circle, or just laugh at our faith.

The call to be faithful

The taunt which Satan made against Job was that he would do anything to save his own skin. In fact that was not true, and Job remained faithful to God despite his suffering.

The threat of persecution can be more frightening than any other suffering, but the apostles and many Christians since have shown that it is just as possible to remain faithful to God under these conditions.

God wants us to remain faithful to him, even if that means not doing what other people want. He promises to give us wisdom to know what to do, and has said that he is always honoured when we stand up for him.

Resisting, even to death

Being faithful to God meant death on the cross for Jesus. In fact, that was why he came to earth – to die for our sins.

But for some of his followers death came

TO THINK ABOUT ...

Take some time to find out about Christians in another part of the world who are being persecuted because of their faith in Jesus Christ.

- What can they teach you about following Jesus? How does persecution affect the faith of Christians?

Now compare their situation with your own experiences as a Christian.

- Have you ever experienced persecution or intense pressure to give up on your faith? What forms of persecution might you face today?
- Do you find it difficult or easy to stand up for Jesus?

early, too, because they loved him. Stephen was stoned to death for sharing his vision of Jesus with the religious leaders, and became the first Christian martyr.

Ever since, people have willingly been murdered rather than deny the truth of Christianity. For most of us, it will not come to that, but the challenge to remain faithful, under pressure, right up to the moment we die, remains.

BIBLE CHECK

The gospel offends people John 15:18-27; 1 Corinthians 1:20-25

The ways they attack Matthew 10:16-39; Acts 4:1-4

The call to be faithful Acts 4:16-20; Mark 13:9-13

Resisting, even to death John 16:1-4; Acts 7:54-60; Hebrews 2:1-4

POSTSCRIPT

Sometimes, Christians can bring persecution on themselves by being tactless or by making too much of secondary or less important truths.

- How can the Spirit help you?
- Do you ever think it would be easier to face death than the ridicule of friends and relatives, or the indifference of society? Is it harder to remain faithful to God when the persecution is subtle?

Thank God for the glorious hope of living with him eternally in his new world! Ask him to help you be faithful to him, whatever situation you are in, so that you will hear his "well done" at the end of your life.

THE PROMISE OF PEACE

"Cast all your anxiety on him because he cares for you" (1 Peter 5:7) is one of the most memorable of the Bible's many guidelines. One of the strongest witnesses to the reality of our faith is the inward peace which Jesus gives when we obey that instruction.

A peace beyond words

Jesus promised his peace to his followers before he died (John 14:27). He said it would be unlike anything the world had to offer. It would not be like the temporary release from anxiety which drugs or strong drink may give, because they deal only with our feelings, and not with the real problem.

Rather, his peace would be an underlying sense of confidence that all our circumstances are in God's capable hands, and that his purposes for us are always good even if very hard or even painful.

A peace despite trouble

The Jewish word for peace, "shalom", means "wholeness" as well as "tranquillity". It reminds us that peace is dependent on our relationship with Jesus. We already have peace with God (Romans 5:1-5) in the sense that everything which makes us his enemies has been dealt with by Jesus' death on the cross.

So, whenever there is turmoil around us, we have an opportunity, firstly, to experience the peace which is the gift of God's Spirit within us (Galatians 5:22). But, secondly, we can also use that sense of peace to help us become peacemakers in that situation, helping others to be reconciled to each other (Matthew 5:9).

WINNING

Jesus is king

KEY TRUTH

The whole universe is already in Jesus' power, and he will one day bring all its rebellious parts to order.

He conquered sin

"Sin" describes both the attitude and actions of people which go against God's laws and purposes. People are cut off from God by sin.

Jesus conquered sin in two ways. First, by living a perfect life on earth, he showed it was possible for people to avoid sinning and obey God.

But most of all, he conquered it through his death on the cross. There, he suffered the punishment – death itself – which each sinful person deserved, so that we could know God and receive his new life which lasts for ever.

He conquered death

"The soul who sins is the one who will die": that was the Bible's judgement until Jesus came to earth. Here more than physical death was implied: it involved spiritual separation from God.

But death could not defeat Jesus, because he was the creator of life! Although his body died completely, God raised him from the dead to demonstrate his total victory over the grave.

In so doing, God broke the curse which had plagued the human race for centuries. He opened up the way to heaven, so that although we, too, will have to pass through death, it cannot hold us in its clutches and keep us from everlasting life.

He conquered evil

Because God gave every person freedom to choose whether or not they would obey him, some people have chosen to do what is wrong. In addition, there are evil powers in the world

trying to overthrow God's kingdom.

When he died on the cross, Jesus mortally wounded the forces of evil, because he conquered their ultimate weapon, death.

Now Satan is in his last days. He knows he will be totally destroyed when Jesus returns to earth. Meanwhile, he attempts to hinder God's people, but he can never harm those who trust themselves entirely to Jesus.

He will conquer the world

In three of Paul's letters – Ephesians, Philippians and Colossians – he bursts into exclamations of praise at the greatness of Jesus' victory.

Jesus promises to do nothing less than conquer the whole world with his love and his truth.

He will do it in two ways. First, he will do it through his people. We are called to take and live out his message in every place. Secondly,

---

TO THINK ABOUT ...

Make a list of some of the people, movements and ideas that seem to be in charge of the world today.

- How do they try to control the world? What powers do they use?
- What does it mean for these "rulers of the world" that Jesus is king?

Jesus' rule over the world was established by his death and resurrection.

- What was so important about Jesus' death and resurrection? What did Jesus accomplish by them?
- How can Jesus' rule as king be seen today? How can your life show that Jesus is king?

he will do it completely when he returns to earth to create a new world in which peace, love and truth are supreme.

BIBLE CHECK
He conquered sin Matthew 9:1-8; Romans 8:1-3; 1 Peter 2:21-25
He conquered death Luke 24:1-9; 1 Corinthians 15:20-28
He conquered evil Luke 13:10-17; Colossians 1:13,14; Revelation 20:7-10
He will conquer the world Philippians 2:9,10

POSTSCRIPT
Because Jesus is king, nothing happens which he cannot use in some way for his own good purposes, even if events stem from evil sources rather than from him.

- What does Jesus' rule mean for the future of the world? What will that mean for you personally?
- Do you find it easier to accept Jesus' rule as a present or as a future reality? Why is it important that he is king both now and then?

Thank God that in Jesus he has conquered the powers of sin, death and evil. Pray that the Spirit would help you to let Jesus rule as king in your life.

BIBLE SUMMARY
JESUS' COSMIC PLAN
Sometimes, Christians talk as if God's plan to give them eternal life was simply a personal, individual matter. In fact, it has a much greater dimension. His plan includes the whole world, which he loves and cares for (John 3:16-18). It has been slowly unfolding through the years (Colossians 1:19,20).

The role of the church
The church may seem weak and powerless in the world today, but in fact it is God's new family (1 Peter 2:9). Jesus is its head, and God's new world will be filled by those who have loved and served him in this life (Ephesians 1:18-23). Those who seem great in the world will not be there, unless they too have trusted Jesus (Matthew 19:28-30; 20:1-16).

The rest of creation
The whole universe will be renewed (Ephesians 1:9,10), held together by Jesus with a new perfection and beauty. All things are out of harmony with God because of the massive impact human sin has had on the physical world. But one day everything will be reconciled to God, just as we have to believe in him (Romans 8:22; Colossians 1:19,20).

In other words, God plans a whole new creation (Revelation 22:1-5, compare 2 Corinthians 5:17-19), in which everyone will know that he is the true king, the creator of all things who alone is worthy to be worshipped and served (Revelation 4:11).

WINNING

Victory is certain

KEY TRUTH

Because Jesus has already shown his power in conquering evil and death, we can be certain of his ability to help us to honour God in every situation.

No need to sin

We are faced with all kinds of temptations to disobey God every day. Sometimes those temptations come from our own weakness, from our circumstances, or directly from Satan.

But whatever their source, and whatever their strength, those temptations are never more powerful than the Holy Spirit who is active in our lives. He is steadily making us more like Jesus, who resisted all temptations.

Prayer helps in overcoming temptation. We can ask God to make us more alert and sensitive, so that we see temptation coming. Also, we can pray for the Holy Spirit's power at the time we need it: to claim Jesus' victory over sin as our own, and to act as if we have already overcome it – and we will!

No need to fear

Fear of any kind can cripple a Christian as much as a physical handicap. Like one animal being attacked by another, we may be paralysed by fear and therefore do nothing until it is too late.

But Christians have nothing to fear, even in frightening situations, for two reasons. First, Jesus is always there, ready to help. Second, he can deal with the fears of those who love and trust him fully, so that they can serve him effectively.

No need to doubt

One of the most remarkable stories of Jesus' life was when he stayed behind while his closest followers crossed a lake in a boat. A storm blew up, and Jesus walked across the water to them.

Peter, impulsive as ever, asked if he too could walk on the water. Jesus said yes, but as soon as Peter had taken a few steps, he saw the waves and felt the wind, doubted, and began to sink.

Yet his own experience had already proved that he could walk on the water – and Jesus had told him to! Our past experience (and that of others) and Jesus' own instructions encourage us to do whatever he wants.

No need to falter

Many Christians are tested almost to breaking point. It might be constant temptation; it could be human suffering of some kind.

TO THINK ABOUT ...

Think of times when you have faced temptation, fear, doubt or suffering.
- When these times come, what happens to your faith in God? Do you become anxious? Why?
- What does Jesus' victory mean in each situation?

Make a list of some promises God makes to the Christian. Note down what situations they would be appropriate for (eg 1 Corinthians 10:13 for temptation).
- Is it possible not to sin? How does God promise to help you? How can you live in the light of this?

It is easy to grow tired, not only physically, but spiritually, too. Battling with evil can be very wearing.

But the Spirit within us will carry us through. He will give that energy we need, that extra will-power and determination to press on. God's love for us never falters, so we, too, can love and serve him consistently.

BIBLE CHECK

No need to sin Mark 11:24; Luke 11:13; 1 John 4:4

No need to fear Psalm 34:4-6; Matthew 10:26-33; 2 Timothy 1:6,7

No need to doubt Matthew 14:22-33; 21:18-22

No need to falter Isaiah 40:27-31; Galatians 6:9; Hebrews 12:3

POSTSCRIPT

There can never be any excuse for not enjoying Jesus' victory. Yet if we do fail him, we know he will not fail us, but will always forgive and renew us.

- Why do you not have to fear the enemies of the Christian life?
- Are you ever like Peter? In what situations do you find it difficult to keep trusting Jesus' power?
- Should your Christian life be marked by victory or defeat? Why?

Memorise some of God's promises you noted down so you can pray them in your times of need. Thank God that he has already won the victory, and is ready to help you when you call on him.

BIBLE SUMMARY

HE IS ABLE

The New Testament is full of confidence about all that God can do. Here are some of its assertions.

Able to keep us

We know that he is able to forgive our sins and give us eternal life; Hebrews 7:25 reminds us that he is able to do this for ever. No matter what century people live in, God can save them.

And once we belong to him, he is able to keep us from falling away (Jude 24). That means victory over sin, and a certain place in heaven.

Able to help us

Jesus reminds Paul in 2 Corinthians 12:9,10 that the strength he is able to give is wholly adequate.

We experience that strength when he enables us to overcome temptation (Hebrews 2:18), and when he keeps his promises to us (Romans 4:20,21).

Able to support us

God shows his power especially by doing all kinds of things for us, through us and within us – things we often do not even expect (Ephesians 3:20,21).

He is able to provide us with whatever we need – spiritual resources and physical resources, too – so that we can do his work in his way (2 Corinthians 9:8).

Right in the heart

KEY TRUTH
The secret of living a successful Christian life is to ensure that our thoughts and attitudes reflect those of God.

Jesus comes first
During his life on earth, Jesus frequently told people that if they really wanted to be his followers, he had to have first place in their lives.

Just as the Old Testament commandment said, "You shall have no other gods before me," so Jesus cannot fully work out his purposes for us if we value anything or anyone more highly than him.

And although that may sound a hard requirement, it is in fact the gateway to success. With Jesus first in our lives, he is free to do many great things, and we are free to enjoy them.

Thinking straight
Proverbs 23:7 is a difficult verse to translate and appears in one Bible version as, "As he thinketh in his heart, so is he." In other words, what we are like inside is what will show outwardly, however much we try to hide it. Jesus said the same thing.

Living a Christian life is not about doing certain good deeds and avoiding bad ones. It is about being in a right relationship with God, from which certain ways of behaving will come naturally.

So the Bible encourages us to let God's Spirit set our thinking straight. To help him do this, we can concentrate our thoughts on God, his goodness and his purposes.

Pure motives
It is perfectly possible to do the right thing for the wrong reason. We can try to help someone, for example, not so much out of concern for them, but because we want to exercise power over them.

Or we can do something right in order to persuade others that we are good, unselfish people, while in fact we are just the opposite, and know it.

Ananias and Sapphira were like that. They sold some land and pretended to give all the money to the church, but held some back. They did not need to give it all, in fact, but the act of pretence was seen to be very serious.

Love determines action
Love for others is the golden rule of the New Testament. Our actions are to be determined by it; we are to do for others only – and everything – what we hope they would do for us.

So before doing something, it is often worth asking both what Jesus would do in the

---

TO THINK ABOUT ...
Read Paul's list of excellent Christian qualities in Philippians 4:8.
- Why does Paul tell his readers to fill their minds with these things? What will the result be (see Philippians 4:9)?
- Do your thoughts ever stray from these qualities?
- What practical steps can you take to keep your mind on these things?
- How do you think your thoughts influence your actions and attitudes?

situation and what we would like done if we were on the receiving end.

But love is not soft. It sincerely desires only what will help, encourage and benefit others. Sometimes that may mean gently helping them come to terms with some sin or fault in their life or faith. Love stems from a deep and genuine concern for the other person's welfare.

BIBLE CHECK

Jesus comes first Exodus 20:3; Luke 9:23-26,57-62; 1 Timothy 6:6-16

Thinking straight Proverbs 23:7(KJV); Mark 7:14-23; Philippians 4:8

Pure motives Acts 5:1-11; 1 Peter 2:1-3

Love determines action Luke 6:27-36; 1 Corinthians 13

POSTSCRIPT

Developing right attitudes is a good example of how we are to co-operate with God: he promises to change our attitudes, but we have to recognise where they need changing, and ask him to deal with them.

Jesus told his disciples that the greatest commandment was love for God, along with love for others.

- What does "love" mean in this context?
- What are some of the motives that drive your life? How can you make sure that you do everything out of love for God and others?
- Would it be helpful to describe the Christian life as "single-minded"?

Thank God that his Spirit transforms your life by renewing your heart. Pray that the Spirit will fill you with love for God and for others, and give you strength to keep your mind focused on all that is excellent.

BIBLE SUMMARY
NOT I, BUT CHRIST

A mistake which many make is to try to live a Christian life largely by their own efforts, and only sometimes drawing on God's help. Paul's example was rather different: for him, being a Christian was to allow Jesus' life to fill and flow through him at all times (Galatians 2:20).

Many things are beyond our complete understanding, and this is one of them. "Christ in you, the hope of glory" (Colossians 1:27), is a mystery, says Paul, but it is true just the same.

So he prays that the Christians in Ephesus may know Christ dwelling in their hearts, and so base their lives firmly on love, and begin to understand the immensity of God's purposes (Ephesians 3:14-19).

Christ changing us

When we allow Jesus to "live through us" we are relying totally on him, but also need consciously to clear away the things which will hinder him (Ephesians 4:22-24). We are encouraged to live consistently with the new nature he has already put in us to make us like him (Colossians 3:5-17).

Overcoming evil

KEY TRUTH

God wants his people to share practically in Jesus' conquest of evil, and to conquer it in their own experience.

Be sure of your ground

We cannot effectively fight evil if we are unsure either about the nature of evil itself, or of the resources we can draw on.

That is why it is important to grow in our knowledge of the Bible. Through it we discover just what a Christian can believe and do, and what is untrue and wrong.

The most effective fighters in any battle are the ones who have the confidence that they will never be defeated. We can have that confidence, because despite the intensity of our fight against evil, God can never be defeated – and nor need we be.

Depend on God's power

With God, nothing is impossible. Furthermore, he wants to show how great and powerful he is, by doing things which we could never do ourselves.

In fact, the person most able to receive and enjoy God's power to overcome evil is the one who is most conscious of their need and weakness. God is then free to work, without being hindered by our self-confidence.

Whenever we face temptation or opposition as Christians, we need to renew our trust in Jesus, rely on his promises, and receive in faith his power to speak or act wisely.

Learn to say no

One of the problems about some kinds of sin is that they seem very attractive. They do not always appear bad. Sometimes they appeal to our natural desire for comfort or excitement.

The secret of conquering any kind of temptation is never to argue about it, or even consider it to be a possible course of action.

If we learn to say no in small things, it will be easier to stand against bigger ones. But saying no to them is only part of our saying yes to Jesus and the far better things he offers.

Tell Satan to go

Satan is sometimes like a very noisy dog. He barks loudly to frighten us away from doing God's will, but in fact if we press on in God's power, Satan will not be able to harm us.

Sometimes, a word of command will make him stop his activity when it is seriously endangering God's work. But we can order

TO THINK ABOUT ...

Name the different types of evil you recognise today. Some evil may be personal or local; other evil may be a worldwide problem.

- How powerful is evil? How does it influence you?
- What does God think about evil?

Jesus dealt decisively with evil in his death and resurrection.

- If Jesus has already defeated evil, why does it still remain in the world?
- What does God want you to do when you are faced with evil? Should you simply run away from it in order to keep yourself pure, or does God want you to fight it in some

him to stop interfering only in the name of Jesus Christ, God's Son, praying for his authority and victory.

We must be specially careful about tangling with the forces of evil, expecially if a non-Christian appears to be controlled by them. In those cases, the way forward may be for several mature Christians to pray for that person's release from Satan's hold.

BIBLE CHECK

Be sure of your ground 1 Corinthians 3:10-15; 1 Timothy 6:11-16

Depend on God's power Mark 13:9-11; Luke 18:27; Philippians 4:13

Learn to say no Matthew 16:21-23; 1 Peter 5:8,9

Tell Satan to go Luke 10:17-20; Acts 13:4-12; 19:11-20

POSTSCRIPT

Fighting evil is not a game, but a deadly serious business. We need not fear evil forces, but we should not belittle their strength or intentions.

way? Is every situation the same?
- Are you able to fight evil on your own? What resources does God give?
- How can you fight evil in God's strength this week?

Even though you may fight against evil, it is only God who can give the ultimate victory. Thank him for his power, and pray for help to overcome evil in your own life, the society around you, and even in the wider world.

THE ARMOUR OF GOD

In Ephesians 6:10-20 Paul reminds his readers that the battle Christians face is not against people so much as against great armies of spiritual forces which influence many people (often without them knowing it) and which control many of the world's institutions and governments (v.12).

In order to deal with them effectively, he tells us to "put on the full armour of God" (vs.11,13). Then he lists the spiritual resources we can draw on, using the picture of a Roman soldier, ready for battle.

Hold to the basics

The basic armour for the soldier was a breastplate, helmet, belt and shoes. For the Christian, our basic protection against evil is the truth of God, his righteousness, and the complete salvation Jesus gives, together with the good news which brings us peace with God and eternal life (vs.14,15,17).

Keep alert and active

In battle, the flaming arrows that were shot at soldiers were intercepted by their shields. So, our faith is something which can be held up to deflect the dangerous arrows of temptation which will be flung at us (v.16).

We also have a "sword" which will cut the enemy to pieces more effectively than any real weapon of war. It is the Bible, which contains God's word for every situation (v.17). And as we use these two pieces of battle equipment, we also need to keep in touch with God our commander through prayer, ready to receive and obey his instructions (v.18).

Resisting pressure

KEY TRUTH

The Christian is called by God, not only to overcome any opposition, but also to resist subtle pressures which would weaken our witness.

The pressure to conform

No one likes to be different from others. We all want to be considered part of a community, club or group of friends. And so we usually adapt our behaviour to what is acceptable to that group. But that may not always be acceptable to God. If we follow him faithfully, we shall sometimes want to be different from other people.

There is also a temptation to conform to the world around us by not bringing the Bible to bear on every aspect of our life. So, for example, some Christians tried to prevent the abolition of slavery in the nineteenth century, simply because it was a part of the society they knew.

The pressure to compromise

There are two dangers here. One is to water down our beliefs under the pressure of teachers or preachers who deny some important truth or to modify our behaviour to include something which God has clearly forbidden, just because it is easier to do so.

The other danger is for us to bring pressure on others by insisting that our way of doing things or our understanding of some problems is the only one possible. However, Christians do sometimes differ, in love, over secondary matters.

In the first case, we must simply stand our ground and obey God: in the second, we should obey our conscience, and learn to respect those who differ.

The pressure to complain

It is always easier to complain about something or someone than to try to put matters right. It is also easy to complain against God or our church leaders when things become difficult.

The new nation of Israel complained bitterly once they had left Egypt under the leadership of Moses and found themselves hungry and thirsty in the nearby desert. They had been keen enough to set off, but were not prepared to follow God through the hard ways as well as the exciting ones.

But the Christian way is always to show love, consideration and faith, rather than shout slogans. In his own kind way, Jesus tells us to get on with our business of living and serving him. We can let him be the judge of what is best for us, and of other people's actions.

The pressure of complacency

Sometimes, the Christian life is quite straightforward. There are no big problems to face, no

---

TO THINK ABOUT ...

Pressures can be so subtle that often you may not be aware that you are giving in to them. Spend some time thinking about your life and try to identify what pressures you face.

- Do you think pressures are as dangerous for your Christian life as temptations and opposition? Why, or why not?
- Are there any situations in which you find it easier to conform to an accepted pattern of behaviour, rather than living according to the pattern of Jesus' life?
- When you meet people who believe or act differently from you, what things are you tempted to compromise on? What should you hold to firmly?

great temptations bearing down on us.

That is just the time when we can slip into complacency. We can become content with our comfortable life and so miss all kinds of opportunities to serve Jesus, by caring for others or speaking for Jesus.

And older Christians, too, can sometimes ease up after many years of devoted service to Christ. To all comes Paul's challenge to press on.

BIBLE CHECK

The pressure to conform Romans 12:1,2; Ephesians 2:1-7

The pressure to compromise 1 Corinthians 8:7-13; 10:23-31; 1 Timothy 4:1-10

The pressure to complain Exodus 17:1-7; Matthew 18:15-22

The pressure of complacency Proverbs 6:6-11; Luke 17:7-10; Philippians 3:12-14

POSTSCRIPT

The example of Jesus, who loved even unlovable people, and for whom nothing was ever too much trouble, is the one we are called to follow, even when many subtle pressures may put us off.

- Do you ever complain? What steps can you take to make your words more peaceful and encouraging?
- What is the difference between rest and complacency?
- How can other Christians help you to resist pressure?

Ask the Spirit to help you identify the pressures on your life. Pray for strength not to give in to them, and receive the Spirit's power into your life.

BIBLE SUMMARY

UNITED WE STAND

One of the functions of the church – the local group of Christians who meet together for worship and fellowship – is to help one another stand firm in the faith (Philippians 1:27,28).

That cannot happen if we are always arguing among ourselves, and the weaker brother or sister may easily slip away from God because of our neglect of their spiritual or other needs (1 Timothy 5:13-15; 2 Timothy 2:22-26).

So the New Testament is always urging us to offer support to one another, so that we may win our battles and overcome the dangers which face us as a group (1 Thessalonians 5:14).

The need for wisdom

In order to stand together on the truth of Jesus, we need to be "wise about what is good, and innocent about what is evil" (Romans 16:17-20).

That means growing in our knowledge of how to live according to the Bible, and at the same time giving evil a wide berth (Ephesians 5:3-6).

It also means sorting out our differences swiftly and maturely, so that we can get on with our main task of proclaiming God's word in the world (1 Corinthians 6:1-8). Jesus promised that, in united prayer, God is able to work mightily when we are all agreed (Matthew 18:19).

Onward Christian soldiers

KEY TRUTH

The Christian life consists, not only in overcoming evil, but also in doing important things in the world for God.

Building the kingdom

The "kingdom of God" was a phrase used by Jesus to describe the extent of God's direct rule on earth over his people, and of their influence for him in the world.

This kingdom is slowly growing in size and extent. Jesus said it was like a tiny seed which grows into a large shrub.

It is also growing in effectiveness. Its members are like seeds sown in good, fertile soil, said Jesus in one of his parables. Each one yields a crop of the "fruit" of his Spirit: we each have some influence for God in our community.

Salt in the world

Salt is an important ingredient in almost everyone's diet. A small amount has a great effect.

Salt was used in Jesus' time to preserve foods like meat in order to stop them going bad when they were stored. It was also used to bring out the flavour of foods.

Jesus said that was how he wanted his people to be in the world. Our influence will help prevent human society going completely bad. For example, God promised to hold back his judgement of Sodom in the Old Testament because of the righteous people there. And we can bring joy and hope into the world, where they are so often lacking.

Light for the world

Light is often used in the Bible as a picture of God, because of the total contrast with sin and evil, which is often described as "darkness".

Jesus said he was the light of the world. He came to show up the deeds of evil people, and to make clear the way to God.

We are to reflect his light, share his love and reveal his life wherever we go. Then others will see that his ways are good and his laws right.

Winning enemy territory

In human warfare, armies not only defend themselves against each other, but also try to capture each other's territory.

In the spiritual battle, God has called us to go with him into the world which is under Satan's influence, and see God himself slowly extend his kingdom.

Together with all God's people we can take

TO THINK ABOUT ...

Make a list of some parables that describe what the kingdom of heaven is like.

• What does "the kingdom of heaven" mean? Is this just another way of talking about the church, or is it something more?
• What does the kingdom of heaven do in relation to the world?

Think of a particular area or situation where you especially want God's kingdom to appear.

• How does God's kingdom grow? Is the growth the result of God's activity, or your activity, or both?

the good news of eternal life in Jesus Christ to those who have never known him. We may see people who were once in Satan's grip released to serve God. We may see individuals, families and even whole communities changed by the power of God's word.

BIBLE CHECK
Building the kingdom Matthew 13:1-9,24-32
Salt in the world Genesis 18:26-33;
Matthew 5:13; Colossians 4:6
Light for the world Matthew 5:14-16;
John 1:4-13; 8:12
Winning enemy territory Acts 8:4-8,26-40

POSTSCRIPT
We have been told to expect to see God at work through the witness of our churches. If nothing seems to be happening it may be because we are not obeying him fully.

- If Jesus is the king of this kingdom, who are you?
- What tasks do all Christians share in as part of this kingdom?
- How might God's kingdom begin to grow in the area or situation you thought about just now? Are there any special tasks that God wants you to do?

Thank God that he uses you to bring his life to the world. Ask for his kingdom to come through your prayers and actions, on earth as it is in heaven.

WHAT IS THE KINGDOM OF GOD?

The kingdom, or rule, of God, was what Jesus came to proclaim (Matthew 4:17), and he sent his followers out to proclaim it, too (Luke 10:8,9).

His kingdom is not a country as we know it, however (John 18:36), and does not have actual land. Rather, it consists of people all around the world who love and obey him (Luke 14:15-24).

Parables of the kingdom
Many of Jesus' parables were about the kingdom of God. It would grow, he said, like seed in the ground (Matthew 13:1-9, 31-32). However, there would be people who did not really belong to it but who seemed to be part of it (Matthew 13:36-43).

The kingdom would have a good but often unnoticed effect on the world, like yeast in a loaf of bread (Matthew 13:33). It is like a precious stone, or treasure; it is worth selling everything in order to get into it (Matthew 13:44-46).

Present and future
The kingdom of God already exists (Luke 17:20,21) wherever God's people are. But it also has a future dimension, and Jesus will establish it finally at the end of time (Matthew 25:31-40).

Called to serve

KEY TRUTH
God wants every Christian to take part in his work in the world.

Called by God
When we became Christians by asking God's forgiveness for our sins and trusting him to give us eternal life, we also became Christian workers.

God has brought us into his worldwide family of people who love him. As in every family, there are lots of jobs to be done if life is to run smoothly. No one is expected to be lazy and do nothing.

God has also put us in the place in the world where he wants us to show his love and spread his truth. We are called by him to be his servants, to do his will wherever we are.

Compelled by love
The first Christians could never have been accused of being halfhearted. They were almost reckless in the way they threw themselves into their service for Jesus. The reason was quite simple. They were so amazed at the love of God for them, that nothing was too hard or too much trouble for them to do in gratitude to him.

The love that resulted in Jesus laying aside all the beauty and perfection of heaven, to share in the limitations of human life, and then to be killed without cause by sinful people, is so great that he rightly deserves all our energy and devotion.

Committed through faith
Part of being a Christian is a willingness to do whatever God wants.

He wants to change our lives so that we become more like Jesus. For this to happen we need to accept his instructions and rebukes.

Since we are already committed to letting him work in our lives, he now wants us to follow his instructions one step further, and commit ourselves to serving him in the world.

Concerned for others
There are many people in every community who have physical or spiritual needs. Some of them may need help just to live more comfortably – people such as the poor and disabled.

Others are lonely and need human friendship; most probably the majority of them still need to find Jesus as their Saviour and friend.

It is easy for us to be so concerned with ourselves that we are blind to the needs of others. But God wants us to grow more sensitive to the needs of others and to help them whenever we can.

TO THINK ABOUT ...
Read the story of Jesus washing his disciples' feet in John 13:1-17.
- How does it make you feel that the Lord of all creation did the work of a household servant?
- How is this a pattern for all Christians? Does it mean you should literally wash feet?
- Why is it important that you see yourself as God's servant? How is this different from being God's employee?
- Are you excited to be a servant, or does it sound like a chore?

Called by God Romans 6:15-19; Ephesians 2:8-10

Compelled by love John 13:34,35; Romans 5:3-5; 2 Corinthians 5:14,15

Committed through faith Matthew 24:45-47; Romans 12:1,2

Concerned for others Matthew 9:36; 14:14; 1 Peter 3:8

POSTSCRIPT

There are many things we could do for God, so we need to pray for his guidance to know exactly what tasks he has for us.

Make a list of the people you meet on a regular basis, and the places you go.

- Have you ever thought of yourself as God's special servant to these people and in these places?
- How would this change the way you behave? Are there things you need to start doing or saying?

Thank God for the privilege of serving him. Pray for the people and places he has called you to serve. Keep praying for them regularly.

BIBLE SUMMARY
PICTURES OF SERVICE

The New Testament writers use a number of pictures to describe God's people as they seek to serve him. Here are a few of them.

Employed on God's business

A frequent description is that of a slave, or servant. In Bible times, slaves were common in society. They worked for one man, and while some of them had a great deal of personal freedom, they were "bound" to their master – they could not leave his service.

Paul regarded himself as the slave of Jesus (Romans 1:1; 1 Timothy 1:12), and said that all Christians were to live as if they were the slaves of God (Ephesians 6:6). Another similar description he uses is that of "stewards", managers of houses and estates, who were required to be honest and faithful to their employer (1 Corinthians 4:1,2).

Working for God's kingdom

Paul sometimes thought of himself as a builder, laying the foundations of faith in Jesus (1 Corinthians 3:10-15), or a farmer who plants seed (the word of God) which others tend and help grow to maturity (1 Corinthians 3:5-9).

He also pictured himself as a soldier, fighting both to defend the truth and defeat evil by bringing others into God's kingdom (1 Timothy 6:12; 2 Timothy 4:7).

Following Jesus' footsteps

Perhaps the most helpful picture is of a "disciple", one who follows in their master's footsteps, always willing to learn and to obey. Jesus' disciples were his pupils and fellow workers (eg Luke 8:9,10; 9:1-6; 11:1).

Power to serve

KEY TRUTH

It is possible to do God's work in God's way only by relying entirely on the power given to us by his Holy Spirit.

Sharing God's work

Christians are called to share in the work God has been doing, and will continue to do, in the world. It is his continuing work, not ours.

That does not mean we can lay aside the skills and knowledge we have gained in the world. But it is easy to assume that God must approve anything we do in connection with telling others about Jesus, or helping in the life of the church. In fact, we can only be sure of what is his work by regularly seeking his guidance. Sometimes, things are done in churches only because they have always been done.

Filled with his Spirit

Whenever the first Christians set out on a new venture, they asked for God's Spirit to fill their lives with the power and wisdom they needed to do his work.

And as they went out in faith, they often discovered that God had already gone ahead, preparing people to receive their message.

When we take part in God's work, we need to do it in his way, and not depend merely on human ideas and methods. Only as we allow the Holy Spirit to flow through us, will we see the results of God's love working in our community or church.

Controlled by his word

God does not want us to go into the world to teach our own ideas about him. He has given us his word – the truth of his nature and our needs – to proclaim and to live out.

That word carries the authority of God himself. However people react to us and our message, we need never doubt its truth and relevance. The living God has stamped it with his power.

However, we are not to be like parrots, repeating key phrases in answer to every question, as some non-Christian sects teach their members. God's word is big and powerful enough to be explained and applied in ways which make sense in our society without losing its truth and authority.

Equipped with his gifts

Jesus told a story about a man who gave his servants money (the coinage was called "talents") to gain profit for the man while he was away on business.

All except one were faithful, and made use of their gifts with varying degrees of success. All were praised, except for the servant who buried his gift in the sand.

TO THINK ABOUT ...

Make a list of the opportunities for service that you have.

- Would you be able to do all or any of them without God's help?
- What would happen if you tried?
- Does God ask you to take every opportunity for service that you come across, or should you learn also when to leave a task for someone else?

God has given us personal abilities to use for him. There are natural talents he gave us when we were born, and there are spiritual gifts he wants us to seek, too. We always have the resources to do whatever he calls us to.

BIBLE CHECK

Sharing God's work John 14:12-14; 2 Corinthians 6:1

Filled with his Spirit Acts 8:26-30; 13:1-4; Ephesians 5:18

Controlled by his word John 17:14; Acts 4:31; 1 Corinthians 2:1-5

Equipped with his gifts Matthew 25:14-30; Ephesians 4:7

POSTSCRIPT

Christian service is as much an act of faith as anything else in the Christian life. We are not called to be timid, but faithful and bold, trusting in God's power.

The Holy Spirit provides you with both the guidance and the strength to use opportunities for service.

- What particular gifts has the Spirit given to you to help you serve God effectively?
- Just because the Spirit gives these gifts, does that mean you have nothing to contribute yourself?
- What can you do to work along with God's Spirit this week?

God equips you for the things he has called you to do. Thank him for his help, and spend some time praying for your opportunities for service.

DOING WHAT COMES NATURALLY

The church is sometimes pictured by Paul as a body. Each person has a particular job to do, just as each part of the human body has its own function.

Working together

So, says Paul, chaos would rule if the foot thought itself useless because it was not a hand, or if the head told the feet they were not needed (1 Corinthians 12:14-21).

In fact, he goes on, God has given the apparently weaker parts of both the human body and "the body of Christ" an indispensable role (vs. 22-26). The Bible gives no justification for creating a hierarchy of jobs in Christian service according to the power or status they are thought to carry. We have one master – Jesus – and all are called to serve him (Matthew 23:8-12).

Being ourselves

Everyone likes to be well thought of by others, and respected for their abilities. Christians are to respect one another for what each has to offer, recognising that all have something of value to give (see Philippians 2:3,4).

Therefore we can be free to do whatever God wants – whether it is leading a church or counting the money, speaking at meetings or providing refreshments – without feeling at all inferior or superior.

And that means the hypocrisy which Jesus so strongly condemned need never appear in our churches (see, for example, Matthew 23:1-7,13-15,23-28). God is then free to do just what he wants through us – which is always a great deal!

Serving in the church

KEY TRUTH

There are as many things to do for one another in the church as there are members of it.

The first shall be last

When two of Jesus' twelve apostles came to him to ask for the best seats in heaven, the rest of the group were naturally upset.

Jesus took the opportunity to explain to them all that, in his kingdom, the greatest person was in fact the one who was slave to the rest. In other words, service to God is more important than human praise.

Jesus taught that the really great people are often those who are despised by others because they are humble rather than ruthless or ambitious, or because they are not very fortunate or gifted.

Lending a hand

Some churches probably have too much organisation – too many committees and planning meetings and administrative tasks. Such things can easily get in the way of our calling to teach and live out the simple message of God's love.

But every church must have some organisation, because God wants us to reflect his character, which brings order out of chaos.

There are all kinds of things to be done today, just as there were in the early church. Everyone can help with cleaning or making things, looking after buildings or children, and arranging activities or meetings.

Caring for the needy

Love, expressed by caring for the poor, the ill, the disabled, the sorrowful, the weak and the homeless has always been a characteristic of the Christian church.

There are people in every congregation who have needs which others can meet. They may require help to buy food or keep their homes tidy. They may be lonely, sad or afraid, and need the comfort and security of someone else's friendship.

Sometimes, this care demands special skills of counselling to help people apply Jesus' truth to their deepest needs. But often it is just a matter of being available to others to let the love of Jesus flow through us.

Speaking God's word

This is often, and wrongly, regarded as the most important aspect of Christian service. It is important, but should not be allowed to overshadow other aspects.

There are many ways we can speak God's word. Some will have opportunities to teach or preach at meetings. Others will be able to contribute to discussions. A few may be given,

---

TO THINK ABOUT ...

Spend some time thinking about your local church.

- Who is the most important person in the church? Should there be a "most important person" in the church?
- Are there any jobs in your church that no one ever wants to do? Why do people avoid them? Could you serve in this way?
- Are there any people in your church who are often overlooked? Do they have needs that you could help with? Could you at least talk with them and pray for them?
- Why is it wrong to leave the communication of God's message only to "the professionals"?

by the Spirit, God's special word of encouragement or warning to the church, which others must test by the Scriptures.

But there are also gifts of singing, writing, acting, dancing, painting and so on, which can all speak God's word in some way. And above all, so too can our daily conversations with friends, neighbours and work colleagues.

BIBLE CHECK

The first shall be last Mark 9:35-45; Matthew 19:29,30

Lending a hand Acts 6:1-3; Romans 12:7,8,13

Caring for the needy 1 Thessalonians 5:14; James 2:14-17

Speaking God's word 1 Corinthians 14:3-5,29-32; 2 Timothy 4:1-5

POSTSCRIPT

Just as each person has something to give, so we also each have something to receive. Christian service is mutual: we must be as willing to be helped as we are to help.

The Christian life calls for mutual service.

- Are you willing to let other people serve you? If not, why not?
- What needs do you have that could be opportunities for service for others in your church?

Thank God for the care you receive from other Christians. Ask him to show you ways that you can serve him and bless others in your local church.

BUILDING COMMUNITY

God intended that all human beings should live in a community of giving and receiving, and of mutual sharing; it is not possible to live a fully human life alone (Genesis 2:18).

The world has long since become a very selfish place, in which everyone fends for themselves, and rarely helps others at their own expense (Luke 11:37-42; 16:19-31).

The church, however, is meant to be the place where God's new community, his kingdom, is made visible to the world as an example of true love and care (see 1 Peter 2:9,10).

Growing together

This ideal can only be reached as Christians learn to share their lives together as fully as possible. That involves more than meeting together regularly, important as that is (Hebrews 10:23-25).

In addition, we need to get to know one another in such a way that we can function like a fit and mature body, without limping or stumbling (1 Corinthians 12:25-27). To achieve this, our church life will become much more than a pastime; it will be the centre of our life.

Into the world

KEY TRUTH

God wants his people to show through their behaviour, speech and church life the difference Jesus has made to them.

A life that is different

A Christian is a human being like everyone else. That means we all share the same emotional, spiritual and physical needs. If we pretend to be above these needs, we shall appear cold and inhuman – something Jesus never was.

But at the same time we are different. God's Spirit is active in our lives. We belong to God's kingdom, which has a different set of values from our human society.

The Christian life is based on love for God and our neighbour. This is meant to result in caring deeply for others, and in avoiding all kinds of sin. We will not need to be like the Pharisees in Jesus' day who tried to impress people by their good deeds. People will simply see Jesus in us.

Lips that are pure

It is always much easier to speak harshly than kindly. And it is easier to curse than to bless, to lie than to tell the truth.

But all these easier things spring from our selfish nature and not from God. We are his representatives in the world, so our conversation should reflect his attitudes. This means that swearing, boasting, lying (even small, "white" lies) and impatient anger are out. Rather, he wants us to be loving, gracious, truthful and patient.

Little things count

There is a false idea that the only things that really count for God are the big, important actions and decisions.

That is the devil's own lie; with God little things are extremely important. Only when we are faithful to him in them can we hope to be faithful in larger issues.

So Jesus and his followers said that the little actions of love, and seemingly unimportant words of help or encouragement, are vital. They are ways of showing God's care for the details of life.

Loving our enemies

Christian love is demanding and far-reaching. Jesus said that most people love those who are kind to them, but that his followers were to love their enemies as well.

This kind of love was to take two forms. There was "going the second mile" – doing

TO THINK ABOUT ...

Think of someone you know or meet regularly who is not yet a Christian.

- Do you think they notice anything different about your life? What makes you different?
- Do any of the differences in your life point people to Jesus? Or do they just make you seem strange?

Living a Christian life in the world is not just about avoiding certain things, but also about living a distinctive life that radiates the life of Jesus!

- How should your Christian faith affect the way you speak with other people?

more for people than they insisted on. And there was also the attitude of being kind and forgiving towards those who insulted or persecuted Christians. Jesus showed us an example of that by praying for the forgiveness of those who were nailing him to the cross.

BIBLE CHECK
A life that is different Matthew 6:1-14; Ephesians 5:3-20
Lips that are pure Ephesians 4:25-32; 1 Peter 3:8-12
Little things count Matthew 10:40-42; Colossians 3:17
Loving our enemies Matthew 5:38-48; 26:48-54; Luke 23:34

POSTSCRIPT
The Christian life does not consist simply of following set patterns of conduct; God wants our total lifestyle to reflect his character so that the world may truly recognise him.

- What actions can you do this week to express your love for God?
- Do you have any "enemies"? How can you follow Jesus' command to love them?

Thank God that the world is his world. Pray that he will help you to live as he intended you to live – full of his life, peace and joy! Pray that God's Spirit will use your life to point others to Jesus.

BIBLE SUMMARY
PILGRIMS IN A STRANGE LAND

Every Christian is a member of God's kingdom. The rest of the world is not. We are, therefore, in this life like "strangers and pilgrims" in a foreign land. Our way of life reflects the love and laws of God (see 1 Peter 2:11,12).

Residents of the world
We are not told to form our own separate communities – cut off from the rest of the world (John 17:15; 1 Corinthians 5:9-13). That would be almost impossible, and would restrict our witness for God.

The Bible encourages Christians to observe the laws of the land and pay their taxes, always bearing in mind they cannot obey a law which prevents them doing what God commands, or orders them to do something wrong. (See Jesus' example in Matthew 17:24-27; his teaching in Matthew 22:15-22, and in the apostles' application of it in Romans 13:1-7; 1 Peter 2:13-17.)

Citizens of heaven
Despite this, Jesus reminds us that we are not of the world (John 17:16) – our citizenship is now in heaven (Philippians 3:20). Therefore we are God's "ambassadors" on earth (2 Corinthians 5:20), living out our new life in a sometimes hostile environment among people who do not know God. But at the same time, we are to tell them about him.

Sharing good news

KEY TRUTH

Jesus has told his people to take his message of new, eternal life and forgiveness to the whole world.

A message for everyone

There is no message the world needs to hear more than the message of Jesus. Everyone needs to hear about him. Their only certain hope of enjoying his love now and for ever is to trust him, just as we have done.

No one is too old, young, clever or illiterate to be able to know Jesus for themselves. His death on the cross was for everyone who would accept it.

So important is the "gospel", the good news, that one of the last things Jesus told his followers was to travel everywhere to proclaim it.

Talking about Jesus

After the first wave of persecution in the early church, the followers of Jesus scattered across several countries. Wherever they went, they told people about Jesus.

In some ways it is natural to tell people about things that mean a lot to us – special events which have happened, new people we have met. So it should be natural to tell them about Jesus and what he has done for us.

Some Christians find it hard to put their faith into words, because it is a deeply personal thing. But there is usually something we can say, at the right moment – a comment, perhaps, about how Jesus promises to deal with some difficulty people are talking about, or just a verse from the Bible which is relevant to a conversation.

Letting God work

There is "a time to be silent and a time to speak", advises a wise Old Testament writer.

While most of us probably do not speak enough about Jesus, sometimes we may choose the wrong moment or manner.

God uses our words, but sometimes we need to be patient, and let his word, through his Spirit, work in a person's mind or heart.

God has gifted certain people in telling others about Jesus and leading them to him. They need our prayers and financial support. We may just be able to interest someone enough to encourage them to meet or hear an evangelist.

Telling the neighbourhood

Paul, in the New Testament, is well known for his missionary strategy. He did not work without a plan. He went to important places and people to proclaim Jesus, leaving behind him a group of Christians who would be able to tell others in their district and beyond.

His example is a good one to follow. There

TO THINK ABOUT ...

Think of a recent event that you were eager to share with other people.

- Do you find it easier to share your own good news or the good news of Jesus Christ? Why do you think this is?
- Do you need special skills to tell people about Jesus?
- Are words the only way to pass the good news on?

The good news of forgiveness and new life in Jesus Christ is for everyone!

- Are there any people in your area who have no Christian witness at the moment? Is there a reason for this?
- What could you do to share the good news

may be groups of people in an area who will be specially open to the gospel. Or there may be areas where there is no witness, to which we could reach out.

The work of evangelism – telling the good news – is something we can all share in by our own personal witness, by delivering leaflets, visiting the homes of others, helping with special church services, and so on.

BIBLE CHECK

A message for everyone Matthew 28:18-20; John 3:16,17; Acts 4:11,12

Talking about Jesus Acts 8:4-8; 9:10-19

Letting God work Ecclesiastes 3:7; John 12:20-23; Luke 1:76-79; 3:4

Telling the neighbourhood Acts 17:16-18; 18:1-4

POSTSCRIPT

It is easy to be discouraged by a lack of response to our efforts, and so concentrate on our church fellowship. But Jesus calls us to keep on proclaiming him, with the methods which are most appropriate in our area.

with these people?

- How does the Holy Spirit help when you are sharing the message about Jesus? Why is the Spirit's work essential?
- What should you do if there seems to be no response from people?

Thank God for his immense love for you. Pray for those who do not yet know him as Saviour and Lord. Pray for opportunities to share the good news with them, and the courage for you to do so.

BIBLE SUMMARY
ALL THINGS TO ALL PEOPLE

Paul told the Corinthians that in his task of proclaiming the good news of Jesus, he became "all things to all men" (1 Corinthians 9:22). The phrase is sometimes used to describe people who are unreliable; just as a chameleon changes the colour of its skin to blend in with its surroundings, they adapt their words or actions so they will always be accepted.

Identifying with people

However, that was not what Paul meant. Rather, he did all he could to identify closely with the people he went to, so that he could make his message totally relevant to their needs or culture.

So to the Jews, he proclaimed Jesus in the context of being the "King of the Jews", the promised Messiah (v.20). To non-Jews, he emphasised the fact that Jesus came to save the whole world, and that God is not concerned with racial differences (v.21).

To people in personal need, Paul preached the tenderness and care of Jesus, which he himself knew and experienced (v.22). His reason was not to change the message, but to adapt the way he taught it to the needs of the moment.

Jesus' own example

In doing this, he was following Jesus' own example. His favourite name for himself was "Son of Man" (eg Luke 5:24), through which he closely identified with us. He, too, adapted his methods. He used parables for some people and direct teaching for others (for example Matthew 13:10-18).

Service for life

KEY TRUTH

Every Christian is in full-time service for Jesus; there are no part-timers or reservists in God's "army".

Ready for change

The Holy Spirit is dynamic – he is always on the move, always working. We, on the other hand, usually prefer a quiet life which is secure and stable.

When Jesus spoke to the church in Ephesus, he said that while they had been faithful to him, they had lost their first love. They needed to be open to change, ready to follow him wherever he led, just as they had once done.

That has always been a challenge to Christians. We need to ask frequently, "Lord, what do you want me to do?"

Giving everything to Jesus

In one sense, we have already given everything to Jesus – our whole selves, our lives, in return for his forgiveness and new life.

But there may be a further way in which he wants us to give ourselves to him; by being willing to give up our jobs and join the staff of a church or missionary society, or enter some other form of Christian work.

Our commitment to him may also be expressed in our willingness to give up more of our spare time to take on church responsibilities. However, if we have families, it is important not to neglect them.

Supporting his workers

"The worker deserves his wages" is a New Testament principle which reminds us that church leaders and workers, some of whom have given up well-paid jobs to serve Jesus in the church, need food to eat and clothes to wear.

And if we do not provide those things for them, they will be hungry and cold. God expects us to share their ministry to us by sharing our earnings and goods with them.

Paul considered that such support was a right. In Corinth, however, he did not exercise that right, to avoid being a burden on the church. Instead, he earned money by making tents. But that was his personal decision, and did not alter the principle on which he usually worked.

Praying for God's servants

Some people do not seem to have much to give in the way of Christian service. They may be old, infirm, poor or with little time to give to the church.

But of course, they can love and care about others. And above all, as with everyone else, they can give time to prayer.

God works the world over through the

TO THINK ABOUT ...

- How has your Christian service changed already over the time you have been a believer? What caused those changes?
- What is your service like at the moment? Do you need to find fresh ways to serve God? Or do you need to renew your enthusiasm for your current activities?
- Is God calling you to some form of Christian work? How can you test this call?

You should also look for opportunities to support other Christian workers.

- Are there any people you know who need your support at the moment?

prayers of his people. Moses, the Jewish leader, once needed someone to support him physically as he led Israel in battle; through prayer, we support spiritually those who are on the front line of spiritual warfare. Without us, the going would be tougher.

BIBLE CHECK
Ready for change Revelation 2:17; John 3:8
Giving everything to Jesus Jeremiah 1:4-10;
Luke 10:1-12; Romans 10:14-17
Supporting his workers Luke 10:7;
1 Corinthians 9:3-18
Exodus 17:10-13; Colossians 1:9; 4:2-4

POSTSCRIPT
Christian service is a work of love. It is hard work, and it is more effective when it stems from our love for Jesus and his people.

• What steps can you take to find out about their needs, so that you can pray for them and give to them more effectively?

In the world of work, retirement comes when a person reaches a certain age.
• Does a Christian ever retire? How does this make you feel?

Thank God that he will always have work for you to do, whatever stage of life you are at. Pray for strength to serve him faithfully to the end.

BIBLE SUMMARY
PAUL, A SERVANT OF GOD

In some respects Paul the apostle was an exceptional person. The amount of work he got through would have killed a lesser person (2 Corinthians 11:23-29)! But despite that, his service for Jesus remains an inspiring model for us to follow.

Dedicated to Jesus
Paul did not believe in doing things by halves. Jesus had given everything for him, so he gave everything for Jesus (Galatians 2:20). Such was his dedication that he never slackened, right up to when he died (2 Timothy 4:6-8). That is the basis of all Christian service – we cannot expect to achieve great things for God unless we are ready to follow him fully.

Controlled by God's word
Before his conversion, Paul was a Jewish scholar (Galatians 1:14) with a good knowledge of the Old Testament Scriptures. After his conversion, God revealed the full truth about Jesus to him (Galatians 1:11,12), which was in full agreement with what the other apostles had been teaching (Galatians 2:1,2).

All his teaching was firmly built on the basic facts of who Jesus was and what he had done on the cross, and Paul firmly resisted all attempts to alter that gospel or add to it (Galatians 1:6-9; 2 Timothy 1:11-14). That is a key to effective Christian service; we cannot expect to win others for Jesus or to help other Christians to grow, if we ourtselves are not firmly teaching and applying his truth.

On the road to heaven

KEY TRUTH

Christians always have heaven in their sights.

Heaven on earth

Every person who has recognised that Jesus Christ's death on the cross was God's way of offering forgiveness and eternal life and who has personally asked for that forgiveness and life will without doubt go to heaven when they die.

For us, eternal life has already begun; God's love has broken into our earthly life. His Holy Spirit has started the process of turning our sinful nature into something pure and perfect which will be completed in heaven.

And the Spirit brings the life of heaven to us by giving us both confidence (or assurance) that we belong to Jesus and his power to overcome sin and evil. Sometimes, too, in our prayers we will become specially conscious that we are no longer bound to earth but are bound for heaven.

Life in perspective

Most people live as if this life were all that mattered. They spend lots of energy and time gathering possessions or working to achieve status or recognition in the world. But Jesus taught that life on earth is important, precisely because it is the period of time we have been given to come to terms with God's purposes for us.

Those purposes embrace the whole world and the whole of eternity. That gives our life now a small but still significant place in his plans. And it puts a comparatively short earthly life into a new perspective: eternity never ends!

Aiming for the goal

We all need an aim in life, otherwise we drift about and are never satisfied. The aim of the Christian life is to please Jesus.

But there is also another goal to aim for, which we cannot miss, but which should determine how we go about pleasing him. That goal is to spend eternity in his presence. If that is where we are going, then every thought, word and deed in this life deserves to be worthy of his presence.

Ready for Jesus

Human nature is the same all over the world. Jesus was aware that a Christian could be as lazy as anyone else. So several of his parables about the end of time showed how we should live now in readiness for the next life.

In one story he showed how five girls did not bother to prepare themselves for a

TO THINK ABOUT ...

Think about the things that people hope for in their lives. Perhaps you could ask a few of your friends for their thoughts on this.

• What do Christians hope for? How is this different from other hopes and dreams for your life?
• How will eternal life in God's new creation be different from the eternal life you have now in Jesus Christ? How will it be the same?
• What are you especially looking forward to?

marriage festival, so that when it happened, they were not allowed in.

And in another, a servant decided to live selfishly and to hurt others, because his master was away and seemed to delay in returning home. He thought it would not matter, but he was punished. Jesus concluded. "You must be ready, for you do not know when the Son of Man is coming."

BIBLE CHECK
Heaven on earth Ephesians 3:14-21;
   Titus 3:3-7
Life in perspective Luke 9:24,25; 16:19-31
Aiming for the goal 1 Corinthians 9:24-27;
   Philippians 3:8-17
Ready for Jesus Matthew 24:45–25:13

POSTSCRIPT
There are two uncertainties in life: one is the time of our death, the other is the time of Jesus' return to earth. The Bible tells us to be ready for both.

The Christian faith is not "a heavenly train ticket", so that all you have to do is wait around on earth for heaven to come along.
- What do Jesus' parables teach about the time of waiting?
- What things should you do this week because of your Christian hope?
- How does the thought of eternal life with God put your life now in perspective?

Thank God for the wonderful future he has for you and for all believers. Pray for his Spirit to help you live in hope now, and bring you safely to his eternal kingdom.

BIBLE SUMMARY
HOPE SPRINGS ETERNAL

When hope dies, life becomes almost impossible (Job 19:10). Everyone needs something to look forward to, to work for, to spur them on. Whether the Christian life for us is very hard or comparatively trouble-free, the hope of eternal life with Jesus is said in the New Testament to be the spur we need in order to be faithful to him, who is faithful to us.

Hope in God's promises
Hope is closely linked to faith in the Bible (eg 1 Corinthians 13:13). Hope, like faith, is confidence that God will fulfil his promises. "Against all hope, Abraham in hope believed" that God would make him, a childless husband, the ancestor of many nations (Romans 4:18-21). Similarly, when we experience difficulty or testing, hope is strengthened as we endure suffering by the power of God: we see what he can do, and his love gives hope that he will continue to sustain us (Romans 5:1-5).

Hope in God's provision
Most of all, hope is something the New Testament writers link to eternal life (Titus 1:2). Hope is the basis of our faith in Jesus (Ephesians 1:18-20; 1 Peter 1:3); we look forward to what God has prepared for us in heaven, which is far better than the best things the world has to offer. Therefore, our life now can be one of self-sacrifice (Colossians 1:4,5), because our hope outweighs any inconvenience we may experience. We cannot see our hoped-for home with Jesus (Romans 8:24,25), but we wait for it patiently, while Jesus' life within us fuels that hope and keeps it alive (Colossians 1:27).

ARRIVING

Coping with bereavement

KEY TRUTH
Jesus brings a new perspective of hope to the sad experience of bereavement.

Coping with our grief
"Jesus wept." That is the shortest verse in the Bible. But the words sum up the deep feelings of Jesus at the tomb of one of his closest friends, Lazarus.

The customs of showing grief in public vary from country to country, but the feelings of grief are very natural and it is not weak or un-Christian to mourn the death of those we love. After all, they have given much to us, for which we are deeply grateful.

But Christians need not grieve "like the rest of men, who have no hope". Sad though the loss is to us personally, we can also rejoice that a believing person has gone to be with the Lord for ever. Yet the loss of unsaved loved ones is an agony beyond words.

Coping with our loss
A time of bereavement is a time of conflicting emotions. The bereaved person wants to be alone, yet they also want the company of friends.

It can easily turn into a time of bitterness when we complain that God has robbed us of someone we love. But of course, our loss means their blessing in his presence.

His perfect plan has allowed for the right time of death for each person, hard as that may sometimes be to understand. One day those who belong to Christ will be reunited; meanwhile, we have the loving presence of Jesus.

Coping, with Jesus' help
Because Jesus has experienced both bereavement and death itself, he knows how to comfort those who mourn. He always showed deep concern and sympathy with the bereaved. Because he never changes, he offers his peace to the troubled, his joy to the sorrowful, and his presence to the lonely.

That does not mean we will suffer no pain at all. But it does mean that because he has kept us here in this life for a little longer, he still has something useful for us to do.

Helping others to cope
In New Testament times, the church always had a special place for widows. This was partly because there was always a welcome for the lonely, but mainly because without husbands they would become very poor.

So the church organised collections to help pay for food, clothes and shelter. There are

---

TO THINK ABOUT ...

Read the story of Jesus at the tomb of Lazarus in John 11.

• Why did Jesus weep (11:35)? What does this tell you about what he thought of death?

• What comfort did he give to Lazarus' sisters?

• How is it different to cope with the death of a Christian and someone who did not believe in Jesus? Should this affect Christian funeral services?

---

always things which the bereaved need help with, even in countries where they are not short of money. Most of all, they need fellowship – the deep caring and sharing of Christians who are able to love and grieve together, and offer human spiritual support.

BIBLE CHECK
Coping with our grief John 11:28-37; 1 Thessalonians 4:13-18
Coping with our loss 2 Corinthians 5:1-8; Revelation 7:9
Coping, with Jesus' help Lamentations 3:19-33; Luke 7:12,13; John 14:27
Helping others to cope 1 Timothy 5:3-16; James 1:27

POSTSCRIPT
An important element in coping with bereavement is being prepared to surrender those we love to Jesus, just as we have surrendered ourselves.

Bereavement can last a very long time. Even though life may go on, you may still feel the loss of a loved one deeply.
• What continued comfort does God offer to those who mourn?
• Are there people who can share your loss? Are there others in your church who need your support and prayers at the moment?
• How is the fellowship of the church important? What can you do to increase this depth of fellowship in your church?

Ask God to give comfort to those you know who are feeling the pain and sadness of bereavement.

BIBLE SUMMARY
WHY MUST WE DIE?

Death is unpleasant, sometimes painful, and always sad. And that in itself partly answers the question as to why it happens. Death is a result of the imperfection and fallenness of humanity (Genesis 3:19; 1 Corinthians 15:56).

No exceptions
Because we all share in the sinfulness of the world, we all have to die (Ezekiel 18:4; Romans 6:23). Death has been called the great leveller; the best and the worst people all have to go through it.

The Bible records only a couple of instances of "translation" – the sudden transformation from this life to the next without death. One was Enoch (Genesis 5:24; Hebrews 11:5) and the other Elijah, who was seen being taken into heaven in a whirlwind (2 Kings 2:11).

The only other exceptions will be when Jesus returns to earth. Christians who are alive then will be taken direct to heaven (1 Corinthians 15:51,52; 1 Thessalonians 4:17).

Death defeated
Death is no longer the unconquerable enemy it once was. Jesus has defeated it by dying and being raised to life. While we must still experience death, a continued life with Jesus is waiting beyond it for all who have accepted his death as God's way of dealing with their sins (See Romans 5:12-21).

ARRIVING

Facing death

KEY TRUTH
Because of Jesus' death and resurrection, we can face our own death with confidence rather than fear.

Life completed
There is no guarantee that a person will live for a certain length of time. Sometimes people die from disease, accident or violence long before we think they should.

That is part of the tragedy of a sinful world. Some people do not have the opportunity to do all they could usefully accomplish. Therefore, we always need to be ready to return to God who made us.

But he alone knows how useful we really are, and his purposes will never be defeated by premature death. When he calls us to be with him for ever, we know that we will have done our part for him on earth.

Saying goodbye
Our attitude to death will depend very much on our attitude to life – which is as good a reason as any to prepare ourselves for it.

If we have been largely selfish, allowing ourselves to be dominated by possessions, wealth, privileges and human status, it will be very hard to let go of these things as death approaches.

But if our life his been characterised by giving, sharing and loving, then it will not be so hard to say goodbye. We can be sure that the Lord who will look after us in eternity will also look after the people we leave behind.

A place for repentance
Sometimes, when death approaches, people are very conscious of all the wrong things they have done in their life. They remember the hasty words, the unkind actions, the forgotten promises and neglected duties. While it is never too late to repent and be saved or experience restored relationships with God or others we have wronged, it is sad to learn so late the joy that reconciliation brings.

The aim for every Christian should be to confess each sin as it happens all through life, in order to keep close to Jesus and experience his love and help.

The doorway to heaven
Death, for the Christian, is not the end of life but, as it were, the gateway through which they pass to experience a new phase of the eternal life Jesus has given. Much of the fear of death arises because both it, and what lies beyond it, are largely unknown.

But Jesus has been through it – and come back again. The heaven he spoke of, and which was revealed to some Bible writers, is not a place to fear but to look forward to.

TO THINK ABOUT ...
Many people talk about the things they want to do before they die.
- Are there certain things you want to accomplish in your life? Why are they important to you? How would you feel if you knew now that you would be unable to do them because of infirmity or death?

Psalm 31:15 says, "My times are in God's hands".
- What does this tell you about the length of your life? Does it necessarily mean your life will end without trouble or pain?

Life completed Philippians 1:19-26;
2 Timothy 4:6-8
Saying goodbye Job 1:21; Psalm 68:5,6;
Mark 10:17-31
A place for repentance Psalm 103:1-14;
Isaiah 53:1-12
The doorway to heaven 1 Corinthians
15:3-19; Revelation 7:16,17

POSTSCRIPT
Death, like life, is God's gift. The Bible does not allow us to take our own or anybody else's life even though, as believers, we may be certain of eternal life.

• How can you be prepared for death? What do you need to change about your behaviour or speech so that when you die, you will have lived a life to the praise of God? Are there any things you need to put right, or arrangements you need to make?
• Should a Christian be afraid of death?

Thank Jesus that he has already gone ahead of you, through death, into God's resurrection life. Pray for the Spirit's help to live your life well, so that whenever and however it ends, your life and death will point others to God.

BIBLE SUMMARY
LIFE'S LAST CHANCE

Jesus once told a story about men who were employed to work in the fields. Some were hired in the morning, others at midday, and still others only a short while before dusk. Yet each received the same wage (Matthew 20:1-16).

The story was intended to show that it does not matter when a person becomes a Christian. All receive the same gift of eternal life, however much of their life has been spent working for Jesus. Christ made the point strongly when he promised that same gift to the thief who was crucified beside him, and who repented just before his death (Luke 23:39-43).

No second chances
However, it is in this life that we are called on to turn away from our sins and look to Jesus for eternal life. There is only one verse in the Bible which implies that those already dead may have a second chance, and it seems to apply only to those who lived in the years before Jesus came to earth (1 Peter 3:18-20).

Because the date of our death is uncertain, and because Jesus came into this world precisely to tell us the way to God in this life, the Bible message is always "now is the day of salvation" (John 1:10-13; 3:14-18; 2 Corinthians 6:2).

Action replay

KEY TRUTH

Every person who has ever existed will have their life judged by God at the end of time.

Nothing is hidden

Adam and Eve tried to do the impossible by hiding themselves from God. And Jesus once said that some religious leaders of his day were like whitewashed tombs – seemingly clean on the outside, but rotten inside.

What we really are, and what we really have or have not done, will be brought to light when the world is judged by God.

Christians need not fear this judgement, because it cannot cost them their place in heaven – that is already secure. But it does remind us that we cannot abuse our gift of eternal life by living carelessly.

The fire test

The major test for everyone is not how they have lived, because no one can enter heaven just because of the good things they have done. The question God will ask each one is, "How did you treat my Son? Did you receive him or reject him?"

However, all Christians will have their lives assessed by God, to see how valuable they have been for him. Paul says some people's lives will be like wood, hay and stubble: they have done nothing worthwhile for God and his kingdom, and it will be as if their work just goes up in smoke.

Others' lives, however, will be like gold, silver and precious stones. They will survive the "fire test" – the searching scrutiny of God's pure love and law – and will be built into the new heavens and earth.

Well done!

Christians will be spared the detailed judgement that others will face. Instead, after their assessment spoken of above, they will be welcomed and praised by Jesus himself.

The detail of Jesus' parables cannot be pressed too far, but in one of them God is pictured as giving his faithful servants degrees of responsibility in heaven, as a reward for their service on earth. Each reward exactly suits their abilities and achievements.

Paul also speaks of another reward – a "crown", a symbol of victory and conquest over evil, which everyone will receive.

A place for you

Heaven is beyond imagination. Some people feel terrified at the thought of a huge mass of people all together; others cannot understand how we shall get on with each other! But Jesus' promise to the individual is that there is a

TO THINK ABOUT ...

Many people, if they believe in heaven at all, think that they will "get in" because they have been nice people or done good things.

- Why is this a dangerous idea?
- What will God's standard of judgement actually be?
- Does it matter what you do in your life, or only what you believe?
- What do you think will happen to those who have never heard about Jesus Christ?

tailor-made place actually waiting for us to fill. He has gone ahead to get it ready for us.

One day, he is coming back to earth. Then, all Christians who have died will be raised from the dead, and they and the Christians still alive will be taken to be with Jesus.

BIBLE CHECK
Nothing is hidden Luke 12:1-3; 2 Corinthians 5:6-15; Hebrews 9:27,28
The fire test 1 Corinthians 3:10-15; 1 John 4:16-19
Well done! Matthew 25:14-30; 1 Corinthians 6:2,3; 2 Timothy 4:8
A place for you John 14:1-7; 1 Thessalonians 4:16,17

POSTSCRIPT
Although this part of our Christian life lies in the future, it will be no less real than our current experience. The Bible is full of predictions which have come to pass, and we can be confident these will too.

Make a list of as many different aspects and activities of your life as you can. Now read 1 Corinthians 3:10-15.
• Which parts of your life are "wood, hay and straw"? Which parts are "gold, silver and costly stones"? How do you think your life will stand in God's refining fire?
• What can you do this week to build your life with quality material?

Thank God for the assurance of his acceptance of you in Jesus Christ. Confess to him the parts of your life that are poor quality, and ask for the help of his Spirit to become more like Jesus.

BIBLE SUMMARY
THE EVENTS OF THE END

The precise order of events surrounding Jesus' return to earth, and the end of the present world, is not entirely clear in Scripture. This has led some people to do precisely what Jesus warned us against: attempting to predict the precise date, and speculate about certain events (Matthew 24:4,36,44; 2 Thessalonians 2:1-4).

Short of grappling with the symbolism of Revelation, the best basic guide to "the end" is Jesus' teaching in Matthew 24 (and parallel passages in Mark 13:1-31 and Luke 21:1-33). Other teaching can then be fitted into that structure.

A time of suffering
The end days will be characterised by great suffering in the whole world (Matthew 24:6-8). This will be followed by intense persecution of Christians (vs.9-13), with false accusation, torture and murder. But the gospel still has to be preached in every part of the world before Jesus can return (v.14).

The "abomination that causes desolation" (v.15) could relate to the anti-Christ spoken of by Paul (2 Thessalonians 2:3-12), a figure of great power who claims to be divine (see also v.24), but who is very evil.

Jesus takes over
After that "great tribulation" the coming of Jesus will be seen by everyone (vs.27,30). He will come to judge the world, and demonstrate his great power in gathering to himself all his own people (v.31). Then he will create a new heaven and new earth, to be occupied only by those who have trusted him as their Saviour from sin and Lord of their life (Revelation 21:1).

Welcome home!

KEY TRUTH

Heaven is the Christian's final home, where we shall live for ever with Jesus and all his people.

A place of peace

Heaven is a real place. Paul teaches that all Christians go straight to be with Jesus when they die, but that we do not take our final place in heaven until it is finally established at the end of the world.

But peace reigns as soon as we die. Our struggles are over. We are with Jesus in a closer, more personal way than we have ever experienced on earth.

In heaven, there is no war. There are not even any arguments. And that is not because people have lost their personalities; it is because they have become perfectly human, as Jesus was when he lived on earth.

A place of joy

Heaven is a very joyful place. There is nothing there to be sad about!

But the joy is not a selfish kind of relief that evil and sin and suffering are a thing of the past. Rather it is rejoicing in the greatness, glory and love of God, which fill heaven.

Worship will be a major activity. It will not be like an unending church service; rather it will be genuine praise from the hearts of people who have come to see more clearly the wonderful gift of eternal life given to them because of Jesus' death on the cross.

A place of beauty

Heaven is a brand-new creation by God for his people. It will replace everything which existed before, although nothing that God originally made will be wasted.

It is therefore hard to imagine. Whenever the Bible writers describe it, they use picture language.

It is certainly a place of beauty and perfection – far better than anything humanity has ever built. It is full of light and colour. Beyond that, we cannot imagine it – but no one will be disappointed by it!

A place of justice

Heaven is where justice will be seen to have been done. Everyone who truly belongs there will be there. And no one who has rejected Jesus and lived in selfishness and evil will be allowed to enter.

TO THINK ABOUT ...

Make a list of the things that make somewhere a "home".

- Will these things be present in God's new creation? How will they be different from your experience of them here and now?

The Bible speaks of a new heaven and a new earth. Have a look at the word picture of this new world in Revelation 21–22.

- What does this tell you about the eternal life you will enjoy for ever?

God's presence in this eternal home will transform everything! He promises to dwell with his people for ever (see Revelation 21:2-3).

Then we shall see that wrongs have been put right – that will be part of our "reward" – and that wrongdoers have received the punishment they deserved.

That state of peace, joy, beauty and justice will never end. No one can imagine what eternity really means, except that it makes our human life and all its concerns seem quite small.

BIBLE CHECK
A place of peace Compare Philippians 1:23 with 1 Thessalonians 4:17; Revelation 21:4-7
A place of joy Revelation 4:8-11; 7:9-12
A place of beauty Revelation 21:9-27; 22:1-5
A place of justice Romans 12:17-21; Revelation 20:11-15; 21:8,27; 22:12-15

POSTSCRIPT
People who believe in heaven are not excused from working to create peace, joy, beauty and justice on earth, where the first signs of God's kingdom are to be built.

- Are you excited by this prospect? Why?
- How will God's new creation be a place of justice and healing?
- Do you often think about this hope? Should you? Why?
- Is it true that some Christians can be so heavenly-minded that they are no earthly good?

Thank God that he is preparing a home for you and for all Christians, in which he will live with you for ever. Pray that he will prepare you to live in this new home for ever!

BIBLE SUMMARY

WHAT HAPPENS TO NON-CHRISTIANS?

Despite the beauties and attractions of heaven, Jesus spent much time talking about the fate of those who rejected him. He did not paint a very pretty picture.

Excluded from God's presence
Jesus often used the picture of "outer darkness" where there will be "weeping and gnashing of teeth" (eg Matthew 24:30). It is a picture of people cut off for ever from the presence of God, from the warmth, love, peace and joy of heaven.

He also used the picture of an unquenched flame. It speaks of a place of frustration and unfulfilled desire, with people consuming themselves with anguish and sorrow. (See Mark 9:42-48; Luke 16:23,24,28; Revelation 20:14,15.)

The implication is that this state, usually called hell, lasts for ever. Certainly its effect is everlasting because there can be no transfer from it to heaven (Luke 16:26).

Jesus, the hope for the world
There is only one certain way of receiving eternal life, and that is to trust our lives entirely to Jesus Christ (John 14:6). That is why we are told to preach the gospel everywhere.

As for those who die without hearing about Jesus, Paul reminds us that God is always just and fair in his judgement of them (Romans 2:14-16). We cannot assume, however, that sinful people can attain that level of total faithfulness to what they have perceived of God's nature; hence the urgency of the missionary task.

ARRIVING

Life's new beginning

KEY TRUTH

The Christian's life has no end; death is the beginning of a new experience of life, love, peace and joy.

All things new

"I am making everything new!" Those are some of the last recorded words of Jesus in the New Testament.

And "everything new" means what it says: the physical earth, no longer corrupt and subject to decay; the organisations and systems which have controlled people's lives, no longer oppressive but creating order and freedom.

Everything which has existed will in some way be renewed and restored, for God wastes nothing. Only truly evil things will be totally destroyed. And this new creation depends as much on Jesus' death on the cross as our own eternal life does.

A new body

When Jesus appeared to his closest followers after his death, he was usually recognisable. Some people even saw the marks of the nails which had fixed him to the cross. But his body was different, so that he seemed no longer bound to the earth by natural laws.

His resurrection body is the prototype of ours. The Bible says we will receive new bodies in heaven. Through them we shall express our true self; without them we would be frustrated spirits, like those in hell who do not receive new bodies.

It seems as though we shall recognise one another in heaven – but of course, all the old disabilities and infirmities will have been taken away.

A new understanding

If you add up everything that is known in the world, it still only comes to a tiny proportion of what could be known. And each one of us only knows a tiny amount of the knowledge which does exist.

We are promised that when we get to heaven, we will understand much that has puzzled us on earth. However, even then we are not promised that we shall know everything – only God can be like that.

We may well understand some mysteries of our life – why God allowed this problem, or seemed not to answer that prayer – unless such issues are no longer of significance!

A new kind of life

Heaven has often been wrongly pictured – usually by those who make fun of it. Some people think of it as an unending holiday, or an everlasting party.

TO THINK ABOUT ...

Think of some of the ways people talk about, and often caricature, heaven.

- How have some people missed the real point of eternal life with God?
- Can you think of anything that you say or do as a Christian that gives a misleading image of what God's future is all about?

God's new creation may still be in the future, but Jesus' resurrection has already given Christians a glimpse of what it will be like.

- What can you learn by looking at the risen Jesus? What will be absent in heaven? What will be present?

In a sense it is, but that is only a part of the truth. The person who never wants to work will not be happy in heaven.

There will be lots to do, see, learn and experience. We will not cease to be human – in fact, we will have become truly human for the very first time. That means our life will be truly satisfying and stimulating – which a long period of idleness could never be. It is certainly something to look forward to!

BIBLE CHECK

All things new Romans 8:19-23; Colossians 1:19-20; Revelation 21:5-7

A new body John 20:19-29; 1 Corinthians 15:35-54

A new understanding 1 Corinthians 13:12; 1 Timothy 3:16; Revelation 7:13,14

A new kind of life Matthew 22:1-13; Revelation 21:22-27

POSTSCRIPT

If Jesus is to make all things new in the future, he will not be content to leave us unchanged in the present; the change starts now.

- Will you have a body in the new creation? Is this important?
- Why do you think God wants to reconcile and renew the world, rather than start from scratch? What does this tell you about creation?
- What will you be doing for eternity?

Praise God for his great plan to renew the whole creation! Thank him for including you in his plan, and for the sure hope of living with him for ever. Pray that you will begin to live today in the power of Jesus' resurrection.

BIBLE SUMMARY
HE IS RISEN!

If Jesus did not rise from the dead, there is no guarantee that we shall rise either. That is Paul's confident – and logical – comment in 1 Corinthians 15:12-20.

Paul believes in eternal life because he is convinced by the evidence that Jesus really did rise.

The empty tomb

The major piece of evidence is the empty tomb (John 20:1-8). The disciples saw the head bandages had been lifted off, and the rest of the bandages were undisturbed – and empty.

The Jews had placed a guard over the tomb (Matthew 27:62-66). At least they took seriously Jesus' prophecy about rising from the dead, even if the disciples did not! But the guards saw nothing criminal, although Matthew 28:4 says they saw something supernatural. So the Jews spread a rumour that the disciples had stolen the body (Matthew 28:11-15). But no one was able to produce it to prove that the resurrection was false.

Many witnesses

Jesus appeared several times to his followers (eg Luke 24:28-53). Once, he appeared to over 500 people at once (1 Corinthians 15:3-8) – no vision or delusion!

Notice what happened to the disciples after the Day of Pentecost (Acts 2:14,37-41). The cowards who had run from the cross now fearlessly preached that Jesus was risen from the dead. They could never have continued with that message if they had known it to be a lie.

Jesus is risen: and his love and power have been poured out through his Spirit to all who trust him and who ask for it – whoever they are.

Bible Reference Resource

The final key section of this handbook is designed as a reference to help you get even more out of your Bible. It contains: a summary of key Bible people and places, including maps of Abraham's journeys and of Jerusalem; a guide to what the Bible has to say about life issues; a guide to the Old Testament prophecies of the Messiah and their fulfilment in Jesus Christ; a guide to where to find help in the Bible in times of personal need; a daily Bible reading plan to give you a balanced diet to take in God's word; and an index to the subjects, people and places in this book.

Key People
and Places

Aaron

Brother of Moses; appointed as his spokesman (Ex 4:14-16; 7:1,2). Held up Moses' hands in battle (Ex 17:12). Consecrated as priest (Ex 28:1-4; 29; Lev 8; Heb 5:4). Made golden calf (Ex 32); opposed Moses (Nu 12:1-3). Priesthood challenged (Nu 16); staff budded as confirmation of his call (Nu 17). With Moses, excluded from Canaan (Nu 20:12). Death (Nu 20:22-29).

Abarim, Mountains of

Mountain range east of the Jordan and Dead Sea. Includes Mount Nebo at its northern point. From here Moses viewed the Promised Land (Nu 27:12; Dt 32:49) and the death of Jehoiakim was proclaimed (Jer 22:20).

Abednego

Formerly Azariah; member of Jewish nobility taken to Babylon with Daniel, Meshach and Shadrach (Da 1:3-7). Refused unclean food (Da 1:8-16); appointed as administrator (Da 2:49). Refused to worship golden image; kept safe in fiery furnace (Da 3).

Abel

Second son of Adam. Shepherd (Ge 4:2); offered sacrifice acceptable to God (Ge 4:4; Heb 11:4); killed by his brother Cain (Ge 4:8).

Abiathar

Son of Ahimelech; priest in time of Saul and David. Escaped Saul's massacre of priests who helped David (1Sa 22:20-23). Faithful to David (1Sa 23:6; 2Sa 15:24-29). Supported Adonijah (1Ki 1:7); deposed by Solomon (1Ki 2:26).

Abigail

1. David's sister (1Ch 2:16,17).
2. Wife of Nabal (1Sa 25:3); entreated David to spare his life (1Sa 25:14-35). Married David after Nabal's death (1Sa 25:40-43); mother of Kiliab (Daniel) (2Sa 3:3; 1Ch 3:1).

Abimelech

1. King of Gerar in time of Abraham. Took Sarah, Abraham's wife, thinking she was his sister (Ge 20). Made covenant with Abraham (Ge 21:22-34).
2. King of Gerar in time of Isaac. Rebuked Isaac for deceit (Ge 26:8-10); later made covenant with him (Ge 26:26-31).

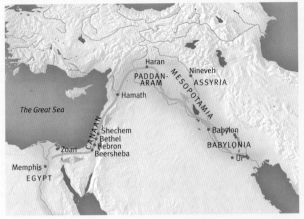

ABRAHAM'S JOURNEYS

Abraham and his family group's journey from Ur in southern Mesopotamia took him through the fertile river plains where their flocks could find pasture. While most of the group settled in Paddan-Aram, Abraham obeyed God's call and travelled on with his own family to Canaan. A visit to Egypt provided respite during a time of famine.

3. Son of Gideon (Jdg 8:31). Murdered brothers (Jdg 9:5); crowned king at Shechem (Jdg 9:6). Death (Jdg 9:54).

Abishai

Son of David's sister, Zeruiah; brother of Joab (1Sa 26:6; 1Ch 2:16). One of David's leading warriors (1Ch 11:15-21; 18:12; 2Sa 18:2; 20:6). Wanted to kill Saul (1Sa 26:7,8), Shimei (2Sa 16:9; 19:21).

Abner

Saul's cousin and commander of his army (1Sa 14:50; 17:55). Made Ishbosheth king after Saul's death (2Sa 2:8,9). Killed Asahel, Joab's brother (2Sa 2:18-25). Defected to David (2Sa 3:6-21). Murdered by Joab and Abishai to avenge Asahel's death (2Sa 3:26-30).

Abraham

Formerly Abram ("exalted father"). Descendant of Shem and son of Terah (Ge 11:10-27); married to Sarah (Ge 11:29). With Terah, travelled from Ur to Haran. Obeyed God's call to continue journey to Canaan (Ge 12:1-5). In Egypt (Ge 12:10), passed Sarah off as his sister (Ge 12:11-20). Divided the land with his nephew, Lot (Ge 13:5-17); settled at Hebron (Ge 13:18). Rescued Lot (Ge 14:1-16); blessed by Melchizedek (Ge 14:18-20). Name changed to Abraham ("father of many" Ge 17:5; Ne 9:7). Father of Ishmael by Hagar (Ge 16). Entertained angelic visitors (Ge 18:1-8); promised a son by Sarah (Ge 18:9-15; 17:16). Pleaded for Sodom (Ge 18:22-32). In Gerar (Ge 20:1), passed Sarah off as his sister (Ge 20:2-18). Father of Isaac (Ge 21:1-7); dismissed Hagar and Ishmael (Ge 21:8-14). Made treaty with Abimelech (Ge 21:22-34). Tested by God's command to sacrifice Isaac (Ge 22). Secured wife for Isaac (Ge 24). Death (Ge 25:7-11). God's covenant with (Ge 12:1-3; 15; 17; 22:15-18; Ex 2:24; Lk 1:72,73; Heb 6:13-15).

Abraham is revered as founding father of both Arab and Jewish nations

Example of faith (Heb 11:8-12); faith credited as righteousness (Ge 15:6; Ro 4:3; Gal 3:6-9). Described as father of God's people (Isa 51:2; Ac 13:26; Gal 3:26-29); God's servant (Ge 26:24); God's friend (2Ch 20:7; Isa 41:8; Jas 2:23).

Absalom

Son of David (2Sa 3:3). Had Amnon killed for raping his sister, Tamar (2Sa 13:23-29); fled from David (2Sa 13:37,38). Returned (2Sa 14:21-23); reconciled to David (2Sa 14:33). Conspired against David (2Sa 15:1-12); proclaimed king (2Sa 16:15-22). Defeated, killed by Joab (2Sa 18:6-10); mourned by David (2Sa 18:33).

Achaia

Roman province, with capital Corinth (2Co 1:1); governed by a pro-consul (Ac 18:12). Linked with Macedonia to denote the whole of Greece (Ac 19:21; Ro 15:26; 1Th 1:7,8); may refer specifically to Corinth. Christians from here contributed to Paul's collection for the poor in Jerusalem (Ro 15:26,27). Visited by Paul (Ac 18:1-18) and Apollos (Ac 18:27). The household of Stephanas were the first converts here (1Co 16:15).

Achan

Sinned by keeping spoils after conquest of Jericho thus causing Israel's defeat at Ai; stoned as punishment (Jos 7).

Achish

King of Gath, with whom David sought refuge and feigned insanity (1Sa 21:10-15), and later feigned loyal service (1Sa 27:2-12).

Achor, Valley of

Not far from Jericho at the entrance to the Promised Land. Name, meaning "trouble", given because Achan and family were killed here for hoarding spoil from Jericho (Jos 7:24-26). Becomes a symbol of hope for God's restored people (Hos 2:15; Isa 65:10).

The seal of Queen Jezebel, wife of King Ahab and enemy of the prophet Elijah

Adam

First man. Created by God (Ge 1:27); placed in Eden (Ge 2:15); given Eve as helper (Ge 2:19-24). Disobeyed God (Ge 3; Ro 5:14) and so brought sin into world (Ro 5:12,15-19). Jesus is described as "the last Adam"; (1Co 15:45).

Adonijah

1. Son of David, by Haggith (2Sa 3:4; 1Ch 3:2). Attempted to succeed David as king (1Ki 1); killed by Solomon's order after he requested Abishag for his wife (1Ki 2).
2. Levite and teacher of the Law (2Ch 17:8,9).

Adullam

Canaanite city whose king was defeated by Joshua (Jos 12:15). Allotted to the tribe of Judah (Jos 15:35), it was fortified by Rehoboam as part of his southern defences (2Ch 11:7). David and his men hid from Saul in Adullam's caves (1Sa 22:1; 2Sa 23:13; 1Ch 11:15).

Agrippa

1. Herod Agrippa I, grandson of Herod the Great. Jewish king, killed apostle James and imprisoned Peter (Ac 12:1-4); sudden death (Ac 12:20-23).
2. Herod Agrippa II, son of Herod Agrippa I, before whom Paul appeared at Caesarea (Ac 25:13–26:32).

Ahab

1. Son of Omri; evil king of Israel (1Ki 16:29.30). Married Jezebel; encouraged worship of Baal (1Ki 16:31-33). Opposed by Elijah (1Ki 17:1; 18:17-20). Defeated Arameans (1Ki 20); condemned for sparing Ben-Hadad (1Ki 20:42). Murdered Naboth and stole his vineyard (1Ki 21). Opposed by Micaiah (1Ki 22:1-28); killed (1Ki 22:34-38).
2. False prophet (Jer 29:21,22).

Ahaz
Son of Jotham; king of Judah (2Ki 16). Worshipped foreign gods (2Ki 16:3,4,10-18; 2Ch 28:2-4,22-25). Attacked by Aram and Israel (2Ki 16:5,6; 2Ch 28:5-8). Turned for help to Assyria rather than God (2Ki 16:7-9; 2Ch 28:16; Isa 7:3-17).

Ahimelech
1. Priest at Nob who helped David (1Sa 21:1-9); killed by Saul (1Sa 22:9-19).
2. One of David's soldiers (1Sa 26:6).

Ahithophel
David's counsellor; gave support to Absalom (2Sa 15:12; 16:21-23). Hanged himself when his advice was ignored (2Sa 17).

Ai
1. Canaanite town east of Bethel, near to Abram's camp and altar (Ge 12:8; 13:3,4). Attacked and finally defeated by Joshua (Jos 8) although Achan's sin led to earlier failure (Jos 7:4,5). Also called Aiath (Isa 10:28) and possibly Aija (Ne 11:31). See **Achor.**
2. Ammonite city east of the Jordan in Moab (Jer 49:3). Exact location unknown.

Alexandria
Port on west of Nile delta on Mediterranean coast. Capital city of Egypt in Greco-Roman period; second city of Roman Empire with large Jewish community. Jews who argued with Stephen came from here (Ac 6:9) as did Apollos (Ac 18:24).

Amasa
David's nephew (1Ch 2:17). In charge of Absalom's army (2Sa 17:24,25); made commander of David's army (2Sa 19:13); treacherously killed by Joab his cousin (2Sa 20:9,10; 1Ki 2:5).

Ammon
Territory inhabited by Ammonites east of the Jordan between Arnon and Jabbok rivers; with capital Rabbah. Western part captured by the Amorites, later occupied by Israel (Dt 2:21-23; Jdg 11:13-23). Its inhabitants frequently warred against the Israelites (1Sa 11:1; 2Sa 10:6-14; 12:26-28; 2Ch 27:5) and its destruction is prophesied (Jer 49:1-6; Eze 21:28-32; Am 1:13-15; Zep 2:8-11).

Amnon
David's firstborn son (2Sa 3:2). Raped Absalom's sister, Tamar (2Sa 13:1-22); killed by Absalom's men (2Sa 13:23-29).

Amos
1. Prophet from Tekoa (Am 1:1); spoke against Israel (Am 7:10-17).
2. Ancestor of Jesus (Lk 3:25).

Ananias
1. With wife Sapphira, died for lying to God (Ac 5:1-11).
2. Disciple, sent to heal and baptise Saul (Paul) in Damascus (Ac 9:10-19).
3. High priest before whom Paul appeared (Ac 22:30–23:5; 24:1).

Anathoth
Levite village north-east of Jerusalem, in Benjamin territory (Jos 21:18). Home of Abiezer (2Sa 23:27), Jehu (1Ch 12:3), Abiathar (1Ki 2:26) and Jeremiah (Jer 1:1; 29:27). Its inhabitants threatened Jeremiah and so faced God's punishment (Jer 11:21-23). During Babylonian siege of Jerusalem, God instructed Jeremiah to purchase a field here as an assurance of eventual redemption (Jer 32:1-15). The Assyrian army passed through here en route to Jerusalem (Isa 10:30).

Andrew
Apostle; brother of Simon Peter (Mt 4:18-20; 10:2; Mk 1:16-18,29); introduced boy with loaves and fish to Jesus (Jn 6:8,9); brought Greeks to Jesus (Jn 12:22). Former disciple of John the Baptist (Jn 1:35-40); brought Simon to Jesus (Jn 1:41).

Anna
Widow; prophetess of the tribe of Asher; recognised the baby Jesus as the Messiah when he was brought into the temple (Lk 2:36-38).

Annas
High priest (Lk 3:2). Questioned Jesus (Jn 18:13,19-24); questioned Peter and John (Ac 4:5-7).

The term "Christian" was first used in Antioch, in northern Syria. Today it is still a bustling metropolis

Antioch

1. Cosmopolitan capital city of Roman province of Syria, on bank of River Orontes, about 15 miles inland from Mediterranean port of Seleucia. Home of Nicolas, one of the first "deacons" (Ac 6:5). Persecuted believers arrived from Jerusalem to evangelise Jews (Ac 11:19), and Greeks (Ac 11:20,21). Barnabas and Paul also came here (Ac 11:22-26). Term "Christian" first used here (Ac 11:26). Became the base for Paul's three missionary journeys (Ac 13:1-3; 15:35-41; 18:23). Dispute arose here about circumcision (Ac 15:1,2), which was later decided at the council of Jerusalem.

2. City in province of either Pisidia or Phrygia (disputed) in southern Asia Minor. On first missionary journey, Paul preached in its synagogue, and though many Gentiles were converted, he experienced Jewish opposition and was expelled (Ac 13:14-51). Paul returned on his way home (Ac 14:21), and possibly again on his second journey (Ac 16:6). He refers to his persecution here in a letter to Timothy (2Ti 3:11).

Antipatris

See **Aphek 1**.

Aphek

1. City on coastal Plain of Sharon whose king was defeated by Joshua (Jos 12:18). Used as a Philistine encampment (1Sa 4:1; 29:1). Later rebuilt as Roman city Antipatris, where Paul was

taken on his way to Caesarea (Ac 23:31).

2. Town east of Galilee, where Ahab overcame the Aramean army (1Ki 20:26-30). Elisha predicted another Aramean defeat at Aphek (2Ki 13:17).

3. Canaanite city (also known as Aphik) in Asher's territory (Jos 19:30,31; Jdg 1:31,32).

Apollos

Disciple from Alexandria, well versed in the Scriptures (Ac 18:24,25); instructed by Priscilla and Aquila in Ephesus (Ac 18:26). Ministered in Corinth (Ac 18:27–19:1; 1Co 1:12; 3:5-9) and on Crete (Tit 3:13).

Aquila

See **Priscilla**.

Arabah

Valley stretching from Mount Hermon in the north to the Gulf of Aqaba in the south, including the Sea of Galilee, River Jordan and Dead Sea. On their journey to the Promised Land, the Israelites travelled and camped in this region (Dt 2:8). Sea of Arabah (Dt 3:17, etc) = Dead Sea.

Aram
Region north of Palestine, from Lebanon to beyond the River Euphrates. Known also as Paddan Aram and Aram Naharaim and by its Greek name Syria. Named after son of Shem (Ge 10:22), whose descendants spread rapidly around this area. Rebekah, Leah, Rachel and Jacob lived here (Ge 25:20; 27:43,44; 28:2; 29:16-28). Balaam came from here (Nu 23:7; Dt 23:4). The Israelites often served its gods (Jdg 10:6; 2Ch 28:23), and suffered at the hand of its army (1Ki 11:25; 2Ki 6:8; 13:4). At one stage Judah and Syria teamed up against Israel (1Ki 15:18-20) but at other times Israel and Syria joined together against Judah (2Ki 16:5). Its downfall was prophesied (Isa 7:1-8; Am 1:5). Roman province in NT times (Mt 4:24) of which Quirinius was governor (Lk 2:2). Paul travelled through here (Ac 15:41; 18:18; 21:3).

Aram Naharaim
See **Aram**; **Mesopotamia**.

Ararat, Mountains of
Range between Black Sea and Caspian Sea, from which streams converged to form Rivers Tigris and Euphrates. Traditionally the resting place of Noah's ark (Ge 8:4). Sennacherib's two sons fled here after murdering him (2Ki 19:37; Isa 37:38). One of the kingdoms God would use to punish Babylon (Jer 51:24-27).

Arnon
Swift river stream running from the mountains of Gilead into the Dead Sea. It separated Moab from the Amorite kingdom (Nu 21:13; 22:36; Jdg 11:18), and later Moab and Israel (Nu 21:25,26; Dt 2:24; 3:8,16; Jos 12:1,2; Jdg 11:21,22). After Moab's destruction fugitives fled here (Isa 16:2-4).

Aroer
1. Amorite city on northern bank of Arnon Gorge (Dt 2:36; 4:48; Jos 12:2). Captured by Israel and given to Reuben and Gad (Dt 3:12). Taken during Jehu's reign by King Hazael of Syria (2Ki 10:32,33).
2. Town in Gilead, facing Rabbah, on the boundary between Gad and the Ammonites (Jos 13:25). Restored and enlarged by descendants of Gad (Nu 32:34). 20 towns between Aroer and Minnith destroyed by Jephthah (Jdg 11:32,33). Exact location unknown.
3. Town in southern Judah (1Sa 30:28). Possibly the same place as Adadah (Jos 15:22) or modern Ararah (12 miles south-east of Beersheba).

Artaxerxes
King of Persia. Stopped work on walls of Jerusalem (Ezr 4:17-23). Provided resources for temple worship under Ezra (Ezr 7); reversed earlier decision to allow rebuilding of walls under Nehemiah (Ne 2:1-10).

Asa
King of Judah (1Ki 15:9,10). Removed idols and reformed worship (1Ki 15:11-15; 2Ch 14:2-5; 15). Rebuilt Judah's cities (2Ch 14:6,7). Relied on God against the Cushites (2Ch 14:9-15); relied on Aram, instead of God, against Israel, rebuked by Hanani the seer (1Ki 15:15-22; 2Ch 16). Death (2Ch 16:12-14).

Asahel
David's nephew; brother of Joab and Abishai (1Ch 2:16). One of David's leading warriors (2Sa 23:24; 1Ch 11:26; 27:7). Killed by Abner after a rash pursuit (2Sa 2:18-23); avenged by Joab (2Sa 3:26,27).

Asaph
1. Levite, in charge of music in the tabernacle and temple (1Ch 6:39; 15:17-19; 16:4-7,37; 1Ch 25:6; Ne 12:46). Composed several psalms (2Ch 29:30; Ps 50; 73-83). His sons set apart for musical and prophetic ministry (1Ch 25; 2Ch 20:14; 35:15; Ezr 2:41; 3:10; Ne 11:17).
2. Keeper of the king's forest (Ne 2:8). **3.** Hezekiah's recorder (2Ki 18:18,37; Isa 36:3,22).

Ashdod

Probably the capital of the five Philistine cities, 3 miles from the Mediterranean coast and 20 miles north of Gaza. Its inhabitants survived Joshua's advances against them (Jos 11:22). Its people suffered punishment when the captured ark of the covenant was placed in Dagon's temple here (1Sa 5:1-7). Captured by King Uzziah of Judah (2Ch 26:6), but generally remained independent. Amos prophesied against it (Am 1:8), and Sargon of Assyria attacked and captured it (Isa 20:1). Later prophets also predicted its fall (Jer 25:20; Zep 2:4; Zec 9:6). Its inhabitants opposed the rebuilding of Jerusalem (Ne 4:7,8), and Israelites were rebuked for intermarrying with them (Ne 13:23-25). Later known as Azotus, and evangelised by the deacon Philip (Ac 8:40).

One of the many lions made from glazed brickwork that decorated the palace throne room in Babylon

Asher

1. Son of Jacob by Zilpah (Ge 30:12,13; 35:26; Ex 1:4; 1Ch 2:2); blessed by Jacob (Ge 49:20).
2. Tribe descended from Asher. Blessed by Moses (Dt 33:24,25). Included in census (Nu 1:40,41; 26:44-47); apportioned land (Jos 19:24-31; Eze 48:2). Supported Gideon (Jdg 6:35; 7:23) and David (1Ch 12:36) but not Deborah (Jdg 5:17).
3. Territory along Mediterranean coast of Palestine, between Tyre and Mount Carmel. Its boundaries and towns were clearly listed (Jos 19:24-31). Allotted to descendants of Jacob's eighth son, who failed to drive out all the Canaanites (Jdg 1:31,32).
4. Town east of Shechem and west of River Jordan, in territory of Manasseh (Jos 17:7).

Ashkelon

One of the five Philistine cities, on the Mediterranean coast about 12 miles north of Gaza. It posed a regular threat to the judges of Israel, though the men of Judah captured it for a while (Jdg 1:18). Samson later killed 30 of its men (Jdg 14:19). Named in David's lament about Saul and Jonathan's deaths (2Sa 1:20). Amos prophesied its destruction (Am 1:8), which saw fulfilment when Sargon of Assyria attacked and captured it (Isa 20:1).

Asshur

See **Assyria**.

Assyria

Originally a city on the west bank of River Tigris, also known as Asshur (Ge 2:14), probably named after a son of Shem (Ge 10:22). It grew into a powerful empire with capital city Nineveh. Its king, Tiglath-pileser III invaded Israel (2Ki 15:19), and deported Israelites (2Ki 15:29), and this continued under Sargon (2Ki 17:6,23). Then Sennacherib invaded Judah (2Ki 18:13), but this

ultimately failed (2Ki 19:35,36; Isa 37:36,37). The prophets predicted its fall (Isa 10:12; 30:31; Mic 5:4-6; Zep 2:13).

Athaliah
Daughter of Ahab; wife of Jehoram, king of Judah; mother of Ahaziah (2Ki 8:18,26; 2Ch 22:2). Encouraged idolatry (2Ki 8:18,27). After Ahaziah's death, killed royal family (except Joash) and reigned for six years (2Ki 11:1-3; 2Ch 22:10-12). Killed by order of Jehoida, who made Joash king (2Ki 11:4-16; 2Ch 23:1-15).

Athens
Political and cultural centre of Greek state of Attica visited by Paul. Paul argued with the Athenians about their idolatry (Ac 17:16-32).

Babylon
1. City on the Euphrates in the Land of Shinar, founded by Nimrod (Ge 10:10). Became capital city of Babylonian Empire; known for its great splendour (Da 4:30). Its destruction was prophesied (Isa 47; Jer 50). The city was taken by the Persians.
2. Name used generally for Babylonia.
3. Used figuratively for Rome to emphasise its opposition to God (Rev 14:8; 16:19).

Babylonia
Located on the plain between the Euphrates and Tigris Rivers. Also called "land of Shinar" (Ge 10:10) and "land of the Chaldeans" (Jer 24:5).

Following the fall of Jerusalem, the people of Judah were exiled here (2Ki 25:21; 2Ch 36:20) just as Isaiah had prophesied (2Ki 20:16-18; Isa 39:5-7). They left here 50 years later (Ezr 1).

Balaam
Prophet, requested by Balak to curse Israel (Nu 22:4-11; 2Pe 2:15); forbidden by God (Nu 22:12); rebuked by his donkey (Nu 22:21-34). Curse turned to blessing (Nu 23–24; Dt 23:4,5; Jos 24:9,10). Advice led to Israel's seduction (Nu 31:15,16). Killed in Israel's defeat of Midianites (Nu 31:8; Jos 13:22).

Barabbas
Criminal, released by Pilate instead of Jesus (Mt 27:15-26; Mk 15:6-15; Lk 23:18-25; Jn 18:40).

Barak
Summoned by Deborah to lead Israel against Canaanites (Jdg 4–5; 1Sa 12:11; Heb 11:32).

Barnabas
Name (meaning "son of encouragement"); given to Joseph, a disciple from Cyprus (Ac 4:36). Apostle (Ac 14:14) and missionary (Gal 2:9). Introduced Paul to Jerusalem apostles (Ac 9:27). Sent to Antioch where he worked with Paul (Ac 11:22-26). With Paul on first missionary journey (Ac 13–14) and at Council of Jerusalem (Ac 15:2-35); parted company over his cousin John Mark (Ac 15:36-40).

Bartholomew
One of the twelve apostles (Mt 10:2,3; Mk 3:16-18; Lk 6:13,14; Ac 1:13). May also have been known as Nathanael.

Bartimaeus
Blind beggar healed by Jesus (Mk 10:46-52; Lk 19:35-43; Mt 20:29-34).

Baruch
Secretary and companion of Jeremiah. Wrote down Jeremiah's prophecies and read them to the people (Jer 36). Jeremiah gave him deeds of field in Anathoth (Jer 32:12-16). Accused of influencing Jeremiah; taken with him to Egypt (Jer 43:1-7). God's word to (Jer 45).

Bathsheba
Wife of Uriah; committed adultery with David and became his wife (2Sa 11). Secured succession for her son, Solomon (1Ki 1:11-40). Included in Jesus' genealogy (Mt 1:6).

Beersheba
Chief city of the Negev, in territory of Simeon (Jos 19:1,2). Site of well where Abimelech made an oath with Abraham (Ge 21:31), and Isaac (Ge 26:32,33). Hagar (Ge 21:17-19), Abraham (Ge 21:33), Isaac (Ge 26:23,24) and Jacob (Ge 46:1-4) encountered God here. It became a focus for pilgrimage (Am 5:5), rivalling Bethel and Gilgal. Samuel's sons were judges here (1Sa 8:1,2); Elijah passed through as he fled from Jezebel (1Ki 19:3).

Belshazzar

King of Babylon at time of its overthrow by Darius. Downfall announced by Daniel, who interpreted writing on the wall (Da 5).

Belteshazzar

Name given to Daniel in Babylon (Da 1:7).

Benjamin

1. Jacob's youngest son; second by Rachel, who died in childbirth (Ge 35:16-18,24; 46:19). Jacob's favourite after loss of Joseph. Father reluctant to allow him to go to Egypt (Ge 42:38; 43); brothers' concern about him led Joseph to make himself known (Ge 44–45). Blessed by Jacob (Ge 49:27).
2. Tribe descended from Benjamin. Blessed by Moses (Dt 33:12). Included in census (Nu 1:36,37; 26:38-41). Apportioned land (Jos 18:11-28; Eze 48:23); did not

take full possession (Jdg 1:21). Almost destroyed by other tribes (Jdg 20–21). Tribe of Saul (1Sa 9:1); followed Ishbosheth (2Sa 2:8,9); later gave support to David (1Ch 12:29; 1Ki 12:21). Tribe of Esther (Est 2:5) and Paul (Php 3:5).
3. Hilly territory west of River Jordan, with Ephraim to the north, Judah to the south, and Dan to the west. Its boundaries and towns were clearly listed (Jos 18:11-28). Allotted to descendants of Jacob's youngest son, who failed to drive out the Jebusites from Jerusalem (Jdg 1:21). Its people were almost destroyed by the other tribes of Israel because of their sin at Gibeah (Jdg 19–21).

Berea

City in Macedonia, about 50 miles south-west of Thessalonica. Paul fled here with Silas after trouble in

Thessalonica (Ac 17:10). Its people were receptive to the gospel and searched the Scriptures daily (Ac 17:11). Jews from Thessalonica followed Paul here, forcing Paul to leave; Silas and Timothy continued the work (Ac 17:13,14). Home of Paul's helper Sopater (Ac 20:4).

Beth Shemesh

1. Town in Valley of Sorek, about 15 miles south-west of Jerusalem, on the border of Judah (Jos 15:10). Probably also called Ir Shemesh (Jos 19:41). Allotted to tribe of Dan and assigned to the Levites (Jos 21:16; 1Ch 6:59). The stolen ark of the covenant was sent here by the Philistines where it remained until it was taken to Kiriath Jearim (1Sa 6:10–7:2). Located in one of Solomon's 12 districts (1Ki 4:9), it was the scene of battle between Jehoash and Amaziah (2Ki 14:11-14; 2Ch 25:21-23). Captured by the Philistines in the time of Ahaz (2Ch 28:18).
2. Town between Mount Tabor and River Jordan, on the border between the territories of Issachar and Naphtali (Jos 19:22).
3. Fortified town in Naphtali (Jos 19:35,38), from which Canaanites were not driven out (Jdg 1:33).

Modern-day well at Beersheba. Abraham, Hagar, Isaac and Jacob each encountered God at a well here

A shepherd watches over his sheep in Bethlehem

Bethany

1. Village on eastern slope of Mount of Olives, about 2 miles east of Jerusalem (Jn 11:18). Home of Mary, Martha and Lazarus (Jn 11:1). Jesus was anointed here in the home of Simon the Leper (Mt 26:6,7; Mk 14:3). Near to the site of Jesus' ascension (Lk 24:50,51).
2. Town on eastern side of the River Jordan where John was baptising (Jn 1:28). Exact location uncertain.

Bethel

1. Town about 12 miles north of Jerusalem, originally known as Luz. Abraham built an altar close by (Ge 12:8; 13:3,4). Jacob renamed the city after his vision (Ge 28:19) and later settled here (Ge 35:1). Conquered by Joshua (Jos 8:17); allotted to Benjamin (Jos 18:22) but taken by the house of Joseph (Jdg 1:22-26). Because the ark of the covenant was kept here (Jdg 20:27), it became a place of divine enquiry (Jdg 20:18; 21:2,3). Centre of worship for northern kingdom, and site for one of Jeroboam's golden calves (1Ki 12:27-29). Denounced for its idolatry (Hos 10:15; Am 5:5,6); Josiah broke down its altar (2Ki 23:15).
2. City in the territory of Simeon near Ziklag (1Sa 30:26-31). Bethul (Jos 19:4) and Bethuel (1Ch 4:30) are probably variants. Exact location unknown.

Bethlehem

1. Town in Judah about five miles south of Jerusalem. Also known as Ephrath (Ge 35:16,19; 48:7), Ephrathah (Ru 4:11; 1Ch 4:4; Ps 132:6) and Bethlehem Ephrathah (Mic 5:2). Rachel buried near here (Ge 35:19; 48:7); book of Ruth set here. David's birthplace where he was anointed (1Sa 16:1-13). Micah predicted Messiah's birth here (Mic 5:2; Mt 2:6), fulfilled by Christ's birth in the "town of David" (Lk 2:11).
2. Town in territory of Zebulun, about 7 miles northwest of Nazareth (Jos 19:15). Probably the home of Ibzan (Jdg 12:8).

Bethphage

Town near Bethany, on slopes of Mount of Olives, near the road from Jerusalem to Jericho. Here the disciples found colt for Jesus to ride into Jerusalem (Mt 21:1; Mk 11:1; Lk 19:29).

Entrance to the amphitheatre, Caesarea

Bethsaida

1. City north of Sea of Galilee, east of River Jordan. Originally a small town, but Philip the Tetrarch raised its status to a city and called it Julias. Home of Peter, Andrew and Philip (Jn 1:44), and possibly James and John (Lk 5:10).

2. City east of the Jordan, about 2 miles north of Sea of Galilee. Site associated with the feeding of the 5000 (Lk 9:10-17), and healing a blind man (Mk 8:22-26). (Possibly these two descriptions relate to the same place.)

Bezalel

Craftsman of the tribe of Judah (1Ch 2:20; 2Ch1:5) chosen, with Oholiab, to organise building of the tabernacle (Ex 31:1-6; 35:30–36:7). Credited with making the ark (Ex 37:1-9).

Bildad

See **Job**.

Boaz

Wealthy and benevolent landowner from Bethlehem; married Ruth, the widow of a relative, fulfilling the responsibility of kinsman-redeemer (Ru 2–4). Ancestor of David (Ru 4:17-22; 1Ch 2:5-15) and of Jesus (Mt 1:5).

Caesarea

Mediterranean port about 30 miles north of Joppa and capital of Judea. Herod Agrippa I died here (Ac 12:19-23); Agrippa II visited with Bernice (Ac 25:13). Home of Cornelius, to whom Peter ministered (Ac 10:1,24), and Philip the Evangelist (Ac 6:5). Paul passed through on his journeys (Ac 9:30; 18:22; 21:8) and was imprisoned here for 2 years before being sent to Rome (Ac 23:23,33; 25:4; 27:1).

Caesarea Philippi

City north of Sea of Galilee, on south-west slope of Mount Hermon. Known as Paneas (after the god Pan) until Philip

Niches in the cliff faces at Caesarea Philippi contained images of the pagan god Pan. It was here that Simon Peter recognised Jesus as "the Christ"

the Tetrarch renamed it. Northernmost limit of Jesus' ministry, where Simon Peter proclaimed him "the Christ" (Mt 16:13-16; Mk 8:27-29).

Caiaphas

High priest at time of Jesus' arrest (Mt 26:57-68; Jn 18:13,24). Unknowingly foretold the significance of Jesus' death (Jn 11:49-52; 18:14). Questioned Peter and John (Ac 4:5-7).

Cain

Eldest son of Adam and Eve (Ge 4:1). Farmer (Ge 4:2); murdered his brother, Abel, when sacrifice not accepted by God (Ge 4:3-8; 1Jn 3:12). Given mark of protection to limit punishment (Ge 4:9-16).

Caleb

One of spies sent to explore Canaan (Nu 13:6); with Joshua encouraged the people to go in

The ruins of a 2nd–3rd C AD synagogue in Capernaum, Jesus' adopted town at the start of his ministry

(Nu 13:30; 14:6-9). Allowed to enter land because of his faith (Nu 26:65; 32:12; Dt 1:36). Given possession of Hebron (Jos 14:6-15; 15:13-19).

Cana

A Galilean village where Jesus changed water into wine (Jn 2:1-11) and healed the son of a royal official (Jn 4:46-54). Home of Nathanael (Jn 21:2).

Canaan

Region between River Jordan and Mediterranean Sea, originally occupied by descendants of Ham's youngest son (Ge 9:18). God promised to give it to Abram and his descendants (Ge 12:1-7), so they settled here (Ge 13:12; 31:18; 33:18). It was

a fruitful land in Moses' time (Nu 13:27-29) but God promised it to the Israelites who captured it under Joshua (Jos 1:1-3), and it became the land of Israel.

Capernaum

City on northern shore of Sea of Galilee, where Jesus resided after leaving Nazareth (Mt 4:13; 9:1). Jesus taught in its synagogue (Mk 1:21; Lk 4:31; Jn 6:59), and performed significant miracles here (Mk 1:34), eg healing centurion's son (Mt 8:5-13; Lk 7:1-10), Peter's mother-in-law (Mk 1:30,31; Lk 4:38,39), a paralytic (Mt 9:1-8; Mk 2:3-12; Lk 5:18-26) and a man possessed by an evil spirit (Mk 1:21-26; Lk 4:31-35). Though a base for Jesus' ministry, he cursed it for its unbelief (Mt 11:23,24; Lk 10:15).

Carmel

1. Wooded mountain range overlooking Mediterranean coast, west of Sea of Galilee. Site of contest between Elijah and prophets of Baal (1Ki 18:19-39). The Shunammite woman found Elisha here (2Ki 4:25). Used figuratively on account of its fruitfulness (SS 7:6; Isa 33:9; 35:2; Jer 46:18; 50:19; Am 1:2; 9:3; Na 1:4).
2. Town in hill country of Judah, about 8 miles south of Hebron. Site of Saul's monument to himself (1Sa 15:12). Home of Nabal's widow Abigail (who David married, 1Sa 25), and one of David's mighty men (2Sa 23:35; 1Ch 11:37).

Cenchrea

Eastern port of Corinth. Paul cut his hair off before sailing from here (Ac 18:18). Phoebe served the church based here (Ro 16:1).

Cilicia

Region along southern coast of Asia Minor; capital Tarsus was the birthplace of Paul (Ac 21:39; 22:3). Cilician Jews argued with Stephen in Jerusalem (Ac 6:9). Paul came here soon after his conversion (Gal 1:21), and again on his second missionary journey (Ac 15:41).

Colossae

City in Phrygia, in Lycus Valley, about 12 miles east of Laodicea. Paul wrote to the church here (Col 1:2), possibly established by Epaphras (Col

Corinth: ruins of the temple of Apollo with the Acro-Corinth behind

1:7; 4:12), and led by Archippus (Col 4:17; Phm 2). Home of Onesimus (Col 4:9).

Corinth

Capital of Achaia, an important trading port between Rome and the East. Paul worked with Aquila and Priscilla here (Ac 18:1,2) and appeared before Proconsul Gallio (Ac 18:12-17). Paul left for Syria (Ac 18:18), and Apollos came to preach (Ac 18:27–19:1). Paul wrote to the church (1Co 1:2; 2Co 1:1), and returned at least twice (2Co 12:14; 13:1-3)

Cornelius

God-fearing Roman centurion stationed at Caesarea (Ac 10:1,2). Sent for Peter (Ac 10:1-8,19-33); heard gospel, received Holy Spirit, baptised (Ac 10:34-48); first Gentile convert.

Crete

Large island in Mediterranean Sea, about 60 miles south of Greece, where Paul's ship sheltered from a storm (Ac 27:8). Titus organised the church here (Tit 1:5).

Cush

1. Country south of Egypt. Land of precious stones (Job 28:19) and tall smooth-skinned people (Isa 18:2,7). Linked with Egypt in war,

Celebrated by some as "the first human rights charter in history", the Cyrus cylinder signals the Persian conquest of Babylon in 539 BC

sometimes against Israel (2Ki 19:9; 2Ch 12:3; Jer 46:9; Eze 38:5). Prophets proclaimed judgement upon Cush (Isa 18:1; Zep 2:12), but some of its inhabitants would join the people of God (Ps 68:31; Isa 11:11; 18:7).

2. Land bordering the Gihon River that flowed from Eden (Ge 2:10-14). Exact location unknown.

Cyprus

Large island in Mediterranean Sea, about 60 miles west of Syria. Mentioned by Isaiah and Ezekiel (Isa 23:1,12; Eze 27:6). Home of Barnabas (Ac 4:36); refuge for believers (Ac 11:19). Barnabas came here with Paul (Ac 13:4), and then Mark (Ac 15:39). Home of Mnason (Ac 21:16).

Cyrus

King of Persia. Issued edict to allow exiles to return to rebuild Jerusalem temple (2Ch 36:22,23; Ezr 1:1-4; 5:13; 6:3); gave back articles taken from temple (Ezr 1:7-11; 5:14,15; 6:5) and provided funds for building work (Ezr 3:7; 6:4). Place in God's purpose foretold by Isaiah (Isa 44:28–45:7,13).

Damascus

Capital city of Syria (Aram) (Isa 7:8), at foot of Mount Hermon, north-east of Sea of Galilee. Home of Abram's servant Eliezer (Ge 15:2). Base for attacks on Israel; captured by David (2Sa 8:5,6; 1Ch 18:5,6),

but later rebelled (1Ki 11:23). Recaptured by Jeroboam II (2Ki 14:28), but became Rezin's base for attack on Jerusalem (2Ki 16:5). Prosperous (Eze 27:18), due to rivers Abana and Pharpar (2Ki 5:12). Final destruction prophesied (Isa 17:1; Am 1:5), and fulfilled through Assyria. Became part of kingdom of Aretas (2Co 11:32). Saul converted on road to Damascus (Ac 9:1-8), and met Ananias here (Ac 9:10-22). Jewish inhabitants were angered by Paul's preaching (Ac 9:25; 2Co 11:32,33). Paul returned later (Gal 1:17).

Dan

1. Son of Jacob by Bilhah (Ge 30:4-6; 35:25); blessed by Jacob (Ge 49:16,17).

2. Tribe descended from Dan. Blessed by Moses (Dt 33:22). Included in census (Nu 1:38,39; 26:42,43). Apportioned land (Jos 19:40-48; Eze 48:1); unable to take full possession (Jdg 1:34), most of tribe migrated northwards to Laish (Jdg 18). Tribe of Samson (Jdg 13).

3. Territory given to tribe of Dan on Mediterranean coast (hence shipping trade, Jdg 5:17). Smallest portion of land allotted to a tribe (Jos 19:40-48). Due to Amorite activity, some Danites forced to migrate north (Jdg 1:34).

4. City near the sources of River Jordan. As the city at Israel's most northern point it appears to describe the extent

of the land (Jdg 20:1; 1Sa 3:20; 2Sa 3:10; 17:11; 24:2,15; 1Ki 4:25; 1Ch 21:2; 30:5). Known originally as Leshem (Jos 19:47), or Laish (Jdg 18:7). Jeroboam set up a golden calf here (1Ki 12:28-30). Conquered by Ben-Hadad of Aram (1Ki 15:20; 2Ch 16:4).

Daniel

1. Son of David and Abigail (1Ch 3:1).

2. Ancient figure regarded as an outstanding example of righteousness and wisdom (Eze 14:14,20; 28:3).

3. Hebrew of noble descent among those taken as captives to Babylon to be trained in the king's service (Da 1:3-6); renamed Belteshazzar (Da 1:7); refused to eat unclean food (Da 1:8-16). Possessed great understanding (Da 1:17,20); interpreted Nebuchadnezzar's dreams (Da 2:24-45; 4:19-27), writing on wall (Da 5:13-29). Held government posts under Nebuchadnezzar (Da 2:48), Belshazzar (Da 5:29), Darius (Da 6:1,2). Refused to obey king's decree; thrown into lions' den (Da 6). Visions predicting coming of Messianic kingdom (Da 7–12).

Darius

1. Mede, who became ruler of Babylon (Da 5:31; 9:1). Appointed Daniel as leading official (Da 6:2,28). Possibly to be identified with Cyrus.

2. Darius the Great, king of Persia (Hag 1:1; Zec 1:1);

revived Cyrus' edict allowing work on rebuilding temple to continue (Ezr 4:24–6:15).

3. Darius II, king of Persia (Ne 12:22).

David

Israel's second and greatest king; ancestor of Jesus (Mt 1:1; Ro 1:3; Rev 22:16); type of promised Messiah (Isa 11:1; Eze 34:23,24; 37:24,25). Singer of psalms and songs (2Sa 23:1; Am 6:5). Son of Jesse of Bethlehem (Ru 4:17; 1Sa 17:12). Anointed king by Samuel (1Sa 16:1-13). Entered Saul's service as musician (1Sa 16:14-23). Killed Goliath (1Sa 17:32-54). Friendship with Jonathan (1Sa 18:1-4; 19:1-7; 20; 23:16-18; 2Sa 1:25,26). Fled because of Saul's hostility (1Sa 19; 21–23). Spared Saul's life (1Sa 24; 26). Among the Philistines (1Sa 21:10-15; 27–29). Lament for Saul and Jonathan (2Sa 1). Anointed king of Judah at Hebron (2Sa 2:1-7). War with Saul's family (2Sa 2–4). United northern and southern tribes as king over all Israel (2Sa 5:1-4; 1Ch 11:1-3; 12:38-40). Captured Jerusalem from Jebusites (2Sa 5:6-10; 1Ch 11:4-9); installed ark there (2Sa 6; 1Ch 15–16). Promised lasting dynasty by God (2Sa 7; 1Ch 17; Ps 89; 132). Established empire: defeated Philistines (2Sa 5:17-25; 1Ch 14:8-17; 2Sa 21:15-22; 1Ch 20:4-8), Moabites, Arameans, Edomites (2Sa 8:1-14; 1Ch 18:1-13), Ammonites (2Sa 10; 1Ch 19).

Committed adultery with Bathsheba; murdered Uriah (2Sa 11); rebuked by Nathan (2Sa 12:1-14); repented (Ps 51). Married Bathsheba and other wives (1Sa 18:27; 25:39-43; 2Sa 5:13; 11:27); father of Solomon, Absalom, Adonijah, etc. (2Sa 3:2-5; 1Ch 3:1-9). Absalom's revolt (2Sa 15–18). Preparations for temple (1Ch 22; 28–29). Appointment of Solomon as successor (1Ki 1:28-48). Death (1Ki 2:10-12; 1Ch 29:26-28).

Dead Sea

At southern end of Jordan Valley, about 50 miles long and averaging about 10 miles wide. Up to 1,300 feet below sea level with salt and potash deposits more concentrated than in any other lake or sea in the world. Known as Salt Sea, Eastern Sea and Sea of Arabah. Mostly mentioned as a boundary – to the land of Israel (Nu 34:3,12; 2Ki 14:25; Eze 47:18), tribal territory (Dt 3:17; Jos 15:2,5; 18:19), neighbouring kingdoms (Dt 4:49; Jos 12:3). Its source was cut off when Israelites crossed into the Promised Land (Jos 3:16). Israel's enemies will be driven into it (Joel 2:20), and living water will flow into it from Jerusalem (Zec 14:8).

Deborah

1. Prophetess, one of Israel's judges. Appointed Barak to lead Israel against Canaanites (Jdg 4–5).
2. Rebekah's nurse (Ge 35:8).

Delilah

Betrayed Samson (Jdg 16:4-22).

Demas

Fellow-worker with Paul (Col 4:14; Phm 24), who later deserted him (2Ti 4:10).

Demetrius

1. Christian commended by John (3Jn 12).
2. Silversmith who stirred up a riot against Paul in Ephesus (Ac 19:23-41).

Derbe

Town in Asia Minor, about 16 miles east of Lystra. Paul and Barnabas fled here from trouble in Iconium (Ac 14:6), and gained converts (Ac 14:20,21). Paul visited on second missionary journey (Ac 16:1). Home of Gaius (Ac 20:4).

Dinah

Daughter of Jacob by Leah (Ge 30:21; 46:15). Raped by Shechem; avenged by Simeon and Levi (Ge 34).

Dorcas

Also known as Tabitha. Disciple in Joppa, known for her good works (Ac 9:36,39). Died (Ac 9:37); raised to life by Peter (Ac 9:38-42).

Dothan

Town about 12 miles north of Samaria, on trade route between Syria and Egypt. Joseph betrayed by brothers near here (Ge 37:17). Elisha encountered Aramean soldiers here (2Ki 6:8-19).

Ebal, Mount

North of Shechem, facing Mount Gerizim to the south. Highest peak of Samaria, at centre of Canaan. The LORD's

The Judean Wilderness, bordering the Dead Sea

curses were to be proclaimed from here (Dt 11:29), and an altar erected (Dt 27:4). Joshua carried out these instructions (Jos 8:30,33).

Eden

1. Wooded garden including Tree of Life and Tree of Knowledge of Good and Evil (Ge 2:9). First home of Adam and Eve (Ge 2:8) who took care of it (Ge 2:15). River flowed from Eden into the garden, and split into four (Ge 2:10-14). After disobeying God, Adam and Eve banished from here (Ge 3:23,24). Used figuratively for God's paradise (Isa 51:3; Eze 28:13; 31:9; 36:35). Alluded to in vision of New Jerusalem (Rev 22:2,3).
2. Market town providing Tyre

with choice items (Eze 27:23), captured by Assyrians (2Ki 19:12; Isa 37:12). Probably in Mesopotamia.

Edom

1. Another name for **Esau**.
2. Nation descended from Esau (Ge 36).
3. Region south of Dead Sea and east of Arabah, known also as land of Seir and Esau. Home of Esau (also called Edom) (Ge 32:3; 38:8). Esau's descendants expelled the Horites (Dt 2:12,22). During Exodus, Israel not permitted to pass through (Nu 20:14-21; 21:4; Jdg 11:17,18). Its people battled against Saul (1Sa 14:47), but were conquered by David (2Sa 8:13,14; 1Ki 11:15,16), enabling Solomon to develop a port here (1Ki 9:26). Revolted against Jehoram (2Ki 8:20-22), but retaken by Amaziah (2Ki 14:7). Azariah captured port of Elath (2Ki 14:22), but later recaptured (2Ki 16:6). Inhabitants joined with Babylonians against Judah (Ps 137:7; Eze 35:5; 36:5; Ob 10-16), and received prophetic judgement (Isa 34; 63:1-6; Jer 49:7-22; Eze 25:12-14; 35; Joel 3:19; Ob; Mal 1:3-5). Later referred to as Idumea (Mk 3:8).

Egypt

Country lying south of Mediterranean Sea and south-west of Palestine. Habitable land limited to Valley of the River Nile. A place of refuge in time of famine or oppression for Abram (Ge 12:10), Jacob and his sons (Ge 42:1-3; 45:16-20), Hadad (1Ki 11:17), Jeroboam (1Ki 11:40), Uriah (Jer 26:21), Ishmael (Jer 41:15-18), and Mary, Joseph and Jesus (Mt 2:13). Also a place of oppression and servitude for many (eg Joseph (Ge 37:28), Jacob's descendants (Ex 1:1-11), Jehoahaz (2Ch 36:4), and the remnant of Judah (Jer 44:12-14,27)). Jacob and Joseph both died here (Ge 50). Moses led Israelites out of slavery in Egypt (Ex 3–12). They were tempted to return to its relative security (Ex 13:17; 14:11,12; Nu 14:2-4; Ac 7:39). Figuratively a place of false security and hope (2Ki 18:21; Isa 20:5,6; 30:1-3; 31:1-3; 36:6; Jer 2:18; Eze 17:15-17). A centre of idolatry (Lev 18:3; Ezr 9:1; Isa 19:1,3; Eze 20:7,8). Its downfall prophesied (Isa 19; Jer 46; Eze 29–32), but it will eventually turn to the LORD (Isa 19:19; Zec 14:16-19).

Ekron

Most northern of five principal Philistine cities, about 35 miles west of Jerusalem. Not conquered by Joshua (Jos 13:1-3), but allotted to Judah (Jos 15:45), and later Dan (Jos 19:43). Ark of covenant brought here (1Sa 5:10), and the five Philistine rulers return here (1Sa 6:16). Philistine army fled here from Israelite army (1Sa 17:52). Baal-Zebub worshipped, and consulted by Ahaziah who dies as a result (2Ki 1). Its judgement is pronounced (Jer 25:20; Am 1:8; Zep 2:4; Zec 9:5,7).

Elam

Region east of Babylonia, named after son of Shem, ancestor of the Elamites (Ge 10:22; 1Ch 1:17). Capital city is Susa or Shushan (Da 8:2). Its king captured Lot in Sodom (Ge 14:1-17). Some Israelites exiled here by Assyria (Isa 11:11; Ac 2:9) and Elamites settled in Samaria (Ezr 4:9). Its part in Babylon's downfall was prophesied (Isa 21:2; 22:6), but it too would receive God's judgement (Jer 25:15-26; 49:34-39; Eze 32:24,25).

Eleazar

Third son of Aaron (Ex 6:23; Nu 3:2; 1Ch 6:3,4); anointed as priest (Lev 8–9; Nu 3:2-4); leader of Levites, responsible for care of sanctuary (Nu 3:32; 4:16). Succeeded Aaron (Nu 20:28; Dt 10:6); assisted Moses (Nu 26:1-4,63; 27:2; 31:12; 32:2). With Joshua, apportioned land (Nu 32:28; 34:17; Jos 14:1; 19:51). Death (Jos 24:33).

Eli

Priest at Shiloh; blessed Hannah (1Sa 1:9-17), who brought Samuel to him (1Sa 1:24-27); raised Samuel (1Sa 2:11,18-21,26). Wickedness of sons (1Sa 2:12-17,22-25); rebuked by prophet (1Sa 2:27-36). Directed Samuel to the Lord (1Sa 3). Death of Eli and his sons (1Sa 4:10-18).

Re and Horus, Egyptian gods of rebirth and protection, watch over Pharaoh on his journey to the afterlife

Elihu
See **Job**.

Elijah
Prophet; predicted drought in Israel (1Ki 17:1; Lk 4:25; Jas 5:17). Fed by ravens at brook Kerith (1Ki 17:2-6), and by widow of Zarephath (1Ki 17:9-16); raised widow's son (1Ki 17:17-24). Contest with prophets of Baal on Mt Carmel (1Ki 18:18-46). Fled from Jezebel to Horeb (1Ki 19); called Elisha (1Ki 19:19-21). Denounced Ahab over Naboth's vineyard (1Ki 21:17-29). Prophesied God's judgement on Ahaziah and called down fire (2Ki 1:1-17). Divided Jordan (2Ki 2:7,8); taken up to heaven in chariot of fire and whirlwind (2Ki 2:11,12); mantle taken by Elisha (2Ki 2:9,10,13-15). Appeared with Moses at Jesus' transfiguration (Mt 17:2,3; Mk 9:2-4; Lk 9:28-31). Return prophesied (Mal 4:5,6; Mt 17:10; Mk 9:11); identified with John the Baptist (Mt 11:13,14; 17:11-13; Mk 9:12,13; Lk 1:17).

Eliphaz
See **Job**.

Elisha
Prophet; succeeded Elijah (1Ki 19:16-21); took his cloak and divided Jordan (2Ki 2:13,14). Purified bad water (2Ki 2:19-22); cursed youths who mocked him (2Ki 2:23-25); helped defeat Moab (2Ki 3:11-19); provided oil for widow (2Ki 4:1-7); raised Shunammite woman's son (2Ki 4:8-37); purified food (2Ki 4:38-41); fed 100 men with 20 loaves (2Ki 4:42-44); healed Naaman (2Ki 5); made axe-head float (2Ki 6:1-7). Captured Arameans (2Ki 6:8-23). Life threatened (2Ki 6:31-33). Prophesied end of siege of Samaria (2Ki 7:1,2). Visit to Damascus (2Ki 8:7-15). Sent prophet to anoint Jehu as king (2Ki 9:1-3). Death (2Ki 13:14-20); miracle with bones (2Ki 13:21).

Elizabeth
Wife of Zechariah; mother of John the Baptist (Lk 1:5-25,57-60). Related to Mary (Lk 1:36); blessed Mary when she visited (Lk 1:39-45).

Emmaus
Village in Judea about 7 miles from Jerusalem (Lk 24:13). After his resurrection, Jesus appeared to Cleopas and another disciple on the Emmaus road (Lk 24:15). He explained Scriptures concerning himself but was not recognised until he broke bread at the evening meal (Lk 24:30,31). Exact location unknown.

Endor
Town about 4 miles south of Mount Tabor, allotted to tribe of Manasseh (Jos 17:11). Home of the medium whom Saul consulted (1Sa 28:7). Fleeing Midianites perished here (Ps 83:10).

Enoch
1. Cain's first son; city named after him (Ge 4:17,18).
2. Descendant of Seth; father of Methuselah (Ge 5:18-21). Prophesied (Jude 14,15); walked with God, and taken by him (Ge 5:22-24).

Epaphroditus
Christian from Philippi; brought gifts from Philippians to Paul (Php 4:18); fellow-worker with Paul; almost died serving Christ (Php 2:25-29).

Ephesus
Capital city and important port of Asia Minor, opposite island of Samos. Famous for temple of Artemis (Ac 19:35). Paul visited on second missionary journey leaving Priscilla and Aquila here (Ac 18:19). Apollos joined them (Ac 18:24-26). Paul returned on third missionary journey (Ac 19:1) and stayed for between two and three years (Ac 19:10; 20:31), preaching in the synagogue (Ac 19:8), in the school of Tyrannus (Ac 19:9) and in private homes (Ac 20:20). His preaching threatened reputation of Artemis and associated trade (Ac 19:23-27), and trouble ensued (Ac 19:28-41). Paul wrote to Corinth from here (1Co 16:8; 15:32). He left Timothy, Onesimus and Tychicus to continue his work (1Ti 1:3; 2Ti 1:18; 4:12), and wrote to the church (Eph 1:1). One of the seven letters of Revelation is addressed to

Ephesus (Rev 1:11), in which the church receives praise and criticism (Rev 2:1-7).

Ephraim

1. Joseph's second son (Ge 41:52); blessed by Jacob as firstborn (Ge 48:13-20).
2. Tribe descended from Ephraim. Blessed by Moses (Dt 33:13-17). Included in census (Nu 1:32,33; 26:35-37). Apportioned land (Jos 16:1-9; Eze 48:5); unable to take full possession (Jos 16:10; Jdg 1:29). Occupied prestigious position among tribes (Jdg 8:2,3).
3. Territory west of River Jordan, between Manasseh and Benjamin. Allotted to the descendants of Joseph's younger son. Territories of Ephraim and Manasseh, often treated together (Jos 16:1–17:2). Canaanites not driven out (Jos 16:10), but enslaved (Jos 17:13). Known for its beauty and fertility, contrasting with its moral decay (Isa 28:1,4; Hos 9:13; 10:11; 12:8).
4. Became synonym for northern kingdom (Ps 78:9-16,67,68; Isa 7:1-17; Jer 7:15; Hos 5; 11).
5. Town where Jesus withdrew with his disciples (Jn 11:54). Exact location unknown, probably also known as Ophrah.

Ephrath
See **Bethlehem 1**.

Ephrathah
See **Bethlehem 1**.

Statue of Artemis (Diana of the Ephesians): the focus of Ephesian devotion

Esau
Also known as Edom (Ge 25:30). Son of Isaac; older twin of Jacob (Ge 25:24-26); hunter, favoured by Isaac (Ge 25:27,28). Sold birthright (Ge 25:29-34; Heb 12:6); lost blessing as eldest son (Ge 27). Married foreign wives (Ge 26:34,35; 28:8,9; 36:2,3). Reconciled to Jacob (Ge 32:3-21; 33:1-16). Occupied land of Seir (Ge 36:8; Dt 2:4-12); ancestor of Edomites (Ge 36:9-43). Rejection by God contrasted with gracious choice of Jacob (Mal 1:2,3; Ro 9:13).

Esther
Jewess living in Persia, also called Hadassah; brought up by cousin Mordecai (Est 2:7).

Became Xerxes' queen (Est 2:8-18). Persuaded by Mordecai to help foil Haman's plot to destroy Jews (Est 3–4); risked life by approaching Xerxes (Est 4:9-11; 5:1-8); revealed Haman's plans (Est 7). Encouraged Jews to slaughter enemies; initiated feast of Purim in celebration (Est 9).

Ethiopia
See **Cush 1**.

Euphrates, River
Longest river of western Asia (about 1,780 miles), which joins with the River Tigris. Known as the River (Ex 23:31) and the Great River (Ge 15:18). Babylon and Ur situated on its bank. One of the four rivers of Paradise (Ge 2:14); the north-east boundary of the Promised Land (Ge 15:18; Dt 1:7; Jos 1:4). David fought here (2Sa 8:3; 1Ch 18:3), and Josiah was killed here (2Ch 35:20-24). It features in prophecies about the exile (Isa 11:15; Jer 46:6; 51:63) and in John's vision (Rev 9:14; 16:12).

Eve
First woman; created from Adam as wife and helper (Ge 2:20-24). Deceived by serpent (Ge 3:1-6; 2Co 11:3; 1Ti 2:13,14). Punished (Ge 3:16). Mother of Cain and Abel (Ge 4:1,2).

Ezekiel
Member of priestly family; deported to Babylon with Jehoiachin (Eze 1:1-3). Vision and call to be prophet to exiles

(Eze 1:4-28; 2–3). Listened to, but words not acted upon (Eze 8:1; 14:1; 20:1; 33:30-32). Sudden death of wife (Eze 24:15-18). Visions: idolatry of Jerusalem (Eze 8–11); valley of dry bones (Eze 37); new temple (Eze 40–47). Prophetic symbolism (Eze 4–5; 12). Oracles: against Israel (Eze 13–24; 33); against nations (Eze 25–32; 35; 38–39); of restoration (Eze 34; 36).

Ezra
Priest and teacher of the Law of Moses (Ezr 7:6,10-28); commissioned by Artaxerxes to lead a return of exiles to Jerusalem, to provide resources for temple worship and to establish observance of Law (Ezr 7–8). Addressed problem of intermarriage (Ezr 9–10); read Law at Feast of Tabernacles (Ne 8); took part in dedication of city walls (Ne 12:36).

Gabriel
Angel; sent to Daniel to interpret vision (Da 8:15-26) and deliver prophetic message (Da 9:20-27); announced birth of John the Baptist (Lk 1:11-20) and of Jesus (Lk 1:26-38).

Gad
1. Son of Jacob by Zilpah (Ge 30:9-11; 35:26); blessed by Jacob (Ge 49:19).
2. Tribe descended from Gad. Blessed by Moses (Dt 33:20,21). Included in census (Nu 1:24,25; 26:15-18).

Apportioned land east of Jordan (Nu 32; 34:14,15; Jos 18:7; 22); crossed into Canaan to fight alongside other tribes (Nu 32:16-32). Place in restored land (Eze 48:27,28).
3. Territory east of River Jordan, with Manasseh to the north, and Reuben to the

Queen Esther's courage enabled the Jewish people to survive Haman's plot to destroy them. A Purim festival tableau is a reminder that Haman was hung on his own gallows as a punishment

south. Its boundaries and towns were listed (Jos 13:24-28; Nu 32:34-36). Allotted to the descendants of Jacob's seventh son, who liked it for its good grazing (Nu 32:1).
4. Seer at David's court (1Sa 22:5; 2Sa 24:11-19).

Galatia
Central region of Asia Minor. Paul passed through on second missionary journey (Ac 16:6)

and due to illness stayed and preached (Gal 4:13,14). Returned during third journey (Ac 18:23), and sent letter here (Gal 1:2; 3:1). Crescens left Paul to go here (2Ti 4:10). Peter addressed his first letter to Galatian church (1Pe 1:1).

Galilee
1. Lake situated 60 miles north of Jerusalem, measuring approximately 13 by 8 miles, fed by River Jordan. Known as Sea of Galilee (Mt 4:18), Sea of Kinnereth (Nu 34:11), Sea of Tiberias (Jn 6:1), and Lake of Gennesaret (Lk 5:1). In OT mentioned as a boundary (Nu 34:11; Jos 12:3; 13:27). Fishing industry thrived here: Jesus called some fishermen to become disciples (Mt 4:18; Mk 1:16); he made use of boats (Lk 5:3; Jn 6:1); he provided disciples with a large catch of fish (Jn 21:1-6); he calmed a storm (Mk 4:35-41).
2. Region between the Lake and Mediterranean Sea. Contained refuge city of Kedesh (Jos 20:7; 21:32). Solomon gave 20 of its towns to Hiram (1Ki 9:11). It was later captured by Tiglath-pileser of Assyria (2Ki 15:29), and flooded with immigrants (2Ki 17:24). It became known as Galilee of the Gentiles. It would be honoured through the coming Messiah (Isa 9:1; Mt 4:15). Jesus lived and ministered here (Mt 2:22; 4:12,13; Lk 23:5; Ac 10:37). He became known as Jesus of Galilee (Mt 26:69).

Gamaliel

1. Leader from Manasseh; helped Moses with census (Nu 1:10; 2:20; 7:54-59; 10:23).
2. Pharisee and respected Rabbi and teacher of the law who intervened in trial of apostles (Ac 5:34-40). Acknowledged by Paul as his teacher (Ac 22:3).

Gath

One of five chief cities of the Philistines, about 10 miles east of Ashdod (Jos 13:3; 1Sa 6:17). Inhabited by the Anakim, even after Joshua had driven them out of the hill country of Judah (Jos 11:22). Home to Goliath (1Sa 17:4) and another giant (2Sa 21:20). Its inhabitants were struck by plague when ark of covenant brought here (1Sa 5:8,9), so sent a guilt offering to Israel (1Sa 6:17). David took refuge here (1Sa 21:10; 27:2-4), and later captured it (1Ch 18:1). Rehoboam fortified it (2Ch 11:8), but Hazael of Aram captured it (2Ki 12:17). Was destroyed by the time of Amos (Am 6:2). Exact location unknown.

Gaza

Most southern of five principal Philistine cities, and the oldest, having been a Canaanite border town (Ge 10:19). Reached during Joshua's conquests (Jos 10:41), but not subdued (Jos 11:22). Captured briefly by men of Judah (Jdg 1:18), but back in Philistine hands when Samson

Upper Galilee, north of Lake Galilee: a region of lush countryside and beauty

tormented its people (Jdg 16:3,21,30). Destruction was prophesied (Jer 25:20; Am 1:6,7; Zep 2:4; Zec 9:5). Ethiopian eunuch converted on road from Jerusalem to here (Ac 8:26).

Gehazi

Elisha's servant. Suggested Shunammite woman be rewarded with a son (2Ki 4:14); obtained money from Naaman falsely, contracted leprosy as punishment (2Ki 5:19-27); recounted Elisha's raising of Shunammite's son (2Ki 8:1-6). May be unnamed servant (2Ki 4:43; 6:15).

Gerar

Border town between Egypt and Philistia (Ge 10:19), where Abraham stayed and pretended Sarah was his sister (Ge 20:1-7). Isaac dug wells here (Ge 26). Asa's army pursued the Cushites to here, killing them and plundering the surrounding villages (2Ch 14:13,14).

Gerizim, Mount

South of Shechem, facing Mount Ebal to the north. Place where the LORD's blessings were to be announced (Dt 11:29; 27:12), fulfilled by Joshua (Jos 8:33-35). Place where Jotham addressed the people of Shechem (Jdg 9:7). In Jesus' day the Samaritans worshipped here (Jn 4:20,21).

Gibeah

1. City in territory of Benjamin (Jos 18:28; Jdg 19:14); inhabitants brutalised the concubine of a Levite of Ephraim (Jdg 19:22-25). War with the Benjamites ensued (Jdg 20:12-48). Occupied by Philistines for a while (1Sa 10:5). Also Saul's home (1Sa 10:26; 15:34), and base (1Sa 11:4; 22:6; 23:19; 26:1). Spirit of God came upon Saul here (1Sa 10:10) and seven of his descendants killed here by Gibeonites (2Sa 21:6).

2. Town south-east of Hebron in territory of Judah (Jos 15:57). Exact location unknown.

3. Town in territory of Phinehas, where Aaron's son Eleazar was buried (Jos 24:33).

Gibeon

Chief of four fortress cities, inhabited by the Hivites (Jos 9:17) and allotted to the tribe of Benjamin (Jos 21:17). Gibeonites tricked Joshua into signing a peace treaty, but they became Israel's woodcutters and watercarriers (Jos 9). Joshua defended them from the Amorite alliance; during the battle the sun stood still (Jos 10:1-14). Saul violated treaty (2Sa 21:1), so his descendants killed by Gibeonites (2Sa 21:9). Place where Saul's and David's men fought (2Sa 2:12-16); David slaughtered the Philistines (2Sa 5:25; 1Ch 14:6) and Solomon offered sacrifices (1Ki 3:3-5; 1Ch 16:39; 21:29; 2Ch 1:3-5,13). Inhabitants helped rebuild Jerusalem (Ne 3:7; 7:25). Home of Hananiah (Jer 28:1).

Gideon

Judge, called to save Israel from Midianites (Jdg 6:11-24). Broke down altar of Baal (Jdg 6:25-32). Sign of fleece (Jdg 6:36-40); army reduced to 300 (Jdg 7:2-8); defeated Midianites (Jdg 7:16–8:28). Refused throne (Jdg 8:22,23); ephod made from spoil became source of idolatry (Jdg 8:24-27). Death (Jdg 8:32).

Gilboa, Mount

Range between plain of Jezreel and River Jordan. Site of battle between Israelites and Philistines (1Sa 28:4), when Israel was defeated (1Sa 31:1; 1Ch 10:1), and Saul and his

View from Mt Gerizim across the valley to Mt Ebal

sons killed (1Sa 31:8; 1Ch 10:8). Cursed by David (2Sa 1:21).

Gilead

1. Mountainous region east of River Jordan, between Sea of Galilee and Dead Sea. Place of refuge for Jacob from Laban (Ge 31:21), Israelites from the Philistines (1Sa 13:7), and David from Absalom (2Sa 17:22,26). Midianite merchants, who bought Joseph, were travelling from here (Ge 37:25). Ideal region for raising livestock, so Reuben and Gad desired it (Nu 32:1). Half was allotted to them and the rest to Manasseh (Dt 3:12,13).
2. A city of wicked men (Hos 6:8). Location unknown.
3. Mountain in the Jezreel valley, where Gideon had to reduce the size of his army (Jdg 6:2,3).

Gilgal

1. First encampment for Israelites in Promised Land, on the eastern side of Jericho (Jos 4:19). Monument set up as a memorial (Jos 4:19,20): here Israelites were circumcised and celebrated Passover (Jos 5:2-10). Israelite base camp for Joshua's conquest (Jos 6:11; 10:15; 14:6), until it moved to Shiloh (Jos 18:1). Here the Gibeonites tricked Joshua (Jos 9:6), and from here he marched to their aid (Jos 10:7). Samuel held court here (1Sa 7:15,16), it became a sanctuary (1Sa 10:8; 13:8-10; 15:21). Here

A satellite view of the Nile Delta reveals its richness. The family of Jacob settled and flourished on the north-eastern side of the delta in Goshen

Agag died (1Sa 15:33), and Saul was both proclaimed king (1Sa 11:15) and rejected as king (1Sa 15:12-23). David was greeted here by the men of Judah (2Sa 19:15). Became a centre of idolatry (Hos 4:15; 9:15; 12:11; Am 4:4; 5:5).
2. Village from which Elijah travelled (2Ki 2:1). Elisha visited here (2Ki 4:8). Probably in hill country of Ephraim, near Bethel and Shiloh.
3. Royal city associated with Dor (Jos 12:23), about 5 miles north of Antipatris.

Goliath

Philistine giant (1Sa 17:4-7); challenged Israel (1Sa 17:8-11,23-26); killed by David (1Sa 17:32-50). Sword kept at sanctuary at Nob; given to David (1Sa 21:9).

Gomorrah

City in Valley of Siddim (Ge 14:2,3), usually paired with

Sodom. Its king and army were defeated by a Mesopotamian alliance (Ge 14:8-11). Faced God's judgement on account of gross sin (Ge 18:20,21; 19:24,25). Used to exemplify human depravity and God's judgement (Dt 29:23; Isa 13:19; Jer 23:14; 49:18; Am 4:11; Mt 10:15; Ro 9:29; 2Pe 2:6). See Sodom.

Goshen

1. North-eastern region of Nile Delta in Egypt. Jacob's family brought here by Joseph during famine (Ge 45:10; 46:28,29,34; 47:1,4,6). They flourished here (Ge 47:27), and Jacob died here (Ge 49:33). It was protected from the plagues (Ex 8:22; 9:26).
2. Region of southern

Palestine, between Gaza and Gibeon. Joshua's conquests reached to here (Jos 10:41; 11:16).

3. Town in the mountains of south-west Judah (Jos 15:51).

Great Sea
Known today as the Mediterranean Sea, it was called the Great Sea (Nu 34:6,7; Jos 1:4; 9:1; 15:12,47; 23:4; Eze 47:10-20; 48:28), the Western Sea (Dt 11:24; 34:2; Joel 2:20; Zec 14:8), and the Sea of the Philistines (Ex 23:31). Formed a natural boundary so often used as a territorial marker.

Habakkuk
Prophet to Judah (Hab 1:1; 3:1).

Hagar
Sarah's Egyptian maidservant given to Abraham as his wife (Ge 16:1-3). Became pregnant; fled from Sarah (Ge 16:4-8); encouraged by God (Ge 16:9-14). Gave birth to Ishmael (Ge 16:15,16; 25:12); driven away by Sarah (Ge 21:9-21). Symbol of those in slavery through dependence on law for justification (Gal 4:21-31).

Haggai
Prophet; encouraged returned exiles to continue rebuilding temple (Ezr 5:1; 6:14; Hag 1:1-11; 2).

Ham
Son of Noah (Ge 5:32; 6:10; 1Ch 1:4). Saved in ark (Ge 7:13; 9:18,19). Father of Canaan, Cush (Ethiopia), Put (Libya) and Mizraim (Egypt) (Ge 9:18; 10:6; 1Ch 1:8). Dishonoured Noah by looking at his nakedness; brought curse on Canaan (Ge 9:20-27). Associated with Egypt (Ps 78:51; 105:23,27; 106:22).

Haman
Agagite, honoured by Xerxes (Est 3:1,2). Angered by Mordecai's defiance (Est 3:3-5; 5:9-14); planned to exterminate Jewish people (Est 3:6-15). Ordered to honour Mordecai (Est 6:1-12). Plot exposed by Esther (Est 7:1-7); hanged on gallows built for Mordecai (Est 7:9,10).

Hamath
City and region in Syria on southern bank of River Orontes. Its king congratulated David for defeat of Hadadezer (2Sa 8:9,10; 1Ch 18:9,10). Solomon controlled it, and built storage depot there (2Ch 8:4). Was lost to Israel but recovered by Jeroboam (2Ki 14:28). After Assyrian capture, some inhabitants moved to Samaria (2Ki 17:24; Isa 36:18,19; 37:13), and some Israelites moved to Hamath (Isa 11:11). Its people worshipped Ashima (2Ki 17:30), and were guilty of syncretism (2Ki 17:29-33). In Amos' time the city was in ruins (Am 6:2).

Hannah
Wife of Elkanah; childless (1Sa 1:1-8). Prayed for a child (1Sa 1:9-18); gave birth to Samuel (1Sa 1:19,20); dedicated Samuel to God (1Sa 1:21-28). Her prayer (1Sa 2:1-10). Blessed with other children (1Sa 2:19-21).

Haran
City in northern Mesopotamia, where Terah and Abram stayed and Terah died (Ge 11:31,32; Ac 7:2,4). Abram received God's promise here (Ge 12:1-4). Here Jacob fled (Ge 28:10), then found and married Rachel (Ge 29:4-28). Captured by Assyrians (2Ki 19:12; Isa 37:12). Its merchants traded with Tyre (Eze 27:23,24).

Hebron
Town in the highlands of Judah, between Beersheba and Jerusalem. Originally known as Kiriath Arba (Ge 23:2; Jos 14:15). Abram's home, where he built an altar (Ge 13:18), received promise of birth of Isaac (Ge 18:1-15), and where Sarah died (Ge 23:2). Isaac and Jacob lived here (Ge 35:27) and Moses' spies came here (Nu 13:22). Joshua killed its king (Jos 10:3-27), Caleb drove out its inhabitants (Jos 14:12-15). Designated a city of refuge (Jos 20:7). Abner killed and buried here (2Sa 3:27-32). David made king here (2Sa 5:1-5); base for Absalom's rebellion (2Sa 15:7-12). Fortified by Rehoboam (2Ch 11:10-12).

Hermon, Mount

At the most northerly point conquered by Joshua (Dt 3:8; Jos 11:3,17; 12:1,5; 13:5,11), also known as Mount Sirion, Mount Senir (Dt 3:9; 1Ch 5:23), Mount Siyon (Dt 4:48) and Mount Baal Hermon (Jdg 3:3; 1Ch 5:23) because of its role in Baal worship. Used figuratively in Hebrew poetry (Ps 42:6; 89:12; 133:3; SS 4:8). (Possibly the site of Jesus' transfiguration.)

Herod

1. Herod the Great. King of Judea at time of Jesus' birth (Mt 2:1; Lk 1:5). Received Magi (Mt 2:1-8); slaughtered infants in attempt to kill Jesus (Mt 2:16-18).
2. Son of Herod the Great, also called Antipas. Tetrarch of Galilee. Arrested and executed John the Baptist (Mt 14:1-12; Mk 6:14-29; Lk 3:19,20; 9:7-9);

The Western Wall in Jerusalem is part of the original temple built by King Herod. Today it is a holy place for Jews where prayers are offered

questioned Jesus (Lk 23:6-12,15).
3. See **Agrippa**.

Herodias

Granddaughter of Herod the Great. Divorced Philip to marry his brother Herod Antipas, bringing condemnation from John the Baptist (Mt 14:3,4; Mk 6:17-19); prompted daughter to ask for John's head (Mt 14:6-12; Mk 6:21-29).

Heshbon

Capital city of Sihon, king of Amorites (Nu 21:26), situated about 25 miles east of northern Dead Sea. Captured by Israelites when Sihon blocked their path (Nu 21:25-30; Dt 2:24-33; Jos

13:10-27). Allotted to Gad and Reuben, who rebuilt it (Nu 32:37), became a Levite town for the Merarites (Jos 21:39). Occupied by Moabites (Isa 15:4; Jer 48:34,45) and Ammonites (Jer 48:2; 49:3). Known for its pastures (Nu 32:1-4), vineyards (Isa 16:8,9) and pools (SS 7:4).

Hezekiah

King of Judah; outstanding for piety (2Ki 18:5,6; 2Ch 31:20,21). Reformed Judah's religious life (2Ki 18:3,4; 2Ch 29-31). Rebelled against Assyria (2Ki 18:7); sought and received help from God (2Ki 19:1-4,14-37; Isa 37:1-7,14-38). Healed (2Ki 20:1-11; Isa 38:1-22; 2Ch 32:24). Built up Jerusalem's defences (2Ch 32:2-5,30). Isaiah challenged dependence on human resources (Isa 22:8-11) and pride in displaying wealth to envoys from Babylon (2Ki 20:12-18; 2Ch 32:31; Isa 39:1-8); repented (2Ch 32:26). Included in Jesus' genealogy (Mt 1:9,10).

Hinnom Valley

Deep ravine on southern slope of Jerusalem, known also as Ben Hinnom. Part of boundary between Judah and Benjamin (Jos 15:8; 18:16; Ne 11:30). Scene of abominable practice of sacrificing children to Molech (2Ch 28:3; 33:6; Jer 7:31,32; 19:6; 32:35), which Josiah tried to prevent (2Ki 23:10) and Jeremiah denounced (Jer 19:2-6).

Hiram

King of Tyre. Helped with building of David's palace (2Sa 5:11,12; 1Ch 14:1). Made treaty with Solomon (1Ki 5:12); provided materials and expertise for building temple (1Ki 5; 2Ch 2) and navy (1Ki 9:26,27; 2Ch 8:18; 1Ki 10:22; 2Ch 9:21).

Hor, Mount

1. On border of Edom (Nu 20:23; 33:37), where Aaron died (Nu 20:22-29; 33:38,39; Dt 32:50).
2. On northern border of Palestine, exact location unknown (Nu 34:7,8).

Horeb

See **Sinai**.

Hormah

Canaanite town near Ziklag in southern Judah (Jos 12:14). Originally called Zephath, until renamed by either the

Israelites (Nu 21:3) or the men of Judah and Simeon (Jdg 1:17). Israelites defeated near here by the Amalekites and Canaanites (Nu 14:45; Dt 1:44). Allotted to Simeon, though in the territory of

Modern watchtower in the Judean hills. The prophets were appointed by God as watchmen to sound warnings to the nation

Judah (Jos 19:14; 1Ch 4:30). David sent a share of Amalekite spoils to here (1Sa 30:30).

Hosea

Prophet to Israel. Relationship with unfaithful wife, Gomer, and readiness to forgive her mirrored the relationship between God and unfaithful Israel (Hos 1–3).

The expulsion of Ishmael and his mother. Illustration by Gustav Doré

Hoshea

1. Former name of Joshua.
2. Last king of Israel. Assassinated and succeeded Pekah (2Ki 15:30). Imprisoned when withheld tribute from Assyria; Israel was invaded and king and people exiled (2Ki 17:3-6; 18:9-12).

Iconium

Capital city of Lycaonia in Asia Minor. Visited by Paul and Barnabas who enjoyed successful ministry here until Jews forced them out (Ac 14:1-7) and pursued Paul to Lystra to stone him (Ac 14:19). Paul later returned (Ac 14:21) and was well received (Ac 16:2), but he remembered the persecution (2Ti 3:11).

Isaac

Son of Abraham and Sarah. Birth announced by God (Ge 17:15-19; 18:10-15; 21:1-7); heir through whom God's promises to Abraham

continued (Ge 17:19,21; 21:12; 26:2-5; Ro 9:6-9; Heb 11:9); patriarch (Ge 50:24; Ex 3:6; Dt 29:13; Mt 8:11). Offered by Abraham (Ge 22; Heb 11:17-19; Jas 2:21). Married Rebekah (Ge 24); father of Esau and Jacob (Ge 25:21-26; 1Ch 1:34). In Gerar, passed Rebekah off as his sister (Ge 26:6-11). Made treaty with Abimelech (Ge 26:26-31). Deceived by Rebekah; blessed Jacob as firstborn (Ge 27:1-29; 28:1-4). Death (Ge 35:28,29).

Isaiah

Prophet to Judah (Isa 1:1); commissioned by God (Isa 6). Married prophetess (Isa 8:3), had two sons whose names were clues to message (Isa 7:3; 8:3). Warned Ahaz; gave sign of Immanuel (Isa 7). Called for trust in God rather than human resources (Isa 7:9; 22:7-11; 31:1); rebuked Hezekiah's pride (2Ki 20:12-18; 2Ch 32:31; Isa 39:1-8). Announced deliverance from Assyria (Isa 10:12-19,24-27; 14:24-27; 36–37; 2Ki 19). Hezekiah's sickness and recovery (2Ki 20:1-11; 2Ch 32:24-26; Isa 38). Recorded Judah's history (2Ch 26:22; 32:32).

Ishmael

1. Son of Abraham by Hagar (Ge 16:15; 1Ch 1:28); circumcised (Ge 17:23-26); blessed by God, but not as heir of promise (Ge 17:19-21; 21:10-13; Gal 4:21-30). Hostility towards Isaac (Ge

16:12; 21:9; 25:18; Gal 4:29); driven away by Sarah (Ge 21:10-14); cry heard by God (Ge 21:15-21). With Isaac, buried Abraham (Ge 25:9). Children (Ge 25:12-16; 1Ch 1:29-31). Death (Ge 25:17).
2. Son of Nethaniah; killed Gedaliah, governor of Judah, and his followers (2Ki 25:22-26; Jer 40:7-9; 41:1-16). Pursued by Johanan; escaped to Ammon (Jer 41:10-15).

Israel

The new name given to Jacob (Ge 32:28; 35:10), was soon used of the land where his descendants settled (Ge 34:7; 49:7), giving rise to the 12 tribes of Israel (Ge 49:28). While in Egypt and the wilderness, it was used only of the people (Ex 5:2), but once resettled in Canaan it was used of the land and kingdom (Lev 20:2; 22:18; Dt 17:4,20; 18:6; Jdg 5:2,7). It reached its full potential (Nu 34:1-15; Eze 47:13-21) under the reigns of David and Solomon. After the kingdom divided it designated the ten tribes of the northern kingdom (1Ki 11:31,35), as opposed to Judah in the south (which had absorbed Simeon). For two centuries Israel was in conflict with Judah (1Ki 12:19), until it fell to the Assyrians (2Ki 17). Re-unification was prophesied (Jer 3:18; Eze 37:16,17).

Issachar

1. Son of Jacob by Leah (Ge 30:17,18; 35:23); blessed by Jacob (Ge 49:14,15).
2. Tribe descended from Issachar. Blessed by Moses (Dt 33:18,19). Included in census (Nu 1:28,29; 26:23-25). Apportioned land (Jos 19:17-23; Eze 48:25).
3. Fertile territory south-east of Sea of Galilee, with Naphtali to the north, and Manasseh to the south. Allotted to the descendants of Jacob's ninth son. Its towns were listed, but its borders were rather vague (Jos 19:17-23).

Jabbok

An eastern tributary of River Jordan, about 22 miles north of Dead Sea. Jacob crossed at its ford, before wrestling with an angel (Ge 32:22-24). It was a natural boundary (Nu 21:24; Dt 2:37; 3:16; Jos 12:2; Jdg 11:13,22).

Jabesh Gilead

Town in Gilead about 10 miles south-east of Beth Shan, 2 miles east of the Jordan. Its people would not fight against Benjamin, so they were put to the sword (Jdg 21:8-15). It was besieged by the Ammonites, but rescued by Saul (1Sa 11:1-11). Its people later rescued Saul's body from the Philistines and gave him a proper burial here (1Sa 31:1-13; 1Ch 10:11,12). Also known by abbreviated name Jabesh (1Ch 10:12).

Jacob

Son of Isaac; younger twin of Esau (Ge 25:21-26). Favoured by Rebekah (Ge 25:27,28). Bought birthright from Esau (Ge 25:29-34); tricked Isaac into blessing him as firstborn (Ge 27); fled to Haran (Ge 27:41–28:5).

Dream at Bethel (Ge 28:10-22); heir to promises of Abrahamic covenant (Ge 28:13-15; 48:3,4; Lev 26:42; Heb 11:9); patriarch (Ex 3:15,16; Jer 33:26; Mt 22:32; Mk 12:26). Gracious choice by God contrasted with rejection of Esau (Mal 1:2,3; Ro 9:13).

Worked for Laban to win Rachel; tricked into marrying Leah; married Rachel in return for further labour (Ge 29:16-30). Children (Ge 29:31–30:24; 35:23-26; 1Ch 2–9). Wealth increased (Ge 30:25-43); returned to Canaan (Ge 31); wrestled with God; called Israel (Ge 32:22-32); reconciled to Esau (Ge 33). Returned to Bethel (Ge 35:1-15).

Showed favouritism to Joseph (Ge 37:3,4). Sent sons to Egypt for food (Ge 42:1-5). Settled in Egypt with family (Ge 46; Ex 1:1-5). Blessed Ephraim and Manasseh (Ge 48:8-20; Heb 11:21); blessed sons (Ge 49:1-28). Death (Ge 49:29-33); burial in Canaan (Ge 50:1-14).

Jael

Wife of Heber the Kenite; killed Sisera, commander of Canaanite army, after his defeat by Deborah and Barak (Jdg 4:17-22; 5:24-27).

Jahaz

Town on plains of Moab about 17 miles east of Dead Sea. Sihon the Amorite was defeated by Israel here (Nu 21:23,24; Dt 2:3,-33; Jdg 11:20). Allotted to tribe of Reuben (Jos 13:18) and set aside for the Levites (Jos 21:34-36). Became part of Moab, about which the prophets proclaimed disaster (Isa 15:4; Jer 48:34). Variant name Jahzah (1Ch 6:78; Jer 48:21).

Jairus

Synagogue ruler whose daughter was raised to life by Jesus (Mt 9:18-26; Mk 5:22-43; Lk 8:41-56).

James

1. Apostle; son of Zebedee, brother of John (Mt 4:21,22; 10:2; Mk 1:19,20; 3:17; Lk 5:10). With Peter and John, especially close to Jesus: at raising of Jairus' daughter (Mk 5:37; Lk 8:51); transfiguration (Mt 17:1,2; Mk 9:2; Lk 9:28,29); in Gethsemane (Mt 26:36-38; Mk 14:32-34). Mother's request (Mt 20:20-28; Mk 10:35-45). Killed by Herod (Ac 12:2).
2. Apostle; son of Alphaeus (Mt 10:3; Mk 3:18; Lk 6:15; Ac 1:13).
3. Brother of Jesus and Jude (Mt 13:55; Mk 6:3; Gal 1:19; Jude 1); saw risen Lord (1Co 15:7) and with disciples before

Jericho, the "City of Palms", is 825 ft below sea level

Pentecost (Ac 1:13); leader of church in Jerusalem (Ac 12:17; 15:13-21; 21:18; Gal 2:9); wrote letter (Jas 1:1).

Japheth

Son of Noah (Ge 5:32; 6:10; 1Ch 1:4). Saved in ark (Ge 7:13; 9:18,19). Blessed by Noah (Ge 9:27); descendants (Ge 10:2-5; 1Ch 1:5-7).

Jazer

Town east of the Jordan, in the south of Gilead. Captured by Israel from Amorites (Nu 21:32). Both Gad and Reuben laid claim to it (Nu 32:1-3), but Gad was given it, and fortified it (Nu 32:35; Jos 13:25). Later designated as a Levite town (Jos 21:39; 1Ch 6:81). Included in David's census (2Sa 24:5; 1Ch 26:31). Became part of Moab, about which the prophets proclaimed disaster (Isa 16:8,9; Jer 48:32).

Jehoiachin

King of Judah; succeeded father, Jehoiakim; after three months taken as captive to Babylon (2Ki 24:8-17; 2Ch 36:8-10); removed from prison to royal palace (2Ki 25:27-30; Jer 52:31-34).

Jehoiakim

King of Judah. Son of Josiah, formerly called Eliakim; made king by Pharaoh Neco (2Ki 23:33-36; 2Ch 36:4). Killed prophet Uriah (Jer 26:20-23; burned Jeremiah's scroll (Jer 36). Became Babylonian vassal; subsequent rebellion brought invasion; died on way into captivity (2Ki 24:1-4; 2Ch 36:5-8; Da 1:1,2).

Jehoshaphat

King of Judah; son of Asa (1Ki 22:41). Devoted to God; removed idols; sent officials to teach Law (2Ch 17:3-9). Strengthened kingdom (2Ch 17:2,10-19). Allied with Israel (1Ki 22:44; 2Ch 18:1; 20:35,36); helped Ahab against Aram (1Ki 22:1-33; 2Ch 18:1–19:1) and Joram against Moab (2Ki 3). Alliances rebuked (2Ch 19:1,2; 2Ch 20:35-37). Appointed judges (2Ch 19:4-11). Trusted God for victory over Moab and Ammon (2Ch 20:1-30). Death (2Ch 21:1).

Jehu

1. Prophet; rebuked Baasha (1Ki 16:1-7) and Jehoshaphat (2Ch 19:1,2).
2. King of Israel. Choice by God announced to Elijah (1Ki 19:16,17); anointed by servant of Elisha; instructed to destroy Ahab's house (2Ki 9:1-13). Killed Joram, Ahaziah (2Ki 9:14-29), Jezebel (2Ki 9:30-37), Ahab's family (2Ki 10:1-17), ministers of Baal (2Ki 10:18-29). Succession promised for four generations (2Ki 10:30). Death (2Ki 10:34-36).

Jephthah

Judge. Social outcast, called on to deliver Israel from Ammonites (Jdg 11:1-32). Rash vow led to sacrifice of daughter (Jdg 11:30-40). Victory over Ephraim (Jdg 12:1-6). Death (Jdg 12:7). Example of faith (Heb 11:32-34).

Jeremiah

Prophet to Judah (Jer 1:1-3). Called by God while still young (Jer 1). Persecuted (Jer 11:18-23; 12:6; 18:18); put in stocks (Jer 20:2); threatened with death (Jer 26:7-11); scroll burned (Jer 36); imprisoned (Jer 37); thrown into cistern (Jer 38:6-13). Warned of Babylonian exile (Jer 25:8-11; 34:1-3); challenged false prophets (Jer 6:10-15; 23:9-40; 28). Promised restoration (Jer 25:12-14; 30; 33); announced new covenant (Jer 31); bought field (Jer 32). Taken to Egypt with fleeing remnant (Jer 43).

Jericho

One of the oldest and lowest-lying cities in the world, situated in Jordan Valley, about 15 miles north-east of Jeru-salem. The Israelites camped opposite here, before crossing the Jordan (Nu 22:1; 26:3,63; 31:12; 33:48,50; 35:1; 36:13; Dt 32:49; 34:1,3; Jos 3:16; 13:32). Joshua's spies focused on this city and escaped with Rahab's help (Jos 2:1-7). Israel's army camped near here to prepare for battle (Jos 4:13), and defeated the city (Jos 6).

Allotted to the tribe of Benjamin (Jos 18:21). David's men waited here while their beards grew back (2Sa 10:5; 1Ch 19:5). Joshua's curse was fulfilled on Hiel who rebuilt Jericho (Jos 6:26; 1Ki 16:34). It became a community of prophets (2Ki 2:5). Known also as the City of Palms (2Ch 28:15). Zedekiah was captured by the Babylonians near here (Jer 39:5; 52:8). Place where Jesus healed blind men (Mt 20:29; Mk 10:46; Lk 18:35) and met with Zacchaeus (Lk 19:1). Referred to in a parable (Lk 10:30).

Jeroboam

1. Israel's first king. Former official of Solomon; rebelled and fled to Egypt (1Ki 11:26-40). After Solomon's death, led northern tribes in rebellion against Rehoboam (1Ki 12:1-20; 2Ch 10). Established idolatrous worship (1Ki 12:25-33); set evil example for successors (1Ki 15:34; 16:19,26,31; 22:52). Rebuked by prophets (1Ki 13–14). Death (2Ch 13:20). **2.** Jeroboam II. Son of Jehoash. Restored Israel's boundaries; brought economic prosperity (2Ki 14:23-29). Spiritual decay challenged by Amos (Am 1:1; 2:6-8; 5:21-24; 6:1-8; 7:9-11).

Jerusalem

City in northern Judea, about 18 miles west of Dead Sea. Its king was defeated by Joshua (Jos 10:1-26; 12:10). Allotted to tribe of Judah, and later Benjamin, but they could not expel the Jebusites (Jos 15:63; 18:28; Jdg 1:21). Chosen by David as capital of his kingdom (2Sa 5:5; 1Ch 3:4) and captured from the Jebusites. He put the ark of the covenant here (2Sa 6:12-15). He planned to build a great temple for the LORD here (2Sa 7; 1Ch 17), but this was Solomon's task (2Ch 2–7). Known as the City of David (2Sa 5:7) it remained capital of Judah after the kingdom split, until it was destroyed by the Babylonians (2Ki 25:10). Since the time of David the word "Zion" has been used to refer to either the hill on which the temple stood or Jerusalem in its entirety. The prophets and the Psalms use "Zion" to convey the idea that Jerusalem is the central place of Israelite religion and as a special place of God's presence it has security and renown (Ps 48; Isa 2:2-4). Historically the city of Jerusalem was rebuilt by Nehemiah after the exile (Ne 2:5); the temple rebuilt by Zerubbabel (Ezr 6:13-15). In NT times Jerusalem was associated with kings (Mt 2:1,2), and another temple stood in place of Zerubbabel's. Jesus came here at 12 years old (Lk 2:41,42), and later confronted the temple sellers (Lk 19:45,46). He entered the city triumphantly (Lk 19:28), but was soon arrested (Lk 22:47), tried (Lk 22:66–23:25)

A market by the Damascus Gate.
The citadel and tower of David: part
of Herod's fortifications

Jerusalem in the Old Testament

Tower of Hananel
Fish Gate
Fish Gate
Old Gate
KIDRON VALLEY
Muster Gate
TEMPLE AREA
East Gate
Mount of Olives
Probable site of Solomon's Palace
LOWER CITY
UPPER CITY
SECOND QUARTER
CHEESEMAKER'S (CENTRAL) VALLEY
Valley Gate
Gihon Spring
Water Gate
CITY OF DAVID
Hezekiah's Tunnel
KIDRON VALLEY
Fountain Gate
HINNOM VALLEY
Dung Gate
Old Pool
Lower Pool

— Zion city walls
— Extended in the time of the Kings
— Eastern wall, built by Nehemiah

Jerusalem was founded by
David on the site of Jebus. It
was extended to the north by
Solomon then westward by
later kings. King Hezekiah
provided added security by
cutting a hidden tunnel to
bring water from the Gihon
Spring inside the city walls.
The city was destroyed by the
Babylonians in 586 BC.
Rebuilding started after the
return from exile, most
notably under Nehemiah.
Further fortification was
added to the west by the
Maccabees.
The exact siting of the city
walls is disputed.

The garden tomb, Jerusalem, traditional site of Jesus' burial and resurrection

The Via Dolorosa, on the route that Jesus was taken to be crucified

Jerusalem in Jesus' Time

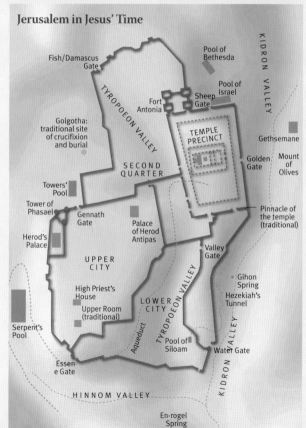

- Pool of Bethesda
- KIDRON VALLEY
- Fish/Damascus Gate
- Pool of Israel
- TYROPOEON VALLEY
- Fort Antonia
- Sheep Gate
- Golgotha: traditional site of crucifixion and burial
- TEMPLE PRECINCT
- Gethsemane
- Golden Gate
- Mount of Olives
- SECOND QUARTER
- Towers' Pool
- Tower of Phasael
- Pinnacle of the temple (traditional)
- Gennath Gate
- Palace of Herod Antipas
- Herod's Palace
- Valley Gate
- UPPER CITY
- Gihon Spring
- High Priest's House
- Hezekiah's Tunnel
- LOWER CITY
- Upper Room (traditional)
- TYROPOEON VALLEY
- Serpent's Pool
- Aqueduct
- Pool of Siloam
- Water Gate
- KIDRON VALLEY
- Essene Gate
- HINNOM VALLEY
- En-rogel Spring

Herod the Great was responsible for a vast rebuilding programme, turning Jerusalem into a beautiful Roman-style city. The temple was rebuilt on an extended precinct overlooking the two north-south valleys, but with a Roman fortress adjoining. Some wall positionings are uncertain.

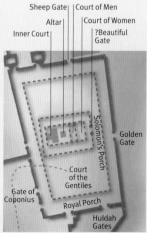

- Sheep Gate
- Court of Men
- Altar
- Court of Women
- Inner Court
- ?Beautiful Gate
- Solomon's Porch
- Golden Gate
- Court of the Gentiles
- Gate of Coponius
- Royal Porch
- Huldah Gates

and crucified (Lk 23:26-55). After Stephen was martyred here (Ac 7:59) many believers left and scattered (Ac 8:1). It remained the place for settling disputes (Ac 15:2). In AD 70 the city was destroyed fulfilling Jesus' prophecy (Lk 19:41-44). A new Jerusalem is envisioned at the heart of God's new kingdom on earth inhabited by Christ and the church (Rev 3:12; 21:2,10).

Jesse

From Bethlehem; father of David (Ru 4:17,22; 1Sa 16; 17:12-20; 1Ch 2:12-17; Isa 11:1,10; Ro 15:12).

Jesus

LIFE: Genealogy (Mt 1:1-17; Lk 3:23-38); birth (Mt 1:18–2:12; Lk 1:26-38; 2:1-20); presented in temple (Lk 2:21-40); fled to Egypt (Mt 2:13-18). Brought up in Nazareth (Mt 2:19-23); visited Jerusalem temple (Lk 2:41-52). Baptised by John (Mt 3:13-17; Mk 1:9-11; Lk 3:21-23; Jn 1:29-34); tempted (Mt 4:1-11; Mk 1:12,13; Lk 4:1-13); began public ministry (Mt 4:12-17; Mk 1:14,15; Lk 4:14-30); called first disciples (Mt 4:18-22; Mk 1:16-20; Lk 5:2-11; Jn 1:35-51); preached in Galilee (Mt 4:23-25; Mk 1:39). Appointed and sent out disciples (Mt 9:35–10:16; Mk 3:13-18; 6:7-11; Lk 9:1-6; 10:1-17). Acknowledged by Peter as Christ (Mt 16:13-23; Mk 8:27-33; Lk 9:18-22). Transfigured (Mt 17:1-8; Mk 9:2-8; Lk 9:28-36). Set out for Jerusalem (Mt 16:21; 20:17-19; Mk 10:32-34; Lk 18:31-34). Last week in Jerusalem: entered city (Mt 21:1-11; Mk 11:1-11; Lk 19:29-44; Jn 12:12-15); cleared temple (Mt 21:12,13; Mk 11:15-19; Lk 19:45-48; Jn 2:13-16); anointed at Bethany (Mt 26:6-13; Mk 14:3-9); shared Last Supper (Mt 26:17-30; Mk 14:12-26; Lk 22:7-23); washed disciples' feet (Jn 13:1-17); prayed in Gethsemane (Mt 26:36-46; Mk 14:32-42; Lk 22:40-46);

A souk (traditional market area) in a narrow street in the old city of Jerusalem

arrested and tried (Mt 26:47-68; 27:11-26; Mk 14:43-65; 15:1-15; Lk 22:47-53; 22:66–23:25; Jn 18:1–19:16); crucified and buried (Mt 27:27-66; Mk 15:16-47; Lk 23:26-56; Jn 19:17-42). Raised to life; appeared to followers (Mt 28; Mk 16; Lk 24; Jn 20–21; Ac 1:1-4; 1Co 15:1-8); commissioned disciples (Mt 28:16-20; Ac 1:4-8); ascended (Lk 24:50-53; Ac 1:9).

MIRACLES: Healed: crowds (Mt 4:23,24; 8:16; Mk 1:32-34; Lk 4:40,41; Mt 14:14; Lk 9:11; Mt 15:29-31; Lk 6:17,18); those with leprosy (Mt 8:2-4; Mk 1:40-45; Lk 5:12-16; 17:11-19); centurion's servant (Mt 8:5-13; Lk 7:1-10); Peter's mother-in-law (Mt 8:14,15; Mk 1:29-31; Lk 4:38,39); demon-possessed (Mt 8:28-34; Mk 5:1-20; Lk 8:26-39; Mt 9:32-34; 12:22; Lk 11:14; Mt 17:14-18; Mk 9:17-27; Lk 9:38-43; Mk 1:23-26; Lk 4:33-35); paralysed man (Mt 9:1-8; Mk 2:3-12; Lk 5:18-26); woman with bleeding (Mt 9:20-22; Mk 5:25-34; Lk 8:43-48); blind (Mt 9:27-31; 20:29-34; Mk 10:46-52; Lk 18:35-43; Mk 8:22-26; Jn 9:1-7); man with shrivelled hand (Mt 12:9-14; Mk 3:1-6; Lk 6:6-11); deaf mute (Mk 7:31-37); crippled woman (Lk 13:10-17); man with dropsy (Lk 14:1-4); high priest's servant (Lk 22:50,51); official's son (Jn 4:46-54); man at pool of Bethesda (Jn 5:1-9). Raised to life: Jairus' daughter (Mt 9:18-26; Mk 5:22-43; Lk

8:41-56); widow of Nain's son (Lk 7:11-17); Lazarus (Jn 11:1-44). Stilled storm (Mt 8:23-27; Mk 4:35-41; Lk 8:22-25); fed 5,000 (Mt 14:15-21; Mk 6:35-44; Lk 9:12-17; Jn 6:5-13); walked on water (Mt 14:25-33; Mk 6:47-52; Jn 6:18-20); fed 4,000 (Mt 15:32-39; Mk 8:1-10); money from fish (Mt 17:24-27); cursed fig-tree (Mt 21:18,19; Mk 11:12-14,20-22); catches of fish (Lk 5:1-11; Jn 21:4-6); changed water to wine (Jn 2:1-11).

TEACHING: Announced God's kingdom (Mt 4:17; 10:7; 12:24-29; Lk 11:14-22; Mt 16:28; Mk 1:15; 9:1; Lk 4:43; 9:11); Sermon on the Mount (Mt 5-7; Lk 6:20-49); pronounced woe on Pharisees (Mt 23; Lk 11:37-54); signs of the end of the age (Mt 24; Mk 13; Lk 21); conversations with Nicodemus (Jn 3), Samaritan

A Byzantine mosaic on the floor of a chapel built in the 4th C AD at Tabgha, Galilee, recalling Jesus' multiplication of the loaves and fish

woman (Jn 4); the bread of life (Jn 6:25-58); the good shepherd (Jn 10:1-20); discourse in Upper Room (Jn 13-17).

PARABLES: wise and foolish builders (Mt 7:24-27; Lk 6:47-49); sower (Mt 13:3-23; Mk 4:2-20; Lk 8:4-8); weeds (Mt 13:24-30); mustard seed and yeast (Mt 13:31-33; Mk 4:30-32; Lk 13:18-21); hidden treasure, pearl, net, houseowner (Mt 13:44-52); lost sheep (Mt 18:12-14; Lk 15:4-7); unmerciful servant (Mt 18:23-34); workers in vineyard (Mt 20:1-16); two sons (Mt 21:28-32); tenants (Mt 21:33-41; Mk 12:1-9; Lk 20:9-16); banquet (Mt 22:2-14; Lk 14:16-24); ten virgins (Mt 25:1-13); talents (Mt 25:14-30;

Lk 19:12-27); sheep and goats (Mt 25:31-46); growing seed (Mk 4:26-29); good Samaritan (Lk 10:30-37); rich fool (Lk 12:16-21); cost of discipleship (Lk 14:28-33); lost coin, lost son (Lk 15:8-32); shrewd manager (Lk 16:1-8); rich man and Lazarus (Lk 16:19-31); persistent widow (Lk 18:2-8); Pharisee and tax collector (Lk 18:10-14).

Jethro

Father-in-law of Moses (Ex 3:1; 4:18), also called Reuel (Ex 2:18). Visited Moses at Horeb; advised him to delegate administration of justice (Ex 18).

Jezebel

1. Daughter of Sidonian king; wife of Ahab (1Ki 16:31). Encouraged his sin (1Ki 21:25): promoted worship of native god, Baal (1Ki 16:32,33; 18:19); killed Lord's prophets (1Ki 18:4,13); threatened Elijah (1Ki 19:1,2); had Naboth killed (1Ki 21). Death prophesied by Elijah (1Ki 21:23); killed by Jehu (2Ki 9:30-37).
2. Designation of prophetess in church at Thyatira who was leading believers astray (Rev 2:20).

Jezreel

1. City in hill country of Judah (Jos 15:56), where Ahinoam was probably born (1Sa 25:43; 27:3). Exact location uncertain.
2. City in northern Israel, about 56 miles north of Jerusalem (Jos 19:18), in a valley named after it (Jos 17:16), with nearby spring (1Sa 29:1). Ahab had a palace here, overlooking Naboth's vineyard (1Ki 21:1-16). Joram recovering from battle was visited by Ahaziah here (2Ki 8:29; 2Ch 22:6). Place of bloodshed during Jehu's revolt (2Ki 9:1–10:11). Hosea's son named Jezreel to announce God's judgement on the house of Jehu (Hos 1:4,5).

Joab

Nephew of David; brother of Abishai and Asahel (1Ch 2:16). Led David's army against Abner (2Sa 2:13-32); killed

The view across the Valley of Jezreel, with Mt Tabor in the distance

Abner to avenge death of Asahel (2Sa 3:26,27,30). Led attack on Jerusalem (1Ch 11:4-6); made commander-in-chief (2Sa 8:16; 18:2; 20:23). Defeated Ammon (2Sa 10:7-14; 1Ch 19:8-15), Rabbah (2Sa 12:26,27). Followed David's order to kill Uriah (2Sa 11:14-17); killed Absalom (2Sa 18:14,15); killed Amasa (2Sa 20:9,10). Supported Adonijah (1Ki 1:17-19); killed by Benaiah (1Ki 2:5,6,28-34).

Joash

1. Father of Gideon (Jdg 6:11,29-31; 8:32).
2. King of Judah; son of Ahaziah. Hidden from Athaliah (2Ki 11:1-3; 2Ch 22:10-12); crowned king by Jehoida (2Ki 11:4-21; 2Ch 23). Repaired temple (2Ki 12; 2Ch 24:1-14); returned to idolatry after Jehoiada's death (2Ch 24:17-24). Defeated by Aram (2Ch 24:23,24); murdered by officials (2Ki 12:20; 2Ch 24:25).

Job

1. Wealthy, God-fearing man from Uz (Job 1:1-8). Uprightness tested by Satan, with God's permission (Job 1:6-12; 2:1-6). Suffered loss of family and wealth (Job 1:13-19), and physical affliction (Job 2:7,8). Remained patient (Job 1:20-22; 2:9,10); protested when innocence challenged by friends (Job 3–31). Rebuked by the Lord (Job 38–41); finally vindicated, healed and restored to greater wealth (Job 42:7-17).

2. Job's friends: Eliphaz (Job 4–5; 15; 22), Bildad (Job 8; 18; 25) Zophar (Job 11; 20) and Elihu (Job 32–37). Came to offer sympathy (Job 2:11-13); tried and failed to explain Job's suffering in terms of conventional wisdom.

Joel

Prophet (Joel 1:1). Saw plague of locusts as depiction of God's judgement (Joel 1:2–2:12); called for repentance (Joel 2:13-17). Future blessing included pouring out of Spirit (Joel 2:18-32; Ac 2:16-21).

John

1. The Baptist; son of Zechariah and Elizabeth (Lk 1:5-25,57-80). Prepared way for Jesus (Mt 3:1-12; Mk 1:3-8; Lk 3:2-17; Jn 1:6-8,15,19-36; 3:27-30); baptised Jesus (Mt 3:13-15; Mk 1:9; Lk 3:21). Opposed Herod's marriage to Herodias; arrested (Mt 14:3-5; Mk 6:17,18); reassured and commended by Jesus (Mt 11:2-19; Lk 7:18-35). Executed (Mt 14:6-12; Mk 6:21-29). Identified with Elijah (Mt 11:14; 17:11-13; Mk 9:12,13; Lk 1:17).
2. Apostle; son of Zebedee; brother of James. With Peter and James, especially close to Jesus: at raising of Jairus' daughter (Mk 5:37; Lk 8:51); transfiguration (Mt 17:1,2; Mk 9:2; Lk 9:28,29); in Gethsemane (Mt 26:36-38; Mk 14:32-34). Mother's request (Mt 20:20-28; Mk 10:35-45). Called "the disciple whom

Jesus loved": close to Jesus at Last Supper (Jn 13:23; 21:20); at crucifixion (Jn 19:25-27). Leader in Jerusalem church (Gal 2:9; 2Jn 1; 3Jn 1). Wrote fourth gospel, letters, book of Revelation (Rev 1:1,9; 22:8; Jn 20:2; 21:7,24).
3. See **Mark**.

Jonah

Prophet during reign of Jeroboam II (2Ki 14:25). Ran from God's call to preach against Nineveh (Jnh 1:2,3,10). God sent storm; thrown overboard; swallowed by fish (Jnh 1:4-17). Prayed; disgorged onto dry land (Jnh 2); deliverance a "sign" prefiguring Jesus' death and resurrection (Mt 12:39-41; Lk 11:29-32). Obeyed second call (Jnh 3); response to Nineveh's repentance rebuked (Jnh 4).

Jonathan

Eldest son of Saul (1Sa 13:16; 14:49; 1Ch 8:33). Courageous warrior (1Sa 14:1-23; 2Sa 1:22,23). Violated Saul's oath (1Sa 14:24-45). Friendship with David (1Sa 18:1-4; 19–20; 23:16-18; 2Sa 1:26). Killed (1Sa 31:1,2); mourned by David (2Sa 1:19-27).

Joppa

Mediterranean seaport about 35 miles north-west of Jerusalem, important for trade. Allotted to the tribe of Dan who had difficulty possessing it (Jos 19:46,47). Solomon and Zerubbabel used the port when building their temples

(2Ch 2:16; Ezr 3:7). Jonah sailed from here when fleeing the LORD (Jnh 1:3). Home of Tabitha, whom Peter restored to life (Ac 9:36-40). While staying with Simon the tanner, Peter had a vision from God (Ac 10:5-17).

Jordan, River

Largest river in Palestine, with principal source near Mount Hermon. Flows southwards from Sea of Galilee through a deep valley into the Dead Sea. Lot desired the fertile land around it (Ge 13:10,11). A natural boundary crossed to escape enemies, eg by Jacob (Ge 32:10), and David (2Sa

17:21,22). Israelites camped to its east (Jos 3:1), before crossing it on dry ground to take the Promised Land (Jos 3:11-17). Used strategically in battle by Ehud (Jdg 3:28), Gideon (Jdg 7:24) and the Gileadites (Jdg 12:5). Elijah and Elisha crossed it on dry ground (2Ki 2:8,14), and Elisha instructed Naaman to wash in it (2Ki 5:10). Mentioned in Isaiah's Messianic prophecy (Isa 9:1), and is the site of Jesus' baptism (Mt 3:13; Mk 1:9).

Joseph

1. Son of Jacob by Rachel (Ge 30:22-24; 35:24; 1Ch 2:2).

Father's favouritism aroused brothers' hostility (Ge 37:3,4). Dreams (Ge 37:5-11). Sold by brothers (Ge 37:12-36); became slave of Potiphar (Ge 39:1-6). Resisted attentions of Potiphar's wife; falsely accused; imprisoned (Ge 39:7-23). Interpreted dreams of cup-bearer and baker (Ge 40); Pharaoh (Ge 41:1-36). Put in charge of Egypt (Ge 41:37-57). Tested brothers when came to buy grain (Ge 42–44); made himself known (Ge 45:1-15); settled family in Egypt (Ge 45:16–47:12). Sons blessed (Ge

Tranquillity on the River Jordan

48); received Jacob's blessing (Ge 49:22-26). Death (Ge 50:22-26; Ex 13:19; Jos 24:32; Heb 11:22). Descendants divided into tribes of Ephraim and Manasseh (Jos 14:4; 16–17; Eze 47:13); blessed by Moses (Dt 33:13-17).

2. Husband of Jesus' mother, Mary (Mt 1:16,18-25; Lk 1:27); descendant of David (Lk 2:4); carpenter (Mt 13:55). Dreams (Mt 1:20-23; 2:13,19,20).

3. Disciple from Arimathea; member of Jewish council. Asked for Jesus' body; gave tomb for burial (Mt 27:57-60; Mk 15:42-46; Lk 23:50-54; Jn 19:38-42).

4. See **Barnabas**.

Joshua

1. Son of Nun, formerly called Hoshea (Nu 13:8,16; 1Ch 7:27). Fought Amalekites (Ex 17:9-14). Moses' assistant: on Sinai (Ex 24:13; 32:17); at tent of meeting (Ex 33:11). One of spies sent to explore Canaan (Nu 13:8); with Caleb encouraged people to go in (Nu 14:6-9); so allowed to enter land (Nu 26:65; 32:12). Succeeded Moses (Dt 1:38; 3:28; 31:1-8; 34:9). Commissioned and encouraged by God (Jos 1:1-9); crossed Jordan (Jos 3–4). Victory at Jericho (Jos 5:13–6:27); defeat then victory at Ai (Jos 7–8); renewed covenant at Mt Ebal (Jos 8:30-35); deceived by Gibeonites (Jos 9); sun stood still to enable victory over five kings at Gibeon (Jos 10); conquered southern

Canaan (Jos 10:29-43), northern Canaan (Jos 11). Apportioned land among tribes (Jos 13–22). Gave final instructions (Jos 23); renewed covenant at Shechem (Jos 24:1-27); death (Jos 24:29-31; Jdg 2:8,9).

2. High priest at time of restoration (Hag 1:1); encouraged by Haggai to finish work on temple (Hag 1:12–2:9). Representative of sinful Israel saved by God's grace (Zec 3); crowning foreshadowed reign of Messiah (Zec 6:9-15).

Josiah

King of Judah; son of Amon (2Ki 21:26; 1Ch 3:14; 2Ch 33:25). Birth prophesied (1Ki 13:2). Godliness commended (2Ki 22:2; 2Ch 34:2,3; Jer 22:15,16). Removed idols (2Ch 34:3-7); repaired temple (2Ki 22:3-7; 2Ch 34:8-13). Repented, following discovery of Book of the Law (2Ki 22:8-20; 2Ch 34:14-28); renewed covenant (2Ki 23:1-3; 2Ch 34:29-32); purified temple (2Ki 23:4-12); destroyed high places (2Ki 23:13-20,24,25; 2Ch 34:33). Celebrated Passover (2Ki 23:21-23; 2Ch 35:1-19). Killed fighting Pharaoh Neco (2Ki 23:29.30; 2Ch 35:20-27).

Judah

1. Son of Jacob by Leah (Ge 29:35; 35:23; 1Ch 2:1). Urged brothers to sell, not kill, Joseph (Ge 37:26,27). Father of Perez and Zerah, by daughter-in-law,

Tamar (Ge 38). Offered himself in place of Benjamin (Ge 44:18-34). Blessed by Jacob as ruler (Ge 49:8-12).

2. Tribe descended from Judah. Blessed by Moses (Dt 33:7). Included in census (Nu 1:26,27; 26:19-22). Apportioned land (Jos 15; Eze 48:7); unable to take full possession (Jos 15:63; Jdg 1:1-20). Anointed David as king (2Sa 2:4); remained loyal to Davidic kings (1Ki 12:21; 2Ch 11:12). Tribe of Jesus (Mt 1:3; Heb 7:14).

3. Southern kingdom of Judah. Following the breakdown of relationships between the northern and southern tribes, Palestine was divided (about 931 BC) and Judah suffered 2 centuries of conflict with the northern kingdom of Israel (1Ki 12–2Ki 17). Judah survived because Israel fell to the Assyrians (2Ki 17:18). But Judah itself fell to the Babylonians about 134 years later (2Ki 25) and the people of Judah were exiled. Following the fall of Jerusalem (586 BC) Judah lost its kingdom status and became a small province of the Persian empire. By NT times this area was known as Judea, an annex of the Roman province of Syria, in which Jesus was born (Mt 2:1).

Judas

1. Brother of Jesus (Mt 13:55; Mk 6:3); also called Jude, author of letter (Jude 1).

2. Apostle; son of James (Lk

6:16; Jn 14:22; Ac 1:13); also known as Thaddaeus (Mt 10:3; Mk 3:18).

3. Apostle; also called Iscariot; known as Jesus' betrayer (Mt 10:4; Mk 3:19; Lk 6:16; Jn 6:71; 12:4); treasurer for disciples (Jn 12:6; 13:29). Agreed to betray Jesus for 30 silver pieces (Mt 26:14-16; Mk 14:10,11; Lk 22:3-6); kissed Jesus to identify him (Mt 26:47-49; Mk 14:43-45; Lk 22:47,48); filled with remorse; committed suicide (Mt 27:3-5; Ac 1:16-25).

4. Prophet; also called Barsabbas. Sent, with Silas, by apostles in Jerusalem to Antioch with decision about circumcision (Ac 15:22-34).

Jude
See **Judas**.

Judea
See **Judah**.

Kadesh Barnea
Oasis town in northern Sinai 50 miles south of Beersheba. Originally known as En

Mishpat and abbreviated to Kadesh. Kedorlaomer defeated the Amalekites and Amorites here (Ge 14:7). An angel appeared to Hagar near here (Ge 16:14), Abram settled close by (Ge 20:1) and the people camped here during the exodus (Nu 20:1; 33:36; Dt 1:19,46). Here Miriam died and was buried (Nu 20:1), the spies reported back (Nu 13:26; Jos 14:7), the people complained (Nu 20:2-5) and messengers were dispatched to Edom and Moab (Jdg 11:17).

Kebar, River
Runs through Babylonia; the exiled people lived along its banks (Eze 1:1; 3:15); Ezekiel received his vision here (Eze 1:3; 3:23; 10:15,20,22; 43:3).

Keilah
Town about 18 miles southwest of Jerusalem allotted to Judah (Jos 15:44). David rescued it from Philistine attack (1Sa 23:1-5), then left here to escape from Saul (1Sa 23:7-14). In Nehemiah's time it

had two rulers who helped rebuild Jerusalem (Ne 3:17,18).

Kerith Ravine
An almost dry river bed east of the Jordan. Elijah hid here (1Ki 17:2,3,5), was fed by ravens and drank from the small brook (1Ki 17:4). When the brook dried up, he went to Zarephath (1Sa 17:7-9).

Kidron Valley
On eastern slope of Jerusalem, towards Mount of Olives, through which flows a small brook. David crossed here to escape from Absalom (2Sa 15:23), and so did Shimei, in disobedience of Solomon (1Ki 2:37-46). Here Asa burned Maacah's Asherah pole (1Ki 15:13; 2Ch 15:16), and the priests burned and tipped articles dedicated to Baal and Asherah (2Ki 23:4,6,12; 2Ch 29:16; 30:14). It became the site of a cemetery (2Ki 23:6; Jer 31:40). Nehemiah inspected the walls of Jerusalem from here (Ne 2:15). Jesus crossed it to reach Gethsemane (Jn 18:1).

Kir
1. Region of Mesopotamia to which Tiglath-pileser deported the Arameans (2Ki 16:9) and from which God later rescued them (Am 9:7). Appears in prophecy about Jerusalem (Isa 22:6).

2. Walled city of Moab that withstood Israelite attack (2Ki

Saints and disciples gathered in heaven. Early Renaissance fresco on a church wall, Italy

View down the Kidron Valley

3:25) but would be destroyed (Isa 15:1; 16:7,11; Jer 48:31,36). Also known as Kir Hareseth.

Kiriath Jearim

One of four Gibeonite fortress cities (Jos 9:17), also known as Baalah (Jos 15:9), Kiriath Baal (Jos 15:60) and Kiriath (Jos 18:28). First allotted to Judah (Jos 15:60) then to Benjamin (Jos 18:28). 600 Danites camped here on their way to attack Laish (Jdg 18:12). After the Philistines returned the ark of the covenant it was kept here in Abinadab's house for 20 years (1Sa 6:21–7:2). Home of Uriah the prophet (Jer 26:20).

Kiriathaim

1. City of refuge in territory of Naphtali, assigned to the Levites (1Ch 6:76). Also

known as Kartan (Jos 21:32).
2. Town east of Dead Sea, in hill country of Moab. The Emites were expelled from here (Ge 14:5). Taken by the Israelites and allotted to Reuben (Jos 13:19), who fortified it (Nu 32:37). Became Moabite territory, sharing in its downfall (Jer 48:1,23; Eze 25:9).

Kishon

River flowing north-east from Mount Gilboa, past Mount Carmel to the Mediterranean Sea. Scene of Deborah's victory over Sisera (Jdg 4:7,13; Ps 83:9), when the Canaanite chariots became bogged down by the flooded river (Jdg 5:21). Elijah brought the prophets of Baal here to be slaughtered (1Ki 18:40).

Korah

1. Son of Esau; Edomite chief (Ge 36:5,14,18).
2. Grandson of Kohath (1Ch 6:22); ancestor of group of musicians (Ps 42; 44–49; 84; 85; 87; 88) and temple gatekeepers (1Ch 9:19; 26:1,19); led rebellion against Moses; killed by God (Nu 16; 26:9-11; Jude 11).
3. Son of Hebron (1Ch 2:43).

Laban

Brother of Rebekah (Ge 24:29); gave permission for sister to marry Isaac (Ge 24:50,51). Received Jacob (Ge 29:13,14); gave daughters, Leah and Rachel, in exchange for service (Ge 29:15-30). Deceived by Jacob (Ge 30:25–31:21);

pursued and made covenant with him (Ge 31:22-55).

Lachish

Canaanite royal city in the lowlands of Judah near Libnah. Its king joined the alliance against Joshua but the alliance was defeated and the city was taken (Jos 10:1-35). Allotted to Judah (Jos 15:39). Fortified by Rehoboam (2Ch 11:5-9). Amaziah fled here from Jerusalem (2Ki 14:19; 2Ch 25:27). Captured by Sennacherib, it became base for negotiations with Hezekiah (2Ki 18:13-17; 2Ch 32:9; Isa 36:1,2). It was one of two fortified cities left in Judah during the Babylonian invasion (Jer 34:7). Denounced by Micah for its sin (Mic 1:13).

Laodicea

City in Phrygia, in the Lycus Valley, about 12 miles west of Colossae. Its church was probably not established by Paul (Col 2:1; 4:12,13), but he addressed a letter to them (Col 4:16). Accused of being lukewarm in one of the seven letters of Relevation (Rev 3:14-22).

Lazarus

1. Beggar in Jesus' parable (Lk 16:19-31).
2. Brother of Mary and Martha; raised to life by Jesus (Jn 11:1–12:11).

Leah

Daughter of Laban; wife of Jacob (Ge 29:16-23); bore six sons and one daughter (Ge 29:31-35; 30:16-21; 34:1; 35:23).

Lebanon

Mountainous region to the north of Palestine, along the Mediterranean coast. Regarded as part of the Promised Land (Dt 1:7; 3:25; 11:24; Jos 1:4; 13:5,6; 1Ki 9:19; Zec 10:10), but occupied by the Hivites (Jdg 3:3-5; 1Ki 9:20,21; 2Ch 8:7,8). Renowned

The siege of Lachish, recorded on a Babylonian fresco

for its forests of cedar and cypress (Jdg 9:15; 1Ki 4:33; 2Ki 14:9; 19:23; 2Ch 25:18), which were used by Solomon (1Ki 5; 7:2; 2Ch 2:8,16), and Zerubbabel (Ezr 3:7). Used figuratively to speak of righteousness (Ps 92:12), pride (Isa 2:13), glory (Isa 60:13), security (Hos 14:5), etc.

Levi

1. Son of Jacob by Leah (Ge 29:34; 35:23); with Simeon killed Shechemites to avenge rape of sister Dinah (Ge 34); blessed by Jacob (Ge 49:5-7).
2. Tribe descended from Levi. Blessed by Moses (Dt 33:8-11). Numbered separately (Nu 1:47-49; 3:14-39; 26:57-62); responsible for tabernacle (Nu 1:50-53; 3:14-37; 4; 8; 18:2-4); dedicated to God in place of firstborn (Nu 3:11-13,40,41). Given towns (Nu 35; Jos 21) but not land (Nu 18:20-24; 26:62; Dt 10:9; Jos 13:14); allocated land in new division (Eze 48:13,14).
3. See **Matthew**.

Libnah

1. A place where the Israelites camped during the exodus from Egypt (Nu 33:20,21).
2. Canaanite town in lowlands of Judah, near Lachish. Captured by Joshua (Jos 10:29-32,39), allotted to Judah (Jos 15:42) and designated a Levitical city (Jos 21:13; 1Ch 6:57). Participated in revolt against Jehoram (2Ki 8:22; 2Ch 21:10) and attacked by Sennacherib (2Ki 19:8; Isa 37:8).

Home of Hamutal, the mother of Jehoahaz and Zedekiah (2Ki 23:31; 24:18; Jer 52:1).

Lod

City in Plain of Sharon, 11 miles south-east of Joppa. Built by the sons of Elpaal (1Ch 8:12) and occupied after the exile by the Benjamites (Ne 11:35). Known later as Lydda, Peter healed Aeneas here (Ac 9:32-35).

Lot

Nephew of Abraham (Ge 11:27); accompanied him from Haran (Ge 12:4,5; 13:1). Settled in Sodom (Ge 13:5-13); rescued by Abraham (Ge 14), and by two angels (Ge 19; 2Pe 2:7,8). Wife became pillar of salt (Ge 19:26). Fathered Ammon and Moab by his two daughters (Ge 19:30-38).

Luke

Doctor; co-worker and close companion of Paul (Col 4:14; 2Ti 4:11; Phm 24). Writer of third Gospel and Acts.

Luz

See **Bethel**.

Lydda

See **Lod**.

Lydia

God-fearing woman living in Philippi; accepted Paul's message; baptised; offered hospitality (Ac 16:14,15,40).

Lystra

City in Lycaonia 18 miles from Iconium. Paul and Barnabas fled here (Ac 14:6) and healed a crippled man (Ac 14:8-10). Jews from Pisidian Antioch and Iconium arrived to stone Paul, but he survived and left for Derbe (Ac 14:19,20), returning later (Ac 14:21,22). Timothy lived here (Ac 16:1). Paul reminded Timothy of the persecution here (2Ti 3:11).

Macedonia

Country north of Greece, with capital Philippi. Paul visited here after being invited in a vision (Ac 16:9,10); also Silas and Timothy (Ac 18:5) and

The Philippi valley. Lydia met Paul and Silas here, by the Gangitis River

Erastus (Ac 19:22). Home of Paul's companions Gaius and Aristarchus (Ac 19:29). Paul returned during his third journey (Ac 19:21; 20:1-6; 1Co 16:5; 2Co 1:16; 2:13; 7:5) and may have returned again later (1Ti 1:3). The church here was generous in supporting Jerusalem (Ro 15:26; 2Co 8:1-5; Php 4:15-18) and Paul himself (2Co 11:9).

Mahanaim

Town in Gilead, east of the Jordan, on the south bank of the Jabbok. Named by Jacob when he saw the angels of God (Ge 32:1,2). On border between Manasseh and Gad (Jos 13:26,30); assigned to the Levites (Jos 21:38; 1Ch 6:80). Here Ish-Bosheth reigned (2Sa 2:8,12,29) and David found refuge from Absalom (2Sa 17:24,27; 19:32; 1Ki 2:8). Became capital of one of Solomon's districts (1Ki 4:14).

Makkedah

Canaanite royal town (Jos 12:16) in the lowlands of Judah. Joshua captured the city and its inhabitants. The five Amorite kings were executed after hiding in a cave nearby (Jos 10:16-27). Allotted to Judah (Jos 15:41).

Malachi

Prophet; name means "my messenger" (Mal 1:1).

Malta

Island in Mediterranean, between Sicily and Africa where Paul was shipwrecked (Ac 28:1). He stayed for three months surviving a snake attack, healing the sick and receiving hospitality (Ac 28:1-11).

Mamre

Wooded area north of Hebron where Abram set up camp and built an altar (Ge 13:18). Here Abram heard of Lot's capture (Ge 14:13) and received promise of a son (Ge 18:1,10). He bought a field and cave here (Ge 23:17): the burial site for Sarah (Ge 23:19), Abraham (Ge 25:8,9), Isaac (Ge 35:27-29), Rebekah, Leah and Jacob (Ge 49:29-33; 50:12,13).

Manasseh

1. Joseph's elder son (Ge 41:51; 46:20); blessed by Jacob but not as firstborn (Ge 48:13-20). **2.** Tribe descended from Manasseh. Blessed by Moses (Dt 33:13-17). Included in census (Nu 1:34,35; 26:29-34).

Apportioned land on both sides of Jordan: east (Nu 32:33,39-42; Jos 13:8,29-31); west (Jos 17:1-11; Eze 48:4); failed to fully possess (Jos 17:12,13). **3.** Territory to the west and to the east of River Jordan south of the Sea of Galilee. Allotted to the descendants of Joseph's older son. Territories of Manasseh and Ephraim often treated together (Jos 16:1–17:1,14). Its towns and borders were listed, to the east (Jos 13:8,29-31), and to the west (Jos 17:7-11). Territory divided by the Jordan, so its inhabitants were treated as two half-tribes (Jos 13:6-8). The eastern half had good grazing (Nu 32:1). In the western half the Canaanites were not driven out but enslaved (Jos 17:12,13). **4.** King of Judah; son of Hezekiah (2Ki 20:21; 2Ch 32:33). Led Israel into idolatry (2Ki 21:2-9; 2Ch 33:2-9); sin held responsible for exile (2Ki 21:10-15; Jer 15:3,4). Deported to Babylon; repented; carried out limited reform (2Ch 33:10-19). Death (2Ki 21:18; 2Ch 33:20).

Mark

Also called John (Ac 12:12). Cousin of Barnabas (Col 4:10). Accompanied Paul and Barnabas (Ac 12:25) but later deserted them (Ac 13:13). Cause of disagreement (Ac 15:37-39). Reconciled to Paul (2Ti 4:11) and a fellow-worker

(Phm 24); close to Peter (1Pe 5:13). Wrote second Gospel.

Martha

Sister of Mary and Lazarus (Lk 10:38,39; Jn 11). Concerned with practical things (Lk 10:40,41; Jn 12:2).

Mary

1. Mother of Jesus; husband of Joseph (Mt 1:16-25; Lk 1,2). Visited by Gabriel (Lk 1:26-38); praised God (Lk 1:46-55). With Jesus at wedding in Cana (Jn 2:1-11). Witnessed crucifixion (Jn 19:25); entrusted to John's care (Jn 19:26,27). With disciples after resurrection (Ac 1:14). **2.** Magdalene. Demoniac delivered by Jesus (Lk 8:2; Mk 16:9). At crucifixion (Mt 27:55,56; Mk 15:40,41,47; Jn 19:25); visited tomb (Mt 28:1; Mk 16:1; Lk 24:1-10; Jn 20:1); met by risen Jesus (Jn 20:10-18). **3.** Sister of Martha and Lazarus (Lk 10:38,39; Jn 11); commended for devotion (Lk 10:39-42); anointed Jesus' feet (Jn 12:3; 11:2). **4.** Mother of James and Joses; wife of Clopas. At crucifixion (Mt 27:55,56; Mk 15:40,41,47; Jn 19:25); visited tomb (Mt 28:1; Mk 16:1; Lk 24:1-10). **5.** Mother of John Mark whose home used by one Jerusalem church (Ac 12:12-17). **6.** Believer in Rome (Ro 16:6).

Matthew

Apostle; tax collector, also called Levi (Mt 9:9-13; Mk

2:14-17; Lk 5:27-32; Mt 10:3; Mk 3:18; Ac 1:13). Wrote first Gospel.

Media

Mountainous country south of Caspian Sea. Some people of Samaria deported here (2Ki 17:6; 18:11). Darius searched its city Ecbatana for Cyrus' decree to rebuild Jerusalem (Ezr 6:2). Absorbed into Persian Empire, its military leaders were invited to dine with King Xerxes (Est 1:3,14). Mordecai's greatness was recorded in its annals (Est 10:2). Its defeat of Babylonian Empire was prophesied (Isa 13:17; 21:2; Jer 51:11,28; Da 5:28) and its own eventual defeat by Greece (Jer 25:25; Da 8:20,21). Its people were in the crowd at Pentecost (Ac 2:9). See **Persia**.

Mediterranean Sea

See **Great Sea**.

Satellite image of the Mediterranean area

Megiddo

Canaanite royal town, southeast of Carmel, on trade route between Egypt and Syria. Conquered by Joshua (Jos 12:21), allotted to the tribe of Manasseh (Jos 17:11; 1Ch 7:29). Scene of Deborah's victory over Sisera (Jdg 5:19). One of Solomon's 12 districts (1Ki 4:12) and fortified by him (1Ki 9:15). Ahaziah fled here from Jehu (2Ki 9:27). Josiah was mortally wounded here (2Ki 23:29.30; 2Ch 35:20-24). Zechariah prophesies that a great battle would take place near here (Zec 12:11), often identified with the battle of Armageddon (Rev 16:16).

Melchizedek

King of Salem and priest of God Most High who blessed Abraham and received tithe from him (Ge 14:18-20; Heb 7:1-10). Presented as a type of Christ (Ps 110:4; Heb 5:6,10; 6:20; 7:11-17).

Memphis

Egyptian royal city on west bank of the Nile, about 13 miles south of Cairo. Referred to by the prophets as a place of false hope (Isa 19:13; Jer 2:16; 44:1; 46:14,19; Eze 30:13,16; Hos 9:6).

Mephibosheth

1. Son of Jonathan; also called Merib-Baal (1Ch 8:34; 9:40). Crippled by a fall (2Sa 4:4); shown kindness by David (2Sa 9:1-13). Slandered by Ziba (2Sa 16:1-4); reconciled to David (2Sa 19:24-30).
2. Son of Saul, executed by the Gibeonites (2Sa 21:8,9).

Meribah

1. Place of a spring near Rephidim, in the Desert of Sin. Means "strife". Here the Israelites grumbled against Moses because of lack of water and God provided water when Moses struck a rock (Ex 17:1-7). Also known as Massah (Ex 17:7; Dt 6:16; 9:22; 33:8; Ps 95:8).
2. Place of a spring near Kadesh, in the Desert of Zin. Once again the Israelites grumbled about lack of water, and water was provided despite Moses' rebellion (Nu 20:1-13). Also known as Meribah Kadesh (Nu 27:14; Dt 32:51).

Meshach

Formerly Mishael; member of Jewish nobility taken to

Babylon with Daniel, Shadrach and Abednego (Da 1:3-7). Refused unclean food (Da 1:8-16); appointed as administrator (Da 2:49). Refused to worship golden image; kept safe in fiery furnace (Da 3).

Mesopotamia

Means "between the rivers", used in the NT to refer to the region around the Euphrates and Tigris. In the OT it was known as Aram Naharaim, Paddan Aram or simply as "beyond the river". Original home of Abraham, where he worshipped other gods (Jos 24:14,15) and where God first appeared to him (Ac 7:2; Jos 24:2,3). Home of Rebekah (Ge 24:10; 25:20), Leah and Rachel (Ge 28:2,5-7; 29:1-28) and several sons of Jacob (Ge 35:26; 46:15). Jacob lived here for a time (Ge 27:43,44; 28:2) but left to return to Canaan (Ge 31:17,18; 33:18). Home of Balaam (Dt 23:4). Its armies fought with Aram (Jdg 3:8; 2Sa 10:16; 1Ch 19:16), defeating the Israelites (Isa 7:20), and scattering them across this region (1Ki 14:15). Its people were in the crowd at Pentecost (Ac 2:9).

Methuselah

Son of Enoch; grandfather of Noah; lived to be 969 (Ge 5:21-27; 1Ch 1:3; Lk 3:36,37).

Micah

1. Prophet from Moresheth (Jer 26:18,19; Mic 1:1)
2. Ephraimite whose idols and priest were taken by migrating Danites (Jdg 17–18).
3. Micaiah. Prophet (1Ki 22:4-28; 2Ch 18:1-27).

Michael

Archangel (Jude 9). Heavenly guardian of Israel against power of Greece and Persia (Da 10:13,21; 12:1). Defeated Satan and cast him from heaven (Rev 12:7-9).

Michal

Daughter of Saul (1Sa 14:49). Became David's wife (1Sa 18:20-29); warned him of Saul's plot (1Sa 19:11-17). Given to Paltiel (1Sa 25:44); returned to David (2Sa 3:13-16). Despised David (2Sa 6:16-23; 1Ch 15:29).

Michmash

A town of Benjamin north of Jerusalem. Scene of battle between Israel and the Philistines where Jonathan's men won a great victory (1Sa 13:2,5-7; 14:4-15,31). The Assyrians stored supplies here (Isa 10:28).

Midian

Land inhabited by Midian's descendants (Ge 25:1,2; 1Ch 1:32,33), on eastern side of Gulf of Aqaba. Moses fled here (Ex 2:15; Ac 7:29) and married Zipporah (Ex 2:16-21). Here God spoke to Moses from a burning bush (Ex 3:1-10; 4:19).

Its elders were consulted by the Moabites about the approaching Israelites (Nu 22:4). Israel defeated its army (Nu 31:7-12) but its people soon recovered and oppressed Israel (Jdg 6:2,6,7). God used Gideon to save the Israelites (Jdg 6:11–8:28) and the victory was remembered in later poetry (Ps 83:9; Isa 9:4; 10:26; Hab 3:7).

Migdol

Fortified town in the north-east of Egypt, where the Israelites camped after leaving Egypt (Ge 14:2; Nu 33:7) and Jewish refugees moved after Jerusalem was destroyed (Jer 44:1). Its downfall was foretold (Jer 46:14).

Miletus

Seaport on eastern coast of Asia Minor, about 37 miles south of Ephesus. Paul visited here (Ac 20:15). He summoned Ephesian elders and addressed them here (Ac 20:16-38). Possibly Paul revisited it leaving Trophimus sick here (2Ti 4:20).

Miriam

Sister of Moses and Aaron (Nu 25:59; 1Ch 6:3). Watched Moses in bulrushes; suggested mother as nurse (Ex 2:4-8). Prophetess; led dancing and sang at Red Sea (Ex 15:20,21); criticised Moses, became leprous (Nu 12:1-15; Dt 24:9). Death (Nu 20:1).

Reeds on the banks of the River Nile. Moses was found by Pharaoh's daughter among reeds on the riverbank

Mizpah

1. A town of Benjamin (Jos 18:26), where the Israelites assembled before the LORD (Jdg 20:1,3; 21:1,5,8). Here Samuel and the Israelites defeated the Philistines (1Sa 7:5,7,11) and Saul was proclaimed king (1Sa 10:17-25). Fortified by Asa (1Ki 15:22; 2Ch 16:6) who built a cistern which was used by Ishmael for Gedaliah and others whom he slaughtered (Jer 41:1-9). **2.** Town in Gilead, east of Jordan, where Jacob set up a memorial to his covenant with Laban (Ge 31:48,49). Probably an Israelite camp (Jdg 10:17) and home of Jephthah (Jdg 11:11,34). Also known as Ramath Mizpah (Jos 13:26). **3.** Region near foot of Mount Hermon, where Jabin's allies the Hivites lived (Jos 11:1-3) whom Joshua defeated (Jos 11:8). **4.** Town in Moab, where David took his parents for safety from Saul (1Sa 22:3).

5. Town in the lowlands of Judah (Jos 15:38).

Moab

Country east of the Dead Sea, inhabited by descendants of Lot's son (Ge 19:36,37). Also called the plains of Moab; captured by the Amorites before the Israelites conquered it (Nu 21:17-31). Here God instructed Moses how to allot the Pomised Land (Nu 33:50–36:12), Moses expounded the commandments (Nu 36:13; Dt 1:5) and made the covenant with God (Dt 29:1). Moses viewed Promised Land from Moab's Mount Nebo before he died here (Nu 27:12-23; Dt 34:1-6). Birthplace of Ruth (Ru 2:6). Its people were defeated by Israelites under Ehud (Jdg 3:29.30), Saul (1Sa 14:47) and David (2Sa 8:2). The tension continued under Jehoshaphat (2Ch 20:1-23), Jehoram (2Ki 3:4-27) and Jehoiakim (2Ki 24:2). The prophets announced its destruction (Isa 15–16; Jer 48).

Mordecai

1. Benjamite exile; brought up cousin, Esther, as own daughter (Est 2:5-7,15,20). Reported plot to kill Xerxes (Est 2:21-23). Refused to bow to Haman resulting in plot against Jews (Est 3:1-6); mourned; persuaded Esther to help (Est 4). Honoured (Est 6); given Haman's position as next in rank to king (Est 8:1,2; 10). Saved Jews; instituted feast of Purim (Est 8–9). **2.** Jewish exile who returned with Zerubbabel (Ezr 2:2; Ne 7:7).

Moriah, Mount

Abraham was instructed by God to sacrifice Isaac here (Ge 22:2). Exact location unknown, but visible after a three-day journey from Beersheba (Ge 22:4). Probably also the site of Solomon's temple at Jerusalem (2Ch 3:1).

Moses

Levite; brother of Aaron (Ex 6:20; 1Ch 6:3). Put into Nile in basket; found and raised by Pharaoh's daughter; killed Egyptian; fled to Midian; married Zipporah (Ex 2; Ac 7:20-29). Called by God at burning bush (Ex 3–4; Ac 7:30-36); confronted Pharaoh (Ex 5:1-4; 7:1-13); plagues (Ex 7–11; Ps 105:26-36). Led people out of Egypt (Ex

12–13), through Red Sea (Ex 14). Brought water from rock (Ex 17:1-7); raised hands to enable victory over Amalekites (Ex 17:8-16); appointed judges (Ex 18; Dt 1:9-18). Given Law on Mt Sinai (Ex 19–23); spoke to people; confirmed covenant (Ex 19:7,8; 24:1-11; Heb 9:19); returned to mountain to receive stone tablets (Ex 24:12-18; 31:18). Broke tablets over golden calf (Ex 32:15-19; Dt 9:7-17); interceded for people (Ex 32:10-14; Dt 9:25-29). Saw God's glory (Ex 33:18-23); given new tablets (Ex 34; Dt 10:1-5); face shone (Ex 34:29-35).

Supervised building of tabernacle (Ex 35–40; Heb 8:5); consecrated Aaron and sons as priests (Ex 28–29; Lev 8–9). Took census (Nu 1–4; 26). Opposed by Aaron and Miriam (Nu 12), Korah (Nu 16; Jude 11). Sent spies into Canaan (Nu 13; Dt 1:19-25). Forbidden to enter Canaan for striking rock (Nu 20:12; 27:12-14; Dt 3:27; 32:48-52). Lifted up bronze snake (Nu 21:4-9). Allocated land east of Jordan (Nu 32). Last words to Israel (Dt 31–33); death (Dt 34); succeeded by Joshua (Dt 3:28; 34:9; Jos 1:1-9). Faithfulness as God's servant commended (Heb 3:3-5). Prayer of Moses (Ps 90); songs of Moses (Ex 15:1-18; Dt 32; Rev 15:3,4).

Naaman
Commander-in-chief of Aramaean army; leprosy healed by Elisha (2Ki 5).

Naboth
Jezreelite, killed by Jezebel so Ahab could take possion of his vineyard (1Ki 21:1-16).

Nahum
Prophet; spoke against Nineveh (Na 1:1).

Nain
Town in south-west Galilee where Jesus raised to life a widow's son (Lk 7:11-15).

Stained glass window in Lincoln Cathedral, UK, showing Jesus raising the son of a widow of Nain to life

Naomi
Mother-in-law of Ruth. With husband Elimelech, moved from Bethlehem to Moab during famine; returned with Ruth after death of husband and sons (Ru 1). Encouraged Ruth's marriage to Boaz (Ru 2:19-3:6); nursed Ruth's son (Ru 4:16,17).

Naphtali
1. Son of Jacob by Bilhah (Ge 30:8; 35:25; 1Ch 2:2). Blessed by Jacob (Ge 49:21).
2. Tribe descended from Naphtali. Blessed by Moses (Dt 33:23). Included in census (Nu 1:42,43; 26:48-50). Apportioned land (Jos 19:32-39; Eze 48:3); unable to take full possession (Jdg 1:33).
3. Territory to the west of Sea of Galilee, with Zebulun and Asher to the west, and Issachar to the south. Allotted to the descendants of Jacob's fifth son. Its towns and borders were clearly listed (Jos 19:32-39). Canaanite inhabitants not driven out but enslaved (Jdg 1:33). Conquered by Assyria before fall of Samaria and its people deported (2Ki 15:29). Isaiah predicted great honour for this land (Isa 9:1), fulfilled in Jesus' ministry there (Mt 4:13-16).

Nathan
1. Prophet; announced God's promise to David of lasting dynasty (2Sa 7:1-17; 1Ch 17:1-15); rebuked David's sin with Bathsheba (2Sa 12:1-14). Supported Solomon's succession (1Ki 1:8-40). Chronicled reigns of David and Solomon (1Ch 29:29; 2Ch 9:29).
2. Son of David (2Sa 5:14; Zec 12:12); included in Jesus' genealogy (Lk 3:31).

Nathanael
Apostle from Cana in Galilee; brought to Jesus by Philip (Jn

Sheep graze peacefully on a hillside overlooking Nazareth

1:45-51; 21:2). Possibly to be identified with Bartholomew, who is also linked with Philip (Mt 10:3).

Nazareth

Town in Galilee between Sea of Galilee and Mediterranean. Home of Mary and Joseph (Lk 1:26; 2:4,39); home of Jesus (Mt 2:23; 21:11; Lk 2:51), which he left to begin his preaching (Mt 4:13-17; Mk 1:9). Jesus returned here (Lk 4:16) but was rejected (Lk 4:29). He was often called Jesus of Nazareth (Mt 26:71; Mk 1:24; 10:47; Lk 4:34; 18:37; 24:19; Jn 1:45; 18:5,7; 19:19; Ac 2:22; 3:6; 4:10; 6:14; 10:38; 22:8; 26:9) or the Nazarene (Mt 2:23; Mk 14:67; 16:6). The town had a poor reputation (Jn 1:46).

Nebo

1. Mountain of the Abarim Range in Moab (Nu 33:47). Here Moses viewed the Promised Land then died (Dt 32:49,50; 34:1-6).
2. Town in Moab allotted to and rebuilt by tribe of Reuben (Nu 32:3,37,38; 1Ch 5:8). Named by the prophets in their laments (Isa 15:2; 46:1; Jer 48:1,22).
3. Possibly a town in Judah whose inhabitants returned from exile (Ezr 2:29). Called by Nehemiah "the other Nebo" (Ne 7:33).

Nebuchadnezzar

King of Babylon. Defeated Egyptians at Carchemish (Jer 46:2); invaded and subdued Judah; took exiles to Babylon; destroyed Jerusalem (2Ki 24—25; 2Ch 36; Jer 39; Da

1:1-5). Dreams interpreted by Daniel (Da 2; 4); fiery furnace (Da 3); madness and restoration; worshipped God (Da 3:28,29; 4:34,35).

Neco

Pharaoh. Reluctantly fought and killed Josiah, who opposed support for Assyria (2Ki 23:29.30; 2Ch 35:20-25). Deposed Jehoahaz, appointed Jehoiakim as vassal (2Ki 23:31-35; 2Ch 36:2-4). Defeated by Nebuchadnezzar at Carchemish (Jer 46:2).

Negev

The southern desert region of Judah (Jos 15:21). Abraham (Ge 12:9; 13:1,3; 20:1) and Isaac (Ge 24:62) camped here.

Twelve spies approached Canaan from this direction (Nu 13:17,22). The home of the Canaanite King Arad (Nu 21:1; 33:40). Part of the Promised Land (Dt 1:7; 34:3) which Joshua conquered (Jos 10:40; 11:16; 12:8). Land here given by Caleb to his daughter (Jos 15:19; Jdg 1:15), and some land was re-allocated to the tribe of Simeon (Jos 19:8). It was prone to attack from Amalekites (1Sa 30:1,14), and Philistines (2Ch 28:18). Included in David's census (2Sa 24:7). Used poetically to portray difficulty

King Nebuchadnezzar in his period of insanity, acting like a wild animal. Illustration by William Blake

and hardship (Ps 126:4; Isa 30:6) and referred to by the prophets (Jer 13:19; 17:26; 32:44; 33:13; Ob 19,20; Zec 7:7).

Nehemiah

Cupbearer to Artaxerxes (Ne 1:10). Prayed over state of Jerusalem (Ne 1); allowed to return to rebuild city walls (Ne 2–6); appointed governor (Ne 5:14; 8:9). Called Ezra to read Law (Ne 8); confessed nation's

sin (Ne 9); dedicated wall (12:27-47); made other reforms (Ne 13).

Nicodemus

Pharisee, member of Sanhedrin who visited Jesus at night (Jn 3:1-15). Argued against condemning Jesus without a hearing (Jn 7:50,51). With Joseph anointed and buried Jesus (Jn 19:38-42).

Nile, River

Running about 3,500 miles from central Africa, northwards to the Egyptian delta on the Mediterranean coast. Appears in Pharaoh's dream that Joseph interpreted (Ge 41:1,3,17). All Hebrew baby boys were to be drowned here (Ex 1:22); Moses escaped and was discovered by Pharaoh's daughter (Ex 2:5-10). During the plagues its water was turned to blood (Ex 4:9; 7:17-25; Ps 78:4), and its frogs invaded the land (Ex 8:3,9,11). Used symbolically by the prophets because of its importance and regular

flooding (Isa 19:7,8; 23:3,10; Jer 46:7,8; Eze 29:3,9; 30:12; Am 8:8; 9:5; Na 3:8; Zec 10:11).

Nineveh

City on bank of River Tigris, built by Nimrod, in Assyria (Ge 10:11,12). Sennacherib's capital city, where he was murdered by his sons (2Ki 19:36; Isa 37:37,38). God instructed Jonah to preach here; its people repented and turned to God (Jnh 1:2; 3:2-10; 4:11). Nahum pronounced God's judgement upon it (Na 1:1,8,11,14; 2:1,8; 3:7); Zephaniah foretold its destruction (Zep 2:13). Jesus compared its people in Jonah's time with his own stubborn generation (Mt 12:41; Lk 11:32).

Noah

Righteous man (Ge 6:8,9; 7:1; Eze 14:14,20; Heb 11:7). Obeyed God's command to build ark (Ge 6:11-22). God's covenant with (Ge 6:18; 9:8-17). Planted vineyard; became drunk, dishonoured

The River Nile, near Thebes

by Ham (Ge 9:20-23); cursed Canaan; blessed Shem and Japheth (Ge 9:24-27). Death (Ge 9:28,29).

Nob

Priestly town (1Sa 22:19) in territory of Benjamin (Ne 11:32), about 2 miles east of Jerusalem. David fled here from Saul (1Sa 21:1) and was given consecrated bread and Goliath's sword (1Sa 21:1-9). All of its priests were then executed by Saul (1Sa

22:11-19). The Assyrian army camped here before assaulting Jerusalem (Isa 10:32).

Obadiah

1. Official in charge of Ahab's palace; believer; hid 100 prophets from Jezebel (1Ki 18:1-16).
2. Prophet; spoke against Edom (Ob 1).

Oholiab

See **Bezalel**.

Looking east along the high plateau region of the Negev desert

Olives, Mount of

East of Jerusalem, across the Kidron Valley. David climbed it on hearing of Absalom's revolt (2Sa 15:30). In the end times the LORD will stand here, and it will split in two from east to west (Zec 14:4). In Jesus' time Bethany and Bethphage were located here (Mt 21:1; Mk 11:1; Lk 19:29). Jesus talked with his disciples here (Mt 24:3; 26:30; Mk 13:3; 14:26; Lk 19:37; 21:37; Jn 8:1), and prayed here on the night of his arrest (Lk 22:39). Probably the site of Jesus' ascension (Ac 1:12).

Omri

King of Israel; father of Ahab (1Ki 16:30). Army commander, appointed king after Zimri assassinated Baasha (1Ki 16:15-28). Sinned against God (1Ki 16:25,26).

On

Town in Egypt about 20 miles north-east of Memphis, east of River Nile. Home of Joseph's

Ancient olive trees in the Garden of Gethsemane

wife Asenath (Ge 41:45,50; 46:20). Later known by its Greek name Heliopolis (Eze 30:17), when its capture by Nebuchadnezzar was foretold.

Onesimus

Runaway slave belonging to Philemon; converted by Paul and dear to him (Col 4:9; Phm 10-16).

Ophir

Region famous for gold and precious stones; location is uncertain. Reached by sea (1Ki 9:28; 10:11; 22:48; 2Ch 8:18), its gold was brought to Solomon for his building projects (1Ki 9:28; 10:10-21; 1Ch 29:4; 2Ch 8:18; 9:10).

Slave shackles – a reminder of the cruel nature of slavery

Used figuratively on account of its great wealth (Job 22:24; 28:16; Ps 45:9; Isa 13:12).

Ophrah

1. City of Benjamin (Jos 18:23), attacked by Philistines (1Sa 13:17). Probably also known as Ephraim (Jn 11:54) and Ephron (2Ch 13:19). Exact location unknown.
2. City of Manasseh, occupied by Abiezrites (Jdg 6:11). Here Gideon built an altar (Jdg 6:24), placed the golden ephod (Jdg 8:27) and was buried (Jdg 8:32). Abimelech came to his father's home here and murdered 70 sons of Jerub-Baal to take the throne (Jdg 9:5). Exact location unknown.

Paddan Aram

See **Aram**; **Mesopotamia**.

Pamphylia

Province along southern coast of Asia Minor, between Lycia and Cilicia. Capital city was Perga (Ac 13:13). Its people were represented in Jerusalem at Pentecost (Ac 2:10). Paul's point of entry into Asia Minor on his first journey (Ac 13:13,14); he returned on his way back to Jerusalem (Ac 14:24-26). Paul sailed near here on his way to Rome (Ac 27:5).

Paphos

Port on south-western coast of Cyprus. Paul and Barnabas visited here, and its governor was converted (Ac 13:6-13). From here they sailed to Perga in Pamphylia (Ac 13:6-13).

Paran

1. Wilderness region in Sinai Peninsula, known also as El-Paran (Ge 14:6). Here Hagar fled with Ishmael (Ge 21:21) and the Israelites stayed after leaving Egypt (Nu 10:12; 12:16). From here the spies were sent into Canaan (Nu 13:3,26).
2. Mountain in Seir (Edom), associated with God coming to help his people (Dt 33:2; Hab 3:3). Hadad passed through

View across the island of Patmos

here on his way to Egypt (1Ki 11:18).

Patmos

Island in the Aegean where the Romans banished criminals. Here John wrote the book of Revelation (Rev 1:9).

Paul

Apostle (Gal 1:1); also called Saul (Ac 13:9). From Tarsus (Ac 9:11; 21:39; 22:3; Php 3:5); Pharisee (Ac 23:6; 26:5; Php 3:5); taught by Gamaliel (Ac 22:3).

Approved of Stephen's death (Ac 7:58; 8:1); persecuted church (Ac 8:3; 9:1,2; 1Co 15:9; Gal 1:13). Saw Jesus on Damascus road (Ac

9:3-9; 22:6-11; 26:12-18); healed and baptised by Ananias (Ac 9:17-19; 22:12-16). Into Arabia (Gal 1:17); escaped from Damascus in a basket (Ac 9:23-25; 2Co 11:32,33). Introduced to apostles in Jerusalem by Barnabas; sent to Tarsus (Ac 9:26-30; Gal 1:18-21). Brought to Antioch by Barnabas (Ac 11:22-26). Visited Jerusalem; message and commission confirmed by apostles (Ac 11:30; Gal 2:1-10). First missionary journey, with Barnabas, (Ac 13–14). Stoned at Lystra (Ac 14:19,20). At Council of Jerusalem (Ac 15). Disagreed with Barnabas over Mark (Ac 15:36-39). Second missionary journey, with Silas

The theatre at Ephesus, where the town clerk had to appeal to the crowd for the safety of Paul and his companions

(Ac 15:40–18:22). Called to Macedonia (Ac 16:9,10); miraculously released from prison in Philippi (Ac 16:16-40); in Athens (Ac 17:16-34); in Corinth (Ac 18). Third missionary journey (Ac 18:23). In Ephesus (Ac 19); raised Eutychus to life (Ac 20:7-12); farewell to Ephesian elders (Ac 20:13-37). Travelled to Jerusalem (Ac 21); arrested (Ac 21:27-36); appealed as Roman citizen (Ac 22:25-29); before Sanhedrin (Ac 22:30–23:10). Taken to Caesarea (Ac 23:12-35); before

Felix, Festus and Agrippa (Ac 24–26). Journeyed to Rome (Ac 27–28); shipwrecked on Malta (Ac 27:27–28:10); under house arrest in Rome; preached gospel (Ac 28:16-31). Letters: Romans, 1 & 2 Corinthians, Galatians, Ephesians, Philippians, Colossians, 1 & 2 Thessalonians, 1 & 2 Timothy, Titus, Philemon.

Peniel

Place along the Jabbok where Jacob wrestled with God (Ge 32:22-32; Hos 12:4); means "the face of God". Its inhabitants refused to give Gideon bread for his men, so he destroyed the city and its

tower (Jdg 8:8,9,17). Later fortified by King Jeroboam (1Ki 12:25).

Perga

Capital city of Pamphylia, on southern coast of Asia Minor. Paul and Barnabas passed through here twice. John Mark left them during the first visit (Ac 13:13,14); they returned later to preach (Ac 14:25).

Pergamum

Capital city of Asia Minor where Antipas was martyred (Rev 2:13). One of the seven letters of Revelation was addressed to the church here which was praised for its faithfulness and warned about false teaching (Rev 2:12-15).

Persia

Ancient empire that began east of Persian Gulf, but under Cyrus absorbed Media and Babylonia (2Ch 36:20). Its kings allowed the exiled Jews to return to Jerusalem to rebuild the temple (2Ch 36:22,23; Ezr 1:1-11; 7:1-28; 9:9). Its military leaders were guests of King Xerxes (Est 1:3,14). Mordecai's greatness was recorded in their kings' annals (Est 10:2). Persians served in the armies of Tyre (Eze 27:10) and Magog (Eze 38:5). Its defeat of the Babylonian Empire was prophesied (Da 5:28), as was its own eventual defeat by Greece (Da 10–11). See **Media**.

Magnificent craftsmanship in a griffin-headed bracelet from the Oxus Treasure: Persian, 5th–4th C BC

Peter

Name means "rock"; in Aramaic, Cephas (Jn 1:42). Apostle; brother of Andrew, also called Simon (Mt 4:18; Mk 1:16-18; Lk 5:3-11; Jn 1:40-42; Mt 10:2; Mk 3:16; Lk 6:14; Ac 1:13). With James and John, especially close to Jesus: at raising of Jairus' daughter (Mk 5:37; Lk 8:51); transfiguration (Mt 17:1,2; Mk 9:2; Lk 9:28,29); in Gethsemane (Mt 26:36-38; Mk 14:32-34). Confessed Jesus as Christ (Mt 16:13-20; Mk 8:27-30; Lk 9:18-21). Caught fish with coin (Mt 17:24-27). Denial predicted (Mt 26:33-35; Mk 14:29-31; Lk 22:31-34; Jn 13:37,38). Followed Jesus after arrest (Mt 26:58; Mk 14:54; Jn 18:15); denied Jesus (Mt 26:69-75; Mk 14:66-72; Lk 22:54-62; Jn 18:17-27). Commissioned by Jesus after resurrection (Jn 21). Exercised leadership in early church (Ac 1:15; 2:14; 5:3-11). Preached on day of Pentecost (Ac 2). Healed lame man at temple gate (Ac 3); before Sanhedrin (Ac 4). In Samaria (Ac 8:14-25). Received vision; went to Cornelius (Ac 10); supported Gentile mission (Ac 11; 15:7-11); lapsed and rebuked by Paul at Antioch (Gal 2:11-21). Miraculously released from prison (Ac 12). Wrote 1 & 2 Peter.

Philadelphia

City of the province of Lydia in western Asia Minor. One of the seven letters of Revelation was addressed to its church which was praised for its endurance (Rev 3:7-13).

Philemon

Co-worker with Paul (Phm 1); owner of runaway slave, Onesimus (Phm 8-11).

Philip

1. Apostle (Mt 10:3; Mk 3:18; Lk 6:14; Ac 1:13); from Bethsaida; brought Nathaniel to Jesus (Jn 1:43-45).
2. Deacon (Ac 6:1-7). Evangelist (Ac 21:8); in Samaria (Ac 8:4-13); spoke to Ethiopian official (Ac 8:26-40).

Mount Hermon, Syria, the traditional site of Jesus' transfiguration before Peter, James and John

Philippi

City in eastern Macedonia, near northern shore of the Aegean. Paul stayed here several days and preached to the women including Lydia, who believed and was baptised (Ac 16:12-15). A fortune-teller was released from spirit possession by Paul resulting in his own imprisonment and the jailer's conversion (Ac 16:16-34). Paul wrote to the Christians here expressing fondness for them (Php 1:1-8).

Philistia

Also known as "the land of the Philistines" or "the region of the Philistines". It extended from the River Shihor (Brook of Egypt) northwards to Ekron (Jos 13:2,3). The term "Philistia" is common in poetry (Ex 15:14; Ps 60:8; 87:4; 108:9; Isa 11:14).

Phinehas

1. Son of Eleazar; grandson of Aaron (Ex 6:25). Priest (Nu 31:6; Jdg 20:28). Held back God's judgement by killing Israelite and pagan Midianite woman (Nu 25:6-11; Ps 106:28-31); zeal rewarded by everlasting covenant of priesthood (Nu 26:12,13). In charge of temple gatekeepers (1Ch 9:20).

2. Disreputable son of Eli (1Sa 1:3; 2:12-17). Condemned with his brother (1Sa 2:34). Both died in battle (1Sa 4:11).

Phrygia

Mountainous region of Asia Minor, between Asia and Galatia. Its people were represented in Jerusalem on the Day of Pentecost (Ac 2:10). Paul travelled through this province on his journeys (Ac

Pilate's name inscribed on a block of limestone, Caesarea, most probably from the time when he was governor there

16:6; 18:23), but does not appear to have founded the churches here (Col 2:1).

Pilate
Roman governor of Judea (Lk 3:1). Questioned Jesus (Mt 27:11-14; Mk 15:2-5; Lk 23:2-5; Jn 18:33-38); gave way to crowds: freed Barabbas; washed hands and gave Jesus up to be crucified (Mt 27:15-26; Mk 15:6-15; Lk 23:13-25; Jn 19). Released Jesus' body to Joseph (Mt 27:57,58; Mk 15:43-46; Lk 23:50-54); allowed guard on tomb (Mt 27:62-66).

Pisgah
Headland near Mount Nebo in the Abarim range, where Moses viewed the Promised Land (Nu 21:20; Dt 3:17,27; 4:49; 34:1). Probably a sacred "high place"; Balaam built seven altars here (Nu 23:14). Originally ruled by King Sihon (Jos 12:3), but eventually allotted to tribe of Reuben (Jos 13:20).

Potiphar
Egyptian official who bought Joseph (Ge 37:36; 39:1) and made him chief steward (Ge 39:2-6). Sent him to prison (Ge 39:7-20).

Priscilla
Also called Prisca. Wife of Aquila. Disciples from Rome (Ac 18:2); co-workers with Paul (Ro 16:3; 1Co 16:19; 2Ti 4:19), accompanied him to Ephesus (Ac 18:18,19); instructed Apollos (Ac 18:26).

Rabbah
1. Chief city of the Ammonites on eastern border of the territory of Gad (Dt 3:11; Jos 13:24,25; 2Sa 12:26; 17:27; Jer 49:2; Eze 21:20). Uriah the Hittite was slain here under orders from David (2Sa 11:1,15). Eventually conquered by David (2Sa 12:27-31; 1Ch 20:1). Its eventual destruction was prophesied (Jer 49:2,3; Eze 21:20; 25:5; Am 1:14).
2. City in the Judean hill country, mentioned with Kiriath Jearim (Jos 15:60). Exact location unknown.

Rachel
Daughter of Laban (Ge 29:9-13); became Jacob's wife (Ge 29:28); mother of Joseph and Benjamin (Ge 30:22-24; 35:16-18,24); died in childbirth; buried by Jacob (Ge 35:16-20; 48:7).

Rahab
1. Prostitute in Jericho; sheltered Israelite spies and helped them escape (Jos 2; Jas 2:25); spared when city fell (Jos 6:22-25; Heb 11:31). Mother of Boaz (Mt 1:5).
2. Female chaos monster (Job 26:12; Ps 89:10; Isa 51:9); figurative name for Egypt (Ps 87:4; Isa 30:7).

Ramah
1. Town in territory of Benjamin (Jos 18:25), near Gibeah (Jdg 19:13,14). Deborah held court between here and Bethel (Jdg 4:5). On border between the divided kingdoms, so was heavily fortified (1Ki 15:17; 2Ch 16:1), but Judah weakened its defences (1Ki 15:22; 2Ch 16:6). On Nebuchadnezzar's invasion route (Isa 10:29; Hos 5:8); he detained Jewish captives here (Jer 31:15; 40:1).
2. Town in territory of Ephraim, exact location unknown. Known also as Ramathaim (1Sa 1:1). Home and burial place of Samuel (1Sa 7:17; 25:1), where the people demanded a king (1Sa 8:4-6). David fled here from Saul (1Sa 19:18).
3. Town on border of territory of Asher (Jos 19:29). Exact location unknown.
4. Fortified town in territory of Naphtali (Jos 19:36).
5. Town in territory of Simeon in the Negev (Jos 19:8). Exact location unknown.

Ramathaim
See **Ramah 2**.

Ramoth Gilead
Fortified city in territory of Gad, about 25 miles east of River Jordan. Designated as a town of refuge (Dt 4:43; Jos 20:8), and assigned to the Levites (Jos 21:38; 1Ch 6:80). Its people received Amalekite plunder from David (1Sa 30:27), and it was one of Solomon's 12 districts (1Ki 4:13). Ahab tried to retake the city from the Arameans, rejecting Micaiah's advice and was killed by a random arrow (1Ki 22:1-38; 2Ch 18:2-34; 22:5,6). Ahab's son Joram also

Marine life in the Red Sea

Rehoboam
Son of Solomon; succeeded him as king (1Ki 11:43; 2Ch 9:31). Refusal to ease burden on people led to breaking away of northern tribes under Jeroboam (1Ki 12; 2Ch 10). In his evil reign temple plundered by Egyptians (1Ki 14:21-28; 2Ch 12:9-16).

Reuben
1. Jacob's firstborn, by Leah (Ge 29:32; 35:23; 46:8). Wanted to save Joseph (Ge 37:19-30). Lost position because slept with Bilhah (Ge 35:22; 49:4). Blessed by Jacob (Ge 49:3,4).
2. Tribe descended from Reuben. Blessed by Moses (Dt 33:6). Included in census (Nu 1:20,21; 26:5-11). Apportioned land east of Jordan (Nu 32; 34:14,15; Jos 18:7; 22); crossed into Canaan to fight alongside other tribes (Nu 32:16-31). Place restored in land (Eze 48:6).
3. Territory east of Dead Sea, and south of territory of Gad. Allotted to the descendants of Jacob's eldest son, who liked it for its good grazing (Nu 32:1). Its towns and borders were clearly listed (Jos 13:15-23).

Riblah
1. Town on River Orontes, between Hamath and Damascus. Pharaoh Neco put Jehoahaz in chains here to prevent him from ruling in Jerusalem (2Ki 23:33). During his siege of Jerusalem, Nebuchadnezzar established

fought the Arameans here and was injured (2Ki 8:28,29). Jehu was anointed king here (2Ki 9:1-6).

Rebekah
Sister of Laban (Ge 25:20); left Haran with Abraham's servant to marry Isaac (Ge 24). Mother of Esau and Jacob (Ge 25:21-26). In Gerar, pretended to be Isaac's sister (Ge 26:1-11). Helped Jacob deceive Jacob and steal blessing (Ge 27).

Red Sea
Sometimes called "Sea of Reeds" as this is an alternative translation of the Hebrew expression. Stretch of water separating Arabia from Egypt and Ethiopia. Locusts sent upon Egypt were carried away to here (Ex 10:19). When Moses led the Israelites out of Egypt, its waters parted for them to cross over (Ex 14:16; Jos 2:10; 4:23) and then returned to drown the pursuing Egyptians (Ex 15:4; Dt 11:4; 24:6,7). The southern border of the Promised Land (Ex 23:31) and an important trade route for Israel (1Ki 9:26).

Statue of St Paul in a niche of the church of St Paul Outside the Walls, Rome

his base here (2Ki 25:6,20,21; Jer 39:5,6; 52:9,10,26,27).
2. Landmark given by Moses for the eastern boundary of Israel, between Shepham and the Sea of Kinnereth (Nu 34:11).

Rimmon
1. Town in the Negev region of southern Judah (Jos 15:32; Zec 14:10), later reassigned to the tribe of Simeon (Jos 19:7; 1Ch 4:32).
2. Town marking the eastern border of the territory of Zebulun (Jos 19:13).
3. A rock in the territory of Benjamin, where 600 of the tribe found refuge from the other Israelite tribes, after they had sinned at Gibeah (Jdg

20:45,47). They were eventually offered peace (Jdg 21:13).

Rome
Capital city of Roman Empire, about 15 miles from Mediterranean coast of Italy. Its inhabitants were at Pentecost (Ac 2:10). Aquila and Priscilla were ordered out of here by Claudius (Ac 18:2). Paul possessed Roman citizenship (Ac 16:37; 22:28) and resolved to preach here (Ac 19:21; 23:11; Ro 1:15; 15:24). After appealing to Caesar for justice (Ac 25:11) he was brought here as a prisoner (Ac 25:24,25; 28:16). The fall of Rome is anticipated in Revelation (Rev 17–18).

Ruth
Moabitess at time of Judges; widow of Naomi's son, Mahlon (Ru 1:4,5; 4:10). Refused to leave Naomi; accompanied her to Bethlehem (Ru 1:11-22). Gleaned in field of Boaz and treated kindly (Ru 2). Claimed protection from Boaz as kinsman-redeemer (Ru 3). Married Boaz; gave birth to Obed, grandfather of David (Ru 4).

Salt Sea
See **Dead Sea**.

Samaria
1. City built by King Omri on hill of Samaria, which he bought from Shemer (1Ki 16:24). It replaced Tirzah as capital of northern kingdom (1Ki 16:23,28,29), and

Samaria was denounced by the prophets for following foreign gods, as depicted by this Baal figurine from Ugarit

remained the royal residence until the Assyrian conquest (2Ki 17:5,6). Site of ornate palace built by Ahab (1Ki 22:39; Am 3:15), and also his temple to Baal (1Ki 16:32,33). Prophets condemned its pride and idolatry (Isa 9:9; Jer 23:13; Eze 16:46-55; Am 6:1; Mic 1:1). The prophets Elisha (2Ki 5:3) and Oded (2Ch 28:9) lived here. Site of assassinations of Ahab's sons (2Ki 10:1-17), Shallum (2Ki 15:14) and

Pekahiah (2Ki 15:25). Twice under Syrian siege (1Ki 20:1; 2Ki 6:24), but did not fall until the Assyrian conquest. Became inhabited by refugees from other conquered countries (2Ki 17:24); led to intermarriage with remaining Jews, and the birth of a despised people (Jn 4:9). Philip preached here (Ac 8:5) and Peter and John were sent to support the new church (Ac 8:14; 9:31).

2. The name of the city extended to include the surrounding region, which became a province under Roman occupation (Lk 17:11; Ac 1:8; 8:1; 9:31; 15:3).

Samson

Judge. Birth promised (Jdg 13:2,3); set apart as Nazirite (Jdg 13:4-7); great strength linked with uncut hair (Jdg 16:17,22). Married Philistine (Jdg 14); killed lion, 30 Philistines (Jdg 14:6,19). Took vengeance on Philistines when wife given away (Jdg 15); killed 1,000 with jaw-bone (Jdg 15:15,16). Carried off gates of Gaza (Jdg 16:1-3). Betrayed by Delilah and captured (Jdg 16:4-21); died when bringing temple of Dagon down on Philistines (Jdg 16:23-30).

Samuel

Judge and prophet (Ac 3:24; 13:20). Born to Hannah, who vowed to dedicate him to God (1Sa 1:9-20). Taken to temple to be raised by Eli (1Sa 1:21-28; 2:11,18-21). Called by God

(1Sa 3). Led Israel to victory over Philistines (1Sa 7). Asked by people for a king (1Sa 8); anointed Saul (1Sa 9–10). Farewell speech (1Sa 12). Rebuked Saul (1Sa 13:8-14; 15); and announced his rejection by God (1Sa 13:13,14; 15:22-26). Anointed David (1Sa 16:1-13); protected David (1Sa 19:18-24). Death (1Sa 25:1). Spirit called up by Saul (1Sa 28:11-19).

Sanballat

Horonite; governor of Samaria; leading opponent of Nehemiah in his task to rebuild walls of Jerusalem (Ne 2:10,19; 4:1-9; 6).

Sarah

Wife of Abraham; formerly Sarai; barren (Ge 11:29.30). Taken by Pharaoh when pretending to be Abraham's sister (Ge 12:10-20). Gave Hagar to Abraham (Ge 16:1-3). Name changed; promised a son (Ge 17:15-21; 18:9,10; Ro 9:9; Heb 11:11); laughed in disbelief (Ge 18:10-15). Taken by Abimelech when pretending to be Abraham's sister; returned (Ge 20:1-18). Gave birth to Isaac (Ge 21:1-7); sent away Hagar and Ishmael (Ge 21:8-14). Death and burial (Ge 23).

Sardis

Capital city of Lydia in Asia Minor, situated on River Pactolus east of Smyrna. One of the seven letters of Revelation was addressed to

the church here (Rev 1:11), which was encouraged to turn from complacency (Rev 3:1-6).

Saul

1. Benjamite; Israel's first king. Chosen by God (1Sa 9:15,16); anointed by Samuel (1Sa 10:1); acknowledged publicly (1Sa 10:17-25). Defeated Ammonites (1Sa 11). Rebuked by Samuel, when offered sacrifices (1Sa 13) and for disobedience (1Sa 15); rejected as king (1Sa 13:13,14; 15:23,26-28; 28:17). Defeated Philistines (1Sa 14). Troubled by evil spirit; soothed by David's playing (1Sa 16:14-23). Sent David to fight Goliath (1Sa 17). Gave David his daughter Michal as wife (1Sa 18:20,21). Became jealous; tried to kill David (1Sa 18:1-11; 19:1-10). Anger at Jonathan (1Sa 20:26-34). Pursued David; killed priests at Nob (1Sa 22); life spared by David (1Sa 24; 26). Consulted medium at Endor; rebuked by Samuel's spirit (1Sa 28). Defeated by Philistines on Mt Gilboa; wounded, took own life (1Sa 31; 1Ch 10). Mourned by David (2Sa 1:19-27). Children (1Sa 14:49-51; 1Ch 8).
2. See **Paul**.

Seir

See **Edom**.

Sennacherib

King of Assyria. Attacked Judah and laid siege to Jerusalem (2Ki 18:13–19:13; Isa 36:1–37:13; 2Ch 32). Pride

A double-shekel coin from Sidon, dated 400–350 BC, depicting a Persian king at the time of Persian conquest

brought God's judgement (Isa 10:12-19).
Fall prophesied by Isaiah, following Hezekiah's prayer (2Ki 19:14-34; Isa 37:14-35); defeat and death (2Ki 19:35-37; Isa 37:36-38).

Shadrach
Formerly Hananiah; member of Jewish nobility taken to Babylon with Daniel, Meshach and Abednego (Da 1:3-7). Refused unclean food (Da 1:8-16); appointed as administrator (Da 2:49). Refused to worship golden image; kept safe in fiery furnace (Da 3).

Sharon
1. Large plain on Mediterranean coast of Palestine, stretching from the foot of Mount Carmel to Joppa. Rich in pasture (1Ch 27:29; Isa 65:10) and known for its fruitfulness and beauty (SS 2:1; Isa 33:9; 35:2). Peter enjoyed a fruitful ministry here (Ac 9:35).
2. District to the east of River Jordan, occupied by tribe of Gad; boasted good pasture land (1Ch 5:16).

Sheba
1. City in territory of Judah, assigned to tribe of Simeon (Jos 19:2).
2. Kingdom of the Sabeans, location uncertain but probably in south-west Arabia. Its queen travelled to Jerusalem to test Solomon's reputed wisdom (1Ki 10:1-13; 2Ch 9:1-12; Mt 12:42; Lk 11:31). Renowned for the quality of its goods (Job 6:19; Ps 72:10,15; Isa 60:6; Jer 6:20; Eze 27:22,23).

Shechem
1. Son of Hamor, a ruling Hivite (Ge 34:2). Raped Jacob's daughter, Dinah, and asked to marry her (Ge 34:2-12). Shechemites treacherously killed by Simeon and Levi in revenge (Ge 34:13-31).
2. Town in hill country of Ephraim, between Mounts Ebal and Gerizim. Where the LORD promised Abram the land (Ge 12:6,7). Abram erected an altar, so it became an important sanctuary (Ge 12:7). Jacob built an altar here to mark his return from Paddan Aram (Ge 33:18-20), and later buried foreign gods under its great oak tree (Ge 35:4). Jacob gave it to Joseph for his burial site (Jos 24:32; Ac 7:16). Allotted to tribe of Ephraim; became a city of refuge (Jos 20:7; 1Ch 6:67). Here Joshua drew up the covenant and laws (Jos 24). Home of Abimelech (Jdg 8:31; 9:1) who was crowned here after executing the sons of Jerub-Baal (Jdg 9:1-6). Jotham chastised its people for this (Jdg 9:7-20), and so they revolted against Abimelech (Jdg 9:22-57). Rehoboam was crowned here (1Ki 12:1; 2Ch 10:1). Jeroboam made it the capital of the northern kingdom (1Ki 12:25). After the exile, inhabited by Samaritans, and became Sychar, where Jesus met a woman at Jacob's well (Jn 4:5-40).

Shem
Son of Noah (Ge 5:32; 6:10; 1Ch 1:4). Saved in ark (Ge 7:13; 9:18,19). Blessed by Noah (Ge 9:26); descendants (Ge 10:21-31); ancestor of Abraham (Ge 11:10-32).

Shiloh

City in hill country of Ephraim, north of Bethel, and east of the road that connects Bethel to Shechem (Jdg 21:19). The Tent of Meeting was first set up here; it became an important sanctuary (Jos 18:1,8-10; 19:51; 21:2; 22:9,12; Jdg 18:31; 21:12,19,21). Samuel grew up here under Eli's care (1Sa 1:24-28; 3:19-21). The ark of the covenant was kept here until it was captured by the Philistines (1Sa 4:1-22), and it never returned (2Sa 6:2-17). Base for Ahijah the prophet (1Ki 14:2,4), who pronounced the downfall of Jeroboam (1Ki 14:7-16). Laid in ruins during the time of Jeremiah's ministry (Jer 7:12-14; 26:6,9).

Shittim

An abbreviation of Abel Shittim. Israel's last encampment east of River Jordan, before entering the Promised Land (Nu 33:49,50). Here the Israelites sinned (Nu 25:1-3) and were punished with a plague (Nu 25:4-9). Joshua sent out spies from here (Jos 2:1) before all the people left to cross the River Jordan (Jos 3:1; Mic 6:5).

Shunem

Town in territory of Issachar (Jos 19:18), where the Philistines camped before meeting Saul in battle (1Sa 28:4). Home of Abishag, who cared for the aged David (1Ki 1:3). Elisha occasionally lodged here with a wealthy couple, and foretold the birth of their long-desired son (2Ki 4:8-17). He later restored the boy to life (2Ki 4:32-37).

Shur

Desert region between Egypt and the Negev. Hagar was on her way here when the angel found her (Ge 16:7). Abraham stayed near here (Ge 20:1). Ishmael's descendants settled here (Ge 25:18). Moses led the Israelites through this parched land (Ex 15:22). Saul pursued the Amalekites this far (1Sa 15:7); David attacked its inhabitants (1Sa 27:8).

Sibmah

Town east of Jordan, near Heshbon. Probably also known as Sebam. One of the towns requested by the Reubenites and Gadites (Nu 32:1-3). Eventually allotted to the tribe of Reuben, who rebuilt it (Nu 32:37,38; Jos 13:19). Renowned for its vines (Isa 16:8,9; Jer 48:32).

Sidon

Ancient city on Mediterranean coast of Lebanon, about 20 miles north of Tyre, founded by the son of Canaan (Ge 10:15; 1Ch 1:13). Israel pursued the defeated Canaanites to here (Jos 11:8); it formed the northernmost border of Asher's territory (Jos 19:28). Asher failed to drive out its Canaanite inhabitants (Jdg 1:31) and Israel was punished for serving their gods (Jdg 10:6,12). The city's importance grew so the King of Tyre was known as "king of the Sidonians" (1Ki 16:31), and its name was used for that whole area (1Ki 17:9). Despite its power, wealth and security (Ezr 3:7; Isa 23:2), the prophets emphasised its fragility (Isa 23:12; Jer 27:3,6; 47:4; Eze 28:21-26; Joel 3:4-8; Zec 9:1-4). Jesus spoke of it more favourably than some of the towns of Galilee (Mt 11:21,22; Lk 4:26; 10:13,14). Here he praised a Canaanite woman's faith and healed her daughter (Mt 15:21-28; Mk 7:24-31). Its people went to Galilee to hear Jesus preach (Mk 3:8; Lk 6:17); they sought peace with King Herod (Ac 12:20); and Paul found kind hospitality here (Ac 27:3).

Silas

Prophet and a leader in Jerusalem church; sent to Antioch from Council of Jerusalem (Ac 15:22-32). Accompanied Paul on second missionary journey (Ac 15:40–18:22; 2Co 1:19). Assisted Peter with first letter (1Pe 5:12); and Paul (1Th 1:1; 2Th 1:1).

Simeon

1. Son of Jacob by Leah (Ge 29:33; 35:23; 1Ch 2:1). With Levi killed Shechemites to avenge rape of sister Dinah (Ge 34). Left in Egypt as hostage (Ge 42:24–43:23). Blessed by Jacob (Ge 49:5-7).
2. Tribe descended from Simeon. Included in census (Nu 1:22,23; 26:12-14). Given territory in restored land (Eze 48:24).

3. Territory at southernmost end of Palestine, in the Negev Desert. Allotted to the descendants of Jacob's second son, taken from Judah's territory which was more than was needed (Jos 19:1-9).

4. Righteous and devout man in Jerusalem; recognised the child Jesus as the Messiah when he was brought into the temple (Lk 2:25-35).

Simon

1. See **Peter**.
2. Apostle; called "the Zealot" (Mt 10:4; Mk 3:18; Lk 6:15; Ac 1:13).
3. Brother of Jesus (Mt 13:55; Mk 6:3).

4. Leper from Bethany, in whose house Jesus was anointed with oil (Mt 26:6; Mk 14:3).

5. Pharisee, in whose house Jesus' feet were washed with tears (Lk 7:40).

6. Man from Cyrene, forced to carry Jesus' cross (Mk 15:21).

7. Sorcerer, who amazed Samaritans with his magic (Ac 8:9-11). Believed Philip and was baptised (Ac 8:12,13); rebuked by Peter for trying to buy spiritual power (Ac 8:18-24).

8. Tanner, with whom Peter lodged (Ac 9:43).

The Sinai desert near Hazeroth, where Miriam was struck with leprosy as punishment for her unbelief

Sin, Desert of

Wilderness area "between Elim and Sinai" (Ex 16:1), near the Red Sea and Dophkah (Nu 33:11,12), exact location unknown. Here the Israelites grumbled to Moses, but were fed with quails and manna (Ex 16).

Sinai

1. Mountain situated in Sinai Peninsula, also known as Horeb, exact location unknown. Here God spoke to Moses from the burning bush

(Ex 3:1-4; Ac 7:30), and later provided water for the Israelites (Ex 17:6). God appeared here again after the exodus (Ex 19; Nu 3:1), revealing to Moses the law (Ex 31:18; 34:29; Lev 7:38; 25:1; 26:46; 27:34; Nu 28:6; Ne 9:13; Ac 7:38). Used figuratively by Paul when writing about slavery to the law (Gal 4:24,25).

2. Wilderness area around the mountain (Ex 19:1), where the Israelites camped while God met with Moses (Ex 19:2; Lev 7:38). Here the Tent of Meeting was set up (Nu 1:1) in which Moses was instructed to take a census of the people (Nu 1:2,19; 3:14; 26:64). Two of Aaron's sons were struck down for making an unauthorised offering (Nu 3:4). The people celebrated Passover (Nu 9:1,5) before moving on (Nu 10:12). They returned to this place later (Nu 33:15,16).

Smyrna

Wealthy city in western Asia Minor, about 40 miles north of Ephesus. One of the seven cities John addressed in which they are described as "in poverty" due to their afflictions and are encouraged to persevere (Rev 2:8-11).

Sodom

City in Valley of Siddim (Ge 14:2,3), at south end of the Dead Sea, exact location unknown. Often paired with Gomorrah as a place of wickedness. Lot and his family chose to settle near here (Ge 13:12). When its king and army were defeated by a Mesopotamian alliance (Ge 14:8-11), Lot was captured (Ge 14:12) and then rescued by Abram (Ge 14:14-16). God threatened to destroy it (Ge 18:20,21) but Abraham pleaded on its behalf (Ge 18:23-33). It was destroyed because of its depravity but Lot and his daughters survived (Ge 19:1-29). Frequently used as an example of man's depravity and God's judgement (Dt 29:23; Isa 1:9,10; Jer 23:14; La 4:6; Eze 16:46-56; Am 4:11; Zep 2:9; Mt 10:15; Lk 10:12; Ro 9:29; 2Pe 2:6; Jude 7; Rev 11:8). See **Gomorrah.**

Solomon

Third king of Israel; son of David and Bathsheba (2Sa 12:24). Appointed by David; anointed by Nathan and Zadok (1Ki 1; 1Ch 29:21-25). Given charge by David (1Ki 2:1-9); had Adonijah, Joab and Shimei killed (1Ki 2:13-46). Asked God for wisdom (1Ki 3:5-15; 2Ch 1:7-12); gave wise judgement (1Ki 3:16-28); noted for his wisdom (1Ki 4:29-34; 10:23,24). Wrote proverbs (1Ki 4:32; Pr 1:1; 10:1–22:16; 25–29); psalms (Ps 72:1; 127:1); Song of Songs (SS 1:1). Built temple (1Ki 5–7; 2Ch 2–4); brought ark; prayer of dedication (1Ki 8–9; 2Ch 5–7). Established trading fleet (1Ki 9:26-28; 2Ch 8:17).

Visited by Queen of Sheba (1Ki 10:1-13; 2Ch 9:1-12; Mt 12:42; Lk 11:31). Acquired great wealth (1Ki 10:14-29; 2Ch 1:14-17; 9:13-28). Foreign wives turned his heart from God (1Ki 11:1-10), causing him to break covenant with God and so to lose part of kingdom (1Ki 11:11-13,29-39). Death (1Ki 11:41-43; 2Ch 9:29-31).

Stephen

Deacon (Ac 6:5,6). Performed miracles; aroused opposition; arrested (Ac 6:8-15). Defence to Sanhedrin (Ac 7:1-53); killed by stoning (Ac 7:54–8:1; 22:20).

Succoth

1. Town east of the Jordan in territory of Gad (Jos 13:27), where Jacob stayed after reconciliation with Esau (Ge 33:16,17). Gideon punished its inhabitants for not helping his troops when they pursued the Midianites (Jdg 8:5-16). Solomon had foundries in this valley (1Ki 7:46; 2Ch 4:17). The Psalmist mentions it to emphasise God's sovereignty (Ps 60:6; 108:7). Exact location unknown.

2. Region where the Israelites first encamped having left Egypt (Ex 12:37; 13:20; Nu 33:5,6). Located in the north-east of the Egyptian delta, close to Rameses.

Susa

Capital city of Elam, situated about 150 miles north of the

Persian Gulf. Favoured by the kings of Persia as a winter residence, and therefore is the backdrop to the book of Esther. Some of its deported officials wrote to Artaxerxes warning of the rebuilding of Jerusalem (Ezr 4:9,10). Here Nehemiah served as Artaxerxes' cupbearer (Ne 1:1) and Daniel received his vision about Belshazzar (Da 8:2).

Sychar

City in Samaria near Jacob's well where Jesus spoke with a Samaritan woman (Jn 4:5-43). Probably built on the site of the ancient town of Shechem (Ge 33:18).

Syria

See **Aram**.

Taanach

Royal city of the Canaanites, situated in the hills south of Valley of Jezreel, about 5 miles south-east of Megiddo. After its defeat by Joshua (Jos 12:21), it was allotted to the tribe of Manasseh (Jos 17:11; 1Ch

Jesus said that even Solomon, with all his finery, could not compete with the beauty of the "lilies of the field"

7:29) and assigned to the Levites (Jos 21:25). Its Canaanite inhabitants were never driven out, so it retained some independence (Jdg 1:27). Canaanite kings fought against Deborah and Barak here (Jdg 5:19). Part of one of Solomon's 12 districts (1Ki 4:12).

Tabitha

See **Dorcas**.

Tabor

1. Isolated mountain on the border between Issachar, Zebulun and Naphtali (Jos 19:22), about 6 miles east of Nazareth. Here Barak gathered his troops to attack the Canaanite army of Sisera (Jdg 4:6,12,14), and Gideon's brothers were killed by the Midianite kings (Jdg 8:18,19). Its greatness was equated with Mount Carmel (Jer 46:18) and

Mount Hermon (Ps 89:13), but it became a sanctuary for idolatry (Hos 5:1).
2. Levite city in the territory of Zebulun (1Ch 6:77).
3. Site of a great tree where Samuel told Saul he would receive a sign of God's favour (1Sa 10:3).

Tahpanhes

City on the eastern side of the Nile Delta, often associated with Memphis (Jer 2:16; 44:1; 46:14). The Judeans fled here after the murder of Gedaliah (Jer 43:7) and Jeremiah was instructed by God to warn the people against putting their faith in Egypt, for it too would fall (Jer 43:7-13; Eze 30:18,19).

Tamar

1. Married in turn to Judah's sons Er and Onan (Ge 38:6-10). Pretended to be prostitute and became pregnant by Judah when he withheld third son (Ge 38:11-30). Mother of Perez and Zerah (Ge 38:27-30; Ru 4:12).

Susa, a major city of the Persian empire, was destroyed by the invading Assyrians in 647 BC

Mount Tabor: where Barak gathered his army to attack Sisera

2. Daughter of David. Raped by Amnon; avenged by brother Absalom (2Sa 13).

3. Town at south end of the Dead Sea. Precise location unknown but near the border of Judah and Edom. It would form part of the southern boundary of the restored land (Eze 47:19). Also known as Tadmor (1Ki 9:18; 2Ch 8:4), which Solomon rebuilt.

Tarshish
City or territory at western end of Mediterranean Sea, possibly in southern Spain, renowned for its shipping (Ps 48:7; Isa 23:1,14; 60:9; Eze 27:25) and valuable merchandise (Ps 72:10; Jer 10:9; Eze 38:13). Jonah tried to flee here from God's call to Nineveh (Jnh 1:3; 4:2).

Tarsus
Principal city of Cilicia in Asia Minor. Birthplace of Paul (Ac 9:11; 21:39; 22:3), he was sent here to escape a Jewish death threat (Ac 9:30). Barnabas fetched him and took him to Antioch (Ac 11:25).

Tekoa
Town in hill country of Judah, about 6 miles south of Bethlehem, and 10 miles south of Jerusalem. Home of the wise woman used by Joab to bring reconciliation between David and Absalom (2Sa 14:2-21). Also home of David's bodyguard Ira (2Sa 23:26). Rehoboam fortified it (2Ch 11:6) because it was a strategic warning point overlooking Jerusalem (Jer 6:1). Birthplace of Amos, where he received his call from God (Am 1:1).

Teman
Town and region in the south of Edom, probably named after one of Esau's grandsons (Ge 36:11; 1Ch 1:36). Its inhabitants were famous for their wisdom (Jer 49:7; Ob 8), one being Job's advisor (Job 2:11). Its destruction was foretold along with all of Edom (Eze 25:13).

Ruins of the Agora, Thessalonica: a city for whose church Paul had deep respect

Thaddaeus

See **Judas**.

Thebes

City in Upper Egypt, on eastern bank of the Nile, also known as No or No-Amon. Its destruction was foretold (Jer 46:25; Eze 30:14-16), to emphasise that no city, however great, could escape God's judgement (Na 3:8).

Thessalonica

Chief seaport of province of Macedonia. Paul established a church here (Ac 17:1-4; 1Th

Sunset over Lake Galilee. Thomas was at the waterside when the miraculous catch of fish was made

1:9,10). A deep affection grew between Paul and the church (1Th 2:1-12). Home of two of his co-workers, Aristarchus and Secundus (Ac 20:4; 27:2), Demas moved here after deserting Paul (2Ti 4:10).

Thomas

Apostle (Mt 10:3; Mk 3:18; Lk 6:15; Ac 1:13); called Didymus, the Twin (Jn 11:16). Asked where Jesus was going (Jn 14:5). Doubted resurrection (Jn 20:24,25); saw Jesus alive;

confessed him as Lord and God (Jn 20:26-29). Present at miraculous catch of fish after resurrection (Jn 21:2-14).

Thyatira

Town in province of Lydia in western Asia Minor. Home of Lydia, a dealer in purple cloth (Ac 16:14). Though not large, this town was known for its thriving manufacturing industry and the pagan customs of some of its trade guilds. One of the seven letters of Revelation was addressed to its church warning against the immoral teaching of Jezebel (Rev 2:18-29).

Tiberias

City on the western shore of the Sea of Galilee, which is sometimes referred to as the Sea of Tiberias (Jn 6:1; 21:1). Some of its inhabitants travelled to hear Jesus (Jn 6:23-25) but there is no record of Jesus visiting here.

Tigris, River

Major river in south-west Asia (about 1,150 miles), which with the River Euphrates gives Mesopotamia its name. One of the four rivers of Paradise (Ge 2:14). Daniel was standing on its banks when he received his vision (Da 10:4-7).

Timnah

1. Town in hill country of Judah (Jos 15:57) where Judah was going when he was tricked by Tamar (Ge 38:12-18).
2. Town on border of territory of Judah (Jos 15:10), belonging

to Dan (Jos 19:43). Here Samson met and married a Philistine woman (Jdg 14:1-8), who was subsequently killed by her own people (Jdg 15:6). The town was captured and occupied by the Philistines (2Ch 28:18).

Timothy

Disciple from Lystra (Ac 16:1); convert of Paul (1Ti 1:2), probably during first missionary journey (2Ti 3:10,11). Circumcised by Paul and taken with him on second missionary journey (Ac 16:2–18:22; 2Co 1:19). Ministry confirmed by prophetic utterances (1Ti 1:18) and laying on of hands (1Ti 4:14; 2Ti 1:6). Sent by Paul to Thessalonica (1Th 3:2); Macedonia (Ac 19:22); Corinth (1Co 4:17). Accompanied Paul to Jerusalem (Ac 20:4-16). Remained in Ephesus to give leadership to church (1Ti 1:3). Imprisoned and released (Heb 13:23).

Timid (1Co 16:10,11; 2Ti 1:7), needing encouragement (1Ti 4:12; 2Ti 1:8; 2:1); but warmly commended by Paul as co-worker and son in the faith (Ro 16:21; 1Co 4:17; Php 2:19-22; 1Th 3:2; 2Ti 1:1-5). Associated with Paul in the writing of the letters to the Thessalonians (1Th 1:1; 2Th 1:1) and to Philemon (Phm 1).

Tirzah

Ancient Canaanite town about 8 miles east of Samaria and five miles north-east of Shechem. Captured by the Israelites under Joshua (Jos 12:24). It replaced Shechem as the capital of the northern kingdom, and remained so until Omri moved his capital to Samaria (1Ki 16:23-28). From this base Menahem launched his coup against King Shallum in Samaria (2Ki 15:14). Known for its beauty (SS 6:4).

Titus

Gentile convert and companion of Paul (Tit 1:4; 2Ti 4:10; 2Co 8:23). Accompanied Paul and Barnabas to Jerusalem (Gal 2:1-3). Sent to Corinth to deal with difficulties; brought good news to Paul in Macedonia (2Co 7:6-16). In Corinth again to complete collection (2Co 8:6,16,17). Left by Paul in Crete to consolidate work (Tit 1:5).

Troas

Port on coast of Mysia in north-western Asia Minor. Paul had a vision here and was called to Macedonia (Ac 16:8-11). On his travels he revisited here, the first time hoping to find Titus (2Co 2:12,13), and the second time reviving a man from a fatal accident (Ac 20:5-12). He probably returned on at least one further occasion (2Ti 4:13).

St Paul's Beach, Crete. Titus took charge of the church in Crete at Paul's direction in order to hold it to sound doctrine

Tyre

Important sea port on Mediterranean coast, about 25 miles south of Sidon and 35 miles north of Carmel. A fortress built upon a rock (Eze 26:4,14) with a commanding position over the sea (Eze 26:17; 27:3). Renowned for its strength and prosperity (Ps 45:12). Good trade relations existed between Tyre and Israel at the time of David and Solomon's building works (2Sa 5:11; 1Ki 5:1; 7:13,14; 9:11,12; 1Ch 14:1; 2Ch 2:3,11-14), and during Zerubbabel's rebuilding (Ezr 3:7). Its dramatic fall was foretold by the prophets because of its pride and faithlessness (Isa 23; Eze 26-28; Joel 3:4; Am 1:9,10; Zec 9:2,3). Despite its wickedness, Jesus spoke of it more favourably than some of the towns of Galilee (Mt 11:21,22; Lk 10:13,14). While visiting he praised a Canaanite woman's faith and healed her daughter (Mt 15:21-28; Mk 7:24-31). Many of its people went to Galilee to hear Jesus (Mk 3:8;

Lk 6:17). Its people sought peace with King Herod (Ac 12:20), and Paul used its port on his third missionary journey (Ac 21:3,7).

Ur

City in southern Mesopotamia, home of Abram's family (Ge 11:28-32), from which God brought him to the Promised Land (Ge 15:7; Ne 9:7).

Uriah

Hittite. Husband of Bathsheba; killed on David's order (2Sa 11).

Uzziah

Also called Azariah. King of Judah; son of Amaziah (2Ki 14:21,22; 15:1,2; 2Ch 26:1-3). Commended, though failed to remove high places (2Ki 15:3,4; 2Ch 26:4,5). Extended power and prestige; strengthened Jerusalem's defences (2Ch 26:6-15). Pride in assuming priestly authority led to affliction with leprosy and isolation (2Ki 15:5; 2Ch 26:16-21). Death (1Ki 15:7; 2Ch 26:23; Isa 6:1).

Vashti

Queen of Persia; wife of Xerxes. Deposed for refusal to appear at banquet (Est 1). Replaced by Esther (Est 2:1-17).

Xerxes

King of Persia (Ezr 4:6; Est 1:1,2); father of Darius (Da 9:1). Deposed Vashti; married Esther (Est 1–2). Assassination attempt uncovered by

Mordecai (Est 2:21-23). Gave assent to Haman's edict to kill Jews (Est 3); allowed Esther to see him without being called (Est 5:1-8); hanged Haman (Est 7). Exalted Mordecai (Est 8:1,2; 9:4; 10); allowed Jews to defend themselves (Est 8–9).

Zacchaeus

Tax collector; climbed tree to see Jesus (Lk 19:2-10).

Zadok

Priest; descendant of Aaron (1Ch 6:3-8). With Abiathar, served David (2Sa 8:17; 1Ch 15:11; 16:39,40); in charge of ark (2Sa 15:24-29). Anointed Solomon as David's successor when Abiathar supported Adonijah (1Ki 1:8,32-48). Descendants served as chief priests (2Ch 31:10; Eze 40:46; 43:19; 44:15).

Persian guards on a frieze at the entrance to the palace of King Xerxes at Persepolis

Zarephath

City on Mediterranean coast, between Tyre and Sidon. Here Elijah was given hospitality by a widow whose son he restored from death (1Ki 17:9-24). Jesus praised this widow's faith, and contrasted it with the faith of those from his home town (Lk 4:26).

Zebulun

1. Son of Jacob by Leah (Ge 30:20; 35:23; 1Ch 2:1). Blessed by Jacob (Ge 49:13).
2. Tribe descended from Zebulun. Blessed by Moses (Dt 33:18,19). Included in census (Nu 1:30,31; 26:26,27).
3. Mountainous territory at northern end of Palestine, between Asher and Naphtali. Allotted to the descendants of Jacob's tenth son, its towns and borders were clearly listed (Jos 19:10-16). Its former Canaanite inhabitants were not driven out but enslaved (Jdg 1:30). Isaiah predicted a time of great honour for this land (Isa 9:1). This was fulfilled in the coming of Christ (Mt 4:13-16).

Zechariah

1. King of Israel; son of Jeroboam II; assassinated (2Ki 14:29; 15:8-12).
2. Prophet who, with Haggai, encouraged rebuilding of temple (Ezr 5:1; 6:14; Zec 1:1).
3. Priest; father of John the Baptist; struck dumb because of unbelief at the angel Gabriel's announcement of the birth of a son (Lk 1:5-22,59-79).

Zedekiah

1. Last king of Judah. Son of Josiah, formerly Mattaniah. Installed by Nebuchadnezzar (2Ki 24:17,18). Evil denounced (Jer 24:8-10; Eze 21:25); dealings with Jeremiah (2Ch 36:12; Jer 37; 38:14-28). Rebellion and broken oath led to fall of Jerusalem (2Ki 24:20–25:7; 2Ch 36:13-21; Jer 39; Eze 17:12-15).
2. Leader of false prophets at Ahab's court (1Ki 22:11-24; 2Ch 18:10-23).

Zephaniah

Prophet during reign of Josiah; descended from Hezekiah (Zep 1:1).

Zerubbabel

Leader of returning exiles (Ne 12:1; Hag 1:1; 2:2); began work on temple (Ezr 3); after delay, encouraged to continue by Haggai (Ezr 5:1,2; Hag 1:2-15; 2) and Zechariah (Zec 4:6-10).

Ziklag

Town in the Negev, about 10 miles north of Beersheba. Allotted by Joshua to the tribe of Judah (Jos 15:31), but later assigned to Simeon (Jos 19:5; 1Ch 4:30). Achish gave it to David as a refuge from Saul (1Sa 27:6; 1Ch 12:1,20). Here the Amalekites took captive Israelite wives and children (1Sa 30). After Saul's death David stayed here for two days (2Sa 1:1) executing the man who claimed he had killed Saul (2Sa 1:8-15). After the exile it was occupied by Judeans (Ne 11:28).

Zin, Desert of

Desert region south of the Negev, through which the Israelites wandered on their way from Egypt to the Promised Land (Nu 13:21; 33:36). Here Miriam died and was buried (Nu 20:1), and Moses and Aaron disobeyed God's instructions (Nu 27:14; Dt 32:51). Part of it was included in the Promised Land (Nu 34:3,4), and was eventually allotted to the tribe of Judah (Jos 15:1,3).

Zion

See **Jerusalem.**

Ziph

1. Town in southernmost corner of Judah, on the border with Edom (Jos 15:21,24).
2. Town in hill country of Judah, about 4 miles southeast of Hebron. Probably named after Caleb's grandson (1Ch 2:42), and later fortified by Rehoboam (2Ch 11:8). Saul searched for David here, after a tip-off from some of its inhabitants, but he did not find him (1Sa 23:19,24).
3. Desert region surrounding 2 above, where David hid to escape Saul's pursuit (1Sa 26:1,2), and where Jonathan brought him encouragement (1Sa 23:14,15).

Zipporah

Daughter of Jethro; wife of Moses (Ex 2:21,22; 18:2); circumcised son to save Moses' life (Ex 4:20-26).

Zoan

Ancient city in Egypt, on the north-east side of the Nile Delta. Its people witnessed the miracles of God at the exodus (Ps 78:12,43), and its wise men were counsellors to Pharaoh (Isa 19:11,13). However, God's power and wisdom surpasses any found within Egypt (Isa 30:1-5; Eze 30:14).

Zoar

City in Jordan Valley, south of the Dead Sea, near Sodom and Gomorrah (Ge 13:10). Originally known as Bela (Ge 14:2,14), God refrained from destroying it along with Sodom and Gomorrah, so that Lot could find refuge there (Ge 19:22,23). Lot did not stay long, however, preferring the safety of the mountains (Ge 19:30). A landmark at the southernmost point of the Promised Land (Dt 34:3), on the border with Moab (Isa 15:5; Jer 48:34).

Zophar

See **Job**.

Zorah

City in the lowlands of Judah near Eshtaol (Jos 15:33), in territory of Dan (Jos 19:41). Home of Manoah and his son Samson (Jdg 13:2,3,24), who were both buried between here and Eshtaol (Jdg 16:31).

Its warriors were sent to spy out Laish for the Danites (Jdg 18:2,8,11). Later Rehoboam strengthened its fortifications (2Ch 11:10).

What the Bible Says About...

What follows is a concise introduction to subjects, especially practical and pastoral matters. The Bible references included here are not exhaustive but we hope they will lay a good foundation for further reflection. When interpreting the Scriptures, it is important to remember that each Scripture should be interpreted in the light of its immediate context and also within the wider context of biblical theology.

Ability

God has created and supernaturally gifted us all with different abilities. We are to use all our abilities humbly and for the benefit of others. Ex 36:1-2; Mt 25:14-30; Ac 14:3; 1Co 12:1-14:1.

Abortion

Abortion is the deliberate termination of a human foetus before birth, usually at an early stage of pregnancy. Job 31:15; Ps 139:13-16; Ecc 11:5; Jer 1:5; Mk 10:14.

Accountability

One of the ways we express love for our Christian brothers and sisters is to gently but firmly hold them to account for their lifestyle. Pr 27:6, 17; Mt 18:15-17; Heb 10:24; Jas 5:19-20.

Addiction

An addiction is a persistent pattern of behaviour, usually destructive, that has become deeply ingrained and difficult to alter. Pr 25:28; Ro 6:11-23; 1Co 6:12; Tit 3:3-7; 2Pe 2:19.

Adultery

Adultery (or marital unfaithfulness) occurs when a married person engages in sexual activity with someone other than his or her marriage partner. Ex 20:14; Pr 6:32; Mal 2:13-15; Mt 19:9; Jn 8:1-11; Heb 13:4.

Alcohol

Whilst Christians are free to enjoy alcohol in moderation, we should avoid drunkenness and be sensitive to the attitudes of our brothers and sisters who abstain totally from drinking alcohol. Ps 104:15; Pr 23:30-32; Jn 2:1-10; Gal 5:19-21; 1Ti 5:23; 1Pe 4:3.

Ambition

Ambition is the desire to achieve great things perhaps for personal recognition (selfish ambition) or, more positively, for God's honour or the benefit of others. Ecc 2:1-26; Ro 15:20; Php 2:3; 1Th 4:11; Jas 3:16.

Angels

Angels appear frequently in the Scriptures usually bearing

"God made the wild animals according to their kinds, the livestock according to their kinds, and all the creatures that move along the ground according to their kinds. And God saw that it was good."
Genesis 1:25

appearance. Such judgements are shallow and sometimes misleading; God is more interested in what is in our hearts. 1Sa 16:7; Isa 53:1-12; Mt 23:28; Lk 6:41-45; Jn 7:24.

Arguments
Our fallen human is such that disagreements often turn into arguments. Whilst standing strong for gospel truth, Christians should make every effort to avoid arguments. Pr 15:1; Ro 12:17-18; Gal 2:11-16; 5:16-26; 2Ti 2:23; 1Pe 3:15.

Assurance
The normal condition of genuine Christians is to have a deep sense of God's love and forgiveness of sin. Theologians term this "assurance" of salvation. Ro 8:1-39; 2Co 13:14; Heb 10:19-22; 1Jn 3:11-24; Jude 21.

messages or practical care for God's people. We should respect these spiritual beings but never worship them. Ps 91:11; Mt 18:10; Ac 5:17-20; Heb 1:14; 13:2; Rev 5:11.

Anger
We feel anger in response to a sense of injustice inflicted on ourselves or others. It usually leads to a desire for retribution. Ex 34:5-7; Pr 29:11; Na 1:2-8; Eph 4:26; 1Ti 2:8; Jas 1:19-20.

Animals
The animals have been created by God to provide a source of food and companionship. Within this overall purpose we must treat them with respect. Ge 1:20–2:20; 9:1-3; Ps 104:1-30; Pr 12:10; Ac 10:9-16.

Anxiety
Anxiety is a natural human response to a perceived threat to our security or status. Christianity counteracts this impulse by emphasising God's concern for us. Pr 12:25; Mt 6:25-34; Lk 21:34; Php 4:6-7; 1Pe 5:7. See also **Worry**.

Appearance
We often judge one another based upon external

Attitudes
We should be careful to guard our attitudes; it is only too easy for selfish and negative attitudes to gradual dominate our thinking. Ge 31:1-5; Eph 4:22-24; Php 2:5-11; 4:8; Heb 4:12; 1Pe 5:5.

Authority
Christians should respect all forms of authority as a gift from God. Nevertheless, we

must not follow instructions contrary to God's will revealed in Scripture. Mk 12:13-17; Ac 4:1-22, Ro 13:1-7; Heb 13:17; 1Pe 2:13-17.

Baptism

Whilst approaches differ, all Christians recognise that undergoing baptism is a command of the Lord Jesus signifying repentance, forgiveness and inclusion in God's family. Mt 28:18-20; Ac 2:22-41; 8:12, 26-40; 1Co 12:12-13.

Blasphemy

Blasphemy is deliberate defiance and hardness of heart towards God. Blasphemy invites God's judgement and Jesus made clear that it is spiritually dangerous. Ex 20:7; 2Ch 32:10-23; Isa 37:14-38; Mt 12:30-32; Ro 2:17-24.

Body

Our physical bodies are gifts from God which become home to the Holy Spirit upon conversion. We will be resurrected with a superior new body. Ro 6:19; 1Co 6:13-20; Gal 2:20; Php 3:20-21; 1Th 4:4; 5:23.

Calling

God calls all people into his kingdom through the message of the gospel and furthermore to follow and serve him single-mindedly in holiness and love. 1Sa 3:1-10; Mt 4:18-20; Ac 13:1-3; Eph 1:18; Php 3:14; 2Ti 1:8-9.

Celibacy

Celibacy is abstinence from sexual relations. It is God's universal requirement outside of marriage and in some cases a special gift and lifelong calling. Mt 19:10-12; 1Co 6:18-20; 7:1-38; 1Th 4:3-8; Heb 13:4.

> "Because of the LORD's great love we are not consumed, for his compassions never fail. They are new every morning; great is your faithfulness."
>
> **Lamentations 3:22-23**

Change

Whatever changes we face, God is unchanging in his faithfulness. Nevertheless, God's unchanging faithfulness to us causes him to change and renew our circumstances. La 3:19-23; Mal 3:6; Lk 5:36-39; 2Co 5:17; Jas 1:17; Rev 21:5.

Character

The ability to bear up under pressure is often described as character. Character is often developed by learning to respond positively to suffering or opposition. Ru 3:11; Pr 12:4; Ro 5:1-4; 1Co 15:33; 1Pe 1:3-7.

Children

Children are a gift from God and bring great joy and vibrancy. Christians must care for children, lovingly discipline them and lead them to Christ. Ex 12:24-27; Dt 11:18-21; Ps 78:1-6; 127:3-5; Mk 10:13-16; Col 3:20-21. See also **Parent(s)**.

Choices

We all have to make many choices. Sometimes the Lord will guide us into a particular decision he wants us to make. Ex 28:30; Ps 23:1-3; 48:14; Pr 3:5-6; Jn 16:13; Ac 1:15-26.

Church

Christianity is a team sport. The Lord expects every Christian to join, passionately serve and encourage a local community of fellow disciples of Christ. Mt 16:18; Ac 2:42-47; 1Ti 3:14-15; Heb 10:24-25

Church leadership

Each local church has leaders, gifted and called by God to serve the members. The leaders also encourage the different gifts the members can contribute. Ac 20:28, Ro 12:7; 1Co 12:28; Eph 4:11-12; Heb 13:17; 1Pe 5:2

Citizenship

Christians should be loyal citizens of their country. Nevertheless, we should never forget that we owe a deeper allegiance to our spiritual citizenship. Mk 12:13-17; Ac 10:34-35; Eph 2:11-22; Php 3:20; 1Pe 2:9.

Complaining

The Scriptures encourage Christians to have a positive attitude towards our circumstances recognising that we are not victims of chance but the recipients of God's loving providence. Ex 16:1-8; Nu 11:1; Isa 40:27-31; 1Co 10:9-10; Php 2:14; Jas 5:9.

Compromise

Whilst we should never compromise commitment to gospel truth, and principles of righteousness and holiness, it is often necessary to give ground on non-essential issues. Mt 5:25-26; 1Co 9:19-23; 2Th 2:15; Jude 3.

Confidence

Christians have the privilege of a God-given confidence in all areas of their lives. Above all this is because they have unconditional fellowship with him. Pr 3:26; Isa 32:17; Jer 17:7; Heb 10:19-22; 1Jn 3:19-22; 4:17.

Conflict

In Christ we are reconciled with God and our fellow believers. Because of our humanity conflicts will inevitably arise, but God gives us the resources to deal with them. Ge 13:5-12; Mt 18:15-17; 2Co 2:5-7; Php 4:2; Col 3:13.

Commitment

God calls us to have a total loving commitment to him and his people, the church. Our inspiration is Jesus' limitless commitment to us. Mt 22:37; Jn 15:12; Ro 12:1; 2Co 5:14-15; 9:8; 2Ti 4:7.

Compassion

Compassion is one of God's most appealing of attributes. Jesus demonstration of a compassionate ministry is a pattern for us to follow today. Ex 34:6-7; Mt 9:36; Col 3:12; Jas 5:11; 1Pe 3:8.

Conscience

God has given us consciences to guide our behaviour. Our consciences are not perfect and we should educate them through Scripture and the indwelling Spirit. Ps 51:1-15; Ac 24:16; Ro 2:14-15; 9:1; 1Co 4:4; 1Ti 1:5.

Courage

The Lord Jesus displayed great courage in his earthly ministry. God has not only revealed his will, but gives us the courage to carry it out. Jos 1:5-9; Jdg 7:15-18; 1Sa 17:37; 1Co 16:13; 2Co 11:26-27; Heb 11:32-34; Rev 12:11.

Creativity

We know that God is wonderfully creative and he has instilled many different forms of creativity within human beings. Ge 1:1, 27; Ex 35:30-36:4; 1Ch 28:21; Ps 139:13-14; Ro 12:6-8.

Criticism

Criticism is an inevitable experience for us all. We must be gracious when we are criticised and ensure that any criticism we offer is properly motivated and expressed. Mt 7:1-5; 1Co 16:14; 2Co 8:18-21; Gal 5:15; Eph 4:15.

Death

Everyone has to face the reality of death. Through Jesus' death and resurrection he both suffers with us and gives us hope of new life. Ecc 12:7; Lk 23:46; 1Co 15:55-56; 1Th 4:13, 16; 2Ti 4:6.

> "... speaking the truth in love, we we will in all things grow up into him who is the Head, that is, Christ."
>
> **Ephesians 4:15**

Debt

God graciously provides for our needs, so that we can help others. We should act prudently, keeping our financial commitments within our ability to pay. Mt 6:31-33; 2Co 9:8; 2Th 3:11-12; 1Ti 6:6-10.

Demons

Demons, or evil spirits, seek to enslave humans through temptation, deception or even sickness. The power of the demonic world was subdued by Jesus Christ. Christians have power to resist them in the name of Jesus. Mt 8:16; Lk 8:26-39; 9:1; Ac 8:7; 16:16-18; Ro 8:38. See also **Satan**.

Depression

Depression is a form of mental disorder typically experienced as deep feelings of hopelessness and associated symptoms. It may be treated with medication or therapy. 1Ki 19:3-18; Isa 35:1-10; Eze 37:1-14; 1Th 5:11; 2Th 2:16-17

Despair

God unreservedly promises to take loving personal control of our lives. Circumstances may drive us to despair, but he causes us to conquer and triumph. Ps 23:4; 34:19; 42:11; Ro 8:37; 2Co 1:9; 2:14.

Discipline

Where necessary, God disciplines us in order to train us in righteousness. Church leaders are called to exert loving discipline over the church. Ps 94:12; Pr 15:32; 1Co 5:1-13; Gal 6:1; Heb 12:5-11; Rev 3:19.

Discouragement

We all get discouraged at times. God wants us to receive his encouragement from the Scriptures, his Spirit and our brother and sisters in Christ. Ps 10:17; Ac 9:31; 11:22-24; Ro 1:11-12; 15:4-5; 1Th 5:11. See also **Encouragement**.

Divisions

It is not uncommon for churches to become divided. This usually causes great sadness and hurt, but worse, it undermines the gospel message of reconciliation. Ro 16:17; 1Co 1:10-12; 3:1-23; 11:17-34; 12:12-26; Eph 4:1-16; Tit 3:10. See also **Unity**.

Divorce

Marriage is intended to be the lifelong union of a man and a woman. Sadly, however, some marriages don't last permanently. Whilst God's standard is that marriage should be lifelong, Jesus made provision for divorce in cases of "unfaithfulness". Dt 24:1-4; Mal 2:16; Mt 19:3-12; 1Co 7:1-40; Heb 13:4. See also **Marriage**.

Doubt

God is bigger than our doubts! When plagued by doubts then we should pray and read the Scriptures but also seek wisdom from mature Christian. Ecc 1:1-2; Mt 14:31; Mk 9:24; 11:23; Jn 20:24-29, Jude 22. See also **Assurance**.

Dreams

Everyone experiences the natural activity of dreaming. In addition, however, throughout the Scriptures, God sometimes reveals his purposes to individuals through dreams. Ge 37:5-11; 1Ki 3:5; Ecc 5:3; Isa 29:8; Mt 2:13, 19, 22; Ac 2:17.

Education

As Christians we must not put our confidence in our education or intellect but we should use our God-given abilities, taking appropriate opportunities for education. Ecc 1:12-18; 12:11-12; Da 1:3-4, 17; Ac 22:3; 1Co 8:1-3.

Encouragement

We all need encouragement from time to time. The Scriptures give us examples to follow and teaching to obey in this area. Isa 1:17; Ac 4:36-37; 9:31; 20:1-2; Ro 15:4-6; 1Co 14:3-5; 2Th 2:16.

Endurance

See **Perseverance**.

Women's education programme, Ghana

Environment

The world God has given to us is beautiful and reveals the Creator. Our responsibility is to honour God by caring for his creation. Ge 1:31; 2:9-15; Ps 8:1-9; Isa 35:1-2; Ro 8:18-22; Rev 22:1-2.

Equality

Each Christian enjoys equal standing as children of God. This is a privilege (others respect and help us) and responsibility (we respect and help others). 1Co 12:7-27; 2Co 8:13-15; Gal 3:28; Heb 8:11; Jas 2:1.

Evangelism

Whilst every Christian is called to bear witness to the gospel of Christ by word and deed, some individuals have a particular gift of evangelism. Mt 28:18-20; Ac 5:41-42; 11:19-21; 2Co 9:13; Eph 4:11-12.

Failure

See **Mistakes**.

Faith

As we exert faith in Christ Jesus, our sin is forgiven. We can then have faith in the Lord for every aspect of the future. Hab 2:4; Mt 6:30-34; Mk 2:3-12; Ro 1:16-17; 3:22-4:16; Heb 4:14.

Faithfulness

God's faithfulness is a key aspect of his character that he seeks to reproduce in his children. Hence faithfulness is a fruit of the Spirit. Ex 34:5-7; 1Sa 26:23; Ps 36:5; Pr 3:3; Gal 5:22.

Family

Christians place a good deal of importance on family relationships. We also become part of the family of God – the church, both local and universal. Mk 3:31-35; Eph 3:14-15; 5:22-6:4; 1Ti 3:1-5; 5:3-4, 8, 16; 1Jn 3:1.

Fasting

Fasting is an important aspect of Christian spirituality. It usually involves abstaining from food (and possibly liquids) for a time to concentrate on prayer. Ne 1:1-2:9; Da 9:1-19; Mt 6:16-18; Ac 13:1-2; 14:23.

Favouritism

Favouritism is the failure to treat people as equals. It is unjust and therefore alien to God's character and standards for human behaviour. Ge 37:1-11; Lev 19:15; Ac 10:34-35; 1Ti 5:21; Jas 2:1-9.

Fellowship: students discussing the Bible together

Fear

Christians suffer fear like anyone else. When this happens our remedy is in God's almighty power. Fear is dispelled as we pray and believe his promises. Ps 46:1-2; Pr 3:24-25; Isa 12:2; Lk 12:32; 1Pe 3:14. See also **Courage**.

Fellowship

Christians enjoy fellowship with God himself and with brothers and sisters in Christ. This is a great privilege and an essential part of Christian experience. Ac 2:42; 1Co 1:9; 2Co 13:14; Gal 2:9; Php 2:1-4; 1Jn 3:1-7.

Food

God has provided plants and animals as a source of food for human beings. We are to receive and enjoy them with gratitude to him. Ge 1:29; 9:3-4; Mt 4:4; Jn 6:27; Ac 14:17; Jas 2:15-16.

Foolishness

Foolishness is very close to sinfulness in Scripture. Typically the fool arrogantly ignores the Lord, pays no attention to instruction and lacks self-control. Ps 14:1; Pr 1:7; 12:15; 29:11; Mt 7:26-27; 1Co 1:18-2:5.

Forgiveness

Because Jesus died in our place, God freely offers us forgiveness from our sins on the condition that we extend forgiveness to others. Ex 34:6-7; Jer 31:31-35; Mic 7:18-19; Mt 6:9-15; 18:23-35; 1Jn 1:9.

Freedom

The gospel message offers freedom – material freedom from oppression and spiritual freedom from sin and Satan. Our challenge is to bring that freedom to others. Ex 6:6-8; Ps 146:7; Isa 58:6; Lk 4:18; Ro 6:1-23; Rev 1:5b-6.

Friendship

God has created human beings with a social nature; friendships are a source of growth and joy. Christians must extend friendship to others without favouritism. 1Sa 20:42; Pr 17:17; Ecc 4:10; Jn 15:13.

Fruit of the Spirit

When we become Christians, God's indwelling Spirit starts to reproduce his character in our lives. We work out that character in practice. Jer 31:33; Jn 15:5,8; Ro 5:5; Gal 5:22-23; Col 3:12-15.

Future

Christians face the future with confidence that God is in control and that nothing can happen which he cannot ultimately turn to our benefit. Ps 37:37; Pr 23:18; Jer 29:11; Ro 8:38.

Gender

Despite emerging from within various patriarchal cultures, the Bible allows a surprising level of freedom for women and stresses the equality of the sexes. Ge 1:27; Ac 2:17-18; Ro 16:12; Gal 3:28; Php 4:2-3.

Generosity

Christians should be open-handed with money and possessions, recognising that God gives us everything we have and we, like him, should be generous. Ex 35:4-29; 1Ch 29:1-20; Mal 3:10; Mk 12:41-44; Ac 4:32-35; 2Co 8:1–9:15.

Gentleness

Gentleness is a fruit of the Holy Spirit's presence in our lives. It should not be mistaken for weakness – it is actually strength under control. Pr 15:1; 25:15; Mt 11:29; Gal 5:22-23; Col 3:12; 1Ti 6:11; 1Pe 3:15.

Giving

See **Generosity**.

Godliness

See **Holiness**.

> "A perverse man stirs up dissension, and a gossip separates close friends"
>
> **Proverbs 16:28**

Goodness

Christians are called to emulate the goodness of the Lord. It is a simple challenge yet one that runs to the heart of spiritual living. Ps 34:14; Lk 6:27-36; Ac 10:38; Gal 5:22; 6:9-10; Eph 2:10.

Gossip

Whilst it is normal to talk to others about those we know, it is not acceptable to share secrets or rumours or unfairly criticise others. Lev 19:16; Ps 15:1-3; Pr 16:28; 20:19; 2Co 12:20.

Grace

God's grace is his unmerited kindness to us in working his saving purpose in us. We respond by gratefully and humbly accepting this free gift. Pr 3:34; Jnh 2:8; Jn 1:14-17; Ro 3:21-28; 5:1-2; 2Co 9:8. See also **Mercy**.

Gratitude

As recipients of God's unmerited kindness, Christians' response to God should be marked by heartfelt gratitude. This gratitude should also mark our attitude to others. Ps 28:6-7; 30:1-12; 100:1-5; Eph 5:19-20; Col 3:15-16; Rev 7:9-12.

Greed

Greed might be defined as the impulse to accumulate and consume more than is good for us. God calls us to live generously not greedily. Ecc 5:10-11; Lk 12:15-34; Eph 5:3; Col 3:5; 1Ti 6:6-10,17-19.

Grief

Grief is the particularly deep and painful type of sadness that we experience when we lose someone who was very dear to us. Ge 37:34-35; Ps 23; Isa 53:3; Mt 5:4; 26:36-44; Ro 12:15; Rev 21:1-4.

Guidance

God graciously guides us in many ways including (most importantly) the Scriptures, times of prayer, advice from a mature Christian and, on occasion, the gentle whispers or nudges of God. Ge 24:12-27; 1Ki 19:11-12; Ps 119:105; Pr 3:6; Isa 40:11; Ac 13:1-3; 2Ti 3:14-17.

Guilt

Guilt is both God's judgement and the uncomfortable emotional state that results from our sinfulness. Christians rejoice that God's forgiveness results in freedom from guilt. Isa 52:13-53:12; Na 1:3; Jn 16:5-11; Ro 8:1; Heb 10:19-22; Jas 2:10.

Hard-heartedness

If we ignore God and sin repeatedly and uncaringly, we may become dangerously hard-hearted towards God, no longer sensing his disapproval of our actions. Ps 95:6-8; Pr 28:14; Jer 4:3-4; Zec 7:12; Eph 4:17-19.

Health

It is easy to take our health and strength for granted but Christians recognise that we should cherish, safeguard and use them for God's glory. Ps 29:11; Pr 20:29; Isa 40:29-31; Jer 9:23-24; 3Jn 2.

Healing

When we are unwell we should pray for God's healing and also get appropriate medical care. Supernatural healings speak of God's amazing power and love. 2Ki 20:1-11; Ps 103:1-3; Mt 8:14-17; Ac 3:1-16; 1Co 12:7-11; Rev 22:1-2. See also **Medicine**.

Holiness

Holiness is literally a state of separation for God's purposes; separation from sin, but also separation from all that distracts from God's purposes. Lev 22:31-33; Ro 6:19-23; 12:1-2; Heb 12:1-2; 2Pe 3:8-14; Rev 4:1-11.

Homosexuality

A homosexual person is sexually attracted to others of the same gender. Whilst the Scriptures denounce homo-erotic activity, Christians should not harass, but should be sympathetic and kind towards, homosexual people. Lev 18:22; Ro 1:18-32; 1Co 6:9-11.

Hope

One of the great benefits of Christian faith is that it enables hopeful living. The promise of resurrection life ultimately overthrows all suffering and despair. Ro 8:1-39; 1Co 15:1-58; Eph 2:11-13; Tit 1:1-2; 1Pe 1:3-4; Rev 21:1-7.

Hospitality

Offering hospitality to others is basic to Christian spirituality. Hospitality may take many forms, most usually table fellowship and providing accommodation. Isa 58:6-7; Mt 25:31-40; Lk 14:12-14; Ro 12:13; 1Ti 3:1-2; Heb 13:2.

Humility

The gospel is fatal to human pride since it requires us to acknowledge our need of forgiveness and our inability to live righteously without God's help. Mic 6:8; Mt 18:2-4; Ro 12:16; Php 2:3; Jas 4:6, 10; 1Pe 3:8. See also **Pride**.

Hypocrisy

Jesus reserved his strongest words for hypocritical religious leaders. Christians must ensure that their private lives and standards should reflect their values embraced in public. Pr 26:23-26; Isa 29:13; Mt 23:1-36; Ro 2:1, 17-24; Tit 1:16.

Idolatry

The Scriptures warn us that God requires us to honour him above everything else. A failure to do so (deliberate or otherwise) is condemned as idolatry. Ex 32:1-8; Isa 44:6-20; Jer 19:3-6; Ro 1:18-25; Col 3:5; 1Jn 5:21.

> "Follow justice and justice alone, so that you may live and possess the land the LORD your God is giving you."
>
> **Deuteronomy 16:20**

Illness

See **Sickness**.

Integrity

Integrity is a very attractive Christian virtue. It may be costly at times to "walk our talk" but it reaps a harvest of inner peace. 1Ch 29:17; Ps 25:21; Pr 10:9; 2Co 8:21; 1Ti 1:5; Tit 2:7-8.

Romania: a radio is given to a woman so that she can listen to gospel broadcasts in her own home

Injustice

The Scriptures make clear that God expects us to treat each other fairly. Christians are therefore called to challenge injustice and support its victims. 2Ch 19:7; Pr 13:23; Ecc 3:16-17; Isa 58:6; Jer 22:13; Am 5:12. See also **Justice**.

Jealousy

A powerful and destructive emotion, jealousy is the illicit and insecure desire to have someone else's gifts, achievements or lifestyle in preference to your own. Ex 20:17; Ecc 4:4; Ac 5:17-18; Ro 13:13-14; 1Co 3:3; Gal 5:19-21.

Joy

The Holy Spirit brings joy to God's children. Eternal life and God's friendship make our joy secure despite the difficulties and sadnesses we may face. Ne 8:10; Ps 30:11; Mt 13:44; Jn 15:11; Ro 15:13; Gal 5:22.

Judgement

The Bible issues many stern warnings about the dangers of making wrong judgements about fellow Christians. We must remember that only God makes perfect judgements. Ps 9:7; 119:66; Jn 7:24; Ro 14:13; Heb 9:27-28; Jas 2:12-13.

Justice

God is committed to justice. Jesus took upon himself the punishment for injustice so that God might grant forgiveness without compromising his commitment to justice. Ge 18:25; Dt 16:19; Ps 103:6; Ac 17:30-31; Ro 3:21-26; Rev 19:11.

Kindness

Kindness is a mark of the Spirit's presence in our lives. God has shown great kindness to us and we should extend this to others. Jer 31:3; Gal 5:22; Eph 2:7; Col 3:12; Tit 3:4-5; 2Pe 1:5-8.

Laziness

Whilst we should take proper rest from our work, we should ensure that we are industrious in the calling God has laid upon us. Pr 6:6-11; 24:30-34; Ro 12:11; 2Th 3:11-13; Heb 6:9-12.

Leadership

See **Church leadership**.

Legalism

Legalism is the attempt to please God by obedience to the Law. The gospel teaches that we can only live righteously through trusting in Jesus Christ. Ro 2:28-29; 3:9-28; 7:6; Gal 2:21; 5:4; Php 3:4-11.

Listening

One of the most important ways in which we show love to God and to our neighbour is by listening carefully to everything they say. Pr 12:15; 18:15; Mk 9:7; Jn 10:27; Ac 10:33; Jas 1:19.

Loneliness

Loneliness is a painful reaction to a lack of companionship. It may be overcome through the friendship of God and involvement in a local church. Ge 2:18; 24:67; Ps 25:16; Pr 18:24; Ecc 4:10; Isa 66:13.

Lord's Supper

A celebration of God's forgiveness and Christian fellowship, the Lord's Supper commemorates the sacrifice of Jesus Christ on the cross. It is a vital part of our spirituality;

every Christian should make it a priority. Mt 26:17-29; Mk 14:12-25; Ac 2:42-47; 20:7; 1Co 10:14-22; 11:17-34.

Love
Love is the primary fruit of the Spirit and the central quality that God wishes to develop in his people. In faithfully loving God and our neighbour we fulfil all righteousness. Mk 12:28-34; 1Co 13; Gal 5:22; 1Ti 1:5; 1Jn 5:2-3; Jude 21.

Loyalty
Loyalty is a noble quality which Christians should demonstrate within every relationship, particularly within marriage, but only God can command our undivided loyalty. 1Ch 29:18; Ps 78:8, Pr 20:6; Php 4:3.

> "Do not let this Book of the Law depart from your mouth; meditate on it day and night, so that you may be careful to do everything written in it."
>
> Joshua 1:8

Lust
Fallen human nature often hungers after things which God has prohibited. Lust refers to any ungodly appetite, usually of a sexual nature. Job 31:1; Mt 5:27-28; Eph 4:17-19; Col 3:5; 1Th 4:4-8; 1Jn 2:16.

Marriage
Marriage is the lifelong union of a man and a woman. It provides companionship, the only proper setting for sexual love and a secure environment for the raising of children. Ge 2:18; Mal 2:13-16; Mt 19:3-6; 1Co 7:1-40; Eph 5:21-33; Heb 13:4.

Maturity
Just as our physical bodies mature with proper nutrition, so Christians should also mature in faith, growing into God and demonstrating greater understanding of his will. Lk 8:14; Eph 4:11-16; Col 4:12; Heb 5:11-6:3; Jas 1:2-4.

Medicine
Modern medicine offers successful treatment and care for many illnesses. Christians should joyfully and prayerfully receive these treatments as part of God's healing purpose. Isa 38:21; Mk 2:17; Lk 10:33-34; Col 4:14; 1Ti 5:23. See also **Healing**.

Meditation
An important aspect of our personal time with God is to quietly and prayerfully meditate on the Scriptures and their significance to our situation. Jos 1:8; Ps 1:1-2; 48:9; 77:12; 119:48; 143:5.

Mercy
Closely related to grace, mercy is the gift of kindness instead of judgement. God is merciful and he expects to find this quality in his people. Ex 33:19–34:7; Ps 51:1-19; Isa 55:7; Mic 6:8; Mt 5:7; Heb 4:16. See also **Grace**.

Mind
See **Thinking**.

Ministry
See **Service**.

Miracles
Miracles are significant events where God acts directly in a way that is beyond human understanding and testifies to his power and kindness. Dt 4:32-40; 1Ch 16:12; Ps 77:11; Mt 11:20-24; Jn 10:25; Ac 4:23-31; Ro 15:17-20.

Mission
All Christians are called to participate in the mission of God – to win people for God's kingdom by Spirit-inspired, faithful testimony and loving actions. Mt 28:16-20; Lk 4:14-21; 15:4-7; Jn 20:19-22; Ac 1:8; Ro 1:1, 8-17.

Mistakes
Mistakes may simply be unintentional errors or due to insensitivity or even deliberate sinfulness. In any case, we should apologise before mistakes corrode our relationships. Nu 15:22-28; Job 6:24; Ecc 5:1-7; Isa 1:15-18; Mk 12:24.

Motives
The Scriptures teach us that the Lord is seeking people whose obedience will spring from zealous devotion to him and warm acceptance of our neighbour. 1Ch 28:9; Pr 16:2; 1Co 4:5; 1Th 2:3-4; Jas 4:3.

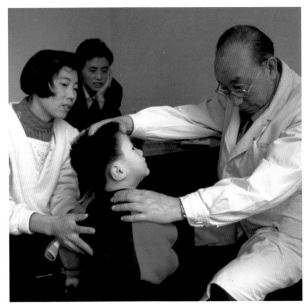

message, but inevitably disagreements arise. We must contend for gospel truth but preserve unity over secondary issues. Pr 18:2; 1Co 13:12; Gal 2:11-21; Php 3:15; Jude 3.

Opposition

Loving, Godly opposition can spare us from mistakes and help shape our character. Other forms of opposition, including spiritual opposition, need to be prayerfully resisted. Nu 16:19-21; Pr 27:6; Ac 6:9-10; Gal 2:11-21; Php 1:27-30; Heb 12:3.

Pain

Nobody enjoys pain and Christians should be sensitive to the pain of others. Nevertheless it cannot be avoided and can provide opportunity for spiritual renewal. Ps 38:1-22; 69:29; Ro 12:15; Heb 12:11; Rev 21:4. See also **Suffering**.

Parent(s)

Parents are responsible to God to love, care for and disciple their children particularly when they are young. Children should love and respect their parents. Ex 20:12; Pr 1:8; Mt 15:4-6; Eph 6:4; Col 3:20-21; 1Th 2:6-12. See also **Children**.

Murder

Murder is the intentional, unlawful killing of another human being. It is a particularly heinous sin which cries out to God for judgement. Ge 4:1-16; Ex 20:13; Pr 28:17; Mt 5:21-26; 1Jn 3:11-15.

Nature

All of nature has been created by God and reflects something of his nature in its beauty and its amazing diversity and functionality. Ge 1:1-2:3; Ps 19:1-6; Ro 1:20; 8:19-21; Col 1:15-17.

Obedience

The presence of the indwelling Holy Spirit enables us to obey God. We must co-operate energetically with the righteous desires he stirs within us. 1Sa 15:22; Ro 1:5;

6:15-18; 16:19; 2Co 9:13; 1Pe 1:1-2.

Occult

The word occult refers to magical techniques by which secrets may be revealed or events caused to occur. The Bible prohibits involvement with occult activities. Lev 19:26; Dt 18:10, 14; Dt 29:29; Ac 19:17-20; Gal 5:19-21.

Old age

Aging is an inevitable and challenging process in this sin cursed world. Nevertheless, Christians must have great respect for the wisdom that comes with age. Lev 19:32; Job 12:12; Ps 92:12-15; Pr 16:31; Ecc 12:1-7; Isa 46:4.

Opinions

Christians share a commitment to the gospel

Past

Prayerful reflection on the past is encouraging for the present and the future. Past sins need not condemn us; God offers free and complete forgiveness. Dt 5:15; Ecc 3:15; Ro 15:4; Heb 8:12; 2Pe 1:5-9; 3:2.

Patience

Patience – being able to bear with the behaviour of others – is an important aspect of Christian discipleship and a mark of the Holy Spirit's presence in our lives. Pr 19:11; Ecc 7:8; 2Co 6:3-10; Gal 5:22; Heb 6:12; Jas 5:7-11.

Peace

A consequence of the work of the Spirit in the life of the Christian will be internal peace and peaceful relationships with others. Nu 6:22-26; Ps 4:8; 29:11; Mt 5:9; Jn 14:27; Gal 5:22.

Peer pressure

We are tempted to measure our achievements or personal worth by comparison to our peers. Additionally we may feel pressured to conform to their standards. Ex 23:2-3; Est 3:2; Mt 14:9; Lk 23:13-25; Ro 12:1-2.

Persecution

Many of God's people have been called upon to suffer for their faith. Their example of selfless commitment to God is inspiring for us all. Jer 38:1-6; Mt 5:11-12; 24:1-13; Ac 3:1-4:31; 5:41; 11:19-21.

Perseverance

Christians are called to persevere in the faith. The Lord will sometimes allow trials to come into our life to test and strengthen our perseverance. Mt 24:13; Lk 8:15; Ro 5:3-5; Heb 3:6; Jas 1:2-4; 2Pe 1:3-11.

Planning

Whilst God is active in his world, he usually works in and through human activity. So we

"Let us throw off everything that hinders and the sin that so easily entangles, and let us run with perseverance the race marked out for us."
Hebrews 12:1

are called to pray, plan and act conscientiously. Ps 20:1-4; Pr 14:22; 16:9; 21:30; Lk 14:25-33; Jas 5:13-17.

Popularity

Whilst it is a good thing to have good friends, the

Christian is called to serve God rather than living for the praise of others. Pr 19:4; Lk 14:12-14; Jn 12:42-43; Ro 2:28-29; 1Th 2:6.

Possessions

God wants us to enjoy the things he entrusts to our use; nevertheless, we must not be controlled by what we own, or desire. Ecc 5:19-20; Lk 12:15-34; Ac 4:32; Heb 10:33-34; 1Jn 3:16-18; Rev 3:14-18.

Poverty

Poverty is an affront to God's standards of justice. It has many causes, but may be alleviated through enterprise, hard work and fairness in trade. Ex 23:10-11; Lev 19:10; Dt 15:11; Pr 6:9-11; 29:7; Lk 4:18-19.

Power

Power often corrupts our frail humanity. God offers something more fulfilling and less corrupting – Holy Spirit power for dynamic and yet humble and loving service. Ac 1:8; 2Co 13:4; Eph 1:15-23; Col 1:28-29; 2Th 1:11-12; 2Ti 1:6-7.

Praise

Christians are committed to expressing their love for God in song. We offer God spiritual, authentic praise for his mighty plan of creation and redemption. Ps 33:1-22; Mk 14:26; 1Co 14:26; Eph 5:19-20; Col 3:16; Jas 5:13.

Prayer

Prayer is one of the great privileges of the Christian. We can give God all our concerns knowing that he listens and responds to us. Mt 6:5-15; Lk 5:16; 18:1-14; Ac 2:42; Ro 8:26-27; Eph 6:18.

Prejudice

Prejudice, making self-centred decisions based upon an inadequate understanding, is a common human failing. Christians are called to be sensitive and accepting towards each other. Mk 6:1-4; Lk 10:25-37; Ac 10:34-35; Ro 15:7; Gal 3:26-28; Jas 2:1-9.

> "Cleanse me with hyssop, and I shall be clean; wash me, and I shall be whiter than snow. Let me hear joy and gladness."
>
> **Psalm 51:7-8**

Pressure

Christianity alleviates a good deal of pressure, not by encouraging laziness, but by asserting that the basis for activity is the unconditional acceptance of God. Mt 11:29; Mk 6:30-31; 2Co 1:8-11; 11:28; 1Pe 5:7; 1Jn 3:19-20.

Pride

Pride is at the root of human wickedness. It is essentially selfish, asserting the right of the individual above the claims of God and others. 1Sa 2:3; 2Ch 26:16-21; Pr 11:2; Ro 12:16; 1Co 13:4; 1Pe 5:5-6. See also **Humility**.

Priorities

Success in any walk of life is ultimately about keeping the main thing the main thing. Christians are committed to keeping God's priorities in mind. 2Ch 1:1-12; Pr 3:5-6; Mic 6:8; Mt 6:25-34; 23:23; Mk 12:28-34.

Punishment

Christ has taken upon himself all the punishment we deserved from God for our wrongdoing; consequently we must release others from any wrongdoing against us. Ge 3:1-24; Pr 10:16; Isa 53:6; Ro 6:23; 12:17-21; 1Jn 4:13-18.

Purity

When we are born again God purifies us and gives us his Holy Spirit to inspire and enable us to live in purity, in defiance of our sinful nature. Ps 24:3-4; 51:1-19; Mt 5:8; 2Co 6:3-7:1; 1Jn 1:7-9; 3:1-3.

Rebellion

The Lord expects us not to be rebellious, but rather to submit to him and to the leaders he places in authority over us. Ex 34:4-7; Jos 1:16-18; 1Sa 15:22-23; Pr 24:21; Ro 13:1-2; Heb 13:17.

Reconciliation

In his crucifixion and resurrection the Lord Jesus reconciled us to God. Consequently, we must now work that reconciliation out in all our human relationships. Mt 5:21-24; Lk 12:58; Ro 5:10-11; 2Co 5:16-21; Eph 2:13-22; Col 1:3-23.

Rejection

Everybody experiences rejection to some extent. God accepts everyone who comes to him; his people are called to show that same acceptance to each other. Jdg 11:1-3; Lk 4:24; Jn 1:10-11; 3:16; 6:37; Ro 15:7.

Reliability

Christian people should be like the One they serve. God is utterly reliable; he never fails to follow through on a promise. Ps 33:4-5; Pr 25:19; Isa 50:10; Jn 8:26; 2Ti 2:1-2; 1Jn 4:16.

Renewal

Because of our human frailty our passion for God and his purposes often ebbs away and we need the Holy Spirit to renew our love for God. Ps 51:1-19; Isa 40:28-31; La 5:21; Eze 37:1-14; 2Co 4:16; Eph 5:18.

Repentance

Repentance is a deep-seated change in attitude and behaviour. The Scriptures call us to repent of our sin and our lack of reverence for God. 2Ch 32:24-26; Isa 59:20; Mt 3:1-12; Mk 1:14-15; Lk 5:29-32; Ac 2:38.

Respect

The Scriptures teach that Christians should demonstrate a proper respect for those in authority as we ourselves endeavour to become people worthy of respect. Lev 19:3, 32; Pr 11:16; Ro 13:7; 1Th 4:11-12; 5:12; 1Pe 2:17.

Responsibility

Christians are responsible to please God and fulfil the calling he has given us. Those who fulfil minor responsibilities may be given more significant ones. Mt 25:14-30; Lk 12:47-48; 16:10-12; Ac 6:1-7.

Rest

Human beings need a rhythm of work and rest. God has established a rhythm of six days of work followed by one day of rest. Ge 2:2-3; Ex 20:8-11; 23:12; Ps 62:1, 5; Mt 11:28-30; Mk 6:31.

Restitution

Whilst Jesus has paid the price for all of our sin, it is good where possible and wise, to make restitution to those we have wronged. Ex 22:1-15; Lev 6:1-7; Nu 5:5-8; Lk 19:1-10.

Resurrection

The resurrection of Jesus was the great overture of the new creation. It guarantees the future physical resurrection of all who have faith in Christ. Jn 11:25; Ro 1:1-4; 6:5; 1Co 15:1-58; Php 3:10-11; 1Pe 1:3.

Revenge

Christians are not to take revenge. The Scripture teaches that we should leave the execution of justice to God and to the legitimate authorities. Lev 19:18; Mt 5:38-39; Lk 17:3-4; Ro 12:17-21.

Rewards

God promises to reward us for good deeds. The Christian life demands sacrifice, but God promises to compensate us in this life and the next. Ge 15:1; Ps 62:11-12; Pr 14:14; Mt 5:11-12; 6:1-18; Rev 22:12.

Riches

See **Wealth**.

Risk

Whilst Christians should not be reckless, we must not hesitate to step out boldly in faith. Getting the balance right requires faith, prayer and wisdom. Ps 138:1-3; Pr 14:16; 28:1; Mk 11:22-24; Jn 14:12-13.

> "Be strong in the grace that is in Christ Jesus. And the things you have heard me say in the presence of many witnesses entrust to reliable men who will also be qualified to teach others."
>
> **2 Timothy 2:1-2**

"The LORD is with me; I will not be afraid. What can man do to me?"
Psalm 118:6

Holy Spirit as he leads us towards greater self-discipline and control. Pr 25:28; 1Co 9:24-27; Gal 5:23; 1Pe 5:8; 2Pe 1:5-9.

Self-esteem

Worldly culture places great emphasis upon self-esteem. Christians know that they are selfish sinners but, nevertheless, have overwhelming value as children of Father God. Lk 15:1-30; 18:9-14; Eph 5:1-2; 2Th 2:15-17; 1Jn 3:1; Jude 1.

Selfishness

The natural condition for fallen humanity is to be more focussed on oneself than others. This selfishness is radically challenged and condemned by the Scriptures. Lev 19:18; Ps 119:36; Mt 22:34-40; Gal 5:14; Php 2:3; Jas 2:8.

Sensitivity

As we develop into Christian maturity, an instinctive sensitivity to the needs of others should grow. This indicates that we are overcoming our natural self-centredness. Job 2:11-13; Eph 4:2; 1Th 2:7; 5:14.

Service

Just as Christ humbly served his disciples, Christians are called to serve God and his people, in the power he gives us, with humility and enthusiasm. Dt 10:12-13; Mk

Sabbath

See **Rest**.

Sacrifice

Jesus' breathtaking sacrifice entirely fulfilled the Old Testament sacrificial system; in response Christians must be prepared to live our lives in sacrificial obedience and worship. Lev 1:1-7:38; 1Sa 15:22; Ro 12:1; Eph 5:1-2; Heb 10:1-18; 13:15-16.

Salvation

Christians have been saved by the grace of God through the death and resurrection of the Lord Jesus. We are to offer this salvation to others. Ex 15:2; Ac 4:8-12; Ro 1:16-17; 1Ti 2:1-4; 2Ti 2:10; Tit 2:11-14.

Satan

Christians should be aware of their spiritual enemy, the devil or Satan, and be prepared for the schemes, temptations and trials he uses against us. Ge 3:1-15; Job 1:1-2:10; Mt 4:1-11; Ac 10:37-38; Eph 6:10-20; 1Pe 5:8-9.

Security

Christians are not immune from insecurities and anxieties. Knowing that God's love for us is overwhelming, we can place our confidence in him for this life and the next. Pr 3:26; Eph 3:7-12; Php 1:3-6; Heb 6:13-20; 13:6; 1Jn 4:17-18.

Self-control

As we grow into mature Christian discipleship, we learn to cooperate with the

10:45; Lk 22:26-27; Gal 5:13; 1Ti 1:12; 1Pe 4:10-11.

Sex

Sex is a beautiful and powerful gift from God. The Scriptures teach us that sex shouldn't be treated casually; it should be reserved for marriage. Mt 5:27-28; Eph 5:3; Col 3:5; 1Th 4:3; Heb 13:4. See also **Marriage**.

Shame

Shame is a powerful sense of humiliation and unease due to our sinfulness or inadequacy. Forgiveness for sin and empowerment for Christian living overcome this debilitating emotion. Ge 2:25; Ps 27:1; Ro 10:11; 2Co 4:2; 1Ti 1:5; Heb 12:2.

> "There wil be no more death or mourning or crying or pain, for the old order of things has passed away."
>
> **Revelation 21:4**

Sickness

While God provides a number of avenues for healing, sickness and pain are usually a reflection in our bodies of the consequences of fallen creation. 2Ki 13:14; Ro 8:22-23; Php 2:26-30; 1Ti 5:23; Jas 5:14-16. See also **Healing**.

Simplicity

This attractive quality relates both to teaching which is easy to understand and to a transparent lack of guile in Christians living and attitude. Ps 116:6; 131:1-3; Ro 16:17-19; 2Co 1:13; 11:3; 1Ti 1:3-5.

Sin

Humanity's wilful disobedience of God is the root cause of death. Christ's atoning death, however, brings God's gift of justification and eternal life. Ro 3:9-26; 5:12-14; 6:15-23; 1Co 15:3; Heb 9:27-28; 1Jn 1:8-9.

Singleness

Although commended by Scripture as a true alternative to marriage, singleness can be a lonely lifestyle and churches should demonstrate sensitivity to unmarried members. Ps 25:16; 68:6; Mt 19:8-12; 1Co 7:1-40.

Social justice

Social justice, including political fairness, reflects the Christian concern to love our neighbour. For the Christian, doing good includes attending to our fellow citizen's well-being. Am 2:6-8; Zec 7:9-10; Mt 23:23; Gal 2:10; 6:10; Tit 3:1.

Sorrow

Sorrow arises from a great variety of causes. God offers present comfort and a permanent end to sorrow in the new creation. Ps 119:28; Jer 31:13; 2Co 7:10; Php 2:27; 1Th 4:13-18; Rev 21:4.

Speech

See **Words**.

Drop-in centre, Greece

Spiritual gifts

These are gifts from the Spirit for the benefit of all. We are to seek these gifts. Ro 12:6-8; 1Co 12:1-14:40; 1Th 5:19-21; 1Ti 1:18; 4:14; 2Ti 1:6-7.

Spiritual warfare

The New Testament often describes discipleship in terms of spiritual warfare. Satan and his demonic army contend against us; we must be ready for battle. Mt 16:18; 2Co 10:4-5; Eph 6:10-20; 1Ti 6:12; 1Pe 5:8-9.

Status

Seeking achievement or high rank is a natural human impulse, but should not control Christians. Never-theless, God uses high status people if they will humble themselves. Ge 41:41; Jer 45:5; Ac 13:1; Ro 16:23; 1Co 1:26-31; 1Jn 2:16-17.

Stress

Stress occurs when spiritual, mental, emotional or physical pressures become more than we can comfortably cope with. We can rely on God in such circumstances. Ge 31:38-42; 2Co 1:8-9; 4:8; 11:28-29; Php 4:12-13; 1Ti 2:2.

Stubbornness

Stubbornness is an unattractive quality that reflects the inflexibility and unyieldedness of sin. Jesus found the stubbornness of the religious leaders of his day deeply disturbing. Jer 16:12; 18:12; Eze 2:4; Mk 3:5; 16:14; Ro 2:5.

Success

Though our efforts may not always seem successful we can be sure that our work for the kingdom is not futile and will not go unrewarded. Jos 1:6-9; Pr 16:3; 19:21; Isa 41:13-15; 1Co 15:58; Jas 4:13-16.

Suffering

Like their master, the Lord Jesus, Christians are often called to suffer. In responding to suffering faithfully then there is opportunity for much growth in grace. Ac 14:22; Ro 8:17-23, 36-39; 2Co 12:7-10; Php 3:10; 1Pe 2:20-21.

Sunday

See **Rest**.

Swearing

Swearing means both the formal taking of oaths and simple bad language. These should be avoided; Christian speech should be truthful, wholesome and pure. Pr 8:13; Mt 5:33-37; Eph 4:29; Col 3:8-9; Jas 3:1-12; 5:12.

Teamwork

When we work together towards God's purposes with love and cohesion, the overall impact of the team is greater than the sum of the individuals. Ezr 5:2; Ne 4:6; Ecc 4:9-12; Lk 10:1; 1Co 12:14-20; Php 4:3.

Temptation

Temptation is Satan's primary weapon; he deceives our sinful nature by presenting sin as attractive. God grants us power through his Spirit to resist temptation. Mt 6:13; Lk 4:1-13; 1Co 10:13; 2Co 11:3; 1Th 3:5; Jas 1:12-15.

Thankfulness

See **Gratitude**.

Thinking

Thinking is a key feature of human behaviour. As Christians, redemption involves our mind, and our thought lives are part of our dedication to Christ. Jer 31:31-34; Mt 22:37; Ro 1:21; 12:2; Eph 6:13-18; Php 4:8; Heb 8:10. See also **Meditation**.

Time

God is eternal whilst humans are time bound. God has plans for the future; our first priority must be to serve him in the present. Ps 90:10, 12; Ecc 3:1-8; Mt 6:34; Heb 4:16; Jas 5:13-17; 1Pe 5:6; Rev 3:3.

Tithing

See **Generosity**.

Trust

Trust is the confidence and belief we place in one another; it peaks in the joyful confidence we can place in God and his word. Ps 13:5; 118:8-9; Isa 12:2; Jn 14:1; Ro 15:13; 1Co 4:2.

Truthfulness

It is fundamental to God's character that he cannot lie and that everything he says is truthful and trustworthy. Our speech should reflect his truthfulness. Nu 23:19; Ecc 12:10; Zec 8:16; Jn 14:6; Eph 4:15, 25; 1Ti 3:14-15.

Unity

Jesus prayed that the unity of the Trinity should be reflected among his followers. We are all "one in Christ" and aspire to fulfil this in Christian fellowship. Ps 133:1-3; Jn 17:20-23; 1Co 12:12-13; Gal 3:28; Eph 4:3-6, 11-13.

Violence

Violence is characteristic of fallen human nature. Worldly kingdoms establish and defend themselves through violence but the kingdom of God "is not of this world". Ge 6:11; Isa 53:9; 58:4; Jn 18:36; Tit 1:7.

> "I will put my law in their minds and write it on their hearts.
> I will be their God, and they will be my people."
>
> Jeremiah 31:33

"Praise the LORD.
How good it is to sing praises to our
God, how pleasant and fitting to
praise him!"
Psalm 147:1

Vision

Christian leaders need God-
given insight, foresight and
conviction to inspire his
people to action. Jesus
criticised his hearers for their
lack of this quality. Jos 1:10,
16-18; 1Ch 28:2, 8; Ne 2:17-18;
Lk 12:54-56; Jn 4:35-36; Ro
15:30-32.

Visions

God grants supernatural
revelation to his people via
visions. Following the
Pentecost gift of the Holy
Spirit visions are a possible
experience for every Christian.
Ge 15:1; Nu 12:6; Da 7:1-2; Ac
2:17; 10:9-16; Rev 1:9-16.

Vows

Vows are binding and solemn
promises. They are more
common in the Old Testament
because the New Testament
focuses upon straightforward,
Spirit-inspired commitment to
others. Nu 6:1-21; Ps 66:13-14;
Pr 20:25; Ecc 5:1-7; Ac 18:18;
21:20-24.

War

Jesus taught that we should
love our enemies. Christians
should therefore only
participate in war after very
serious consideration. Some
Christians believe in pacifism,
advocating the pursuit of
peaceful methods as an
alternative to war. Ps 120:6-7;
Mic 4:1-3; Mt 5:38-48; 26:52;
2Co 10:3-6.

Weakness

God's power is often displayed
in weakness: in the crucifixion;
in relying on him when we are
weak; and in helping others in
their weakness. Ac 20:35; Ro
8:36; 1Co 1:27; 9:22; 2Co
12:8-10; 13:4.

Wealth

Whereas the Old Testament
equates wealth with God's
blessing, the New Testament
considers wealth spiritually
dangerous. Nonetheless,
wealthy Christians have an
important part to play in God's
purposes. Ps 112:3; Pr
31:10,16,24; Mk 10:23; 1Ti
6:3-10, 17-19; Jas 2:1-7.

Wisdom

While worldly wisdom is a
snare, true Godly wisdom is
something God wants every
Christian to demonstrate.
Jesus was especially noted for
his wisdom. 1Ki 4:29; Pr 4:5-9;
Lk 2:52; 1Co 1:18-29; Jas 1:5;
Rev 5:12.

Words

Our words reflect the quality of our walk with God and should reveal the Lordship of Christ. Christian speech should have a wholly positive effect. Pr 16:24; Isa 50:4; Mt 12:33-37; Ro 10:8-10; Col 3:17; Jas 3:1-12.

> "And whatever you do, whether in word or deed, do it all in the name of the Lord Jesus, giving thanks to God the Father through him."
>
> **Colossians 3:17**

Work

Work, though often frustrating, is an essential part of life, reflecting the activity of God. We must complete the tasks God calls us to diligently. Ge 2:2; 3:23; Pr 12:14; Eph 1:11; 6:5-9; Php 2:25-30; 2Th 3:10-13.

Worry

Over-anxiousness is a corrosive problem. Learning to conquer anxiety through trust in God's faithfulness is a liberating and joyful victory for the Christian. Jer 17:7-8; Mt 6:25-34; Lk 10:38-42; Php 4:6-7; 1Pe 5:7. See also **Anxiety**.

Worship

The first duty of the Christian is to worship God for creation and redemption, in prayer and praise (words) and in all our actions (deeds). Ps 95:1-11; Hos 14:2; Jn 4:19-24; Ro 12:1-2; Heb 13:15-16; Rev 5:6-14.

Youth

Youth is a time of physical strength and enjoyment but with the potential for spiritual waywardness. Jesus set young people a good example to follow. Ps 25:7; Pr 1:1-4; Ecc 11:9-12:1; Lk 2:52; 1Ti 4:12; 1Jn 2:13-14.

Zeal

Zeal is a commendable spiritual quality. Misdirected zeal, however, as in the case of Paul before his conversion, needs to be informed by gospel truth. Pr 19:2; Jn 2:17; Ac 22:3-8; Ro 10:1-3; 12:11; Gal 4:17-18.

Prophecies of the Messiah

FULFILLED IN JESUS CHRIST

	Old Testament prophecy	New Testament fulfilment

Children of the serpent	"I will put enmity
	  between you and the woman,
	and between your offspring and hers;
	  he will crush your head,
	  and you will strike his heel."
	Genesis 3:15
		But when the time had fully come, God sent his Son, born of a woman, born under law, to redeem those under the law, that we might receive the full rights of sons.
		Galatians 4:4-5

Abraham's children	"I will bless those who bless you.
	  and whoever curses you I will curse,
	and all peoples on earth
	  will be blessed through you."
	Genesis 12:3
		A record of the genealogy of Jesus Christ the son of David, the son of Abraham.
		Matthew 1:1

God's promise through Isaac	Then God said, "Yes, but your wife Sarah will bear you a son. And you will call him Isaac. I will establish my covenant with him as an everlasting covenant for his descendants after him." **Genesis 17:19**	… Judah, the son of Jacob, the son of Isaac, the son of Abraham, the son of Terah, the son of Nahor. **Luke 3:33-34**

Jacob's ancestor	"I see him, but not now;
	  I behold him, but not near.
	A star will come out of Jacob,
	  a sceptre will rise out of Israel.
	He will crush the foreheads of Moab,
	  the skulls of all the sons of Sheth."
	Numbers 24:17
		Abraham was the father of Isaac,
		  Isaac the father of Jacob,
		  Jacob the father of Judah and his
		    brothers.
		Matthew 1:2

From the tribe of Judah	The sceptre will not depart from Judah
	  nor the ruler's staff from between his
	    feet,
	until he comes to whom it belongs
	  and the obedience of the nations is
	    his.
	Genesis 49:10
		… Nahshon,
		the son of Amminadab, the son of
		  Ram,
		the son of Hezron, the son of Perez,
		the son of Judah …
		Luke 3:32-33

	Old Testament prophecy	New Testament fulfilment

Heir to David's throne	Of the increase of his government
	    and peace
	    there will be no end.
	He will reign on David's throne
	    and over his kingdom,
	    establishing and upholding it
	    with justice and righteousness
	    from that time on and for ever.
	The zeal of the LORD Almighty
	    will accomplish this.
	Isaiah 9:7
		"He will be great and will be called the Son of the Most High. The Lord God will give him the throne of his father David, and he will reign over the house of Jacob for ever; his kingdom will never end."
		Luke 1:32-33

Born in Bethlehem	"But you, Bethlehem Ephrathah,
	    though you are small among the
	      clans of Judah,
	out of you will come for me
	    one who will be ruler over Israel
	whose origins are of old,
	    from ancient times."
	Micah 5:2
		So Joseph also went up from the town of Nazareth in Galilee to Judea, to Bethlehem the town of David, because he belonged to the house and line of David. He went there to register with Mary, who was pledged to be married to him and was expecting a child. While they were there, the time came for the baby to be born, and she gave birth to her firstborn, a son.
		Luke 2:4-7

The time of Messiah's birth	"Know and understand this: From the issuing of the decree to restore and rebuild Jerusalem until the Anointed One, the ruler, comes, there will be seven 'sevens', and sixty-two 'sevens'. It will be rebuilt with streets and a trench, but in times of trouble." **Daniel 9:25-26**	In those days Caesar Augustus issued a decree that a census should be taken of the entire Roman world. (This was the first census that took place while Quirinius was governor of Syria.) **Luke 2:1-2**
Born of a virgin	"Therefore the Lord himself will give you a sign: the virgin will be with child and will give birth to a son, and will call him Immanuel." **Isaiah 7:14**	In the sixth month, God sent the angel Gabriel to Nazareth, a town in Galilee, to a virgin pledged to a man named Joseph, a descendant of David. The virgin's name was Mary. But the angel said to her, "Do not be afraid, Mary, you have found favour with God. You will be with child and give birth to a son, and you are to give him the name Jesus." **Luke 1:26-27,30-31**

	Old Testament prophecy	New Testament fulfilment
Escape to Egypt	"When Israel was a child, I loved him. and out of Egypt I called my son." **Hosea 11:1**	So he [Joseph] got up, took the child and his mother during the night and left for Egypt, where they stayed until the death of Herod. And so was fulfilled what the Lord had said through the prophet: "Out of Egypt I called my son." **Matthew 2:14-15**
Innocent children slaughtered	This is what the LORD says: "A voice is heard in Ramah, mourning and great weeping, Rachel weeping for her children, and refusing to be comforted, because her children are no more." **Jeremiah 31:15**	When Herod realised that he had been outwitted by the Magi, he was furious, and he gave orders to kill all the boys in Bethlehem and its vicinity who were two years old and under, in accordance with the time he had learned from the Magi. Then what was said through the prophet Jeremiah spoke was fulfilled: "A voice is heard in Ramah, weeping and great mourning, Rachel weeping for her children, and refusing to be comforted, because they are no more." **Matthew 2:16-18**
The one who prepared the way	"See, I will send my messenger, who will prepare the way before me. Then suddenly the Lord you are seeking will come to his temple; the messenger of the covenant, whom you desire, will come," says the LORD Almighty. **Malachi 3:1**	After John's messengers left, Jesus began to speak to the crowd about John. "What did you go out into the desert to see? A reed swayed by the wind? ... This is the one about whom it is written: "'I will send my messenger ahead of you, who will prepare your way before you.'" **Luke 7:24,27**
Declared as God's Son	I will proclaim the decree of the LORD: He said to me, "You are my Son; today I have become your Father." **Psalm 2:7**	And a voice from heaven said, "This is my Son, whom I love; with him I am well pleased." **Matthew 3:17**

Old Testament prophecy	New Testament fulfilment
His ministry in Galilee Nevertheless, there will be no more gloom for those who were in distress. In the past he humbled the land of Zebulun and the land of Naphthali, but in the future he will honour Galilee of the Gentiles, by the way of the sea, along the Jordan – The people walking in darkness have seen a great light, on those living in the land of the shadow of death. a light has dawned. **Isaiah 9:1-2**	Leaving Nazareth, he went and lived in Capernaum, which was by the lake in the area of Zebulun and Naphtali – to fulfil what was said through the prophet Isaiah: "Land of Zebulun and land of Naphtali, the way to the sea, along the Jordan, Galilee of the Gentiles – the people living in darkness have seen a great light; on those living in the land of the shadow of death a light has dawned." **Matthew 4:13-16**
Raised up as a prophet The LORD your God will raise up for you a prophet like me from among your own brothers. You must listen to him. **Deuteronomy 18:15**	"… and that he may send the Christ, who has been appointed for you – even Jesus. … For Moses said, 'The Lord your God will raise up for you a prophet like me from among your own people; you must listen to everything he tells you.'" **Acts 3:20,22**
Come to heal the broken-hearted The Spirit of the Sovereign LORD is on me, because the LORD has anointed me to preach good news to the poor. He has sent me to bind up the broken-hearted, to proclaim freedom for the captives and release from darkness for the prisoners, to proclaim the year of the Lord's favour and the day of vengeance of our God. to comfort all who mourn. **Isaiah 61:1-2**	"The Spirit of the Lord is on me, because he has anointed me to preach good news to the poor. He has sent me to proclaim freedom for the prisoners and recovery of sight for the blind, to release the oppressed, to proclaim the year of the Lord's favour." **Luke 4:18-19**

	Old Testament prophecy	New Testament fulfilment

Spoke in parables	O my people, hear my teaching,
	    listen to the words of my mouth.
	I will speak in parables,
	    I will utter hidden things, things
	        from of old –
	what we have heard and known,
	    what our fathers have told us.
	Psalm 78:1-3
		Jesus spoke all these things to the crowd in parables; he did not say anything to them without using a parable. So was fulfilled what was spoken through the prophet:
		"I will open my mouth in parables,
		    I will utter things hidden since the
		        creation of the world."
		Matthew 13:34-35

Rejected by his own people	He was despised and rejected by men,
	    a man of sorrows, and familiar with
	        suffering.
	Like one from whom men hide their
	    faces
	    he was despised, and we esteemed
	        him not.
	Isaiah 53:3
		He came to that which was his own, but his own did not receive him.
		John 1:11

The stone the builders rejected	The stone the builders rejected
	    has become the capstone;
	the LORD has done this,
	    and it is marvellous in our eyes.
	Psalm 118:22-23
		"'The stone the builders rejected
		    has become the capstone;
		the Lord has done this,
		    and it is marvellous in our eyes'?"
		Mark 12:10-11
		
		"He [Jesus] is
		'The stone you builders rejected,
		    which has become the capstone.'"
		Acts 4:11
		
		Now to you who believe, this stone is precious. But to those who do not believe,
		"The stone the builders rejected
		    has become the capstone."
		1 Peter 2:8

A priest of the line of Melchizedek	The LORD has sworn
	    and will not change his mind;
	"You are a priest for ever,
	    in the order of Melchizedek."
	Psalm 110:4
		But God said to him,
		"You are my Son.
		    Today I have become your Father."
		And he says in another place,
		"You are a priest for ever,
		    in the order of Melchizedek."
		Hebrews 5:5-6

Every ten years the story of Jesus'
passion is enacted in full by the
villagers of Oberammergau, Germany

	Old Testament prophecy	New Testament fulfilment
Entered Jerusalem as a king	Rejoice greatly, O Daughter of Zion! Shout, Daughter of Jerusalem! See, your king comes to you. righteous and having salvation, gentle and riding on a donkey. on a colt, the foal of a donkey. **Zechariah 9:9**	When they brought the colt to Jesus and threw their cloaks over it, he sat on it. … Those who went ahead and those who followed shouted, "Hosanna!" "Blessed is he who comes in the name of the Lord!" "Blessed is the coming kingdom of our father David!" "Hosanna in the highest!" Jesus entered Jerusalem and went to the temple. **Mark 11:7,9-11**
Betrayed by a friend	Even my close friend, whom I trusted, he who shared in my bread, has lifted up his heel against me. **Psalm 41:9**	While he was still speaking a crowd came up, and the man who was called Judas, one of the Twelve, was leading them. He approached Jesus to kiss him, but Jesus asked him, "Judas, are you betraying the Son of Man with a kiss?" **Luke 22:47-48**
Sold for 30 silver coins	I told them, "If you think it best, give me my pay, but if not, keep it." So they paid me thirty pieces of silver. **Zechariah 11:12**	Then one of the Twelve – the one called Judas Iscariot – went to the chief priests and asked, "What are you willing to give me if I hand him over to you?" So they counted out for him thirty silver coins. **Matthew 26:14-15**
Accused by false witnesses	Ruthless witnesses come forward; they question me on things I know nothing about. **Psalm 35:11**	Then some stood up and gave this false testimony against him: "We heard him say, 'I will destroy this man-made temple and in three days will build another, not made by men.'" **Mark 14:57-58**
Refused to defend himself	He was oppressed and afflicted, yet he did not open his mouth, he was led like a sheep to the slaughter, and as a sheep before her shearers is silent, so he did not open his mouth. **Isaiah 53:7**	So again Pilate asked him, "Aren't you going to answer? See how many things they are accusing you of." But Jesus still made no reply, and Pilate was amazed. **Mark 15:4-5**

Old Testament prophecy	New Testament fulfilment

Spat upon and beaten

I offered my back to those who beat me,
my cheeks to those who pulled out
my beard,
I did not hide my face
from mocking and spitting.
Isaiah 50:6

Then they spat in his face and struck him with their fists. Others slapped him and said, "Prophesy to us, Christ! Who hit you?"
Matthew 26:67

Hated for no reason

Let not those who gloat over me
who are my enemies without cause;
let not those who hate me without
reason
maliciously wink the eye.
Psalm 35:19

"If I had done among them what no one else did, they would not be guilty of sin. But now they have seen these miracles, and yet they have hated both me and my Father. But this is to fulfil what is written in their Law: 'They hated me without reason.'"
John 15:24-25

Sacrificed in our place

But he was pierced for our
transgressions,
he was crushed for our iniquities;
the punishment that brought us peace
was upon him,
and by his wounds we are healed.
Isaiah 53:5

You see, at just the right time, when we were still powerless, Christ died for the ungodly. Very rarely will anyone die for a righteous man, though for a good man someone might possibly dare to die. But God demonstrates his own love for us in this: While we were still sinners, Christ died for us.
Romans 5:6-8

Crucified along with criminals

Therefore I will give him a portion
among the great,
and he will divide the spoils with the
strong,
because he poured out his life unto
death,
and was numbered with the
transgressors.
For he bore the sins of many,
and made intercession for the
transgressors.
Isaiah 53:12

They crucified two robbers with him, one on his right hand and one on his left.
Mark 15:27

Given vinegar and gall to drink

They put gall in my food
and gave me vinegar for my thirst.
Psalm 69:21

There they offered Jesus wine to drink mixed with gall, but after tasting it, he refused to drink it.
Matthew 27:34

	Old Testament prophecy	New Testament fulfilment
Scorned and mocked	All who see me mock me, they hurl insults, shaking their heads. "He trusts in the LORD. Let the LORD rescue him. Let him deliver him, since he delights in him." **Psalm 22:7-8**	The people stood watching, and the rulers even sneered at him. They said, "He saved others; let him save himself if he is the Christ of God, the Chosen One." **Luke 23:35**
Prayed for his enemies	In return for my friendship they accuse me, but I am a man of prayer. **Psalm 109:4**	Jesus said, "Father, forgive them, for they do not know what they are doing." **Luke 23:34**
Soldiers gambled for his cloak	They divide my clothes among them and cast lots for my clothing. **Psalm 22:18**	When they had crucified him, they divided up his clothes by casting lots. And sitting down, they kept watch over him there. **Matthew 27:35-36**
Not one bone broken	He protects all of his bones, not one of them will be broken. **Psalm 34:20**	The soldiers therefore came and broke the legs of the first man who had been crucified with Jesus, and then those of the other. But when they came to Jesus and found that he was already dead they did not break his legs. ... These things happened so that the scripture would be fulfilled; "Not one of his bones will be broken." **John 19:32-33,36**
Hands, feet and side pierced	"And I will pour out on the house of David and the inhabitants of Jerusalem a spirit of grace and supplication. They will look on me, the one they have pierced, and they will mourn for him as one mourns for an only child, and grieve bitterly for him as one grieves for a firstborn son." **Zechariah 12:10**	Instead, one of the soldiers pierced Jesus' side with a spear, bringing a sudden flow of blood and water. ... and, as another scripture says, "They will look on the one they have pierced." **John 19:34,37** Then he said to Thomas, "Put your finger here; see my hands. Reach out your hand and put it into my side. Stop doubting and believe." **John 20:27**

	Old Testament prophecy	New Testament fulfilment
Buried in a rich man's tomb	He was assigned a grave with the wicked, and with the rich in his death, though he had done no violence, nor was any deceit in his mouth. **Isaiah 53:9**	As evening approached, there came a rich man came from Arimathea, named Joseph, who had himself become a disciple of Jesus. Going to Pilate, he asked for Jesus' body, and Pilate ordered that it be given to him. Joseph took the body, wrapped it in a clean linen cloth, and placed it in his own new tomb that he had cut out of the rock. He rolled a big stone in front of the entrance to the tomb and went away. **Matthew 27:57-60**
Resurrected from the grave	Therefore my heart is glad and my tongue rejoices; my body will also rest secure, because you will not abandon me to the grave, nor will you let your Holy One see decay. **Psalm 16:10** But God will redeem my life from the grave, He will surely take me to himself. **Psalm 49:15**	"Don't be alarmed," he said. "You are looking for Jesus the Nazarene, who was crucified. He has risen! He is not here. See the place where they laid him. But go, tell his disciples and Peter, 'He is going ahead of you into Galilee. There you will see him, just as he told you.'" **Mark 16:6-7** … he was buried … he was raised on the third day according to the Scriptures … **1 Corinthians 15:4**
Ascended to God's right hand	When you ascended on high, you led captives in your train; you received gifts from men, even from the rebellious – that you, O LORD God, might dwell there. **Psalm 68:18**	After the Lord Jesus had spoken to them, he was taken up into heaven and he sat at the right hand of God. **Mark 16:19** That is why it says: "When he ascended on high, he led captives in his train and gave gifts to men." **Ephesians 4:8**

In Times of Need...

What follows is a brief listing of some key Bible references, which we hope will be helpful in different experiences of life. The references are not exhaustive but we hope they will lay a good foundation for further reflection. When interpreting the Scriptures, it is important to remember that each Scripture should be interpreted in the light of its immediate context and also within the wider context of biblical theology.

When considering...

Approaching a friend about sin:
Matthew 7:2-4;
18:15-17;
Galatians 6:1

Baptism:
Matthew 3:13;
Mark 1:4;
Romans 6:4

Children:
Genesis 1:28;
Psalm 127:3-5; 139:13-16

Coming back to God:
Jeremiah 15:19;
Hosea 14:4;
Luke 15:22-24

Divorce:
Malachi 2:15-16;
Matthew 19:1-11;
1 Corinthians 7:10-16

Fasting:
Joel 2:12-13;
Matthew 6:16-18;
Acts 13:1-3

Generosity:
Psalm 112:5;
Proverbs 11:25; 22:9

God's sovereignty:
Proverbs 16:1-4;
Isaiah 55:8-9;
Romans 9:10-21

God's word:
Ephesians 6:17;
2 Timothy 3:16-17;
Hebrews 4:12

How to be a good daughter:
Exodus 20:12;
Ephesians 6:1;
Colossians 3:20

How to be a good father:
Ephesians 6:4;
1 Timothy 3:4;
Titus 2:6

How to be a good husband:
Genesis 2:23-24;
Ephesians 5:25-33;
Colossians 3:19

How to be a good mother:
Proverbs 22:6; 29:15;
Titus 2:4-5

How to be a good son:
Exodus 20:12;
Proverbs 13:1;
Colossians 3:20

How to be a good wife:
Proverbs 31:10-31;
Ephesians 5:22-24;
1 Peter 3:1-6

Lord's Supper:
Luke 22:14-20;
1 Corinthians 10:14-21;
11:17-34

Marriage:
Proverbs 18:22;
Ecclesiastes 4:9-12;
2 Corinthians 6:14-18

Righteous behaviour:
Psalm 37:21; 97:12;
Proverbs 11:6

Taking revenge:
Leviticus 19:18;
Nahum 1:2;
Romans 12:19

The burdens of others:
Psalm 68:19;
Galatians 6:2;
1 John 3:16-20

The elderly:
Leviticus 19:32;
1 Timothy 5:3, 17

Tithing:
Leviticus 27:30;
2 Chronicles 31:5-6;
Malachi 3:8-12

Your conduct:
Ephesians 4:1-6;
Philippians 1:27;
1 John 1:5-10

Your money:
Proverbs 13:11;
Ecclesiastes 5:10;
Matthew 6:19-24

"Every word of God is flawless;
he is a shield to those who take
refuge in him."
Proverbs 30:5

Your priorities:
Matthew 16:24-27;
Luke 10:27;
Acts 20:35

Your speech:
Proverbs 12:17-19;
Proverbs 15:1-4;
James 3:1-12

When experiencing...

Awe:
Job 25:2;
Psalm 119:120;
Hebrews 12:28

Depression:
Psalm 37:23-24;
Isaiah 41:10;
John 16:33

Fear:
Deuteronomy 31:6;
Joshua 1:9;
Psalm 118:6

Grief:
Matthew 5:4;
1 Thessalonians 4:13-14;
Revelation 21:4

Joy:
Psalm 33:1-3; 118:15-16;
Isaiah 44:23;
Luke 10:21;
Philippians 4:1-9

Loneliness:
Deuteronomy 31:8;
Isaiah 41:10;
John 14:18

Suffering:
Romans 5:3; 8:17;
2 Corinthians 1:5

Unbelief:
Mark 9:24;
John 6:29; 20:29

When feeling...

Afraid:
Psalm 27:1; 56:3;
Isaiah 44:8

Angry:
Ephesians 4:31-32;
Colossians 3:8;
James 1:19-21

Bereaved:
Psalm 23; 71:1-3; 116:1-7;
John 14:1-4

Betrayed:
Psalm 41:4-13;
52:1-5;
Proverbs 19:5

Confused:
Psalm 107:17-22;
1 Corinthians 13:12;
14:33

Despair:
Proverbs 3:24;
Romans 8:38-39;
2 Corinthians 1:3-4

Discouraged:
Ephesians 6:10-13;
2 Thessalonians 2:13-17;
Revelation 19:6-8

Far from God:
Psalm 22:1-11; 42:1-8;
Isaiah 34:1

Gratitude:
Psalm 95:2;
Jonah 2:9;
Colossians 3:17

Hopeless:
Isaiah 40:31;
Romans 5:5;
Hebrews 10:23

Impatient:
Psalm 37:7;
Ecclesiastes 7:8;
James 5:7-8

Insecure:
Deuteronomy 33:12;
Psalm 16:5;
Proverbs 14:26

Judgemental:
Matthew 7:1-2;
John 7:24;
James 4:11-12

Poor:
1 Samuel 2:7-8;
Psalm 34:6-7;
James 2:5

Persecuted:
Matthew 5:10-12;
1 Corinthians 4:10-13;
2 Timothy 3:10-15

Prayerful:
Chronicles 7:14;
Psalm 32:6;
Matthew 6:9-15

Proud:
Proverbs 11:2; 16:18;
1 Peter 5:5-7

Rebellious:
1 Samuel 15:23;
Isaiah 1:19-20;
James 4:7

Sad:
Psalm 119:28;
Ecclesiastes 7:3;
2 Corinthians 7:10-11

Self-confident:
Jeremiah 10:23-24;
Philippians 3:2-11;
2 Thessalonians 3:4

Sleepless:
Psalm 3:3-6; 4:6-8;
Jeremiah 31:25

Stressed:
Proverbs 12:25;
Matthew 11:28;
Philippians 4:6

Tempted:
1 Corinthians 10:13;
Hebrews 2:18;
James 1:12-15

Undecided about God:
Psalm 1:1-6; 127:1-5;
Isaiah 59:1

"Praise be to you, O LORD,
God of our father Israel,
from everlasting to everlasting.
Yours, O LORD, is the greatness
and the power
and the glory and the majesty
and the splendour,
for everything in heaven is yours.
Yours, O LORD, is the kingdom;
you are exalted as head over all.
Wealth and honour come from you;
you are the ruler of all things.
In your hands are strength and power
to exalt and give strength to all.
Now, our God, we give you thanks,
and praise your glorious name."
1 Chronicles 29:10-13

Weak:
Psalm 72:12-14;
Isaiah 40:29;
Mark 14:38

Weary:
Isaiah 50:4;
Jeremiah 31:25;
Matthew 11:28-30;
Galatians 6:9

Worried:
Matthew 6:25; 6:33-34;
Luke 10:38-42

Worshipful:
Isaiah 6:1-8;
Revelation 7:9-17; 19:1-8

When needing...

Assurance of your salvation:
Psalm 62:7; 69:13;
John 6:37;
1 John 2:3,9-10; 3:21-24

Courage:
Deuteronomy 31:8;
Joshua 1:6-9;
1 Chronicles 28:20;
1 Corinthians 16:13

Comfort:
Psalm 9:9; 55:22;
Matthew 11:28

Direction:
Psalm 5:8; 143:10;
Isaiah 49:8-13

Forgiveness:
Acts 2:38;
2 Corinthians 2:10;
1 John 2:12

Freedom from sin:
Ezekiel 36:25-26;
Romans 6:6-7;
2 Corinthians 5:17

Grace:
Psalm 86:3-8;
2 Corinthians 12:8-10;
Ephesians 2:8-9

Guidance:
Proverbs 11:14;
Isaiah 58:11;
John 16:13

Healing:
Exodus 15:26;
Psalm 147:3;
Isaiah 30:26

Humility:
Proverbs 15:33;
Ephesians 4:2;
James 4:10

Peace:
Psalm 119:165;
Proverbs 16:7;
Isaiah 26:3; 52:7;
Philippians 4:4-7

Protection:
Psalm 91:9-16;
Zechariah 9:14-17;
Ephesians 6:10-20

Provision:
Psalm 111:5; 144:12-15;
Philippians 4:19;
1 Timothy 6:17

Repentance:
Acts 2:38; 3:19;
1 John 1:9

Sobriety:
1 Thessalonians 5:8;
1 Peter 1:13; 5:8

Strength:
Psalm 46:1-5;
Psalm 118:14;
Philippians 4:13

Wisdom:
Psalm 51:6;
Proverbs 4:10-12;
1 Corinthians 2:6-10

When needing to be reminded that...

God is all-powerful:
1 Chronicles 29:11-13;
Psalm 65:5-7;
Amos 4:13

God is eternal:
Deuteronomy 33:27;
Psalm 90:2;
Jeremiah 10:10

God is in control:
Psalm 139:13-14;
Isaiah 46:10;
Jeremiah 29:11

God is just:
Psalm 37:5-6;
73:27-28;
145:19-20

God is love:
Psalm 117;
John 3:16-21;
John 15:9-13;
Romans 5:8

God is unchanging:
Psalm 102:25-27;
Hebrews 1:10-12; 13:8

God knows everything:
Psalm 139:2-6;
Isaiah 40:13-14;
Matthew 10:29-30

When struggling with...

Doubt:
Psalm 27:7-14;
Matthew 14:31;
Romans 4:18-25

Drunkenness:
Proverbs 23:21;
Luke 21:34;
Ephesians 5:18

Envy:
Proverbs 3:31; 27:4;
Romans 13:13

Greed:
Proverbs 15:27; 28:25;
Colossians 3:5

Guilt:
Psalm 103:12;
Romans 3:22-24; 8:1-3

Laziness:
Proverbs 10:4; 12:27;
Ecclesiastes 10:18

Lust:
Proverbs 6:25;
2 Timothy 2:22;
1 John 2:16

Lying:
Proverbs 12:22; 19:22;
1 John 2:22

Receiving discipline:
Job 5:17;
Hebrews 12:11;
Revelation 3:19

Self-image:
Genesis 1:26-27;
Psalm 139:14;
Ephesians 1:4-6

"Lazy hands make a man poor, but diligent hands bring wealth."
Proverbs 10:4

Submission to authority:
Romans 13:1;
Hebrews 13:17;
1 Peter 2:13

Temper:
Proverbs 15:18; 16:32;
2 Peter 1:5-8

Waiting on the Lord:
Psalm 37:34; 130:5-6;
Isaiah 40:27-31;
Proverbs 20:22

Daily Bible Reading Plan

In order to grow in our understanding of God and to feel his heart, we need a balanced diet of taking in God's word. It can be helpful to have a plan to guide our readings.

If you want to try to read through the whole Bible in four years, follow consecutive readings from one vertical list.
If you want to try to read through the whole Bible in two years, follow the readings from two of the vertical lists.
If you're up to trying to read through the whole Bible in one year, follow the readings in all four vertical lists.

> "The unfolding
>   of your words gives light,
> it gives understanding to
>   the simple."
> **Psalm 119:130**

> "Jesus answered,
> 'It is written: "Man does not live
> on bread alone, but on every
> word that comes from the mouth
> of God."'"
> **Matthew 4:4**

> "All Scripture is God-breathed
> and is useful for teaching, rebuking,
> correcting and training in righteousness,
> so that the man of God may be thoroughly
> equipped for every good work."
> **2 Timothy 3:16-17**

JANUARY

	MORNING		EVENING	
1	Ge 1	Mt 1	Ezr 1	Ac 1
2	Ge 2	Mt 2	Ezr 2	Ac 2
3	Ge 3	Mt 3	Ezr 3	Ac 3
4	Ge 4	Mt 4	Ezr 4	Ac 4
5	Ge 5	Mt 5	Ezr 5	Ac 5
6	Ge 6	Mt 6	Ezr 6	Ac 6
7	Ge 7	Mt 7	Ezr 7	Ac 7
8	Ge 8	Mt 8	Ezr 8	Ac 8
9	Ge 9–10	Mt 9	Ezr 9	Ac 9
10	Ge 11	Mt 10	Ezr 10	Ac 10
11	Ge 12	Mt 11	Ne 1	Ac 11
12	Ge 13	Mt 12	Ne 2	Ac 12
13	Ge 14	Mt 13	Ne 3	Ac 13
14	Ge 15	Mt 14	Ne 4	Ac 14
15	Ge 16	Mt 15	Ne 5	Ac 15
16	Ge 17	Mt 16	Ne 6	Ac 16
17	Ge 18	Mt 17	Ne 7	Ac 17
18	Ge 19	Mt 18	Ne 8	Ac 18
19	Ge 20	Mt 19	Ne 9	Ac 19
20	Ge 21	Mt 20	Ne 10	Ac 20
21	Ge 22	Mt 21	Ne 11	Ac 21
22	Ge 23	Mt 22	Ne 12	Ac 22
23	Ge 24	Mt 23	Ne 13	Ac 23
24	Ge 25	Mt 24	Est 1	Ac 24
25	Ge 26	Mt 25	Est 2	Ac 25
26	Ge 27	Mt 26	Est 3	Ac 26
27	Ge 28	Mt 27	Est 4	Ac 27
28	Ge 29	Mt 28	Est 5	Ac 28
29	Ge 30	Mk 1	Est 6	Ro 1
30	Ge 31	Mk 2	Est 7	Ro 2
31	Ge 32	Mk 3	Est 8	Ro 3

FEBRUARY

	MORNING		EVENING	
1	Ge 33	Mk 4	Est 9–10	Ro 4
2	Ge 34	Mk 5	Job 1	Ro 5
3	Ge 35–36	Mk 6	Job 2	Ro 6
4	Ge 37	Mk 7	Job 3	Ro 7
5	Ge 38	Mk 8	Job 4	Ro 8
6	Ge 39	Mk 9	Job 5	Ro 9
7	Ge 40	Mk 10	Job 6	Ro 10
8	Ge 41	Mk 11	Job 7	Ro 11
9	Ge 42	Mk 12	Job 8	Ro 12
10	Ge 43	Mk 13	Job 9	Ro 13
11	Ge 44	Mk 14	Job 10	Ro 14
12	Ge 45	Mk 15	Job 11	Ro 15
13	Ge 46	Mk 16	Job 12	Ro 16
14	Ge 47	Lk 1:1-38	Job 13	1Co 1
15	Ge 48	Lk 1:39-80	Job 14	1Co 2
16	Ge 49	Lk 2	Job 15	1Co 3
17	Ge 50	Lk 3	Job 16–17	1Co 4
18	Ex 1	Lk 4	Job 18	1Co 5
19	Ex 2	Lk 5	Job 19	1Co 6
20	Ex 3	Lk 6	Job 20	1Co 7
21	Ex 4	Lk 7	Job 21	1Co 8
22	Ex 5	Lk 8	Job 22	1Co 9
23	Ex 6	Lk 9	Job 23	1Co 10
24	Ex 7	Lk 10	Job 24	1Co 11
25	Ex 8	Lk 11	Job 25–26	1Co 12
26	Ex 9	Lk 12	Job 27	1Co 13
27	Ex 10	Lk 13	Job 28	1Co 14
28	Ex 11–12:20	Lk 14	Job 29	1Co 15

MARCH

	MORNING		EVENING	
1	Ex 12:21-51	Lk 15	Job 30	1Co 16
2	Ex 13	Lk 16	Job 31	2Co 1
3	Ex 14	Lk 17	Job 32	2Co 2
4	Ex 15	Lk 18	Job 33	2Co 3
5	Ex 16	Lk 19	Job 34	2Co 4
6	Ex 17	Lk 20	Job 35	2Co 5
7	Ex 18	Lk 21	Job 36	2Co 6
8	Ex 19	Lk 22	Job 37	2Co 7
9	Ex 20	Lk 23	Job 38	2Co 8
10	Ex 21	Lk 24	Job 39	2Co 9
11	Ex 22	Jn 1	Job 40	2Co 10
12	Ex 23	Jn 2	Job 41	2Co 11
13	Ex 24	Jn 3	Job 42	2Co 12
14	Ex 25	Jn 4	Pr 1	2Co 13
15	Ex 26	Jn 5	Pr 2	Gal 1
16	Ex 27	Jn 6	Pr 3	Gal 2
17	Ex 28	Jn 7	Pr 4	Gal 3
18	Ex 29	Jn 8	Pr 5	Gal 4
19	Ex 30	Jn 9	Pr 6	Gal 5
20	Ex 31	Jn 10	Pr 7	Gal 6
21	Ex 32	Jn 11	Pr 8	Eph 1
22	Ex 33	Jn 12	Pr 9	Eph 2
23	Ex 34	Jn 13	Pr 10	Eph 3
24	Ex 35	Jn 14	Pr 11	Eph 4
25	Ex 36	Jn 15	Pr 12	Eph 5
26	Ex 37	Jn 16	Pr 13	Eph 6
27	Ex 38	Jn 17	Pr 14	Php 1
28	Ex 39	Jn 18	Pr 15	Php 2
29	Ex 40	Jn 19	Pr 16	Php 3
30	Lev 1	Jn 20	Pr 17	Php 4
31	Lev 2–3	Jn 21	Pr 18	Col 1

APRIL

	MORNING		**EVENING**	
1	Lev 4	Ps 1-2	Pr 19	Col 2
2	Lev 5	Ps 3-4	Pr 20	Col 3
3	Lev 6	Ps 5-6	Pr 21	Col 4
4	Lev 7	Ps 7-8	Pr 22	1Th 1
5	Lev 8	Ps 9	Pr 23	1Th 2
6	Lev 9	Ps 10	Pr 24	1Th 3
7	Lev 10	Ps 11–12	Pr 25	1Th 4
8	Lev 11–12	Ps 13–14	Pr 26	1Th 5
9	Lev 13	Ps 15–16	Pr 27	2Th 1
10	Lev 14	Ps 17	Pr 28	2Th 2
11	Lev 15	Ps 18	Pr 29	2Th 3
12	Lev 16	Ps 19	Pr 30	1Ti 1
13	Lev 17	Ps 20–21	Pr 31	1Ti 2
14	Lev 18	Ps 22	Ecc 1	1Ti 3
15	Lev 19	Ps 23–24	Ecc 2	1Ti 4
16	Lev 20	Ps 25	Ecc 3	1Ti 5
17	Lev 21	Ps 26–27	Ecc 4	1Ti 6
18	Lev 22	Ps 28–29	Ecc 5	2Ti 1
19	Lev 23	Ps 30	Ecc 6	2Ti 2
20	Lev 24	Ps 31	Ecc 7	2Ti 3
21	Lev 25	Ps 32	Ecc 8	2Ti 4
22	Lev 26	Ps 33	Ecc 9	Tit 1
23	Lev 27	Ps 34	Ecc 10	Tit 2
24	Nu 1	Ps 35	Ecc 11	Tit 3
25	Nu 2	Ps 36	Ecc 12	Phm
26	Nu 3	Ps 37	SS 1	Heb 1
27	Nu 4	Ps 38	SS 2	Heb 2
28	Nu 5	Ps 39	SS 3	Heb 3
29	Nu 6	Ps 40–41	SS 4	Heb 4
30	Nu 7	Ps 42–43	SS 5	Heb 5

MAY

	MORNING		**EVENING**	
1	Nu 8	Ps 44	SS 6	Heb 6
2	Nu 9	Ps 45	SS 7	Heb 7
3	Nu 10	Ps 46–47	SS 8	Heb 8
4	Nu 11	Ps 48	Isa 1	Heb 9
5	Nu 12–13	Ps 49	Isa 2	Heb 10
6	Nu 14	Ps 50	Isa 3–4	Heb 11
7	Nu 15	Ps 51	Isa 5	Heb 12
8	Nu 16	Ps 52–54	Isa 6	Heb 13
9	Nu 17–18	Ps 55	Isa 7	Jas 1
10	Nu 19	Ps 56–57	Isa 8:1–9:7	Jas 2
11	Nu 20	Ps 58–59	Isa 9:8–10:4	Jas 3
12	Nu 21	Ps 60–61	Isa 10:5-34	Jas 4
13	Nu 22	Ps 62–63	Isa11–12	Jas 5
14	Nu 23	Ps 64–65	Isa 13	1Pe 1
15	Nu 24	Ps 66–67	Isa 14	1Pe 2
16	Nu 25	Ps 68	Isa 15	1Pe 3
17	Nu 26	Ps 69	Isa 16	1Pe 4
18	Nu 27	Ps 70–71	Isa 17–18	1Pe 5
19	Nu 28	Ps 72	Isa 19–20	2Pe 1
20	Nu 29	Ps 73	Isa 21	2Pe 2
21	Nu 30	Ps 74	Isa 22	2Pe 3
22	Nu 31	Ps 75–76	Isa 23	1Jn 1
23	Nu 32	Ps 77	Isa 24	1Jn 2
24	Nu 33	Ps 78:1-37	Isa 25	1Jn 3
25	Nu 34	Ps 78:38-72	Isa 26	1Jn 4
26	Nu 35	Ps 79	Isa 27	1Jn 5
27	Nu 36	Ps 80	Isa 28	2Jn
28	Dt 1	Ps 81–82	Isa 29	3Jn
29	Dt 2	Ps 83–84	Isa 30	Jude
30	Dt 3	Ps 85	Isa 31	Rev 1
31	Dt 4	Ps 86–87	Isa 32	Rev 2

JUNE

	MORNING		EVENING	
1	☐ Dt 5	☐ Ps 88	☐ Isa 33	☐ Rev 3
2	■ Dt 6	■ Ps 89	■ Isa 34	☐ Rev 4
3	☐ Dt 7	☐ Ps 90	☐ Isa 35	☐ Rev 5
4	■ Dt 8	■ Ps 91	■ Isa 36	■ Rev 6
5	☐ Dt 9	☐ Ps 92–93	☐ Isa 37	☐ Rev 7
6	■ Dt 10	■ Ps 94	■ Isa 38	■ Rev 8
7	☐ Dt 11	☐ Ps 95–96	☐ Isa 39	☐ Rev 9
8	■ Dt 12	■ Ps 97–98	■ Isa 40	■ Rev 10
9	☐ Dt 13–14	☐ Ps 99–101	☐ Isa 41	☐ Rev 11
10	■ Dt 15	■ Ps 102	■ Isa 42	■ Rev 12
11	☐ Dt 16	☐ Ps 103	☐ Isa 43	☐ Rev 13
12	■ Dt 17	■ Ps 104	■ Isa 44	■ Rev 14
13	☐ Dt 18	☐ Ps 105	☐ Isa 45	☐ Rev 15
14	■ Dt 19	■ Ps 106	■ Isa 46	■ Rev 16
15	☐ Dt 20	☐ Ps 107	☐ Isa 47	☐ Rev 17
16	■ Dt 2	■ Ps 108–109	■ Isa 48	■ Rev 18
17	☐ Dt 22	☐ Ps 110–111	☐ Isa 49	☐ Rev 19
18	■ Dt 23	■ Ps 112–113	■ Isa 50	■ Rev 20
19	☐ Dt 24	☐ Ps 114–115	☐ Isa 51	☐ Rev 21
20	■ Dt 25	■ Ps 116	■ Isa 52	■ Rev 22
21	☐ Dt 26	☐ Ps 117–118	☐ Isa 53	☐ Mt 1
22	■ Dt 27–28:19	■ Ps 119:1-24	■ Isa 54	■ Mt 2
23	☐ Dt 28:20-68	☐ Ps 119:25-48	☐ Isa 55	☐ Mt 3
24	■ Dt 29	■ Ps 119:49-72	■ Isa 56	■ Mt 4
25	☐ Dt 30	☐ Ps 119:73-96	☐ Isa 57	☐ Mt 5
26	■ Dt 31	■ Ps 119:97-120	■ Isa 58	■ Mt 6
27	☐ Dt 32	☐ Ps 119:121-144	☐ Isa 59	☐ Mt 7
28	■ Dt 33–34	■ Ps 119:145-176	■ Isa 60	■ Mt 8
29	☐ Jos 1	☐ Ps 120–122	☐ Isa 61	☐ Mt 9
30	■ Jos 2	■ Ps 123–125	■ Isa 62	■ Mt 10

JULY

	MORNING		EVENING	
1	Jos 3	Ps 126–128	Isa 63	Mt 11
2	Jos 4	Ps 129–131	Isa 64	Mt 12
3	Jos 5–6:5	Ps 132–134	Isa 65	Mt 13
4	Jos 6:6-27	Ps 135–136	Isa 66	Mt 14
5	Jos 7	Ps 137–138	Jer 1	Mt 15
6	Jos 8	Ps 139	Jer 2	Mt 16
7	Jos 9	Ps 140–141	Jer 3	Mt 17
8	Jos 10	Ps 142–143	Jer 4	Mt 18
9	Jos 11	Ps 144	Jer 5	Mt 19
10	Jos 12–13	Ps 145	Jer 6	Mt 20
11	Jos 14–15	Ps 146–147	Jer 7	Mt 21
12	Jos 16–17	Ps 148	Jer 8	Mt 22
13	Jos 18–19	Ps 149–150	Jer 9	Mt 23
14	Jos 20–21	Ac 1	Jer 10	Mt 24
15	Jos 22	Ac 2	Jer 11	Mt 25
16	Jos 23	Ac 3	Jer 12	Mt 26
17	Jos 24	Ac 4	Jer 13	Mt 27
18	Jdg 1	Ac 5	Jer 14	Mt 28
19	Jdg 2	Ac 6	Jer 15	Mk 1
20	Jdg 3	Ac 7	Jer 16	Mk 2
21	Jdg 4	Ac 8	Jer 17	Mk 3
22	Jdg 5	Ac 9	Jer 18	Mk 4
23	Jdg 6	Ac 10	Jer 19	Mk 5
24	Jdg 7	Ac 11	Jer 20	Mk 6
25	Jdg 8	Ac 12	Jer 21	Mk 7
26	Jdg 9	Ac 13	Jer 22	Mk 8
27	Jdg 10–11:11	Ac14	Jer 23	Mk 9
28	Jdg 11:12-40	Ac 15	Jer 24	Mk 10
29	Jdg 12	Ac 16	Jer 25	Mk 11
30	Jdg 13	Ac 17	Jer 26	Mk 12
31	Jdg 14	Ac 18	Jer 27	Mk 13

AUGUST

	MORNING		**EVENING**	
1	Jdg 15	Ac 19	Jer 28	Mk 14
2	Jdg 16	Ac 20	Jer 29	Mk 15
3	Jdg 17	Ac21	Jer 30–31	Mk 16
4	Jdg 18	Ac 22	Jer 32	Ps 1–2
5	Jdg 19	Ac 23	Jer 33	Ps 3–4
6	Jdg 20	Ac 24	Jer 34	Ps 5–6
7	Jdg 21	Ac 25	Jer 35	Ps 7–8
8	Ru 1	Ac 26	Jer 36 & 45	Ps 9
9	Ru 2	Ac 27	Jer 37	Ps 10
10	Ru 3–4	Ac 28	Jer 38	Ps 11–12
11	1Sa 1	Ro 1	Jer 39	Ps 13–14
12	1Sa 2	Ro 2	Jer 40	Ps 15–16
13	1Sa 3	Ro 3	Jer 41	Ps 17
14	1Sa 4	Ro 4	Jer 42	Ps 18
15	1Sa 5–6	Ro 5	Jer 43	Ps 19
16	1Sa 7–8	Ro 6	Jer 44	Ps 20–21
17	1Sa 9	Ro 7	Jer 46	Ps 22
18	1Sa 10	Ro 8	Jer 47	Ps 23–24
19	1Sa 11	Ro 9	Jer 48	Ps 25
20	1Sa 12	Ro 10	Jer 49	Ps 26–27
21	1Sa 13	Ro 11	Jer 50	Ps 28–29
22	1Sa 14	Ro 12	Jer 51	Ps 30
23	1Sa 15	Ro 13	Jer 52	Ps 31
24	1Sa 16	Ro 14	La 1	Ps 32
25	1Sa 17	Ro 15	La 2	Ps 33
26	1Sa 18	Ro 16	La 3	Ps 34
27	1Sa 19	1Co 1	La 4	Ps 35
28	1Sa 20	1Co 2	La 5	Ps 36
29	1Sa 21–22	1Co 3	Eze 1	Ps 37
30	1Sa 23	1Co 4	Eze 2	Ps 38
31	1Sa 24	1Co 5	Eze 3	Ps 39

SEPTEMBER

	MORNING		EVENING	
1	1Sa 25	1Co 6	Eze 4	Ps 40–41
2	1Sa 26	1Co 7	Eze 5	Ps 42–43
3	1Sa 27	1Co 8	Eze 6	Ps 44
4	1Sa 28	1Co 9	Eze 7	Ps 45
5	1Sa 29–30	1Co 10	Eze 8	Ps 46–47
6	1Sa 31	1Co 11	Eze 9	Ps 48
7	2Sa 1	1Co 12	Eze 10	Ps 49
8	2Sa 2	1Co 13	Eze 11	Ps 50
9	2Sa 3	1Co 14	Eze 12	Ps 51
10	2Sa 4–5	1Co 15	Eze 13	Ps 52–54
11	2Sa 6	1Co 16	Eze 14	Ps 5
12	2Sa 7	2Co 1	Eze 15	Ps 56–57
13	2Sa 8–9	2Co 2	Eze 16	Ps 58–59
14	2Sa 10	2Co 3	Eze 17	Ps 60–61
15	2Sa 11	2Co 4	Eze 18	Ps 62–63
16	2Sa 12	2Co 5	Eze 19	Ps 64–65
17	2Sa 13	2Co 6	Eze 20	Ps 66–67
18	2Sa 14	2Co 7	Eze 21	Ps 68
19	2Sa 15	2Co 8	Eze 22	Ps 69
20	2Sa 16	2Co 9	Eze 23	Ps 70–71
21	2Sa 17	2Co 10	Eze 24	Ps 72
22	2Sa 18	2Co 11	Eze 25	Ps 73
23	2Sa 19	2Co 12	Eze 26	Ps 74
24	2Sa 20	2Co 13	Eze 27	Ps 75–76
25	2Sa 21	Gal 1	Eze 28	Ps 77
26	2Sa 22	Gal 2	Eze 29	Ps 78:1-37
27	2Sa 23	Gal 3	Eze 30	Ps 78:38-72
28	2Sa 24	Gal 4	Eze 31	Ps 79
29	1Ki 1	Gal 5	Eze 32	Ps 80
30	1Ki 2	Gal 6	Eze 33	Ps 81–82

OCTOBER

	MORNING		**EVENING**	
1	1Ki 3	Eph 1	Eze 34	Ps 83–84
2	1Ki 4–5	Eph 2	Eze 35	Ps 85
3	1Ki 6	Eph 3	Eze 36	Ps 86
4	1Ki 7	Eph 4	Eze 37	Ps 87–88
5	1Ki 8	Eph 5	Eze 38	Ps 89
6	1Ki 9	Eph 6	Eze 39	Ps 90
7	1Ki 10	Php 1	Eze 40	Ps 91
8	1Ki 11	Php 2	Eze 41	Ps 92–93
9	1Ki 12	Php 3	Eze 42	Ps 94
10	1Ki 13	Php 4	Eze 43	Ps 95–96
11	1Ki 14	Col 1	Eze 44	Ps 97–98
12	1Ki 15	Col 2	Eze 45	Ps 99–101
13	1Ki 16	Col 3	Eze 46	Ps 102
14	1Ki 17	Col 4	Eze 47	Ps 103
15	1Ki 18	1Th 1	Eze 48	Ps 104
16	1Ki 19	1Th 2	Da 1	Ps 105
17	1Ki 20	1Th 3	Da 2	Ps 106
18	1Ki 21	1Th 4	Da 3	Ps 107
19	1Ki 22	1Th 5	Da 4	Ps 108–109
20	2Ki 1	2Th 1	Da 5	Ps 110–111
21	2Ki 2	2Th 2	Da 6	Ps 112–113
22	2Ki 3	2Th 3	Da 7	Ps 114–115
23	2Ki 4	1Ti 1	Da 8	Ps 116
24	2Ki 5	1Ti 2	Da 9	Ps 117–118
25	2Ki 6	1Ti 3	Da 10	Ps 119:1-24
26	2Ki 7	1Ti 4	Da 11	Ps 119:25-48
27	2Ki 8	1Ti 5	Da 12	Ps 119:49-72
28	2Ki 9	1Ti 6	Hos 1	Ps 119:73-96
29	2Ki 10	2Ti 1	Hos 2	Ps 119:97-120
30	2Ki 11–12	2Ti 2	Hos 3–4	Ps 119:121-144
31	2Ki 13	2Ti 3	Hos 5–6	Ps 119:145-176

NOVEMBER

	MORNING		**EVENING**	
1	2Ki 14	2Ti 4	Hos 7	Ps 120–122
2	2Ki 15	Tit 1	Hos 8	Ps 123–125
3	2Ki 16	Tit 2	Hos 9	Ps 126–128
4	2Ki 17	Tit 3	Hos 10	Ps 129–131
5	2Ki 18	Phm	Hos 11	Ps 132–134
6	2Ki 19	Heb 1	Hos 12	Ps 135–136
7	2Ki 20	Heb 2	Hos 13	Ps 137–138
8	2Ki 21	Heb 3	Hos 14	Ps 139
9	2Ki 22	Heb 4	Joel 1	Ps 140–141
10	2Ki 23	Heb 5	Joel 2	Ps 142
11	2Ki 24	Heb 6	Joel 3	Ps 143
12	2Ki 25	Heb 7	Am 1	Ps 144
13	1Ch 1–2	Heb 8	Am 2	Ps 145
14	1Ch 3–4	Heb 9	Am 3	Ps 146–147
15	1Ch 5–6	Heb 10	Am 4	Ps 148–150
16	1Ch 7–8	Heb 11	Am 5	Lk 1:1-38
17	1Ch 9–10	Heb 12	Am 6	Lk 1:39-80
18	1Ch 11–12	Heb 13	Am 7	Lk 2
19	1Ch 13–14	Jas 1	Am 8	Lk 3
20	1Ch 15	Jas 2	Am 9	Lk 4
21	1Ch 16	Jas 3	Ob	Lk 5
22	1Ch 17	Jas 4	Jnh 1	Lk 6
23	1Ch 18	Jas 5	Jnh 2	Lk 7
24	1Ch 19–20	1Pe 1	Jnh 3	Lk 8
25	1Ch 21	1Pe 2	Jnh 4	Lk 9
26	1Ch 22	1Pe 3	Mic 1	Lk 10
27	1Ch 23	1Pe 4	Mic 2	Lk 11
28	1Ch 24–25	1Pe 5	Mic 3	Lk 12
29	1Ch 26–27	2Pe 1	Mic 4	Lk 13
30	1Ch 28	2Pe 2	Mic 5	Lk 14

DECEMBER

	MORNING		**EVENING**	
1	1Ch 29	2Pe 3	Mic 6	Lk 15
2	2Ch 1	1Jn 1	Mic 7	Lk 16
3	2Ch 2	1Jn 2	Na 1	Lk 17
4	2Ch 3-4	1Jn 3	Na 2	Lk 18
5	2Ch 5:1–6:11	1Jn 4	Na 3	Lk 19
6	2Ch 6:11-42	1Jn 5	Hab 1	Lk 20
7	2Ch 7	2Jn	Hab 2	Lk 21
8	2Ch 8	3Jn	Hab 3	Lk 22
9	2Ch 9	Jude	Zep 1	Lk 23
10	2Ch 10	Rev 1	Zep 2	Lk 24
11	2Ch 11–12	Rev 2	Zep 3	Jn 1
12	2Ch 13	Rev 3	Hag 1	Jn 2
13	2Ch 14–15	Rev 4	Hag 2	Jn 3
14	2Ch 16	Rev 5	Zec 1	Jn 4
15	2Ch 17	Rev 6	Zec 2	Jn 5
16	2Ch 18	Rev 7	Zec 3	Jn 6
17	2Ch 19–20	Rev 8	Zec 4	Jn 7
18	2Ch 21	Rev 9	Zec 5	Jn 8
19	2Ch 22–23	Rev 10	Zec 6	Jn 9
20	2Ch 24	Rev 11	Zec 7	Jn 10
21	2Ch 25	Rev 12	Zec 8	Jn 11
22	2Ch 26	Rev 13	Zec 9	Jn 12
23	2Ch 27–28	Rev 14	Zec 10	Jn 13
24	2Ch 29	Rev 15	Zec 11	Jn 14
25	2Ch 30	Rev 16	Zec 12:1–13:1	Jn 15
26	2Ch 31	Rev 17	Zec 13:2-9	Jn 16
27	2Ch 32	Rev 18	Zec 14	Jn 17
28	2Ch 33	Rev 19	Mal 1	Jn 18
29	2Ch 34	Rev 20	Mal 2	Jn 19
30	2Ch 35	Rev 21	Mal 3	Jn 20
31	2Ch 36	Rev 22	Mal 4	Jn 21

Index

Authors and Contributors

Creative 3 International

Tony Cantale, designer, is passionate about communicating the message of the good news in print. He has spent his working life exploring ways to present the gospel in relevant forms to ordinary people.

Robert Hicks' first career was as a senior executive in retailing before he moved into publishing, in which he has concentrated on creativity and marketing as well as initiating national enterprises. He has led the distribution of over 100 million Gospels and Gospel extracts, and initiated the annual "Back to Church" campaign which involves thousands of churches.

Martin Manser has been a professional reference book editor since 1980. He has compiled or edited over 180 reference books, particularly English-language dictionaries and Bible-reference titles. He is also a Language Trainer and Consultant with national companies and organisations.

Contributors

David Barratt (*The Bible Book by Book*) was for many years Senior Lecturer in English at the University of Chester. He has also taught in Pakistan and the United States, and is the author of a book on C.S.Lewis. One of his concerns is the interplay of literature and the Christian faith.

Mike Beaumont (*The Bible Book by Book*) is a pastor, lecturer, author and broadcaster. Based in Oxford, he travels widely in many nations and has over 30 years' experience equipping pastors, churches and seminaries. He contributed to the *NIV Thematic Study Bible* and is the author of *The One-Stop Bible Guide* (Lion).

Richard Bewes OBE (*Bible Teaching*), – formerly at All Souls Langham Place, London – travels widely, has written 20 books and is known for his hosting of the on-screen programmes *Open Home Open Bible* and *Book by Book*.

Nicola Bull, editorial assistant, is an Oxford University science graduate and freelance editor, working mainly on Christian books. She is active in her local Baptist church, and is also involved in ecumenical and environmental groups.

James Collins (*What the Bible Says About …*) is currently the pastor of Redhill Baptist Church. He has a PhD from the London School of Theology where he has taught the sociology of religion.

Nicholas Gatzke (*In Times of Need*) is the Senior Pastor of Osterville Baptist Church on Cape Cod, Massachusetts. He gained his PhD in Homiletics from the London School of Theology and holds degrees from Gordon-Conwell Theological Seminary and Moody Bible Institute.

Pieter Lalleman (*The Bible Book by Book*) is tutor of New Testament and Academic Dean of Spurgeon's College, London. A graduate of Utrecht and Groningen universities (the Netherlands), he is an ordained Baptist minister and the author of several books and many articles.

Richard Littledale (*The Bible Book by Book*) is Pastor of Teddington Baptist Church, London. A tutor at the College of Preachers, he has an interest in innovative communication. He has preached on BBC Radio 4, and is a regular contributor to Radio 2's *Pause for Thought*.

Debra Reid (*The Bible Book by Book*) has been a tutor at Spurgeon's College, London, since 1987, having trained at Cardiff, University of Wales. She has been involved with the publication of a variety of Bible editions, new translations and other reference works. She is the author of the *Tyndale Old Testament Commentary* on Esther.

Andrew Stobart (*The Authority and Inspiration of the Bible; The Bible Book by Book; Living the Christian Life*) is a student minister in the Methodist Church, training at Durham University. Previously, he studied Christian theology to doctoral level at London School of Theology and Aberdeen University. His publications include contributions to biblical and theological dictionaries.

Keith White (*The Bible for Today's World*) lectures worldwide in theology and sociology, and chairs the Child Theology Movement. He edited *The Bible (Narrative and Illustrated)*, and recent books include *The Art of Faith* and *The Growth of Love*.

Derek Williams (*The Bible Book by Book; Living the Christian Life*) is a Church of England minister who works as the Bishop of Peterborough's Administrator and Press Officer. He is the author of a number of books, including *The Bible Chronicle* and (with Dr J. I. Packer) *The Bible Application Handbook*.

Acknowledgements

Text and layout

Grateful thanks to Kevin Wade, designer, for assistance on layout in a time of need

Graphics

Maps and charts by Tony Cantale. Consultant Dr Debra Reid. *How the Bible Developed* chart based on The Bible Society *Timeline*, used with permission

Pictures

Illustrations and photography by Tony Cantale unless otherwise stated

Amazon Kindle 19

Artville 244, 248, 319, 655 (top)

Bible Society 28 (de Reina)

Andy Bisgrove 240-241 (illustration)

Todd Bolen 38 (Jordan), 43 (gathering in), 46 (sacrifice), 49 (Sinai), 56–57, 92–93, 116, 176, 240, 581–582, 586, 590, 591, 592 (niches), 593, 594 (Corinth), 597, 602, 603, 607, 612 (tower), 616, 618, 621, 623, 629, 630–631, 633, 634, 636 (Mt Hermon), 643

British Library 27 (codex)

British Museum 30, 32, 33 (chariot), 38 (Nero), 52 (ivory), 54 (duck weight, lion-weight), 55 (measuring), 635, 641

University of Calgary 26 (Septuagint)

The Carey Center 28–29 (Carey)

Digital Stock 216, 332/346–356/455 (mountain)

Digital Vision 38 (comet), 49 (waterfall, stars), 154, 256, 277, 332/430–440/462 (sea), 332/442–452/462 (lightning), 468/520–530 (canoeists), 468/532–542 (sunset), 469/544–564 (runner), 638, 653, 664, 685, 688

Mary Evans 27 (Wycliffe, Bede), 259 (Wesley)

John Foxx 12–13, 31 (Karnak), 39 (Parthenon), 466/484–494 (hard hat), 598

Rex Geissler www.greatcommission.com 26 (jar)

Goodshoot 121

Jesus College Cambridge 129 (John Eliot)

Charles Moore 26–27 (Sinai), 46 (sheep), 73, 194, 219, 237, 584, 606, 610, 612 (market), 613 (both), 614, 615, 632, 636 (inscription), 646, 647 (Thessalonica), 677

Mukti Mission 29 (Pandita Ramabai)

Adrian Nielson 465/466/472–480 (climbers)

Operation Mobilisation 192, 229, 663

Photodisc 27 (Hebrew text), 45 (grapes, menorah), 69, 91, 129, 133, 137, 150, 212, 245, 281, 289, 292, 322, 325/329, 332/358–368/456 (statue), 332/418–428/461 (footprints), 333/382–392/458 (faces), 470/568–578 (father & child), 583 (Jewish man), 620, 645 (flowers)

Isabelle Rozenbaum 284

John Rylands Museum Manchester 26 (fragment)

Tear Fund 29 (reader), 141, 253, 469/556–566 (clinic), 655 (bottom), 657, 683

Rachel Todhunter 467/496–506 (drink-break)

Trans World Radio 287, 661, 667

Ukraine Plus Group 26 (scroll)

WEC International 258, 658, 668

Wellspring 15 (both), 20, 279, 298, 467/508–518 (students), 670

Keith White 17

Wikimedia Commons 28 (Tyndale, Luther, Coverdale), 29 (Qumran), 31 (Hattusha), 33 (discus thrower), 27 (Alexander), 26 (coin), 27 (Pompey), 39 (Artemis), 43 (Purim), 44 (Gezer calendar), 52 (temple, frieze), 130 (Xerxes), 201, 259 (Luther, Augustine), 600, 608, 627, 630 (Nebuchadnezzar), 639 (figurine), 647 (Lake Galilee), 649 (both)

Wikimedia Commons: alex.ch 687; Almog 601; Aviceda 77; Ciar 158; CNG www.cngcoins.com 53 (coins rows 2,3,4,5,6); Gryffindor 588; Jannisch 55 (stadium); Jastrow 53 (top), 594 (cylinder); Ravil Kayumov 596; NASA 250, 604, 625; Pentocelo 130 (Purim); Julius Rückert 208; Keith Schengili-Roberts 54 (jar); The Yorck Project 27 (Jerome); Zereshk 645 (frieze); Zunkir 159

Wycliffe Bible Translators 18

Simon Zisman 184, 583 (Arab)